D1558845

AFTER THE
DELUGE

AFTER THE EMPIRE:
THE FRANCOPHONE WORLD AND
POSTCOLONIAL FRANCE

Series Editor
Valérie Orlando, Illinois Wesleyan University

Advisory Board
Robert Bernasconi, Memphis University
Alec Hargreaves, Florida State University
Chima Korieh, Central Michigan University
Françoise Lionnet, UCLA
Obioma Nnaemeka, Indiana University
Kamal Salhi, University of Leeds
Tracy D. Sharpley-Whiting, Hamilton College
Frank Ukadike, Tulane University

Dedicated to the promotion of intellectual thought on and about the Francophone world, *After the Empire* publishes original works that explore the arts, politics, history, and culture that have developed in complex negotiations with the French colonial influence. The series also looks at the Hexagon and its borders, and at the transgressions of those borders that problematize notions of French identity and expression.

Of Suffocated Hearts and Tortured Souls: Seeking Subjecthood through Madness in Francophone Women's Writing of Africa and the Caribbean, by Valérie Orlando

Francophone Post-Colonial Cultures: Critical Essays, edited by Kamal Salhi

In Search of Shelter: Subjectivity and Spaces of Loss in the Fiction of Paule Constant, by Margot Miller

French Civilization and Its Discontents: Nationalism, Colonialism, Race, edited by Tyler Stovall and Georges Van Den Abbeele

After the Deluge: New Perspectives on Postwar French Intellectual and Cultural History, edited by Julian Bourg with an Afterword by François Dosse

Remnants of Empire in Algeria and Vietnam: Women, Words, and War, by Pamela A. Pears

Packaging Post/Coloniality: The Manufacture of Literary Identity in the Francophone World, by Richard Watts

The Production of the Muslim Woman: Negotiating Text, History, and Ideology, by Lamia Ben Youssef Zayzafoon

AFTER THE DELUGE

New Perspectives on the Intellectual and Cultural History of Postwar France

Edited by Julian Bourg

LEXINGTON BOOKS

Lanham • Boulder • New York • Toronto • Oxford

LEXINGTON BOOKS

Published in the United States of America
by Lexington Books
An imprint of The Rowman & Littlefield Publishing Group, Inc.
4501 Forbes Boulevard, Suite 200, Lanham, Maryland 20706

PO Box 317
Oxford
OX2 9RU, UK

Copyright © 2004 by Lexington Books

All rights reserved. No part of this publication may be reproduced,
stored in a retrieval system, or transmitted in any form or by any
means, electronic, mechanical, photocopying, recording, or otherwise,
without the prior permission of the publisher.

British Library Cataloguing in Publication Information Available

Library of Congress Cataloging-in-Publication Data

After the deluge : new perspectives on the intellectual and cultural history of postwar
France / edited by Julian Bourg.
     p. cm. — (After the empire)
  Includes bibliographical references and index.
  ISBN 0-7391-0791-7 (cloth : alk. paper) — ISBN 0-7391-0792-5
(pbk. : alk. paper)
 1. France—Civilization—1945– 2. France—Intellectual life—20th century. 3.
France—Social life and customs—20th century. 4. France—Politics and
government—1945– 5. France—Social conditions—1945– I. Bourg, Julian, 1969 II.
Series.
DC33.7.A6 2004
194—dc22

                                        2004010874
Printed in the United States of America

♾™ The paper used in this publication meets the minimum requirements of
American National Standard for Information Sciences—Permanence of Paper for
Printed Library Materials, ANSI/NISO Z39.48–1992.

CONTENTS

ACKNOWLEDGMENTS

An edited collection is a collaborative enterprise, and an editor's work is made gratifying, dare I say enjoyable, by the quality of the contributions that arrive. It has been my good fortune to have worked with fourteen exemplars of thorough, thoughtful, and relevant scholarship, and I thank the authors for their comments and criticisms, patience with endless requests, and timely replies. Serena Krombach believed in this project and brought it to light—I am indebted to her, full stop.

I am furthermore grateful to Robert Carley, Kimberly Ball Smith, and the rest of the Lexington Books staff. Martin Jay brought his usual rapid-fire acumen to a draft of the introduction, and Marie-Pierre Le Hir's assessment of the entire manuscript improved it considerably. A Mellon Postdoctoral Fellowship in Interdisciplinary Studies at Washington University in St. Louis provided the basic support for this project, and I would like to thank Mechelen Dachshund, Daniel Geary, Jennie Sutton, the good folks at Kaldi's, and my colleagues at Wash U—John Bowen, Howard Brick, David Ciepley, Gerald Izenberg, Martin Jacobs, Hillel Kieval, Linda Nicholson, and Steven Zwicker—for their stimulation and encouragement. This volume, or my part in it, is dedicated to my parents.

INTRODUCTION

Julian Bourg

Few figures of contemporary history have been as booed and ballyhooed as the postwar French intellectual. The authors of incomprehensible babble, the last-standing fashioners of critical dissent and sublime insight, the supercilious inhabitants of the Parisian left bank, the sexy heroes of anti-authoritarian free thought—French intellectuals gained a reputation, an aura, in the twentieth century that preceded, accompanied, and even seems to have outlasted them. As a matter of Western cultural stereotype, America, one might say, has had the dollar, England a queen, Germany cars, and France a set of products exported alongside its famous cheeses and wines, namely, men and women who think and write (or paint or make films) and who sometimes take public stands on politics. The successive waves are familiar to many. There was 1950s existentialism and, with others, the dominating though squat Jean-Paul Sartre delivering philosophy from the seminar room to the corner café. Then came 1960s and 1970s "French theory," its staggering success driving the once-swollen, now-deflated term postmodernism. If by the late twentieth century there was a precipitous decline in the international influence of French intellectuals, coupled with a sustained breast-beating in France about the crisis and malaise of domestic intellectual life, nevertheless, for large stretches of the recently past "short century," French thinkers and their ideas circulated throughout the world with an untold influence on academic and popular culture.

The passing of an era invites re-examination. After trends and fashions have faded and passions have cooled, it is possible to revisit a time and place with the patient will to understand as well as decide what is worth remembering. At a glance, French intellectual and cultural life already seems so obviously familiar and well known. There has been, as we will see below, no shortage of commentaries on the endangered species, the *intellectuel français*. And yet familiarity has a way of blocking comprehension. The animal and its habitat remain under study. Perhaps we've been too close to see them clearly, or better, the understanding of postwar French intellectual and cultural history is evolving, just as that history itself evolved. Knowledge accumulates, and appreciations shift. The early twenty-first century seems an opportune moment for gauging the shape of a historical period that has passed and for taking stock of its significance. The character of the internationally renowned French intellectual who flourished in the latter half of the twentieth century may no longer be actual, in the sense of existing at the current moment. If this is the case, then it is possible in new ways to avoid uncritical reception, hypercritical polemic, and other forms of *analyses à chaud*, or analyses too close to see clearly, that interfere with balanced explanation and judicious evaluation. It goes without saying that assessing how that history looks now means that in years to come it will appear different. But at the present there are new perspectives on postwar French intellectual and cultural history. These are some of them.

After the Deluge marks the arrival of a new historiographical and generational sensibility. This volume showcases recent work, much of it by younger scholars, that historicizes key debates, figures, and turning points in post-1945 French culture. Written by authors hailing from Italy, France, the United Kingdom, and the United States, the following articles show that, since World War Two, French intellectual and cultural history has involved much more than a few infamous thinkers and concepts. The contributors are motivated by the impulse to fill the many gaps in our understanding of postwar French intellectuals and culture (turning over unturned rocks), by the desire to explain why certain ideas arose when they did and how they fit with their times, by a preference for attentive detail and skillful storytelling, by the will to test the continuing relevance of certain thinkers and ideas, and, as scholars are wont to do, by the inclination to challenge existing interpretations. Relying on primary and archival sources and taking seriously the historian's mission to narrate and contextualize, the authors of *After the Deluge* add significant depth and breadth to our knowledge of postwar French intellectual and cultural history.

The title *After the Deluge* refers indirectly to Madame de Pompadour's quip, traditionally ascribed to her lover Louis XV, "After us, the deluge"— *Après nous, le déluge.* This phrase has long been understood as a callous dismissal of the effect Louis's decadent regime would have on his subjects; some have taken it as a hapless prophecy of the French Revolution. Here, "deluge" refers to two historical situations: first, French intellectuals and culture after the stormy caesura of World War Two. Where many French intellectuals had looked east of the Rhine for inspiration during the interwar years, after the war, France replaced Germany as the intellectual center of Continental Europe, even if German thought continued to influence French thinkers in important ways. The shame and guilt of defeat and collaboration, as well as the hopes and possibilities introduced by the experience of resistance, continued to reverberate in the country for the rest of the century.

The second meaning of deluge refers to emerging historical scholarship on postwar French intellectuals and culture after the Anglo-American academy in particular has been inundated with French theory for nearly three decades. It was difficult to get a liberal arts education in parts of the West during the 1980s and 1990s without at some point being exposed to the poststructuralist and postmodernist theories that so fundamentally transformed North American and European scholarship. Such theories were the French version of the Beatles invasion. A number of the contributors to this volume came to study postwar French history by way of earlier engagements with French theory; and this path characterizes a distinctive generational ethos. By the 1990s, of course, exhaustion with French theory had set in. "If I hear the name 'Foucault' one more time," one imagines a typical professor in the humanities or social sciences saying, "I'm going to fall out of my chair." When its partisans themselves declare the era of French theory to be closed, you know it is time to call in the historians.[1]

Historians of postwar French intellectual and cultural life might be compared to a crew of janitors who enter a ballroom after a very large party the previous night. A good time was had by all, and now there is a mess to clean up. These janitors, though, while mopping up, sift through the remains in order to reconstruct what had taken place the night before. Historians are janitors or detectives or anthropologists of the recent past.

Claims for new perspectives need to be offset by a frank acknowledgment of preceding and reigning analyses. One might distinguish among three available approaches—the history of intellectuals, intellectual history, and cultural history—and further among recent French, American, and

British treatments of these aspects of postwar French history. Briefly
sketching the outlines of these methods and national differences might be
helpful in situating this volume.

The history of intellectuals focuses on social and political actors, on men
and women who perform certain types of work and also play particular roles
in society. There is wide consensus that the modern notion of the intellectual
emerged in France. The story of the novelist Emile Zola's late-nineteenth-
century defense of Captain Alfred Dreyfus has been repeated often, having
become the genesis account of a social type. When Dreyfus was accused of
treason on trumped up charges fueled by anti-Semitism, Zola wrote his famous article, *J'Accuse*, in which he defended the soldier according to principles of universal truth and justice. Zola lived by his pen and turned his literary talents toward the public sphere, entering politics as a writer who claimed
to see further and hope for more than politicians, the military, or the legal system seemed capable. The universalizing intellectual was born. The title,
though, has been awarded posthumously to those before Zola who produced
culture and who took public stands on public issues.

The history of French intellectuals has touched on the domestic tradition
of *belles lettres* since at least the eighteenth century, on the corporatist spirit
of those whose profession was intellectual or artistic work, on the relative
importance of institutions (in the broad sense) ranging from universities to
newspapers to the public sphere, and on the cultural self-identification of
intellectuals from the avant-garde to the reactionary rearguard. The history
of intellectuals contends with the political stands of writers and artists,
stands that in France ranged from Zola's rallying around the Third Republic to extreme splits between Left and Right intellectuals during the interwar period to the predominance of left-wing intellectuals in the thirty years
after World War Two, when the Right coped with discredit. Finally, the history of intellectuals borrows heavily from the sociology of intellectuals, pioneered by Karl Mannheim's sociology of knowledge in the 1920s and exemplified in France by Pierre Bourdieu before his death in 2002. The
sociology of intellectuals ultimately turned attention from ideas and individuals to social types, classes, groups, generations, and collective phenomena. Centering on either heroic individuals or the broader social field, the
history of intellectuals method has seemed most firmly established in
France.[2]

In contrast to the history of intellectuals, intellectual history is more interested in ideas than in socio-political actors and structures. At least, it
privileges ideas instead of reducing them. Intellectual history studies ideas
in time and across time, situating them in their local contexts and following

their travels outside those local contexts. Ideas have coherent logics and can themselves be characters in a story. But they also bear an inevitable relationship of tension to their times; while thought defies reduction to its milieu, it cannot be understood historically apart from that situation. Intellectual history differs from the history of ideas because the former believes that context is unavoidably pertinent if not decisive. In France, intellectual history in this sense has no real tradition, largely because philosophers have maintained control of the history of philosophy and historians have preferred to consider mentalities.[3] Setting aside the British case for a moment, in the United States several prominent schools of European intellectual history developed in the postwar period. Viewed broadly, Arthur Lovejoy's history of ideas was less interested in local contexts than in epic careers of big concepts. H. Stuart Hughes's social history of ideas paid more attention to context, finding cohorts of thinkers working on similar problems at the same time, often without being in dialogue with one another. Carl E. Schorske took contextual issues even more seriously, sometimes seeing certain ideas as epiphenomenal symptoms of broader social and political tensions, and he also helped bring methods of psychology and psychoanalysis to historical writing. Hughes and Schorske were furthermore significant since they trained a number of intellectual historians who have flourished since the 1970s.[4]

This most recent generation of European intellectual historians working in the United States is worth mentioning for a variety of reasons. To begin with, several of them wrote early, generally sympathetic accounts of postwar French intellectuals and their critical (usually Marxist) theories.[5] Such accounts were early in the sense that they were written close to the thinkers studied. European intellectual historians have furthermore played an important role in keeping Continental thought alive as American philosophy departments, famously, moved decisively toward analytic philosophy. But the 1980s and 1990s also witnessed a serious challenge to American practitioners of European intellectual history. This challenge came in two related forms: methodological debates about the "linguistic turn" and cultural historians' charge that intellectual history was elitist and therefore politically undemocratic and epistemologically narrow. Significantly, both these developments had to do with the reception of French theory. In 1982, Dominick LaCapra and Steven L. Kaplan noted "a far-reaching change" underway in the discipline of intellectual history due to "the recent invasion of new theoretical perspectives and research practices from Europe."[6] They had in mind the importation of French theory and the related "linguistic turn" in scholarship then underway. For their part, advocates of cultural history, building on social history, the *Annales* school's history of mentalities, anthropology, and French theory, put intellectual history squarely in their sights.[7] Cultural historians were perhaps less hostile to intellectuals and their texts than social historians had been, and the emergence of "discourses" and "representations" as objects of historical concern facilitated a general hermeneutics of meaning that cut across distinctions between high and low culture.[8] Still, until the end of the twentieth century intellectual history was on the defensive; the "age" belonged to culture.[9] Though virtually all the essays in this volume contextualize intellectuals and their ideas, the inclusion of the adjective *cultural* in the title is a bow to the contemporary reality of historical writing: one cannot avoid the fact that intellectual history deals with distinctive kinds of cultural practices, representations, and meanings. Genres are included in the species of which they are part.

The point of this disciplinary digression is to raise the questions of what has happened in recent years to historical writing on postwar French intellectual and cultural life and what warrants the assertion that new perspectives and sensibilities may be emerging. With a number of notable exceptions I will discuss below, in the 1990s, established historians in the United States largely ceased to write as historians about postwar French intellectual and cultural life. Methodological worries generally did not pay returns in the historical understanding of the above-mentioned "invasion." The issue of contextualization, crucial to Hughes and Schorske's generation, seemed to have gone away. Scholars such as LaCapra and Mark Poster, who wrote early studies of postwar intellectual history, have in subsequent years more often applied French theories than taken them as objects of research. Sherry Turkle and Michael S. Roth have moved on to other fields. Even someone like Martin Jay, who has written a hefty historical survey of "anti-ocular" discourse in twentieth-century France, has elsewhere described his technique as situated "between intellectual history and cultural critique." A New Press series on postwar French thought published primary source material, but the availability of such spindles of thread has not, as it were, made the looms of historians hum. Sande Cohen has noted the virulent attacks on French theories by some historians unable to consider those theories as "objects of *research*."[10]

There is a counterpoint case, centered in the United Kingdom but with echoes in the United States. French cultural studies have thrived in the United Kingdom in ways that do not seem to have precluded the study of postwar French intellectuals and their ideas. In the hands of Margaret Atack, David Drake, Patrick Ffrench, Jeremy Jennings, Michael Kelly, Brian Rigby, Keith Reader, and Douglas Smith, among others, studies of postwar

French intellectual and cultural life have thrived.[11] True, the aims of cultural studies are not always those of historical explanation, contextualization, and narrative, and scholars working in French studies do not necessarily have the same disciplinary orientations as historians. The point is not to grumble about disciplinary boundaries; this is the era of interdisciplinary studies. But historians do ask certain kinds of questions, or certain kinds of questions are historical. Insofar as French theories have contributed to development of French cultural studies, their British reception appears to have been accompanied by research into their origins, development, and crises. Perhaps due to proximity and exchange, English-language translations of essays by French scholars on postwar intellectual and cultural life in France have mostly appeared in the United Kingdom. A corollary field of scholarship exists in American departments of French and Comparative Literature, but again one can point to differences between the aims of literary-textual and historical scholarship.[12]

A moment ago I mentioned that there are a number of notable exceptions to the decline of historical writing on postwar French intellectual and cultural life. In addition to the cultural studies crowd, the most significant and influential historiographical trend in the past decade has been the neoliberal school. Suspicious of postwar French intellectuals and especially of their commitment to Marxism, authors in this field have celebrated the return to political liberalism. Tony Judt's provocative indictment of postwar French intellectuals' attachment to communism, *Past Imperfect: French Intellectuals, 1944–1956* (1992), set the tone.[13] Published at the end of the Cold War, his account condemned certain French intellectuals for their blindness toward Soviet totalitarianism. His dismissal of the French Left in favor of Anglo-American liberalism was polemical, an example of explanation driven by belief. As editor with Thomas Pavel of Princeton's New French Thought series since 1994 and as commentator in his own right, Mark Lilla has similarly encouraged a revision of postwar intellectual history by championing French thinkers who have since the 1980s rethought the liberal and Republican traditions.[14] Samuel Moyn has noted that this school has ignored the methodological worries of those scholars who grappled with the invasion of French theory and that they have tended to judge intellectuals and their ideas according to very particular anti-Marxist and anti-totalitarian political standards.[15] By implication they have generally ignored the study of French theorists who were more skeptical about the liberal and French Republican traditions, and they have surrendered the intellectual historian's mission to explain and understand thinkers and their ideas, not simply condemn them or dissolve them in their context.

Several of the essays in this volume respond to the neo-liberal school directly or implicitly.

Receiving the torch passed by earlier historians, the multinational contributors to *After the Deluge* combine the methods of the history of intellectuals with those of intellectual and cultural history. They exemplify the spirit of interdisciplinarity: setting forth from various academic departments (French, geography, history, philosophy, and political science) to approach a shared research field with overlapping and consonant questions and approaches. They avoid tedious theoretical loftiness and polemic for the more modest craft of historicizing one of the most fascinating moments of the twentieth century. *After the Deluge* is organized into three sections: on the historicization of French intellectual culture, on individual thinkers, and on the interstices between culture and politics. The articles in each section, of course, inevitably resonate with others in the volume.

The chapters in part I view the postwar intellectual and cultural field with wide-angled lenses. Issues of context and transformation predominate here. Historicizing postwar French intellectual culture as a whole means contending with well-known as well as overlooked characters, and it requires weaving together interpretive threads of varying thicknesses and densities: from the international down to the interpersonal. Examples of the much-maligned-and-lauded domain of French theory make their appearance, but they do so as part and parcel of broad milieu and middle-term narratives. Intellectuals are not disembodied heads. They have to eat. As socio-political creatures, what intellectuals write and say is related, as the following three essays demonstrate, to the institutional, economic, and national contexts in which they thrive. Shifts in intellectual and cultural life inevitably point to changing social, material, and political circumstances.

Alan D. Schrift is out to challenge reigning orthodoxies, especially in the United States, about what "French philosophy" was supposed to have been. In addition to insisting on the crucial importance of French educational institutions for understanding French thought, he criticizes three "myths" about twentieth-century French thought, myths about the French reception of German phenomenology, the conflict between existentialism and structuralism, and the view of French philosophy as Gallic Heideggereanism. Against the view that phenomenology simply yielded existentialism before it was vanquished by structuralism, in a heroic clash of great ideas, Schrift notes that phenomenology also contributed to the French epistemological tradition. Against the impression that twentieth-century French philosophy culminated in Martin Heidegger's two children—Jean-Paul

Sartre and Jacques Derrida—Schrift points out that some of the most important philosophical developments in France had little to do with Heidegger (for example, in analytic philosophy as well as in a persistent Spinozist Marxism).

Addressing the political and intellectual economies of postwar France, William Gallois argues that pervasive French critiques of capitalism were often vague and that many theorists had an implicit if curious convergence with political leaders such as Charles de Gaulle, himself no friend to market capitalism. Everyone, it seemed, was against capitalism, but few paragons of French theory criticized the distinctive *dirigiste* form of French capitalism. Gallois claims that an exception can be found in Jean-François Lyotard. Writing on Algeria in the early 1960s, Lyotard, in a refreshingly concrete criticism, said that French "big capital" was eager to dispense with the colonies because their expense stifled economic growth. Lyotard's views had a certain resonance in the 1980s when François Mitterrand liberalized the French economy.

Warren Breckman examines the passage from Marxism to post-Marxism. Attempting to go beyond Marxism while using it as a compass, in the 1980s, Ernesto Laclau, originally from Argentina but working in England, and Chantal Mouffe, a Belgian working in France, made use of poststructuralist critiques of meaning and subjectivity to rethink leftist politics. Where some commentators have argued that postmodernism is marked by a melancholy born of the infinite deferral of meaning, Breckman argues that these post-Marxists discovered in the alleged contingency and openness of the social world a principle of hope and a new framework for radical politics. Laclau and Mouffe's project can be explained in part by the different histories of the intellectual Left in postwar France and Great Britain. The British context made possible a different response to the crisis of Marxism than in France, where post-Marxism has often meant anti-Marxism. The eclipse of constructive engagement with the Marxian legacy in 1980s France, Breckman suggests, reveals something of the more censorious side of the much-praised liberal turn in recent French thought.

The chapters in part II treat particular figures, those who have generally been overlooked as well as those who will be familiar to students of postwar French intellectual culture. Discussions of persons who have been largely neglected—Kostas Axelos, Cornelius Castoriadis, Daniel Guérin, Guy Hocquenghem, and Kostas Papaioannou—add to our understanding of the independent French Left. The treatments of two more recognizable figures—Emmanuel Levinas and Raymond Aron—nuance and round out existing accounts of their contributions to postwar French intellectual life. Between texts and contexts, intellectual biographies of these thinkers inevitably refer to themes raised elsewhere on intellectual fields, cultural politics, and periodization.

Christophe Premat follows the careers of three Greek intellectuals who, fleeing a country in turmoil, arrived in France on the same ship in December 1945. Because of their experiences of fascism and Stalinism in their native land, Cornelius Castoriadis, Kostas Axelos, and Kostas Papaioannou spent their mature years criticizing the politics of domination, notably bureaucratism and communist-distorted Marxism. Castoriadis's emphasis on "self-management" or Axelos's on "planetary thought" were original contributions to postwar French reflections on politics. Their criticisms emerged from within the radical tradition, warning of the dangers inherent in all political life but holding out the possibility of yet-unrealized emancipatory politics.

Stuart Elden traces the itinerary of the aforementioned Kostas Axelos. Finding himself at the center of some of the most innovative theoretical work of the 1960s, Axelos was translator of Georg Lukács and Martin Heidegger, editor of the non-communist Left journal, *Arguments*, and director of an influential publication series at the Éditions de Minuit. In addition to following Axelos's trajectory in dialogue with his contemporaries, Elden assesses Axelos's Heideggerean-Marxist notion of "world," a notion with continuing critical pertinence in the era of globalization.

David Berry sketches the intellectual biography of the largely forgotten Daniel Guérin. Anarchist, correspondent with Leon Trotsky, pioneer in post-colonial theory, godfather to contemporary French gay liberation, Guérin cut a swath through much of the twentieth century. Berry trails him from the late 1930s until his death in 1988, from attraction to and disillusionment with Trotskyism, to his historical studies on the French Revolution, to his conversion to anarchism and search for a way to blend it with Marxism in a libertarian communism, to his anti-colonial activism since the 1930s and his post-1968 engagement with sexual politics.

From a different generation, Guy Hocquenghem also found himself at the center of the 1968-era cultural revolution. Ron Haas follows Hocquenghem's career from 1968 through the early 1970s, arguing that he never hesitated to criticize other leftists for their intransigence or narrowmindedness. Even as the heat of revolution cooled for many of his fellow militants, Hocquenghem the writer and critic continued to promote a French cultural revolution in its varied, kaleidoscopic expressions. His positions on the significance of 1968, maintained until his death twenty years later, reveal neglected dimensions in French cultural memory and raise questions about the unresolved conflicts of what Jean-Pierre Le Goff has called May 1968's "impossible inheritance."

In the first of the two chapters on characters who have received far greater attention in past years, Ethan Kleinberg, like Schrift, attacks a prevalent myth about his subject, Emmanuel Levinas. This myth is the suggestion some have made that Levinas, known as both a phenomenological philosopher and a Talmudic commentator, provides a direct link with the prewar Jewish culture of Lithuania. Drawing on biographical and textual evidence from the 1910s until the 1960s, Kleinberg insists this cannot be true, since Levinas had no formative exposure to the Talmud as a young man and turned to it only after the Holocaust. Against the myth of a lost and irretrievable past, Kleinberg demonstrates how Levinas used his own version of the Jewish tradition to criticize, rethink, and rehabilitate Western philosophy.

Lucia Bonfreschi's chapter on Raymond Aron similarly bridges the years on either side of World War Two. Though exposed to the dangers of nationalism while a visiting student to Germany during the 1930s, in exile in London during the war, Aron argued for nations as communities that needed to defend themselves. During the "schism of the universe" that was the Cold War, Aron championed the Atlantic alliance while holding out hope that Europe could find a post-national and unified identity. Bonfreschi shows how during the 1950s Aron advocated the construction of European institutions as a prelude to the emergence of more organic and popular European sentiment.

Demonstrating the overlaps and crosscurrents between culture and politics, the chapters in part III address the impact of international political events on French intellectuals, the contested legacies of cultural memory, the role of the state as facilitator of French culture, and the transcendent or religious bases for political legitimation. Politics appear both as events that provoke responses and as forms that are put in question. Culture emerges as one privileged sphere where struggles among agonistic elements take place. As producers of and ruminators on culture, intellectuals reflect on the meaning, possibilities, and limits of the political, and in doing so refract its energies and conflicts.

When Soviet tanks arrived in Budapest in 1956, many French intellectuals questioned their commitment to Moscow and Marx. Michael Scott Christofferson examines the conflicted responses of the communist-controlled Comité national des écrivains to the Hungarian Revolution. Its feeble response to Soviet repression caused the group to lose members and relevance. In contrast, non-communist Left intellectuals who founded the Comité Tibor Déry actively worked to free imprisoned Hungarian writers

and thinkers while maintaining a belief that socialism and liberty could ultimately be united.

Samuel Moyn takes up the politics of French memory of the Holocaust.
Until the 1960s, Nazi totalitarianism was understood in France along lines
defined by David Rousset, who said that the camps in the East where Jews
were murdered were more extreme cases of the camps in the West—all
were part of the same "concentrationary universe." Resistance to or victim-
ization by the Nazis was understood in terms of antifascist politics. In 1966,
however, Jean-François Steiner published his account of the rebellion at
Treblinka. Underscoring the Jewish identities of those who rebelled,
Steiner insisted that death camps were different from concentration camps
because the Holocaust targeted Jews in particular. The book proved to be a
turning point for French understandings of the Holocaust, notably that of
the eminent historian Pierre Vidal-Naquet.

Centering his analysis on French state cultural policy from the election
of Mitterrand to the present, Philippe Poirrier explores shifts and controversies around government sponsorship of national culture. In the 1980s,
Mitterrand's Minister of Culture, Jack Lang, instituted a policy of "cultural
democracy," focusing on artists and culture industries and breaking with
André Malraux's earlier vision of national patrimony. However, market liberalization and the growing importance of the media raised serious questions about the state's capacity to steward national culture. By the time the
Right came to power in 1993, a tension had developed between the liberal
imperative to cut budgets and the impulse to protect French culture from
dilution in the era of globalization.

In the last chapter in this section, Michael Behrent traces the itineraries
of two thinkers—Régis Debray and Marcel Gauchet—as they have developed an appreciation for the importance of religion in political life. Rethinking the conditions of political life in light of 1968-era frustrations, both
Debray and Gauchet came to see that politics had perhaps always been
haunted by the religious imagination. In the 1980s, each in his own way, they
both embraced French Republicanism as a new religion, and in the 1990s
they argued that traditional religion had a positive role to play in the public
sphere and civil society. Behrent demonstrates how Debray and Gauchet
have consistently made a case that politics requires a relation to transcendence, even if the ways they have expressed that insight have changed.

Finally, in his afterword, François Dosse assesses the practice of intellectual history in France. He notes the factors that have previously impeded
this field as well as developments, such as the relatively recent arrival of a
historiography on intellectuals, conducive to the emergence of intellectual

history. The waning of the particular historical type of the French critical intellectual has invited historical investigation. Using his own two-volume *History of Structuralism* (1991–92) as an example, Dosse makes the case for an intellectual history that splits the difference between internalist and externalist explanations and that contributes to broader conversations about the cultural and political possibilities of the present—not in order to reduce the past to the present, but to make the past relevant.

These chapters overlap in both form and content. Many of them handle their subjects with a high degree of factual care. While the word "empiricism" has long had negative connotations for some students of culture, including historians of intellectual life, it is worth noting that many of the authors in this volume make skillful use of archival and previously neglected sources in their attempt, basic to the historian's craft, of getting the story right. There's no question of definitive interpretations here, or of closing debate on the who, what, how, and why of French intellectual culture. One might even argue that the contributors gathered here step through doors opened by the recent generation of cultural historians and literary scholars; such work remains intertextual (texts are used to shed light on other texts) and rhetorical (arguments are made). And yet, one is struck by the way these chapters are unafraid to answer questions of context, to rely on familiar narrative strategies, and to engage in the modest task of explanation. There are also differences in the interpretive styles of the various nationalities represented here. Such differences should not be exaggerated, no more than the differences in national scholarly temperament discussed earlier; still, variety in everything from narrative structures to the value of footnotes are apparent. To my eye, tediously predictable tropes of cultural studies and identity politics and of complication for the sake of complication are absent here. At the same time, and this is not estimable, this volume generally elides matters of race and gender. Additionally, the French Right has virtually no representation here, intellectuals on the Left monopolizing the conversation. These absences have something to do with the research field itself, but as editor, I also take responsibility for choices made.

The contributions to this volume also unsettle expected ways of periodizing postwar French intellectual and cultural history, whether according to schools and movements, cohorts and crises, or before and after World War Two. For example, Schrift complicates the phenomenology-begot-existentialism-begot structuralism story; Premat describes an émigré cohort by national origins left behind but not forgotten; Behrent follows the shared thematic paths of two, otherwise quite different thinkers; Berry, Kleinberg, and Bonfreschi explain postwar developments in light of prewar circumstances. They slice the pie of periodization differently, allowing for narratives to emerge that fit the particular figures, themes, and debates under study. There is thus a local, case study character to many of these chapters, grasping episodes in French intellectual and cultural life in all their texture, color, and drama.

Beyond formal or methodological considerations, these chapters also converge on a number of subjects and concerns. First of all, the role of World War Two as a dividing moment remains capital, qualifications notwithstanding. The dual legacy of the experiences of fascism and resistance showed up, often indirectly, in numerous cultural forms. Moyn's study of the dynamic of Holocaust memory is a case in point. Furthermore, the famous dates of 1956 and 1968 similarly retain their explanatory force. Secondly, half the chapters in this volume deal with Marx in some way. Pride of place is given to noncommunist, independent Left intellectuals who sought to integrate, as both Christofferson and Berry point out, socialism and liberty. One might wonder if the emergence of new studies of French Left intellectuals signals an attempt to answer the neo-liberal historiographical school, discussed above, or if it is part of a larger renaissance of social thinking, which would include a Marx forced to face up to the totalitarian crimes committed in his name but whose questions remain unanswered and perhaps timely. There are enough reconstructive treatments of Left intellectuals here to take the possibility seriously. Historians are not antiquarians after all. Then again, half the chapters in this volume have nothing to do with Marx. Thirdly, with the exception of Schrift, Gallois, and Breckman, none of the authors deal directly with familiar figures of French theory, a silence perhaps explained by fatigue, lack of interest, or the urge to change the subject. Maybe we are still too close to see clearly, or maybe this is what things look like after the deluge. The history of French theory remains to be written.[16] Two other themes to note in passing are religion and French exceptionalism. The theme of religion—from the historicity of religious communities to the place of religion in French history—appears in several chapters. While Christianity and Islam figure here, Judaism and the secular "religion" of Republicanism command special attention. Finally, the specificity of France is probed—the uniqueness of its institutions (Schrift), *dirigiste* capitalism (Gallois), and persistent providential state (Poirrier); its flourishing, 1968-era counterculture speaking in Marxist-revolutionary tongues (Haas); and its differences with other nations like the United Kingdom (Breckman).

It is not unreasonable to ask, Why should we care? Why is postwar French intellectual history important? Hasn't the devaluation of French intellectual and cultural life simply been a necessary market correction? And what of the field of intellectual history—hasn't it, too, been replaced as out of date? The contributors to this volume don't think so. They are not alone.[17] Intellectual history plays crucial roles in the academy; in monitoring changes in prevailing winds; in explaining origins, continuities, and ruptures in thought; and in reflecting on the relationship between scholarship and citizenship. More specifically, it seems possible in new ways to revisit postwar French culture as a whole, climb into its detailed corners, and understand its complexity, conflicts, and contributions. This volume helps us know better the sources of contemporary realities—the project of European unification, for instance, or talk of globalization—and how transformations in the recent past occurred—many French thinkers had been critically reflecting on Marxism for a long while. On the whole, the study of intellectual and cultural life contributes to intellectual and cultural life. It keeps alive ideas that might otherwise be forgotten. It shows how ambiguity, error of judgment, insight, and innovation appear in all historical moments. It testifies to the courage others have had to interpret their world and to try to change it, others who thought deeply about their times and the possibilities they believed available to them. In our own thoughtless era, we need such lessons and examples.

NOTES

1. Michael Payne and John Schad, eds., *Life After Theory: Jacques Derrida, Frank Kermode, Toril Moi, and Christopher Norris* (London: Continuum, 2003); Terry Eagleton, *After Theory* (New York: Basic Books, 2003).

2. Pierre Bourdieu, *La Distinction: critique sociale du jugement* (Paris: Éditions de Minuit, 1979); *Distinction: A Social Critique of the Judgment of Taste*, trans. Richard Nice (Cambridge, Mass.: Harvard University Press, 1984). Following Bourdieu have been Christophe Charle, *Naissance des "intellectuels," 1880–1900* (Paris: Éditions de Minuit, 1990); and Christophe Prochasson, *Les Intellectuels, le socialisme et la guerre, 1900–1938* (Paris: Seuil, 1993). See also Rémy Rieffel, *Les Intellectuels sous la Ve République*, 3 vols. (Paris: Calmann-Lévy, 1993); and Niilo Kauppi, *French Intellectual Nobility: Institutional and Symbolic Transformations in the Post-Sartrean Era* (Albany: The State University of New York Press, 1996).

Writing less in the spirit of Bourdieu than as political historians or journalists, other French works in the history of intellectuals include Pascal Ory and Jean-François Sirinelli, *Les Intellectuels en France de l'affaire Dreyfus à nos jours* (Paris: Armand Colin, 1992); Sirinelli, *Deux intellectuels dans le siècle: J.-P. Sartre et R.*

Aron (Paris: Fayard, 1995); François Hourmant, *Le Désenchantement des clercs: figures de l'intellectuel dans l'après-Mai 68* (Rennes: Presses universitaires de Rennes, 1997); Olivier Mongin, *Face au scepticisme: les mutations du paysage intellectuel (1976–1998)*, 2nd ed. (Paris: Hachette, 1998); Michel Winock, *Le Siècle des intellectuels*, rev. ed. (Paris: Seuil, 1999); Bernard Brillant, *Les Clercs de 68* (Paris: PUF, 2003).

Elisabeth Roudinesco's studies on Jacques Lacan and French psychoanalysis point toward French intellectual culture more generally. Roudinesco, *La Bataille de cent ans: histoire de la psychanalysme en France*, 2 vols., rev. ed. (Paris: Fayard, 1994); volume 2 translated as *Jacques Lacan & Co.: A History of Psychoanalysis in France, 1925–1985*, trans. Jeffrey Mehlman (Chicago: The University of Chicago Press, 1990). Roudinesco, *Jacques Lacan: esquisse d'une vie, histoire d'une système de pensée* (Paris: Fayard, 1993); *Jacques Lacan*, trans. Barbara Bray (New York: Columbia University Press, 1997).

3. François Dosse, "De l'histoire des idées à l'histoire intellectuelle," in *L'Histoire des intellectuels aujourd'hui*, eds. Michel Leymaire and Jean-François Sirinelli (Paris: PUF, 2003), 161. Dosse's work does walk the line between the history of intellectuals and intellectual history, if sticking close to the in's and out's of Parisian family dramas. See notably his *Histoire du structuralisme*, 2 vols. (Paris: La Découverte, 1991–92); *History of Structuralism*, trans. Deborah Glassman, 2 vols. (Minneapolis: Minnesota University Press, 1997); *La Marche des idées: histoire des intellectuels–histoire intellectuelle* (Paris: La Découverte, 2003); and his "Afterword" in this volume. For philosophers as historians, see Vincent Descombes, *Le Même et l'autre* (Paris: Éditions de Minuit, 1979); *Modern French Philosophy*, trans. L. Scott-Fox and J. M. Harding (Cambridge: Cambridge University Press, 1980); Dominque Lecourt, *Les Piètres Penseurs* (Paris: Flammarion, 1999); *The Mediocracy: French Philosophy since the Mid-1970s*, trans. Gregory Elliott (London: Verso, 2001). An American example would be Gary Gutting, *French Philosophy in the Twentieth Century* (Cambridge: Cambridge University Press, 2001).

4. Hughes taught Gerald N. Izenberg, Martin Jay, Dominick LaCapra, David Luft, Paul A. Robinson, and John E. Toews. Schorske taught Peter Jelavich, Harry Liebersohn, Peter Loewenberg, William J. McGrath, Michael S. Roth, and Debora Silverman. David L. Schalk studied with Schorske as an undergraduate at Wesleyan and with Hughes at Harvard as a graduate student. One might also consider the influence of Jacques Barzun, Crane Brinton, Peter Gay, Leonard Krieger, Frank E. Manuel, George Mosse, and Fritz Ringer.

5. Mark Poster, *Existential Marxism in Postwar France* (Princeton: Princeton University Press, 1975). Dominick LaCapra, *A Preface to Sartre* (Ithaca: Cornell University Press, 1978). Arthur Hirsch, *The French New Left: An Intellectual History from Sartre to Gorz* (Boston: South End Press, 1981). Michael S. Roth, *Knowing and History: Appropriations of Hegel in Twentieth-Century France* (Ithaca: Cornell University Press, 1988).

6. Dominick LaCapra and Steven L. Kaplan, "Preface," in *Modern European Intellectual History: Reappraisals and New Perspectives*, eds. LaCapra and Kaplan (Ithaca: Cornell University Press, 1982), 7. See Sande Cohen, "Structuralism and the Writing of Intellectual History," *History and Theory* 17 (1978). John E. Toews, "Intellectual History after the Linguistic Turn: The Autonomy of Meaning and the Irreducibility of Experience," *American Historical Review* 92, no. 4 (October 1987). See also Russell Jacoby's exchange with LaCapra in the *American Historical Review* 97, no. 2 (April 1992).

7. Roger Chartier, "Intellectual History and the History of Mentalités," in *Cultural History: Between Practices and Representations* (Ithaca: Cornell University Press, 1988). Lynn Hunt, ed., *The New Cultural History* (Berkeley: University of California Press, 1989). Robert Darnton, "Intellectual and Cultural History," in *The Kiss of Lamourette: Reflections in Cultural History* (New York: Norton, 1990).

8. William Bouwsma, "Intellectual History in the 1980s: From the History of Ideas to the History of Meaning," *Journal of Interdisciplinary History* 12, no. 2 (1981).

9. "Symposium on Intellectual History in the Age of Cultural Studies," *Intellectual History Newsletter* 18 (1996).

10. Sherry Turkle, *Psychoanalytic Politics: Jacques Lacan and Freud's French Revolution*, 2nd ed. (New York: The Guilford Press, 1992); *Life on the Screen: Identity in the Age of the Internet* (New York: Simon & Schuster, 1995). Michael S. Roth, *Knowing and History; The Ironist's Cage: Memory, Trauma, and the Construction of History* (New York: Columbia University Press, 1995). Martin Jay, *Downcast Eyes: The Denigration of Vision in Twentieth-Century French Thought* (Berkeley: University of California Press, 1993); *Force Fields: Between Intellectual History and Cultural Critique* (New York: Routledge, 1993). Jacques Revel and Lynn Hunt, eds., *Postwar French Thought*, vol. 1, *Histories: French Constructions of the Past* (New York: The New Press, 1995). Denis Hollier and Jeffrey Mehlman, eds., *Postwar French Thought*, vol. 2, *Literary Debate: Texts and Contexts* (New York: The New Press, 1999). Cohen, "Research Historians and French Theory," in *French Theory in America*, eds. Sylvère Lotringer and Sande Cohen (New York: Routledge, 2001), 300.

11. Michael Kelly, *Modern French Marxism* (Baltimore: The Johns Hopkins University Press, 1983). Keith Reader, *Intellectuals and the Left in France since 1968* (New York: St. Martin's Press, 1987). Jeremy Jennings, ed., *Intellectuals in Twentieth-Century France: Samurais and Mandarins* (New York: St. Martin's Press, 1993). Patrick Ffrench, *The Time of Theory: A History of Tel Quel (1960–1983)* (Oxford: Clarendon Press, 1995). Douglas Smith, *Transvaluations: Nietzsche in France 1872–1972* (Oxford: Clarendon Press, 1996). Margaret Atack, *May '68 in French Fiction and Film: Rethinking Society, Rethinking Representation* (Oxford: Oxford University Press, 1999). Christopher Flood and Nick Hewlett, eds., *Currents in Contemporary French Intellectual Life* (New York: St. Martin's Press, 2000). David Drake, *Intellectuals and Politics in Post-War France* (Houndmills: Palgrave, 2002).

For cross-cultural dialogue on cultural studies, see André Kaenel, Catherine Lejeune, and Marie-Jeanne Rossignol, eds., *Études culturelles–Cultural Studies* (Nancy: Presses universitaires de Nancy, 2003).

12. Allan Stoekl, *Agonies of the Intellectual: Commitment, Subjectivity, and the Performative in the 20th Century French Tradition* (Lincoln: University of Nebraska Press, 1992). Kristin Ross, *Fast Cars, Clean Bodies: Decolonization and the Reordering of French Culture* (Cambridge, Mass.: The MIT Press, 1995). Danielle Marx-Scouras, *The Cultural Politics of Tel Quel: Literature and the Left in the Wake of Engagement* (University Park, Pa.: Pennsylvania State University Press, 1996). Alice Yaeger Kaplan, *The Collaborator: The Trial & Execution of Robert Brasillach* (Chicago: The University of Chicago Press, 2000). Ross, *May '68 and Its Afterlives* (Chicago: The University of Chicago Press, 2002).

13. Tony Judt, *Past Imperfect: French Intellectuals, 1944–1956* (Berkeley: University of California Press, 1992). See also, Judt, *The Burden of Responsibility: Blum, Camus, Aron, and the French Twentieth Century* (Chicago: The University of Chicago Press, 1998); and Sunil Khilnani, *Arguing Revolution: The Intellectual Left in Postwar France* (New Haven: Yale University Press, 1994).

14. Mark Lilla, ed., *New French Thought: Political Philosophy* (Princeton: Princeton University Press, 1994); *The Reckless Mind: Intellectuals and Politics* (New York: The New York Review of Books Press, 2001). From a slightly different orientation, Richard Wolin's attacks on French intellectuals have resonated with this current. See his *Labyrinths: Explorations in the Critical History of Ideas* (Amherst: University of Massachusetts Press, 1995); and "The Grandeur and Twilight of French Philosophical Radicalism," in Flood and Hewlett, eds., *Currents in Contemporary French Intellectual Life*. Cf. Martin Jay, "Lafayette's Children: The American Reception of French Liberalism," in *Refractions of Violence* (New York: Routledge, 2003).

15. Samuel Moyn, "Intellectual History after the Liberal Turn" (paper delivered at Columbia University, 31 October 2003).

16. On the American reception of French theory, see Ieme van der Poel et al., eds., *Traveling Theory: France and the United States* (Madison, N.J.: Fairleigh Dickinson University Press, 2000); Jean-Philippe Mathy, *Extrême Occident: French Intellectuals and America* (Chicago: The University of Chicago Press, 1993); Mathy, *French Resistance: The French-American Culture Wars* (Minneapolis: The University of Minnesota Press, 2000); Lotringer and Cohen, eds., *French Theory in America*; *SubStance*, special issue on "The American Production of French Theory," 31, no. 1 (2002); and François Cusset, *French Theory: Derrida, Foucault, Deleuze et Cie. et les mutations de la vie intellectuelle aux États-Unis* (Paris: La Découverte, 2003).

17. The first issue of the new journal, *Modern Intellectual History*, edited by Charles Capper, Anthony J. La Vopa, and Nicholas T. Phillipson, appeared in 2004.

I

HISTORICIZING FRENCH INTELLECTUAL CULTURE

1

IS THERE SUCH A THING AS "FRENCH PHILOSOPHY"? OR WHY DO WE READ THE FRENCH SO BADLY

Alan D. Schrift

Is there such a thing as "French philosophy"? At the start of the twentieth century, there was little doubt how that question should be answered. Victor Delbos, a scholar of Benedict de Spinoza, Immanuel Kant, and post-Kantian philosophy, and the author of the first French publication on Edmund Husserl, gave a course on this theme at the Sorbonne in 1915–1916 that set out to demonstrate that there was indeed a national identity to philosophy in France—independent of German and English influences—that must be preserved and defended.[1] This identity, he claimed, which began with René Descartes and could be traced through Blaise Pascal, Nicholas Malebranche, Voltaire, the Encyclopedists, Jean-Jacques Rousseau, the Ideologues, Maine de Biran, Auguste Comte, into the present, distinguished itself in particular from German philosophy by means of its commitment both to clarity and to the cultivation of the human spirit.

Fourteen years later, in his preface to the first French text to examine twentieth-century German philosophy—Georges Gurvitch's *Les Tendances actuelles de la philosophie allemande* (1930)—neo-Kantian Léon Brunschvicg, the dominant academic philosopher of the day, also affirmed the idea of a specific national identity to philosophy. While no less committed than Delbos to the idea of a philosophy's national identity, Brunschvicg's views were not, like Delbos's, motivated by the desire to offer a patriotic response to Germany's aggression in World War One. As a consequence, Brunschvicg took a more dialogic view of the relations between French and

German philosophy: French philosophy, he wrote, could be traced to Descartes and the Cartesian commitment to the unity of reason, while German philosophy had its origins in Kant's bifurcation of reason between the analytical and the dialectical.[2] Rather than preserving and defending the French philosophical tradition against foreign interventions, Brunschvicg argued that a dialogue between the French and German philosophical traditions was essential for each tradition's self-elaboration.

By the end of the twentieth century, however, a different argument was being offered for the identity of French philosophy. Pierre Macherey, for example, writes that although there are no unifying features in terms of which one could identify a uniquely "French" philosophy, it still makes sense to speak about French philosophy in terms of two institutional forms: the French language and the French tradition of public instruction.[3] Both emerged in their modern forms following the French Revolution, and both continue to this day to mark the practical activity of philosophizing in France.

My perspective inclines more toward Macherey's view than those of Delbos and Brunschvicg. To speak of "French philosophy" is not to speak of a unified tradition that shares certain philosophical assumptions. It is, rather, to speak of a historical unfolding of philosophical discourse that took place in the French language in the twentieth century and that was marked by certain events and developments, both historical and intellectual. In what follows, then, there is no assumption of a single set of shared properties, shared philosophical commitments, or shared goals. There is only the empirical fact that the figures discussed below, whether or not born in France or native French speakers, did their philosophical work in the French language and were engaged with and informed by the institutional practices of the French academic world. That is to say, I want to argue that there is such a thing as French philosophy, but that this thing is not to be understood in terms, say, of a commitment to empiricism or the rigorous analysis of language, as one might identify British philosophy, or the sympathy to dialectical thinking and logic, as a feature that unites most German philosophizing. Instead, I want to suggest that the intellectual and philosophical formation of virtually every well-known French philosopher in the twentieth century who completed their education prior to 1968 has been marked by certain institutional practices unique to the French academic world.

Let me give a few quick examples. Until the 1960s, it was virtually a requirement for academic success in France for one to attend the École normale supérieure (ENS) on the rue d'Ulm in Paris, and this was particularly true for academic success in a department of philosophy. So, of the philosophers likely to have been heard of by English-speaking philosophers, Paul Ricoeur, Gilles Deleuze, and Jean-François Lyotard are perhaps the only major French philosophers of the past half century to have had successful academic careers and *not* to have studied at the École normale. (In Ricoeur's and Lyotard's cases, because they were unable to pass the competitive entrance exam. Deleuze, on the other hand, appears to be one of the very few important French philosophers not to have tried to enter the ENS.)

The size of the entering class at the ENS has always been quite small, with the result that often quite intense friendships and rivalries develop. To give a sense of this, consider that the 1924 entering class at the École normale included, among the twenty-nine students admitted in arts and letters, Raymond Aron, Georges Canguilhem, Daniel Lagache, Paul Nizan, and Jean-Paul Sartre; Jean Hyppolite and Maurice de Gandillac entered the following year, and Maurice Merleau-Ponty entered the year after that. The limited places at the ENS are won by means of a grueling competitive examination—the *concours*—for which students prepare over two years following their *baccalauréat*, in classes designed specifically for the entrance examinations (known in ENS slang as the *hypokhâgne* and *khâgne*). While students from all over France compete for these limited places, the vast majority of students admitted have traditionally come from Paris, and among these, about 90 percent come from the *khâgne* in two particular Latin Quarter *lycées*: Louis-le-Grand and Henri-IV.[4] Again to mention some names, among the alumni of Louis-le-Grand are Alain Badiou, Jean Beaufret, Jacques Derrida, Vladimir Jankélévitch, Lyotard, Merleau-Ponty, Sartre, and Jean Wahl, while Henri-IV's alumni include Georges Canguilhem, Deleuze, Mikel Dufrenne, Michel Foucault, Étienne Gilson, and Jacques Maritain.

Beyond these educational institutions, the most important and unique French institutional practice that has had a significant impact on French philosophy, one with no equivalent in the English-speaking academic system, is the *agrégation*. The *agrégation* was established in 1766 under Louis XV as a competitive examination to certify secondary school teachers, and since 1825, there has been a specific philosophy *agrégation* that licenses students for teaching philosophy in secondary schools.[5] The content of the exam is chosen by a *jury d'agrégation*, acting under the auspices of the Ministry of Public Instruction (now the Ministry of National Education), on the basis of the philosophy *Programme* determined for the preceding year. The structure and content of the philosophy *agrégation* has been a subject of almost constant review and debate throughout the twentieth century.[6] In the early years of the twentieth century, the exam consisted of two parts: a written part, itself consisting of three essays, each allotted seven hours, often scheduled for a single week, with two questions on general philosophy and one on the history of philosophy. Following the written examination, of which only one in four applicants typically passed, several oral examinations were required. In the first oral examination, applicants were given three philosophical texts with one hour each to prepare a thirty-minute explication. The second oral exam required applicants to prepare a "lesson" on an assigned topic; examinees were given six hours access to the Sorbonne library to prepare the lesson. The number of applicants who ultimately were admitted into the *agrégation* was determined by the state in accordance with the number of posts available. The *agrégation* results of 1913 are typical of these early years: of sixty-six students who registered for the exam, seventeen passed the written examination and were "admittable" to the oral examination; of these, ultimately seven passed the oral examination and were admitted as *agrégés*. In its more recent incarnations, both the length of the written exams and the number of oral presentations have been reduced, in part in response to claims that the examination was too difficult, in part in response to the need for more individuals to fill the available posts.

I have gone into such detail concerning the *agrégation* because I think it has had an enormous impact on developments within French philosophy. For one thing, the *Programme* has always concentrated on canonical figures from the history of philosophy, with few figures from the nineteenth century and almost none from the twentieth.[7] When a philosopher's work appears on the *Programme* for the *agrégation*, this means that all students that year who hope for a career in philosophy will spend two years reading that philosopher's work intensively. Not surprisingly, spending two years concentrating on a figure often results not just in subsequent publications on that figure, but it results equally often in that figure being a constant intellectual resource for one's subsequent career. Equally important, there has been a tendency for university professors to "teach to the exam," that is, in an effort to ease the burden on students preparing for the *agrégation* examination, topics of university courses are often chosen in terms of topics announced or anticipated on future exams. As a consequence, not only advanced students but the work of the professoriat as well is determined in response to the *Programme* of the *agrégation*. It is thus important who serves on the jury that selects the figures to appear on the *Programme*, and equally important which figures, like Plato, Kant, Aristotle, George Berkeley, or Spinoza, appear frequently on the *Programme* and which other figures, like Locke or Hegel, appear significantly less frequently. Likewise, it is important to know when figures disappear from the *Programme* after having been frequently represented in previous years, and when new figures are introduced. So, to take an example that seems particularly significant to me, Friedrich Nietzsche's *On the Genealogy of Morals* appears on the reading list in 1958, the first time a work of his appears on the *Programme* in over thirty years. Might this, and his subsequent appearances, be correlated with the explosion of interest in Nietzsche in the '60s , and the appearance of numerous texts and essays on his work in the years shortly following his appearance on the *Programme*, while there were almost no books on Nietzsche published in France by philosophers in the preceding four decades (the only one I am aware of is Angèle Kremer-Marietti's 1957 doctoral thesis *Thèmes et structures dans l'œuvre de Nietzsche*)?[8]

Finally, to note one final indication of the "smallness" and centralization of the French academic world, while it might be well known that Sartre, Simone de Beauvoir, and Merleau-Ponty worked closely as the founding editors of the journal *Les Temps modernes*, or that Hélène Cixous collaborated with Gerard Genette and Tvetan Todorov to found the literary journal *Poétique*, it may be less well known, for example, that in spring 1929, the philosophy faculty at the Lycée Janson-de-Sailly in Paris's sixteenth arrondissement included Beauvoir, Claude Lévi-Strauss, and Merleau-Ponty; or that Foucault and Cixous became close friends in 1968, both having been invited by Georges Canguilhem to organize the faculty in the departments of philosophy and English, respectively, at the experimental university at Vincennes (University of Paris VIII). Deleuze was Foucault's first selection, but because of his poor health, he would not in fact join the faculty for two years, by which time Foucault had already left. Others Foucault invited who did join the faculty included Alain Badiou, Étienne Balibar, François Châtelet, Daniel Defert (a controversial choice, given his relationship with Foucault and relative lack of philosophical credentials at the time), Judith Miller (daughter of Jacques Lacan), Jacques Rancière, René Schérer, and Michel Serres.

These unique academic institutions, the uniformity of philosophical instruction, and the intimacy of the French academic world, centered as it is in Paris, should be kept in mind in what follows, as I challenge some of what I regard as the orthodox view of French philosophy as it has been conceived within the English-speaking philosophical community. Much of this challenge is directed toward the way the French tradition has been taught in philosophy graduate programs in the United States. In particular, I want to highlight three of the more widespread myths concerning philosophy in France in the twentieth century that I think continue to inform both graduate education in Continental philosophy and the general understanding English-speaking Continental philosophers have of French philosophy. These myths are what I'll call "The Monolith of Phenomenology"; the view of existentialism vs. structuralism as a Hegelian battle to the death enacted in the polemic between Sartre and Lévi-Strauss; and the construal of French philosophy as a kind of Gallic Heideggerianism that has promoted a "cult of personality" focused in particular on Sartre and Derrida. The picture that will emerge will challenge certain assumptions about who were the major influences on developments in French philosophy over the past century, as it will challenge the tendency of each subsequent French generation to downplay its own origins out of the seminar rooms and lecture halls in which the preceding generations taught them.

THE MONOLITH OF PHENOMENOLOGY

The third and fourth decades of the twentieth century saw a significant change in philosophical sensibilities in France, as the three schools that dominated the early decades—positivism, associated with Émile Durkheim at the Sorbonne; idealism, associated with Léon Brunschvicg at the Sorbonne and Émile Boutroux at the École normale supérieure; and spiritualism associated with Henri Bergson at the Collège de France and Maurice Blondel at the University at Aix-en-Provence—began to fall out of favor. The turn away from idealism and spiritualism was taken up explicitly by Jean Wahl in his 1932 work *Vers le concret*. Wahl argued in successive chapters on William James, Alfred North Whitehead, and Gabriel Marcel, that we see in their works a dialectic between thought and its object that refuses to lose touch with the real. The principal enemy for James, Whitehead, and Marcel is "mental aridity [*sécheresse mentale*]," and because they each retain an attention to the body and to lived experience, their dialectics, unlike Hegel's, remain oriented toward the concrete.[9] We see a similar motivation driving Alexandre Kojève's historical and materialist reading of Hegel's master-slave dialectic as he argues that "History is the history of the working Slave" who will become free by transcending himself through labor.[10] And, perhaps most significantly, this is a fundamental motivation for those who, like Sartre and Merleau-Ponty, were turning to Husserl and Martin Heidegger, whose method of phenomenological description and account of Being-*in*-the-world were just what they needed to turn away from Brunschvicg and Bergson and turn, in the words of Wahl's text, *toward the concrete*.[11]

As young philosophy students turned away from France's four B's—Bergson, Blondel, Boutroux, and Brunschvicg—and discovered German philosophy's three H's—Hegel, Husserl, and Heidegger—they turned from spiritualism to phenomenology and from idealism to existentialism. The introduction of German philosophy was facilitated by the immigration to France of several Eastern European philosophers, most notably the Russian Alexandre Koyré in 1919, who was the first person to introduce Husserlian phenomenology to the French; fellow Russian Alexandre Kojève in 1927, mentioned above, whose lectures on Hegel at the École pratique des hautes études from 1933–1939 played a major role in the French Hegel revival; and the Lithuanian Emmanuel Levinas, who became a naturalized French citizen in 1931, the year he co-translated, with Gabrielle Peiffer, the first edition of Husserl's work to appear in French, the 1931 *Méditations cartésiennes: introduction à la phénoménologie*, and the year after he published the first French book devoted exclusively to Husserl's thought.[12]

It is difficult to establish a precise chronology during these transitional years, but several influential events can be noted which mark the transformation of French philosophy away from the spiritualistic metaphysics of Bergson and Brunschvicg and toward the more rigorous rationalism of phenomenology. First and foremost is the introduction of phenomenology itself, first in the presence of Max Scheler (1874–1928), then Husserlian phenomenology, and soon thereafter the renaissance of Hegel studies in France. Scheler, who in the early '20s was regarded in Germany as second only to Husserl in importance within the phenomenological movement, was the first of the leading phenomenologists to be invited to visit France, in 1924 and again in 1926. His 1923 text *Wesen und Formen der Sympathie* (*The Nature of Sympathy*) was in 1928 the first work of phenomenology to appear in French translation.[13] Husserl himself was invited to Paris in 1929 by the Institut d'études germaniques and the Société française de philosophie, and he delivered two lectures entitled "Introduction to Transcendental Phenomenology" (the so-called Paris Lectures) at the Sorbonne on February 23 and 25.[14] Although Husserl's own presentation at the Sorbonne did not overwhelm his audience, and the reviews of his *Méditations cartésiennes* in the two leading philosophical journals were unfavorable,[15] the reception of his work in the early '30s by the younger generation was anything but, as indicated by the oft-quoted story related by Simone de Beauvoir in the first volume of her autobiography, in which she recalls how Raymond Aron returned to Paris in 1932 for a break from his studies at the French Institute in Berlin and first introduced Sartre and Beauvoir to Husserl's phenomenology at a Montparnasse café.

Aron said, pointing to his glass: "You see my dear fellow, if you are a phenomenologist, you can talk about this cocktail and make philosophy of it!" Sartre
turned pale with emotion at this. Here was just the thing he had been longing
to achieve for years—to describe objects just as he saw and touched them, and
extract philosophy from the process. Aron convinced him that phenomenology exactly fitted in with his special preoccupations: by-passing the antithesis
of idealism and realism, affirming simultaneously both the supremacy of reason and the reality of the visible world as it appears to our senses.

Later that evening, Sartre stopped at a bookshop on Boulevard Saint-
Michel and purchased Emmanuel Levinas's new book on Husserl, which
Beauvoir tells us he was so eager to begin that he leafed through the vol-
ume as he walked along, without even having cut the pages.[16]

The introduction of Husserlian phenomenology was followed in short
order by a renewal of interest in Hegel's philosophy and, in particular, in
Hegel's *Phenomenology of Spirit*. Jean Wahl's *La Malheur de la conscience
dans la philosophie de Hegel* (1929) marks the beginning of the Hegel
renaissance in France as it offered a reading of Hegel that was more "existential" and less focused on "System." Shortly thereafter, first Koyré and
then Kojève lectured on Hegel at the École pratique des hautes études,
and Kojève's seminar in particular, which ran from 1933–1939, attracted
an audience that included several individuals who would dominate the
French intellectual scene for much of the twentieth century, including
among others Raymond Aron, Georges Bataille, André Breton, Aron Gur-
witsch, Jacques Lacan, and Maurice Merleau-Ponty. Sartre is often included among those who attended Kojève's Hegel seminars, but the
records of registered students kept by the École pratique do not mention
him. That said, it is clear that Sartre was familiar with Kojève's reading of
Hegel, perhaps through his friendships with Aron or Merleau-Ponty, and
Kojève's influence on several formulations found in Sartre's *Being and
Nothingness* (1943) is readily apparent. The third major figure in the
French Hegel renaissance, Jean Hyppolite, published his French translation of Hegel's *Phenomenology of Spirit* in two parts between 1939–1941,
following this with his monumental commentary on the *Phenomenology*
in 1946, which to this day remains perhaps the dominant interpretation of
Hegel in French philosophy.[17]

This rapid transformation of the French philosophical scene was truly remarkable. In 1930, Koyré reported to the first philosophical congress on
Hegel in The Hague that, unlike the situations in Germany, England, and
Italy, a tradition of Hegel studies had never developed in France and there
was little to report in terms of French Hegel scholarship. For all practical

purposes, Koyré concluded, there were no Hegelian studies in France.[18] But sixteen years later, following Kojève's lectures, the appearance of *Being and Nothingness*, and the recent appearance of Hyppolite's translation and commentary, the situation had been so transformed that Merleau-Ponty could comment, in the essay "Hegel's Existentialism," that "All the great philosophical ideas of the past century—the philosophies of Marx and Nietzsche, phenomenology, German existentialism, and psychoanalysis— had their beginnings in Hegel; it was he who started the attempt to explore the irrational and integrate it into an expanded reason which remains the task of our century."[19]

Heidegger, the third of the German influences, also was introduced into France in the early '30s. Although *Being and Time* would not be translated into French until 1985, translations of Heidegger's essays "What is Meta-physics?" and "On the Essence of Reasons" both appeared in French jour-nals in 1931.[20] It is often difficult to distinguish Heidegger's influence from Husserl's in these years, as most of those who read their works (Levinas, Wahl, Sartre, Merleau-Ponty, Ricoeur) tended to interpret each through the other. Although it may be apocryphal, Herbert Spiegelberg relates the following anecdote that speaks to this point: "When asked soon after the War about his early acquaintance with Sartre, Heidegger did not first remember him by name; then he identified him as 'the Frenchman who had always confused him with Husserl'."[21] It is clear, however, that as the young philosophers of the '30s were looking elsewhere than idealism and spiritualism in their desire to make philosophy more concrete, they felt great sympathy toward Heidegger's ontological description of Being-in-the-world and Husserl's phenomenological method for describing that world. As Merleau-Ponty put this in the preface to the *Phenomenology of Percep-tion*, the experience of reading Husserl or Heidegger was not so much an experience "of encountering a new philosophy as of recognizing what [we] had been waiting for."[22]

Thus far, we see that the story of the importation of phenomenology into France, first via Husserl, and then via Heidegger, overlooks the fact that for much of the '20s, Scheler is at least as important a phenomenological pres-ence in France as is Husserl. This fact gains in significance when we recall that in the thirties, it was Gabriel Marcel who was the best known French representative of the phenomenological approach to philosophy. Moreover, for the French themselves, the appearance of phenomenology was not nec-essarily identified primarily with Husserl or Heidegger; indeed, in the '30s, the case could be argued that the major phenomenological presence in France was Hegel's.

As we move into the '40s, a new story takes shape, as phenomenology transforms into existentialism. The standard English-language history of French philosophy sees the years between the appearance of *Being and Nothingness* in 1943 and the emergence of structuralism in the late '50s to be years totally dominated by Sartrean existentialism. According to this history, Sartre is the master thinker, the leading man, as it were, while Maurice Merleau-Ponty, Simone de Beauvoir, and Albert Camus are relegated to roles as supporting cast. This, I think, is mistaken on several counts.[23] While there is little question that Sartre was the dominant intellectual in France during these years, and *Les Temps modernes* the dominant cultural journal, it is not at all clear that Sartre was the dominant *philosophical* presence. That is to say, while Sartre was indeed a dominant cultural presence who had a profound influence on the reading public through his essays and plays as well as his imprimatur,[24] insofar as Sartre remained almost entirely outside the academic, and in particular, the university world, several others had as much if not more impact on developments in the evolution of French philosophy. First among these is Merleau-Ponty, whose teaching at the École normale, the Sorbonne, and the Collège de France had a profound influence on many of the dominant philosophers in the second half of the twentieth century.

I will return in a moment to the role played by Merleau-Ponty, but first I want to indicate that there is in fact an entire tradition in French philosophy that developed alongside the emergence of existentialism and that, while largely unrecognized in the English-speaking philosophical world and not well-known outside French academic circles, has been widely recognized in France as playing a major role in the ultimate unseating of existentialism as a dominant philosophical position in the second half of the century. In his 1978 introduction to the English translation of Georges Canguilhem's *The Normal and the Pathological*, Michel Foucault tells a story of the rise of "contemporary philosophy in France" that is worth recalling here. According to Foucault's story, there are in fact two modalities of philosophizing that emerge from the introduction of Husserlian phenomenology in France in the late twenties. On the one hand, there is what he calls the "philosophy of experience, of sense and of subject" that he identifies with Sartre and Merleau-Ponty. But in addition to this philosophy of the subject that emphasizes reflexivity and consciousness, there was, according to Foucault, another Husserlian trajectory, one associated with formalism, intuitionism, and the theory of science. This second modality of French philosophizing produced "a philosophy of knowledge, of rationality and of concept" that Foucault associates with the work of Gaston Bachelard, Jean Cavaillès, and Georges Canguilhem.[25]

What the French refer to as *"épistémologie"* is largely associated with this second modality, and the importance of this tradition can be seen through the rise of structuralism and what followed structuralism in France.[26] And as Foucault correctly notes, this tradition first appeared in France at the same time as did existentialism. Bachelard submitted his *thèse d'Etat, Essai sur la connaissance approchée* in 1927—the year Gabriel Marcel published what is widely regarded as the first existentialist philosophical text of the twentieth century, his *Metaphysical Journal*—and Canguilhem was a *normalien* with Sartre and submitted his first thesis, on Comte, in 1926 and his second thesis, *Essay on Some Problems Concerning the Normal and the Pathological*, in 1943, the year Sartre published *Being and Nothingness*. Like existential phenomenology, this epistemological tradition arose in response to the spiritualist tendencies of French philosophy in the late nineteenth and early twentieth century. But unlike existentialism, the orientation of this epistemological tradition pointed less toward the problems of classical metaphysics and more toward the physical and natural sciences. And where Sartre and Marcel chose to work and had large followings outside the dominant French educational institutions, Bachelard and Canguilhem were major figures within these institutions, as they occupied in succession the position of director of the Institut d'histoire des sciences et des techniques and chair in the history and philosophy of science at the Sorbonne from 1940 to 1971.

Jean Cavaillès, for his part, at the age of twenty-eight came to occupy the influential position of *agrégé-répétiteur* ("*caïman*" in ENS slang)—the instructor responsible for preparing students to take the *agrégation*—at the École normale supérieure. More so than either Bachelard or Canguilhem, Cavaillès was deeply interested in phenomenology, as his interest in mathematics led him to Husserl, in particular, the latter's *Formal and Transcendental Logic* and *Logical Investigations*. While not denying that phenomenology offered a philosophy of consciousness, insofar as each act of consciousness appeared conjoined to an object of consciousness, Cavaillès concluded that phenomenology provided not only "a philosophy of consciousness but [also] a philosophy of the concept which can provide a theory of science."[27] Cavaillès had a profound influence on many of the students with whom he worked in his four years as *caïman*. Had he lived longer—Cavaillès was a Resistance leader executed by the Nazis in 1944—and had the influence on subsequent generations of *normaliens* that others in his position exercised (think of Louis Althusser, who served as *caïman* from 1948–1980), one must wonder whether someone like Foucault, who clearly situates himself in the tradition of the "philosophy of the concept," would have come to be as hostile to phenomenology as he was.[28]

Foucault's distinction between a philosophy of the subject and a philosophy of the concept, between a tradition that attends to reflexivity and one that focuses on epistemology, is important for several reasons. First, it accurately reflects the fact that existentialism was not the only French philosophy in the years between Sartre's and Marcel's early works and the 1960s. Second, it acknowledges that there were, in fact, two distinct receptions of Husserlian phenomenology in France, one that attended to the Husserl of *Ideas I* and gave rise to the existential phenomenology of Sartre and Merleau-Ponty and the phenomenological hermeneutics of Ricoeur, and another that attended to the Husserl of *Formal and Transcendental Logic* and *Logical Investigations* and gave rise to phenomenological reflections on science and mathematics that are much more sympathetic to the concerns of analytic philosophy than to Heidegger. In addition to Cavaillès, this "other" phenomenological tradition is associated more recently with Jean-Toussaint Desanti (1914–2002), Jules Vuillemin (1920–2001), and Gilles-Gaston Granger (1920–), and it is worth noting here that the latter two, Vuillemin and Granger, while virtually unknown in the English-speaking world, were the philosophers elected to occupy the chairs at the Collège de France following the deaths of Merleau-Ponty and Foucault, respectively.[29] Third and finally, Foucault's distinction acknowledges that there was already an indigenous philosophical tradition in France to which the supporters of structuralism could appeal as they sought to challenge the hegemony of existentialism and the philosophy of the subject.

EXISTENTIALISM VS. STRUCTURALISM, OR SARTRE VS. LÉVI-STRAUSS

The year 1960 is often seen as the year that existentialism as a living philosophy in France ended: Albert Camus, who was still largely associated with the existentialist movement, died in a car accident on January 4; and Sartre, who remained the dominant presence in existentialist philosophy, published *The Critique of Dialectical Reason*, which he himself described as a "structural, historical anthropology."[30] But focusing on the events of 1960 would be in some respects deceptive, because the intervention of structuralism was, by 1960, already well under way, as was the diminishing of the influence of philosophy in general. That is to say, by 1960 structuralism had already emerged as a dominant intellectual paradigm, and the institutional importance of the Department of Philosophy at the Sorbonne was already being challenged by the more interdisciplinary departments at the École normale supérieure and the centers of research in the human sciences at the École pratique des hautes études.

The emergence of structuralism as a dominant intellectual force can be tied to many factors, not least a number of political and historical events—the end of World War Two and the beginnings of the Cold War, the Soviet invasion of Hungary, colonial unrest in Vietnam and Algeria—that left many politically active students dissatisfied with the relatively ahistorical and otherwordly reflections of the Sorbonne philosophers. Some, following a path taken earlier by Lévi-Strauss, left philosophy altogether. Others, intrigued by the seminars and figure of Lacan, thought a psychoanalytic understanding of language and the unconscious could make better sense of events than traditional philosophical reflection.

That students of philosophy would turn to the human sciences is not so strange when one recalls the proximity of philosophy and the human sciences in the French educational system. Until the 1960s, to receive a teaching credential in philosophy required one to undertake advanced work and be certified in one of the sciences, whether hard (physics, mathematics, chemistry, biology) or soft (psychology, ethnology, and what the French call "prehistory").[31] In addition, because the field of sociology was not a discipline recognized for advanced degrees in France until 1958, many of the great French sociologists and anthropologists, including Émile Durkheim, Lucien Lévy-Bruhl, Claude Lévi-Strauss, Raymond Aron, Henri Lefebvre, and Pierre Bourdieu, had their educational training and advanced degrees in philosophy and, for those working at universities, taught within departments of philosophy. But once both a *licence* and *Doctorat de troisième cycle* were approved in sociology in April 1958, it became possible for students interested in the theoretical study of society to completely avoid doing advanced work in departments of philosophy. In fact, according to Bourdieu and Jean-Claude Passeron, ten years after the creation of the *licence* in sociology, there were "in Paris as many students registered for this new degree . . . as there [were] candidates for the Degree in Philosophy."[32]

In addition to these institutional features that facilitated the emergence of structuralism in France, there is also an important philosophical development that was at work, one that had its analogue in the previous emergence of existentialism. For, as the transformation from spiritualism to existentialism was motivated by the discovery of three German philosophers—Hegel, Husserl, and Heidegger—a philosophical opening for structuralism was cleared by the rediscovery of three other German

thinkers, those named by Paul Ricoeur in 1965 the "masters of suspicion"—
Marx, Nietzsche, and Freud.[33] While these thinkers are more commonly associated with French philosophy after structuralism, it was really the structuralists' desire to locate the underlying structures of kinship, society, or the
unconscious that lead them to read Marx, Nietzsche, and Freud as kindred
spirits who sought to decipher the superstructural world in terms of underlying infrastructural relations of economic forces and class struggle, relations of normative forces and wills to power, and relations of psychic forces
and unconscious libidinal desires, respectively.[34]

The emergence of structuralism is often explained in terms of the appearance of several master thinkers—Lévi-Strauss, Lacan, Roland Barthes,
Althusser—whose work revolutionized how one thought about the human
sciences, psychoanalysis, literature, and Marx. That those thinkers who are
most closely identified with the so-called death of the subject should have
become themselves the subjects of fascination bordering on hero worship is
an irony that few have recognized. Some of these individuals—most notably
Lacan—certainly cultivated the mystique that surrounded them and used it
to further their theoretical projects. But that structuralism could emerge so
apparently quickly and eclipse the enormous intellectual presence of
Sartrean existentialism should not be explained by these cults of personality surrounding these master thinkers. While the stories recounting the
polemics between Sartre and Lévi-Strauss in their books[35] and the media,
or between Sartre and Althusser for the hearts and minds of young Marxist
students, have been retold for the past four decades, the focus on high visibility personalities obscures the impact of the institutional forces that were
at work and the personal interactions that took place in the French academy during the years that Sartre, Beauvoir, and *Les Temps modernes* were
so influential outside the academy.

In this history of the development of structuralism in France, a major
role is played by the Russian linguist Roman Jakobson (1896–1982). One of
the founders of the Moscow Circle and a leading figure of Russian formalism, Jakobson left Russia for Prague in 1920, and his turn away from for-
malist and toward structuralist linguistics is marked by the founding of the
Linguistic Circle of Prague (the "Prague School") in 1926. In his collabora-
tions with other linguists, most notably fellow Russian emigré Nikolai Trou-
betzkoy (1890–1938), he was largely responsible for the development of
phonology. It was in Prague that Jakobson first learned of Ferdinand de
Saussure's *Course in General Linguistics* (1916). In fact, while Saussure's
Course makes frequent reference to a science that will study language as a
"system," it was in Jakobson's presentation in Prague at the First Interna-

tional Congress of Slavists in October 1929 that the word "structuralism" first appears:

> Were we to comprise the leading ideas of present-day science in its most var-
> ious manifestations, we could hardly find a more appropriate designation than
> *structuralism*. Any set of phenomena examined by contemporary science is
> treated not as a mechanical agglomeration but as a structural whole, and the
> basic task is to reveal the inner, whether static or developmental, laws of this
> system.[36]

In 1941, Jakobson emigrated to the United States, where he taught first in New York at the École libre des hautes études. Jakobson's linguistic interests extended to ethnography and folklore and, in 1942, the dean of this French university-in-exile, fellow Russian émigré Alexandre Koyré, introduced Jakobson to another exile, Claude Lévi-Strauss. The two became friends, and from Jakobson, Lévi-Strauss learned the basic principles of Saussurean linguistics. More importantly, their encounters in New York led Lévi-Strauss to recognize that the Saussurean analysis of sign systems could be extended beyond linguistic sign systems. With this realization, structuralism as a general method of analysis began.

Jakobson played an equally important role in the career of Jacques Lacan, to whom he was introduced by Lévi-Strauss in Paris in 1950 and with whom he became good friends. Like Lévi-Strauss, Lacan first learned of Saussurean linguistics from Jakobson and, again like Lévi-Strauss, he quickly realized that the structuralist methods of linguistic analysis could be extended to psychoanalysis and the sign systems of the unconscious. Where Lévi-Strauss had argued, in *Structural Anthropology*, that "the kinship system is a language,"[37] Lacan, for his part, would claim that, for example, psychoanalytic interpretation is based "on the fact that the unconscious is structured in the most radical way like a language, that a material operates in it according to certain laws, which are the same laws as those discovered in the study of actual languages, languages that are or were actually spoken," and that "what the psychoanalytic experience discovers in the unconscious is the whole structure of language."[38]

Among the institutional forces that facilitated the rise of structuralism, and a factor that has not been sufficiently recognized, is the important academic positions during the fifties occupied by someone whose name is more commonly associated with the existentialists than the structuralists. I refer here to none other than Maurice Merleau-Ponty, who played a major role in the success of structuralism. In his teaching at the École normale, Merleau-Ponty encouraged his philosophy students to explore psychoanalysis, child psychology, and linguistics, and he was one of the first to indicate the importance of the work of Saussure. His 1951 lecture, "On the Phenomenology of Language," presented at the First International Phenomenology Colloquium in Brussels, credits Saussure for noting that the elements in a language do not individually signify anything and should not be considered as vehicles for the transmission of meaning; rather "each of them signifies only its difference in respect to the others . . . and as this is true of them all, there are only differences of signification in a language."[39] In his inaugural lecture at the Collège de France in 1952, he noted that the theory of signs that was developed in modern linguistics perhaps offers a conception of historical meaning that gets "beyond the opposition of *things* versus *consciousness*" and that Saussure "could have sketched a new philosophy of history."[40]

In addition to introducing the thought of Saussure into the academy, Merleau-Ponty was also a strong supporter of the work and career of Claude Lévi-Strauss. Shortly after his own election in 1952 to the Collège de France, he played a major role in Lévi-Strauss's election to the chair in Social Anthropology, and his subsequent essay, "From Mauss to Claude Lévi-Strauss," strongly defended Lévi-Strauss's reading of Mauss and his approach to anthropology while making clear Merleau-Ponty's own appreciation of what structuralism had to offer philosophy:

> This notion of structure, whose present good fortune in all domains responds to an intellectual need, establishes a whole system of thought. For the philosopher, the presence of structure outside us in natural and social systems and within us as symbolic function points to a way beyond the subject-object correlation which has dominated philosophy from Descartes to Hegel. By showing us that man is eccentric to himself and that the social finds its center only in man, structure particularly enables us to understand how we are in a sort of circuit with the socio-historical world.[41]

While Merleau-Ponty saw structuralism and phenomenology as compatible, with the former providing an objective analysis of underlying social structures that would complement the latter's description of lived experience,[42] the structuralists themselves were much less convinced of the need for or value of phenomenology as they engaged in their various structuralist enterprises. In part, this was due to their association of phenomenology with a philosophy of the subject, a philosophy that their theoretical antihumanism had to oppose. But in part, this was also a consequence of their polemic against the figure of Sartre, a figure associated with both existentialism and phenomenology and one who each of the four dominant structuralist thinkers chose to establish as the other (sometimes an other who looks more like a caricature of Sartre) against whom their theoretical projects were the required alternative. We thus find Lévi-Strauss, most notably in the closing chapter of *The Savage Mind* (1962)—a work we should recall that was dedicated "To the memory of Maurice Merleau-Ponty"—setting Sartre up as the definitive representative of humanism against whom he puts forward the rhetoric of the "death of the subject," writing that "I believe the ultimate goal of the human sciences to be not to constitute, but to dissolve man."[43] But we should also note that Althusser, Barthes, and Lacan all saw fit to challenge Sartre's hegemony as they put forward their own views.[44]

Let me close this section by returning to the point with which it began: although there was a clear polemic between the structuralists and Sartre, structuralism's replacing existentialism as the dominant intellectual paradigm in the early '60s had less to do with the charismatic force of a Lévi-Strauss, Althusser, or Lacan, or Lévi-Strauss's definitive victory in the polemic against Sartre, and more to do with other features of French academic institutions. That is to say, the legitimation of the human sciences within the academy and the turn away from philosophy in general that this legitimation facilitated, a turn furthered in part by Merleau-Ponty's own acceptance and introduction of structuralism within the centers of academic power, were the primary reasons for existentialism's fall from grace. And it was not just existentialism that suffered, nor was Sartre the only philosopher whose work was displaced by the challenge to philosophy raised by the advances in the human sciences. In general, the '50s and '60s saw philosophy turn away from questions of value, and for several decades, little attention was paid to the work of aesthetic thinkers like Mikel Dufrenne or ethical thinkers like Vladimir Jankélévitch (who for most of his twenty-six years at the Sorbonne was the only professor to hold a chair in moral philosophy) or Emmanuel Levinas. One might, as an aside, wonder whether the recent turn to ethics and religion in French philosophy is not itself a consequence of the turn away from Marxian political philosophy which for many years was the only normative philosophy tolerated in France and which was to some extent discredited both by the failure of the French Left to live up to the promise of May '68 and by the Left's disappointment with the Mitterrand presidency.

FRENCH PHILOSOPHY AS GALLIC HEIDEGGERIANISM, OR THE CULT OF PERSONALITY

I have already alluded to this last myth, so I will here only briefly address it by way of concluding that French philosophy is badly misunderstood if it is

seen simply as a succession of "master thinkers" who Oedipally destroy
their predecessors. Such a view, which some of the French "masters" themselves have clearly cultivated, tells the story of the French century as a story
in which Bergson is vanquished by the tough-nosed and phenomenologi-
cally informed *normaliens* Sartre and Merleau-Ponty, who themselves are
vanquished by the antihumanist structural horde led by Lévi-Strauss and
Althusser, only to give birth to a generation who will post them in the form
of new master thinkers like Derrida, Foucault, or Deleuze. At the very
least, such an Oedipal tale plays fast and loose with the generational history:
Merleau-Ponty, Sartre, Canguilhem, and Lévi-Strauss were all roughly the
same age (born between 1904 and 1908), while Althusser was closer in age
to Deleuze and Foucault than to Lévi-Strauss or Lacan. More importantly,
such a tale overlooks both the other "master thinkers" who the "official
story" now ignores—think, for example, of Brunschvicg, Marcel, Gilson,
Aron, Bachelard—while overlooking the impact that the "master teachers"
had on successive generations of students at the Sorbonne, École normale,
or École pratique des hautes études—again, Brunschvicg,[45] Alain, Wahl,
Koyré, Kojève, Canguilhem, Hyppolite, Desanti, Beaufret—as well as the
centralized educational system run by the Ministry of Public Instruction
(now the Ministry of Education) and monitored through the *agrégation*.

This cult of personality takes a particularly American form when the
dominant personalities are determined insofar as they can be framed as a
response and reaction to a number of significant German philosophical
thinkers. In particular, I would argue that the American reception of
French philosophy has grossly overestimated the role that Heidegger's philosophy has played, with the result that for much of the twentieth century,
French philosophy meant Sartre, and when it no longer meant Sartre, it
meant Derrida. While Sartre and Derrida are both significant philosophical
voices, they are not the only voices, nor were they ever the exclusive French
voices or, in Derrida's case, even a dominant voice. Because the American
reception has been so heavily invested in Heidegger and a certain version
of the phenomenological tradition, what has resulted is an almost total
blindness to important trends within French philosophy that are not
amenable to being framed as Gallic Heideggerianism.

Most notable here is the French epistemological tradition, represented by
Bachelard, Canguilhem, Cavaillès, and more recently, Michel Serres, a major French philosopher whose work is virtually ignored by American Continental philosophers. Serres, by the way, is the author of more than thirty
books, and is only the tenth philosopher to be elected to the Academie
Française since 1900, and the only one since 1979. The English-speaking

philosophical community's relative indifference and inattention to Serres is reflected as well by its failure to note that some of the most influential philosophers of the last two decades of the twentieth century work in what can only be called the analytic tradition. In fact, since Foucault's death in 1984, all of the chairs in philosophy at the Collège de France have been held by philosophers who work in the analytic tradition:[46] Jules Vuillemin, Gilles-Gaston Granger, Jacques Bouveresse, Anne Fagot-Largeault, and Ian Hacking, the last two the initial holders of new chairs created in 1999 in "Philosophy of the Biological and Medical Sciences" and "Philosophy and History of Scientific Concepts" respectively. Even more telling, since Merleau-Ponty's death in 1961, the only chairs in philosophy at the Collège de France held by philosophers who in the English-speaking philosophical world would be commonly associated with "French" philosophy were those occupied by Foucault (1970–1984) and Jean Hyppolite (1960–1968).

Beyond this blindness to the French epistemological tradition, there have been other consequences of the general view of philosophy in France as Gallic Heideggerianism that inform the way French philosophy has been read and taught in the last half of the twentieth century. Bergson, for example, has been largely overlooked, with the notable exception of those who follow Deleuze's work, for whom Bergson is an essential reference. And Deleuze, for his part, was "discovered" by English-speaking philosophers long after his impact on French thought was made. Where Derrida's early works of the '60s were translated into English usually within five to ten years of their appearance in France, Deleuze's major works took three to four times as long to appear in English. For example, Derrida's *Of Grammatology*, *Speech and Phenomena*, and *Writing and Difference*, all published in France in 1967, appeared in English translation six, nine, and eleven years later. By contrast, although Deleuze's early text on Proust appeared in English in 1972, eight years after its French publication, none of Deleuze's important historical studies of the 1960s (on David Hume, Nietzsche, Kant, Bergson, and Spinoza) appeared in English less than twenty-one years after their French publication, and his two major works, *Difference and Repetition* (1968) and *The Logic of Sense* (1969) appeared in English translation in 1994 and 1990, respectively twenty-six and twenty-one years after their French publication.[47] And while the translation of Deleuze's book on Proust was initially well-received and continues to be an important resource for scholars of French literature, his series of historical monographs on Hume, Nietzsche, Kant, Bergson, and Spinoza, which offer as significant a re-reading of modern philosophy as has appeared in recent years, is largely overlooked by those philosophers who consider themselves specialists in recent French philosophy. Even Foucault, who would be regarded as the most dominant philosophical presence in France in the latter half of the twentieth century, was initially far less enthusiastically read by American "Continental" philosophers than he was by historians, social scientists, and feminist theorists. In fact, much of the early *philosophical* reception of Foucault's works came precisely from philosophers whose interests were in feminist theory.[48] But the fact that feminist philosophers as well as other feminist theorists were interested in Foucault's work from its first appearance does not alter the fact that the "mainstream" Continental philosophical establishment and most of the large graduate programs in Continental philosophy were slow to warm to Foucault's importance; his position in these programs is far less important than the position of several other French philosophers who are more easily assimilated into the phenomenological-Heideggerian tradition, broadly construed.

One last significant philosophical development that has received little attention outside France, again because it does not fit the dominant model of what the English-speaking philosophical community considers "French" philosophy, is the work that brings a Spinozist approach to Marxian theory. This work reflects the long tradition of Spinoza scholarship in France in the twentieth century, beginning with Alain, Jules Lagneau, Delbos, and Brunschvicg,[49] and continuing in more recent years with the teaching and writing of Ferdinand Alquié, Martial Guéroult, Gilles Deleuze, and Louis Althusser.[50] Spinoza has been throughout the century one of the authors whose works were most often part of the required reading for the *agrégation*,[51] and while today the English-speaking philosophical world has all but given up on political theories that don't in some way ground themselves in Kant, whether in a Habermasian or Rawlsian guise, many of the politically engaged students who came under Althusser's influence in his years at the École normale have followed his turn away from Kantian transcendental philosophy and toward a Spinozist immanentism. One place to locate this turn from Kant to Spinoza is in terms of how the French Spinozists avoid the Kantian assumption that the individual autonomy of the isolated subject is the *summum bonum*, an assumption that leads to the modern idea that politics begins with the problem of balancing the rights of the individual against the needs of society. For Deleuze as well as French Marxists like Althusser, Alain Badiou, Jacques Rancière, Pierre Macherey, Pierre-François Moreau, Alexandre Matheron, or Étienne Balibar, the political attractiveness of Spinoza is in part because his metaphysics of the subject can avoid this problem by allowing the subject to see him or herself as *one* with the public rather than a *part* of the public. As Antonio Negri has argued, in a

book well-known in French philosophical circles, contrary to the rigid individualism that characterizes seventeenth-century thinkers like Hobbes,[52]
Spinoza understands human individuality constructing itself as a collective
entity.[53] "By singular things," Spinoza writes in the *Ethics*, "I understand
things that are finite and have a determinate existence. And if a number of
individuals so concur in one action that together they are all the cause of
one effect, I consider them all, to that extent, as one singular thing."[54] This
understanding of individual and collective, which Spinoza elaborates in his
political works in terms of his concept of the multitude,[55] departs from both
the Kantian and contract-theory traditions, and it has facilitated a continued
attraction to Marxian theory that one sees in the works of Badiou, Rancière,
Balibar, Macherey, and others. But insofar as these thinkers work out of a
tradition that is alien both to the Heideggerian-phenomenological tradition
that has dominated English-language Continental philosophy and to the
neo-Kantian tradition that dominates current English-language social and
political theory, their work has been all but ignored.

As I have tried to suggest throughout this chapter, were one familiar with
the institutions that govern philosophy and the indigenous developments in
philosophy in France in the nineteenth and twentieth centuries, it would be
harder to ignore some of the philosophical positions that have been obscured
by the English-language, and particularly the American reception, of a few
"master thinkers." While it might not be surprising for philosophy, which has
often understood itself to be the most transcendent of disciplines, to see itself
as distinct from the institutional practices that form its practitioners, it is
ironic that followers of trends in twentieth-century French philosophy, who
pride themselves on their attentiveness to history, should be guilty of the
same conceit.[56] And, to return to an idea suggested at the outset, I hope that
it is now clear that it makes sense to speak of "French philosophy" and mean
by that something more than simply the philosophy that is written in France
or in the French language. For while there may be no unifying themes that
describe what one would identify as uniquely "French" philosophy, there are
certain institutions—the *lycée* education and the *classe de philosophie*, the
preparation for and study at the École normale supérieure, the preparation
for and admission into the *agrégation*, the tradition of public instruction at
the University of Paris, the institutional practices at the Collège de France
and the École pratique des hautes études—that throughout the last century
and continuing to this day have marked the activity of philosophizing in
France. And these institutions have created a unique philosophical sensibility that does allow one to identify developments in "French philosophy" that
distinguish it from its German, British, and American counterparts.

Why so many of the English-speaking "specialists" in French philosophy are unaware of these institutions and their effects on French philosophical sensibilities is a question worth asking. As is the following: How much does the fixation with Heidegger, and with French philosophy as Gallic Heideggerianism, still explain who and what is read by English-language, and especially American Continental philosophers? What role does it play in the continuing fascination with Derrida and the recent celebrity of Levinas or Jean-Luc Nancy? And what role does it play in the continuing lack of attention to Deleuze and indifference to Serres, Bourdieu, or Badiou? I will leave these questions rhetorical, and close with the hope that more attention will be spent examining the academic institutionalization of philosophy in France, and in the United States, with rather less spent awaiting the next appearance of a master discourse from a master thinker.

NOTES

1. See Maurice Blondel's preface to Victor Delbos, *La Philosophie française* (Paris: Librairie Plon, 1919), i. In "Husserl: Sa critique du psychologisme et sa conception d'une Logique pure," *Revue de métaphysique et de morale* (1911), Delbos discussed the first volume of Husserl's *Logical Investigations*.

2. See Léon Brunschvicg, "Préface," in Georges Gurvitch, *Les Tendances actuelles de la philosophie allemande* (Paris: Librairie Vrin, 1930), 6.

3. See Pierre Macherey, "Y a-t-il une philosophie française?", in *Histoires de dinosaure: faire de la philosophie 1965–1997* (Paris: PUF, 1999), 313–22.

4. From 1921 to 1956, of the 1,082 students admitted into the ENS Lettres section, 799 (73.8 percent) did their *khâgne* in Paris, 283 in the provinces. And from Paris, 461 of those admitted did *khâgne* at Lycée Louis-le-Grand and 251 at Lycée Henri-IV. These figures come from *Revue universitaire* 65, no. 5 (November–December 1956): 290–91.

5. André Cheval, *Histoire de l'agrégation: contribution à l'histoire de la culture scolaire* (Paris: Éditions Kimé, 1993), 18. Most of the following details concerning the history of the *agrégation* come from this work.

6. For a fascinating discussion of the philosophy *agrégation*, see the proceedings of the May 7, 1938, meeting of the Société française de philosophie, which was devoted to this topic: "L'Agrégation de philosophie," *Bulletin de la Société française de philosophie* 38 (1938): 117–58. Participants included Brunschvicg, Désiré Roustan, Dominique Parodi, Célestin Bouglé, and Maurice Merleau-Ponty.

7. Arthur Schopenhauer, Friedrich Nietzsche, and Auguste Comte are the most frequent nineteenth-century thinkers on the *Programme*. Among twentieth-century philosophers whose oeuvre is required for the written examination, only

Henri Bergson appears prior to 1965 (four times in the 1950s); Gaston Bachelard appears in 1974 and 1975, and Edmund Husserl in 1994.

8. Angèle Kremer-Marietti, *Thèmes et structures dans l'œuvre de Nietzsche* (Paris: Lettres modernes, 1957).

9. Jean Wahl, *Vers le concret* (Paris: Vrin, 1932), 13. Although this text is comprised of three studies of James, Whitehead, and Marcel, the notes in the preface make clear that Wahl's orientation toward the concrete is guided by his reading of Martin Heidegger's *Being and Time*.

10. Alexandre Kojève, *Introduction to the Reading of Hegel*, ed. Raymond Queneau, trans. James H. Nichols, Jr. (New York: Basic Books, 1969), 20.

11. Sartre mentions Wahl's text as enjoying a "great success" among his generation in *Search for a Method*, trans. Hazel Barnes (New York: Alfred A. Knopf, 1963), 19.

12. Edmund Husserl, *Méditations cartésiennes: introduction à la phénoménologie*, trans. Gabrielle Peiffer and Emmanuel Levinas (Paris: Armand Colin, 1931). These "Cartesian Meditations" differ significantly from the further revised German text *Cartesianische Meditationen*, published following Husserl's death in 1950 as the first volume of Husserl's collected works: *Husserliana 1: Cartesianische Meditationen und Pariser Vorträge*, ed. Stephen Strasser (The Hague: Martinus Nijhoff, 1950/1973; English translation: *Cartesian Meditations: An Introduction to Phenomenology*, trans. Dorion Cairns [The Hague: Martinus Nijhoff, 1960]). Husserl was apparently not satisfied with the original French translation, which was strongly criticized by his former student Roman Ingarden (Ingarden's criticisms are published in *Husserliana 1*, 203–18), and this likely influenced his decision to rework the text before its eventual German publication as the first volume of the *Husserliana*.

13. Max Scheler, *Nature et formes de la sympathie: contribution à l'étude des lois de la vie émotionnelle*, trans. M. Lefebvre (Paris: Payot, 1928).

14. English translation: *The Paris Lectures*, trans. Peter Koestenbaum (The Hague: Martinus Nijhoff, 1964).

15. In the *Revue de métaphysique et de morale* 39 (1932), and *Revue philosophique de la France et de l'étranger* 115 (1933). For an account of Husserl's reception in France, see Gene H. Frickey, *The Origins of Phenomenology in France, 1920–1940* (Ph.D. diss., Indiana University, 1979). See also Herbert Spiegelberg, *The Phenomenological Movement: A Historical Introduction*, 3rd rev. ed. (The Hague: Martinus Nijhoff, 1982), 431–35.

16. Simone de Beauvoir, *The Prime of Life*, trans. Peter Green (New York: World Publishing Co., 1962), 112.

17. Jean Hyppolite, *Genèse et structure de la "Phénoménologie de l'esprit" de Hegel* (Paris: Aubier, 1946); trans. Samuel Cherniak and John Heckman as *Genesis and Structure of Hegel's Phenomenology of Spirit* (Evanston, Ill.: Northwestern University Press, 1974).

18. See Alexandre Koyré, "Rapport sur l'état des études hégéliennes en France," in *Études d'histoire de la pensée philosophique* (Paris: Éditions Gallimard, 1971), 225–49. The substance of Koyré's report is a discussion of some of the reasons why

French philosophy, which had welcomed Kant, J. G. Fichte, and Friedrich Schelling, had been so unreceptive to Hegel up to that point.

19. Maurice Merleau-Ponty, "Hegel's Existentialism," in *Sense and Non-Sense*, trans. Hubert L. Dreyfus and Patricia Allen Dreyfus (Evanston, Ill.: Northwestern University Press, 1964), 63. Merleau-Ponty's essay appeared originally in *Les Temps modernes* 1, no. 7 (April 1946): 1311–19. Two years later Georges Canguilhem makes a similar comment: "Contemporary philosophical thought is dominated by Hegelianism." Canguilhem, "Hegel en France," *Revue d'histoire et de philosophie religieuses* 27 [1948]: 284.

20. "Was ist Metaphysik?" appeared in *Bifur*, and "Vom Wesen des Grundes" appeared in *Recherches philosophiques*; both were published originally in German in 1929.

21. Herbert Spiegelberg, *The Phenomenological Movement: A Historical Introduction* (The Hague: Martinus Nijhoff, 1960), 2: 463 n. 2. Interestingly, this comment does not appear in the third revised edition of Spiegelberg's text, published in 1982.

22. Merleau-Ponty, *Phenomenology of Perception*, trans. Colin Smith (London: Routledge and Kegan Paul, 1962), viii.

23. I am not here able to address the place of existentialism prior to 1943. That story would show that Gabriel Marcel, and not Sartre, was thought by many to be the dominant French existentialist thinker of the thirties.

24. See, for example, Sartre's contribution to the emergence of post-colonial criticism in his prefaces for Frantz Fanon's 1961 *The Wretched of the Earth*, trans. Constance Farrington (New York: Grove Press, 1968), Albert Memmi's 1957 *The Colonizer and the Colonized*, trans. Howard Greenfeld (New York: Orion Press, 1965), and Léopold Senghor's *Anthologie de la nouvelle poésie nègre et malgache de langue française* (Paris: PUF, 1948).

25. Michel Foucault, "Introduction" to Georges Canguilhem, *The Normal and the Pathological*, trans. Carolyn R. Fawcett in collaboration with Robert S. Cohen (New York: Zone Books, 1991), 8–9.

26. One might wonder whether, outside France, the existential-phenomenological tradition's initial dismissal of structuralism and hostility toward poststructuralists like Foucault, Deleuze, or Derrida is related to its almost total lack of awareness of the role played by this "epistemological" tradition in the education of all students of philosophy at the Sorbonne or École normale supérieure from the mid-1940s onward.

27. Jean Cavaillès, "On Logic and the Theory of Science," in *Phenomenology and the Natural Sciences*, eds. Joseph Kockelsman and Theodore Kisiel (Evanston, Ill.: Northwestern University Press, 1970), 409.

28. See, here, Foucault's comment in the foreword to *The Order of Things* (New York: Random House, Inc., 1970), xiv, where he both denies that he adheres to the methods of structuralism and specifies phenomenology, insofar as it "gives absolute priority to the observing subject" and leads to a transcendental consciousness, as

the one (and only?) philosophical position toward which he has no sympathy. Cf. however the contrasting statement in Foucault, "What is Critique?", trans. Kevin Paul Geiman, in *What is Enlightenment? Eighteenth-Century Answers and Twentieth-Century Questions*, ed. James Schmidt (Berkeley: University of California Press, 1996), 390.

29. In 1962, Merleau-Ponty's chair was renamed the "Chair in the Philosophy of Consciousness" upon the election of Vuillemin, who held the chair until his retirement in 1990. After Foucault's death, his chair was redefined with the election of Granger in 1986 as the "Chair in Comparative Epistemology." Granger retired in 1991.

30. Sartre, *Search for a Method*, xxxiv. One should note, however, that Sartre refrains from using the adjective "*structurale*," which one finds in Lévi-Strauss's *Anthropologie structurale*, using instead what one might regard as a Heideggerian ontic term "*structurelle*."

31. Prehistory is defined in André Lalande's *Vocabulaire technique et critique de la philosophie* (Paris: PUF, 1928) as: "Part of history that is too ancient to be known by written documents or traditions, and that can only be induced from existing material traces, or reconstructed by reasoning from a priori considerations." See Michel Serres (with Bruno Latour), *Conversations on Science, Culture, and Time*, trans. Roxanne Lapidus (Ann Arbor: University of Michigan Press, 1995), 35. This explains, in part, why Merleau-Ponty and Foucault wrote their first works in conjunction with research in psychiatry and psychiatric hospitals, and why a number of the important French philosophers, including among others Jean Cavaillès, Gilles Deleuze, Michel Serres, and Alain Badiou, are familiar with and make use of advanced concepts in mathematics.

32. Pierre Bourdieu and Jean-Claude Passeron, "Sociology and Philosophy in France Since 1945: Death and Resurrection of a Philosophy without a Subject," *Social Research* 34, no. 1 (Spring 1967): 193.

33. See Paul Ricoeur, *Freud and Philosophy: An Essay on Interpretation*, trans. Denis Savage (New Haven: Yale University Press, 1970), 32. As was mentioned earlier, Nietzsche begins to appear on the *Programme* for the *agrégation de philosophie* in the late 1950s and 1960s. Charles Soulié suggests that his appearance might "constitute a concession of the *jury d'agrégation* to modernity" insofar as Nietzsche was the "most canonical" of the three "masters of suspicion." Charles Soulié, "Anatomie du goût philosophique," *Actes de la recherche en sciences sociales* 109 (October 1995): 12.

34. For a good account of what resources the structuralists found in Nietzsche, Freud, and Marx, see Michel Foucault, "Nietzsche, Freud, Marx," trans. Alan D. Schrift, in *Transforming the Hermeneutic Context: From Nietzsche to Nancy*, eds. Alan D. Schrift and Gayle L. Ormiston (Albany: SUNY Press, 1990), 59–67.

35. See in particular Sartre's *Search for a Method* and the concluding chapter of Claude Lévi-Strauss's *The Savage Mind* (Chicago: University of Chicago Press, 1966).

36. Originally published in the Czech weekly ČIN (31 October 1929), Jakobson cites this remark at the start of his essay, "Retrospect," in Roman Jakobson, *Selected Writings*, vol. 2 (The Hague: Mouton, 1971), 711.

37. Claude Lévi-Strauss, *Structural Anthropology*, trans. Claire Jacobson and Brooke Grundrest Schoepf (New York: Basic Books, 1963), 47.

38. Jacques Lacan, *Écrits*, trans. Alan Sheridan (New York: Norton, 1977), 147, 234.

39. Merleau-Ponty, "On the Phenomenology of Language," in *Signs*, trans. Richard C. McCleary (Evanston, Ill.: Northwestern University Press, 1964), 88.

40. Merleau-Ponty, *In Praise of Philosophy*, trans. John Wild and James M. Edie (Evanston, Ill.: Northwestern University Press, 1963), 54–55.

41. Merleau-Ponty, "From Mauss to Claude Lévi-Strauss," in *Signs*, 123.

42. See Merleau-Ponty, "From Mauss to Claude Lévi-Strauss," in *Signs*, 119.

43. Lévi-Strauss, *The Savage Mind*, 247.

44. See, for example, Louis Althusser's essay, "Marxism is not a Historicism," in Althusser and Étienne Balibar, *Reading Capital*, trans. Ben Brewster (London: NLB, 1970), 119–44, or his "Reply to John Lewis," in *Essays in Self-Criticism*, trans. Grahame Lock (London: NLB, 1976); Roland Barthes, *Writing Degree Zero*, trans. Annette Lavers and Colin Smith (New York: Hill and Wang, 1968); or Jacques Lacan, "The Mirror Stage as Formative of the Function of the I as Revealed in Psychoanalytic Experience," in *Écrits*.

45. To take just one example here of the sort of influence certain figures had within the very closed French academic world: in the 1919–1920 academic year, every student at the École normale supérieure who was to take the *agrégation* lists taking Brunschvicg's course on "La conscience." Centre d'accueil et de recherche des archives nationales [CARAN], Paris, carton AJ/61/192.

46. While I am characterizing these philosophers as "analytic," this means something different in the French context than the American one. Where Anglo-American analytic philosophy has since its beginnings been committed to empiricism and a method of linguistic analysis grounded in (both formal and informal) logic, the French philosophical tradition has since Descartes been more comfortable with rationalism than empiricism, and with mathematics rather than logic. As a consequence, while both French and Anglo-American philosophy in the twentieth century can be characterized as having made a linguistic turn, both Vuillemin and Granger are, as Pascal Engel has noted, for different reasons not easily situated within more mainstream analytic philosophy. Engel, "Continental Insularity: Contemporary French Analytical Philosophy," in *Contemporary French Philosophy*, ed. A. Phillips Griffiths (Cambridge: Cambridge University Press, 1987), 6–7.

47. Even more striking is the reception of Derrida's later works, which often appear in English before they appear in French or are translated almost immediately after their French publication, and would seem to have a far larger audience of English than French readers.

48. I am thinking here of the work of people like Linda Alcoff, Sandra Bartky, Judith Butler, Nancy Fraser, and Jana Sawicki, among others.

49. Alain [Émile-Auguste Chartier], *Les Philosophes* (Paris: Delaplane, 1901); Victor Delbos, *Le Problème moral dans la philosophie de Spinoza et dans l'histoire du spinozisme* (Paris: F. Alcan, 1893); Léon Brunschvicg, *Spinoza* (Paris: F. Alcan, 1894), and *Spinoza et ses contemporains* (Paris: F. Alcan, 1923).

50. Ferdinand Alquié, *Nature et vérité dans la philosophie de Spinoza* (Paris: Centre de documentation universitaire, 1965), and *Le Rationalisme de Spinoza* (Paris: PUF, 1981); Martial Guéroult, *Spinoza*, vol. 1, *Dieu (Éthique, I)* (Paris: Aubier-Montaigne, 1968), and *Spinoza*, vol. 2, *L'Âme (Éthique, II)* (Paris: Aubier-Montaigne, 1974).

51. From 1900 to 1958, Spinoza's texts, sometimes in French and sometimes in Latin, were part of the program for the *concours* thirty-one times. Only Plato and Kant (who appear almost every year), Aristotle (44 times), Descartes (41 times), Leibniz (33 times), and Hume (32 times) appear on the program more frequently. The somewhat unexpected presence of Hume is in part a consequence of selections from Hume's *Treatise on Human Nature* being a choice for the English-language oral explication every year from 1946 to 1958. Spinoza's centrality to the French canon should be compared to his role in American philosophical instruction, where he is by far the most often marginalized or overlooked among modern philosophy's "Gang of Seven": Descartes, Leibniz, Spinoza, Locke, Berkeley, Hume, and Kant.

52. C. B. Macpherson's *The Political Theory of Possessive Individualism: Hobbes to Locke* (Oxford: Clarendon Press, 1962) is the *locus classicus* for this account of individualism in seventeenth-century thought.

53. Antonio Negri, *The Savage Anomaly: The Power of Spinoza's Metaphysics and Politics*, trans. Michael Hardt (Minneapolis: University of Minnesota Press, 1991), 135.

54. Benedict de Spinoza, *Ethics*, Book II, Definition 7.

55. See Negri, *The Savage Anomaly*, 194–210; and Étienne Balibar, "Spinoza, the Anti-Orwell," in *Masses, Classes, Ideas: Studies on Politics and Philosophy Before and After Marx*, trans. James Swenson (New York: Routledge, 1994), 3–37.

56. Soulié comes to a similar conclusion at the end of his "Anatomie du goût philosophique."

2

AGAINST CAPITALISM?
FRENCH THEORY AND THE ECONOMY
AFTER 1945

William Gallois

This chapter investigates connections between the French economy and theory in the postwar period through a concentration on the theme of capitalism. A resistance to capitalism was a major premise of much postwar French thought, but it is the suggestion of this chapter that the nature of that resistance was remarkably vague and elusive, and in most cases uninterested in the specificities of French capitalism. I do not wish to suggest that French economists and social scientists ignored the particularities of French capitalism, but, rather, that many partisans of what has become known as "French theory" offered evasive appraisals of the domestic scene. This indistinctiveness of French theoretical writing on capitalism afforded it a certain global currency, but it also allowed for a convenient coalescence in France, in both political and theoretical circles, around the idea that France and the French economy were *not quite capitalist*.[1] This alliance of ambivalence was most obvious in the Fifth Republic, when both Charles de Gaulle and many French theorists used the language of Marx to speak publicly "against capitalism." There existed, of course, a major disjuncture between such statements on de Gaulle's part and the dynamism of the technocratic capitalist economy he supervised. My suggestion here is that the *"anti-capitaliste"* stance adopted by de Gaulle, and many theorists, had been conceived in the nineteenth century as a means of describing the particular *dirigiste* form of capitalism that developed in France. In this chapter I will suggest that Jean-François Lyotard has been unique among French theorists in his attendance to this conceit that France is somehow *not quite capitalist*.[2]

This chapter therefore draws out links between the manner in which the remarkable success of postwar French theory and the French economy were bound together in their ambivalent stances toward capitalism. It traces the movement of a particular French idea of capitalism from its origins in the nineteenth century, and its development as a frequently unacknowledged French way of practicing capitalism, through a more direct articulation of this particularly French compromise under de Gaulle, to its seeming demise in the 1980s, and its evident continuance well beyond that decade.

In developing this argument, I will clearly not be able to look at particular theorists or the French economy in as much detail as I would like, so I hope that this chapter will be seen as an initial sketch of a curiously ignored problem in French intellectual history. The justification for this current volume is the idea that a new intellectual space has opened up "after the moment of French theory," which provides an opportunity for theoretically attuned historians to return to interrogate that culture which provided them with many of the tools for their critical practice.

In order to clarify the approach of this chapter, let me say that in using the term "French theory" I mean to refer to that group of postwar French writers whose work—which tends to both cross disciplines and be applied across disciplines—managed to be both globally successful and to take part in a common conversation in France that moved through various stages of Marxism, phenomenology, structuralism, post-Marxism, psychoanalysis, feminism, and post-structuralism. In other words, this cast of French theorists includes Jean-Paul Sartre, Simone de Beauvoir, Maurice Blanchot, Louis Althusser, Pierre Macherey, Jacques Derrida, Lyotard, Michel Foucault, and Jean Baudrillard. While there are major differences among the work of such writers, it is the contention of this chapter that in spite of a common opposition to capitalism, the resistance of many of these writers tended to be defiantly unspecific and uninterested in the particularities of the French capitalist economy. As we shall see, the major exception to this rule was Lyotard, and it is through his work that I criticize the tendency of such French writers to prefer the safety of theory to an engagement with the very distinct capitalist culture they saw around them.

THE CURIOUS ABSENCE OF CAPITALISM
FROM FRENCH THEORY

One can, I think, say with some confidence that most French theorists have been "against capitalism." Conceived of as the economic laws of the free market, capitalism has obviously been rejected as a dehumanizing system, a means of structuring inequality in modern societies, and a force that has blocked the development of better ways of organizing human cultures. Such sentiments underpin the politics of many theoretical texts, and it would seem reasonable to believe that an opposition to capitalism has been a tenet of French theory.[3] Such a position clearly meshes with the broad political orientation of theory to "the Left" in the postwar period, and the development of educational cultures in the social sciences and humanities (in philosophy most of all) where an understanding of Marx was regarded as essential in the grounding of a certain unified form of intellectual.[4]

Capitalism, we might also note, would seem to have been an ideal subject matter for French theory, since the best forms of the critique of capitalism could aspire to merge the theoretical (looking at the conceptual architecture of capitalism as an economic and social system), the practical (descriptions of the way in which actions in society can be read as capitalist—and, potentially, anti-capitalist—political action), and the personal (how the actions of the writer relate to the broader organizing system of the society). As French critical theory and philosophy were essentially concerned with the phenomenological and ontological questions which arose from consideration of the connections between selves, texts, and the world in the postwar period, what better object of study could there have been than capitalism?

Yet, in spite of its worldwide success, postwar French theory has not generally been successful in developing new or compelling descriptions or critiques of capitalism. There are many possible reasons as to why this has been the case:

a. Postwar French theorists tended to have little education in economics and presumed a knowledge of certain strands of Marxist critique to be equivalent to a more general understanding of economics.
b. The aspiration of theory toward generality provided convenient reasons why the specific situation of French capitalism could be ignored. Conversely, the belief in capitalism as an increasingly global phenomenon served as another justification for non-specific forms of criticism, and certainly proved a self-serving prophecy as the generality of French theory acquired global recognition.
c. Much theory was, of course, about theory. When one revisits classic French Marxist theoretical texts from the postwar period, it is in many ways impressive how involved the works are in a common conversation, and how interconnected are their arguments.[5] Yet it is also striking how

the realm of theory takes precedence over the social and economic realities of France at that time.

d. In the critique of "master narratives" (Lyotard's *grands récits*), certain elusive and poetic qualities have been prized in French theoretical writing. While such qualities have sometimes offered novel views of capitalist culture, the prized isolation of such ideas has blocked more relentless forms of critique.

e. This observation also points to a broader issue which is that the philosophical orientation of so much French postwar thought was epistemological, and driven in the case of much structuralist and poststructuralist thought by attempts to question the very bases of theory and intellectual work. There is no denying the importance of such writing, but it is clear that such stances implied that social and political questions would be better addressed after the regrounding of theory upon sounder epistemological foundations. A more sympathetic view would be to suggest that French theory, though antifoundational, believed it could address social and political questions through epistemological ones.

f. The Cold War posed a difficult problem for French theorists since there was an instinctive reluctance to be seen to be too close to the orbit of either the Soviet Union (with its political repression neutering its value as a direct opponent of capitalism) or the United States (with its repressive foreign policy and crassly seductive culture, as well as its notionally laissez-faire capitalist economy). In the face of such a choice, French theory conceived of itself as operating in an *other* position (in spite of the pretty serious ontological problems this raised), analogous to de Gaulle's "third way" between capitalism and socialism. A shared sense of "grandeur" accompanied these cultural and political positions.

g. It might even be argued that the curiously consensual attitude toward capitalism among postwar French political classes generated a situation in which it was relatively hard for theorists to know what they were reacting *against*. When confronted by heads of state such as de Gaulle who used Marxist language to criticize capitalism, in a way with which many theorists must have felt comfortable, one can understand why a certain vagueness on the subject of capitalism—or a concentration on "structural questions"—seemed attractive.

h. French theory's failure to confront capitalism adequately might simply be indicative of a broader failing of the academy to seriously advance understanding of capitalism in the postwar period. We might

ask how much more advanced the analysis of capitalism has become
since Marx, and whether the disciplinary structure of the modern
academy has afforded the opportunity to develop comprehensive critiques of capitalism. It does not seem hard to argue that the more unified thinkers of the period 1850–1900 deepened our understanding of
capitalism far more than thinkers of the twentieth century.

Before moving on to consider some common misconceptions regarding
French capitalism, I want to make it clear that while this chapter is critical
of French theory's abnegation of real engagement with capitalism, it is not
my intention to criticize French theory more generally, or to ignore the very
real gains that it made in areas such as phenomenology, psychoanalysis,
feminism, and literary analysis.

WRITING THE HISTORY OF FRENCH CAPITALISM

It has proven far easier for historians to write the history of French capitalism in the nineteenth century than it has to describe that phenomenon in
the twentieth century. It is in fact remarkable how rarely the *specificity* of
France's capitalism has been invoked in studies of the twentieth century as
compared with its predecessor.[6] I do not mean to say that capitalism itself—
as a broader, global phenomenon—has been systematically ignored in
French culture, but that there almost seems to have been an assumption
that the economy, society, and culture of modern France cannot quite be
described as capitalist. Various reasons might be advanced for this, most
centered on the particular orientation of the *dirigiste* French state, and its
wide involvement in the control and direction of the French economy. Yet
the adoption of such a critical position is completely untenable in that it
confuses capitalism as a form of pure economic theory (where free trade
and the invisible hand rule over all) with the reality of capitalism as practice
(which includes a place for strong states, whose actions are not wholly motivated by drives to growth and profit).

If it was the case that French national culture was somehow assured by
prevalent anti-capitalist ideas in the postwar period, then it is interesting to
ask where this commonality of interests came from. The answer to that
question, I think, lies partly in the specific political conditions that per-
tained to Western Europe at the end of World War Two, but mainly to the
particular character of French capitalism that had developed since the revolutionary period.

In discussing the European political climate in 1945, I am referring to that continental instinct which saw that an opportunity existed for the remaking of European societies along new lines after the traumas and losses of the war. The global fight for freedom against fascism and the roles played by mass populations in that victory needed to be reflected in new social and political institutions that would somehow more fully reflect the ideals for which the Allies had fought. In Britain this was demonstrated by the surprising electoral victory of the Labour Party in 1945, the establishment of the National Health Service, and the nationalization of coal and many other key industries. In France, one might say that the Fourth Republic attempted to bring to fruition that vision of an energetic, reforming state that had been articulated by the Popular Front in 1936–1938, and, of course, so disparaged by the wartime Vichy government of collaboration.[7] Yet we should also acknowledge that the wave of nationalizations and labor reforms which emerged in the immediate postwar period also had their roots in the established political classes' fear of the strength of the Parti communiste française (PCF).

However, the will to temper the excesses of free-market capitalism and the enthusiasm for the state's place in directing the market in France in 1945 were not solely functions of the new political space opened up at a time of liberation. They were also restatements of a traditional French stance toward the development of a capitalist society in which the state played a major role as a producer, director, and regulator of the economy. This system had arguably emerged in the revolutionary period and had then been refined through the nineteenth century.

Looked at in a very general economic and cultural sense, one might make the claim that the key shift inaugurated by the French Revolutions of 1789 and 1793 was the move from an autocratic economy to an economy where power was more broadly dispersed, in other words, to a capitalist economy. It was, after all, in France that the term *capitaliste* had emerged in the late eighteenth century to describe those new bourgeois figures who preferred a culture of risk and financial speculation to the Ancien Régime's intentionally undynamic supervision of an economy where wealth was held in the form of land, the stability of which was prized over its potential to generate extraordinary profits.[8] This is not the place to look in more depth at class-based interpretations of the revolutionary period,[9] but what does need to be remarked upon is the legacy of that period in terms of the Napoleonic synthesis of (1) the bourgeois drive to expansion and an economy of risk, with (2) a powerful, centralizing political state.

A nineteenth-century example of the particularity of the development of French capitalism can be found in the establishment of the national railway network.[10] Following the British example, railway building began in France in the 1830s and accelerated in the following decades. At the inception of the railways a fascinating series of debates took place in the Chambre des Députés regarding the structure and development of a national rail network. These discussions were especially interesting for the insights they revealed into the strange alliances that went into making up what would become the rather consensual character of French *dirigiste* capitalism—conflicts between capital and organized labor notwithstanding. In the 1830s, the belief of the deputies was that there was a central political and economic choice to be made in the case of the establishment of a railway system between the establishment by private entrepreneurs, on the one hand, or by the state, on the other hand. Those in favor of private financing could generally be described as liberals, while against them were arrayed a formidable alliance of socialists, centrists, and nationalists. Socialists (such as Pierre-Joseph Proudhon) and nationalists naturally made the statist case on different grounds: with the nationalists emphasizing national security and foreign policy priorities (in other words, fear of Prussia) and the socialists highlighting the need for the state to control the commanding heights of the economy in order to combine growth with social justice.

Ultimately, what would become a familiar synthesis was arranged for the railways, in which the statists won out in terms of organization, while private enterprise prospered in terms of the distribution of revenues. The French railway network was to be planned and directed by the state, with individual lines run by private concessions for fixed-term periods. Yet the aim of this solution was certainly not the creation of a free market in rail provision, for it quickly became apparent that an oligopoly of six firms was being established to operate the regional branches of the French railway system. This cartel had the support of the French government—evidently many of its personnel came from the political elites—and in a short space of time, a very French solution to the problem of railway development had been found.

What was interesting about this technocratic French solution (which we can see in many of the other French oligopolies of the nineteenth century, such as coal and department stores) was that while it was seen as an effective arrangement in many ways, it could clearly be criticized on the grounds of economic and other inefficiencies.[11] In fact, once developed, the major inefficiency of the network was perceived to be its very poor safety record, which critics such as Pierre Larousse attributed to the cartelization of the railways in France, the interpenetration of governments and railway companies by elite figures, and the lack of competition in the market as compared with other industrializing countries.[12]

POSTWAR FRANCE

A question which therefore arises in postwar French intellectual history is whether the governments of de Gaulle and the Fourth and Fifth Republics changed or developed French capitalism in any new ways. It is the contention of this chapter that they did not really do so, and that it was not coincidental that the moment which saw the rise and predominance of French theory took place at the same time as the ultimate refinement of French *dirigiste* capitalism. The two phenomena coincided temporally and spatially. It should thus not be seen as surprising that there was a relative decline in the status of French theory at precisely that time, under François Mitterrand's tenure and especially after 1989, when the "French solution" to capitalism seemed to be increasingly incapable of dealing with new problems in the global capitalist economy.[13]

Looking back on the economic history of the postwar world, it does seem remarkable how little credit France received for its economy's consistent outperformance of other industrialized nations, especially given France's traditional reputation as a "blocked society," or *"société bloquée,"* and the difficulties the French political classes had in dealing with the economic crises of the 1930s.[14] Taking economic growth as a key indicator, France can be seen to have outperformed other G7 states consistently in the postwar period, right until the early 1980s.[15] In the period 1960 to 1967 the French annual growth rate was 5.4 percent, as compared with a G7 average of 5.0 percent (with the latter figure incorporating the exceptional growth of Japan); from 1968 to 1973 France moved even further ahead of the G7 average, with its rate of 5.5 percent as against the G7 average of 4.4 percent; while in the more globally depressed markets of the 1970s, France grew at 2.8 percent each year in the period 1974–1979, as compared with 2.7 percent across the G7 states. While such a measure only assesses relative performance—and it might be claimed that France found itself starting from a lower base position than her rivals in 1945—it is clear that the *trente glorieuses* of the postwar period (as the years of economic boom between the Liberation and the oil crisis of 1973 became known) were ones of spectacular economic performance. My assertion is that the extent of the postwar French economy's success and the role played by the particular character of French capitalism in that success have been underestimated and understated outside of France, notably among devotees of French theory.[16]

In the immediate postwar period it was clear that anti-capitalist sentiment was motivated by a desire to create a new French political economy that avoided the lethargy and the partisanship of politics and economic management of the interwar period, while allowing for national solutions to economic problems which originated outside France. Policies of nationalization and other such strategies were also intended to neuter the unprecedented political support received by the PCF in the immediate postwar period. In a sense, such tempered forms of state socialism represented a rare engagement with ideology in French politics, for in spite of the appearance of a political system containing a wide spectrum of political views, it can be suggested that in the nineteenth and twentieth centuries, French political culture was decidedly *apolitical* in many ways— that is, not captivated by systematic ideologies. Compared with neighboring countries such as Germany and Great Britain, France had traditionally experienced governments that were reactive in nature, rather than driven by ideological programs, and other than the burst of anticlerical legislation of the 1870s, it had been remarkable how little the early French republics had sought to change France. We might call this the legacy of the Radicals, for that party summed up the existence of a political culture where battles were fought on local issues and personalities, rather than in the realm of ideas or idea-driven politics.[17]

It has been argued that the introduction of more ideologically driven politics contributed to the collapse of the Third Republic, for there seems little doubt that the explicitly leftist Popular Front coalition of 1936–1938 undertook a program of social change unprecedented in modern France.[18] However, equally driven ideological forces of rightist reaction of the 1930s were to contribute to that regime's downfall. That collapse was, of course, quickly followed by catastrophic defeat in World War Two and the creation of the Vichy regime, which sought ideological vengeance against the spirit of the Popular Front. It was in this context, then, that the Fourth Republic came into being after a time of unusual ideological foment in French politics. Nationalizations and the elaboration of the *dirigiste* state could be justified both in terms of the expanded political scope offered by this ideological atmosphere, and also by recourse to more traditional French technocratic strategies where governments took the major role in the direction of the national economy.[19]

Had that spirit of the early Fourth Republic continued for a longer period of time, perhaps the regime would have lasted rather longer than thirteen years. Interestingly, in addition to particular problems such as Algeria, the Fourth Republic ultimately collapsed because of a willingness of French political classes to return to the rather apolitical culture of the pre-Popular Front period. Once the threat of the PCF began to recede, French politicians retreated to parties founded upon personality and instinct, rather than any coherent ideological foundations. De Gaulle himself withdrew from politics after the foundation of the Fourth Republic.

This notion of a political culture beyond ideology—of a politics beyond politics if you like—found its intellectual counterpart in the career of the theorist Alexandre Kojève.[20] Before World War Two, Kojève had led one of the most influential philosophical seminars in twentieth-century France. He taught Hegel's *Phenomenology of Spirit* at the École pratique des hautes études to some of the most important figures of interwar and postwar intellectual life, including Raymond Queneau, Jacques Lacan, Georges Bataille, and reportedly, Jean-Paul Sartre.

The originality of Kojève's reading of the *Phenomenology* was founded on his identification of a very specific form of teleology in Hegel's writing, in which the "End of History" came at that time when the ultimate form of political organization was founded in the modern nation-state. According to Kojève, Hegel had identified this moment as taking place in 1806 when—in defeating the Prussians—Napoleon had overcome the final serious rival to the hegemony of the model of the French revolutionary state as the basis for national politics in Europe and, ultimately, the world.[21] Hegel was not claiming that the Napoleonic state was a perfect realization of a political end-state, but his assertion was that its being founded upon democratic ideas institutionalized a concept that would ultimately be impossible for other political systems to ignore, for in some significant ways democracy was a more perfect and satisfying form of political organization than any of its rivals. Now, this is not to say that Kojève believed that Hegel was enthusiastic about such changes, merely that he regarded them as inevitable.

The relevance of this description to the argument of this chapter comes in the fact that after World War Two, Kojève concluded that Hegel had been right in identifying an End of History in which a post-political culture would emerge, but simply wrong in his dating of the event. After the defeat of the Nazis and the containment of the communist bloc, Kojève reasoned that it was much more apt to claim that an End of History and a post-ideological era had begun after World War Two. To this end, the prewar philosopher abandoned intellectual work in the academy to become one of the founding architects of the European Union while working at the French Ministry for Economic Affairs. Kojève concluded that the chief responsibility of the intellectual in the post-historical age was to assist in the development of states and structures which could best manage democracies. In effect what this project could also justify was a form of politics that accepted capitalism as an economic corollary of democracy and that

viewed the essential task of politics as being the assurance of economic stability and growth.

When Kojève's admirer, Francis Fukuyama, restated his mentor's thesis
in 1990, there was considerable disquiet from across the academy with the
idea that history could be "ended."[22] Yet if we now look back at postwar
Europe there does not seem any real reason for favoring Fukuyama's date
for the End of History over that of Kojève. Crucially, in terms of the thesis of this chapter, Kojève propagated the idea that capitalism was a social
system that could only be ameliorated and managed, rather than challenged and replaced. Whether the acceptance of such an idea came
through a reception of Kojève's work or not, one characteristic of postwar
French engagement with capitalism was its tendency to criticize capitalism
in theory, but to not truly be *against capitalism in practice*. Again, my focus here is not on those in industry, government, unions, and parties who
certainly contended with the practical-policy dimensions of the French
economy, but on those many whose criticized capitalism in theory while
overlooking the uniqueness of the French situation. In France, intellectuals worked in a culture where political elites were often dismissive of capitalism in the public sphere, even if one might contend that the realities of
French economic growth did not quite square with such rhetorical resistance to capitalism.

CHARLES DE GAULLE AND CAPITALISM

Charles de Gaulle's belief in the possibility of finding "third ways" between
conventional, polarized political choices could be seen in a range of areas:
in his opening of a distinct French foreign policy between the positions of
the Cold War foes, in his initial aim to enable an "Algerian solution" that lay
between independence and French rule, in his conception of a presidency
"beyond politics" and a shift away from the destructiveness of party politics,
and, of course, in his belief that France could enjoy an economic and social
system between and beyond capitalism and communism. In all these fields,
de Gaulle's basic pragmatism was somewhat hidden by the grand idealism
with which he managed to imbue the idea of third ways and uniquely
French solutions.

In the case of capitalism, we might question to what extent de Gaulle's
opposition to it, and his intention to move beyond it, were ever translated
into policies which would have achieved those goals. After all, de Gaulle
supervised a good deal of perhaps the most dynamic period of French

twentieth-century economic growth, and looked at cursorily, this growth would seem to have been achieved by precisely the kind of technocratic capitalism which had been developed in France in the early nineteenth century, with the government playing a major role in facilitating the formation of limited numbers of relatively uncompetitive enterprises, and in fact acting as a leading producer in its own right.

Where de Gaulle did perhaps differ from his predecessors was in his ability to theorize and speak clearly about the particularity of this French solution to capitalism:

> Capitalism says: the level of general social well-being will rise in a society driven by the profit motive, for this drive generates more and more wealth, which is then distributed by the free market. Yet we must recognize that the property and profits generated by the capitalist system return only to the holders of capital! Those without wealth find themselves in a state of alienation, inside a system which they contribute to making. I say to you, "No, capitalism does not offer a satisfying solution to the organization of human society."[23]

In essence, all de Gaulle is doing here is restating a Marxist critique of capitalism, yet his solutions to the iniquities of this system which produced so many layers of alienation were evidently very different to those envisioned by Marx. Where Marx ultimately foresaw the abandonment of capitalism, de Gaulle's "third way" was essentially meliorist in its attempt to harness the power of capitalism through state direction of production and the valorization of the concepts of "participation" and "association." These latter concepts were realized as policies in the Fifth Republic—in terms of the development of greater worker involvement in industrial decision-making, and through political referenda—though it seems hard to conclude that the French public of the 1960s saw such policies as offering a true way of life outside capitalism.[24] More realistically, one might say that the social and work-based reforms introduced by de Gaulle institutionalized many of the aspirations to social involvement and cohesion of the Popular Front, serving as an equivalent process to that period of Liberal social reform in 1900s England, after which there was little option of wholly returning to the excesses of the era of monopoly capitalism. Thus, the relatively strong culture of workers' rights apparent in contemporary France can be said to have some of its roots in de Gaulle's policies.

Looking back, however, at economics texts from the 1960s, it is plain that the French mode of capitalism was seen by outsiders as being unusual. Vera Lutz, for instance, notes:

> We have seen that in France, even during the long period of stable govern-
> ment under the Fifth Republic, the *régime* has so far hesitated to make a clear
> choice between liberalism and *dirigisme*, or between "classical" capitalism and
> some more "modern" form of capitalism. Instead, it has sometimes appeared
> to be moving in one direction, sometimes in the other, and sometimes in both
> at once.[25]

In fact, Lutz's description of French capitalism's moving in the direction of
liberalism and *dirigisme* "both at once" in the Fifth Republic seems a ver-
dict that could have been applied to the history of French capitalism more
generally. Lutz was, though, surely right in her assertion that pressure
would be placed on this compromise, with calls for "clear choices" in order
to move toward some "more 'modern'" form of capitalism. One might argue
that the moment at which that pressure was realized was during the first
years of François Mitterrand's presidency when, after a decade of major
exogenous shocks, the French compromise began to lose its comparative
advantage over other states. At that point Mitterrand found himself in a position whereby his move toward a more "modern" *dirigisme* was rejected by
global financial markets more convinced of the "modern" qualities of
Reaganomics and neo-liberalism.

   While most French theoretical writing at that time avoided the specificities of this particular capitalist culture in France (concentrating primarily
on the general structures of capitalism and modes of interpreting such
structures), the work of Jean-François Lyotard and Pierre Bourdieu addressed French capitalism in much more concrete detail. Significantly, both
writers had produced a great deal of work on Algerian society and were able
to see the particularity of French culture from a comparative perspective.[26]
   Lyotard's work is unusual among French theorists for the way it addressed in a systematic fashion both capitalism in theory and the specificities of French capitalism from the 1960s to the present. Capitalism is everywhere in Lyotard's writing, though—in the manner of language in Ludwig
Wittgenstein's thought—the universality of capitalism does not mean that
its description is obvious, for there are many frustrations that come from
describing what is all around us. In addition to his attendance to changes in
French capitalism, Lyotard is unique in his identification of the connections
between de Gaulle's limited anti-capitalism, the French model of *dirigiste*
capitalism, and theory's tendency to avoid the realities of French capitalism
through generalization. These themes came together in his essay, "The
State and Politics in the France of 1960."[27]

There Lyotard stresses an underlying economic motivation behind the major changes in France and Algeria between the Fourth and the Fifth Republics, claiming that de Gaulle's re-ascension to power and his formation of a much more personalized regime were driven by a desire to modernize the interests of the French economy in favor of what Lyotard describes as "big capital."[28] Lyotard centers both "the Algerian crisis" and the move from the Fourth to the Fifth Republics around problems in French capitalism. Specifically, he alleges that de Gaulle's Fifth Republic was formed as a means of renewing French capitalism—which had gone astray under the Fourth Republic—and abandoning France's position at the head of an economically uncompetitive empire.[29]

According to Lyotard, it was the Algerian question that ultimately served as a motor for change, since, there, the starkness of the choice facing French capitalism was clearest. There one saw that, "The adversary that big capital had to defeat immediately was not the working class, but the bloc of the colonels and the extreme right." The threat posed by such forces was the cost to the nation of fully integrating Algeria "into the *métropole*"—with the creation of a market from "Dunkirk to Tamransett"—when France's economic resources would have been better devoted to competing with "the modern capitalist countries," which were of course mostly unburdened of their empires by this time.[30]

In other words, "big capital" saw a choice between the consequences of integrating Algeria fully into the French economy or integrating France into that European market which Kojève had already identified as a historical end-state. Writing in 1961 Lyotard was confident that, "in the absence of a massive intervention of the workers, French capitalism is capable of carrying out a transition to the structure required of the modern world."[31]

THE MARKETS AGAINST MITTERRAND

The "modernization" of French capitalism along lines envisaged by Lutz and Lyotard in the 1960s took place in the early 1980s.[32] François Mitterrand was elected on an interventionist, *dirigiste* mandate, but he found himself confronted with both a major global recession and financial markets firm in their belief that Keynesian, *dirigiste* strategies were not a "modern" option for capitalist development. This ultimately forced Mitterrand's government to reverse its inclinations, and it appeared as though France was being pushed into the new, global orthodoxy of the neo-liberal, mixed capitalist economy.

Such decisions came as no surprise to Lyotard who had forecast in 1961 that "the socialists will clash head-on with hostile owners and managers of capital; they will have to give up after two years, once they have lost the confidence of their electoral constituency, and the hour of Jacques Chirac will have come."[33] Chirac's accession to power took slightly longer than Lyotard had imagined, but his central predictions about the changing character of French capitalism were, of course, absolutely correct, and they were intimately connected to those changes in the French political economy which he had described in the 1960s.

The jolt that came from the realization of France's place in the global capitalist sphere in the early 1980s began a refiguration of capitalism in French theoretical writing.[34] Writing about the 1970s formation of one of French theory's great American presses, *Semiotext(e)*, Sylvère Lotringer later commented, "What happened is that we forgot that capitalism even exist[ed]. It ha[d] become invisible because there [wa]s nothing else to see."[35] Such paradoxical claims that capitalism became more invisible as its omnipresence grew became less and less tenable when it became increasingly apparent that the character of French capitalism seemed to change rapidly during the Mitterrand presidency. Yet Lyotard's work remained unique in France for the manner in which it maintained its relentless focus on capitalism. Equally distinct, as Hans Bertens observes, was the manner in which Lyotard's theoretical orientation from the 1950s to the 1980s was diametrically opposed to that of French theory in general: where theory moved from a central concern with "language and structure" to concerns with "power and desire," Lyotard moved in the opposite direction.[36] Yet Lyotard's shift toward questions of language and structure did not signify an abnegation of the specific (French capitalism) in favor of the general (global capitalism), as I am suggesting had been the case in much French theory before the 1980s.

When Lotringer expressed a certain futility at capitalism's invisible universality, Lyotard set out to generate a conceptual description of the structures of capitalism in France, and capitalism more generally, by deploying the thought of writers such as Sigmund Freud and Wittgenstein. Such critics helped Lyotard describe capitalism in a fashion which reflected both its systemic qualities and the lived experience of capitalist society. By the 1980s Lyotard had arguably followed Kojève in seeing capitalism as an end-state, albeit one which he believed could be transformed if only it could be better understood. This was made plain in the 1982 essay "The Differend," where he argued that "the logic of capital is essentially the logic of *Capital*, without its dialectical framework."[37] In other words, one

might say that Lyotard advocated a belief in Marxian economics without a
faith in Marxist politics. He went on to say that he did "not mean that there
are no contradictions in the functioning of the capitalist economy but only
that nothing results from these contradictions that signifies or announces
the obsolescence of capitalism."[38]

Yet Lyotard's realism as to the seeming permanency of the capitalist condition did not preclude liberational tendencies in his writing. Like Wittgenstein's work on language, Lyotard's work on capitalism is full of frustration
at the difficulties that arise from trying to see one's subject clearly, but also
a sense of hope in the ability of critical work to demystify the subject. Unlike Kojève, Lyotard believed in the possibility of theory generating resistance to capitalism, but unlike most French theorists, he used notions of
epistemology and "self-reflexivity" not as means of evading a real engagement with French capitalism (with the excuse that such branches of theory
revealed the imperfections of "naive" action), but as realistic starting points
for the critique of the political economy of France and Canada.[39]

Wittgenstein's writing on language provided Lyotard with an epistemological solution to the phenomenological doubt that plagued most French
theory.[40] Wittgenstein's notion of the "language game" stressed the specificity of local action, but it did this in a way that connected speech to a
larger world of practice that could be conceived in rough, conceptual terms,
even if it could not be seen through a clearer, theoretical lens. This model
of language served a double purpose for Lyotard: it served as a means of in-
vestigating capitalism, and it also mirrored the structure of capitalism, in
which local actions form part of a larger system which is ill-defined by theoretical writing.[41]

In making these observations, Lyotard described a similar target of investigation as that confronting other French theorists, but his approach and
the heritage which he drew on to generate that approach set him apart from
French theory more generally. Taking Baudrillard as an example, one can
certainly identify major differences between his and Lyotard's writing
against capitalism, even though they had been cast notionally not only as
French critical theorists, but as fellow postmodernists or poststructuralists.
Where Lyotard follows Wittgenstein in sharing a faith in the knowledge that
can come from the analysis of ordinary language,[42] Baudrillard follows "the
Saussure of the anagrams, where words seem to emerge mysteriously, and
almost magically, through the letters, which is more in keeping with the way
language works."[43] Where Lyotard can still conceive of theory as a means to
change (however difficult this might be), Baudrillard seems more concerned in clarifying the ontological status of man and his thoughts with the

world through a decisive rejection of the possibility of there being connections between the "theoretical" and the "real."[44] Theory, according to Baudrillard, must become more thoroughly detached from the impure character of the present, for "It must tear itself from all referents and take its pride only in the future. Theory must operate on time at the cost of a deliberate distortion of present reality."[45] The nihilism of such claims—which serve as an extreme representative of a major trend within French theory—make an interesting contrast to the specificity of the present in Lyotard's writing on capitalism from the 1960s to the 1990s. While it is true that Baudrillard and Lyotard share commonalties both in terms of their stress on "language and structure" and the potentially mystificatory belief in a "spirit of capitalism," they are in the end separated by hope; more specifically, Baudrillard's lack of intellectual hope, and the hope which both feeds into and comes out of Lyotard's commitment to reading the capitalism of his present.

WAS THERE A NEW WORLD AFTER 1989?

For French capitalism, as was the case in other Western states, the 1980s were a decade of considerable change. While in the 1970s global crises were cushioned by the country's continued outperformance of its economic rivals, the following decade seemed to confirm the inexorable move toward the kind of "modern," liberal capitalism noticed by Lutz in the early 1960s. The decade began with a global recession and the abandonment of Keynesian orthodoxies, and it ended in a collapse of the Soviet bloc that was commonly interpreted as a victory for neo-liberal capitalism. Kojève's End of History seemed to be progressing on many fronts, for as well as the fall of communism/victory of capitalism, there was an expansion of the European Union and a reorientation within leftist parties away from Marxist or socialist rhetoric and toward aspirations for good societies that were to be achieved through prudent economic management. Historians of French capitalism, such as Patrick Fridenson and André Strauss, were able to assert that, "In a short space of time, everything has changed. No longer are international norms and constraints denied: the *dirigiste* state has been called into question, while the ideas of competition, free enterprise, and management are being viewed more positively."[46]

The drive in France to liberalize economically was undeniably strong, for after decades of outperforming her rivals, the French economy barely grew in the 1980s, and it began to lag behind other Western economies (in the period 1980–1988 France grew at 1.9 percent p.a. against a G7 average of

2.8 percent).[47] In addition to this cycle of low growth, France began to suffer high levels of long-term unemployment and regional malaises of a kind that had been unknown in the earlier postwar period, and for which the nation was not prepared in the manner that it had been in previous global crises. In earlier recessions, such as that of the early 1930s, there is considerable evidence that the country's huge agricultural sector initially eased the impact of recession, as unemployed workers moved to the country to live with relatives or to undertake casual agricultural work. Of course, by the early 1980s, such options no longer existed, for while France had been the last of the major Western powers to have more than half of its workforce in agricultural production, by that time France's patterns of employment were roughly similar to those of other major Western economies.[48]

Yet if we look at France from the 1990s and at the question of whether serious shifts took place within French capitalism that moved the country decisively away from *dirigisme* toward liberalism, one might begin to wonder whether the "modern" capitalism of the 1980s might not simply have been a recasting of the traditional French capitalist solution.[49] In other words, were Fridenson and Strauss right to assert that "Everything ha[d] changed"?

While there have been privatizations in France from the 1980s onward, it is still the case that the French state has a relatively unusually high level of involvement in areas of industry such as defense and power production as well as a major stake in emblematic firms such as France Telecom, Air France, and Renault.[50] Although membership in the European Union has lowered trade barriers, France has argued hardest for the protection of cultural industries (in France and in Europe more generally) in trade rounds with the United States, with an explicit defense of the Habermasian notion of the separation of social spheres, and the need to ensure that the laws of the market are not allowed to penetrate the cultural sphere.[51] Similarly, while neo-liberals were relentless in their insistence that the "freeing of labor markets" and the relaxation of workers' rights were essential in the generation of fast-growing, competitive economies, it has been France which has defended most vocally the virtues of the thirty-five hour working week, which arguably makes sense not only in terms of quality of life issues, but also in the attempt to reduce long-term unemployment and to expand the size of the labor force. It should also be noted that there have been signs of considerable dynamism in the twenty-first century French economy, especially as compared with states such as Germany and Japan, which also enjoyed postwar economic miracles.[52]

In many ways the collapse of the Soviet Union and revived debates on the End of History were easier to deal with in French theory than in other European cultures. Given the fact that Marxism had undergone a sustained critique in France from psychoanalytic and feminist theoretical perspectives, given the crucial place that was accorded a rejection of the "*grands récits*" in poststructuralist thought, and given the undermining of Marxism in post-Marxist debates on totalitarianism, it was perhaps not surprising that 1989 was perceived as less of a challenge to the theoretical status quo in France than in other Western states.[53]

In fact, the atmosphere of the 1990s was in some way reminiscent of the 1960s in that there was again real political interest in maintaining a distinct brand of capitalism in France, and again a sensation that there was a commonality of interest between political and intellectual classes in their being against capitalism; or, as we should now say, being against a particular liberal brand of capitalism. I am not arguing that there was a planned or public confluence of ideas; instead I want simply to point out the convenient character of the manner in which two seemingly divergent cultural groups arrived at the same critical position.

At this very moment of accommodation, one also began to see a variety of French critical theorists discover the analysis of capitalism as a subject, in part because of its novel visibility after the end of the Cold War. Chief among the theorists taking a more public, engaged stance on political questions, and most especially on capitalism, was Jacques Derrida. In *L'Autre cap* (whose name plays on the many linguistic allusions of the word "cap," not least that of ending and capitalism, and thus the reputed capitalist end of history), Derrida throws off the relatively apolitical nature of his earlier work, to talk of "the need for a new culture which will invent another way [*une autre manière*] of reading and analyzing *Capital*, Marx's book, and capital in general."[54] Such a statement can be read with varying degrees of cynicism. Interpreted in a positive fashion, one might applaud the spirit of resistance of Derrida when he wrote those words in 1991, for at that time he stood, as a representative of deconstruction and French theory more generally, in opposition to the seemingly utterly dominant neo-liberal orthodoxy then loudly and globally proclaiming its victory as an end-state in intellectual and politico-economic terms. Yet if one were to adopt a more skeptical reading of this grand demand of Derrida's for a "new culture," one might question why it was not until 1991 that this issue had become pressingly important. Was it not the case that the rediscovery of capitalism, and the loud claims for new readings and understandings of it, served both to cloak the relative failure of French theory's analysis of capitalism and also to justify the idea that there truly had been some kind of "End of History" in 1989? In *L'Autre cap*, Derrida went on to stress the novelty of the post-1989 world, calling for "courage and lucidity in a new critique of the new effects of capital," yet one might fundamentally challenge such a view by asking what really was new about French or global capitalism after 1989.[55] Following Lyotard's critique of capitalism—which had always sought to connect theory to the realities of French capitalism—one could build a much more convincing case that what has been needed in the period since 1989 have been readings of French capitalism that stress its continuities and its resistance to change.

CONCLUSION

In the absence of a significant literature on the history of postwar French capitalism, this chapter has sought to show that there have been considerable continuities in the structure of French capitalism in and beyond this period, and to suggest that French theory's general failure to critique capitalism partly derived from a certain commonality in the stances toward capitalism by French political and cultural spheres. Theorists such as Lyotard have worked from a number of directions to try to engender more specific critical theories of capitalism, but such work has had relatively little impact compared with the influence of those diverse voices which seem to have either called for or tacitly accepted a distinctly French form of capitalism.

   In the postwar period many theoretical voices have implicitly accepted Hegel and Kojève's teleology, and it is for this reason that when we review the history of postwar French capitalism, it appears rather more consistently "modern" than many critics believed at the time. France arguably had a post-ideological and a post-political state[56] well ahead of more general Western trends moving in those directions, and in economic terms the French capitalist synthesis looks far more mainstream in 2004 than it did in the 1980s, now that the vigor of neo-liberalism in Europe has somewhat waned.

NOTES

   1. For a more general Marxist critique of the convenient proximity of French political and intellectual elites see: Nicos Poulantzas, *State, Power, Socialism*, rev. ed. (London: Verso, 2000), 61–62.
   2. Jean-François Lyotard's writing on French capitalism initially came partly from his involvement with the Socialisme ou Barbarie group whose leading members also included Claude Lefort and Cornelius Castoriadis. There was certainly no absence of

specific readings of French capitalism in the group's journal, which ran from 1949–1965, and among the various publications of the circle's adherents. A very useful introduction to the range and specificity of the group's work can be found in: Cornelius Castoriadis, *Capitalisme moderne et révolution*, 2 vols. (Paris: Union générale d'éditions, 1979). My intention in this chapter, however, is to concentrate on Lyotard's reading of French capitalism from the 1960s to the 1990s. Without wanting to diminish the achievements of the *Socialisme ou Barbarie* group, my suggestion is that Lyotard's work on French capitalism had great breadth and depth in its connection of theory with empirical observation over such an extended period of time.

3. See, for example, Louis Althusser, Jacques Rancière, Pierre Macherey, Étienne Balibar, and Roger Establet, *Lire "Le Capital,"* 2 vols. (Paris: Maspéro, 1965); Pierre Macherey, *Pour une théorie du production littéraire* (Paris: Maspéro, 1966); and Jean-Paul Sartre, *Critique de la raison dialectique* (Paris: Gallimard, 1960).

4. I do not mean to imply that all French theory was Marxist, merely that an engagement with Marx was regarded as being central to postwar theorists (in an intellectual and personal sense in most cases, especially from the 1960s). Marx was, as Sartre put it, "the unsurpassed horizon" for French thought.

5. For example, Althusser, *Pour Marx* (Paris: Maspéro, 1965); or Althusser et al., *Lire "Le Capital."*

6. For the nineteenth century see: Pierre Guiral, *La Vie quotidienne en France à l'Age d'Or du capitalisme 1852–1879* (Paris: Hachette, 1976); Charles H. Pouthas, *Démocraties et capitalisme (1848–1860)* (Paris: PUF, 1948); Guy P. Palmade, *Capitalisme et capitalistes français au XIXe siècle* (Paris: Armand Colin, 1901); and Walter Benjamin, *Paris: capitale du XIXe siècle: le livre des passages* (Paris: Les Éditions du Cerf, 1989).

7. I am grateful to Julian Bourg for helpfully pointing out the Gaullist desire to renew France and to lay the foundations for a "new man" at the Liberation.

8. Raymond Williams, *Keywords* (London: Fontana, 1983).

9. Georges Lefebvre, *The Coming of the French Revolution*, trans. R. R. Palmer (Princeton: Princeton University Press, 1947). Albert Soboul, *The French Revolution, 1787–1799: From the Storming of the Bastille to Napoleon*, trans. Alan Forrest and Colin Jones (New York: Vintage, 1975).

10. For a more detailed treatment of this theme see William Gallois, *Zola: The History of Capitalism* (Bern: Peter Lang, 2000).

11. See Charles E. Freedeman, *The Triumph of Corporate Capitalism in France, 1867–1914* (Rochester, N.Y.: University of Rochester Press, 1993), 130.

12. See the essay on "Les chemins de fer," in Pierre Larousse, ed., *Grand Dictionnaire Universel du XIXe siècle* (Paris: Larousse, 1866–76).

13. An alternative date might be 1984, the year in which Michel Foucault died and in which Mitterrand turned away from *dirigisme* toward privatization.

14. Michel Crozier, *La Société bloquée* (Paris: Seuil, 1971).

15. Economic growth data taken from: online.stcharles.ac.uk/courses/business/economic_growth.htm (11 March 2004). For another positive account of French

economic performance in the nineteenth and twentieth centuries, see Raymond Aron, *France Steadfast and Changing: The Fourth to the Fifth Republic* (Cambridge, Mass.: Harvard University Press, 1960).

16. See also Jean Fourastié, *Les Trentes glorieuses* (Paris: Pluriel, 1975).

17. Gordon Wright, *France in Modern Times*, 5th ed. (New York: W.W. Norton, 1995), 246–47.

18. Wright, *France in Modern Times*, 363–65.

19. In 1946 industries such as coal, gas, and electricity, as well as major banks and insurance companies, were nationalized, and a new social security system was introduced. Wright, *France in Modern Times*, 402.

20. A very good reading of Kojève's work is found in Perry Anderson, *A Zone of Engagement* (London: Verso, 1992), 309–24.

21. Alexandre Kojève, *Introduction à la lecture de Hegel: leçons sur la Phénoménologie de l'Esprit* (Paris: Gallimard, 1947), 172.

22. See, for example, Christopher Bertram and Andrew Chitty, eds., *Has History Ended? Fukuyama, Marx, Modernity* (Aldershot, Eng.: Avebury, 1994).

23. Charles de Gaulle, *Discours et Messages*, 5 vols. (Paris: Omnibus/Plon, 1993), 5: 1088.

24. Wright, *France in Modern Times*, 415–17.

25. Vera Lutz, *Central Planning for the Market Economy: An Analysis of the French Theory and Experience* (London: Longman, 1969), 187.

26. While I will concentrate on the work of Lyotard in this chapter, mention should be made of Bourdieu's long-standing engagement with French capitalism, which also bridges theory and commentary on French capitalism. See, for example, Pierre Bourdieu, ed., *La Misère du Monde* (Paris: Seuil, 1993); and John Lechte, *Fifty Key Contemporary Thinkers: From Structuralism to Postmodernity* (London: Routledge, 1994), 45. Other French theorists whose work on capitalism is undoubtedly of great value, in spite of their tendency toward critiques of capitalism in general, rather than works capitalism in France include: Guy Debord, *La Société du spectacle*, 3rd ed. (Paris: Gallimard, 1992); and Gilles Deleuze and Félix Guattari, *A Thousand Plateaus: Capitalism and Schizophrenia* (London: Continuum, 1988). On a specific, though anthropological, level, Georges Bataille's work on expenditure, general economy, and gifts is also of considerable importance. See *The Bataille Reader*, eds. Fred Botting and Scott Wilson (Oxford: Blackwell, 1997).

27. Jean-François Lyotard, *Political Writings* (London: UCL Press, 1994), 252–76.

28. Similar observations on the interpenetration of political and economic elites in France can be found in the work of Lyotard's forebears: Emile Zola, Charles Baudelaire, and Walter Benjamin.

29. Lyotard, *Political Writings*, 253.

30. Lyotard, *Political Writings*, 254.

31. Lyotard, *Political Writings*, 257.

32. The gap between the prediction of "modernization" and its actual arrival might be partly explained by some combination of global economic trends, the time lag be-

tween the critique of Keynesian orthodoxies in economic theory and its acceptance within mainstream politics, and the force of the events of 1968, which encouraged, for some and if only rhetorically at times, adherence to statism over liberalism.

33. Lyotard, *Political Writings*, 257.

34. Although I am concerned here with the evasion of French capitalism in particular kinds of theoretical texts, there have been a number of works of popular economics in France over the past thirty years which have addressed French capitalism directly. See, for example, Henry Coston, *Les 200 familles au pouvoir* (Paris: Henry Coston, 1977); Alain Cotta, *Le Capitalisme dans tous ses états* (Paris: Fayard, 1991); Viviane Forrester, *L'Horreur économique* (Paris: Fayard, 1996); and Alain Minc, *www.capitalisme.fr* (Paris: Grasset, 2000).

35. Chris Kraus and Sylvère Lotringer, *Hatred of Capitalism: A Semiotext(e) Reader* (Los Angeles: Semiotext(e), 2002), 8.

36. Hans Bertens, *The Idea of the Postmodern: A History* (London: Routledge, 1995), 134.

37. Lyotard, *Political Writings*, 8.

38. Lyotard, *Political Writings*, 8.

39. Lyotard, *The Postmodern Condition: A Report on Knowledge* (Manchester: Manchester University Press, 1984).

40. See Lyotard, *Political Writings*, 21–22: "It should be easily understood that the principal difficulty is neither that of the state nor of 'civil society,' as is often thought, but consists in the functioning of capital, which is a regime of linking phrases far more supple and far more 'inhuman' (oppressive, if you will) than any political or social regime. Wages, profits, funds for payment and credit, investment, growth and recession, the money market: it would indeed be interesting to analyze these objects as moves or rules proceeding from various language games. And what if capital were a multiform way of dominating time, of linking?"

41. I realize that the claimed differences between the "conceptual" and the "theoretical" may seem tendentious here, but it is clear that for Wittgenstein the abandonment of theory need not imply the rejection of all modes of general interpretation. I also want to note that Lyotard's emphasis on language did not preclude his interest in the notion that there was a particular "spirit" of capitalism. See Lyotard, *Political Writings*, 25. It seems to me that this particular notion represents one of the most problematic aspects of Lyotard's analysis of capitalism and an area scarcely differentiated from the work of other theorists. Conversely, while an emphasis on language might seem to connect French theory in general and Lyotard in particular, I would argue that Lyotard's adoption of a Wittgensteinian "linguistic turn" marked him out from his French contemporaries.

42. Some might argue that an equivalent might be Foucault's stress on the local in his micro-politics.

43. Lechte, *Fifty Key Contemporary Thinkers*, 233.

44. Jean Baudrillard, "Why theory?" in Kraus and Lotringer, *Hatred of Capitalism*, 129–31.

45. Jean Baudrillard, "Why theory?" in Kraus and Lotringer, *Hatred of Capitalism*, 130.

46. Patrick Fridenson and André Strauss, eds., *Le Capitalisme français XIXe–XXe siècles: blocages et dynamismes d'une croissance* (Paris: Fayard, 1987), 7.

47. online.stcharles.ac.uk/courses/business/economic_growth.htm (11 March 2004).

48. Wright, *France in Modern Times*, 259.

49. Fridenson and Strauss, *Le Capitalisme français*, 8.

50. www.eurofound.eu.int/emire/FRANCE/NATIONALIZATION-FR.html (11 March 2004).

51. www.lib.bke.hu/gt/2000-4/towse.pdf (11 March 2004). See also Philippe Poirrier, "French Cultural Policy in Question, 1981–2003," in this volume.

52. In the year 2000, France enjoyed economic growth of 3.6 percent. www.pbs.org/wgbh/commandingheights/lo/countries/fr/fr_economic.html (11 March 2004).

53. See Bertram and Chitty, eds., *Has History Ended?* for evidence of the agonizing in British Marxist circles over the fall of the Berlin Wall and the implications of Fukuyama's "End of History."

54. Jacques Derrida, *L'Autre cap* (Paris: Éditions de Minuit, 1991), 56. See also, Derrida, *Specters of Marx* (London: Routledge, 1994).

55. Derrida, *L'Autre cap*, 56.

56. By "post-political" I mean a political state where parties are generally driven by practical and personal questions, rather than by ideological or theoretical debate. Politics is thus conceived as a limited form of social and economic management, rather than as a means of social transformation.

3

THE POST-MARX OF THE LETTER

Warren Breckman

In a late text, Louis Althusser urged his readers to give "the crisis of Marxism" a "completely different sense from collapse and death." Instead of writing the epitaph for Marxism, he insisted, it was necessary to show "how something vital and alive can be liberated by this crisis and in this crisis."[1] This missive went unanswered by Althusser's French readers, and in fundamental ways it remains unanswered in French to this day. Indeed, by the time Althusser dispatched his call in 1977, the French intelligentsia was in "the process of full de-Marxification."[2] With the left-wing parties and unions compromised by their response to the events of May 1968, the 1970s had witnessed the fragmentation of the Left followed by the near wholesale collapse of the miscellany of Maoists, Trotskyists, *autogestionnaires*, anarchists, and so on. The leading edge of radicalism had passed to the philosophers of desire and the postmodern critics of normativity, metanarratives, and metaphysical "humanism." The podium of moral declamation had been seized, albeit briefly, by the ex-Marxist *Nouveaux Philosophes*, while more quietly and more profoundly, the ground was shifting toward liberal democratic pluralism, a sea change that would thrust into prominence older figures like Claude Lefort and François Furet and prepare the way for younger talents like Marcel Gauchet and Pierre Rosanvallon. In such a climate, not only was Althusser's call unheeded, but also his once extraordinarily influential brand of structural Marxism, his so-called theoretical practice, was permanently eclipsed.

If the call went unanswered in France, it was heard in England; or at least the spirit of a call that was not Althusser's alone animated a great deal of English intellectual labor of the late 1970s and 1980s. The contrast between the two intellectual cultures during that period is striking. For even though the post-1968 British Left entered a period of crisis that only escalated with the success of Thatcherism in the early 1980s, the desire to liberate something "vital and alive" from this crisis remained powerful. Perhaps the most original, intellectually engaging, and influential of all such efforts was Ernesto Laclau and Chantal Mouffe's 1985 book *Hegemony & Socialist Strategy*. Yet it was undoubtedly also one of the most controversial, for Laclau and Mouffe sought to restore the theoretical dignity of Marxism by articulating a "post-Marxism without apologies."[3] Their double gesture of going beyond Marxism while incorporating it as a legacy and moral compass—signaled concisely in their claim to be both "*post*-Marxist" and "post-*Marxist*"—thematized the ambiguity of their intervention in relation to the various discourses that claimed patrimony from Marx. Yet another ambiguity resided in the fact that Mouffe and Laclau sought to rethink leftist politics using precisely the poststructuralist conceptual tools that in France had operated simultaneously as cause and symptom of the collapse of Marxist politics in the 1970s.

Laclau and Mouffe's post-Marxism belongs to the intellectual history of France after 1968, and that for two reasons: first, because they continued a trajectory launched in France but all but fully arrested there; and second, because the deflection of that trajectory into England offers an outstanding example of both the persistent importance of local context *and* the ultimate insufficiencies of the national paradigm in the study of intellectual history.[4] When we are dealing with a project firmly grounded in French poststructuralism, addressed to the international crisis of the Left, and articulated in Paris by a Belgian woman educated in France and in England by her husband teaching at the University of Essex and drawing on his formative political experience in the Argentinian Left, the question arises, just where *is* "French" thought in the decades after 1968?

THE INTERNATIONAL CAREER OF HEGEMONY

When Jacques Derrida addressed Marxism's collapse in his 1993 book *Specters of Marx*, he spoke of a sense of déjà vu that made the question of Marxism's fate resonate like "an old repetition."[5] Similarly, Mouffe and Laclau placed themselves in relation to a genealogy of distress within Marxism. As Laclau emphasized in a 1988 interview in response to Robin Black-burn, "post-Marxism" is not a deviation from a pure source, but a radical-ization of "the ambiguity of Marxism—which runs through its whole his-tory" and is present even in Marx himself. "The act of constitution of post-Marxism is not different from its genealogy: that is, from the complex discourses through which it has been gradually gestating, including the Marxist tradition."[6] A substantial part of *Hegemony & Socialist Strategy* is devoted to this genealogical reconstruction of the conflict in twentieth-century socialist thought between a deterministic social metaphysics grounded in the essentialist categories of class and economy and the con-tingencies and exigencies of historical existence. Gramsci holds pride of place in this history because of his radical reworking of the idea of hege-mony that he had inherited from Russian debates about the gap between the "necessary laws of history" and the actual political demands of the Rus-sian situation. Gramsci's emphasis upon the importance of consent in the formation of bourgeois domination shifted the proletarian struggle onto the ideological terrain of civil society; at the same time, his conception of the materiality of ideology identified ideology not merely with ideas or mental representations, but with "an organic and relational whole, embod-ied in institutions and apparatuses, which weld together a historical bloc around a number of basic articulatory practices. This precludes the possi-bility of a 'superstructuralist' reading of the ideological."[7] Finally, and most importantly for Mouffe and Laclau, Gramsci's recognition of the historical and contingent character of the working class's assertion of its claims and identity subverted the essentialist determinist logic of Marxist thinking about class. Gramsci thereby pointed toward a new recognition of "social complexity as the very condition of political struggle," and thus his concep-tion of hegemony "sets the basis for a democratic practice of politics, com-patible with a plurality of historical subjects."[8]

Laclau and Mouffe's appropriation of the Gramscian concept of hege-mony came as they distanced themselves from their earlier attachment to Althusser. In an online interview in 1998, Mouffe, who had been a student of Althusser's in Paris, explained that "I became a Gramscian when I ceased to be an Althusserian." Gramsci offered her a way out of an "Althusserian kind of dogmatism" that Althusser's followers were then putting into prac-tice.[9] Laclau's attachment was more tenuous than that of his wife. Although the theory of ideology offered in his 1977 book, *Politics & Ideology in Marxist Theory*, contains a strong Althusserian dimension, Laclau empha-sized in a 1988 interview that it was only insofar as Althusser seemed to sub-vert the totalizing character of Marxist discourse that his work attracted him. This disruptive resource lay in Althusser's "overdetermined contradiction," a concept of psychoanalytic provenance that opened the way for Laclau and Mouffe's break with the economistic reductionism of classic Marxism. Yet, as Laclau has often noted, the non-reductionist theory suggested in Althusser's *For Marx*, the 1965 collection of his articles from the early 1960s, was belied by the tendency toward a closed structuralist system already discernible in *Reading Capital*, also published in 1965.[10] Given Althusser's increasing rigidity, Laclau maintained in the 1988 interview, it was not surprising that the Althusserian school "had little time to mature intellectually in a post-Marxist direction—the '68 wave created a new historical climate that turned obsolete all that analytical-interpretative lucubration around Marx's holy texts; but in the second place . . . the Althusserian project was conceived as an attempt at an internal theoretical renewal of the French Communist Party—a project that gradually lost significance in the seventies."[11] Althusser's own development may have been arrested by both his own internal impasses and the development of post-1968 politics, but Laclau acknowledged that "a great deal of my later works can be seen as a radicalization of many themes already hinted at in *For Marx*."[12] The recovery of Gramsci played an indispensable dimension of this process of radicalization.

In thus turning to Gramsci, Laclau and Mouffe were in fact participants in an international surge of engagement with the Italian theorist. In England, the influence of Gramsci can be found as early as the post-1956 thaw, when de-Stalinization and the formation of the New Left found a resource in the 1957 edition of *The Modern Prince and Other Writings*.[13] The cultural and historical analysis pioneered by scholars like Raymond Williams and Edward Thompson drew on Gramsci, as did Tom Nairn and Perry Anderson's theoretical analyses of the British state and the labor movement. In the mid-1970s, Gramsci's influence strengthened, as Gramscians gained considerable influence in the British Communist Party and played a crucial role in the emergence of a Eurocommunist majority at the party's Thirty-Fifth Congress in 1977. On a different plane, the cultural Marxist appropriation of Gramsci begun by figures like Thompson and Williams gained new momentum in cultural and media studies, most importantly at the Centre for Contemporary Cultural Studies at Birmingham University and the Popular Culture group at the Open University. Surveying the continent in 1977, Chantal Mouffe and Anne Showstack Sassoon argued that the end of the 1960s marked an important turning point in French and Italian Gramscian studies because the parochial and dogmatic treatment of Gramsci as the theorist of the Italian Communist Party had broken down. Freed from the narrow reading of the

Italian communists, Gramsci had emerged as the "theoretician of the revolution in the West." Mouffe and Sassoon reserved special praise for the works of Leonardo Paggi and Christine Buci-Glucksmann, who offered compelling readings of Gramsci as the theorist of the superstructures. Even more importantly, both Paggi and Buci-Glucksmann used Gramsci to criticize Althusser's insistence upon distinguishing "ideology" and "science" as well as his characterization of Marxist philosophy as the "theory of theoretical practice." Gramsci rejected the notion of philosophy as a "science with a specific object" and recognized philosophy as a vital political action in the ideological struggle.[14] In Mouffe and Sassoon's reading, Gramsci emerges as a kind of post-Althusserian. As Mouffe wrote, "If the history of Marxist theory during the 1960s can be characterized by the reign of 'Althusserianism,' then we have now, without a doubt, entered a new phase: that of 'Gramscism'."[15] In Britain, too, the decline of Althusserianism coincided with the rise of Gramsci, as structuralist analysis gave way to awareness of the need for historical modes of analysis to account for the "surging conservative revival coalescing around the person of Margaret Thatcher."[16]

Mouffe's 1977 contribution to her edited volume on *Gramsci and Marxist Theory* points toward important dimensions of *Hegemony & Socialist Strategy*, but it remained within a Marxist framework as did most of the international engagement with Gramsci. In the intervening years leading up to the publication of *Hegemony*, Mouffe and Laclau became convinced that Marxism was not only inadequate but was an obstacle to the need to understand the post-1968 proliferation of new social movements—"feminisms, ecology, peace, Third World solidarities, gay-lesbian rights, and antiracism, as well as squatting and the broader alternative scenes"—and the distinctive forms of democratic politics that had emerged after 1968.[17] Gramsci offered a promising resource for this project, but only if his ideas were detached from his own ultimate reliance upon the essentialist core of Marxism: its reliance upon the foundational status of the material base. Hence, Laclau and Mouffe grafted the notion of hegemony onto the stem of French poststructuralism, seeing hegemony as the process whereby the social world is constructed through discourse. The relationship between workers and socialism, for example, is not a necessary relationship, but rather the outcome of a process of articulation and political contestation. Social agents do not discover their common interests in an underlying shared essence, but forge them through "articulatory practices" that construct discourses operating within a political space that is itself not determined by the logic of anything exterior to it. "[T]he relation of articulation is not a relation of necessity," wrote Laclau and Mouffe. "What the discourse of 'historical interests' does

is to *hegemonize* certain demands. . . . Political practice constructs the interests it represents."[18]

This detachment of interests from some anterior social base might alone
have been sufficiently blasphemous to draw the wrath of many Marxists,
but the real novelty and radicalism of Laclau and Mouffe came from their
appropriation of poststructuralism. Following Derrida's deconstructive
strategy, they argued that there is no "transcendental signified," no "eidos,
arché, telos, energia, ousia, alétheia, etc."[19] Lacking a point of anchor,
meaning is purely relational, emerging out of a mobile play of differences,
presences, and absences. Insofar as society is discursively constructed, this
differential element ensures that society itself can never be a closed, fixed
system of meaning. "Society" is *impossible*, in the strict sense that society
can never be fully present as an objective field, "a sutured and self-defined
totality."[20] But Mouffe and Laclau were also careful to insist that if society
is not "totally possible, neither is it totally impossible."[21] This play of possibility and impossibility within an overdetermined field opens up the possibility of hegemonic politics. Hegemony works by establishing equivalential
links among entities within a field of difference. Hence, for example, the articulation of the "rights of man and citizen" opens further arguments that
those rights require an extension to people of color as well as to women,
thereby displacing democratic discourse from the field of political equality
among citizens to the field of equality between the sexes or between races.
Hegemony is not "an irradiation of effects from a privileged point," but "basically metonymical: its effects always emerge from a surplus of meaning."[22]
Hegemony combines elements around a core, what Mouffe and Laclau
named a *point de capiton*, borrowing Lacan's term for the "privileged signifiers that fix the meaning of a signifying chain" and thereby establish the positions that make predication possible.[23] In a key statement, Mouffe and
Laclau wrote: "The practice of articulation, therefore, consists in the construction of nodal points which partially fix meaning; and the partial character of this fixation proceeds from the openness of the social, a result, in
its turn, of the constant overflowing of every discourse by the infinitude of
the field of discursivity."[24]

In the 1990s, Laclau's work became increasingly stamped by Lacan, inspired in part by Slavoj Zizek's efforts to fully integrate post-Marxism into
the field of Lacanian psychoanalysis.[25] In *Hegemony & Socialist Strategy*,
however, Lacan was just one resource underlying Laclau and Mouffe's insistence that the "meaning-giving" human subject cannot be defended as
the last redoubt of essentialism. Having abandoned the straitjacket of Marxism, Laclau and Mouffe refused to have their identities bounded by any

specific theoretical frontier. Many theoretical legacies tattoo the body of their text. Hence, they located themselves in a continuum with Friedrich Nietzsche, Sigmund Freud, Ludwig Wittgenstein, Martin Heidegger, and, of course, the French poststructuralists in contesting the view of the subject as an "agent both rational and transparent to itself" and the "conception of the subject as origin and basis of social relations."[26] In place of "subjects," they spoke of "subject positions" formed within a discursive structure. The subject is another *point de capiton*, a nodal point that is itself implicated *within* and created *by* the practices of articulation. As with every other element of the discursive field, the subjectivity of the agent is penetrated by the same precariousness and polysemy that overflow all attempts to conceal or "suture" the indeterminacy of meaning. Ultimately then, hegemonic politics is about the struggle for the creation of new subjects, or more precisely, new subject positions, through the practices of articulation. The distance from Marxism is clear; as with any other social identity, class identity is a subject position created through articulation. The classic socialist struggle over the relations of production has no primacy, but is itself the outcome of a certain discursive practice. Indeed, even though Mouffe and Laclau went to great lengths to emphasize that the preoccupations of traditional socialist politics remain important dimensions of democratic struggle, they become just one dimension of "radical democracy," the concept offered by Laclau and Mouffe to describe the political project opened by the much more fractured, pluralistic, and mobile front of new social movements contesting social, sexual, racial, and gender hierarchies.

Laclau and Mouffe's concept of the construction of the subject through language "as a partial and metaphorical incorporation into a symbolic order" has led some critics to argue that they were insufficiently detached from Althusser's view of the subject as passively produced through the process of ideological interpellation.[27] Laclau went to some lengths to dispel this view in a 1988 interview. While acknowledging that his first works had drawn on Althusser's "Spinozan notion of a 'subject effect,' which merely stems from the logic of the structures," he emphasized that the production of subjects through interpellation works only if the individuals thus being hailed *identify* with ideology. Given this view, he and Mouffe conceived interpellation "as part of an open, contingent, hegemonic-articulatory process which can in no sense be confused with Spinozan 'eternity'."[28] Laclau and Mouffe's resistance to Althusser found a striking expression in their intervention in the debate prompted by Edward Thompson's attack on the Althusserians in *Poverty of Theory*.[29] In opposition to Thompson's essentialist humanism, Laclau and Mouffe emphasized

the complexity of the discourses that have produced the modern subject
and hence the fragility and incompleteness of the project of "humanism";
and contrary to Althusser's relegation of humanism to the field of ideology,
they insisted not only on the effective power of humanist discourse in
emancipatory struggles since the eighteenth century, but also on the forms
of overdetermination that always put subjects in excess of any symbolic order.[30] Between the essentialism of the humanist "subject" and the excessive swing of poststructuralist thought toward the metaphor of dispersal,
Laclau and Mouffe insisted that an analysis of subjectivity "cannot dispense with the forms of overdetermination of some positions by others," a
conception of relation that resists both dispersal and suture.[31]

   This intervention offers a striking instance of the contextual hybridity of
Laclau and Mouffe's text. They act here as *mediators* in the conflict between "humanists" and "anti-humanists," which in France reached something of an apex in Alain Renaut and Luc Ferry's *La Pensée 68*, published
the same year as *Hegemony*.[32] The fact that their mediation comes through
a commentary on the climactic clash between the British Marxist humanism and Althusser, or at least his British proxies, suggests the multiple levels at which Laclau and Mouffe acted as cultural *brokers* standing at the
point of exchange between two intellectual and political traditions.

MOURNING OR MELANCHOLY?

Post-Marxism reinvents social struggle in terms of postmodernism's general
critique of logocentrism and essentialism. Post-Marxism thereby taps directly into a main intellectual trend in French thought since the 1960s. After 1968, when orthodox Marxism and the Parti communiste français (PCF)
revealed their bankruptcy in the streets, French theorists turned to new
forms of critical thought emphasizing the importance of contingency, micro-
resistance, cultural rebellion, and a conception of the political no longer
bounded by the state. Waves of theory ceased to refer to Marx and socialism
and celebrated new forms of liberation instead. Hence, the schizo-politics of
Deleuze and Guattari, the micro-politics of Foucault, the gaming of Lyotard,
the aesthetic "play" of Derrida, and Baudrillard's celebration of the hyper-
real simulacrum.

   In an essay entitled "The Apocalyptic Imagination and the Inability to
Mourn," Martin Jay has explored the double meaning of these febrile ges-
tures of postmodernism. Jay takes his point of departure from Eric Sant-
ner's suggestion that much postmodernism represents itself as a healthy

mourning for the lost hopes of the modernist project. However, drawing on Freud's distinction between mourning and melancholia, Jay points toward the apparent endlessness of postmodern mourning. The insistence on the inability of language to achieve a plenitude of meaning leads to "a valorization of repetition that is closer to melancholy than mourning *per se*."[33] As Jean Baudrillard wrote in 1981, "Melancholy is the quality inherent in the mode of disappearance of meaning, in the mode of volatilization of meaning in operational systems. And we are all melancholic."[34] In Freud's famous discussion, Jay writes, the work of mourning is "conscious of the love-object it has lost," and "it is able to learn from reality testing about the actual disappearance of the object and thus slowly and painfully withdraw its libido from it. The love-object remains in memory, it is not obliterated, but it is no longer the target of the same type of emotional investment as before."[35] Instead of gradually withdrawing his libidinal attachment from the lost object, the melancholic internalizes the object as a form of self-identification. According to Freud's model, the melancholic ego's regressive narcissistic identification with the lost object couples with guilt to produce alternating states of manic elation and self-punishing low esteem. From this perspective, it might be suggested that postmodernism's celebration of excess is the manic side of a melancholia that manifests itself in fantasies of obliteration and endless dispersal. Martin Jay argues that this vacillation helps to explain the peculiarity of the postmodern apocalyptic imagination, which works with only one side of the apocalyptic tradition: the threat of destruction, but not the promise of revelation.

Post-Marxism would seem to compound the sources of melancholy, as it not only inhabited the loss of meaning but also the specific loss of Marxism as a privileged object, intellectual investment, and emotional cathexis. The language of mourning is not absent from post-Marxism. Laclau and Mouffe viewed Marxism as a tradition, a culture, a collective memory, a personal past, and a personal identity. As Laclau said in 1988, "The loss of collective memory is not something to be overjoyed about. It is always an impoverishment and a traumatic fact. One only thinks *from* a tradition."[36] Jacques Derrida, who entered this discussion in 1993 with the book *Specters of Marx*, oriented the discussion of Marxism toward bereavement. Derrida wrote of an uncanny situation in which Marx has vanished but continues to haunt us. The specter of Marx becomes a way for Derrida to activate the *trace* of meaning as a political principle; the ghostly presence of Marx's demand for justice disrupts the seamlessness of contemporary time. It orients Derrida's call for justice toward the ghosts of those who were and those yet to be. The logic of spectrality, further, furnishes Derrida with a weak—a deliberately weak—hold on the Marxian tradition, or at least a "certain spirit of Marxism." That is to say, a dimension of "radical critique" and a "certain emancipatory and messianic affirmation" of a democracy that is always a "promise that can only arise in . . . failure, inadequation, disjunction, disadjustment, being 'out of joint'."[37]

Although *Specters of Marx* is elegiac in tone, it aims to further the work of mourning by seeking to preserve Marxism's radical spirit while rejecting the *strong* messianism, determinism, and ontological foundationalism that overburdened the Marxist tradition. In a lengthy 1999 response to his Marxist critics, Derrida sharply distanced his book from despair or nostalgia. He insisted that "one can discuss the work of mourning, analyze its necessity and political effects across the globe (after the alleged 'death of Marx' or of the communist idea)—one can be constrained to do so for all kinds of reasons, without therefore relinquishing a certain gaiety of affirmative thinking. Even without recalling the many texts and talks I have devoted to this possibility, I think it fair to say that *Specters of Marx* is anything but a sad book."[38]

Despite their admission of trauma, Laclau and Mouffe do not write in the elegiac mode. Indeed, their post-Marxism reverses many of the signs of postmodern melancholia. Where the indefinite deferral of meaning had fed a "tone of dread and hysteria" that Derrida described in the 1980 article, "Of an Apocalyptic Tone Recently Adopted in Philosophy," the "impossibility of society" furnished a source of optimism for Laclau and Mouffe. Hence, Laclau insisted in 1990 that the poststructuralist critique of the rationalism of the project of modernity does not undermine the emancipatory project linked to it. Instead, he argued that the renunciation of the Enlightenment's "rationalistic epistemological and ontological foundations" and a true acceptance of our historicity and contingency expand the democratic potentialities of the Enlightenment tradition, while "abandoning the totalitarian tendencies arising from the [Enlightenment] reoccupation of the ground of apocalyptic universalism."[39] The arrested apocalypse of the postmodern imagination thus furnishes an unexpected principle of hope. As Laclau wrote, "this final incompletion of the social is the main source of our political hope in the contemporary world: only it can assure the conditions for a radical democracy."[40] Recognition of ontological openness, as the condition for the articulation of multiple contestatory subject positions, performs the work of mourning. The post-Marxist can disengage from the lost object of Marxism and form a new cathexis to the self-constituting community of radical democracy. It allows the post-Marxist to "restore Marxism to its theoretical dignity" by creating a genealogy of post-Marxism "from the complex discourses through which it has been gradually gestating, including the Marxist tradition. In this sense, post-Marxism restores to Marxism the only thing that can keep it alive: its relation with the present and its historicity."[41]

At its most fundamental, this post-Marxist principle of hope rests on the recovery of "historicity," that is, the liberation of the historical world from determinism. Derrida's *Specters of Marx* reminds the reader of deconstruction's basic critique of "the onto-theo- but also archeo-teleological concept of history—in Hegel, Marx, or even in the epochal thinking of Heidegger." This is to be a critique, Derrida wrote, undertaken for the sake of "thinking another historicity . . . another opening of event-ness as historicity that permit[s] one not to renounce, but on the contrary to open up access to an affirmative thinking of the messianic and emancipatory promise as promise: as *promise* and not as onto-theological or teleological program or design."[42] Laclau and Mouffe likewise urge a "radical historicism" based on an "acceptance of our contingency and historicity."[43] Ultimately, both Derrida and the post-Marxists invoke an ontological condition wherein the impossibility of closure defines our "historicity" as the condition of all "history," event-ness the condition of the specificity of the event.

Yet if they all draw on a conception of ek-stasis that is ultimately of Heideggerean provenance, they move from there in quite different directions. In a very perceptive essay on *Specters of Marx*, Laclau agreed with much of what Derrida had to say, but he sharply parted company over the ethico-political consequence to be drawn from Derrida's "hauntology." Laclau wrote: "The illegitimate transition is to think that from the impossibility of a presence closed in itself, from an 'ontological' condition in which the openness to the event, to the heterogenous, to the radically other is constitutive, some kind of ethical injunction to be responsible and to keep oneself open to the heterogeneity of the other necessarily follows." For one thing, if the "promise implicit in an originary opening to the 'other'" is an "'existential' constitutive of all experience," then it is always already there, and an injunction would be superfluous. More importantly, Laclau could discern no necessary link between the "impossibility of ultimate closure and presence" and "an ethical imperative to 'cultivate' that openness or even less to be necessarily committed to a democratic society."[44] For Laclau, the consequences of deconstruction for politics and ethics could be developed only if deconstruction truly radicalizes undecidability as the "condition from which no necessary course of action follows." And this requires freeing deconstruction from the ethics of Levinas, "whose proclaimed aim," he wrote, "to present ethics as *first* philosophy, should from the start look suspicious to any deconstructionist."[45] In short, Derrida's ethico-political injunction must itself enter into a hegemonic logic if it is to become politically operative.

Similar concerns animate Zizek's recent critique of Derrida's *Specters of Marx*, which he conducts in a text whose title—in Zizek's typically vaudevillian way—shines a light down one path leading from the French exit from Marxism: "MELANCHOLY AND THE ACT in which the reader will be surprised to learn that anyone who is not a melancholic, or does not agree that we are thrown into a contingent finite universe, can today be suspected of 'totalitarianism'."[46] Zizek offers a drastic redefinition of the melancholic, whom he no longer sees as "primarily the subject fixated on the lost object, unable to perform the work of mourning it, but, rather, the subject who *possesses* the object, but has lost his desire for it, because the cause which made him desire this object has withdrawn, lost its efficacy." Melancholia "occurs when we finally get the desired object, but are disappointed with it."[47] Derrida's spectral turn to a "certain spirit of Marxism" may indeed be melancholic in this way; or even better, it may be a melancholic prophylaxis insofar as the messianic promise of a democracy *à venir* remains irreducibly distant from all positive incarnations of democracy. Watching Derrida address his Marxist critics in "Marx & Sons," one shares his irritation at the proprietary and censorious tones of unreconstructed hardliners like Terry Eagleton, but it is hard not to be struck by his double prohibition—against bringing his vision into focus, let alone acting upon it. Derrida's affirmative gaiety seems a very different affair from the recognizably *political* contours of Laclau's hegemonic logic, not to mention from Zizek's call for specific "economico-political measures" to address poverty and other injustices.[48]

THE NATIONAL CONTEXTS OF MARXISM'S CRISIS

Supporters and critics of poststructuralism alike have frequently imputed a specific politics to it. In response, Laclau has insisted that "there is nothing that can be called a 'politics of poststructuralism'." Rejecting the idea that there are philosophical systems with "unbroken continuities" that go from metaphysics to politics, Laclau maintained in an interview that "the correct question . . . is not so much which is *the* politics of poststructuralism, but rather what are the *possibilities* a poststructuralist theoretical perspective opens for the deepening of those political practices that go in the direction of a 'radical democracy'."[49] Likewise, in his review of *Specters of Marx*, Laclau maintained that "with any deconstruction worthy of the name, there is a plurality of directions in which one can move."[50] Certainly, if one looks to the early 1980s, when Laclau and Mouffe were composing their book, there can be no question of the lability of deconstructive politics. Derrida may have praised Laclau and Mouffe in 1993 for their "novel elaboration, in a 'deconstructive' style, of the concept of *hegemony*,"[51] but in the early 1980s, the most prominent deconstructive variation on the much-remarked "return of the political" in France was the work of Jean-Luc Nancy and Philippe Lacoue-Labarthe and the Center for Philosophical Research on the Political that they founded in 1980. For Nancy and Lacoue-Labarthe, politics is, à la Heidegger, implicated in the long history of humanism's forgetting of Being. Tying political action to the human subject's "exorbitant" drive toward unity, essence, and domination, Nancy and Lacoue-Labarthe could at best offer the paradoxical ideal of the "inoperative community," a *being-in-common* that only works so long as it does not work. Ruling out all exercise of will as a recuperation of the totalitarian mania for fusion, communion, and substance, Nancy could only invoke *Gelassenheit*, or resignation, as the means by which the inoperative community would be "exposed" as "this strange being-the-one-with-the-other."[52] The contrast to Laclau and Mouffe grows sharper if one measures their different perspectives on *autogestion*, the political goal that had first been articulated by Cornelius Castoriadis and Socialisme ou Barbarie in the 1950s and that returned as an ideal of student activists in 1968 and then of the *Deuxième Gauche*, the post-1968 leftist tendency that repudiated the bureaucratized politics of the PCF in favor of direct democracy. Where Laclau and Mouffe criticized "self-management" only because they believed that shop-floor politics should not be limited to workers themselves but should be articulated hegemonically with the interests of other political agents, Lacoue-Labarthe acknowledged the politics of self-management as the only viable "provisional politics" in the broken landscape of the Left, but he worried that councilist politics focus "unduly on what could indisputably lead to 'Marxist metaphysics,' on the motif of *self*-organization, and that is to say on the conception of the proletariat as Subject."[53]

We may readily accept Laclau's claim that undecidabilty and contingency accompany the moves that political thinkers make, but does that mean there are no other considerations that might contribute to an understanding of the specific moves that Laclau and Mouffe chose to make? Here, it is necessary to expand the discussion of the contextual complexities of their intervention. *Hegemony & Socialist Strategy* is a hybrid product, drawing on various theoretical legacies and responding to various contexts. Differences between the French and English contexts, the remaining pages of this section will argue, help to explain the differences in tone and project that we have noted in the contrast between Laclau and Mouffe, on one side, and figures like Derrida, Lacoue-Labarthe, and Nancy on the other.

The Soviet invasion of Hungary in 1956 had some similar effects among both English and French leftist intellectuals. For many, a wave of revulsion and disillusionment brought an end to their attachment to the respective communist parties and the birth in both countries of the New Left, although that term is at best a flag of convenience raised over a fragmented terrain. In France, Socialisme ou Barbarie, founded in 1948, witnessed a marked rise in membership after the Hungarian invasion, although the group's historian, Philippe Gottraux, gives equal weight to the radicalizing effects of the Algerian War.[54] Other anti-Stalinist groups like the Situationist International and the Arguments circle emerged as a direct response to the Soviet aggression. However prescient these groups might look from our present vantage point, it was, ironically, Althusserian Marxism that benefited most from the disenchantment of leftist intellectuals with the PCF. François Furet suggested in an important article of 1967 that the triumph of structuralism in the 1960s stemmed directly from "the dislocation of Marxist dogmatism."[55] As to the curious fact that structuralism served as both an exit strategy for disillusioned leftists who turned to anthropology and the eternal verities of peoples without history or to psychoanalysis and the timeless unconscious, *and*, in Althusser, as a way of rescuing Marxism, the historian François Dosse writes: structural Marxism "was one response to the need to abandon an official, dogma-bound, post-Stalinist Marxism with an onerous past. . . . [Althusser] offered the exciting challenge to a militant generation that had cut its teeth in anticolonial combats of resuscitating a scientific Marxism freed of the scoria of regimes that had ruled in the name of Marxism."[56] Or, from Furet's closer and more jaundiced view, "the structuralist 'deideologizing' of Marxism undoubtedly offers a way of living through the end of the ideologies inside the Communist world."[57]

May 1968 shook Althusserianism, as it did structuralism as a whole.[58] Nonetheless, as Dosse notes, the second wind of Marxism among intellectuals after 1968 actually raised Althusser's stock to unprecedented highs. With Althusser enjoying a growing readership, new enthusiasts, academic consecration, and official PCF recognition, the Althusserians resumed their long march through the structures. Yet "the triumphal period" proved to be as "ephemeral as it was exciting."[59] Indeed, the intellectual Left unraveled with stunning speed, and episodes like Althusser's self-criticism, an act of self-destruction that he considered more radical than suicide, or the scathing critique of the Althusserian apostate Jacques Rancière were local events within a larger story that includes the effects of the "Common Program" that brought the PCF and the Socialist Party into an electoral alliance in 1972, the French publication of Alexander Solzhenitsyn's *The Gulag Archipelago*, and the paradoxical effects of François Mitterrand's electoral victory in 1981 upon the leftist sympathies of intellectuals.[60] The rise of the *Nouveaux Philosophes*, the apotheosis of Raymond Aron, the impact of François Furet and Claude Lefort, the revival of political liberalism in the 1980s, the hyperallergic reaction of postmodernists to all forms of totalizing thought—all these mark a reversal that is stunning in its suddenness and depth.

The causes for this sea change are too complex to explore in detail here, but I do want to mention two possible factors. First, numerous commentators have remarked the loaded historical relationship between the state and the political intellectual in France. From at least Emile Zola through to Jean-Paul Sartre, the politically engaged intellectual, the universal intellectual who speaks as the voice of reason or of the people was an icon in French culture, intimately tied to French national identity and the horizons of possible political action. Historically, this defense of universal values had moved in close step with the Jacobin ideal of the republican state as the agency for the realization of the general will. Identification with this ideal of a power that fully manifests democratic unity combined with commitment to a revolution that would realize this goal at a stroke. This affective-intellectual constellation exercised a powerful hold on the political imagination of the French Left even as its object shifted from the French to the Bolshevik Revolution, from Republicanism to Marxism. It tended to produce an "ideological manichaeism" that became intense in moments of crisis from the Dreyfus Affair, the 1930s, defeat and resistance in the 1940s, the Cold War, and up to 1968.[61] Indeed, we may see its continuation into the 1970s in the *Nouveaux Philosophes*, in whom Dosse sees "equally violent thinking, the same propensity for exaggeration in other directions, as Althusser had counseled, in order to be heard."[62] The melancholic impasses so common to French poststructuralism seem yet another expression of this Manichean form. It would assign too much power to one writer to say that François Furet led the French beyond this impasse, but his 1978 declaration that the French Revolution is "over" was symptomatic of a shift in intellectual mood and in French politics.[63] Furet's conviction that Jacobin-Bolshevism had given way to a liberal consensus and a "normalized" liberal democratic state seemed confirmed in 1986, when a socialist president and a conservative government proved capable of cohabitation in the name of centrist pragmatism. By the 1989 bicentenary of the revolution, an editorial in *Le Point* could write that "the revolutionary dream of a change of society is abandoned" and celebrate the advent of a "pacified, banalized republic shorn of its passions."[64]

It has become customary to date the decline of the iconic figure of the French intellectual to the development of the liberal consensus and the centrist republic. However, a second factor that might help explain the abrupt reversal of intellectual leftism runs in a somewhat different direction. In a 1983 interview, Michel Foucault evoked wistfully the exciting currents of left-wing thought that had existed since at least 1960 but had disappeared by the early 1980s. Foucault ventured that the crisis of Marxism was not the result of the disappearance of the public intellectual, but rather of the democratization of the intellectual function. New circumstances since the 1960s had given "university activity an echo which reverberated widely beyond academic institutions or even groups of specialists, professional intellectuals."[65] Although he acknowledged some gains in terms of public awareness, he essentially endorsed Régis Debray's influential argument that French intellectual life had entered a "media cycle" by the 1970s. As Debray wrote, "Marx called France the land of ideas. The Atlantic world lives in the era of the scoop. Atlantic France has manufactured the ideological scoop. It teaches newsmen nothing, still less men of thought. But it satisfies a certain 'national intellectual personality'."[66] Under the pressure of the mass media, Foucault argued,

> a fairly evolved discourse, instead of being relayed by additional work which perfects it (either with criticism or amplification), rendering it more difficult and even finer, nowadays undergoes a process of amplification from the bottom up. Little by little, from the book to the review, to the newspaper article, and from the newspaper article to television, we come to summarize a work, or a problem, in terms of slogans. This passage of the philosophical question into the realm of the slogan, this transformation of the Marxist question, which becomes "Marxism is dead," is not the responsibility of any one person in particular, but we can see the slide whereby philosophical thought, or a philosophical issue, becomes a consumer item.[67]

In a context unusual for the extent of the centralization of education, intellectual life, the media, and the public sphere, the media could perhaps play a particularly strong role in transforming an unsettled debate into the decided conviction of public opinion. That this amplification effect could stifle debate is made clear by Derrida's announcement at a conference in 1981 that he had maintained "a silence with respect to Marxism—a blank signifying . . . that Marxism was not attacked like such and such other theoretical comfort." This blank, Derrida insisted, was a "perceptible political gesture" at a time when critical reflection on Marx would simply get sucked into the "anti-Marxist concert."[68]

In his recently published memoir, Eric Hobsbawm recalls with distaste the "militant and ill-tempered anti-communism of so many of the formerly left-wing 'intellocrats'" in the France of the 1980s and 1990s. He writes "As a by now quite well-known Marxist historian, I found myself for a while a champion of the embattled and besieged French intellectual Left."[69] Although Hobsbawm, a self-described "heterodox communist" to this day, is by no means typical of contemporary British leftists, his remarks suggest something of the relevant comparison between France and Britain in the post-1968 period. Without question, the British Left entered an open-ended period of crisis, defined by the defeat of the Labour Party, the disastrous miners' strikes, eighteen years of Conservative rule, and the return to power in the late 1990s of a Labour Party transformed almost beyond recognition, led by a man whom Hobsbawm calls "Thatcher in trousers."[70] The 1980s saw much discussion around the question, "What's Left?" Despairing as that question was, however, it did not suggest a massive rejection of left-wing allegiances among the intellectuals who continued to pose and explore it. In fact, although the 1980s were politically disastrous for the British Left, a left-wing intellectual culture continued in Britain. Lin Chun, a historian of the British New Left, details the growth of left-wing publications and activities during the 1970s. She writes, "All these developments had combined to transform the environment of the intellectual work of the Left. By the end of the decade, Marxist traditions had been much strengthened in some fields in this notoriously parochial country, in sharp contrast to the collapse of Marxist strongholds on the continent at exactly the same time."[71]

To overcome British parochialism had been one of the stated goals of the younger generation of New Leftists. Perry Anderson's "Origins of the Present Crisis" was instrumental in opening this direction in the mid-1960s when he lamented the inability of the New Left to develop any "structuralist analysis of British society" and traced the older New Left's intellectual style to Britain's antitheoretical empiricist culture. The poverty of cultural and intellectual life in Britain became a recurrent theme for the contributors to *New Left Review*, and the effort to fill what Anderson called the "absent centre" of British society and culture increasingly took the form of a widening engagement with continental Western Marxism. After 1968, the turn toward Western Marxism deepened as the *New Left Review* group worked to acquaint English readers with the writings of European Marxist thinkers, *terra incognita* with the exception of Gramsci and, since the mid-1960s, Althusser. Through translations, anthologies of critical essays, and books like Anderson's measured *Considerations on Western Marxism* (1976), British leftist intellectuals became increasingly conversant with Karl

Korsch, Georg Lukács, Theodor Adorno, Max Horkheimer, Sartre, and Althusser.[72] Looking back from 1990 to this sustained effort to break the British Left's intellectual isolation, Anderson noted that 1968 was not merely a political break, but a "geo-cultural" one as well.[73]

These circumstances bore directly on the British reception of French poststructuralism. According to Antony Easthope, author of the major survey of British poststructuralism, "Whereas the 'new ideas' and the 'new criticism' were assimilated in America to a liberal and libertarian tradition, in Britain they acquired a radical and political force because they were adopted into the British Marxist and left-culturalist inheritance."[74] In America, the reception first began with Derrida and then moved on to Lacan, thus bypassing almost entirely the work of Althusser. In Britain, Easthope shows, the reception began with Althusser in the 1960s and then progressed through the analysis of ideology to Lacan.[75] By the mid-1980s, much of the energy on the intellectual Left had swung back from the French to the native "linguistic turn," with the growth of analytical Marxism; and even at the height of the British enthusiasm for French theory, there were many left-wing dissenters who attacked Althusserian sectarians and regarded structuralism and poststructuralism to be antithetical to the socialist project. One thinks immediately of Edward Thompson, but Perry Anderson can be added to the list of prominent opponents. Despite his willingness to defend Althusser against Thompson, Anderson's *In the Tracks of Historical Materialism* (1983) damns the French theorists; and then, too, there is his rather ill-informed inclusion of Pierre Clastres, Claude Lefort, and Marcel Gauchet among the priests of "Desire," the latest "fashionable philosophy of Parisian irrationalism."[76] Dogged by controversy as British Althusserianism and Lacanianism were, the important point is that French theory unfolded within, not against, the broad culture of the British Left.

Left-wing British intellectuals had often envied the partisan vitality of French intellectual life, the prominence of the public intellectual in France, and the subtleties of French political discussion.[77] Perhaps, however, the more decentralized nature of intellectual life in Britain, the weaker hold of revolution on the political imagination of the Left, the strong orientation of leftist intellectuals to questions of culture, the greater distance of intellectuals from the mass media, indeed, the greater marginality of intellectuals within a culture that remained suspicious of abstraction and never appointed its leading writers to a higher moral tribunal, had the effects of immunizing the British Left against the more extreme swings that accompanied the collapse of Marxism in France. Post-Marxism may have been vigorously attacked by its staunchest British Marxist critics as quite simply "ex-Marxism," but we would miss a crucial dimension of the tone and substance of Mouffe and Laclau's appropriation of poststructuralism if we failed to see it as partly a product of the British context, where the crisis of Marxism was not accompanied by an "anti-totalitarian moment," public rituals of self-abasement, and the manic-depressive tone of so much French thought of the period.[78]

   Hegemony & Socialist Strategy was a relay between two political and intellectual cultures that responded quite differently to the crisis of the Left after 1968. The relay was literal, insofar as the book was co-authored while Chantal Mouffe lived and taught in Paris and her husband taught at the University of Essex. They progressed by exchanging drafts and comments through the mail. Written in the final decade before e-mail, the construction of the post-Marxist argument relied on the cross-channel post. Lest we fall into a simple image of a two-way trade between the British and French elements of this construction, it is important to at least mention yet another context haunting their discourse, namely the impact of their Latin American experiences. Mouffe, who had moved from Belgium to Paris in the mid-1960s, became involved in anti-imperialist movements and Latin American politics. This led her to go to Columbia, where she lectured in philosophy at the National University from 1967 to 1973. Mouffe credits the specific dynamics of Latin American politics with stimulating a critical revaluation of structural Marxism that had begun even before she left Paris.[79] To an even greater extent, Ernesto Laclau's formative experiences were within the Argentinian Socialist Party of the National Left during the 1960s. Within that context, Laclau has emphasized, the classical issues and divisions of the European Left were overshadowed by the political legacy of Juan Peron, who had been elected president in 1946 by "a heterogeneous coalition of the most diverse kind, ranging from the far-left to the far-right."[80] The challenges of left-wing politics in a situation dominated by Peronist populism gave Laclau the "experience of the ambiguity of democratic banners—what we would today call 'floating signifiers'—as well as the recognition of the centrality of the categories of 'articulation' and 'hegemony'." It was unnecessary, Laclau has maintained, to read poststructuralist texts to learn the lessons of contingency and undecidability. "I'd already learnt this through my practical experience as a political activist in Buenos Aires. So when today I read *Of Grammatology*, *S/Z*, or the *Écrits* of Lacan, the examples which always spring to mind are not from philosophical or literary texts; they are from a discussion in an Argentinian trade union, a clash of opposing slogans at a demonstration, or a debate during a party congress."[81] After he came to Europe in 1969, earned a Ph.D. at the University of Essex and began teaching there, these experiences continued as points of reference for a "non-dogmatic" reflection on Marxist theory and politics.

PLACING THE POST-MARXIST INTELLECTUAL

I want to conclude by considering a theme that has run implicitly throughout this chapter. Since the time when Marx declared that the proletariat finds its *intellectual* weapons in philosophy, through the Leninist vanguard, Gramsci's war of position, Sartre's committed writer, and Althusser's "theoretical practice," the Marxist tradition reserved a privileged place for the radical intellectual. In the French context, the Marxist belief in the unity of theory and practice amplified the long association of the French intellectual with the defense of universal values. Although the figure of the *philosophe engagé* has continued to haunt the French imaginary, the collapse of Marxism ushered in an ongoing discussion of the disappearance of the great intellectual as well as a widespread critique of universal values and the *maîtres à penser* (including structuralists like Lévi-Strauss and Althusser) who had spoken for them. The late 1970s and 1980s witnessed numerous efforts to demystify that figure, most notably Pierre Bourdieu's, as well as attempts to reconceptualize the political role of intellectuals, such as Foucault's idea of the "specific intellectual" or Julia Kristeva's notion of the dissident, the latter privileging the Freudian and the avant-garde writer, but *not* the rebel who attacks political power directly.[52] For Mouffe and Laclau, thinkers who situated themselves within the discourses of suspicion directed against the universalism and essentialism that had sustained the traditional intellectual, who yet still claimed, however ambiguously, a legacy in Marxism, what was the fate of the radical intellectual's political vocation?

Post-Marxism would seem to imply a greatly diminished place for the political intellectual. After all, the identity of theory and practice seems to be the first casualty of the post-Marxist critique of historical determinism and foundationalist logics. With no logical historical process to discover and no foundation upon which to articulate normative arguments about justice and the good, the older privilege of the intellectual would seem irretrievably shattered. Laclau addressed this issue directly in a 1988 interview, when he described their role as an extension of Gramsci's idea of the organic intellectual. Like Gramsci, Laclau rejected the definition of intellectuals as a segregated group and instead emphasized "the intellectual function" which establishes "the organic unity of a set of activities, which, left to their own resources, would remain fragmented and dispersed."[53] The intellectual function is thus the practice of articulation. Far from diminishing the intellectual function, the dissolution of rationalist social ontologies like Marxism amplifies it because "hegemonic articulations are not a secondary or marginal effect but the ontological level itself of the constitution of the social." Where the tradition of "great intellectuals" had rested on a claim that the intrinsic truth of things could be recognized by certain persons possessing the means of access, the organic intellectual participates in the construction of a truth that is "essentially pragmatic" and "democratic."[84] The intellectual function thus "consists in the invention of languages. If the unity of historical blocs is given by 'organic ideologies' that articulate into new projects fragmented and dispersed social elements, the production of those ideologies is the intellectual function *par excellence*." Laclau emphasizes that these ideologies are not "utopias" proposed to society, but "inseparable from the collective practices through which social articulation takes place."[85]

This radicalization of the Gramscian organic intellectual raises as many problems as it resolves, however. For one thing, it suffers the dilemma common to pragmatist arguments, for it dispenses with the effort to confirm truth claims in any manner beyond the validation that comes when an argument seems to work politically. A glaring example of this problem comes when they seek support in Georges Sorel's concept of "myth."[86] Even leaving aside the troubling vacillations in Sorel's career and considering only strategic concerns, the Sorelian myth of the general strike seems to illustrate precisely the inadequacy of an articulation that no longer searches for verification beyond the discursive terms set by itself. After all, it can be plausibly argued that the myth of the general strike lulled socialists into complacency, blinded them to their real situation, and impeded their strategic thinking in the years leading up to the outbreak of war in 1914. Laclau and Mouffe's detachment of truth claims from a materialist foundation was, of course, what upset Marxists most. However, even among post-foundationalist political thinkers, one sees a striking contrast. Jürgen Habermas's attempt to develop a discourse theory of democratic legitimation springs immediately to mind; however, even closer to the discursive tradition within which Laclau and Mouffe operate, their position contrasts sharply with a figure like Claude Lefort. Lefort, whose discussion of the dynamics of the democratic revolution that has unfolded ever since 1789 figures prominently in the final pages of *Hegemony & Socialist Strategy*, comes closer to their position when he writes that "the quest for truth and the truth itself are one and the same"; but his argument that both politics and truth depend on utterance, performance, and a "process of questioning" that is implicit in modern social practice opens a different prospect for the intellectual.[87] Lefort describes the intellectual pursuit as requiring a "heroism of mind" animated and haunted by "the 'impossible' task of disclosing that which is—the being of history, of society, of man—and of creating, of bringing forth through the exercise of a vertiginous right to thought and to speech, the work in which meaning makes its appearance."[88] In admittedly quite different ways, Habermas and Lefort each insists upon the intellectual's responsibility to the argument itself as well as the possibility of deliberative capacities within the public(s) construed in the broadest terms. Vexed though the question of validity has become, there remains a compelling need to understand the process whereby we test our claims as something that reaches beyond the pragmatic goal of constructing historical blocs, even if we also recognize the impossibility of foundational guarantees and the untenability of the traditional intellectual's privileged position vis-à-vis truth.

Even on Laclau and Mouffe's own terms, there seems to be a deep division between the organic intellectual's role in inventing languages that will unify fragmented social elements into new political projects and the deconstructive intellectual's understanding of the constitutive impossibility of identity. Social movements, even ones occupying the fragmented political space of postmodernity, do not thrive on a sense of their own impossibility, nor do movements coalesce around a sense of their own arbitrariness and contingency. Indeed, the new social movements have not been without their essentialisms. So, for example, the Women's Peace Camp founded at Greenham Common U.S. Air Force Base in 1981 by the Women for Life on Earth Peace March banned men throughout the thirteen years of its existence. Nature, not nurture, let alone choice, is most likely to figure in gay, lesbian, and transgendered claims for rights. Foucault's caution about queer politics is revealing here, for he saw there a tendency to repeat the essentializing politics of identity that he had spent his career battling. When English activists connected the closure of coal pits with the expansion of nuclear energy in England, and then with the women's protest movement at Greenham Common, the global context of nuclear fuels, and finally antiapartheid and peace groups, and then organized a conference called "Make the Links—Break the Chains" which brought all these groups together in 1986, were they *constructing* the connections or *discovering* them?[89] Viewed analytically, this is a great example of hegemonic articulation within an overdetermined field; however, the agents themselves would likely have been surprised and possibly skeptical to be told that the links were not accurate descriptions of a *real* state of affairs.

Laclau maintained that even after toppling the pillars of Marxist orthodoxies, the concept of ideology could be retained, "even in the sense of 'false consciousness,' if by the latter we understand that illusion of 'closure' which is the imaginary horizon that accompanies the constitution of all objectivity."[90] Yet the constitution of "objectivity" seems to be a condition of all social movements, thereby rendering them all instances of false consciousness. To update a Leninist dictum, by the post-Marxist logic, if left to themselves, political agents will never develop more than a predicative consciousness. But how many social movements could survive in the full light of Laclau and Mouffe's knowledge? There seems to be a clear divide between the organic intellectual of the social movement and the deconstructive analyst who exposes the ontology of the social. Possessed of this knowledge, the post-Marxist seems condemned to what Barthes called "theoretical sociality": "we constantly drift between the object and its demystification, powerless to render its wholeness. For if we penetrate the object, we liberate it but destroy it; and if we acknowledge its full weight, we respect it, but restore it to a state which is still mystified."[91]

This observation brings me to a final point. I have argued in this chapter that Laclau and Mouffe redirected the sources of postmodern melancholia toward the work of mourning. I have tried to delineate their appropriation of poststructuralist theory and suggest reasons—both internal to their own trajectories and related to the contextual hybridity that stamps their work— why they embraced an affirmative stance vis-à-vis the collapse of Marxism, moving beyond a potential impasse into a fruitful theory of social antagonism and the role of discourse in the formation of political movements, in short, why their theory is so French and so very un-French. Yet if the "final incompletion of the social" offers the main source of hope for the project of radical democracy, have the post-Marxists worked through their own mourning at the risk of minimizing a deeper trauma connected to democracy itself? Claude Lefort, whose work represents the best that issued from the French reflection on totalitarianism, speaks of the traumatic core of democracy itself, which was born in the symbolic disincorporation of power. The loss of the visible unity of the body politic, the experience of social division and indetermination haunt the democratic experience. The death of embodied power was the enabling condition of modern democracy, but it also marks an originary scene of loss that still seems to exert power over the psychical life of democracy. "[I]s it not true," Lefort writes, "that in order to sustain the ordeal of the division of the subject, in order to dislodge the reference points of the *self* and the *other*, to depose the position of the possessor of power and knowledge, one must assume responsibility for an experience instituted by democracy, the indetermination that was born from the loss of the substance of the body politic?"[92] Lefort's influence is explicit in Laclau and Mouffe's conception of radical democracy, but the sober tones of Lefort's confrontation with this undercurrent of desire and loss are essentially absent. This is unfortunate. A fuller attempt to reckon with those phantasmatic dimensions of democracy should be a vital measure for a theory that would amplify the experience of indetermination and antagonism in the name of a more radical expression of democracy in an age beyond "Science," "Class," "Party," "Logos," "Human Nature," "Reason," and "God."[93]

NOTES

1. Louis Althusser, "The Crisis of Marxism," in *Power and Opposition in Post-Revolutionary Societies*, trans. P. Camiller (London: Ink Links, 1979), 225.

2. Fredric Jameson, *Late Marxism: Adorno, or, The Persistence of the Dialectic* (London: Verso, 1990), 5.

3. See Ernesto Laclau and Chantal Mouffe, "Post-Marxism without Apologies," in *New Reflections on the Revolutions of Our Time*, ed. Ernesto Laclau (London: Verso, 1990), 97–132.

4. See Malachi Hacohen, "The Limits of the National Paradigm in the Study of Political Thought: The Case of Karl Popper and Central European Cosmopolitanism," in *The History of Political Thought in National Context*, eds. Dario Castiglione and Iain Hampsher-Monk (Cambridge: Cambridge University Press, 2001), 247–79.

5. Jacques Derrida, *Specters of Marx: The State of the Debt, the Work of Mourning, & the New International*, trans. Peggy Kamuf (New York: Routledge, 1994), 14.

6. Laclau, "Theory, Democracy, and Socialism," in *New Reflections*, 236.

7. Laclau and Mouffe, *Hegemony & Socialist Strategy: Towards a Radical Democratic Politics* (London: Verso, 1985), 67.

8. Laclau and Mouffe, *Hegemony & Socialist Strategy*, 71.

9. "An Interview with Chantal Mouffe and Ernesto Laclau" (1999), www.knowtv.com/primetime/conflicting/mouffe.html (July 2003).

10. "An Interview with Chantal Mouffe and Ernesto Laclau" (1999), 4–5.

11. Laclau, "Building a New Left," in *New Reflections*, 178–79.

12. Laclau, "Building a New Left," in *New Reflections*, 178.

13. For discussions, see Don Forgacs, "Gramsci and Marxism in Britain," *New Left Review* 176 (1989): 70–88; Dennis Dworkin, *Cultural Marxism in Postwar Britain: History, the New Left, and the Origins of Cultural Studies* (Durham, N.C.: Duke University Press, 1997); Lin Chun, *The British New Left* (Edinburgh: Edinburgh University Press, 1993).

14. Mouffe and Sassoon, "Gramsci in France and Italy—A Review of the Literature," *Economy and Society* 6 (1977): 53.

15. Mouffe, ed., *Gramsci and Marxist Theory* (London: Routledge, 1977), 1.

16. Dworkin, *Cultural Marxism*, 232–33.

17. Geoff Eley, *Forging Democracy: The History of the Left in Europe, 1850–2000* (New York: Oxford University Press, 2002), 461.

18. Laclau and Mouffe, *Hegemony*, 120.

19. Laclau and Mouffe, *Hegemony*, 112.

20. Laclau and Mouffe, *Hegemony*, 111.

21. Laclau and Mouffe, *Hegemony*, 129.

22. Laclau and Mouffe, *Hegemony*, 141.

23. Laclau and Mouffe translate *point de capiton* as "nodal point," but Zizek's term "quilting point" better conveys Lacan's image of upholstery gathered up and anchored by a button.

24. Laclau and Mouffe, *Hegemony*, 112–13.

25. Slavoj Zizek admired Laclau and Mouffe's book from the moment he reviewed it for the Paris magazine *L'Age* in 1985. For his engagement with their ideas, see especially his essay "Beyond Discourse-Analysis," in *New Reflections*. For discussions, see Andrew Norris, "Against Antagonism: On Ernesto Laclau's Political Thought," *Constellations* 4, no. 9 (December 2002): esp. 558; Elizabeth Bellamy, "Discourses of Impossibility: Can Psychoanalysis be Political?" *Diacritics* 1, no. 23 (Spring 1993): 23–38; and Thomas Brockelman, "The Failure of the Radical Democratic Imaginary: Zizek versus Laclau and Mouffe on Vestigial Utopia," *Philosophy & Social Criticism* 29, no. 2 (2003): 183–208. The development of a more critical relationship between the two thinkers is evident in their contributions to Zizek, Laclau, and Judith Butler, *Contingency, Hegemony, Universality: Contemporary Dialogues on the Left* (London: Verso, 2000).

26. Laclau and Mouffe, *Hegemony*, 115, 121.

27. Laclau and Mouffe, *Hegemony*, 126.

28. Laclau, "Theory, Democracy, and Socialism," 210.

29. E.P. Thompson, *The Poverty of Theory and Other Essays* (London: Merlin, 1978). On the heated debate provoked by *The Poverty of Theory*, see Dworkin, *Cultural Marxism*, 219–45, and, of course, Perry Anderson, *Arguments within English Marxism* (London: Verso, 1980).

30. Laclau and Mouffe, *Hegemony*, 117.

31. Laclau and Mouffe, *Hegemony*, 116.

32. Alain Renaut and Luc Ferry, *La Pensée 68: essai sur l'anti-humanisme contemporain* (Paris: Gallimard, 1985); trans. Mary H. S. Cattani as *French Philosophy of the Sixties: An Essay on Antihumanism* (Amherst: The University of Massachusettes Press, 1990).

33. Martin Jay, "The Apocalyptic Imagination and the Inability to Mourn," in *Rethinking Imagination: Culture and Creativity*, eds. Gillian Robertson and John Rundell (New York: Routledge, 1994), 47 n. 36.

34. Baudrillard quoted in Jay, "The Apocalyptic Imagination," in *Rethinking Imagination*, 35.

35. Jay, "The Apocalyptic Imagination," in *Rethinking Imagination*, 39.

36. Laclau, "Building a New Left," 179.

37. Derrida, *Specters of Marx*, 64

38. Derrida, "Marx & Sons," in *Ghostly Demarcations: A Symposium on Jacques Derrida's Specters of Marx*, ed. Michael Sprinker (London: Verso, 1999), 259. Galilée published Derrida's text in French in 2002 with the same title.

39. Laclau, *New Reflections*, 83.

40. Laclau, *New Reflections*, 82.

41. Laclau, *New Reflections*, 236.

42. Derrida, *Specters of Marx*, 75.

43. Laclau, *New Reflections*, 83.

44. Laclau, "'The Time is Out of Joint,'" in *Emancipation(s)* (London: Verso, 1996), 77.

45. Laclau, "'The Time is Out of Joint,'" 78.

46. Zizek, *Did Somebody Say Totalitarianism? Five Interventions in the (Mis)use of a Notion* (London: Verso, 2001), 141.

47. Zizek, *Did Somebody Say Totalitarianism?* 148.

48. Zizek, *Did Somebody Say Totalitarianism?* 154.

49. Laclau, "Building a New Left," 191.

50. Laclau, "'The Time is Out of Joint,'" 70.

51. Derrida, *Specters of Marx*, 180n31.

52. Jean-Luc Nancy, *The Inoperative Community*, ed. Peter Connor (Minneapolis: University of Minnesota Press, 1991), 121. See also Philippe Lacoue-Labarthe and Jean-Luc Nancy, *Retreating the Political*, ed. Simon Sparks (New York: Routledge, 1997).

53. Nancy, *The Inoperative Community*, 98.

54. Philippe Gottraux, *"Socialisme ou Barbarie": un engagement politique et intellectuel dans la France de l'après-guerre* (Lausanne: Editions Payot Lausanne, 1997), 77–129.

55. François Furet, "French Intellectuals: From Marxism to Structuralism," in *In the Workshop of History*, trans. Jonathan Mandelbaum (Chicago: University of Chicago Press, 1984), 30.

56. François Dosse, *History of Structuralism*, trans. Deborah Glassman, 2 vols. (Minneapolis: University of Minnesota Press, 1997), 1: 294.

57. Furet, "French Intellectuals," 38.

58. For a sharp critique of Alain Renaut and Luc Ferry's linkage between 1960s structuralism and May '68 in their book *La Pensée 68*, see Cornelius Castoriadis, "The Movements of the Sixties," in *World in Fragments: Writings on Politics, Society, Psychoanalysis, and the Imagination*, ed. and trans. David Ames Curtis (Stanford: Stanford University Press, 1997), 50–51.

59. Dosse, *History of Structuralism*, 2: 164–78.

60. See Diana Pinto, "The Left, the Intellectuals, and Culture," in *The Mitterrand Experiment: Continuity and Change in Modern France*, eds. George Ross,

Stanley Hoffmann, and Sylvia Malzacher (New York: Oxford University Press, 1987), 217–28. See more recently Michael Scott Christofferson, *French Intellectuals Against the Left: The Antitotalitarian Moment of the 1970s* (New York: Berghahn Books, 2004).

61. See Natalie Doyle, "The End of a Political Identity: French Intellectuals and the State," *Thesis Eleven* 48 (February 1997): 46.

62. Dosse, *History of Structuralism*, 2: 274.

63. Furet, *Interpreting the French Revolution*, trans. Elborg Forster (Cambridge: Cambridge University Press, 1981).

64. Steven Kaplan, *Farewell Revolution: The Historians' Feud* (Ithaca: Cornell University Press, 1995), 86.

65. Michel Foucault, *Politics, Philosophy, Culture: Interviews and Other Writings, 1977–1984*, ed. Lawrence Kritzman (New York: Routledge, 1988), 44.

66. Régis Debray, *Teachers, Writers, Celebrities: The Intellectuals of Modern France*, trans. David Macey (London: New Left Books, 1981), 87.

67. Foucault, *Politics, Philosophy, Culture*, 44–45.

68. Quoted in Nancy Fraser, "The French Derrideans: Politicizing Deconstruction or Deconstructing the Political?" *New German Critique* 33 (1984): 133–34.

69. Eric Hobsbawm, *Interesting Times: A Twentieth-Century Life* (New York: Pantheon, 2002), 335–36.

70. Hobsbawm, *Interesting Times*, 276.

71. Chun, *British New Left*, 109.

72. Dworkin, *Cultural Marxism*, 110–36. See also Chun, *British New Left*, 110–27.

73. Anderson quoted in Dworkin, *Cultural Marxism*, 124.

74. Antony Easthope, *British Post-Structuralism: Since 1968* (London: Routledge, 1991), xiii. A similar point about the American reception is made by Jean-Philippe Mathy, "The Resistance to French Theory in the United States: A Cross-Cultural Inquiry," *French Historical Studies* 19, no. 2 (Fall 1995): 331–47.

75. Easthope, *British Post-Structuralism*, xiii. The pioneering film studies journal *Screen* played a major role in this mediation. For a superb example of this British Leftist appropriation of Lacan, see Rosalind Coward and John Ellis, *Language and Materialism: Developments in Semiology and the Theory of the Subject* (London: Routledge, 1977).

76. Anderson, *Arguments*, 161.

77. See the remarks of Raymond Aron, *The Opium of the Intellectuals*, trans. Terence Kilmartin (New York: Doubleday, 1957), 219.

78. See Norman Geras, "Ex-Marxism Without Substance: A Rejoinder," in *Discourses of Extremity: Radical Ethics and Post-Marxist Extravagances* (New York: Verso, 1990); and Ellen Meiksins Wood, *The Retreat from Class: A New "True" Socialism* (London: Verso, 1986).

79. See Jacob Torfing, *New Theories of Discourse: Laclau, Mouffe, and Zizek* (Oxford: Blackwell, 1999), 15.

80. Laclau, "Theory, Democracy, and Socialism," 198.

81. Laclau, "Theory, Democracy, and Socialism," 200.

82. Bourdieu, *Homo Academicus* (Paris: Editions de Minuit, 1984); Foucault, "Truth and Power," in *Power/Knowledge: Selected Interviews and Other Writings, 1972–1977*, ed. and trans. Colin Gordon (New York: Pantheon 1980); Julia Kristeva, "A New Type of Intellectual: The Dissident," in *The Kristeva Reader*, ed. Toril Moi (New York: Columbia University Press, 1986).

83. Laclau, "Building a New Left," 195.

84. The links to pragmatism are explicitly thematized in Simon Critchley, Jacques Derrida, Ernesto Laclau, and Richard Rorty, *Deconstruction and Pragmatism*, ed. Chantal Mouffe (New York: Routledge, 1996).

85. Laclau, "Building a New Left," 196.

86. See Laclau, "Theory, Democracy, and Socialism," 232.

87. Lefort, "The Question of Democracy," in *Democracy and Political Theory*, trans. David Macey (Minneapolis: University of Minnesota Press, 1988), 19.

88. Lefort, "How Did You Become a Philosopher?" in *Philosophy in France Today*, ed. Alan Montefiore (New York: Cambridge University Press, 1983), 91.

89. I take these examples from Eley, *Forging Democracy*, 463–67.

90. Laclau, "Building a New Left," 186.

91. Barthes quoted in Dick Hebdige, *Subculture: The Meaning of Style* (London: Metheun, 1979), 140.

92. Lefort, "The Image of the Body and Totalitarianism," in *The Political Forms of Modern Society: Bureaucracy, Democracy, Totalitarianism*, ed. John Thompson (Cambridge, Mass.: The MIT Press, 1986), 305–6.

93. Laclau, "Building a New Left," 189, 194.

II

FIGURES:
OVERLOOKED AND FAMILIAR

4

A NEW GENERATION OF GREEK INTELLECTUALS IN POSTWAR FRANCE

Christophe Premat

The Sun is lost. . . . It's all in pieces. All coherence is gone. . . . This is the world's condition now.

John Donne, *The Anatomy of the World* (1611)

In December 1945, a ship left Athens' harbor Piraeus with several intellectuals on board, including Cornelius Castoriadis, Kostas Axelos, and Kostas Papaioannou. The French Institute of Athens, an organization sponsored by the French Foreign Office and promoting the development of French language and culture abroad, helped these intellectuals escape the chaotic political situation in Greece. A first civil war in 1944 and 1945 had divided Greece between communists who wanted to fight against German, Bulgarian, and Italian invaders and others who were afraid of a communist regime. Then, from 1946 until 1949, a second civil war occurred in Greece, opposing the communists to monarchists helped by the British government.

In this chapter, we will focus on these three left-oriented philosophers—Castoriadis, Axelos, and Papaioannou—and examine what they brought to the postwar French intellectual sphere. As political theorists, these three philosophers played an important role in French postwar debates: they undertook a criticism of the Marxist tradition and its French epigones after World War Two. We will first briefly recall historical events that will help us understand the circumstances of their emigration. Axelos, Papaioannou, and Castoriadis had been engaged in the Greek Communist Party before or during World War Two and took part in the Greek Resistance. Whereas Castoriadis joined the Greek Communist Youth when he was a teenager and quit it in order to be a Trotskyist activist, Axelos and Papaioannou joined the Greek Communist Party. Axelos was responsible for the Resistance Youth during World War Two and was known as a communist theorist. He was sentenced to death by the Germans during that period because of his political engagement.

In the second part of this chapter, we would like to analyze the close relation between these Greek émigrés and the work of Marx. By shaping a dialogue with Marx, they avoided a prevalent enchantment with Stalinism, strong in French society, especially among intellectuals. Having been engaged at a different time in the Greek Communist Party, they had quit it because of its totalitarian tendencies. They returned to Marx in order to analyze the gap between the socialist regimes and Marx's texts and intentions. Instead of rescuing Marx against Marxists, they pointed out the contradictions and the unclear points in his work. They dared to criticize the work of Marx when the Communist Party was a seductive force in France—the French Communist Party had around 30 percent of votes immediately following World War Two, due in part to the mythic role of communists in the French Resistance.

Castoriadis, who will be given particularly close attention here, was not a typical intellectual figure in French society. His political and philosophical engagements were at the opposite of the mainstream of French leftist intellectuals who chose to join the Communist Party. Distinctively, he tried to promote the central role of politics. Asking how past and existing institutions of society worked, he influenced the trend called institutional analysis.[1] In every society, there are social norms that are created by humans in order to live together. These norms are the products of political decisions and are internalized by individuals. The trend of institutional analysis (which exists in ethnology and sociology) analyzes social norms and the way individuals reflect them unconsciously; with time, these norms can be perceived as taboos. According to Castoriadis, individuals should be aware that if these norms were instituted by humans, then humans should be able to transform them. He considered this particular kind of reflection as political action, which is why his writings can be classified as political anthropology.

In the third part of this chapter, we will determine how Castoriadis had an outsider's perspective, which facilitated his criticisms of French intellectual fashions (Marxism, Heideggerianism, and Lacanianism) without taking part in them. Furthermore, Castoriadis never gave up wondering why democracy appeared and how it is threatened by totalitarianism. He was thus led to develop a radical theory of democracy: according to him, democracy is socialism, which means that every individual should take part in all the decisions affecting the social sphere. Ancient Greece offered a rare example of a democratic society where almost every individual citizen could discuss laws and public measures on the *agora*.

In fact, the Greek émigrés discussed here generally explored a philosophical crossroads between modernity and the world of ancient Greece. Greece is indeed a part of our Western world: if this thought is obvious nowadays, we cannot forget that this country was still seen as a part of the Orient in the nineteenth century. Two pivotal events of twentieth-century Greek history occurred in 1936 when John Metaxas led a coup d'état, and between 1941 and 1944, when Greece fought Italy before being invaded by the Germans. Then, in 1944–1945, the first civil war wrecked the country. Leftist ideas were severely repressed in this political context, and the Greek émigrés turned to France in search of freedom of speech and a place where they could explore their ideas without risking their lives. Having experienced the war caught between the West (the United Kingdom and the United States) and East (the Soviet Union and even the Greek Communist Party), these intellectuals expressed very early on the antagonism between totalitarian regimes and the idea of democracy.

Castoriadis was born in Constantinople in 1922, Axelos in Athens in 1924, and Papaioannou in Volos in 1925. We will refer to Castoriadis's biography since he mentioned on several occasions the importance of the political situation of Greece to his own life trajectory.[2] Castoriadis spent all his childhood in Greece with a very Francophile education: his father was very keen on French philosophy and literature and passed this infatuation on to him. It was little wonder Castoriadis chose France when he had to flee the country when the civil war broke out in 1944. When he was a teenager, he joined the Communist Youth in the era of John Metaxas's dictatorship (1936–41). During this period, political meetings were repressed, and it was very difficult to get involved in politics. The international context made Greece's situation even more tragic, when on October 28, 1940, Benito Mussolini delivered a humiliating ultimatum to Metaxas, which the latter refused. Consequently, the future of Greece rested on the outcome of World War Two. Metaxas died in January 1941, and on April 6, 1941, German troops invaded Greece by way of Yugoslavia and Bulgaria. By the beginning of June 1941, the whole of Greece was under German, Italian, and Bulgarian occupation.

Castoriadis found himself studying in Athens at a time when the Germans occupied the city as well as Salonica, Crete, and a number of the Aegean islands (the Bulgarians were permitted to occupy western Thrace and parts of Macedonia, and the Italians controlled the rest of the country). Castoriadis had not been tortured, but some of his friends had been victims of torture under the dictatorship of Metaxas. In his later writings, Castoriadis paid tribute to all his Trotskyist comrades, who had never betrayed him. "After several months," he recalled, "my comrades (I would like here to say their names: Koskinas, Dodopoulos, and Stratis) had been arrested, but though they were savagely tortured, they never denounced me."[3]

The situation was chaotic in Greece, and one of the few ways to resist was to join the Communist Party, which was becoming increasingly Stalinist. At that time, Castoriadis began to become aware that politics might imply a radical rupture with the Marxist party.

> It is not interesting to tell here how a teenager, discovering Marxism, *thought* that he respected it by joining the Communist Youth under the dictatorship of Metaxas. Nor is it interesting to tell why he could believe, after the occupation of Greece and the German attack against Russia, that the chauvinistic orientation of the Greek Communist Party and the formation of the National Liberation Front resulted from a local deviance that could be corrected by ideological struggle within the Party.[4]

Then, Castoriadis, who was attracted by Trotskyism and in 1942 collaborated with the cells of Spiros Stinas (a Greek Trotskyist leader), suffered on two fronts: on the one hand, from the circumstances of the war and the fight against fascism and, on the other hand, from the political repression of the Communist Party which assassinated many Trotskyist activists. Castoriadis was conscious at that time that fighting against fascism within the Greek Communist National Liberation Front (EAM) was not effective. The EAM's leaders claimed that they alone could resist against the invaders. Any other tendency inside the EAM was severely repressed. This communist organization had a particular appeal to young people and to women, to whom it held out the prospect of emancipation in a largely rural and decidedly patriarchal society.

> The war had made possible the revival of the masses' "nationalistic illusions." The masses remained imprisoned by those illusions until the experience of war dispelled them and led the masses to revolution. This war had only achieved the transformation of the Communist Party into a national-reformist party, completely integrated in the bourgeois order—a situation Trotsky had foreseen for a long time.[5]

Castoriadis began to develop his own theories through having experienced the war and the brutality of the Communist Party. He grew deeply suspicious that the Communist Party could help achieve social emancipation, because the party despised any kind of free expression. Castoriadis made this diagnosis very early thanks to the lucidity with which he viewed the Greek situation: "The critique of Trotskyism and my own conception were completely shaped during the first Stalinist attempt of coup d'état in Athens in December 1944." Castoriadis refers to the aborted communist revolution in 1944, which transpired with the help of the Soviet Union. After World War Two, the future of Greece was decided by Stalin and Churchill, the latter wanting to establish a kingdom in Greece, in order to give Great Britain access to the Mediterranean Sea. On October 9, 1944, the USSR and the United Kingdom concluded an agreement on Greece stipulating that the British authorities could control the country. Stalin was not specifically interested in the area since he was focusing more on other Eastern countries like Yugoslavia and Albania. After a war that began in 1944 between the monarchists, helped by the British army, and the communists, a February 1945 agreement signed in Varzika put an end to the first civil war. The communists promised to give up their weapons, and the British authorities agreed to recognize officially the existence of the Communist Party of Greece. In fact, the agreement was never respected, and thousands of communists were arrested. In 1946, elections were organized under the pressure of Great Britain. Many people voted in a menacing climate, and a conservative government was elected. Then, the EAM fought against this conservative government. The rupture between Yugoslavia (a country close to Greece that could send troops easily) and the USSR did not help the Greek communists. The second civil war ended on September 16, 1949, with the defeat of the communists. Castoriadis, Axelos, and Papaioannou did not experience the events of the second civil war since they came to France during the first. Axelos and Papaioannou had fought within the Greek Resistance during the first civil war, whereas Castoriadis was a political activist among Greek Trotskyists who were persecuted both by the monarchists and the communists. A member of the Greek Communist Youth in 1937, after the German occupation of Greece (1941), Castoriadis was the cofounder of a journal attempting to reform the Greek Communist Party. He failed on that point and became a Trotskyist by 1942, avoiding Stalinist and Gestapo agents.

The history of Greece in the twentieth century was rife with coup d'états and dictatorships. One significant tragedy was that Greece had been torn between the possibility of a fascist dictatorship and a communist dictatorship.

As a matter of fact, Castoriadis, Axelos, and Papaioannou experienced in Greece the roots of the totalitarian system. The political problem could not be simply solved by changing a government; it implied reflecting on the conditions of totalitarianism, a politics that had two sides, a Left one (Stalinism) and a Right one (fascism). In Castoriadis's view, Greece had been an interface: first between fascism and Stalinism and then between capitalism (the Western countries) and Stalinism (the Eastern countries). As such, there was no space for a certain kind of autonomy and for political thought. The socialist revolution had to take place in another country where circumstances would be more opportune; the seeds of social autonomy, which emerged in the ancient Athenian society of the eighth century B.C.E., had to be transplanted somewhere else in order to be saved.

For Castoriadis, totalitarianism was characterized by a perfect bureaucratic system of domination. Bureaucracy means a political system that aims at creating two separated spheres, the sphere of executive political-economic power and the sphere of producers. The disconnection between these two spheres contributes to total domination by the executive sphere. In other words, bureaucracy is the name for a system that establishes a total separation of tasks: the workers are separated from the rulers and depend on them. There are different types of bureaucracies: in the USSR, bureaucracy was achieved through the total separation of workers and rulers. The rulers decided all the social questions, and the workers were totally dominated, without knowing exactly the will of the rulers. (This was the strategy of planning, where rulers determined how the production of goods should operate as well as what social goods were).

Fighting in Greece was all the more difficult as the country was caught between West and East.

> If Greece was one thousand kilometers northwards—or France one thousand kilometers eastwards—the Communist Party would have taken power after the war, and this power would have been secured by Russia. What would it have done? The Communist Party would have installed a regime similar to the Russian one, eliminating the existing dominant classes after having absorbed what it could of them, establishing its own dictatorship, placing its men in all the commanding and privileged positions. Certainly, at the time, all those were "if's." But the subsequent evolution of the satellite countries, confirming this prognosis as no other historical prognosis could be confirmed, led me to return to this way of reasoning.[6]

Castoriadis went on to compare the social and historical situations of Greece and France. At the end of World War Two, France found itself in

an ambiguous political situation. The country had known the German occupation and the Vichy government, and then faced the myth of the Communist Party in the French Resistance—a myth all the more striking since
the Communist Party did not appeal early to resistance against the Germans because of the August 1939 Hitler-Stalin pact, even if many communists disobeyed official instructions in order to join the French Resistance.
In Greece, Castoriadis had experienced the contradictions of the Stalinist
project, and when he arrived in France, he became a Sovietologist, studying all the different phases of mutation of Russian bureaucratic organization. He analyzed first the conditions of the Bolshevik Revolution, secondly
the social regime of the USSR, and then the Russian bureaucracy after the
death of Stalin.[7]

In 1948, Castoriadis founded the group Socialisme ou Barbarie with
Claude Lefort in order to rescue the ideas of the young Marx as well as the
revolutionary project that Marx initiated. The group was inaugurated as
part of an explicit critique of Trotskyism and as a scission inside the Trotskyist Fourth International.[8] For the members of Socialisme ou Barbarie,
Trotskyists, including Trotsky himself, had not gone far enough in their critique of Stalinism.[9] For instance, in 1948, French Trotskyists' proposed alliance with Tito, who had broken with Stalin, was unacceptable to Castoriadis and those who followed him. A new movement was necessary.
Socialisme ou Barbarie began to fight for proletarian emancipation outside
bureaucracy. They promoted the topic of self-management [*autogestion*],
which would become popular after the events of May 1968. The idea of
self-management implies that all the workers should be able to take part in
the administration of the factory. Socialisme ou Barbarie, the group and the
review of the same name, lasted until 1967.

The influence of the group was limited, as the Communist Party was
the first political power in France after World War Two. In this context,
Socialisme ou Barbarie was seen as a radical far-left group to be fought.
Castoriadis and his colleagues closely studied the internal changes of the
French political situation and the characteristics of Stalinism in France,
for example, the social basis of the French Communist Party and its tactics linked to the evolution of the USSR.[10] Socialisme ou Barbarie focused on the necessity of rethinking the revolutionary movement. Its
members set out to challenge the assumptions, the practices, and the direction of the entire French Left. They presented their main goals
through a manifesto, modeled on the *Communist Manifesto*, which declared how the workers should organize themselves with a maximum of
autonomy.

One century after the *Communist Manifesto*, thirty years after the Russian Revolution, after huge victories and deep defeats, the revolutionary movement seems to have disappeared, like a river, which, by getting near to the sea, results in swamps and vanishes in the sand. "Marxism," "Socialism," the working class, a new historical period, have never been so current, and at the same time, never has real Marxism been so ridiculed, Socialism regarded with such contempt, and the working class sold and betrayed by those who claim to speak for it. . . ." Socialism" seems to have been accomplished in countries that have four hundred millions of inhabitants, but this "socialism" cannot be separated from concentration camps, from the most intensive social exploitation, from the most frightening dictatorship, and from the most extensive stupidity.[11]

Castoriadis wanted to distinguish two opposing projects in Marx's work: on one hand, the project of autonomy and, on the other hand, a functionalist and somewhat scientific project. There were two moments in Marx's thought, a period when he focuses on social struggles and a period when he theorizes revolutionary *praxis*. Castoriadis wanted to handle the first "Machiavellian moment."[12] When he focused on social struggles, Marx thought of human self-determination outside the frame of the state. Revolutionary humanism aims at destroying any kind of state because the category of the state was created in order to justify political and economic domination.

Unfortunately, Marx ultimately reduced institutions in every society to basic economic needs. He applied a deterministic approach to every society, ignoring more and more the priority of social struggles. In Socialisme ou Barbarie, Castoriadis had two main interests: on the one hand, he analyzed the evolution of Russian society, and on the other hand, he initiated a political debate with Marx. Socialisme ou Barbarie became increasingly critical not only of the so-called Marxist or socialist countries of the Eastern bloc, but also of Marxism itself, with its nineteenth-century scientism. If avowed Marxists were building a strong political apparatus contrary to the emancipation of proletarians, did it mean that Marx had to be saved from the people who invoked him? Perhaps there were some unclear points in Marx's theories that could lead to different interpretations. To grapple with these questions, Castoriadis focused on the actual situation of the proletariat and compared it to Marxist theory. The main problem in France in the 1940s and 1950s was that the working movement was under the influence of the French Communist Party, being led to a kind of apathy without the so-called revolutionary elite being able to understand and change this situation.

As far as Castoriadis was concerned, everything is determined by politics, and citizens should be able to participate in the legitimation of social norms.

The ideas of worker self-management were opposite to what the French Communist Party tried to promote. In this frame, Marxists did not fight against a capitalistic system but enlarged that system's goals. Instead of organizing the proletariat as a contesting force, the Communist Party and trade unions such as the communist Confédération générale du travail divided the working class unity and reduced its power of action. The proletariat was less active, and power was transferred to a class of revolution specialists, as in Leninist theories. Castoriadis could have held onto this point of view and developed a classic Trotskyist theory against Stalinist bureaucracy. Contrary to Althusser, who analyzed the deviance of Marxists from Marx's scientific works, Castoriadis did not hesitate to confront the theories of Marx with contemporary historical reality. He insisted that one should not have to consider Marx a sacred person in order to be able to discuss his theories.

Castoriadis did agree with Marx on two main points: Marx had been right to have explained, first, that the capitalist system had to destroy every former form of production (for example, the medieval mode of production), and second, that capitalism evolved toward a monopolistic phase by assembling capital and getting rid of small producers. Still, Castoriadis pointed out three crucial questions that Marx did not answer:

> What determines the level of exploitation of paid work by capital, what Marx called the rate of exploitation (relation of the total surplus value or the mass of profits to the mass of paid workers), and how did this rate evolve? How to realize economic equilibrium (equality of global supply and global demand) in a system in which production and demand depend on millions of independent acts, and where, above all, relations are constantly upset by accumulation and technological evolution? Finally, what are the long-term tendencies of capitalism's evolution; in other words, how does the functioning of the system progressively modify the structure?[13]

Castoriadis thus criticized the lack of accuracy of certain of Marx's concepts, such as the rate of exploitation. By determining the objective economic conditions of the capitalistic process, Marx tended to underemphasize the fight of the proletariat. By relating real salary to real products in order to explain how the rate of exploitation could increase, Marx considered the working force of the proletarian as merchandise.

Castoriadis maintained that Marx's reductionism showed how he was immersed in the social imagination of his time. For example, he thought in the same way as the capitalists when he wanted to define a constant economic rate of exploitation, ignoring that one hour of work differed from one individual to another. The rise of the rate of exploitation, the elevation of the organic composition of the capital, and the diminution of the profit rate explained for Marx the main crisis of capitalism, especially the crisis of overproduction. He strongly held that there was a law that regulated the rate of exploitation inside capitalism; by pointing out the objective contradictions of the system, he made the mistake of believing that such contradictions do not depend on the actions of individuals. Moreover, to Castoriadis's mind, we read in Marx's work the seeds of an economist interpretation of society, ignoring the impact of social fights and generalizing an institution of society that fits only some Western societies.[14]

Axelos and Papaioannou also shared critical points of view on the work of Marx, even if they were not expressed in the same style. We will treat each of them in turn. Axelos did not neglect the economic and political aspects of Marxist theory but wondered especially if one could talk about a Marxist philosophy. There were three main points to Axelos's critique of Marx: on the economic level, Marxist theory tended to underappreciate new emerging technological and economic processes; politically, it did not solve the problem of power; finally, on the philosophical level, it gave up a questioning thought.

> Marxism gives up the questioning thought, doesn't practice radical questioning, and forgets global interrogation. It leaves thought to absorb itself in scientism, sociologism, and flat and positivistic historicism. It sacrifices all theory to the sole practice—totally indifferent to *logos* and meaning [*sens*]—of the dialectic that turns about like a machine.[15]

Axelos was close to Castoriadis on two points: first, he refused the systematic and mechanical approach of the society that seduced many French intellectuals in the 1950s and 1960s, and secondly, he referred to the necessity of questioning. Politically, the conclusions of Axelos are similar to those of Castoriadis: Marxist theory resulted in the promotion of a bureaucratic society. As he wrote, "The Marxist current, full of contradictions and crevices, calls itself socialist and claims socialism. It ends up in what we can call capitalism and/or State socialism, as a bureaucratic collectivism. . . . It state-a-fies [*étaise*] more than it socializes."[16] These are exactly the theses expressed by Socialisme ou Barbarie. Axelos and Castoriadis thus followed a similar evolution on the necessity of overcoming Marxism.

The Hungarian Revolution of 1956 was a real shock in France and had an important effect on French intellectuals.[17] Indeed, some began to be more critical toward prevailing Marxist discourse, and many intellectuals left the Communist Party. The review *Socialisme ou Barbarie* covered the Hungarian Revolution from the perspective of the working-class challenge to "communist" rule at the very moment that Axelos was helping to found the publication *Arguments*. "We tried an adventure at the end of 1956 and the beginning of 1957," he recalled, "Events in Poland and Hungary seemed to have opened some rifts [*brèches*]."[18] Furthermore, he insisted on the review's isolation among intellectuals, in a way parallel to Castoriadis and Socialisme ou Barbarie, who also broke with existing Left trends. There were significant bonds between Socialisme ou Barbarie and Arguments circles.

To take one example, in 1968, Edgar Morin, a French sociologist who was a member of the Arguments group, wrote with Castoriadis and Lefort a book on the May events.[19] Morin was deeply influenced in his theories by his experience with *Arguments* and the work of Axelos. When he points out the fact that human beings live in a planetary iron age, we perceive the direct influence of Axelos. Morin left us a very interesting and complete testimony on the postwar French intellectual context.[20] Through his experience, we can understand the beliefs and the disillusionment of the postwar French Left. Morin was a member of the Communist Party until 1951. In his book *Autocritique*, he shows exactly how the party built its legitimacy and seduced intellectuals because of the experience of the Resistance. It became a cultural religion with a specific mission: it had to enlighten and guide the proletariat to its destiny. The way the Communist Party worked was similar to the Catholic Church—exclusion of the party felt like excommunication. Furthermore, Morin did not trust communist rule after the myth of Stalingrad. Contrary to other intellectuals who still gravitated toward the party, Morin gave up the communist experience as lost. He saw the work of *Arguments* as an experience of plurality. Its birth had been linked to the events of 1956 in Hungary, a moment at which dialogue and democracy were in demand.

> It was at the end of 1956 and at the beginning of 1957. In this review, without realizing it, we made a kind of Copernican Revolution; our foundation was in fact our plurality. We started, of course, from our common obsession, but we had especially developed an interrogation without limits. Our rule was that we could confront and contradict each other.[21]

If 1956 appeared like an opening onto a new way of thinking and a new way of doing politics, it was in fact a failure, as a large segment of the French intelligentsia of the 1960s was still imprisoned by a Marxist dogmatism.

Axelos had founded the collection "Arguments" in 1960. The review *Arguments* existed for only five years, whereas, as mentioned above, *Socialisme ou Barbarie* lasted until 1967.

> We weren't at home anywhere. We weren't Christians or liberals, social democrats or progressives, anarchists, Surrealists, or existentialists. We were no longer Marxists—should one say, dogmatic?—or Stalinists. And we were no longer writers or scholars, researchers, thinkers, and journalists. . . . We were interrogating, questioning, problematizing [*dans l'interrogation, la mise en question, la problématique*]. We resolved to lay the foundations for a post-Marxism.[22]

In these remarks by Axelos concerning the creation of *Arguments*, we can feel a self-critical position concerning his Marxist engagement, especially when he identifies existing Marxist discourse with Stalinism. In fact, Axelos's originality can be noticed in the way he developed his philosophy at a crossroads between Heidegger and Marx.[23] Like Heidegger, he focused on the phenomenological approach to the category of "world," the necessity of questioning phenomena and of criticizing the domination of *techne*. The essence of technique is not technical, as Heidegger had claimed in a conference given on this topic.[24] If, on the one hand, Marx had explained the evolution of the technical world in its relation to the development of capitalism, Heidegger pointed out that the essence of *technique* was rooted in a certain kind of metaphysics.[25] The capitalistic tendencies of the world were the result of a metaphysics that imposed a way of understanding the world through calculus. According to Heidegger, this particular thought had emerged in G. W. F. Leibniz's theory of sufficient reason, the notion that every effect must have a cause.[26] As far as Leibniz was concerned, the production of phenomena could be analyzed through a strict scheme of logically deducible causality. Leibniz wanted to build a mathematical science of phenomena that would be purely logical. Heidegger claimed that this metaphysical way of controlling Being through determinism was a tendency of the human spirit and dated back to the invention of Western metaphysics.

Instead of metaphysics Castoriadis would have said social imaginary. To his mind, the idea of a bureaucratic institution of life emerged in the thirteenth century with the rise of the merchant class. This social imaginary contradicted the project of autonomy created by the Athenian society between the eighth and the fifth centuries B.C.E. The Athenians created a way of doing politics as well as a way of practicing philosophy. When each citizen can take part in the making of laws or discuss their application, then we have for the first time in history a society that is able to question its mode of existence.[27] This characteristic was very intriguing to Castoriadis, though Greek society had been neither utopian nor perfect. A democratic society is a very difficult venture, and it can never be perfect since its norms can be always discussed.

The category of social imaginary was forged by Castoriadis in order to seize the significant objects that together make an institutional symbolism. This institutional symbolism defines a culture.[28] Heidegger had rejected Western metaphysics without considering such a contradiction between autonomy and bureaucracy, because he did not want to think within a political field. According to Castoriadis, consequently, Heidegger was not able to see the crisis of the contemporary society. "This is obviously one of the numerous consequences of his ignorance of the social dimension of history," Castoriadis concluded, "and of this history as including internal struggles."[29]

Axelos had joined a Marxist perspective with a Heideggerean conceptual frame, and these keys allowed him to decipher the way the world had evolved. Like Castoriadis and (as we will see) Papaioannou, Axelos attempted to think at a global scale, promoting what he called a "planetary thought": "Planetary thought should not present itself as a world perspective; on the contrary, it should understand itself as a global and perhaps even a friendly interrogation, putting everything in question."[30] We will return to this notion of a pure form of philosophy enlightened by a global perspective. According to Axelos, humanity had in fact invented relatively few metaphysical ideas. Three prominent ones could be found in all existing societies: the idea of God, the idea of nature, and the idea of the human being. For him, questioning thought had to modify these concepts and expose them to interrogation. This thought opens up on multidimensionality because nothing is really ever total or achieved, which is why questioning thought has to be fragmented and fluent. This reference to fluidity was very important in the works of our three philosophers: fluidity is what fights against any form of determinism and in that concept we can see a reference to Heraclitus. Such a reference was clear for Axelos, who wrote a book on the philosophy of Heraclitus, but it was more discreet in Castoriadis's work, for example, in the way he constantly referred to the idea of a singular human creation.[31] As Heraclitus suggested in his famous line—"we cannot enter in the same river two times"—the idea of creation contradicts any kind of reproduction. Creation is linked to the alteration of the world. Furthermore, Castoriadis often used the same metaphor of a "river open to the anonymous collective," when he dealt with the democratic experience and the necessity of self-management.[32] There is not an existing rational totality or a metaphysical system that can make us definitively understand the way the world works. With creation, everything evolves and is subject to change—in this perspective, determinism is not possible. For Castoriadis, determinism is on the metaphysical level what bureaucracy is on the political level. The imaginary signification of bureaucracy is control, and a prerequisite to control is a theoretical system closed on itself. History is creation and indeterminacy; it is not governed by a scheme. To Axelos's mind, Marxism had become a new tradition. Like earlier religious and cultural traditions, a Marxist tradition had appeared and defined its codes and values in reference to a set of basic texts. This tradition was now over, and from the point of view of planetary thought, Marxism and its dogmas had to be questioned.

Kostas Papaioannou had a similar career to Castoriadis. After high school, he studied law and, like Axelos, philosophy, especially German philosophy. Papaioannou and Axelos became friends when they met on the boat taking them to France. Resisting the Nazis, Papaioannou had been arrested, put in jail, and tortured for two months.[33] During the civil war, he joined the Greek Communist Party. At the end of 1945, thanks to the French Institute of Athens, he left Greece with a number of left-oriented intellectuals and artists. At that moment, he had already abandoned the Communist Party and denounced Stalinism, when he saw how the party repressed those who did not agree with its directives. Papaioannou finished his studies of philosophy at the Sorbonne and began to write in Greek and later in French. His special focus was on the philosophy of history, which led him to study Hegel and Marx and translate a number of their books.[34] These speculative interests did not prevent him from posing serious political questions, and like Axelos and Castoriadis, he wondered why so many people were living in misery and were the victims of strong dictatorships under the name of Marxist-Leninist theories. How was it that there were so many people fascinated by such theories, especially among the French bourgeois intelligentsia?

Papaioannou's critical confrontation with Marxism was isolated. Few people knew his work well, and it ran against the grain of popular enchantments with historical materialism. The French university largely ignored the work of Marx until World War Two, but after 1945, because of the prestige of the French Communist Party in the Resistance, Marxism was introduced in a generally dogmatic manner. Papaioannou aimed at understanding why Marxist theory would lead to a totalitarian society. Although unsympathetic to Marx and Marxists, it was necessary to read them closely in order to see where the Marxist project turned out to be a deterministic project. He translated the works of the young Marx and wrote on Hegel, whom he preferred.[35] The extraordinary conceptual system that Hegel built inspired him to write a general theory of history, in which he showed the radical gap between Greek antiquity and our modern civilization: whereas Greek society was linked to an eternal *cosmos*, our civilization has affirmed the privilege of history and time.

> The organization of the terrestrial city always remained at the center of the re-flection of Greek poets and philosophers, who were almost always educators and legislators. However, they never thought to situate the true destiny of hu-mankind in the historical world.[36]

With Hegel and Marx, history judges what is worth saving and what is not. With the Marxian perspective, history was seen as the realm of productive forces, a field that determined human activity. However, Papaioannou per-ceived another important contradiction: even if he had aspired to do so, Marx failed to build a monist theory, since he found two moving forces in history, an objectivist conception through the productive forces and a sub-jectivist one through the class struggle. According to Papaioannou, this made two forces, unable to be reunified through dialectics:

> The "objective" description of evolution as a determinism of productive forces and the "subjective" description of historical process as a class struggle do not work together as well as Marx thought.[37]

Papaioannou never wrote his planned major work on Marx and the Marx-ist tradition. Nevertheless, his articles on this topic were gathered in a book published in 1983, two years after he died.[38] Raymond Aron wrote the pref-ace to the book, pointing out the courage of a thinker who had resisted philosophical fashions. Papaioannou had taken part in some of Aron's sem-inars, and both of them shared a familiarity with Marx's work and had a strong sympathy for each other. Papaioannou had been affiliated with a review named *Le Contrat social*, directed by Boris Souvarine, a former rev-olutionary who had denounced early on the deviance of Stalinism and Marxism-Leninism. In fact, the articles from Papaioannou on Marx and Marxism were first published in that review. *Le Contrat social* was active between 1957 and 1968, more or less in the same period as *Socialisme ou Barbarie* and *Arguments*. Souvarine was a source of inspiration for Pa-paioannou and Castoriadis—the latter cited Souvarine as an example of free thought.[39] In 1947 Souvarine had returned from wartime exile in the United States, and he stayed in France until his death in 1984. In short, it is striking to see how the evolution of Castoriadis, Axelos, and Papaioannou held certain parallels, especially with their engagement in critical reviews. If they were active in politics, they tried to rethink the philosophical categories that underlined this practical engagement.

   Throughout his career Castoriadis constantly wondered how a society decided to have democratic institutions. His political engagement in Socialisme ou Barbarie led him to work on a theory of democracy. What he admired in classical Athenian society was that all aspects of social existence were decided by citizens. In fact, there were no social norms existing outside the society that could determine its evolution. Castoriadis wrote a provocative work proving the relation between democracy and tragedy in the former Athenian society.[40] He claimed that Greek tragedy was clearly associated with democracy, and he underlined the fact that Greek tragedy appeared at the same time as philosophy and the interrogation of institutions. Tragedy worked as popular education. In tragedy, even the gods were subject to *hybris*, and the people understood that those gods were products of themselves. Greek tragedy not only was a reflected image of society, it also made people aware that there was nothing outside the social sphere that determined it. The gods had the same passions as individuals; they were neither better nor worse.

   In Socialisme ou Barbarie, Castoriadis went on building this theory of a democratic society.[41] Drawing on his critical dialogue with Marx, he began to challenge some of Plato's basic ideas. At the end of his career, when he taught at the École des hautes études en sciences sociales, Castoriadis got deeper into this debate by affirming that all the philosophy of Plato was a metaphysical and political attempt to destroy democracy. According to Castoriadis, the Platonist philosophy had as its raison d'être proving the inanity of democracy. Plato never mentioned Greek authors like Democritus who promoted the idea of a universe that was self-organized. Democritus had argued that, in physics, matter was self-engendered. Those conclusions could have had a strong political impact, but Plato had never referred to such theories. In contrast, Democritus framed a democratic universe, where human beings realize that the world is the product of their actions and that they can modify laws in order to live together in the political city. For Castoriadis, the idea of self-management and the idea of autonomy were equivalent; they defined democracy (etymologically, of course, democracy signifies in Greek the power of *demos*, the power of the people). Only human beings can draw the limits of their action in order to mobilize a social power—*kratos* in Greek.[42]

Plato wanted a special category of individuals to rule the political city, since they had a specific knowledge of how the city should be ruled. Castoriadis denounced this ideology of specific knowledge ruling the city in the name of the good. This management ought not be reserved to a class of individuals, because no total knowledge of society is possible, even if particular opinions are. A view of society cannot exceed a situated perspective, however well-informed.[43] In democracy, anybody can have an executive role in public affairs or in politics. Plato associated democracy with demagogy; according to him, it is a scene where rhetoricians try to be persuasive in order to come to power. Yet, Castoriadis does not idealize the form of democracy: it is the regime of political risk. The people are afraid of this idea of autonomy, since their actions were not guaranteed by an extra-social foundation like the gods or principles. In the Platonist theory of the specialization of knowledge, one finds the imaginary signification of a bureaucratic institution. Bureaucracy means specialization of tasks and control of these tasks. In democracy, the rotation of roles and collective discussion must avoid this bureaucratic tendency. We have mostly been living under political oligarchies, where politics is centered on a private sphere instead of on collective discussions.

Castoriadis promoted his theory of a radical direct democracy against any form of bureaucratic institution. The postwar context was important here, since he wanted to save democracy against the kind of terrifying bureaucratic institution of life that had and continued to murder countless individuals. Democracy is the only regime where the individuals can experience autonomy. In contrast, Plato affirmed a heteronomous society led by specialists. Instead of specialists, we would rather employ the word "technocrats" nowadays, and it is striking to notice that the dilemma is still largely the same. Castoriadis's main goal was to develop a theory of democracy. It had to be linked to an understanding of how human institutions work. Knowing theoretically that the imaginary rather than reason is what defines the human being would help individuals pursue self-management and build the conditions of social autonomy. Social autonomy is inseparable from individual autonomy. Everything should be discussed in the frame of collective decision. This political view requires lucid individuals. If they understand that laws and principles are human products, then they can influence these laws' evolution. Social autonomy means that the individuals of a society are able to change the rules that govern them. Individuals are responsible for the social order and the rationality that they create, even if sometimes they prefer to delegate it to the gods, God, nature, or the power of ancestors. Castoriadis was very close to Maurice Merleau-Ponty's philosophy of existence when he built this notion of social imaginary.[44] Moreover, Claude Lefort, who was the co-founder of Socialisme ou Barbarie, was also the former student of Merleau-Ponty.[45] Merleau-Ponty was one of the rare French philosophers for whom Castoriadis had respect, contrary to Sartre whom he vigorously denounced as the theorist of French Stalinism.[46] Castoriadis worked on this notion of imagination through encounters with Merleau-Ponty's philosophy.

As a matter of fact, Castoriadis evolved on the margins of the French intellectual field. He thus condemned many main trends of French intellectual life. Castoriadis criticized the Marxist tradition's attempt to go beyond capitalism via bureaucratic means (control of the masses through the apparatus of a strong political party), and also, the fashion of structuralism.[47] He refused to understand human reality through the idea of structure. His anthropology led him to study psychoanalysis before starting to practice it in 1973. He read Freud passionately and attacked the theories of Lacan, who reduced the unconscious to a symbolic structure of language.[48] In his view, Lacan defined a symbolic structure that alienated every individual, explaining that the Other spoke through the individual. For Castoriadis, the implication of Lacan's view was that the existing social order was already present inside the individual. This theory had to be criticized for its political consequences.

Castoriadis, Axelos, and Papaioannou were original figures in French intellectual circles. As leftist philosophers critical of Marx, they maintained a certain lucidity with respect to the political events of their time. This temperament helped them to refuse a dogmatic Marxism prevailing in postwar French society. In a way, Axelos and Papaioannou agreed with the theses of Socialisme ou Barbarie concerning the evolution of the Russian bureaucratic society. The fact that they experienced the absurdity of Stalinist methods in Greece during the civil war gave them this early cautiousness against any kind of determinism or scientism. As a matter of fact, they escaped the sad illusions in which many French intellectuals had fallen because they were attached to a way of questioning phenomena, without being seduced by closed and systematic approaches. History is creation, and neither ideologies nor closed systems can determine the historical process.

> We were thus sent back to philosophy and more than that, to its historical character and to the enigma that it posed. Time is not simply exterior determination for philosophy, and even less a landmark for the ordered succession of philosophers' thoughts.[49]

NOTES

1. His principal book is about the imaginary institution of society and links his political engagement to his philosophical views. See Cornelius Castoriadis, *L'Institution imaginaire de la société* (Paris: Seuil, 1975). The trend of institutional analysis has been influential in pedagogy and the sphere of education. Georges Lapassade, who wrote many books on institutions, was a member of the same political group as Castoriadis, Socialisme ou Barbarie. See Lapassade, *Groupes, organisation et institutions* (Paris: Gauthier-Villars, 1970). René Lourau is also one of the main figures of that trend. See Lourau, *L'Analyse institutionnelle* (Paris: Éditions de Minuit, 1970).

2. Castoriadis touches on his autobiography in *La Société bureaucratique*, vol. 1, *Les Rapports de production en Russie* (Paris: Union générale d'éditions, 1973), 12; *Les Carrefours du labyrinthe*, vol. 4, *La Montée de l'insignifiance* (Paris: Seuil, 1996), 82; and *Les Carrefours du labyrinthe*, vol. 5, *Fait et à faire* (Paris: Seuil, 1997), 21.

3. Castoriadis, *La Montée de l'insignifiance*, 82.

4. Castoriadis, *Les Rapports de production en Russie*, 12–13.

5. Castoriadis, *Les Rapports de production en Russie*, 14.

6. Castoriadis, *Les Rapports de production en Russie*, 15–16.

7. Castoriadis, "Le rôle de l'idéologie bolchevique dans la naissance de la bureaucratie," in *L'Expérience du mouvement ouvrier*, vol. 2, *Prolétariat et organisation* (Paris: Union générale d'éditions, 1974). The articles on Russian bureaucratic society are gathered in Castoriadis, *Les Rapports de production en Russie*, and in *La Société bureaucratique*, vol. 2, *La Révolution contre la bureaucratie* (Paris: Union générale d'éditions, 1973). See also, Castoriadis, "La bureaucratie après la mort de Staline," in *Prolétariat et organisation*, 157–88.

8. Castoriadis, "Lettre ouverte aux militants du PCI et de la IVe internationale," in *Les Rapports de production en Russie*, 185–205.

9. Claude Lefort gathered the articles that he wrote for *Socialisme ou Barbarie* on the critique of bureaucracy in his *Eléments d'une critique de la bureaucratie* (Paris: Gallimard, 1971).

10. Castoriadis, "Sur la question de l'URSS et du stalinisme mondial," in *Les Rapports de production en Russie*, 63–73.

11. Castoriadis, "Sur la question de l'URSS," 139.

12. The expression is used by Miguel Abensour, *La Démocratie contre l'État: Marx et le moment machiavélien* (Paris: PUF, 1997).

13. Castoriadis, *Capitalisme moderne et révolution*, vol. 2, *Le Mouvement révolutionnaire sous le capitalisme moderne* (Paris: Éditions 10/18, 1979), 76.

14. In the second volume of *Capitalisme moderne et révolution*, Castoriadis confronts Marx's theses with the reality of the actual proletarian situation. See Castoriadis, *Le Mouvement révolutionnaire sous le capitalisme moderne*, 47–184.

15. Kostas Axelos, *Vers la pensée planétaire* (Paris: Éditions de Minuit, 1964), 186. Axelos developed the characteristics of this planetary thought in other books. See his *Systématique ouverte* (Paris: Éditions de Minuit, 1984), 93–100.

16. Axelos, *Vers la pensée planétaire*, 199.

17. See Michael Scott Christofferson, "French Intellectuals and the Repression of the Hungarian Revolution of 1956: The Politics of a Protest Reconsidered," in this volume.

18. Axelos, *Vers la pensée planétaire*, 186.

19. Edgar Morin, Claude Lefort, and Jean-Marc Coudray [Cornelius Castoriadis], *Mai 68: La Brèche* (Paris: Complexe, 1988). Moreover, Morin and Castoriadis were close friends, and it is striking to find some elements of Castoriadis's anthropology in Morin's theories on the complexity of human nature, culture, and self-management.

20. See Morin, *Pour sortir du vingtième siècle* (Paris: Nathan, 1981); and *Autocritique* (Paris: Seuil, 1970), esp. chapter 9, entitled, "L'âge de fer planétaire." For Morin, the planetary iron age began in 1492 when America was discovered. Exchanges were henceforth made in all parts of the world, meaning that the globalization of the world was underway. Castoriadis had similar views when he described the characteristics of planetary capitalism.

21. Morin, *Reliances* (Paris: Éditions de l'Aube, 2002), 53.

22. Axelos, *Vers la pensée planétaire*, 186.

23. See Stuart Elden, "Kostas Axelos and the World of the *Arguments* Circle," in this volume.

24. Martin Heidegger, *Essais et conférences*, trans. André Préau (Paris: Gallimard, 1992).

25. Heidegger, *Essais et conférences*, 9.

26. Heidegger, *Le Principe de raison*, trans. André Préau (Paris: Gallimard, 1962).

27. Castoriadis, "La *polis* grecque et la création de la démocratie," in *Les Carrefours du labyrinthe*, vol. 2, *Domaines de l'homme* (Paris: Seuil, 1986), 261–306.

28. Castoriadis, *L'Institution imaginaire de la société*, 493–532. This is the final chapter of the book and deals with the significations of the social imaginary.

29. Castoriadis, *La Création humaine*, vol. 1, *Sujet et vérité dans le monde social-historique: séminaire 1986–1987* (Paris: Seuil, 2002), 299.

30. Axelos, *Vers la pensée planétaire*, 186. See Castoriadis, *Domaines de l'homme*, 165.

31. Axelos, *Héraclite et la philosophie* (Paris: Éditions de Minuit, 1962).

32. Castoriadis, *L'Institution imaginaire de la société*, 533.

33. See the short biography written by Alain Pons at the end of Kostas Papaioannou, *De la critique du ciel à la critique de la terre* (Paris: Allia, 1998), 53–62.

34. For the translations of Papaioannou in French, see Hegel, *La Raison dans l'histoire* (Paris: Union générale d'éditions, 1965). Friedrich Engels and Karl Marx, *La Première Critique de l'économie politique* (Paris: Union générale d'éditions, 1972). Marx, *Critique de l'Etat hégélien* (Paris: Union générale d'éditions, 1976). These two last translations have been presented by Papaioannou in Karl Marx, *Ecrits de jeunesse* (Paris: La République des Lettres, 1994).

35. Papaioannou, *Hegel* (Paris: Agora, 1962).

36. Papaioannou, *La Consécration de l'histoire* (Paris: Ivréa, 1996), 51.

37. Papaioannou, *La Consécration de l'histoire*, 149.

38. Papaioannou, *De Marx et du marxisme* (Paris: Gallimard, 1983).

39. Castoriadis, *La Montée de l'insignifiance*, 82.

40. Castoriadis, "Anthropogonie chez Eschyle et autocréation de l'homme chez Sophocle," in *Les Carrefours du labyrinthe*, vol. 6, *Les Figures du pensable* (Paris: Seuil, 1999).

41. Castoriadis was a researcher and a teacher at the École des hautes études en sciences sociales from 1980 until his death in 1997. See Castoriadis, *Platon, Sur le Politique* (Paris: Seuil, 1999), which were seminars that he gave at the École.

42. We refer here to several texts from Castoriadis besides his courses on Plato: "La démocratie athénienne: fausses et vraies questions," "La culture dans une société démocratique," "La démocratie comme procédure et comme régime," in *La Montée de l'insignifiance*.

43. Castoriadis, "Une interrogation sans fin," in *Domaines de l'homme*, 241–60.

44. Castoriadis, "Merleau-Ponty et le poids de l'héritage ontologique," in *Fait et à faire*, 157–96.

45. Lefort wrote a very penetrating essay on Merleau-Ponty. See his, *Sur une colonne absente* (Paris: Gallimard, 1978).

46. Castoriadis, "Les divertisseurs," in *La Société française* (Paris: Union générale d'éditions, 1979), 223–37. See also Castoriadis, "Sartre, le stalinisme et les ouvriers," in *L'Expérience du mouvement ouvrier*, vol. 1, *Comment lutter* (Paris: Union générale d'éditions, 1974), 179–248.

47. It is worth recalling that the French Communist Party renounced the idea of the "dictatorship of proletariat" only in 1976. Henceforth the democratic route to power was privileged.

48. Castoriadis, *Les Carrefours du labyrinthe* (Paris: Seuil, 1978).

49. Castoriadis, *Les Carrefours du labyrinthe*, 15.

5

KOSTAS AXELOS AND THE WORLD OF THE *ARGUMENTS* CIRCLE

Stuart Elden

At the heart of French intellectual life for over half a century, Kostas Axelos remains a largely unknown figure in the English-speaking world. He was born in Greece in 1924, quickly became a communist, and was active in the National Liberation Front against the Nazi occupation. After Greece was liberated in 1944, and the country descended into civil war, he was sentenced to death by the Royalist government and left on the same ship as Cornelius Castoriadis.[1] Almost immediately on arriving in France he got in touch with the Parti communiste français (PCF).[2] He studied at the Sorbonne, taught at the University of Paris, and researched at the Centre national de la recherche scientifique. Axelos had a wide range of intellectual contacts, including Jacques Lacan, Jean Beaufret, and, through them, Martin Heidegger; Pablo Picasso, whose partner Françoise Gilot, the subject of the 1996 film *Surviving Picasso*, ended up living with Axelos, André Breton, and Georges Bataille.[3] He attended seminars by Karl Jaspers and had his thesis examined by, among others, Paul Ricoeur and Raymond Aron.[4] He is cited approvingly by Jacques Derrida in *Of Grammatology*, and his books were reviewed in *Critique* by Gilles Deleuze and in *Esprit* by Henri Lefebvre.[5] Now in his eighties, Axelos continues to be active: his most recent book was published in 2001, and he participated in a conference to celebrate fifty years of conferences at Cerisy-la-Salle in August 2002 and in one on Heidegger's thought in France in November 2002.[6]

Little of his work—nineteen books and numerous articles—is available in
English.[7] The only book-length translation is of the 1961 study, *Marx
penseur de la technique*, which develops a version of Heideggerian Marxism, also pursued in the German-language collection *Einführung in ein
künftiges Denken: Über Marx und Heidegger*, which would prove important
in the non-Sartrean appropriation of Heidegger's ideas in France.[8] This article will discuss one of his ideas, the notion of "world," in some detail, but
Axelos is perhaps most important in his role as a facilitator and node in an
intellectual network, a world of another kind. This took a range of forms, including his work with the journal *Arguments*, and a book series of the same
name with Éditions de Minuit. Axelos is also known for his French translations of Georg Lukács' *History and Class Consciousness* and Heidegger's
What is Philosophy?, a lecture originally given at Cerisy-la-Salle in 1955
where Axelos acted as Heidegger's interpreter.[9] Over the next few years, Axelos also did this for Heidegger's meetings with René Char and Georges
Braque, and spent several days at Lacan's country house in the company of
Beaufret, Heidegger, and Lacan.[10]

In English-language critical scholarship on Marxism in France, it is only
really in Mark Poster's *Existential Marxism in Postwar France* (1975) that
Axelos has received substantial treatment.[11] My own *Understanding Henri
Lefebvre* (2004) traces some of the interrelations between Lefebvre and Axelos;[12] Michael Kelly's *Modern French Marxism* (1982) simply makes reference to the "greatly overestimated 'Arguments' and 'Socialisme ou Barbarie' groups," the latter being founded by Castoriadis and Claude Lefort.[13]
In France there has been more interest, including a biography, a book by
Lefebvre and Pierre Fougeyrollas, and an edited collection of essays.[14] This
is not to say that the French reception has been all positive. A similar
downplaying of the importance of *Arguments* to that of Kelly is found in
Richard Gombin's *The Origins of Modern Leftism* (1971), for example.[15] Indeed, Lefebvre's biographer Rémi Hess has recently suggested that Axelos's
work merits being rediscovered, arguing that even in his adopted homeland
he is largely ignored.[16] In a sense, though, the Anglophone neglect is a circular problem—the lack of translations means lack of knowledge and interest in his writings; the absence of that interest means translations would be
unlikely to find an audience. While the Pluto series on modern European
thinkers includes a study of his fellow *Arguments* editor, Edgar Morin,[17]
there has been almost no attention paid to Axelos even in Anglophone journal articles. In fact, aside from Poster, the most detailed treatment of Axelos is Ronald Bruzina's introduction to his translation of *Alienation, Praxis,
and Techne in the Thought of Karl Marx*.[18]

THE *ARGUMENTS* JOURNAL

Axelos's role as a facilitator of debate, after his work with Heidegger, was initially in the *Arguments* journal, which he edited between 1958 and 1962, and whose contributors included Lefebvre, Maurice Blanchot, Deleuze, and Lefort.[19] Morin, Roland Barthes, Colette Audry, and Jean Duvignaud were the original figures behind the journal, with Morin the key figure. Barthes was involved for the first five and last six issues.[20] Other figures were part of a fairly fluid editorial team, including François Fejtö and Fougeyrollas. Despite some suggestions, Lefebvre was never an editor of *Arguments*.[21] The journal was linked with and modeled on the Italian journal, *Ragionamenti*, whose editors included Franco Fortini and Roberto Guiducci.[22] As well as sharing intellectual content and aims, *Arguments* borrowed the typographical and stylistic characteristics of *Ragionamenti*: a rather muted and unassuming format. As Morin suggests, the aim was for the impact to come from the content rather than design.[23] The journal also had links with other European publications, such as *Praxis* in Yugoslavia and *Nowa Cultura* in Poland, and directly inspired the German *Das Argument*.[24] The British journal *New Left Review*, which though not formally connected shared some characteristics and had contact with Morin, was launched in 1960.[25]

The date of the first issue was December 1956–January 1957. This is significant, 1956 being the year of Khrushchev's denunciation of Stalin to the Twentieth Congress of the Soviet Communist Party, and events in Hungary, Poland, and Suez.[26] It was, the editors declared, launched at the time of the *éclatement*, the explosion or destruction, of Stalinism.[27] *Arguments* was a journal for those who had left the PCF, such as Morin, or those who were about to, such as Lefebvre. Morin's *Autocritique* and Lefebvre's *La Somme et le reste*, both published in 1959, are classic accounts of the struggle to rid themselves of the accumulated baggage of party membership—in Lefebvre's case lasting almost three decades.[28]

The journal tried very hard to be non-sectarian, including Stalinists, Trotskyists, and even Sartreans among its contributors.[29] But there was a danger that this open Marxism would involve going beyond Marxism, a not-inaccurate description of the tension in the journal as a whole.[30] Taking a lead from some of the ideas proposed by Maurice Merleau-Ponty, especially following his resignation as political editor of *Les Temps modernes* in 1952, *Arguments* was interested in what Western Marxism might be without the Leninist element.[31] Although Kevin Anderson has shown how some of Lenin's work— particularly the notebooks on Hegel—opened up alternatives to orthodox

Marxist-Leninism, this post-Leninist move was part of a reshaping of the French, and more broadly European, Left.[32] Myron Kofman notes that by the end of its run *Arguments* had "drawn contributions from almost all of the leading names of the non-communist Left in France with two significant exceptions: Castoriadis and Sartre." Indeed Kofman suggests that *Les Temps modernes* was "almost as much 'the enemy' as was the PCF."[33]

Axelos's first involvement was as a cotranslator of Lukács in issue number three, and then as a contributor in number four.[34] He was involved in the editing from number five and quickly established his mark on the journal. Morin recalls his arriving "like a meteorite."[35] Although he did not take over as chief editor until 1961, issue twenty-one, *Arguments* was changed quite dramatically by his presence. Instead of its previous form as a research bulletin, originally conceived by Morin as a forum for debate and the exchange of ideas, under Axelos it became much more of a standard journal.[36] The opening lines of the original manifesto, at the head of the first issue, had proclaimed that "*Arguments* is not a review but a bulletin of research, discussions, and clarifications, open to all who place themselves in a scientific and socialist perspective."[37] Axelos recalls the transition somewhat differently, being a move from a concern with communism and the rupture with the PCF to more general questions concerned with life, love, the universe, and language.[38]

Axelos's recollection shows the wide-ranging interests of the journal. Listed at the end of issue number seven, the subject groupings of previous articles are revealing. As well as "Marxist Thought," "Economy and Society," "The Problems of Socialism," and "Lukács," a number of articles had been published on "The Third World," "Culture, Language, and the Theatre," and "The Contemporary Novel." Barthes's piece in the first issue was one of the first discussions of semiology.[39] Subsequent issues would look at a wide range of other concerns: from historical issues, the arts, politics, cosmology, the world and the planet, and, as mentioned by Axelos, love. Indeed, Axelos himself contributed an essay entitled, "L'Errance érotique" to the seventh issue of *Arguments*, a piece later collected in *Vers la pensée planétaire*, and then published as a book in its own right. He had also written the piece "Les marxistes et l'amour" under the pseudonym of Jean de Leyde.[40]

As Axelos recalls, putting together *Arguments* was a very social occasion, with much of the discussion moving from the offices of Éditions de Minuit to meals at the editors' homes. He also notes that it was impossible to estimate how much time he spent on the journal, as the social aspects meshed with the work aspects. He describes the work as "free militancy [*un mili-*

tantisme gratuit] but with a lot of pleasure."[41] As Eric Haviland notes, Axelos's recollections of this period are predominantly happy.[42] It is also worth noting that the managing editor for much of the time was Axelos's wife, Réa Karavas. In a retrospective interview Axelos was asked whether he agreed with the idea that many of the pieces in the journal were sketches or works in progress, rather than finished pieces. He agreed, but denied that this indicated an absence of work on them. Articles were worked on, reworked and re-reworked, but the point was to show thought in movement rather than sedentary positions, hence the appearance of sketchiness.[43]

According to Axelos, around the time of number five or six about 1,000 issues were produced, although circulation eventually climbed to 4,000, and some issues had to be reprinted.[44] Morin notes that this was in large part a Latin Quarter phenomenon, four hundred copies being sold on the boulevard Saint-Michel alone.[45] However, its impact cannot simply be measured in figures. As Rémy Rieffel phrases it, "the existence of *Arguments* was short (1956–1962), but its influence was felt for a long time."[46] *Arguments* not only published some of the key intellectual figures of postwar France, it also introduced the French public to a range of writers in translation. Foremost among these was Georg Lukács, several of whose essays from *History and Class Consciousness* appeared in the journal.[47] These translations drew a fairly harsh response from Lukács, who suggested, via Emile Bottigelli, that "for twenty years, I have, several times, publicly declared that I consider my book *History and Class Consciousness*, published in 1923, as outdated [*pour dépassé*] and, in many respects, wrong."[48] The *Arguments* response was bullish, continuing to publish chapters and then the full text, which also drew a criticism from Lukács, "not for formal reasons concerning author's rights," but because the book was erroneous and "dangerous," being part of Lukács' transition from "the objective idealism of Hegel to dialectical materialism," and therefore only likely to "provoke confusion with readers today."[49] Axelos also played a major role in making other German writers known to a French audience, including Theodor Adorno, Karl Korsch, and the later work of Heidegger.[50]

One of the other things that is notable about the journal is that it was keen not to outstay its welcome. Its end was not due to lack of money or readers.[51] As noted above, the journal had changed from its original format, and it was in danger of being just a collection of papers, without a coherent purpose. Equally, as Morin notes, the team behind the journal were further and further apart, in some cases literally: Duvignaud in Tunisia, Fougeyrollas in Senegal, and Fejtö and Barthes occupied with their own work.[52] In 1962, then, Axelos and Morin closed the journal, Axelos declaring that "with

and without joy and sadness, the *Arguments* review is scuttled by its cap-
tains."[53] Axelos saw the demise of *Arguments* as inevitable given the end of
its intellectual project, which was to open up an intellectual space for variants with French leftism.[54] For Morin, because *Arguments* had been
formed just as Khrushchev's secret speech had opened up the possibility of
plural Marxisms, its demise signaled the end of that project.[55] For Kofman,
"if Axelos said farewell with the passing sorrow of a wanderer, Morin burst
into a lament for a lost love."[56]

In 1963, the Internationale Situationniste (IS) published a tract entitled
"Into the Dustbins of History," which both mocked the demise of the journal they despised and particularly condemned what they saw as the plagiarism of their work on the Paris Commune, in an article by Lefebvre which
appeared in the final issue of *Arguments*.[57] In the pamphlet, reprinted in a
later issue of their own journal, the IS laid their own "Theses on the Paris
Commune" alongside the offending text of Lefebvre's. The details of the
particular case are less important than what it says about the infighting of
the French Left in this period.[58] Accordingly to the IS, *Arguments* was
France's "purest expression" of "the fraudulent carnival of modern
thought."[59] Sometime later, the IS accused Axelos of having invented
"Jacques Darquin," a writer supposedly "briefly a member of the Internationale Situationniste," in order to pen a positive article about himself.[60]
The IS coined the derogatory epithet "Argumentist," which Morin dryly observed was "the nicest compliment that they gave us."[61]

After *Arguments* folded, the *Socialisme ou Barbarie* journal tried to take
on its subscribers, if not its ideas, writing a letter suggesting that "we know
your subscription to *Arguments* testifies to similar preoccupations."[62] Although this is cited critically by the IS, according to Lefebvre, Guy Debord
told him that "our journal, the *Internationale situationniste*, has to replace
Arguments."[63] It did not take long before these journals similarly folded,
Socialisme ou Barbarie three years later, *Internationale situationniste* in
1969. René Lourau has called this the self-dissolution of the avant-gardes,
although he sees the breakups as important for the group-based politics of
1968 and beyond.[64]

The end of *Arguments* was certainly the end of an era, and yet certain aspects of its project continued, both in the book series that bore its name and
in the work of its organizers. Axelos has noted that *Arguments* had an important impact on his subsequent career and work, suggesting that it "was
a great laboratory or fusion of ideas."[65] As Axelos's ex-wife Réa Karavas suggests, several ideas tried out in the journal went on to be "discovered" many
years later.[66] Others went in different directions. Morin moved closer to

Castoriadis and Lefort of *Socialisme ou Barbarie*; and as Olivier Corpet notes, it is interesting that a number of those involved with *Arguments*, including Lefebvre and Duvignaud, were involved in the launch of the journal *Autogestion* in 1966.[67] Sometime collaborators Alain Touraine, François Châtelet, and Fougeyrollas all went on to produce important works. But perhaps most interesting, French Marxism found new stars. Sartre's *Critique of Dialectical Reason* was published in 1960, and, as Kofman notes, just as *Arguments* folded, Althusser's articles began to attract attention.[68]

THE *ARGUMENTS* BOOK SERIES

Just before the journal was terminated, Axelos launched a book series of the same name with Éditions de Minuit. Although Kofman suggests that the series was everything Morin feared the journal would become, Axelos claimed that it both "continued and began a same and different history" [*poursuit et inaugure une histoire même et autre*].[69] Éditions de Minuit was at the forefront of the publication of French thought, along with the Critique series, also paralleling a journal of the same name, edited by Georges Bataille.[70] Its catalogue reads almost like a who's who of French postwar intellectual life, with the *Arguments* series including Deleuze's *Spinoza et le probleme de l'-expression* and his presentation of Sacher-Masoch's *Venus in Furs*, Bataille's *L'Érotisme*, and Blanchot's *Lautréamont et Sade*.[71] The series also published several books by contributors to the journal, including three by Lefebvre, Edgar Morin's work on cinema, and almost all of Axelos's own works.[72] Jean Beaufret's four-volume *Dialogue avec Heidegger*, crucial in understanding the French reception of Heidegger's thought, since Beaufret was the recipient of Heidegger's *Letter on Humanism*; René Lourau's analyses of the state and institutions; and Didier Franck's important studies of Husserl and Heidegger, are some of the other highlights in an extensive backlist.[73] Also important, as with the journal, was the program of translations. A whole range of studies, both within and outside Marxism, appeared in this series: for some writers this was the first time they had appeared in French. Lukács' *Histoire et connaissance de classe* (1960), already mentioned, was the inaugural book, with an important preface by Axelos himself.[74] This translation preceded the English translation, which did not appear until 1971, and therefore served as an early way into the ideas of Lukács.[75] Works by a range of other thinkers, including the dissident Marxism of Karl Korsch and Herbert Marcuse; Louis Hjelmslev and Roman Jakobson's pioneering work on linguistics; and the phenomenology of Karl

Jaspers and Eugen Fink were also included in the series.[76] It is worth noting that if the journal was always a collaborative venture, the book series was almost entirely the work of Axelos.[77]

One of the recurrent themes of the journal, and continued in detail in the book series, was the question of the notion of "world." This seems to me to be the enduring legacy of their work. The fifteenth issue of the journal, in 1959, had a large number of articles devoted to the theme of "the world-wide problem [*le problème mondial*]," including a brief, but suggestive article entitled "Thèses sur la mondialisation," by Fougeyrollas.[78] In this piece Fougeyrollas discusses how the tensions between capitalism and socialism are masking the opportunity of deploying the world's resources to deal with the world's problems, for example starvation and malnutrition. A new universalism, a universalism of the world [*universalisme mondialiste*], must replace the universalist ethics, law, and social structure of, respectively, Christianity, democracy, and Marxism. "To the *mondialisation* of problems we must respond with the *mondialisation* of thought and action"; the West "must propose or offer [*proposer*] to the East and South to make a unity of the human world."[79]

The following issue had a theme section on "the planetary era"; the 1960 manifesto of the journal explained one of its purposes as understanding the "second half of the twentieth century: a planetary age of technology; iron age of a new industrial civilization; new age of the human";[80] and the *Arguments* book series was divided into two divisions, one of which was entitled "The Becoming-Thought of World and the Becoming-Worldly of Thought."[81] This phrase undoubtedly trades on a line from Marx's doctoral thesis, where he suggests that "the world's becoming philosophical is at the same time philosophy's becoming worldly, that its realization is at the same time its loss."[82] Both Axelos and Lefebvre regularly cited this as an aphorism, and for Axelos, it could be said to serve as a guiding theme for his entire work.[83] Marx's point is that in its becoming worldly, that is in its actualization, philosophy is transcended and overcome.[84] What is interesting here, in relation to the book series, is that "philosophy" is replaced by "thought," a very Heideggerian move. So, here, as will become apparent in much of Axelos's work, we have a Marxist theme transfigured through Heidegger. Two books translated in the *Arguments* series particularly contributed to this thinking of the relation between world and thought: Eugen Fink's *Le Jeu comme symbole du monde*—play, or the game, as symbol of the world—and Wilfrid Desan's *The Planetary Man*, to which Axelos contributed an afterword.[85] Fink had been Husserl's assistant for many years, and was the co-organizer, with Heidegger of a 1966–67 seminar on Heraclitus.[86] In the famous fragment 52, Heraclitus had declared that time, the world, or the universe "is like a child playing a game."[87]

THE WORLD AND TECHNOLOGY

It is in this theme of thinking of the world that perhaps we can see the greatest contemporary relevance of Axelos and the *Arguments* circle. The "world" thematic has the potential to act as a valuable correction to current lazy thinking on globalization. The issue of the world, particularly in relation to the notion of play or the game—*le jeu*—was a recurrent concern of Axelos's own writings.[88] In numerous works, notably *Vers la pensée planétaire*, *Horizons du monde*, and *Le Jeu du monde*, Axelos sketched a number of key themes. In the last, which Jacques Sojcher has called his "master-book," and which apparently took fifteen years to write, he pursues the question in considerable detail.[89] In the second half of this chapter I therefore offer some thoughts on Axelos's work in this regard.

The argument is that the 1960s saw a new era of planetary technology and *mondialisation*, a term that can only be loosely translated as "globalization."[90] The stress is on the process of becoming worldly, the seizing and comprehending of the world as a whole, as an event in thought, rather than on the spread of phenomena of economics and politics across the surface of the globe. In other words, the second process, globalization, is in a sense only possible because of this prior comprehending of the world, *mondialisation*. Although the distinction between the two terms has been blurred in more recent French writings, it is important in understanding the concepts in their usage at the time. This issue is explored in much detail in Axelos's writings, and was picked up, for example, in Lefebvre's work on the state and production on the world scale.[91] These are some of the earliest usages of the term in French literature, and predate the discussion of the notion of globalization in English-language scholarship. As Axelos suggested much later, when globalization was much more widely discussed, the term globalization—affecting the globe—misses the "world" and so-called world history.[92]

Axelos suggests that when we talk of an atomic or nuclear era we do so without knowing what we are naming. Both of these designations trade upon the wider context of planetary technology, which is seen as the new destiny of the world.[93] Axelos describes this as the "becoming-worldly of technology, and the becoming-technological of the world," in another twist to the phrase.[94] It is to the world that the crisis facing humanity has risen: if Nietzsche discussed European nihilism, Axelos saw it on the worldwide level.[95] Like Heidegger, who discussed this aspect of Nietzsche's work in his lecture courses,[96] by technology [*technique*] Axelos means something much broader than tools or techniques; he addresses their underlying logic.

> Technology founds, undoubtedly, the possibility and effectiveness of machines, industry, the exploitation of atomic energy and of all other energy, but it goes far beyond apparatuses and machinery. And it is global technology which orders the new worldwide politics, the planetary politics.[97]

Axelos therefore works through in detail the "encounter between global technology and modern humans."[98] The quoted phrase is, of course, Heidegger's, where he uses it to describe the "inner truth and greatness of national socialism," that is the so-called private version of national socialism that he yearned for in the face of the distortion he saw ruling in Germany.[99] For Axelos, the thinking of this encounter is of considerable importance, though his political inclination was a form of dissident, albeit Heidegger-influenced, Marxism. "World" does not simply signify the totality of all that exists; it is concerned with relations, interplay, and the game—*le jeu*.[100] Axelos claims, just as Heidegger does, that the human and world are not one, but neither are they two: "Neither of them is the other, but they cannot act [*jouer*] without the other."[101] Rather, they are something that requires their being thought together, what Heidegger calls being-in-the-world, which should not be understood in a primarily spatial sense, but rather as an integration of the human and the environment.[102] As Axelos puts it, "there is not the human *and* world. The human is not *in* the world."[103] What this means is that we are not so much in the world but *of* the world, just as the world is not in space-time, but is spatio-temporal.[104] Our relation with the world is the crucial issue; it is both something within and outside our control: "The human is the great partner of the play of the world, yet the human is not only the player, but is equally the 'outplayed' [*déjoué*], the plaything [*jouet*]."[105] As well as this thinking of the relation of the human and the world, clearly Axelos's thought on technology is indebted to Heidegger's work in this area.[106] What we have is the interesting contrast between a Nazi party member and someone who was sentenced to death for their role in the Greek resistance.[107]

It is worth noting here that, although Axelos would remain Heideggerian, he did not shy away from the political aspects of Heidegger's career. According to Haviland, he questioned Heidegger about his allegiance to the Nazi party, but never got much beyond straightforward explanations: that

Nazism was not the same at the beginning as it became and that we should not judge 1933 events on the basis of what we think of Nazism now; that "I committed an error, and must pay for it"; and that "but in my work, there is no trace of Nazism." At least the last is palpably false, as Axelos realized.[108] Then, in 1959, Axelos, Beaufret, Châtelet, and Lefebvre debated numerous aspects of Heidegger's work, including his relation to Marx and to his Nazi past.[109] This should give the lie to any suggestion that French Heidegger scholarship was woken from its dogmatic slumbers in 1987 by Victor Farías's book: the question had also been discussed in *Les Temps modernes* in the 1940s.[110] Axelos, just as some of the more intelligent recent discussions of Heidegger and politics have realized,[111] knew that you could be a Heideggerian without being on the political Right, but that this could not be at the expense of a detailed and careful interrogation of the relationship between his politics and his thought.[112]

Axelos interrogates Marx and Marxism through this question of technology. For Lefebvre, this is one of the important characteristics of Axelos: he is "one of a rare breed, if not the only one" who studies, criticizes, and situates Marx within the history of thought.[113] In his book on Marx, Axelos shows how alienation, that great concern of Marx that dominated so much French discussion of his ideas in the twentieth century, has relations to Heidegger's notion of the "forgetting of being."[114] Alienation in Marx, according to Axelos, can be found not only in ideology and economics, but also through technology. In Marx's own writings we find this thought particularly in his work on the labor process, and Axelos reads Marx widely to interrogate this problematic. One of the key passages is found in *The Poverty of Philosophy*:

> Social relations are closely bound up with productive forces. In acquiring new productive forces men change their mode of production; and in changing their mode of production, in changing the way of earning their living, they change all their social relations. The hand-mill gives you society with the feudal lord; the steam-mill, society with the industrial capitalist.[115]

Technology therefore affects the way in which we deal with nature, the world, and the entirety of our social relations.

Axelos describes modern technology as an *échafaudage*, a scaffold or a framework.[116] In *Contribution à la logique* he talks of the "*worldwide technical échafaudage*."[117] Such a metaphor becomes clearer when we recognize that this is the term Axelos suggests be used to translate the Heideggerian notion of *das Ge-stell*, usually translated as "en-framing," or, in French, as *arraissonment* or *dispositif*.[118] Like Heidegger, Axelos thinks that the way that we conceive of the world is founded upon a particular ontological determination of it as calculable, measurable, and therefore controllable and exploitable. "Modernity leads to the planetary era. This era is global and worldwide, errant, leveling and flattening, planning, calculating and combinative" [*Cette ère est globale et mondiale, errante, aplanissante et aplatissante, planificatrice, calculatrice et combinatoire*].[119] The framework which makes modern technology achievable precedes it as a condition of possibility. It follows that Marx's critique of political economy is based upon trying to comprehend the reduction of phenomena to value—use or exchange—a numerical measure of productivity and power. For Axelos therefore:

> The world cannot be reduced either to an ensemble of intraworldly phenomena, nor to "creation," or to the Cosmic Universe, to which is adjoined a social and historical world, nor to the totality of that which human representation understands [*de ce que saisit la représentation humaine*], nor to the total scope of technical activity.[120]

But Axelos, as well as reading the examination of a Heideggerian problematic in Marx, reads Marx in much the same way as Heidegger reads Nietzsche, as the final figure of Western metaphysics, in whom the most radical challenge and the exhaustion of possibilities comes together.[121] Heidegger only briefly acknowledges the role that Marx plays in the final stages of metaphysics.[122] It is interesting to note that the two places where Heidegger does deal with this theme are in relation to French promptings—in the "Letter on Humanism" to Beaufret, and in the "What is Philosophy?" lecture Axelos had translated for the Cerisy-la-Salle audience. When Axelos suggested that Heidegger has not sufficiently dealt with the thought of Marx on technology, or indeed Marx at all, Heidegger replied that he should do it himself.[123] Marx therefore plays the same role for Axelos as Nietzsche does for Heidegger, as the "last philosopher,"[124] where "a great epoch of Western metaphysics, that is, of Greek, Judeo-Christian, and modern metaphysics, reaches a culmination."[125] Like Heidegger, Axelos turns to the pre-Socratics, particularly Heraclitus. As already mentioned, Axelos's secondary thesis was on him, and he translated and edited a collection of his writings.[126] For Lefebvre, against the new Eleatics, the Zenos of structuralism, Axelos is the "new Heraclitus,"[127] because Axelos, like Heraclitus, is a dialectical, historical thinker. Lefebvre thinks that Axelos is the most important thinker to have grasped Heraclitus's teaching of thought *of* the world and thought *in* the world.[128]

As Poster intimates, Axelos was only able to make Marx seem tangled in metaphysics in this way by reading him simply as a philosopher.[129] But Axelos's point is that the way in which Marx thinks various issues—value, alienation, and technique, for example—depends on metaphysical notions. Axelos argues that although Marx wants to "abolish philosophy in a radical way so that it can realize itself in real, material action," to change the world rather than merely interpret it, he remains within the system he seeks to reverse, just as Heidegger claimed with Nietzsche.[130] For Poster, the question of the transcendence of philosophy, and in particular Marx's role in it, especially in an age of technology, was a theme of Fougeyrollas, Lefebvre, Axelos, and François Châtelet: "Looking at their work as a whole, we can say that Axelos and Fougeyrollas tended to be more critical of Marx, while Châtelet and Lefebvre saw less urgency in revising Marx's basic propositions."[131]

TRILOGIES, SYSTEMS, ISOLATION

Axelos viewed most of his output in terms of trilogies. He discusses the relation between them in a number of places, particularly in *Problèmes de l'enjeu*.[132] The books on Marx and Heraclitus, his primary and secondary theses, were partnered by *Vers la pensée planétaire* in the first trilogy. His works on logic and ethics were the first and third volumes of the second trilogy, joining *Le jeu du monde*. The final trilogy comprised *Arguments d'une recherche*, *Horizons du monde*, and *Problèmes de l'enjeu*. Each of these trilogies were given an overall title: the unfolding, unfurling, or deployment [*deploiement*] of *errance*, of the game, and of an inquiry. *Le Jeu du monde* is therefore the central book in the central trilogy.

Axelos was nothing if not ambitious, and the brief summary of his own work here cannot do justice to the range of his concerns. He describes the first trilogy as a certain grasp of the play [*saisie du jeu*] of the history of thought and the thought of history; and the second trilogy as presenting,

Table 5.1. The Trilogy of Trilogies—Axelos's Principal Writings

Le déploiement de l'errance	Le déploiement du jeu	Le déploiement d'une enquête
Héraclite et la philosophie (1962)	Contribution à la logique (1977)	Arguments d'un recherché (1969)
Marx penseur de la technique (1961)	Le Jeu du monde (1969)	Horizons du monde (1974)
Vers la pensée planetaire (1964)	Pour une éthique problematique (1972)	Problèmes de l'enjeu (1979)

without representing, "a systematic of thought: a logic and a methodology; a questioning and encyclopedic ontology, fundamental, and animating regional ontologies; an anthropology and an ethic."[133] Grand themes indeed, and the three trilogies and his other writings are extremely self-referential and have the impression of an almost Kantian architectonic. He was keen, however, to resist the idea that he was building a system. Instead he pursued an "open systematic."[134] Within this systematic the overarching theme had been the question of the world, the play or the game of the world, and the relation of the human to that world of which they are both part and creator.

Axelos is therefore extremely important in terms of his network of contacts and because of the way in which he brought into print a range of texts showing disparate interests. His importance as a facilitator of translation alone is worthy of note. In his own writings the principal interlocutors are Heraclitus, Marx, and Heidegger. Other figures—Hegel and Nietzsche for example—are mentioned, and there are studies of Pascal, Freud, and Rimbaud, but these three are the central ones.[135] His critical reflections on their thought led him to the important thinking through of issues around the notion of world, something which has relevance to contemporary thinking on these issues. What is striking, particularly for someone so well-connected, is the paucity of references to his contemporaries. I opened by listing some of the people who had referred to his work or written about it. Axelos rarely repays the compliment. In *Problèmes de l'enjeu*, for example, he writes about madness without mentioning Foucault and the city without reference to Lefebvre.[136] In fact his engagement with other contemporary writers— with the exception of Heidegger—was usually at the beginning of his career and often in the form of short reviews.[137] He says of Heidegger that he "was not a man of discussion. He debated with texts from the history of thought and poetry, but he did not debate in his seminars."[138] This might almost be said of Axelos's own writing.[139] What we have is the curious paradox of a writer in exile who is both adopted by and helps to fundamentally shape the intellectual and cultural landscape of postwar France, and yet who, in his work, retreats more and more into intellectual isolation.[140] As the world of which he wrote dominated the intellectual horizon, his own world closed in around him.

NOTES

1. On the civil war, see Kostas Axelos, "La guerre civile en Grèce," in *Arguments d'une recherche* (Paris: Éditions de Minuit, 1969), 125–39.

2. Rémy Rieffel, *La Tribu des clercs: les intellectuels sous la Ve République 1958–1990* (Paris: Calmann-Lévy/CNRS Éditions, 1993), 290.

3. Françoise Gilot and Carlton Lake, *Life with Picasso* (New York: McGraw Hill, 1964), 356–57, mentions Axelos briefly.

4. Much of this biographical detail comes from Eric Haviland, *Kostas Axelos: une vie pensée, une pensée vécue* (Paris: L'Harmattan, 1995), especially 41, 65; "Notice Bio-Bibliographique," in Henri Lefebvre and Pierre Fougeyrollas, *Le Jeu de Kostas Axelos* (Paris: Fata Morgana, 1973), 97–99; and Ronald Bruzina, "Translator's Introduction," in Axelos, *Alienation, Praxis, and Techne in the Thought of Karl Marx*, trans. Ronald Bruzina (Austin: University of Texas Press, 1976), ix–xxxiii, xxv.

5. Jacques Derrida, *Of Grammatology*, trans. Gayatri Chakravorty Spivak (Baltimore: Johns Hopkins University Press, 1976), 326 n. 14. Gilles Deleuze, "Faille et feux locaux, Kostas Axelos" [Review of *Vers la pensée planétaire*, *Arguments d'une recherche*, and *Le jeu du monde*], *Critique* 275 (April 1970): 344–51. Henri Lefebvre, "Marxisme et technique," *Esprit* 307 (1962): 1023–28; "Kostas Axelos: *Vers la pensée planétaire: le devenir-pensée du monde et le devenir-homme* [sic] *de la pensée* (Ed. de Minuit)," *Esprit* 338 (1965): 1114–17. See also Lefebvre and Fougeyrollas, *Le Jeu de Kostas Axelos*.

6. Axelos, *Ce Questionnement: Approche—Éloignement* (Paris: Éditions de Minuit, 2001); <http://www.ekemel.gr/deapiliotis5.htm> (May 2003); and Nina Zivancevic, "Letter from Paris," *NY Arts* 8, no. 1 (January 2003), <http://nyartsmagazine.com/72/letter.htm> (11 March 2004).

7. Of these books, two were published in Greek, one in German, and the remainder in French. There are numerous translations of his writings, in over fifteen languages, notably in Italian and Spanish.

8. Axelos, *Marx penseur de la technique: de l'aliénation de l'homme à la conquête du monde*, 2 vols. (Paris: Éditions de Minuit, 1974; org. pub. 1961); trans. *Alienation, Praxis, and Techne in the Thought of Karl Marx*; *Einführung in ein künftiges Denken: Über Marx und Heidegger* (Tübingen: Max Niemeyer, 1966). This last work, Axelos suggests, had its publication delayed due to "orthodox Heideggerians, Marxists, and Progressives." Axelos, *Vers la pensée planétaire: le devenir-pensée du monde et le devenir-monde de la pensée* (Paris: Éditions de Minuit, 1964), 222–23 n. 2. On Axelos's role as a translator and facilitator, see Dominique Janicaud, *Heidegger en France*, 2 vols. (Paris: Albin Michel, 2001), 1: 172–73, 178. The book on Marx was Axelos's thesis, submitted in 1959; his secondary thesis was on Heraclitus, published as *Héraclite et la philosophie: la première saisie de l'être en devenir de la totalité* (Paris: Éditions de Minuit, 1962). See Rieffel, *La Tribu des clercs*, 292. Aside from this book, the only other translations I know of are "Planetary Interlude," trans. Sally Hess, *Yale French Studies* 41 (1968): 6–18; and "Play as the System of Systems," trans. Robert Emmett Chumbley, *Sub-Stance* 25 (1980): 20–24.

9. Georg Lukács, *Histoire et connaissance de classe: essais de dialectique marxiste*, trans. Kostas Axelos and Jacqueline Bois (Paris: Éditions de Minuit, 1960).

Martin Heidegger, "Qu'est-ce que la philosophie?" trans. Kostas Axelos and Jean Beaufret, in Heidegger, *Questions I et II* (Paris: Gallimard, 1968), 317–46.

10. Axelos and Dominique Janicaud, "Entretiens du 29 janvier 1998 et du mars 2000," in Janicaud, *Heidegger en France*, 2: 11–33, 12; Haviland, *Kostas Axelos*, 50.

11. Mark Poster, *Existential Marxism in Postwar France* (Princeton: Princeton University Press, 1975).

12. Stuart Elden, *Understanding Henri Lefebvre: Theory and the Possible* (London: Continuum, 2004).

13. Michael Kelly, *Modern French Marxism* (Baltimore: Johns Hopkins University Press, 1982), 98.

14. Haviland, *Kostas Axelos*; Lefebvre and Fougeyrollas, *Le Jeu de Kostas Axelos*; Jean-Philippe Milet, ed., "Kostas Axelos et la question du monde," Special Issue of *Rue Descartes* 18 (1997). See also Louis Soubise, *Le Marxisme après Marx (1956–1965): quatre marxistes dissidents français* (Paris: Aubier Montaigne, 1967), which treats Axelos alongside Lefebvre, François Châtelet, and Fougeyrollas.

15. Richard Gombin, *The Origins of Modern Leftism*, trans. Michael K. Perl (Harmondsworth: Penguin, 1975), 40–41.

16. Rémi Hess, "Henri Lefebvre et le projet avorté du *Traité de matérialisme dialectique*," in Henri Lefebvre, *Méthodologie des sciences: inédit* (Paris: Anthropos, 2002), v–xxvi, xiii n. 1.

17. Myron Kofman, *Edgar Morin: From Big Brother to Fraternity* (London: Pluto, 1996).

18. Bruzina, "Translator's Introduction."

19. All the issues of the journal have been reissued in a two-volume set, with original pagination and the addition of short prefaces by Axelos, Edgar Morin, and Jean Duvignaud, as *Arguments 1956–1962: édition intégrale* (Toulouse: Privat, 1983). All subsequent references are to the issues found in this collection, although the volume number and pages accord to the original issue. On *Arguments*, see also Olivier Corpet, "Jean, Kostas, François, Edgar et les autres…," in *Arguments pour une méthode (Autour d'Edgar Morin)*, eds. Daniel Bougnoux, Jean-Louis Le Moigne, and Serge Proulx (Paris: Éditions du Seuil, 1990), 57–66; Gil Delannoi, "*Arguments*, 1956–1962 ou la parenthèse de l'ouverture," *Revue française de science politique* 34, no. 1 (February 1984): 127–45; Corpet, "Au fil d'*Arguments*," in "Kostas Axelos et la question du monde," Special Issue of *Rue Descartes*, 115–19.

20. For the role Barthes played in the *Arguments* journal, see Michael Kelly, "Demystification: A Dialogue between Barthes and Lefebvre," *Yale French Studies* 98 (2000): 79–97.

21. Arthur Hirsch, *The French New Left: An Intellectual History from Sartre to Gorz* (Montreal: Black Rose Books, 1982), 89.

22. See Morin, Franco Fortini, Duvignaud, and François Fejtö, "Les origines," *La Revue des revues* 4 (Fall 1987): 12–14, 12; Rieffel, *La Tribu des clercs*, 297. For a discussion, see Mariateresa Padova, "Arguments-Ragionamenti: Un Jumelage Fécond," in *Arguments 1956–1962*, xxv–xxviii.

23. Morin et al., "Les origines," 14.

24. Rieffel, *La Tribu des clercs*, 297. Axelos, *Arguments d'une recherche*, 161.

25. See "Entretien avec Edgar Morin (Paris, 28 September 1978)," in Padova, "Testimonianze su 'Arguments'," *Studi Francesci* 73 (January–April 1981): 46–72, 69.

26. Morin, "La fin d'un commencement," *Arguments* 27–28 (1962): 123–26, 123. Axelos, "Le jeu de l'autocritique," *Arguments* 27–28 (1962): 127–28, 127.

27. "Manifeste," *Arguments* 1 (December 1956–January 1957): 1.

28. Morin, *Autocritique* (Paris: Éditions du Seuil, 2nd ed., 1970; org. pub. 1959). Henri Lefebvre, *La Somme et le reste* (Paris: Méridiens Klincksieck, 3rd ed., 1989; org. pub. 1959).

29. See Poster, *Existential Marxism in Postwar France*, 212.

30. See Kofman, *Edgar Morin*, 44.

30. George Lichtheim, *Marxism in Modern France* (New York: Columbia University Press, 1966), 81, 93.

32. Kevin Anderson, *Lenin, Hegel, and Western Marxism: A Critical Study* (Illinois: University of Illinois Press, 1995).

33. Kofman, *Edgar Morin*, 43–44. On the relation between Sartre and *Arguments* see Gil Delannoi, "Les voyages de la raison: Sartre, 'Arguments,' Morin," *Esprit* 5 (May 1984): 78–97.

34. Georg Lukács, "Qu'est-ce que le marxisme orthodoxe?" *Arguments* 3 (April–May 1957): 1–17, translated by Jacqueline Bois and Axelos; Axelos, "Y a-t-il une philosophie marxiste?" *Arguments* 4 (June–September 1957): 34–36, followed by exchanges between Axelos, Robert Misrahi, and Edgar Morin, 36–40.

35. Morin, "Une tribune de discussion," in "Kostas Axelos et la question du monde," Special Issue of *Rue Descartes*, 121–23, 121.

36. See Kofman, *Edgar Morin*, 45–46; Morin, et al., "Les origines," 12, 14.

37. "Manifeste," 1.

38. Axelos and Corpet, "Le fonctionnement," *La Revue des revues* 4 (Fall 1987): 15–17, 16.

39. Roland Barthes, "Les taches de la critique brechtienne," *Arguments* 1 (December 1956–January 1957): 20–22. See "Entretien avec Roland Barthes (Paris, 3 mai 1979)," in Padova, "Testimonianze su 'Arguments'," 48.

40. Axelos, "L'errance érotique: problématique de l'amour," and "Les marxistes et l'amour," *Arguments* 21 (1961): 16–28, 34–37; repr. in *Vers la pensée planétaire*, 273–96; *L'Errance érotique* (Paris: Éditions de Minuit, 1992); *Arguments d'une recherche*, 86–92.

41. Axelos and Corpet, "Le fonctionnement," 15.

42. Haviland, *Kostas Axelos*, 70.

43. Axelos and Corpet, "Le fonctionnement," 16.

44. Axelos and Corpet, "Le fonctionnement," 17. See Morin, "La fin d'un commencement."

45. Morin, "La fin d'un commencement," 124.

46. Rieffel, *La Tribu des clercs*, 288.

47. Georg Lukács, "Qu'est-ce que le marxisme orthodoxe?"; "Rosa Luxembourg, Marxiste," *Arguments* 5 (December 1957): 20–31; "Le phénomène de la reification," *Arguments* 11 (December 1958): 14–30. These were all translated by Jacqueline Bois and Axelos, who also published other parts in *La Nouvelle Réforme* and *Socialisme ou Barbarie*, and who eventually published a full version of the book.

48. E. Bottigelli, "Une protestation de G. Lukács," *Arguments* 5 (December 1957): 31–32, 31.

49. Letter from Budapest (28 June 1960), in Axelos, "Une déclaration de G. Lukács," *Arguments* 20 (1960): 61. That said, the English translation, Lukács, *History and Class Consciousness: Studies in Marxist Dialectics*, trans. Rodney Livingstone (London: Merlin, 1971), is based on a re-edition of the German, including Lukács' own "Preface to the new edition (1967)," ix–xxxix. See Axelos's note on Lukács in his *Marx penseur de la technique*, 2: 197 n. 1; *Alienation, Praxis, and Techne*, 371 n. 1.

50. Theodor Adorno, "Fragments," and "Hegel et le contenu de l'experience," *Arguments* 14 (1959): 23–25, 26–35 (these selections were preceded by Axelos, "Adorno et l'école de Francfort," 20–22); "Musique et technique, aujourd'hui," *Arguments* 19 (1960): 50–58. Karl Korsch, "Thèses sur Hegel et la révolution," and "Dix thèses sur le marxisme aujourd'hui," *Arguments* 16 (1959): 25, 27–28. These short texts were introduced by Axelos, "Présentation bio-bibliographique de Karl Korsch," 24–25; and Maximilien Rubel, "Présentation des 'Dix thèse sur le marxisme'," 26–27. Heidegger, "Principe d'identité," trans. Gilbert Kahn, *Arguments* 7 (April–May 1958): 2–8; "Le mot de Nietzsche 'Dieu est mort'," trans. W. Brokmeier, *Arguments* 15 (1959): 2–13; "Principes de la pensée," trans. François Fédier, *Arguments* 20 (1960): 27–33; "Au-delà de la métaphysique," trans. Roger Munier, *Arguments* 24 (1961): 35–39.

51. Morin, "La fin d'un commencement," 123.

52. Morin, "La fin d'un commencement,", 125.

53. Axelos, "Le jeu de l'autocritique," 128. On the suicide of the journal see also Fougeyrollas, Axelos, Duvignaud, Morin, and Corpet, "Le sabordage," *La Revue des revues* 4 (Fall 1987): 18–19.

54. See Poster, *Existential Marxism in Postwar France*, 213.

55. Kofman, *Edgar Morin*, 12, 43.

56. Kofman, *Edgar Morin*, 51.

57. Internationale Situationniste (IS), *Aux poubelles de l'histoire* (Paris: IS, 1963), repr. in *Internationale Situationniste* 12 (September 1969): 108–11. All the issues of IS are included in *Internationale Situationniste 1958–1969, edition augmentée*, ed. Patrick Mosconi (Paris: Librarie Artheime Fayard, 1997).

58. Lefebvre's article was "La signification de la commune," *Arguments* 27–28 (1962): 11–19. See also his later book on the issue, *La Proclamation de la Commune* (Paris: Gallimard, 1965). For a longer discussion see Kristin Ross, "Lefebvre on the Situationists: An Interview," *October* 79 (Winter 1997): 69–83; and my *Understanding Henri Lefebvre*, Chapter Four.

59. IS, "Les mois les plus longs (février 1963–juillet 1964)," *Internationale Situationniste* 9 (August 1964): 30–37, 30.

60. IS, "Quand Axelos avait trouvé un disciple," *Internationale Situationniste* 11 (October 1967): 56. The article originally appeared in the *Bulletin of the International Centre of Poetic Studies* (June 1966).

61. Fougeyrollas et al., "Le sabordage," 19.

62. Circular of January 20, 1964, cited in IS, "Les mois les plus longs," 34. Some articles on Socialisme ou Barbarie appeared in *Arguments* 4 (June–September 1957).

63. Ross, "Lefebvre on the Situationists," 78.

64. See René Lourau, *Autodissolution des avant-gardes* (Paris: Éditions Galilée, 1980); *La Clé des champs: une introduction à l'analyse institutionnelle* (Paris: Anthropos, 1997).

65. Axelos and Corpet, "Le fonctionnement," 17.

66. "Lettera di Réa Karavas (Paris, 8 juillet 1979)," in Padova, "Testimonianze su 'Arguments'," 65.

67. Corpet, "Arguments pour une ré-édition d'Arguments," in *Arguments 1956–1962*, xxi–xxiv, xxii n. 6.

68. Kofman, *Edgar Morin*, 8.

69. Axelos, "Arguments et pensées," in "Kostas Axelos et la question du monde," Special Issue of *Rue Descartes*, 111–14, 114. See Kofman, *Edgar Morin*, 46; and Axelos, "Une problématique," in *Arguments 1956–1962*, xii–xiii, xiii.

70. On the early history of the publishing house itself, see Anne Simonin, *Les Éditions de Minuit 1942–1955: le devoir d'insoumission* (Paris: IMEC Éditions, 1994). On the *Arguments* series, see Juliette de Trégomain, "Les Minuit: A Personal Fight, An Independent House," *The Culture of Publishing* 4 (June 2001), <http://www.brookes.ac.uk/schools/apm/publishing/culture/2001/tregomai.html> (11 March 2004).

71. Gilles Deleuze, *Spinoza et le probleme de l'expression* (Paris: Éditions de Minuit, 1968); and *Présentation de Sacher-Masoch: la Vénus à la fourrure* (Paris: Éditions de Minuit, 1967). Georges Bataille, *L'Érotisme* (Paris: Éditions de Minuit, 1957). Maurice Blanchot, *Lautréamont et Sade* (Paris: Éditions de Minuit, 1949). The last two were reissued in this series.

72. Lefebvre, *Introduction à la modernité: préludes* (Paris: Éditions de Minuit, 1962); *Métaphilosophie: prolégomènes* (Paris: Éditions de Minuit, 1965); *La Fin de l'histoire* (Paris: Éditions de Minuit, 1970). Morin, *Le Cinema ou l'homme imaginaire: essai d'anthropologie* (Paris: Éditions de Minuit, 1978).

73. Beaufret, *Dialogue avec Heidegger*, 4 vols. (Paris: Éditions de Minuit, 1973–85). Lourau, *L'Analyse institutionnelle* (Paris: Éditions de Minuit, 1970); and *L'État-inconscient* (Paris: Éditions de Minuit, 1978). Didier Franck, *Chair et corps: sur la phénomenologie de Husserl* (Paris: Éditions de Minuit, 1981); and *Heidegger et le problème de l'espace* (Paris: Éditions de Minuit, 1986).

74. Axelos, "Preface de la presente édition," in Lukács, *Histoire et connaissance de classe*, 1–8.

75. The English translation, *History and Class Consciousness*, cites the Axelos and Bois translation as useful in the preparation of the English version.

76. See, among others, Herbert Marcuse, *Eros et civilisation: contribution à Freud*, trans. Jean-Guy Nény and Boris Fraenkel (Paris: Éditions de Minuit, 1963); and *L'Homme unidimensionel: étude sur l'idéologie de la société industrielle*, trans. Monique Wittig (Paris: Éditions de Minuit, 1968). Louis Hjemslev, *Essais linguistiques* (Paris: Éditions de Minuit, 1971). Roman Jakobson, *Essais de linguistique generale*, trans. Nicolas Ruwet, 2 vols. (Paris: Éditions de Minuit, 1963–1973). Karl Jaspers, *Strindberg et van Gogh, Swedenborg, Hölderlin* (Paris: Éditions de Minuit, 1970). Eugen Fink, *La Philosophie de Nietzsche*, trans. Hans Hildenbrand and Alex Lindenberg (Paris: Éditions de Minuit, 1965); *Le Jeu comme symbole du monde*, trans. Hildenbrand and Lindenberg (Paris: Éditions de Minuit, 1966); and *De la Phénoménologie*, trans. Didier Franck (Paris: Éditions de Minuit, 1975).

77. See "Entretien avec François Fejtö (Paris, 2 mai 1979)," in Padova, "Testimonianze su 'Arguments'," 57.

78. Fougeyrollas, "Thèses sur la mondialisation," *Arguments* 15 (1959): 38–39.

79. Fougeyrollas, "Thèses sur la mondialisation," 38–39.

80. "Manifeste no. 2 (1960)," in *Arguments 1956–1962*, xxx.

81. Axelos, *Arguments d'une recherche*, 164–65. For a discussion, see *Vers la pensée planétaire*, 13, 30.

82. Karl Marx, *Writings of the Young Marx on Philosophy and Society*, eds. Loyd D. Easton and Kurt H. Guddat (New York: Doubleday, 1967), 62.

83. For examples, see Lefebvre, *Marx* (Paris: PUF, 1964), 55; and *Métaphilosophie*, 33. Axelos, *Marx penseur de la technique*, 1: 5, 2: 50, 162; *Alienation, Praxis, and Techne*, v, 202, 271; and *Problèmes de l'enjeu* (Paris: Éditions de Minuit, 1979), 177.

84. On this period of Marx's work, see Lefebvre, "Les rapports de la philosophie et de la politique dans les premières oeuvres de Marx (1842–1843)," *Revue de métaphysique et de morale* 63, nos. 2–3 (April–September 1958): 299–324.

85. Fink, *Le Jeu comme symbole du monde*. Wilfred Desan, *The Planetary Man: A Noetic Prelude to a United World* (Washington, D.C.: Georgetown University Press, 1961); and *L'Homme planétaire: prélude théorique a un monde uni*, trans. Hans Hildenbrand and Alex Lindenberg (Paris: Éditions de Minuit, 1968). Axelos's "Postface: Qui est donc l'homme planétaire," 151–57, is reprinted in *Arguments d'une recherche*, 181–86. For Axelos on Fink, see "Postface: Qui est donc l'homme planétaire," 198. On the relation between Axelos and Fink, see several of the essays in "Kostas Axelos et la question du monde," Special Issue of *Rue Descartes*, especially Françoise Dastur, "Monde et jeu: Axelos et Fink," 25–38.

86. Martin Heidegger and Eugen Fink, *Heraclitus Seminar 1966/67*, trans. Charles E. Seibert (Alabama: University of Alabama Press, 1979).

87. See Hermann Diels, *Die Fragmente der Vorsokratiker*, ed. Walther Kranz, 3 vols. (Berlin-Grunewald: Weidmannsche Verlagsbuchhandlung, 6th ed., 1951), 1: 162. Heidegger discusses this in detail in *The Principle of Reason*, trans. Reginald Lilly (Bloomington: Indiana University Press, 1991). For Axelos's reading, see Her-

aclitus, *Les Fragments d'Héraclite d'Ephèse*, ed. and trans. Axelos (Paris: Éditions Estienne, 1958); Axelos, *Problèmes de l'enjeu; Arguments d'une recherche*, 195–99; and *Vers la pensée planétaire*, 21.

88. In his *Identität und Differenz* (Pfulligen: Neske, 1957), 64, Heidegger suggests that "the essence of being is the game itself [*das Spiel selber*]." This is cited by Axelos in *Vers la pensée planétaire*, 22.

89. Jacques Sojcher, "Jeu en enjeux de l'amour," in Axelos, *L'Errance érotique*, 47–62, 47. Axelos, *Entretiens: "Reéls," Imaginaires, et avec "Soi-Même"* (Montpellier: Fata Morgana, 1973), 17; and *Le Jeu du monde* (Paris: Éditions de Minuit, 1969). Although this book is of the utmost importance in Axelos's thought, its breadth of topics and style make it extremely hard to summarize. Some of the key issues are presented with more conventional clarity in other of his works. The discussion here follows this logic.

90. See Axelos, *Arguments d'une recherche*, 162.

91. See, in particular, Lefebvre, *De l'État*, 4 vols. (Paris: UGE, 1976–78); and for a commentary, Elden, *Understanding Henri Lefebvre*, chapter 6.

92. Axelos, *Ce Questionnement*, 40.

93. On this in detail see "La question de la technique planétaire," in Axelos, *Ce Questionnement*, 15–35.

94. Axelos, *Métamorphoses: Clôture—Ouverture* (Paris: Éditions de Minuit, 1991), 132.

95. Fougeyrollas, "Au-delà du nihilisme," in Lefebvre and Fougeyrollas, *Le Jeu de Kostas Axelos*, 35–96, 77.

96. See especially, Heidegger, *Nietzsche: Der europäische Nihilismus, Gesamtausgabe Band 48* (Frankfurt am Main: Vittorio Klostermann, 1986). A shorter version is translated as the final volume in *Nietzsche*, 4 vols. (San Francisco: Harper Collins, 1991).

97. Axelos, *Vers la pensée planétaire*, 297.

98. Heidegger, *Einführung in die Metaphysik, Gesamtausgabe Band 40* (Frankfurt am Main: Vittorio Klostermann, 1983), 208. As well as the texts mentioned by Axelos, see also *Pour une éthique problématique* (Paris: Éditions de Minuit, 1972), 26–27; *Arguments d'une recherche*, 169.

99. See Elden, *Mapping the Present: Heidegger, Foucault, and the Project of a Spatial History* (London: Continuum, 2001), 30–31, for a note on the textual basis of this phrase.

100. Axelos, *Lettres à un jeune penseur* (Paris: Éditions de Minuit, 1996), 10 n. 1, 13.

101. Axelos, *Lettres à un jeune penseur*, 13.

102. See Heidegger, *Being and Time*, trans. John Macquarrie and Edward Robinson (Oxford: Blackwell, 1962); and for a commentary, Elden, *Mapping the Present*, 15–21.

103. Axelos, *Ce Questionnement*, 56.

104. Axelos, *Lettres à un jeune penseur*, 19. See also, Axelos, *Systématique ouverte* (Paris: Éditions de Minuit, 1984), 40–54.

105. Axelos, *Entretiens*, 53.

106. See, above all, Heidegger, *The Question Concerning Technology and Other Essays*, trans. William Lovitt (New York: Harper & Row, 1977).

107. Heidegger's thought of the world is important in a whole range of appropriations of his work for radical purposes. See, among others, Lefebvre, and the work of Jean-Luc Nancy. In a recent lecture, André Tosel suggested the Nietzschean/Heideggerian understanding of the world is the most interesting of the four alternatives he offered—economic, political/Habermas, and Hardt and Negri being the other three. Tosel, "Les philosophies de la mondialisation" (public lecture, Université René Descartes, Paris V, 7 July 2003).

108. Axelos and Janicaud, "Entretiens," 14; and see Haviland, *Kostas Axelos*, 52–53. As well as the interpreting roles noted above, Axelos stayed with Heidegger in the Black Forest. For an account of his Christmas 1955 visit, see *Vers la pensée planétaire*, 224–25.

109. Axelos, Beaufret, Châtelet, and Lefebvre, "Karl Marx et Heidegger," in Axelos, *Arguments d'une recherche*, 93–105; org. pub. in *France Observateur* 473 (28 May 1959). See also *Vers la pensée planétaire*, 223–25.

110. Victor Farías, *Heidegger and Nazism*, trans. Paul Burrell and Gabriel R. Ricci (Philadelphia: Temple University Press, 1989). See Axelos and Janicaud, "Entretiens," 15. Karl Löwith, "Les implications politiques de la philosophie de l'existence chez Heidegger," *Les Temps modernes* 14 (November 1946): 343–60.

111. See, in particular, Dominique Janicaud, *L'Ombre de cette pensée* (Grenoble: Jérome Millon, 1990).

112. Axelos, *Vers la pensée planétaire*, 224. See also *Métamorphoses*, 16–17 n. 1.

113. Henri Lefebvre, *Qu'est-ce que penser?* (Paris: Publisad, 1985), 167–68.

114. Axelos and Janicaud, "Entretiens," 11.

115. Karl Marx, *The Poverty of Philosophy* (New York: International Publishers, 1963), 109.

116. See, for example, *Problèmes de l'enjeu*, 16, 66.

117. Axelos, *Contribution à la logique* (Paris: Éditions de Minuit, 1977), 80, see 121.

118. Axelos, note to Heidegger, "Principe d'identité," 5 n. 1. Kahn, the translator of the piece, uses *la com-mande*. For a brief discussion of the term in French, see Elden, *Mapping the Present*, 110–11.

119. Axelos, *Arguments d'une recherche*, 174. In *Horizons du monde* (Paris: Éditions de Minuit, 1974), 112–13, this notion is linked to the idea of the end of history. On technology generally, see the essays in *Métamorphoses*.

120. Axelos, *Problèmes de l'enjeu*, 30.

121. Axelos, *Arguments d'une recherche*, 168; *Marx penseur de la technique*, 2: 120–21; and *Alienation, Praxis, and Techne*, 246.

122. For the acknowledgement of Marx, see Heidegger, *What is Philosophy?/Was ist das–die Philosophie?* [English-German edition], trans. William Kluback and Jean T. Wilde (London: Vision Press, 1963), 89; and "Letter on Hu-

manism," in *Pathmarks*, ed. William McNeill (Cambridge: Cambridge University Press, 1998), 239–76, 258–59.

123. Axelos and Janicaud, "Entretiens," 15; and Haviland, *Kostas Axelos*, 56.

124. Axelos, *Marx penseur de la technique*, 2: 270; and *Alienation, Praxis, and Techne*, 331.

125. Axelos, *Marx penseur de la technique*, 2: 120–21; and *Alienation, Praxis, and Techne*, 246.

126. Axelos, *Héraclite et la philosophie*; Heraclitus, *Les Fragments d'Héraclite d'Ephèse*. For a similar agenda by another member of the *Arguments* group, see Châtelet, *Logos et praxis: recherches sur la signification théorique du marxisme* (Paris: Société d'Édition d'Énseignement Supérieur, 1962).

127. Lefebvre, "Au-delà du savoir," in Lefebvre and Fougeyrollas, *Le Jeu de Kostas Axelos*, 11–33, 32.

128. Lefebvre, *Qu'est-ce que penser?* 13; see also "Au-delà du savoir," 24–6.

129. Poster, *Existential Marxism in Postwar France*, 61–62.

130. Axelos, *Marx penseur de la technique*, 1: 13; *Alienation, Praxis, and Techne*, 7; and see *Arguments d'une recherche*, 100–1. The allusion to Marx is the famous eleventh thesis on Feuerbach, but also the eighth, regularly quoted elsewhere by Axelos: "All social life is essentially *practical*. All mysteries which lead theory to mysticism find their rational solution in human practice and in the comprehension of this practice." See "Theses on Feuerbach," in Karl Marx and Friedrich Engels, *The German Ideology*, ed. C. J. Arthur (London: Lawrence & Wishart, 1970), 121–23, 122. Axelos's Heideggerian "Thèses sur Marx" are found in *Vers la pensée planétaire*, 172–77.

131. Poster, *Existential Marxism in Postwar France*, 220.

132. *Problèmes de l'enjeu*, 188–90. For an overall schema of his work, see Haviland, "Le déploiement de l'œuvre," in *Kostas Axelos*, 77–134.

133. Axelos, *Contribution à la logique*, 7.

134. See Axelos, *Systématique ouverte*, esp. 36.

135. In Axelos, *Horizons du monde*, 93, he talks of the "constellation Hegel-Marx-Nietzsche-Freud-Heidegger." See also Axelos, *Einführung in ein künftiges Denken*, vii. In *Notices "autobiographiques"* (Paris: Éditions de Minuit, 1997), 34, he gives a longer list: "After Heraclitus, Sophocles, and Shakespeare, there are Pascal and Rimbaud, Dostoyevsky, Hölderlin, Hegel, and Marx, (Freud), Nietzsche, and Heidegger." See also *Contribution à la logique*, 8. The studies of Pascal, Freud, and Rimbaud are found in *Vers la pensée planétaire*.

136. Axelos, "Le problème de la folie," and "La ville problème," in *Problèmes de l'enjeu*, 97–117, 118–34. The only reference to Lefebvre in his work as a whole is in *Horizons du monde*, 103 n. 1, but this merely cites the latter's *La Fin de l'histoire*, without discussion.

137. An exception is his tribute, "Entre le marxisme, le freudisme, le structuralisme et le nihilisme: Lucien Sebag," in *Arguments d'une recherche*, 114–19.

138. Axelos and Janicaud, "Entretiens," 20.

139. See, however, the collection of interviews *Entretiens*, where Axelos plays the role both of interviewee, interviewer (with Lefebvre and Fougeyrollas), and sometimes both (in the "Imaginary Interview" and the "Interview with Himself").

140. We could also note the almost willful obscurity of *Notices "autobiographiques"*, which, despite its title, gives almost nothing away and is rather a collection of aphorisms and short paragraphs, reminiscent of Nietzsche, concerning the themes of his work.

6

"UN CONTRADICTEUR PERMANENT": THE IDEOLOGICAL AND POLITICAL ITINERARY OF DANIEL GUÉRIN

David Berry

As he once wrote of the fate suffered by anarchism, Daniel Guérin (1904–1988) has himself been the victim of unwarranted neglect and, in some circles at least, of undeserved discredit.[1] Guérin's extensive archives (held at the Bibliothèque de documentation internationale contemporaine in Nanterre) have been mined by many researchers over the years, but most of these have been interested in only one particular aspect of Guérin's work or activism. For although many people know of Guérin, relatively few seem aware of the breadth of his contribution. His writings cover a vast range of subjects, from fascism and the French Revolution to the history of the European and American labor movements; from Marxist and anarchist theory to homosexual liberation; from French colonialism to the Black Panthers; from Paul Gauguin to French nuclear tests in the Pacific—not to mention several autobiographical volumes.[2] Similarly, Guérin was involved in various movements and campaigns: anticolonialism, antiracism, antimilitarism, and homosexual liberation. This is a man who counted François Mauriac, Simone Weil, C. L. R. James, and Richard Wright—to name but a few of the famous names which litter his autobiographies—among his personal friends. His youthful literary efforts provoked a letter of congratulation from Colette; he met and corresponded with Leon Trotsky; and he had dinner "en tête à tête" with Ho Chi Minh. Jean-Paul Sartre judged his reinterpretation of the French Revolution to be "one of the only contributions by contemporary Marxists to have *enriched* historical studies."[3] The gay liberation activist Pierre Hahn believed his own generation of homosexuals owed more to Guérin than to any other person, and the Martinican poet Aimé Césaire paid tribute to his work on decolonization.[4] Noam Chomsky considers Guérin's writings on anarchism to be of great importance to the development of contemporary socialist thought.[5]

Yet despite such assessments, and although there is widespread and enduring interest in Guérin among activists, he has been badly neglected by academic researchers in France and elsewhere. This is doubtless due to a combination of factors: Guérin never held an academic post nor any leadership position (except briefly as director of the Commission du livre at the Liberation); he was consistently anti-Stalinist during a period when the influence of the French Communist Party, both among intellectuals and within the labor movement, was overwhelming; he never fit easily into ideological or political pigeonholes and was often misunderstood and/or misrepresented; and in France in the 1960s and 1970s, his bisexuality was shocking even for many on the Left. Guérin was, in a word, a "troublemaker" [trouble-fête].[6]

The aim of this chapter—part of a longer-term project which is a biography of Guérin—is to help rectify this neglect by outlining Guérin's ideological and political evolution after World War Two. It focuses on his transition from not uncritical Trotskyist in the 1940s to figurehead of resurgent anarchism in the 1960s, and his attempt in the 1970s and 1980s to theorize and promote a synthesis of anarchism and Marxism. I would argue that despite the apparently protean nature of his commitments, Guérin in fact demonstrated a certain ideological and political consistency. He remained a historical materialist all his life, and although it was many years before he found an organization that lived up to his expectations, he was always at heart a libertarian communist, developing an increasingly strong belief in the importance of a "total revolution" which would attach as much importance to issues of race, gender, and sexuality as to workplace-based conflict. Hence his attempts to incorporate these issues into an overarching historical materialist analysis and revolutionary socialist strategy. In several respects, Guérin was ahead of his time.

Given the fact that Guérin's contribution to the rejuvenation of socialist thought and praxis in postwar France was founded initially on his analysis of the state of the Left and the labor movement in the 1930s and 1940s, it will be useful to start with a brief look at his formative years as an activist.

THE 1930s: THE BANKRUPTCY OF
STALINISM AND SOCIAL DEMOCRACY

Heir to the Hachette publishing and book-selling empire, Guérin nevertheless "inherited" antiracist and antimilitaristic attitudes from his liberal,

Dreyfusard family. On a theoretical level, at least, and in the context of the increasingly polarized debates of the period between the far-right and far-left ("Maurras versus Marx"), he identified with the "Marxist extreme-left" from an early age.[7] His "discovery" of the Parisian working class and of the concrete realities of their everyday existence (to a large extent through his homosexual relationships with young workers) reinforced a profound "workerism" which would stay with him for the rest of his life.[8] This workerism would lead him in 1930–1931 to join the syndicalists grouped around the veteran revolutionary Pierre Monatte. It was also responsible for a strong attraction toward the proletarian constituency of the Parti communiste français (PCF), despite his "visceral anti-Stalinism" and what he saw as the party's "crass ideological excesses, its inability to win over the majority of workers, and its mechanical submission to the Kremlin's orders."[9] Yet Guérin was no more impressed with the existing social-democratic alternative, the Section française de l'internationale ouvrière (SFIO), which he found petty-bourgeois, narrow-minded, dogmatically anticommunist, and obsessed with electioneering:

> The tragedy for many militants of our generation was our repugnance at having to opt for one or the other of the two main organizations which claimed, wrongly, to represent the working class. Stalinism and social democracy both repelled us, each in its own way. Yet those workers who were active politically were in one of these two parties. The smaller, intermediate groups and the extremist sects seemed to us to be doomed to impotence and marginalization. The SFIO, despite the social conformism of its leadership, at least had the advantage over the Communist Party of enjoying a certain degree of internal democracy, and to some extent allowed revolutionaries to express themselves; whereas the monolithic automatism of Stalinism forbade any critics from opening their mouths and made it very difficult for them even to stay in the party.[10]

Hence his decision to rejoin the SFIO in 1935, shortly before the creation by Marceau Pivert of the Gauche révolutionnaire (GR) tendency within the party, of which he would become a leading member. Guérin was attracted by Pivert's "Luxemburgist," libertarian, and syndicalist tendencies, and was consistently on the revolutionary wing of the Gauche révolutionnaire and of its successor the Parti socialiste ouvrier et paysan, created when the GR was expelled from the SFIO in 1938. He drew a clear distinction between what he called the "Popular Front no. 1"—an electoral alliance between social democracy, Stalinism, and bourgeois liberalism—and the "Popular Front no. 2"—a powerful, extra-parliamentary, working-class movement, which came into conflict with the more moderate (and more bourgeois) Popular Front government.[11] He viewed the "entryism" of the French Trotskyists in these years as a welcome counterbalance to the reformism of the majority of the SFIO.

Indeed, in the 1930s, Guérin agreed with Trotsky's position on many issues: on the nature of fascism and how to stop it, on war and revolutionary proletarian internationalism, on opposition to the collusion between "social-patriotism" and "national-communism" as well as to any pact with the bourgeois Radicals, and on the need to fight actively for the liberation of Europe's colonies. As Guérin comments after recounting in glowing terms his sole meeting with Trotsky in 1933: "On a theoretical level as well as on the level of political practice, Trotsky would remain, for many of us, both a stimulus to action and a teacher."[12]

Ultimately, Guérin's experience of the labor movement and the Left in the 1930s—as well as his research on the nature and origins of fascism and Nazism[13]—led him to reject both social democracy and Stalinism as effective strategies for defeating fascism and preventing war. Indeed, the Left—"divided, ossified, negative, and narrow-minded" in Guérin's words—bore its share of responsibility and had made tragic errors.[14] The SFIO was criticized by Guérin for its electoralism and for allowing its hands to be tied by the Parti radicale-socialiste, "a bourgeois party whose corruption and bankruptcy were in large part responsible for the fascist explosion"; for its incomprehension of the nature of the capitalist state, which led to the impotence of Léon Blum's government; for its failure to take fascism seriously (and to aid the Spanish Republicans), despite the warnings, until it was too late; and for its obsessive rivalry with the PCF. Guérin criticized the PCF for its blind obedience to the Comintern and the criminal stupidity of the latter's "third period," and for its counter-revolutionary strategy both in Spain and France.[15]

As for Trotsky, Guérin disagreed with him over the creation of the Fourth International in 1938, which, for the reasons we have seen above, seemed to him premature and divisive. More generally, Guérin was critical of what he saw as Trotsky's tendency continually to transpose the experiences of the Russian Bolsheviks onto contemporary events in the West, and of his "authoritarian rigidness." Trotskyism, Guérin argued, represented "the ideology of the infallible leader who, in an authoritarian fashion, directs the policy of a fraction or of a party."[16] What Guérin wanted to see was "the full development of the spontaneity of the working class."[17] Writing in 1963, he would conclude with regard to such disputes over revolutionary tactics:

> The revolutionary organization which was lacking in June 1936 was not, in my opinion, an authoritarian leadership emanating from a small group or sect, but

an organ for the coordination of the workers' councils, growing directly out of the occupied workplaces. The mistake of the Gauche révolutionnaire was not so much that it was unable, because of its lack of preparation, to transform itself into a revolutionary party on the Leninist or Trotskyist model, but that it was unable . . . to help the working class to find for itself its own form of power structure to confront the fraud that was the Popular Front no. 1.[18]

So as Guérin summarized the state of the Left in the 1930s: "Everything made the renewal of the concepts and methods of struggle employed by the French Left both indispensable and urgent."[19] These debates on the Left regarding tactics—working-class autonomy or "Popular Frontism"—and the role of the avant-garde—in syndicalist terms, the "activist minority" [*minorité agissante*]—would recur in the postwar years, and Guérin's position would vary little.

THE 1940s: GUÉRIN AND TROTSKYISM

Despite Guérin's reservations about Trotskyism, his relations with the movement became closer in the 1940s, as he became involved in clandestine political activities with his old friend, Yvan Craipeau, a leading member of the Trotskyist Parti ouvrier internationaliste (POI).[20] The Trotskyists in the French Resistance, in Guérin's eyes, demonstrated "tremendous courage and intelligence," not least because they remained true to their internationalism and to their class politics.[21] They rejected, for instance, the PCF's demagogic nationalism. To Guérin, who was fluent in German, ordinary German conscripts were "the sons of workers and of peasants, who hated the war and Hitler's dictatorship. . . . It is to the honor of the French Trotskyists . . . that they sought to fraternize with the German soldiers, while others simply attacked them from behind."[22] Guérin was thus closely involved with the Trotskyists' attempts to organize extremely dangerous antimilitarist and anti-Nazi propaganda among German soldiers. He also contributed to the activities of a group of Trotskyist workers producing newsletters carrying reports of workplace struggles against both French employers and the German authorities. Invited, on the other hand, to contribute to a clandestine Gaullist paper, Guérin declined: "I intended to remain true to revolutionary internationalism and, since the appeal of 18 June 1940, none of my reservations about the general had been diminished. I would never ally myself with the chauvinists of my country in order to resist Hitler. Their means were not ours."[23] For Guérin, Charles de Gaulle represented "the militarist, imperialist bourgeois Resistance."[24] Indeed, in a letter of February 1945 to Dwight MacDonald, Guérin would write of the persistence of the Pétainism of the bourgeoisie, of their fear of the urban working classes, and of the concessions repeatedly made to the Right by De Gaulle's provisional government: "So there has been no discontinuity in the political direction of the bourgeoisie. Two successive military governments have kept the working class in their place during this critical period. The poor naïve things in the Resistance thought De Gaulle was the opposite of Pétain. They are now beginning to understand that De Gaulle is Pétain's heir."[25] Guérin's profound distrust of De Gaulle's Bonapartist tendencies would persist undiminished into the 1950s and 1960s.

Guérin's undoubted commitment to the Trotskyist movement continued to be tempered by his critique both of its tendency toward dogmatism and its mode of organization. His extended tour of the United States in 1946–1949 seems to have been structured to some extent around visits to branches or prominent militants of the Socialist Workers' Party and the breakaway Workers' Party. Although not all of his experiences of the American Trotksyists were negative—his meetings with his friend C. L. R. James and with Joan London, daughter of Jack, were enjoyable—many were, and the trip represented a turning point in Guérin's "Trotskyism." In a 1948 letter to Marceau Pivert, he commented on his unhappiness with the Trotskyists' tendency to "repeat mechanically old formulae without rethinking them, relying lazily and uncritically on the (undeniably admirable) writings of Trotsky."[26] Looking back thirty years later, he would conclude: "It was thanks to the American Trotskyists, despite their undeniable commitment, that I ceased forever believing in the virtues of revolutionary parties built on authoritarian, Leninist lines."[27]

COLD WAR: NEITHER WASHINGTON NOR MOSCOW

On his return to Paris from his visit to the United States, Guérin found his political position further complicated by the onset of the Cold War, and he became involved in a number of initiatives, some of which were directed at Stalin and some at the imperialist pretensions of American capital. In October 1949, during the final phase of the Stalinization of Eastern Europe and after Tito's break from the Soviet bloc, he was one of the signatories of an appeal addressed to the Hungarian government regarding the trial of the ex-minister László Rajk, accused of conspiring with Tito to overthrow the Stalinist Hungarian regime.[28]

In February 1950, on the other hand, he addressed a letter to the editor of *Le Monde*, accusing the French government of being tied to the apron springs of American bellicists.[29] In July 1950, he joined Claude Bourdet in helping to produce and collect signatures for an "Appel des Français in-dépendants," published in *Le Monde*, which argued that the best way to promote peace in the Far East would be for China to be admitted to the UN.[30] Signed by about thirty individuals, including Sartre and André Gide, this manifesto caused an uproar, given the fact that the Korean War had recently begun, and it brought Guérin into conflict with his old friend and one-time mentor, the "Atlanticist" François Mauriac.[31]

It was also in 1950 that Guérin met and befriended the black American writer, Richard Wright, and attended the constitutive meeting of Wright's "Franco-American Fellowship," the aim of which was to encourage links between the progressive French intelligentsia and black Americans living in Paris. Through Guérin, Wright was invited to give a talk to the editorial group of *L'Observateur*, launched by Bourdet, with Guérin's support, earlier that year. Unfortunately, the fact that Wright had contributed to *The God That Failed* (published in French in 1949) did not go down well with the many "crypto-Stalinists" in the group.[32] Wright was automatically labeled by them as an "anticommunist," similarly to the way in which Guérin tended to be seen as "anti-American."

Unfortunately for Guérin, the first volume of his critical study of the United States appeared shortly after the outbreak of the Korean War.[33] In the hysterical, Cold War atmosphere of the time, Guérin was widely attacked as anti-American and an enemy of democracy, even—most upsettingly for him—by "some ex-comrades whose support would have meant the most to me."[34] In fact Guérin was one of the small number of left-wing intellectuals (mostly associated with *Esprit*, *Le Monde*, and *L'Observateur*) consistently opposed to both Washington *and* Moscow:

> I felt it necessary, in my book [*Où va le peuple américain?*], to claim the right to attack big business, while remaining, as ever, a declared enemy of Stalin's regime and of Russian foreign policy. . . . I demanded the right to criticize the Marshall Plan without being accused of collusion with the Kremlin and its agents or of hostility towards the American people.[35]

But this declaration of intent, unequivocal though it was, would prove to be a waste of effort, and in July 1950 Guérin was refused a visa to visit his wife and daughter in the United States, officially informed by the embassy that he was believed to be a Trotskyist and an anarchist. Despite a letter-writing campaign and support from Eleanor Roosevelt, and notwithstanding an appeal

organized by Clara Malraux and signed by, among others, Sartre, Simone de
Beauvoir, Albert Camus, and Wright, he would remain excluded from the
United States until 1957.[36]

THE CONTEMPORARY RELEVANCE OF THE
FRENCH REVOLUTION

Unlike many on the Left associated with postwar ideological renewal, most
of whom would focus on a revision or reinterpretation of Marxism, often at
a philosophical level (for example, Sartre, Louis Althusser, or Henri Lefebvre), Guérin the historian began with a return to what he saw as the source
of revolutionary theory and praxis: in 1946, he published his study of class
struggle in the First French Republic (1793–1797).[37] His aim, he later recalled, was to "draw lessons from the greatest, longest, and deepest revolutionary experience France has ever known, lessons which would help re-
generate the revolutionary, libertarian socialism of today," and to "extract
some ideas which would be applicable to our time and of direct use to the
contemporary reader who has yet to fully digest the lessons of another revolution: the Russian Revolution."[38] Applying the concepts of permanent
revolution and combined and uneven development, inspired by Trotsky's
History of the Russian Revolution (1930), Guérin argued that the beginnings of a conflict of class interest could already be detected within the revolutionary camp between an "embryonic" proletariat—the manual workers
[*bras nus*], represented by the *Enragés*—and the bourgeoisie—represented
by Robespierre and Jacobinism. For Guérin, the French Revolution thus
represented not only the birth of bourgeois parliamentary democracy, but
also the emergence of "a new type of democracy," a form of working-class
direct democracy as seen, however imperfectly, in the local popular assemblies [*sections*], precursors of the Commune of 1871 and the Soviets of 1905
and 1917. In a later edition of the work he would add "the Commune of
May 1968" to that genealogy.

   Similarly, this interpretation tended to emphasize the political ambivalence of the bourgeois Jacobin leadership which "hesitated continually between the solidarity uniting it with the popular classes against the aristoc-
racy and that uniting all the wealthy, property-owning classes against those
who owned little or nothing."[39] For Guérin, the essential lesson to be drawn
from the French Revolution was thus the conflict of class interest between
the bourgeoisie and the working classes. Bourgeois, social democratic, and
Stalinist interpretations of the revolution, which tended—like those of Jean

Jaurès, Albert Mathiez, and so many others—to maintain the "cult of Robespierre," thus reinforcing the labor movement's dependence on bourgeois democracy, were thus to be rejected.[40]

La Lutte de classes sous la Pemière République, 1793–1797 not only shocked many academic historians of the revolution—especially those with more or less close links to the PCF: Georges Lefebvre, and especially Albert Soboul and Georges Rudé—but also those "politicians who have been responsible for perverting and undermining true proletarian socialism."[41] The fallout was intense and the debate which ensued lasted for many years; indeed, Guérin is still today regarded with distrust by many historians influenced by the Republican and mainstream Marxist interpretations of the revolution as a bourgeois revolution. Guérin brought that whole historiographical tradition into question. The political significance was that the Revolutionary Terror had been used as a parallel to justify Bolshevik repression of democratic freedoms and repression of more leftist movements. Stalin had been compared to Robespierre. The Jacobin tradition of patriotism and national unity in defense of the bourgeois democratic Republic has been one of the characteristics of the dominant tendencies within the French Left, and therefore central to the political mythologies of the Popular Front and the Resistance. Guérin, as Ian Birchall has put it, "was polemicizing against the notion of a Resistance uniting all classes against the foreign invader."[42]

Since 1945, the PCF had been campaigning for unity at the top with the SFIO and in the 1956 elections called for the re-establishment of a Popular Front government. Guérin, as we have seen, argued that alliance with the supposedly "progressive" bourgeoisie in the struggle against fascism was a contradiction at the heart of the Popular Front strategy. His conception of the way forward for the Left was very different. At a time when fascism in the form of Poujadism looked as if it might once more be a real threat, Guérin argued that the "New Left" [Nouvelle Gauche] (of which he was a member) should try to create a "genuine" Popular Front, that is, a grassroots social movement rather than a governmental alliance, a truly popular movement centered on the working classes that would bring together the labor movement and all socialists who rejected both the pro-American SFIO and the pro-Soviet PCF:

And if we succeed in building this new Popular Front, let us not repeat the mistakes of the 1936 Popular Front, which because of its timidity and impotence ended up driving the middle classes towards fascism, rather than turning them away from it as had been its aim. Only a combative Popular Front,

which dares to attack big business, will be able to halt our middle classes on
the slope which leads to fascism and to their destruction.[43]

THE DEVELOPING CRITIQUE OF LENINISM

Guérin's friend and translator, C. L. R. James, wrote in 1958 of the political
significance of Guérin's revisiting the history of the French Revolution:

> Such a book had never yet been produced and could not have been produced
> in any epoch other than our own. It is impregnated with the experience and
> study of the greatest event of our time: the development and then degenera-
> tion of the Russian Revolution, and is animated implicitly by one central con-
> cern: how can the revolutionary masses avoid the dreadful pitfalls of bureau-
> cratization and the resurgence of a new oppressive state power, and instead
> establish a system of direct democracy?[44]

It was in very similar terms that Guérin expressed the central question facing the Left in a 1959 essay, "La Révolution déjacobinisée."[45] This is an important text in Guérin's ideological itinerary, continuing the political analysis he began in *La Lutte de classes sous la Pemière République* and
developed in *La Révolution française et nous* (written in 1944 but not published until 1969) and "Quand le fascisme nous devançait" (1955).[46]

In "La Révolution déjacobinisée," Guérin argued on the basis of extensive
readings of Marx and Engels in the original German that the "Jacobin" traits
in Marxism and particularly in Leninism were the result of an incomplete
understanding on Marx and Engels' part of the class nature of Jacobinism
and the Jacobin dictatorship, to be distinguished according to Guérin from
the democratically controlled "revolutionary coercion" [*contrainte révolutionnaire*] exercised by the popular *sections*. Thus by applying a historical
materialist analysis to the experiences of the French revolutionary movement, Guérin came to argue, essentially, that "authentic" socialism (*contra*
Louis-Auguste Blanqui or Lenin) arose spontaneously out of working-class
struggle and that it was fundamentally libertarian. Authoritarian conceptions
of party organization and revolutionary strategy had their origins in bourgeois or even aristocratic modes of thought.

Guérin believed that when Marx and Engels referred—rather vaguely—
to a "dictatorship of the proletariat" they envisaged it as a dictatorship exercised by the working class as a whole, rather than by an avant-garde detached from the class. But, he continued, Marx and Engels did not
adequately differentiate their interpretation from that of the Blanquists,

advocates of a revolutionary vanguard. This made possible Lenin's later authoritarian conceptions: "Lenin, who saw himself as both a 'Jacobin' and a
'Marxist,' invented the idea of the dictatorship of a party substituting itself
for the working class and acting by proxy in its name."[47] This, for Guérin,
was where it all started to go badly wrong:

> The double experience of the French and Russian Revolutions has taught us
> that this is where we touch upon the central mechanism whereby direct de-
> mocracy, the self-government of the people, is transformed, gradually, by the
> introduction of the revolutionary "dictatorship," into the reconstitution of an
> apparatus for the oppression of the people.[48]

Guérin's leftist, class-based critique of Jacobinism thus had three related
implications for contemporary debates about political tactics and strategy.
First, it implied a rejection of class collaboration and therefore of any type of
alliance with the bourgeois Left (Popular Frontism). Second, it implied that
the revolutionary movement should be more uncompromising, that it should
push for more radical social change and not stop halfway (which, as Saint-Just
famously remarked, was to dig one's own grave), rejecting the Stalinist emphasis on the unavoidability of separate historical "stages" in the long-term
revolutionary process. Third, it implied a rejection both of the Leninist model
of a centralized, hierarchical party dominating the labor movement and of the
"substitutism" (substitution of the party for the proletariat) that had come to
characterize the Bolshevik dictatorship.

This critique clearly had its sources both in Guérin's reinterpretation of
the French Revolution and in the social and political conditions of the time.
La Révolution française et nous was informed by Guérin's critique of social-
democratic and Stalinist strategies before, during, and after the war. "La
révolution déjacobinisée" was written after the artificial national unity of
the immediate postwar years had given way to profound social and political
conflict, as Guy Mollet's SFIO became increasingly identified with the defense of the bourgeois status quo and the Western camp in the Cold War,
as the immensely powerful postwar PCF reeled under the effects of Hungary and the Khrushchev revelations, and as the unpopular and politically
unstable Fourth Republic collapsed in the face of a threatened military
coup. It was this situation which made renewal of the Left so necessary. In
1959, Guérin also picked up on the results of a survey of the attitudes of
French youth toward politics, which indicated to him two facts: first, that
what alienated the younger generation from "socialism" was "bureaucrats
and purges," and second, that, as one respondent put it, "French youth are
becoming more and more anarchist."[49] Ever the optimist, Guérin declared:

Far from allowing ourselves to sink into doubt, inaction, and despair, the time has come for the French Left to begin again from zero, to rethink its problems from their very foundations. . . . The necessary synthesis of the ideas of equality and liberty . . . cannot and must not be attempted, in my opinion, in the framework and to the profit of a bankrupt bourgeois democracy. It can and must only be done in the framework of socialist thought, which remains, despite everything, the only reliable value of our times. The failure of both reformism and Stalinism imposes on us the urgent duty to find a way of reconciling (proletarian) democracy with socialism, freedom with Revolution.[50]

ANTICOLONIALISM

Periodically in French history, moments of social and political crisis have arisen that have challenged the existing political forces, dividing onetime allies, throwing together former enemies, and producing new ideological currents. The Algerian war of independence was one such crisis, and on the far-left anticolonialism was the catalyst for change. Guérin had already been a committed anticolonial campaigner since his twenties. In 1927, he had embarked on a life-changing journey when he was sent by his family to run the Syrian branch of Hachette. Meetings with Emir Khaled, grandson of Abd el-Kader (the Algerian independence pioneer), and Ibrahim bey Hanano (the Syrian politician and patriot) converted him to Arab nationalism. Subsequent visits to Djibouti (1928) and then French Indochina (1929–1930), where he met with the nationalist leader Huynh-Thuc-Khang, provided Guérin with further first-hand experience of the hypocrisy of the West's "civilizing mission" and the double standards of so-called socialists and members of the Ligue des droits de l'homme [Human Rights League] when living in the colonies. By the time he returned to Marseille in 1930, he had made the decision to devote his life to "the struggle for the abolition of this social and colonial scandal"—the social and the colonial always being inextricably linked in Guérin's Marxist perspective.[51] Resolving to abandon all the "superfluous" pastimes of his privileged youth, he burned his unpublished writings and consigned to silence his published poems and novels, ashamed of their very existence.

On his return to France, he contributed articles on the colonies to Henri Barbusse's weekly paper, *Monde*, was an active member of Francis Jourdain's Comité d'amnistie aux indochinois, and would argue for the Popular Front government to grant Algeria independence. In 1952, he undertook a three-month fact-finding trip around North Africa and established connections with nationalists and trade unionists. In 1953, he joined the Comité France-Maghreb, chaired by François Mauriac, but left it in 1955, exasperated by the committee's passivity. In 1954, Guérin published *Au service des colonisés*, the first of several books on colonialism that would appear through the 1950s, 1960s, and 1970s.[52] He was involved in a series of activities in support of the Algerian nationalists and had particularly close links with Messali Hadj, the Marxist and anticolonialist founder of the Mouvement national algérien (MNA). He also met and became friends with the leading Algerian nationalist and historian, Mohamed Harbi.[53]

In France, it was the Trotskyist PCI and the Fédération communiste libertaire (FCL) who were the first to support—in theory and practice—the uprising initiated by the Algerian Front de libération nationale (FLN) in 1954. The far-left—anarchists, Trotskyists, and other revolutionary groups—had been both weak and divided until this point. But through the campaign of opposition to the war against Algerian independence, for the first time in some years and over an extended period, a space was created to the left of the PCF in which the far-left was able to reassert itself as a significant political force. Their campaigns included not only support for the Algerian nationalists, but also support for French military deserters and those refusing to answer conscription, antifascist actions directed at the Organisation d'armée secrète, mass demonstrations, and petitions involving prominent intellectuals. These campaigns and the new profile of the far-left would be important preludes for developments in 1968.

This was a period during which Guérin—building on the work he had done on the French Revolutionary period—had been studying the history of the political conflicts within the First International and, more generally, the relations between anarchism and Marxism. The FCL's ideological stance (libertarian Marxism) and its position on the Algerian war ("critical support" for the nationalist movement in the context of the struggle against French bourgeois imperialism: "Every victory of the proletariat of the colonies is a victory of the French proletariat against its exploiters"[54]) thus proved doubly attractive to Guérin. He also appreciated their refusal to duplicate the sectarian conflict between the MNA and the FLN. In part for these reasons, 1954 represented the beginning of a relationship, notably with Georges Fontenis (leading light of the FCL), which would ultimately take Guérin into the ranks of the "libertarian communist" movement (of which more later). Guérin publicly supported the FCL when its paper, *Le Libertaire*, was seized in November 1954 on the orders of the Minister of the Interior, François Mitterrand. When Mitterrand also prohibited a planned public meeting (organized jointly by the FCL and the PCI) to protest repression in Algeria, Guérin, who was to have chaired the meeting, led a delegation to protest to the minister in person. To Mitterrand's quip that, "Algeria is France" [*L'Algérie, c'est la France*], Guérin replied at a meeting organized by the Comité d'action des intellectuels contre la poursuite de la guerre en Afrique du Nord that "Algeria has never been France" [*L'Algérie n'a jamais été la France*].[55]

Guérin was also one of the first to sign the so-called Manifesto of the 121 in 1960. More than an appeal calling for the right to refuse military service in Algeria, this petition marked a watershed in the campaign against the war. The text's conclusion declared:

> We respect and regard as justified the refusal to take up arms against the Algerian people. We respect and regard as justified the actions of those French citizens who feel it their duty to offer help and protection to Algerians oppressed in the name of the French people. The cause of the Algerian people, who are making a decisive contribution to the destruction of the colonial system, is the cause of all free men.[56]

Guérin himself hid young Frenchmen escaping conscription as well as Algerian militants sought by the police.

After Algerian independence was declared in 1962, Guérin sought actively to persuade the new government formed by the FLN leader Ahmed Ben Bella to ensure the transformation of the struggle for national independence into the struggle for socialism. Toward the end of 1963, he traveled around Algeria studying socialized factories and farms. Guérin argued strongly that these must be systematized and centrally coordinated, and he personally handed a report of his findings to President Ben Bella. He attended the first Congress on Worker Self-Management in Algeria in 1964 and published his *L'Algérie qui se cherche* the same year. After Houari Boumedienne's military coup of 1965, Guérin took part in the defense committee established to support Ben Bella and other victims of the subsequent repression.

The year 1965 would also see the abduction of the leading Moroccan militant, El Mehdi Ben Barka. Having persuaded François Mauriac to resurrect the old Comité France-Maghreb, Guérin played a prominent part in the campaign to establish the truth around Ben Barka's disappearance. The conclusion of his research would be that the abduction was the result of collusion between the CIA, the Moroccan monarchy, and the French authorities.[57]

FROM NEW LEFT TO ANARCHISM

In the mid-to-late 1950s, like other ex- or "critical" Trotskyists as well as ex-militants of the FCL (banned in 1956), Guérin belonged—though "without much conviction"—to a series of left-socialist organizations: the Nouvelle Gauche, the Union de la gauche socialiste, and, briefly, the Parti socialiste unifié.[58] But it was also around 1956 that Guérin discovered anarchism. Looking back on his 1929 boat trip to Vietnam and the small library he had taken with him, Guérin commented that of all the authors he had studied—Marx, Pierre-Joseph Proudhon, Georges Sorel, Hubert Lagardelle, Fernand Pelloutier, Lenin, Trotsky, Gandhi, and others—"Marx had, without a doubt, been preponderant."[59] But having become increasingly critical of Leninism during the 1950s, Guérin discovered the collected works of Mikhail Bakunin, a revelation which rendered him forever "allergic to all versions of authoritarian socialism, whether Jacobin, Marxist, Leninist, or Trotskyist."[60] Guérin would describe the following ten years or so—which saw the publication notably of the popular anthology *Ni dieu ni maître* and of *L'Anarchisme*, which sold like hot cakes at the Sorbonne in May 1968 and which still today is seen by many as the best short book on anarchism—as his "classical anarchist phase."[61] He became especially interested in Proudhon, whom he admired as the first theorist of *autogestion*, or worker self-management; Bakunin, representative of revolutionary, working-class anarchism, close to Marxism yet remarkably prescient about the dangers of statist communism; and Max Stirner, appreciated as a precursor of 1968 because of his determination to attack bourgeois prejudice and puritanism.

The discovery of Bakunin coincided with the appearance of the Hungarian workers' committees and the Soviet suppression of the Hungarian uprising in 1956. These events provoked him into studying the councilist tradition, which, since 1918–20 and its theorization by Antonio Gramsci and others, had come to be seen by many as representing revolutionary socialist direct democracy in contrast to the Bolshevik-controlled *soviets*.

1968 AND LIBERTARIAN COMMUNISM

Early on during the student revolt of 1968, at a time when PCF students were complaining about the disruption to their exams, Guérin, Sartre, De Beauvoir, Michel Leiris, and Colette Audry issued a statement calling on "all workers and intellectuals to give moral and material support to the movement of struggle begun by the students and lecturers."[62] This was one of the first public recognitions of the importance of the student movement.

Ten years before, early in 1958, Guérin had declared during a radio debate on youth that "socialism is still alive in the consciousness of the young, but, in order for it to be attractive to them, it would have to be dissociated from the monstrosities of Stalinism, it would have to appear more libertarian."[63] In 1968, Guérin believed that events now bore out this earlier assessment, and that "this unexpected explosion was in large measure anarchistic."[64] 1968 had its origins, for Guérin, in the critique not only of bourgeois society but also of the influence of "post-Stalinist communism" in the universities. The whole experience represented "a whirlwind apprenticeship in direct democracy."[65] Guérin was keen to pick out the renewed popularity of anarchism, and the unusual (if still relative) degree of "fraternization" between anarchists and Marxists and among different Marxist groups. He was impressed by Daniel and Gabriel Cohn-Bendit's book on *gauchisme*. Since he shared their concern to formulate a new "leftism" transcending both anarchism and Marxism, he no doubt appreciated their unwillingness to dwell on the old conflict between Bakunin and Marx.[66]

Guérin was critical of the way in which virtually all commentators emphasized the originality of May '68. For Guérin, despite the originality of the role of the student movement in the early phase of the events, the second, more radical phase involving strikes and occupations by the working class was far more significant. It was entirely comparable with other general strikes and revolutionary movements in France's history: 1793, 1840, 1848, 1871, 1919, and 1936. The reason so many people were taken aback by 1968, and why so many overestimated—in Guérin's view—the movement's originality, was that the events occurred in "a phase of history in which the idea of revolution, in France, has been emptied of all meaning, in which it has been betrayed, distorted, wiped off the map by two powerful political steamrollers, two machines for crushing all critical thought: Stalinism and Gaullism." This was why 1968 had seemed so audacious, why it had seemed to question everything: "because Stalinism for the last forty years, and Gaullism for the last ten have made the French people lose the habit of radical dissent and the taste for libertarian protest—a habit, a taste, a tradition which had been theirs for nearly one-hundred-and-fifty years."[67] Even the resurgence of anarchism was nothing radically new: it was simply the traditional "anarcho-syndicalism" of the French working class, the "old syndicalist ferment in the consciousness of the workers," bubbling irrepressibly to the surface again, despite the anger of the "bureaucratic liquidators" such as Georges Séguy, communist general secretary of the Confédération générale du travail at the time.[68]

FOR A SYNTHESIS OF MARXISM AND ANARCHISM

Having called himself a "libertarian socialist" in the late 1950s before going through an "anarchist" phase in the 1960s, by 1968 Guérin was advocating "libertarian Marxism," a term he would later change to "libertarian communism" in order not to alienate some of his anarchist friends. In May 1969, with Georges Fontenis and others Guérin launched the Mouvement communiste libertaire (MCL), which attempted to bring together various groups such as ex-supporters of Denis Berger's Voie communiste, former members of the FCL, and individuals such as Gabriel Cohn-Bendit associated with Socialisme ou Barbarie.[69] Guérin was responsible for the group's paper, *Guerre de classes*. In 1971, the MCL merged with another group to become the Organisation communiste libertaire. In 1980, after complex debates notably over the question of trade union activity, Guérin—who rejected ultra-left forms of *"spontanéisme"* which condemned trade unionism as counter-revolutionary—would ultimately join the Union des travailleurs communistes libertaires (UTCL), created in 1978. He would remain a member of this group until his death in 1988.[70]

The attempt to formulate a libertarian communism, both theoretically and practically, was the conclusion of a process of rethinking the Left which Guérin had begun during World War Two. In a letter of 1947 to Marceau Pivert, Guérin had described his reinterpretation of the French Revolution as "an introduction to a synthesis of anarchism and Marxism-Leninism I would like to write one day."[71] It is important to note that Guérin talked of a "synthesis." As Georges Fontenis would write: "For us [the FCL], as for Guérin, 'libertarian Marxism' was never to be seen as a fusion or a marriage, but as a living synthesis very different from the sum of its parts."[72]

Guérin was always keen to emphasize the commonalities in Marxism and anarchism, and underscored the fact that, in his view at least, they shared the same roots and the same objectives. Having said that, his study of Marx led him to suggest that those such as Maximilien Rubel, who saw Marx as a libertarian, were exaggerating and/or being too selective.[73] Reviewing the ambivalent but predominantly hostile relations between Marx and Engels, on the one hand, and Stirner, Proudhon, and Bakunin, on the other, Guérin concluded that the disagreements between them were based largely on misunderstanding and exaggeration on both sides. The date of 1872, when the Bakuninists were expelled from the International Working Men's Association Congress at La Haye, was for Guérin "a disastrous event for the working class, because each of the two movements needs the theoretical and practical contribution of the other."[74]

Libertarian communism was an attempt to "revivify everything that was constructive in anarchism's contribution in the past." The very successful 1965 book on anarchism focused on "social, constructive, collectivist, or communist anarchism."[75] Guérin was more critical of "traditional" anarchism, with its knee-jerk rejection of organization, and particularly its Manichean and simplistic approach to the question of the "state" in modern, industrial, and increasingly internationalized societies. He became interested particularly in militants such as the Spanish anarchist Diego Abad de Santillán, whose ideas on "integrated" economic self-management contrasted with, in Guérin's view, the naïve and backward-looking policy of the Spanish National Labor Confederation (Confederación nacional del trabajo) advocated at its 1936 Saragossa conference by Isaac Puente and inspired by Peter Kropotkin.[76] Such a policy seemed to Guérin to take no account of the nature of modern consumer societies and the need for economic planning and coordination at national and transnational levels. In this connection, Guérin also became interested in the ideas of the Belgian collectivist socialist César de Paepe on the national and transnational organization of public services within a libertarian framework.[77]

On the other hand, libertarian communism did not reject those aspects of Marxism which still seemed to Guérin valid and useful: (1) the notion of alienation, which Guérin saw as being in accordance with the anarchist emphasis on individual freedom; (2) the insistence that the workers shall be emancipated by the workers themselves; (3) the analysis of capitalist society; and (4) the historical materialist dialectic, which for Guérin remained

> one of the guiding threads enabling us to understand the past and the present, on condition that the method not be applied rigidly, mechanically, or as an excuse not to fight on the false pretext that the material conditions for a revolution are absent, as the Stalinists claimed was the case in France in 1936, 1945, and 1968. Historical materialism must never be reduced to a determinism; the door must always be open to individual will and to the revolutionary spontaneity of the masses.[78]

In the 1970s Guérin developed a particular interest in Rosa Luxemburg and played a role in the wider resurgence of interest in her ideas. She was for Guérin the only German social democrat who stayed true to what he called "original" Marxism, and in 1971 he published an anthology of her writings on the pre-1914 SFIO, as well as a study of the notion of spontaneity in her work.[79] The following year he took part in a debate with Gilbert Badia, Michael Löwy, Madeleine Rebérioux, Denis Vidal-Naquet, and others on the contemporary relevance of Luxemburg's ideas.[80] Guérin saw no significant difference between her conception of revolutionary working-class spontaneity and the anarchist one, nor between her conception of the "mass strike" and the syndicalist idea of the "general strike." Her criticisms of Lenin in 1904 and of the Bolshevik Party in the spring of 1918 (regarding the democratic freedoms of the working class) seemed to him very anarchistic, as did her conception of a socialism propelled from below by workers' councils. She was, he argued, "one of the links between anarchism and authentic Marxism."[81]

Guérin was convinced that a libertarian communism which represented a synthesis of the best of Marxism and the best of anarchism would be much more attractive to progressive workers than "degenerate, authoritarian Marxism or old, outdated, and fossilized anarchism."[82] But he was adamant that he was not a theorist, that libertarian communism was, as yet, only an "approximation," not a fixed dogma. "The only thing of which I am convinced is that the future social revolution will have nothing to do with either Muscovite despotism or social-democratic anemia; that it will not be authoritarian, but libertarian and based on self-management."[83]

FOR A DIALECTIC OF SOCIAL REVOLUTION AND SEXUAL REVOLUTION

Other, better-known currents in the postwar New Left—existentialists, revisionists around Henri Lefebvre and the journal *Arguments*, and the Socialisme ou Barbarie group—were all concerned in different ways with questions of subjectivity, consciousness, authenticity, and alienation. The development of Guérin's concerns paralleled these attempts to develop or reinterpret Marxism, and his motivation in certain respects was very much rooted in direct personal experience. Guérin came out of the closet in 1965 with the publication of his first autobiography, *Un Jeune Homme excentrique*.[84] He had begun in the 1950s to write about sexuality and sexual liberation, playing an important role in popularizing the work of Alfred Kinsey in France.[85] In the late 1960s, he published on Charles Fourier and Wilhelm Reich and was attracted by the idea of a synthesis of Marxism and psychoanalysis.[86] By 1968—a turning point in terms of the visibility of homosexuality—Guérin was already seen as the "grandfather" of the gay liberation movement.[87] For a short while a member of the high-profile Front homosexuel d'action révolutionnaire, he soon became disillusioned with the apolitical attitude of most gay activists, however. The homophobia of the Left and of the labor movement had been a source of great personal suffering for Guérin ever since the 1930s, and he became determined in his later years to try to find what he termed a "dialectic of revolution and homosexuality," arguing that "only a true libertarian communism, antiauthoritarian and antistatist, would be capable of promoting the definitive and concomitant emancipation both of the homosexual and of the individual exploited or alienated by capitalism."[88] One of the reasons he joined and stayed in the Union des travailleurs communistes libertaires was its unusually progressive stance on sexuality. As a UTCL pamphlet entitled *Le Droit à la caresse* insisted:

> There can be no liberation of homosexuality other than on the basis of new social relations, in other words other than in a new society, which is why we are allies with the labor movement in its struggle, the labor movement being the only force capable of bringing about the necessary social change. So, if socialism is not to be a caricature of itself, we, as homosexuals, have a role to play in the class struggle.[89]

For the first time in his life, Guérin had found an organization in which he felt entirely at home.

CONCLUSION

It is a strange irony that in Arthur Hirsch's account of the French New Left, half of those individuals discussed as contributors to the rejuvenation of Marxism were ex-Stalinists, whereas Guérin is mentioned only as an example of someone who promoted mechanistic, economistic reductionism— criticized by Sartre, someone who only came to revolutionary politics and Marxism relatively late in life.[90] One cannot help feeling that there is not only a gap in the historical account here, but also an injustice. As Guérin himself wrote regarding Sartre's conversion to anti-Stalinist Marxism after Khrushchev's 1956 speech:

> There are some of us who have to bite their tongue in order not to give vent to their resentment. They could mention the tragedy of a generation of anti-Stalinist Marxists whose lives have been broken by the dreadful taboo of the tyrant now overthrown, who long found themselves practically alone, gagged, crushed between a bourgeoisie which rejected them and a "communist" orthodoxy which poured down insults on them, and who strove with immense difficulty to resolve that awesome contradiction: denouncing Stalinism without falling into the camp of the enemies of the October Revolution.[91]

There were of course overlaps and differences between Guérin and other Marxist "revisionists." Guérin wrote for *Arguments*. He took part with Cornelius Castoriadis, Claude Lefort, and Edgar Morin in a 1965 forum on "Marxism Today" organized by Socialisme ou Barbarie (whose work was described by Morin as representing "an original synthesis of Marxism and anarchism").[92] Members of the Socialisme ou Barbarie group had taken part in the Comité de lutte contre la répression colonialiste established by Guérin in 1954. Ian Birchall has examined the frequent but often problematic relations between Guérin and Sartre, concluding that in the end— and increasingly so as Sartre's politics evolved to resemble Guérin's— "what united them was more important than their differences."[93] The libertarian communist group Noir et Rouge felt that what distinguished Guérin—apart from the fact that he started from Marxist premises and arrived at conclusions very similar to those of many anarchist communists— was his courage and his honesty, "his concern to really rethink a certain number of problems which virtually all other critics do not dare confront or who do so only superficially; this concern, combined with his intellectual rigor, often led him to confront certain 'taboos' . . . and gave him the courage to criticize even the masters of Marxism themselves."[94] There seems little doubt that Guérin's contribution was exceptional and that he was one of the most innovative and interesting figures on the Left in postwar France.

NOTES

1. On Guérin's view of the historiography of anarchism, see "Un procès en réhabilitation," in Guérin, *À la recherche d'un communisme libertaire* (Paris: Spartacus, 1984), 22–23. This collection of articles has just been re-published by Spartacus (2003) with a new introduction by Georges Fontenis.

2. For a bibliography, see my website at: www-staff.lboro.ac.uk/~eudgb/DG. htm (11 March 2004).

3. In *Question de méthode*, quoted in Ian Birchall, "Sartre's Encounter with Daniel Guérin," *Sartre Studies International* 2, no. 1 (1996): 48.

4. "Une lettre du regretté Pierre Hahn," in Guérin, *Homosexualité et révolution* (Paris: Le Vent du ch'min, 1983), 43. Aimé Césaire, "Introduction," in Guérin, *Les Antilles décolonisées* (Paris: Présence africaine, 1956), 9–17.

5. See Chomsky, "Introduction," in Guérin, *Anarchism: From Theory to Practice* (New York: Monthly Review Press, 1970).

6. See Louis Janover, "Guérin, le trouble-fête," *Débattre* 10 (Spring 2000): 11–15.

7. Guérin, *Autobiographie de jeunesse, d'une dissidence sexuelle au socialisme* (Paris: Belfond, 1972), 126–27. Charles Maurras was the leader of the right-wing movement, Action française.

8. For more detail, see my "'Prolétaires de tous les pays, caressez-vous!' Daniel Guérin, the Labour Movement, and Homosexuality," in *Sexualität, Unterschichten-milieu und ArbeiterInnenbewegung*, eds. Paul Pasteur, Sonja Niederacher, and Maria Mesner (Vienna: ITH & Akademische Verlagsanstalt, 2003), 189–203. See also Peter Sedgwick, "Out of Hiding: The Comradeships of Daniel Guérin," *Salmagundi* 58, no. 9 (June 1982): 197–220.

9. Guérin, *À la recherche*, 9; and *Front populaire, révolution manquée? témoignage militant* (Arles: Actes Sud, 1997), 23.

10. Guérin, *Front populaire*, 147.

11. Guérin's *Front populaire* is a classic "revolutionist" interpretation of the Popular Front experience.

12. Guérin, *Front populaire*, 104.

13. Guérin, *La Peste brune a passé par là* (Paris: Librairie du Travail, 1933), trans. *The Brown Plague: Travels in Late Weimar and Early Nazi Germany* (Durham, N.C.: Duke University Press, 1994); and *Fascisme et grand capital* (Paris: Gallimard, 1936), trans. *Fascism and Big Business* (New York: Monad Press, 1973). *Fascism* has been criticized by some for tending toward reductionism. See Claude Lefort, "L'analyse Marxiste et le fascisme," *Les Temps modernes* 2 (November 1945): 357–62. Others regard Guérin's methodology as fundamentally correct. See Alain Bihr's introduction to the 1999 edition of *Fascisme et grand capital* (Paris: Syllepse, 1999), 7–14.

14. Guérin, "Quand le fascisme nous devançait," in *La Peste brune* (Paris: Spartacus, 1996), 21–22.

15. Guérin, "Quand le fascisme nous devançait," 25.

16. Guérin, *Front populaire*, 150, 156–57, 365.

17. Guérin, *Front populaire*, 157.

18. Guérin, *Front populaire*, 213.

19. Guérin, *Front populaire*, 23.

20. See Craipeau's autobiography, *Mémoires d'un dinosaure trotskyste: secrétaire de Trotsky en 1933* (Paris: L'Harmattan, 1999).

21. Interview with Pierre André Boutang in *Guérin*, television documentary by Jean-José Marchandl, FR3 (4 & 11 September 1989), film made in 1985. For more details, see my "'Like a Wisp of Straw Amidst the Raging Elements': Daniel Guérin in the Second World War," in *Vichy, Resistance, Liberation: Festschrift in Honour of H. R. Kedward*, eds. Simon Kitson and Hanna Diamond (Berg, forthcoming).

22. Guérin, *Le Feu du sang, autobiographie politique et charnelle* (Paris: Grasset & Fasquelle, 1979), 100.

23. Guérin, *Le Feu du sang*, 109.

24. Guérin, *Front populaire*, 414.

25. Guérin, *Le Feu du sang*, 270–72.

26. Letter to Marceau Pivert (2 Januaury 1948), Fonds Daniel Guérin, Bibliothèque de documentation internationale contemporaine, Nanterre, F° Δ Rés 688/9/1.

27. Guérin, *Le Feu du Sang*, 149. On Guérin's tour of the U.S., see *Le Feu du Sang*, 143–219. Guérin's researches led to the publication of the two-volume *Où va le peuple américain?* (Paris: Julliard, 1950–51). Sections of this would be published separately as *Décolonisation du noir américain* (Paris: Éditions de Minuit, 1963); *Le Mouvement ouvrier aux Etats-Unis* (Paris: Maspero, 1968); and *De l'Oncle Tom aux Panthères: le drame des noirs américains* (Paris: UGE, 1973). Translations: *Negroes on the March: A Frenchman's Report on the American Negro Struggle*, trans. Duncan Ferguson (New York: George L. Weissman, 1956); and *100 Years of Labor in the USA*, trans. Alan Adler (London: Ink Links, 1979).

28. Guérin, *Le Feu du sang*, 221–22.

29. Guérin, *Le Feu du sang*, 223.

30. Guérin, *Le Feu du sang*, 224, 281–84. *Le Monde*, 5 August 1950.

31. On Guérin's relationship with Mauriac, see the *Autobiographie de jeunesse*, *passim*.

32. The term is Guérin's, in *Le Feu du sang*, 225.

33. Guérin, *Où va le peuple américain?*.

34. Guérin, *Le Feu du sang*, 227. Guérin mentions no names.

35. Guérin, *Le Feu du sang*, 226.

36. Guérin, *Le Feu du sang*, 228–31.

37. Guérin, *La Lutte de classes sous la Pemière République, 1793–1797*, 2 vols. (Paris: Gallimard, 1946; 1968).

38. Guérin, *La Révolution française et nous* (Paris: Maspero, 1976), 7–8. Note that the reference to "libertarian socialism" is in the preface to *La Révolution française et nous*, written thirty years after the main text and after Guérin had moved closer to anarchism.

39. Guérin, *La Lutte de classes* (1968 edition), 1: 31.

40. Guérin, *La Lutte de classes*, 58.

41. Guérin, *La Révolution française et nous*, 7.

42. Birchall, "Sartre's Encounter," 46.

43. Guérin, "Faisons le point," *Le Libérateur politique et social pour la nouvelle gauche* (12 February 1956).

44. C. L. R. James, "L'actualité de la Révolution française," *Perspectives socialistes: revue bimensuelle de l'Union de la gauche socialiste* 4 (15 February 1958): 20–21.

45. Guérin, "La révolution déjacobinisée," in *Jeunesse du socialisme libertaire* (Paris: Rivière, 1959), 27–63.

46. *La Révolution française et nous* was originally intended as the preface to *Lutte de classes*. "Quand le fascisme nous devançait" was originally commissioned for a special issue of *Les Temps modernes* on the state of the Left.

47. Guérin, "La Révolution déjacobinisée," 43.

48. Guérin, "La Révolution déjacobinisée," 43–4.

49. Guérin, "Preface," *Jeunesse du socialisme libertaire*, 7–8.

50. Guérin, "La Révolution déjacobinisée," 30–31.

51. Guérin, *Autobiographie de jeunesse*, 227.

52. Guérin, *Au Service des colonisés: 1930–1953* (Paris: Minuit, 1954); *Les Antilles décolonisées*; *L'Algérie qui se cherche* (Paris: Centre d'étude socialiste, 1964); *Les Assassins de Ben Barka, dix ans d'enquête* (Paris: Guy Authier, 1975); and *Quand l'Algérie s'insurgeait, 1954–1962: un anticolonialiste témoigne* (Paris: La Pensée sauvage, 1979).

53. See Mohammed Harbi, *Une Vie debout: mémoires politiques, tome 1: 1945–1962* (Paris: La Découverte, 2002), 109–12.

54. *Le Libertaire* (organ of the FCL), 15 July 1954, quoted in Georges Fontenis, "L'insurrection algérienne et les communistes libertaires," in *Des Français contre la terreur d'Etat (Algérie 1954–1962)*, ed. Sidi Mohammed Barkat (Paris: Editions Reflex, 2002), 81–90, 84.

55. Guérin, *L'Algérie n'a jamais été la France* (Paris: Published by the author, 1956). Other speakers at this meeting were Aimé Césaire, Jean-Paul Sartre, and Michel Leiris.

56. "Déclaration sur le droit à l'insoumission dans la guerre d'Algérie" [Le Manifeste des 121, 6 February 1960], in *La France du XXe siècle: documents d'histoire*, eds. Olivier Wieworka and Christophe Prochasson (Paris: Seuil, 1994), 497.

57. Guérin, *Les Assassins de Ben Barka*; and *Ben Barka, ses assassins, seize ans d'enquête* (Paris: Plon, 1982).

58. Guérin, *Le Feu du sang*, 233.

59. Guérin, *À la recherche*, 9.

60. Guérin, *À la recherche*.

61. Guérin, *À la recherche*, 10. *L'Anarchisme, de la doctrine à la pratique* (Paris: Gallimard, 1965); and *Ni dieu ni maître, anthologie de l'anarchisme* (Lausanne: La Cité-Lausanne, 1965). Both have been republished several times since, and *L'Anarchisme* has been translated into more than twenty languages. They have been published in English as *Anarchism: From Theory to Practice*; and *No Gods No Masters: An Anthology of Anarchism* (Edinburgh: AK Press, 1998).

62. *Le Monde*, 8 May 1968.

63. Guérin, "Mai 1968," in *À la recherche*, 116.

64. Guérin, "Mai 1968," 117.

65. Guérin, "Mai 1968."

66. Daniel Cohn-Bendit and Gabriel Cohn-Bendit, *Le Gauchisme, remède à la maladie sénile du communisme* (Paris: Seuil, 1968).

67. Guérin, "Mai, une continuité," in *À la recherche*, 119–20.

68. Guérin, "Mai, une continuité."

69. See Fontenis, *Changer le monde: histoire du mouvement communiste libertaire, 1945–1997* (Paris: Le Coquelicot/Alternative libertaire, 2000), 161–62, 255–56.

70. The UTCL's manifesto, adopted at its Fourth Congress in 1986, has recently been republished (with a dedication to Guérin) by the UTCL's successor organiza-

tion, Alternative libertaire: *Un Projet de société communiste libertaire* (Paris: Alternative libertaire, 2002).

71. Letter to Marceau Pivert (18 November 1947), quoted in "Daniel Guérin," special issue of *Alternative libertaire* (2000): 16.

72. Fontenis, *Changer le monde*, 80 n. 1.

73. Guérin, "Anarchisme et marxisme," in *L'Anarchisme* (1981 edition), 250.

74. Guérin, "Anarchisme et marxisme," 248.

75. Guérin, "Anarchisme et marxisme," 237.

76. On Abad de Santillan, see the section on "L'Espagne libertaire," in "Les Anarchistes et l'autogestion," special issue of *Autogestion et socialisme* 18–19 (1972): 81–117, including an introduction by Guérin.

77. See Guérin, *Ni dieu ni maître*, 1: 268–91.

78. Guérin, "Anarchisme et marxisme," 252.

79. Rosa Luxemburg, *Le Socialisme en France, 1898–1912* (Paris: Belfond, 1971), with an introduction by Guérin, 7–48; and *Rosa Luxemburg et la spontanéité révolutionnaire* (Paris: Flammarion, 1971).

80. Gilbert Badia et al., "Rosa Luxemburg et nous: Débat," *Politique aujourd'hui: recherches et pratiques socialistes dans le monde* (1972): 77–106.

81. Guérin, "Anarchisme et marxisme," 233.

82. Guérin, "Anarchisme et marxisme," 252.

83. Guérin, *À la recherche*, 10–11.

84. Guérin, *Un Jeune Homme excentrique: essai d'autobiographie* (Paris: Julliard, 1965).

85. See Sylvie Chaperon, "Kinsey en France: les sexualités féminine et masculine en débat," *Mouvement social* 198 (2002): 91–110; and "Le fonds Daniel Guérin et l'histoire de la sexualité," *Journal de la BDIC* 5 (2002): 10.

86. See *Kinsey et la sexualité* (Paris: Julliard, 1955; repub. EDI, 1967); "Le Nouveau monde amoureux de Fourier," *Arcadie* 168 (1967): 554–60, and *Arcadie* 169 (1968): 16–23; "Hommage à Wilhelm Reich," in *Société et répression sexuelle: l'œuvre de Wilhelm Reich*, eds. Guérin, Boris Fraenkel, Michel Cattler, Constantin Sinelnikoff, Marc Kravetz, and Jacques Delattre (Bruxelles: Editions Liaisons 20, 1968), 3–5; "Wilhelm Reich aujourd'hui" [Introduction à un débat organisé à Bruxelles le 29 novembre 1968 par 'Liaison 20'] (1969); and *Essai sur la révolution sexuelle après Reich et Kinsey* (Paris: Belfond, 1969). Guérin also produced the anthology, Charles Fourier, *Vers la liberté en amour* (Paris: Gallimard, 1975).

87. Frédéric Martel, *Le Rose et le noir: les homosexuels en France depuis 1968* (Paris: Seuil, 2000), 46.

88. Guérin, *Homosexualité et révolution*, 25, 9.

89. Union des Travailleurs Communistes Libertaires, *Le Droit à la caresse: les homosexualités et le combat homosexuel* (Paris: UTCL, n.d.).

90. Arthur Hirsch, *The French New Left: An Intellectual History from Sartre to Gorz* (Boston: South End Press, 1981), 60–61.

91. Guérin, "Sartre et la chute de l'idole," *Combat* (5 April 1956).

92. Edgar Morin, "L'Anarchisme en 1968," *Magazine littéraire* 19 (1968), available at www.magazine-litteraire.com/archives/ar_anar.htm (4 March 2004).

93. Birchall, "Sartre's Encounter," 52. On Guérin's take on 1950s Marxist revisionism, see "Du jeune Marx à Marx," in *Jeunesse du socialisme libertaire*, 67–87.

94. *Noir et Rouge (Cahiers d'études anarchistes révolutionnaires): anthologie 1956–1970* (Paris: Spartacus, 1982), 140.

7

GUY HOCQUENGHEM AND THE CULTURAL REVOLUTION IN FRANCE AFTER MAY 1968

Ron Haas

May 1968–May 1986: Your careers have reached their maturity. The time has come to take an assessment. You would love to avoid this fate; how quickly the time has passed! But I will hold you to it, this two-fold assessment, of eighteen years of radical leftism followed by five years on the Left. The past already out of fashion, you would voluntarily condemn it to oblivion; but to prevent you from making clean slates of yourselves . . . this book will shove your noses in your own shit, throw back in your faces all of your recent ignominies.

Guy Hocquenghem,
Open Letter to Those Who Traded Maoism for the Rotary Club (1986)[1]

A leftist of the French "sixty-eight" generation, Guy Hocquenghem felt so betrayed by his former comrades' compromises during François Mitterrand's first presidency that he decided to publish in 1986, after some hesitation, the *Open Letter to Those Who Traded Maoism for the Rotary Club*. His first intercession in public debates after a number of years of silence, the *Open Letter* is a venomous assault directed at the former leaders of the radical Left, such as Daniel Cohn-Bendit, André Glucksmann, and Bernard Kouchner, who had since climbed to positions of power within the publishing industry, the media, and the newly elected socialist government. Not only had they reneged on their revolutionary promises and been recuperated by the powers they once dreamt of overthrowing, they had become, for

Hocquenghem, that which they despised most in their youth: bourgeois conformists, unscrupulous careerists, and petty seekers of power and wealth. Of the revolutionary conflagration Hocquenghem helped them stoke in 1968 only ashes remained in the 1980s, and paradoxically it was they, the ex-Maoists turned courtiers of the "Mitterrand Restoration," and not the Gaullist reactionaries, who had put out the flames. For Hocquenghem, their politics were neither Left nor Right—they had been equally poised to rally around Giscard d'Estaing—but a synthesis of the worst in both: the Jacobinism of the Left in the service of the *realpolitik* and moral consensus of the Right. If the strength of a democracy can be measured by its internal differences, Hocquenghem writes, then the Maoist-turned-Rotarians were destroying democracy in France by burying its sources of contestation.

For those who were outsiders to the world of Parisian intellectual politics in the 1970s and 1980s, Hocquenghem's *Open Letter* may seem difficult to crack. Deprived since 1982 of any welcoming outlet for his burlesque satire, Hocquenghem used this broadside against the recreant 68ers to settle a few outstanding personal scores. This doubtless helps explain his ruthless portraiture of the court of "Mitterrand the First," which includes, for example, Roland Castro, architect to the king and Hausmann of the suburban housing projects; André Glucksmann and Bernard Henri-Lévy, the king's pro-nuclear crusaders; and a host of other courtiers each "more royalist than the king." It also, unfortunately, provided an easy excuse for his enemies to sanctimoniously dismiss the *Open Letter*. When it appeared in 1986, not one of its main targets responded publicly. Instead, on behalf of the numerous affronted parties, *Libération* editorialist Jean-Michel Helvig denounced the pamphlet as a hateful harangue worthy of the anti-Semitic far-right critics of the 1930s, effectively preempting any further debate.[2]

Hocquenghem predicted such a reaction to his *Open Letter* and seems not to have cared. Introducing the pamphlet, he wrote, "It's true, a realist I am not. And certainly, this book is futile in the era the 'Right-Left-ex-radical-Left' consensus . . . futile maybe, but at the same time necessary: with this book, I banish you from my life and return to the spring of eighteen years past its eternal youth."[3] As he likely knew when he penned it, the *Open Letter* would serve as his final adieu to his generation. A year earlier, in 1985, he tested positive for HIV, and in 1988, he died of AIDS-related illness at the age of forty-two. It may be true, as Helvig wrote in his review, that "Celebrating a fidelity to one's ideas is not necessarily an ode to the intelligence of time."[4] On the other hand, for the generation that is perhaps better known in France today not for having built the barricades of May but for having rebuilt their careers in the late 1970s and 1980s as "New Philosophers," anti-communists, and neo-liberals, self-renunciation is not necessarily a mark of sophistication either. The satire and personal invective aside, this was the underlying message of Hocquenghem's scathing "assessment."

Although he remains something of a legend for veterans of the French homosexual liberation movements in which he played a founding role in the early 1970s, Hocquenghem seems for the most part to have sifted out of his generation's collective memory.[5] Until the 2003 re-edition of the *Open Letter* not one of Hocquenghem's works of nonfiction was still in print in France. In Hervé Hamon and Partrick Rotman's monumental two-volume chronicle of the French Left of the 1960s and 1970s, *Génération*, Hocquenghem appears only in a handful of anecdotes, and in most French histories of the period he receives no mention at all.[6] The wholesale rejection of revolutionary politics and utopian thinking by those who traded Mao for Mitterrand in the 1980s may help explain the general neglect today of Hocquenghem's oeuvre. By his own description, his was a generation that "turned forty from twenty-five with almost no transition."[7] But there may be an even deeper reason behind this neglect, one that has less to do with his quarrels with the Left than with what the sociologist Jean-Pierre Le Goff has referred to as May 1968's "impossible heritage" and the Left's inability to mourn the events of May 1968—a question to which I will return at the end.

Hocquenghem's intellectual itinerary was deeply rooted in the experience and the spirit of May '68, and his influence, like the events themselves, was fierce and short-lived, but to consign him therefore to a few historical footnotes would be unfortunate. To begin with, his talents as an essayist, satirist, and critic rank him among the best of his generation—this not even his enemies would deny him. Whether it was a manifesto, a novel, or one of his famous pamphlets like the *Open Letter*, he always imparted his characteristic tone, which has been aptly described as "less a mark of personality or style than a manner—affective, musical, even gestural—to unsettle conventions," a tone both "caustic and vivifying."[8] When his pen turned to criticism, Hocquenghem respected nothing and spared no one. Words to Hocquenghem, as a militant close to him once put it, were like Kleenex, to be used and thrown out as needed.[9] When these words were aimed at the hypocrisy, conformism, and increasing retrenchment of his former comrades, no one played the role of thorn-in-the-left-side-of-the-Left more skillfully.

But if Hocquenghem used words recklessly, he was not a rebel without a cause. In the first few years following May 1968, he militated among a milieu of *gauchistes* (radical leftists) who demanded everything—"What we want: EVERYTHING!" the masthead of one of their most famous publications read. One of the conclusions they drew from the failures of the 1968 student-worker uprising was that the revolution of the cultural sphere could not wait until after the workers' revolution. Following the Marxist logic of Mao Tse-Tung's Great Proletarian Cultural Revolution, but more in the spirit of the counter-cultural movements of the American West Coast, they sought nothing less than the total revolution—economic, political, and cultural—of French society, and they believed that total revolution was possible only through the politicization of everyday life. Disillusioned and exhausted, many of Hocquenghem's comrades abandoned these utopian aspirations after 1969 and 1970 failed to produce another May 1968. With the social liberalization of the second half of the 1970s under Giscard d'Estaing and the victories of the Left's social agenda under Mitterrand in the 1980s, many others still were incorporated into the politics of the mainstream Left. But Hocquenghem never completely abandoned the idealism of his twenties. His life and his oeuvre reveal a forgotten dimension of the May '68 revolt that was never, perhaps never could have been, taken up by the politics of the Left, but which remains essential for understanding French society after 1968 and many of the dilemmas it continues to face.

Hocquenghem's education was exemplary of the Parisian student Left who led the way in May 1968. After three years at the prestigious Lycée Henri IV, he entered the École normale supérieure (ENS) in 1965. That same year he began militating with the Jeunesse communiste révolutionnaire (JCR), joining the wave of students who were fleeing the Stalinist Communist Party to form their own Marxist splinter groups. When the student movements exploded suddenly in Paris, just weeks after being ignited on the nearby university campus at Nanterre, Hocquenghem raced with his JCR comrades to the Sorbonne, the symbolic seat of student power. In the confusing first days of May, organizational affiliations and intellectual parentages meant little; action meant everything. At the Sorbonne, Hocquenghem joined up with another group of militants, André Glucksmann and Bernard Kouchner among them, to found what is properly considered the first new publication of the '68 generation, appropriately entitled *Action*.

In its first issue, Hocquenghem hazarded an early attempt to give meaning and direction to the student revolt in the centerpiece article entitled, "Why we struggle" [*Pourquoi nous nous battons*]. Though the terminology was largely borrowed from the Marxist lingua franca of the times, Hocquenghem's manifesto describes something close to what Herbert Marcuse had referred to a few years earlier in *One Dimensional Man* as a "great refusal" beginning to emerge.[10] The youth of 1968, Hocquenghem wrote, "refuse the future that the existing society offers them. . . . And when they revolt with violence, they are conscious that they are rendering this refusal more visible and clear."[11] The immediate task of the student movement, too, was clear: "The students are aware that their struggle can only succeed if the workers understand its meaning and wage their own struggle."[12] The prize of every student Marxist circle at the time was the sympathy of the workers, without whose participation, it was believed, no real change was possible.

At the heart of the student revolt may have been this great refusal, but no less important was the student's *prise de parole*, their determination to speak their grievances and make their demands. Within days the Sorbonne had been transformed into a gallery of revolutionary manifestos in the fashion of the famous Chinese *daziboas* of the Cultural Revolution. One day, while Hocquenghem was at the occupied Sorbonne, a handful of posters appeared in the main amphitheatre with the mysterious heading, "Call from the Revolutionary Pederast Action Committee" (Comité d'action pédérastique révolutionnaire or CAPR). The manifesto denounced the repression of homosexuals and demanded freedom of speech and freedom of practice for all sexual minorities. Attacking the well-known double standard in French society whereby homosexuality was tolerated, even admired, among certain figures of the cultural elite and oppressed everywhere else, it proclaimed: "For each glorious Jean Genet, there are a hundred thousand shamed homosexuals, condemned to misery!"[13] The posters were immediately torn down. When the authors of the manifesto later tried to hold a discussion at the occupied Odeon Theater not far away, the response was just as hostile. Summing up the general attitude of the student militants at the time, Guy Chevalier, one of posters' authors, later recalled the response of fellow comrade Philippe Sollers during the Odeon discussion: "But haven't you read Freud? He explained your problem, which is neither political nor revolutionary but personal."[14] Apparently it was not "forbidden to forbid" in May 1968 as the famous slogan goes.

Hocquenghem was not among the small band of CAPR militants, and, like the majority of the Sorbonne's occupants, probably never even saw their manifesto. The general attitude in May 1968, even among those inclined toward tolerance, even among those militants who considered themselves homosexuals, was that the workers' revolution took precedence over every other concern. The students believed at the time, and not without some reason, that they were in the middle of a revolution as important as those of 1789, 1848, 1871, and 1917, and that decisions made and strategies adopted in the immediacy of the moment would have far-reaching consequences. Beneath the festive ebullition of the Latin Quarter, filled with music, dancing, drinking, and poetry, there lay a nucleus of intense discussion, where matters of revolutionary theory and practice were debated with utmost seriousness.

Then, almost as mysteriously as the May revolution had begun, it was over by the end of June. The Gaullists were firmly back in power, most students were preparing to leave Paris for summer vacation, and the vast majority of the workers had gone back to their jobs under the Grenelle Accords brokered by Prime Minister Georges Pompidou. For many student radicals, however, May 1968 was not the end but only the beginning, the initial *prise de conscience*, or awakening, that would lead to a real socialist revolution. Sensing the student radicals' resolve to continue "demanding the impossible," as May's graffiti had urged, the government immediately banned the JCR along with about a dozen other organizations of the radical Left who had participated in the May uprising. When most of what had been the JCR later merged into the Ligue communiste révolutionaire (LCR), the new French section of the United Secretariat of the Fourth International, Hocquenghem was excluded from joining.[15] Hocquenghem's sexuality had on occasion been a source of contention within the group—in his memoirs he recalls having once staunchly denied being a homosexual to his friends in the JCR, an act he would always regret—but this likely had nothing to do with his exclusion.[16] Along with a minority group within the JCR, Hocquenghem was denounced for his supposed adherence to *spontanéiste*, or "direct action," ideas, ideas that were generally associated with the Trotskyists' rivals the Maoists and which would no longer be tolerated in the doctrinally streamlined LCR. The exclusion, in any case, mattered little, as Hocquenghem and his small band of heretics were already moving off in other directions. As he described the mood of the months following May in his memoirs, "one had to be as leftist as possible. Even the Trotskyism to which I had adhered seemed tepid and opportunistic."[17]

Determined to recreate May '68 outside of any doctrinal or organizational affiliations Hocquenghem and his friends left the Latin Quarter after the summer of 1968 to live in a series of communes in working-class suburban neighborhoods around Paris. In Maoist fashion, they formed what was referred to as a *groupe de base*, a kind of grassroots revolutionary cell that met regularly at Censier in Paris and militated in the automobile factories at Sochaux-Flins and Billancourt. There were, of course, practical and financial advantages to living communally if one was a career militant, but it also afforded cover for many *gauchistes* at a time when state repression under Interior Minister Raymond Marcellin was a very real threat.[18] For Hocquenghem, going underground further provided the attraction of living a social experiment. The communes in which he lived were places where workers from the neighborhood came and went freely, where the expenses and the chores were shared by everyone, and where one might stay up until five o'clock in the morning in a room choked with hashish smoke debating whether or not the door on the bathroom stall represented the last vestige of bourgeois privilege and needed to be removed.[19]

From their *groupe de base* at Censier, Hocquenghem and his band of friends assessed the May revolt and tried in 1969 to launch a new revolutionary journal in cooperation with André Glucksmann and his like-minded *groupe de base* at Vincennes. The title of this failed publication aptly expressed the new philosophy: *Révolution culturelle*. The cooptation of the political parties of the Left and the trade unions coupled with the landslide victories of the Gaullists after May '68, Hocquenghem argued, necessitated the rejection of "official" politics and political ideologies for the new forms of struggle born in May '68. "The French situation in 1970 requires the same efforts in creative strategizing that were required of Mao in the face of the peasant problem in China."[20] Although the "cultural revolution" Hocquenghem advocated was ultimately still a struggle for political power, it proceeded by preparing the masses ideologically, by targeting in other words bourgeois ideas, thoughts, and values at the same time that it fought bourgeois power. "The European Cultural Revolution will spare no bourgeois institution or value from the critique of the people," he wrote.[21] Perhaps with the repression of the CAPR at the Sorbonne in mind, Hocquenghem now insisted that every front must be attacked at once; there was no such thing, as the doctrinaire Marxist-Leninists insisted, as "secondary" struggles that could wait until later. Using a turn of phrase that would soon thereafter become a rally cry of the counter-cultural Left, the goal of the revolution had to be in the first instance "to change life" [*changer la vie*]. The task of the cultural revolutionary after May '68 was to synthesize the various struggles emerging throughout France. "The generation of May, despite its tardiness in recognizing the revolt, is not yet disenchanted; to charge it with the task of bringing together the various revolts on all fronts is to point in the direction of a concrete reorganization of everyday life."[22]

Armed with their ideas for a "European Cultural Revolution," Hocquenghem and his Censier comrades also spent a fair amount of time visiting militant groups in Italy and Germany in an effort to forge a kind of "international" but without much result. Their efforts in France at least might have met with more success had it not been for the rapidly growing popularity and visibility during this same period of the newly formed Gauche prolétarienne (GP), the Maoist group that put Maoism on the political map, transforming the term "*mao*" into a synonym for radical militancy in the early 1970s. Hocquenghem was well-acquainted with this group, made up of many of the same Althusserians who, in 1966 and 1967, broke from the French Communist Party to form the first independent student Marxist splinter groups. And although Hocquenghem would later save his most vitriolic passages for the former leaders of the GP in the *Open Letter*, his own outlook at the time was not all that different from theirs. Yet already in late 1968, as the GP's ranks were beginning to swell, its prestige enhanced by the support of such luminaries as Jean-Paul Sartre and Simone de Beauvoir, Hocquenghem found these "*pur et dur*," or hardcore, Maoists too doctrinaire and disturbingly militaristic. Thus, even as many of their close friends flocked to the GP, André Glucksmann and most of the Vincennes *groupe de base* among them, Hocquenghem's circle remained determined to let this bandwagon go by.

Yet they also realized that by remaining independent they risked extinction, so it was with some sadness that the Censier *groupe de base* decided finally to seek out some kind of larger affiliation. On the campus of Nanterre, home of the infamous Movement of 22 March led by Daniel Cohn-Bendit, the true initiators of the May revolt, a different kind of Maoist group was being born. Though they considered themselves to be Maoists of the *spontanéiste* variety like the GP, the Nanterrois Maoists, led by Roland Castro and Tiennot Grumbach and who called themselves Vive la révolution (VLR), seemed more serious about the "cultural" aspect of Mao's "cultural revolution." As they declared in the first issue of *Vive la révolution*, the publication that announced their birth, the time had come to extend the struggle begun in May 1968 "to all aspects of life under capitalist society."[23] The VLR also seemed to be having a lot more fun than the hardcore militants of the GP, being far more open-minded about sex, drugs, and partying, for example—activities for which a committed militant of the GP was supposed to have little time. The VLR represented a "strange kind of Maoism," as Hocquenghem explained in 1974, "whose attraction resulted from its conjunction of numerous different currents that were thought to be irreconcilable: 'respect for and attention to the masses' in the Chinese fashion, individualism in the grand tradition of French anarchism, American-style communitarianism, and soon enough the emerging sexual liberation movements."[24] It was this same chaotic and

self-contradictory confluence of ideas that drew Hocquenghem into the
orbit of the VLR in 1969 and 1970.

What unified the VLR was less a shared philosophy than a common style of
thought and action, a revolutionary "attitude" as they referred to it. They distinguished themselves theoretically from the GP, as well as from the other
Maoist and Trotskyite groups, by contrasting the "isms" of the Left to "Mao
Tse-Tung thinking" [*la pensée-maotsétung*]. Whereas "Leninism," "Maoism,"
and "Trotskyism" signified mindless obedience to foreign revolutionary doctrines, "*la pensée-maotsétung* demands that communists think for themselves,
beginning from concrete circumstances."[25] For the militants of the VLR, then,
it was not so much the model of Chinese society that mattered—most of them
knew and cared little about China—but Mao's insight that, just as China could
not follow the same path to revolution as the Soviet Union, so too must each
nation blaze its own trail toward socialism. All a priori theory was to be thrown
out the window, or, more precisely, theory was supposed to exist in a dialectical relationship with practice; theory emerged from engagement with the
struggles of the people, but always remained secondary and provisional.

In the summer of 1969, Roland Castro invited Hocquenghem and his
friends to bring their ideas and talents to the editorial staff of the organization's new publication, a "*quinzomadaire*" (appearing every fifteen days),
which was to be called *Tout: ce que nous voulons!* (What we want: EVERY-
THING!). The goal of the new publication was not to speak for the voice-
less, but to create a forum "where all disenfranchised, frustrated, and dissenting groups can express themselves . . . [because] in order for the
revolution to succeed, the people need to have an understanding of the
whole of history's movement."[26] Thus, as Hocquenghem and the editorial
staff explained in the first issue, the reader could expect to read less and less
in coming issues from the "intellectuals" in the VLR, and more and more
from the various peoples' movements, none of which took precedence over
any other. At the time, it still seemed to Hocquenghem and the VLR that
the unification of the various groups in nascent revolt—students, workers,
youth, women, immigrants, and so on—was not only possible, but was the
only possibility for the revolution's continuation.

In this spirit, Hocquenghem launched an inner critique of the
gauchistes in the pages of *Tout*, whom he found, on the whole, still too
doctrinaire and conformist and not nearly revolutionary enough with regard to everyday life. Thus, for example, in May 1971, as the movement
for Bengali independence was being suppressed by the Pakistani government with the support of China, Hocquenghem took the Maoists of the
GP to task for withholding all criticism on the premise that "there was not

enough information." Singling out André Glucksmann, at the time a journalist for the GP's *J'Accuse*:

> I'm disgusted to see that our revolutionaries are justifying a massacre following
> China's lead that they would surely otherwise condemn. . . . I believe that there
> is a kind of general sentiment, immediate and intuitive, that is part of politics;
> that one can later make corrections to this impression, but one cannot begin by
> simply denying it. The overwhelming general sentiment is that the Chinese are
> supporting a reactionary government that is committing genocide on a people
> in revolt, and that it is the Chinese who are providing the guns with which the
> Pakistanis are executing the Maoists of the Bengali people.[27]

Interestingly, Hocquenghem accused the Chinese communists and their
French avatars not of being too Maoist, but of not being Maoist enough.
Even before Richard Nixon's historic visit to China in 1972, the beginning
of a rapprochement even the most loyal Maoists had trouble swallowing,
the VLR had begun to question just how revolutionary Chinese society and
the Chinese Cultural Revolution really was. But although the Chinese Cultural Revolution ceased to be a point of reference for Hocquenghem and
the VLR, they continued to take *la pensée maotsétung* seriously. Using *la
pensée maotsétung* meant first of all sparing nothing and no one from criticism. "Criticize Confucius and Lin Bao" as the Chinese newspapers famously proclaimed that same year, but criticize Chairman Mao and the Chinese Communist Party, too. Applying *la pensée maotsétung* furthermore
entailed thinking for oneself and beginning from concrete experience
rather than abstract principles. One of the greatest flaws of *gauchiste* politics, however, "which it seemed to me was beginning to disappear in recent
months but which has forcefully reappeared with the events in Pakistan,"
Hocquenghem wrote, "is that which consists of judging whether or not a
people is revolutionary according to an ensemble of a priori principles, as
though these people did not really exist and did not really suffer."[28]

Another serious flaw of *gauchisme* that Hocquenghem reproached in
the GP was its Jacobin inclination toward demagoguery and cults of personality. In October 1970, Alain Geismar, a former hero of '68 turned
spokesperson for the GP, appeared before a court after a five-month pre-
trial detention for what would become France's version of the trial of the
Chicago Seven. Geismar was arrested for "inciting" a revolt during a
speech in which he called for the release of two GP comrades sentenced
to eighteen-month prison terms in 1969 for their work on the GP's newspaper *La Cause du peuple*. Since then he had been become the universally
recognized leader of the radical Left. But Geismar was only one of hun-

dreds of *gauchistes* imprisoned under Marcellin's severe hand. While expressing his solidarity with Geismar in *Tout*, Hocquenghem also tried to inject a lone discordant note in the Left's paean. Commenting on the Left's encomiastic coverage of the event, he wrote:

> Let's not kid ourselves: Geismar's trial is not the people's trial, and Geismar is not the people. The "people" do not even recognize themselves yet as such, so they certainly do not recognize themselves in those who pretend to symbolize them. . . . Let's liberate Geismar from prison, but also from the role with which we have imprisoned him.[29]

It was also in the pages of *Tout* that Hocquenghem first asserted the revolutionary potential of homosexuality. In its first issue, he reprinted a speech delivered several weeks earlier by the Black Panther Party minister of defense, Huey Newton, in support of the women's liberation and homosexual liberation movements. Newton's argument, coming on the heels of the June 1969 Stonewall protests in New York, was quite simple: regardless of the endlessly debatable nature and causes of homosexuality, the homosexual's history of oppression in capitalist society alone makes him or her a valuable revolutionary partner. Not only could homosexuals be revolutionaries, he insisted; their particularly severe history of oppression makes them "likely to be among the most revolutionary of revolutionaries."[30] In retrospect, the Huey Newton speech may seem like a strange way to have finally broached the issue. In context, however, it made perfect sense. For the *gauchistes*, the central question remained whether or not homosexuals and homosexual liberation could be considered revolutionary—in traditional Marxist wisdom homosexuality was a luxury of the bourgeois, which, ostensibly, would have no place in a socialist society. And if there was any single group whose revolutionary credentials could not be questioned, it was the Black Panthers, idolized as much by the GP as by the VLR for their courageous resistance in the heart of the evil empire itself. For the French radical Left in 1970, Huey Newton publicly defending homosexual liberation was as good as hearing it from Mao himself.

As *Tout* developed into one of the most read and discussed of the new leftist publications—at its peak, its printing of 80,000 copies an issue was hardly sufficient to meet demand—Hocquenghem brought more new topics to the table of revolutionary discussion.[31] In 1969 France began to see a new side of America: "Woodstock Nation." Hocquenghem and the staff of *Tout* tried to translate the emerging ideas and slogans of the American underground, always in the most "revolutionary" possible light—"Do It!"; "Here and Now"; "Drop Out"; "Break on through to the other side."[32] His articles introduced the French to the American LSD and marijuana drug cultures, the philosophy of the Yippies, and the rock and roll of the Doors, Jimi Hendrix, and Janis Joplin. The magazine itself began to take on a new look—the hallucinatory comics of Robert Crumb gradually edged out the political caricatures of French cartoonists Siné and Wolinsky, and colorful images of naked bodies replaced the traditional silhouetted profiles of icons like Marx, Lenin, and Che. A new culture, "youth culture," was spreading through America, and whereas culture in France was still imprisoned in libraries and galleries, in America, Hocquenghem exclaimed, "Everything is passing from books into life."[33] Like the excitement surrounding the Chinese Cultural Revolution, the fascination with "Woodstock Nation" was largely a projection of the French revolutionaries' collective imagination, and by 1972 this enthusiasm had given way to a much more skeptical and selective reception of American cultural trends. But for a brief period at least, the American West Coast seemed to have replaced China as a repository for revolutionary aspirations, breathing new life into a dream that was already beginning to fade.

Moreover, the French cultural revolutionaries understood that France could not simply follow the American model. The peculiar character of the Americans, described by Alexis de Tocqueville a century and a half earlier, seemed to make them better suited to the proliferation of "Woodstock" communities. In France, however, the enormous presence of the "republic" in everyday life meant that the moral order would have to be attacked head on. Hocquenghem defined the task of the "French" cultural revolution perhaps most clearly in a response to a speech made by Georges Pompidou in December 1970, in which the new president attempted futilely to bridge the generation gap. As a countermeasure to the social confusion of the era, Pompidou proposed to bolster the "family," the institution "best situated to resist the shocks, because it is founded on nature, on the law of the species." In the family, Pompidou continued, "everyone finds a way to be both a unique self and part of a whole."[34] Not surprisingly, the president of the Republic's answer for social reconciliation did not persuade anyone in the offices of the VLR. What is surprising is that his message did seem to reach something like a "moral majority," receiving little criticism from the mainstream press and differing little in fact from the discourse at the time of the French Communist Party and the major trade unions.

Hocquenghem perceived in Pompidou's speech and its silent reception on the Left a resurgent nostalgia for the moral order of Maréchal Pétain's Vichy France: Work, Family, Nation [*Travail, Famille, Patrie*]. On the cover of *Tout*'s fifth issue, he struck back: "Pompidou, we will not be your families!"[35] As his response reveals, the French cultural revolution now meant essentially the revolution of everyday life and social relationships. Bourgeois society was still the enemy, and would have to be destroyed before "*our next family,*" a socialist society, could be created, only the strategy now was hardly recognizable as Marxist.[36] Although France had been rid of Pétain for over two decades, the pillars of the *pétainiste* moral order continued to survive. Pétain's continuing presence was especially salient to homosexuals, since it was in fact the Vichy government that drew up France's first laws criminalizing homosexuality, laws that were later taken up whole cloth by Charles de Gaulle in the Fifth Republic. For Hocquenghem, this juridical continuity between Vichy and the Fifth Republic was no aberration, but only one indication that the French moral order had changed little since the Liberation. If there was to be a real revolution in France, this *pétainisme*, resurrected under De Gaulle's pro-natalist vision of a "nation one hundred million strong," would have to be the first victim.

While working on the staff of *Tout* in 1970 and 1971, Hocquenghem once again sensed that the winds of revolution were changing, and if he wanted to remain on the avant-garde, he had to change with them. Just as the Trotskyism to which he adhered as a teenager seemed "tepid" after May '68 in comparison with the Maoist movements, now it was Maoism that seemed old hat. But if Trotskyism had cooled off somewhat after May '68 as it began to resemble more and more the established parties of the Left in organization and ideology, Maoism was beginning to boil over. Over two years had passed since the summer of '68 and the Maoists, despite their tireless efforts, seemed further and further each day from winning over the proletariat for their revolution. Their frustrations, furthermore, were driving certain camps, especially within the GP, in more violent directions. The GP's clandestine commando wing, the Nouvelle Résistance populaire—an allusion to the communist resistance fighters of the German Occupation—had been mostly symbolic up until 1971. Beginning with the imprisonment of the editors of *La Cause du peuple* and trial of Geismar, the Nouvelle Résistance populaire, armed and ready for action, embarked on more daring and dangerous missions, culminating in the famous kidnapping of Renault boss Robert Nogrette in March 1972 after one of their own comrades was shot and killed in a protest at the Renault automobile plant at Billancourt.[37]

Hocquenghem's disaffection with the ever-narrowing and evermore violent vision of the *gauchistes* was even beginning to create problems within VLR, where his insufficient reverence on such occasions as the trial of Geismar and his insufficient attention to the proletariat in *Tout* came under fire from fellow comrades. Also, it appears that Hocquenghem was beginning to sense the limitations of *gauchiste* tolerance regarding homosexuality, even within the notoriously libertarian VLR. As he admitted once in the summer of 1971, his homosexuality, of which his Maoist comrades were more or less aware, had not raised any serious problems until he volunteered to join one of the VLR's committees at the Renault automobile plant at Flins—factory militancy at the time was fairly muscled work, involving frequent physical confrontations with unionists and factory security, and had something of a "macho" aura about it.[38] The *gauchiste* groups in 1971, it seemed to Hocquenghem, were either spent or spinning out of control. On the other hand, the successes of the recently formed French Women's Liberation Movement (Mouvement de libération des femmes or MLF), the American Yippies, and the American Gay Liberation Front following Stonewall seemed to point in a new direction. Though relatively few in number in comparison with the ranks of *établis*, these groups, through guerilla theater shock tactics and "consciousness raising," had managed to muscle their own agendas into the center of public discussion.

Hocquenghem was not just following a new wind; as his detractors within the VLR correctly pointed out, his philosophy of cultural revolution had well outgrown the categories of *gauchiste* thought. The key to revolution, as Hocquenghem increasingly viewed it, no longer lay in the liberation of the proletariat, students, immigrant workers, prisoners, women, or any other oppressed group but in the liberation of desire *tout court*. In his laudatory descriptions of the American counterculture he had already been hinting in this direction. "*Woodstock Nation*, the youth's world of pop festivals," he explained, "teaches us something: the class struggle is also a struggle for the expression of desire, for communication, and not simply an economic and political struggle." The liberation of desire had as a major component the liberation of sexuality from the constraints of bourgeois morality, but sexuality was only one aspect of human social relations that stood to be revolutionized through the emancipation of desire. Hocquenghem's thought was evolving in the direction of what is sometimes referred to as "Freudo-Marxism" or the French "philosophy of desire," an intellectual current inspired by Wilhelm Reich, Herbert Marcuse, the French anti-psychiatry movement, and the Michel Foucault of *The Birth of the Clinic* and represented most notably in Gilles Deleuze and Félix Guattari's opus, *Anti-Oedipus*.[39] Less a coherent philosophy than the critical esprit of the early sexual liberation movements, the "philosophy of desire" rejected the Freudian thesis that human civilization was doomed to its "discontents." The historical emergence of bourgeois capitalism was responsible for human misery, or "schizophrenia" in the language of Deleuze and Guattari, but it remained possible that in a different form of social, political, and economic organization "desire" might flow and flourish unhindered. But if the revolutionary subject, the agent of social change, was not the proletariat, or even really a "subject" for that matter, but desire itself, then how could one mobilize revolution, and what would the new revolutionary avant-garde look like?

As Hocquenghem was once again assessing the radical Left, another group of militants inspired by the successes of the MLF, and with some of the MLF veterans among their ranks, began taking initiative.[40] In March 1971, a small group of men and women stormed and forced off the air a successful French radio show program which had gathered a group of "experts" in medicine, law, and religion to discuss "Homosexuality, the Painful Problem."[41] In the weeks that followed this band of brave militants multiplied their actions, interrupting meetings of the political parties of the Left, and even organizing a raucous cortege for the May 1 Parade. From the far back of the parade, well behind the rest of the trade unions and political parties where parade organizers had placed them, they chanted such slogans as "We are a social scourge!" (*"fléau social"*—in the famous words of Fifth Republic French deputy Paul Mirguet), and "Workers of the world fondle one another!" Among them was a small group of drag queens who called themselves the *"gazolines"* and who had dressed up appropriately for the occasion. The *gazolines* called for the nationalization of the sequin factories and sang the communist anthem *"la lutte finale"* in *bel canto*. In their lewd sense of humor the *gazolines* referred to themselves as the revolutionary "rear-garde," but to Hocquenghem the founders of the Front homosexuel d'action révolutionnaire (FHAR) seemed much more avant-garde than the Marxist-Leninist types with whom he used to keep company.

Hocquenghem soon began attending the FHAR meetings, and in April he proposed to give them several pages in the next issue of *Tout*, an issue he planned to dedicate to sexual liberation. When this collaboration finally appeared on April 23, the cover proclaimed boldly:

Yes, our bodies belong to us!
–Free and legal abortion and contraception
–The right to homosexuality and all sexualities
–The rights of minors to the freedom of their desires and their fulfillment.[42]

A hodgepodge of personal anecdotes, manifestoes, and criticisms of the general treatment of sexuality by the medical, legal, and psychoanalytical "experts," the famous number twelve hardly resembled a *gauchiste* publication—actually, it did not look like anything France had ever seen.

From the women's and sexual liberation movements, Hocquenghem learned the power of calculated provocation. There was no longer any point in hiding behind the Marxist discourses of Mao or even Huey Newton. A couple of weeks earlier some members of the MLF had caused an uproar with a pro-choice manifesto published in *Le Nouvel Observateur* and signed by "343 women who admit to having had an abortion."[43] In a gesture of mocking respect, Hocquenghem included in the number twelve of *Tout*, the "Manifesto of 343 fags who admit to having been fucked by Arabs," daring *Le Nouvel Observateur* to publish it, too—a challenge *Le Nouvel Observateur*, of course, declined. Such acts, Hocquenghem realized, carried more force than the tired slogans of the Maoists.

Responding to the complaints of politicians and magistrates around the country, the government banned the issue and managed to seize 10,000 copies (about one-fifth of the entire printing). The nominal director of publication, Jean-Paul Sartre, was brought up on charges of "obscenity" (*outrage contre bonnes mœurs*), at least one vendor of the magazine in Grenoble was arrested, and the offices of the VLR were raided by Marcellin's vice squad. The issue was universally decried by the press, and perhaps most vehemently by the publications of the Left. The main Maoist bookstore in Paris, Norman Bethune, refused to carry the issue and so did many of the VLR militants. In short, it was an enormous success. At the next meeting of the FHAR in Paris there were a few hundred participants rather than the usual few dozen.

There were four more issues of *Tout* before the VLR disbanded in September 1971.[44] In the year and a half that followed, Hocquenghem dedicated himself fully to exploring the revolutionary potential of the "politics of the self" in the circles of the FHAR and played a key role in drafting both of the FHAR's central texts, published anonymously as *FHAR: Rapport contre la normalité* (Report Against Normality) and *Trois milliards de pervers* (Three Billion Perverts).[45] In January 1972, he published his notorious article in *Le Nouvel Observateur*, "The Revolution of Homosexuals," that would propel him to stardom and forever associate his name with the cause of homosexual liberation. The article reads much more like a personal confession than a manifesto. Beginning modestly—"My name is Guy Hocquenghem. I am 25 years old."—it goes on to relate in intimate detail the story of Hocquenghem's self-discovery as both a militant and a homosexual.[46] In the context of Pompidou's France, where even the most celebrated homosexual literary and cultural giants were cagey about their sexual lives, the article was a bombshell. On the heels of the *Le Nouvel Observateur* article appeared his manifesto of sexual revolution, *Homosexual Desire*.[47] Observing that there was almost nothing in the theoretical repertoire of the day that was directly serviceable for the emerging homosexual liberation movement, Hocquenghem had initially envisioned the project as a collaborative one, along the lines of the extremely influential *Rapport contre la normalité*.[48] Although it was written with the situation in France in 1971 specifically in mind, *Homosexual Desire* remains today his best-known work and is considered a founding text of queer theory.[49] Largely through Hocquenghem's efforts, by mid-1972, there were over a thousand people trying to cram into the FHAR general assemblies.[50] With no leaders, no speakers, and no real program, the meetings of the FHAR soon degenerated into a chaos of erotic frenzy. "Cruising" gradually replaced discussion, and "backrooms" the seminar rooms. Like the movement it aimed to represent in all of its diversity and contradictions, the FHAR had become completely uncontrollable by virtue of its exponential growth.

With the breakup of the FHAR in 1974, the revolutionary posture that had attracted Hocquenghem to the women's and sexual liberation movements in 1971 vanished, too. Even before the dissolution of the FHAR, the general disillusionment with revolution that was beginning to settle in for the 68ers had begun to effect Hocquenghem as well. As some *gauchistes* dug in their heels, modeling themselves after the Marxist-Leninist guerilla movements in Germany and Italy, and as many others deserted the cause of revolution to pursue careers, Hocquenghem's inner critique of *gauchisme* transformed into a cynical indictment. While working on the staff of *Actuel*, a kind of *Pravda* of the French counterculture in the early 1970s, he ran an article on the everyday lives of *gauchiste* leaders, entitled "The Wonderful Life of the Gauchistes," to expose just how those who still proclaimed "changer la vie" went about their own lives—who did their laundry, how much money they made, how many times a week they had sex, etc. Of the fifty surveys he sent out to a who's who list of leftist leaders and countercultural gurus, a list that included the unappreciative editors of *Actuel*, he received only three completed surveys and a dozen or so angry letters. His harsh conclusion: the radical Left had supplanted the bourgeoisie as France's new moral guardians. With this exposé Hocquenghem had found the trademark wit that would mark his writings throughout the 1970s and 1980s, rankling his enemies, editors, and sometimes even his friends.[51]

The close of the revolutionary moment opened up by May, however, did not fundamentally change Hocquenghem's critique of French society or of his former comrades who had given up on overturning it. After 1973, Hocquenghem stopped referring to "cultural revolution," preferring to speak, for example, of multiple "volutions" instead. Explaining himself in a self-critique by that title, which serves as the introduction to a collection of his writings from 1968 to 1973, Hocquenghem wrote:

> What they [the *gauchistes*] hide from us with their mythology of the "revolutionary subject," the "proletariat," and their sacrosanct "strategy" is the manifold of paths unexplored, uncompleted, or too soon abandoned. . . . Rather than measuring the sum of our disruptions against the universal and abstract yardstick of "revolution," which only indicates to the bourgeois the level of the danger, quantifying it, localizing it, and closing it in, we should be moving in all directions, dispersing through the civilizing powers, burrowing, everywhere possible, mining underneath the edifice, always surprising the enemy from behind, never being trapped where they are waiting for us.[52]

As a journalist and polemist Hocquenghem continued throughout the rest of his life to dig away at the bourgeois institutions of *Travail, Famille, Patrie*. (Tellingly, one of the FHAR's earliest slogans was "*Travail, Famille, Patrie*—We do not get off/cum in your system!")[53] In the second half of the 1970s, Hocquenghem wrote more or less regularly for *Libération*, the daily newspaper founded by the GP Maoists in the early 1970s. His tenure on the paper, however, was always a precarious one, and in 1982, after a series of disputes with the editors and after a several month-long suspension from the staff, Hocquenghem left behind the bustle of Parisian intellectual life for a semi-reclusive existence in the suburbs and began focusing his energies on more literary and philosophical pursuits.

In early 1985 Hocquenghem tested positive for HIV.[54] Not long thereafter his health began to deteriorate. That year the venom briefly returned to his plume as he bid adieu to his former revolutionary comrades in the *Open Letter*. The real danger posed by the "Maoist-turned-Rotarians," Hocquenghem argued, stemmed less from their conversion to the liberal consensus than from the way in which they converted. Possessed by the same doctrinaire zeal with which they once preached revolution, they exploited their credentials as 68ers to impose their vision of politics on future generations, silencing their demands and censoring their imaginations. Pointing his finger at his "*rénégation*," as he dubbed them, he wrote:

> There you sit, guarding the door to the future, and like the dog from the parable, the food you could not eat—utopia, the nourishment of spirit—you prohibit others from consuming. . . . Out of your repudiation squared, cubed, you constructed a pyramid which you've pulled yourselves up onto, reaching for

power and money. And there you've remained, occupying all the posts, your networks blocking entry to all newcomers. . . . And from the top of your pyramid of arrogance and hypocrisy you coldly declare, holding down those who would take a look for themselves, that there is nothing to see, just a sad wasteland extending to infinity.[55]

Hocquenghem's cruel sense of humor, honed to perfection in the *Open Letter*, has been the source of much miscomprehension regarding his life and works. (Jean-Michel Helvig's cry of fascism in *Libération*, however, was simply ridiculous.) In a short essay from 1987 Hocquenghem explained how humor for him arises essentially out of a sense of *dégoût* or "disgust."[56] Far from being a simple case of aversion or nausea, the experience of *dégoût* situates an individual in a state of profound disharmony with his surroundings. It is at the same time "noble, misanthropic, [and] comical . . . in short *dégoût* is never just mournful, it is desperate or humorous."[57] Like "melancholy" in Baudelaire's modernist aesthetics, *dégoût* harbors both creative and destructive potential. Creating humor out of *dégoût* was, for Hocquenghem, a form of the "heroism of modern life," to quote Baudelaire's famous phrase, a means of lifting oneself temporarily out of the muck of the modern world.[58] But as Hocquenghem observed, the very capacity to experience *dégoût* had already become a thing of the past. "The man with no disgust, capable of accepting everything . . . is the new fashion." Disgust today is "nothing more than a problem of stress or a case of the blues."[59]

Humor, however, is only one potentiality of *dégoût*. In its complete repulsion of the world as it is, *dégoût* also creates a space for imagining it anew; it is, in other words, a condition for the possibility of utopian thinking. This connection first revealed itself to Hocquenghem in May 1968, when the Parisian students, united only in their "great refusal," rose up and nearly toppled the Gaullist government. Though the May movement failed in its effort to seize political power, it inaugurated a utopian moment whose impact on French culture and society was profound and irreversible. When the "Maoists-turned-Rotarians" tried to seal the lid on this utopian moment in the 1980s, Hocquenghem fought to wedge it back open. He was not so obliviously idealistic, as his critics maintained, that he rejected or denied the enormous achievements of the Left's social and cultural agenda under Mitterrand, but he believed that without that initial experience of *dégoût*, without a space for utopian thinking, something vital had been lost.[60]

The theme of utopia pervades Hocquenghem's entire oeuvre. The same year the *Open Letter* appeared, he also published what might be considered

its philosophical companion text, *L'Âme atomique* [Atomic Soul], a pun on
"atomic weapon" [*l'arme atomique*] in French.[61] Written in collaboration
with his former philosophy professor and lifelong friend René Schérer,
L'Âme atomique begins from the observation that "the fear of the end of the
world prohibits reflection about the ends of this world."[62] Weaving through
two millennia of utopian thought in the West, they investigate the possibilities for restoring "soul" to Cold War Europe, a civilization still reeling from
the horrors of the twentieth century and paralyzed by the fear of the bomb
and ecological disaster. Similarly, in his historical and travel novels from the
1980s, the search for "aborted utopias," those moments when Western civilization might have taken a different turn, dominates his literary sensibility,
whether he is describing the complex first-century society of John the Bap-
tist, the pristine New World of the sixteenth-century Franciscan monk
Brother Angelo, or the rich homosexual underworlds of New York, Ams-
terdam, and Rio de Janeiro.[63]

But the aborted utopia that figures always in the background is the one
he experienced firsthand. In his unfinished memoirs Hocquenghem described the years immediately following May '68 as the only period in which
"humanity, in its long history, ceased to be afraid."[64] This moment, he
wrote, formed a "parenthesis in the history of man when the ancient fears,
culpabilities, and self-limitations receded slightly. A breath a fresh air punc-
tuating a litany of catastrophes, repressions, and societal nightmares."[65]
Cast in the form of a *roman à clef* written from the vantage point of the year
2018, Hocquenghem imagines in his "anticipated memoir" that he has tri-
umphed over AIDS through the miracles of modern science, only to have
settled into the same comfortable lifestyle he derided in his former comrades: a successful writer and novelist, financially secure, and socially sta-
ble. Frail and weak in his seventieth year, he finally sits down to put his life
story to paper. Hocquenghem began his "anticipated memoir" while literally on his deathbed in 1988 and worked furiously on it until he could no
longer move his hand to write.[66] Though it makes numerous allusions to
events that took place in his life after the birth of the FHAR in 1971, the
narrative breaks off suddenly after his experiences in the communes in
1969 and 1970.

Hocquenghem's interrupted autobiography is a fitting final metaphor
for his steadfast refusal to let go of the years of his eternal youth, but it is
also emblematic of the difficulties his entire generation has faced in trying to move beyond May '68. Hocquenghem was early to observe a national dilemma that the sociologist Jean-Pierre Le Goff referred to in the
1990s as the problem of May '68's "unfinished mourning," the conse-

quences of which extend well beyond the '68 generation itself. To the French youth of the 1970s, 1980s, and even 1990s, May '68 has bestowed what Le Goff has referred to as the "impossible heritage."[67] Over thirty years ago the students erected a commune in the Latin Quarter as a microcosm of the revolutionary society to come. This utopian moment remains a foundational myth for much of the French Left, even as its participants continue to oscillate between an attitude of distant nostalgia and one of bitter renunciation, glorifying their courageous efforts to transform society and decrying in the same breath the narcissism, hedonism, and cynicism they see as end results of those efforts. The "Maoists-turned-Rotarians" are still on the forefront of Left politics. They reproach today's youth for their apathy and denounce the disenchanted world in which they live, and yet they would deny them the same passion that once moved them. Perhaps Le Goff is right in asserting that the greatest mistake today would be to call on the youth of today to embrace May '68's spirit of unlimited revolt, as though the bourgeois institutions of *Travail*, *Famille*, and *Patrie* continued to exert the same power and influence they did in the early 1960s. But how can one continue to instill the passion that once inspired the 68ers, only in moderation, circumscribed within democratic institutions? "Is passion without utopia possible? Can it find rooting in a democracy?"[68] For Le Goff, these questions lie at the heart of May '68's "impossible heritage."

One cannot build democratic institutions on a foundation that is constantly being undermined by youth in revolt. But nor, as Hocquenghem reminds us, can they be built without the participation of the youth and without viable spaces for contestation. When the Maoists who became France's "New Philosophers" in the late 1970s exhorted humility and austerity in political thought as a safeguard against catastrophe, Hocquenghem tried to warn against an overdose of their medicine. For his own part, Hocquenghem never apologized for his *gauchisme* when it became popular to do so in the late 1970s and 1980s. When asked in 1988, for example, about the relationship between the early homosexual liberation movement and *gauchisme*, he replied: "It is very simple: because all aspects of life passed through *gauchisme*, we never imagined we could be anything else."[69] When the former leaders of the GP reflected on their earlier *gauchiste* militancy in the 1980s and saw only terror and violence, Hocquenghem tried to evoke another side of *gauchisme*, the revolution of everyday life. The consequences of this revolution escape all easy value judgments and reductive attempts at explanation, in no small part because they are still playing themselves out in French society today.

Hélène Hazera, a friend of Hocquenghem in the days of the FHAR, wrote of his funeral: "There was a huge crowd for Guy. Some people there could not keep themselves from smiling before remembering why they were there and returning to their airs of seriousness . . . with Guy, it was a whole generation we were burying."[70] For many veteran 68ers today, Hocquenghem's name continues to evoke the same heady mixture of nostalgia, bitterness, rancor, and regret associated with the May events themselves. That he has somehow failed to settle into a fixed place in his generation's collective memory is a telling sign that the task of mourning May '68 remains unfinished. Offered the choice between this fate or an assured legacy with continued commercial success, Hocquenghem would have no doubt preferred it this way.

NOTES

For their invaluable input and careful attention to earlier drafts of this chapter I would like to thank Hélène Hazera, Roland Surzur, Lionel Soukaz, René Schérer, Jean-Michel Gerrasi, Douglas Ireland, and Olivier (Marc) Hatzfeld.

1. Guy Hocquenghem, *Lettre ouverte à ceux qui sont passés du col Mao au Rotary*, intro. Serge Halimi (Marseille: Agone, 2003), 33.

2. Jean-Michel Helvig, [Review of Hocquenghem, *Lettre ouverte*], *Libération*, 1 June 1986, 11. For a discussion of the *Lettre ouverte*'s reception in 1986 and a passionate argument for its continuing relevance see Halimi's introduction, 7–28.

3. Hocquenghem, *Lettre ouverte*, 37.

4. Helvig, [Review of Hocquenghem, *Lettre ouverte*], 11.

5. For a discussion of Hocquenghem's role in the French homosexual liberation movement and his contributions to the philosophy of homosexuality and queer theory more generally, see Bill Marshall, *Guy Hocquenghem: Beyond Gay Identity* (Durham, N.C.: Duke University Press, 1997).

6. Hervé Hamon and Patrick Rotman, *Génération*, 2 vols. (Paris: Seuil, 1988). In Jean-Pierre Le Goff, *Mai 68, l'héritage impossible* (Paris: La Découverte, 2002), and Bernard Brillant, *Les Clercs de 68* (Paris: Presses universitaires de France, 2003), to cite two prominent examples, Hocquenghem is not cited or mentioned at all.

7. Hocquenghem, "Faux printemps," repr. in *Oiseau de la nuit* (Paris: Albin Michel, 1998), 103.

8. René Schérer, "Guy Hocquenghem: la passion de l'étranger," *Sociétés* 21 (December 1988): 50.

9. See Élisabeth Salvaresi's portrait, "Guy Hocquenghem" in *Mai en héritage* (Paris: Syros, 1988), 19–26.

10. Herbert Marcuse, *One-Dimensional Man* (Boston: Beacon Press, 1991), esp. chapter 10.

11. "Pourquoi nous nous battons," *Action* 1 (7 May 1968), repr. in Hocquenghem, *L'Après-mai des faunes* (Paris: Grasset, 1974), 45.

12. "Pourquoi nous nous battons."

13. "Appel du Comité d'Action Pédérastique Révolutionnaire," repr. in Jacques Vandemborghe, "Mai 68 dans la Sorbonne Occupée," *Mec Magazine* 1 (1988): 32.

14. Interview with Guy Chevalier, "Le sacerdoce de l'activiste," *Têtu* 54 (March 2001): 98.

15. For a detailed English-language history of Maoism and Trotskyism in France, see A. Belden Fields, *Trotskyism and Maoism: Theory and Practice in France and the United States* (New York: Autonomedia, 1998). On French Maoism, see Christophe Bourseiller, *Les Maoïstes: la folle histoire des gardes rouges français* (Paris: Plon, 1996).

16. Hocquenghem, *L'Amphithéâre des morts: mémoires anticipées*, preface by Roland Surzur (Paris: Gallimard, 1994), 91–92.

17. Hocquenghem, *L'Amphithéâre des morts*, 86–87.

18. For a chronicle of the repression of the radical Left between May 1968 and March 1974, see Maurice Rajsfus, *Mai 68: sous les pavés, la repression (mai 1968–mars 1974)* (Paris: Le cherche midi éditeur, 1998).

19. Hocquenghem, *L'Amphithéâre des morts*, 93–99.

20. "Changer La Vie," *Faire la révolution* 2 (April 1970), repr. in Hocquenghem, *L'Après-mai des faunes*, 59.

21. "Changer La Vie," 52.

22. "Changer La Vie," 62.

23. *Vive la Révolution* 1 (November 1969): 8. For more on the VLR, see Françoise Picq, *Libération des femmes: les années-mouvement* (Paris: Seuil, 1993), 87–111.

24. Hocquenghem, *L'Après-mai des faunes*, 83.

25. *Vive la Révolution* 1 (November 1969): 11.

26. *Tout: ce que nous voulons!* 1 (23 September 1970) : 2.

27. "Vive le Bengale libre," *Tout* 13 (May 1971), repr. in *L'Après-mai des faunes*, 90.

28. "Vive le Bengale libre," 89.

29. "Geismar, c'est Geismar," *Tout* 3 (October 1970), repr. in *L'Après-mai des faunes*, 87–88.

30. *Tout: ce que nous voulons!* 1 (23 September 1970): 6.

31. See François-Marie Samuelson, *Il était une fois Libération . . .* (Paris: Seuil, 1979), 75–93.

32. "Ici et maintenant," *Tout* 2 (October 1970), repr. in *L'Après-mai des Faunes*.

33. "Ici et maintenant," 85.

34. Quoted in "Pompidou, nous ne serons pas tes familles," *Tout* 5 (December 1970), repr. in *L'Après-mai des faunes*, 136.

35. Quoted in "Pompidou, nous ne serons pas tes familles."

36. Quoted in "Pompidou, nous ne serons pas tes familles."

37. The history of the *Nouvelle Résistance populaire* is recounted in Bourseiller, *Les Maoïstes*, 189–229.

38. In the film documentary *FHAR 1971* (Paris: Vidéo Out, 1971), C. Roussopoulos, prod., Centre audiovisuel Simone-de-Beauvoir, Paris.

39. Gilles Deleuze and Félix Guattari, *Anti-Oedipus: Capitalism and Schizophrenia* (Minneapolis: University of Minnesota Press, 1985). For a historical contextualization of "liberation of desire" philosophy see Le Goff, *Mai 68, l'héritage impossible*, part III "Naissance d'une contre-culture," 265–393.

40. The history of the early years of the MLF are recounted in Picq, *Libération des femmes*.

41. The full transcript of Ménie Grégoire's interrupted program, "L'Homosexualité, ce douloureux problème" (10 March 1971), repr. in *La Revue h* 1 (Summer 1996): 52–59. For the history of the *Front homosexuel d'action révolutionnaire*, see Yann Le Goff, "Le FHAR," *Têtu* 54 (March 2001); Françoise D'Eaubonne, "Le FHAR," *La Revue h* 2 (Fall 1996): 18–30; Alain Sanzio, "Une Décennie mouvementée," *Masques* 9/10 (Summer 1981): 99–109; and "FHAR" in *Dictionnaire des cultures gays et lesbiennes*, ed. Didier Eribon (Paris: Larousse, 2003). See also Roussopoulos, *FHAR 1971*.

42. *Tout* 12 (23 April 1971).

43. "Liste des 343 femmes qui ont eu le courage de signer le manifeste 'je me suis fait avorter'," *Le Nouvel Observateur* (5 April 1971).

44. On the history of *Tout* and the VLR's collapse, see Picq, *Libération des femmes*, 87–111.

45. *FHAR: Rapport contre la normalité* (Paris: Champs Libre, 1971). "Trois milliards de pervers: grande encyclopédie des homosexualités," *Recherches* 12 (March 1973).

46. Hocquenghem, *La Dérive homosexuelle* (Paris: Delarge, 1977), 25.

47. Guy Hocquenghem, *Homosexual Desire*, trans. Daniella Dangoor (Durham: Duke University Press, 1993). For an excellent discussion of *Homosexual Desire* see Jeffrey Weeks's preface to the 1978 edition, repr. in the 1993 edition.

48. [Interview with Guy Hocquenghem by Hugo Marsan], *Gai Pied Hebdo* 130–31 (4 August 1984): 54–56, 114.

49. On the importance of *Homosexual Desire* for queer theory see Patrice Maniglier, "Penser la culture gay," *Magazine littéraire* 426 (December 2003): 58–60.

50. One thousand five hundred according to one estimate. See "FHAR: il y a 10 ans," *Gai Pied* 25 (April 1981).

51. *Actuel* 29 (March 1973): 62–65.

52. Hocquenghem, *L'Après-mai des faunes*, 20–22.

53. FHAR Tract no. 2 (1972), 4-WZ-10838, Bibliothèque Nationale François Mitterrand.

54. Among the numerous factual errors and manipulations in Frédéric Martel's *The Pink and the Black: Homosexuals in France since 1968*, trans. Jane Marie Todd (Stanford: Stanford University Press, 1999), is the claim that Hocquenghem re-

fused to test himself for AIDS and did not learn of his condition until he was already ill. This is false. Roland Surzur has the medical record establishing that Hocquenghem learned he was HIV-positive in March 1985, not long, that is, after the test became available. Martel then goes on to characterize a text by Hocquenghem that appeared in *Gai Pied Hebdo* in September 1985 as the bitter complaint of an HIV patient, whereas according to his own account Hocquenghem was ignorant of his condition at the time. For criticisms of Martel's book, see, for example, Hélène Hazera, "Petites prouesses avec des mort: 'Le rose et le noir'," *Libération*, 30 May 1996; La Veuve Cycliste, "Martel en tête, pas en mémoire," *La Revue h* 1 (Summer 1996): 44; and Phillipe Colomb, "Le Rose du destin et le noir de la politique," *La Revue h* 3 (Winter 1996–97): 40.

55. Hocquenghem, *Lettre ouverte*, 45–46. For a recent analysis of the 68ers' role in the construction of the collective memory of May 1968 and a discussion of some of Hocquenghem's main arguments in the *Open Letter*, see Kristin Ross, *May '68 and its Afterlives* (Chicago: The University of Chicago Press, 2002).

56. Guy Hocquenghem, "Le dégoût du siècle," *Traverses* 33–34 (1985): 76–77.

57. Hocquenghem, "Le dégoût du siècle."

58. On Baudelaire's "melancholy" and "heroism of modern life" see Marshall Berman's foundational study of modernism, *All That Is Solid Melts Into Air: The Experience of Modernity* (New York: Penguin Books, 1982), 131–71.

59. Hocquenghem, "Le dégoût du siècle."

60. For a much more measured assessment by Hocquenghem of the Left's social and cultural achievements under Mitterrand see Douglas Crimp, "The New French Culture: An Interview with Guy Hocquenghem," *October* 19 (Winter 1981): 105–17.

61. Guy Hocquenghem and René Schérer, *L'Âme atomique* (Paris: Albin Michel, 1986).

62. Hocquenghem and Schérer, *L'Âme atomique*, 315.

63. See Marshall, *Guy Hocquenghem*, for a complete bibliography and discussion of his literary works.

64. Hocquenghem, *L'Amphithéâtre des morts*, 28.

65. Hocquenghem, *L'Amphithéâtre des morts*, 27–28.

66. See Surzur, "Preface," in Hocquenghem, *L'Amphithéâtre des morts*.

67. Le Goff, *Mai 68, l'héritage impossible*. See, in particular, "Conclusion: L'héritage en question," 457–63.

68. Le Goff, *Mai 68, l'héritage impossible*, 463.

69. "Les premières lueurs du Fhar" (Interview with Hocquenghem), *Gai Pied Hebdo* (12 March 1988): 32.

70. Hélène Hazera, "Enterrements," *La Revue h* 2 (Fall 1996): 59.

8

THE MYTH OF EMMANUEL LEVINAS

Ethan Kleinberg

> I always attribute my difficulties in finding this coherence and this pro-
> found logic of Talmudic speech to the poverty of my means. Perhaps
> nothing should ever be published under the title "Jewish thought" as
> long as this logic has not been rediscovered.
>
> Emmanuel Levinas[1]

In her work *Vilna on the Seine*, Judith Friedlander credits Emmanuel Levinas with introducing the French public "to a style of learning developed by
the legendary Gaon of Vilna in the late eighteenth century and passed down
for generations by rabbis trained rigorously in the scholarly tradition established by this brilliant Talmudist."[2] Other contemporary Jewish intellectuals such as Alain Finkelkraut and Richard Cohen have credited Levinas
with leading them away from "postmodern" philosophy and back to the
Eastern European Jewish traditions that were all but eradicated in the destruction of the Shoah. Benny Lévy's explanation of his own turn to Judaism
and religious learning is exemplary.

> The name of one person is important, a person to whom I must confess my in-
> debtedness, Emmanuel Levinas. Here is someone who had the very same
> philosophical training as Sartre, the same roots in phenomenology and hu-
> manism. He was someone who was very close to Sartre in his philosophical
> language, and yet profoundly different, because he had roots in Talmud.[3]

Statements like this have led to the belief that Levinas himself was "trained rigorously in the scholarly tradition" of the Gaon of Vilna and thus capable of passing on these teachings. Furthermore, Levinas's own self-fashioning through statements regarding his relation to the study of Talmud strengthened this belief. This belief is false. Levinas was not trained as a Talmudic scholar, and the errant assumption that he was is the "myth" of Emmanuel Levinas.

This chapter will attempt to dispel the "myth of Emmanuel Levinas" by presenting a biographical sketch of Levinas's early life in relation to his work, but it will also attempt to understand the origins and meaning of this myth. The most obvious answers lie in the desire of many Jewish intellectuals to retrieve what was lost in the Shoah: through the person of Levinas the Eastern European Talmudic tradition could be reborn. But it may also point to a continuing tension Levinas represents between the desires for assimilation and autonomous Jewish identity. There is a certain guilt in the figure of Levinas, who chose to leave the Talmudic tradition of Eastern Europe to study Western philosophy in France and Germany in the years just prior to that tradition's untimely end. By making Levinas into a "Talmudic" scholar, the complicated fact that he left that culture (as many did) is silently glossed over. Levinas's turn to the Talmud in his later work is not a return to the mitnaggedic tradition of Vilna, nor could Levinas pass on the techniques of a tradition he did not know. Instead, the turn to Talmud speaks to Levinas's own doubts and guilt about the philosophical decisions of his youth and the poverty of the Western metaphysical tradition that allowed for the Shoah. It is my position that Emmanuel Levinas's turn to the study of Talmud represents the inversion of his prewar emphasis on the primacy of philosophy in the investigation of religion. After the war and the Shoah, Levinas came to see the study of Talmud as the precondition for the study of philosophy. But Levinas's authority in reading Talmud was not based on a traditional training in Talmud. Instead it was based on his training in Western philosophy and his understanding of the relationship between Western philosophy and Jewish thought in the years following World War Two. In this sense, Levinas's Talmudic lectures are in keeping with the interpretive nature of the rabbinic chain of tradition (*shalshelet ha-kabbalah*), and I would argue that through his inventive interpretation of Talmud Levinas established a post-rabbinic chain of tradition.[4] But through his students and disciples, largely philosophers, Levinas was transformed into an "authentic" Talmudic master whose authority justified their own turn to Judaism and ability to interpret Talmud. This mythic presentation of Levinas as an "authentic" representative of the mitnageddic tradition of Vilna keeps the reader removed from the interpretive tradition itself and focuses all attention on Levinas as a purely charismatic figure. Here the issue becomes authority and authenticity, and Levinas's own emphasis on interpretation is lost. The danger of the myth of Emmanuel Levinas is that it leads his readers on a nostalgic search for an irretrievable past, rather than to his larger, more challenging, and daunting project of using Jewish thought and commentary to criticize, rethink, and rehabilitate the Western philosophical tradition in the wake of the Shoah. The goal of this paper is to understand the significance of both the man and the myth.

MASKILIM

In 1906, the year of Levinas's birth, Kovno, Lithuania was still very much a part of Czarist Russia. It is true that 30 percent of its 80,000 inhabitants were Jewish and that Kovno and the area surrounding it were known for their yeshivas and their history of Talmudic scholars like the Gaon of Vilna (1720–1797) and Chaim of Volozhin (1749–1821). But equally prevalent was a spirit of enlightenment and an assimilation of Russian and Jewish heritages.[5] The Maskilic, enlightened, Jewish families spoke Russian, rejected orthodoxy, and embraced traditional Russian culture while keeping Kosher and observing the rituals of traditional Jewish life. The Levinas household was just such a family. The tension between the desires for assimilation and autonomous Jewish identity can be seen in the incongruities of the Levinas family's everyday life. They lived outside of the Jewish area, spoke primarily Russian at home, owned a Russian bookstore, and wanted their children to attend Russian schools. Yet they interacted primarily in Jewish circles, kept kosher, celebrated the Jewish holidays, and learned Hebrew, albeit as a modern language.[6] Emmanuel Levinas first encountered the Hebrew Bible as translation material to learn Russian and Hebrew, without the "famous commentaries that would later appear to me as being essential. The silence of these marvelous rabbinical commentaries was also an homage to modernity."[7]

Growing up in Kovno, Levinas was spared the most blatant and violent forms of anti-Semitism that were prevalent in surrounding areas, but he was made well aware of the limits placed on Jews under the Czarist regime. The most glaring example in Levinas's early childhood was the *numerus clauses*, the restriction on the number of Jews allowed in the Russian high school— the cause of his parents' emphasis on academic excellence.

In 1915, the German invasion of Lithuania forced the Levinas family to move out of Kovno. Their original plan was to move to Kiev, but it was closed to Jews at this time so they moved to the Ukrainian city of Kharkov instead. For five years, from age eleven, he followed the Russian school program with its emphasis on Russian culture and literature. He began to study German at school while continuing with Hebrew by means of private lessons. One year after his entrance into the Russian school, the Czar abdicated. He spent his first year of school under the Czarist regime and the following year under the regime of the February Revolution. Levinas was drawn toward the excitement and hope of communism and Leninism, but his parents insisted adamantly that he avoid politics and keep to his studies.[8]

After the German evacuation in 1919, Lithuania declared its independence and formed a republic. In 1920, the Levinases took the "first possible opportunity" to leave Kharkov and the Soviet Ukraine to return to Kovno. But the Kovno to which the Levinas family returned was not the Kovno they had left. The Russian bookstore had been sold. Furthermore, and perhaps more troubling to the Levinas family, the Russian high school had been closed as part of the reformation of the Lithuanian national school system. Emmanuel Levinas returned to the Jewish high school; his hopes of graduating from the Russian high school and entering into the culture of Russia and Europe were dashed. Here we must consider the disappointment of the Levinases as a telling sign of the times. Emmanuel Levinas's parents did not choose to send him to a herder nor yeshiva to study Talmud. Indeed, even the return to the Jewish gymnasium was seen as a setback.

But as one "opening to Europe" and assimilation had been closed, a new path opened. Levinas recalled that the director of the Jewish school, Dr. Moses Schwabe, was a German Jew "who had discovered Eastern European Judaism during his captivity in Russia. He was a doctor of philosophy, and it was he who taught me German."[9] Dr. Schwabe taught courses on German literature, and Levinas became enamored with the works of Goethe. Under the instruction of Dr. Schwabe, Levinas finished high school with an emphasis on Russian literature. Philosophy classes in the traditional sense did not exist in the Russian or Lithuanian school systems, so it was through authors such as Nikolai Gogol, Aleksandr Pushkin, Feodor Dostoyevsky, Mikhail Lermontov, Leo Tolstoy, and Ivan Turgenev that Levinas was introduced to what he termed "metaphysical unease" (*inquiétude métaphysique*).[10] While Levinas was familiar with the Bible and the Jewish traditions, Russian literature was his first step toward the investigation and interrogation of what he later referred to as the "meaning of life" (*sens de la vie*), and not his position in the Lithuanian Jewish community.[11] He had not studied the Talmud, nor the exegetic methods of the Gaon of Vilna or Chaim of Volozhin. He would not come to his love of the

Torah, which he believed was crucial to answering these questions, until much later in life.

Emmanuel's parents had originally planned for him to attend a Russian university, but after the revolution it became clear that this was no longer an option. Given his studies with Dr. Moses Schwabe, his knowledge of German, and the proximity of Germany, the German university system seemed a logical choice. But Emmanuel Levinas decided to venture in 1923 to the University of Strasbourg, "the city in France closest to Lithuania," where he did not speak the language well, and which was certainly more distant than many universities in Germany. Increasing anti-Semitism in Germany, the unstable value of a diploma from a Jewish school in Lithuania, and the reticence of German universities toward admitting Eastern European Jewish immigrants may have determined the choice for him.[12]

PHILOSOPHE

In any event, Levinas's choice was a good one. Strasbourg was a city fluent in German and French, and Levinas was able to use his German while he improved his French. In his second year he enrolled as a student of philosophy in the school of letters. This was Levinas's first foray into the academic world of philosophy. He had no formal training in philosophy, but what he lacked in formal training he more than made up with his knowledge of Russian literature and familiarity with the Torah. His approach was not that of a student brought up studying philosophy in the French school system, nor was it that of a student of Talmud. Instead, as Levinas recollected, his interest in philosophy came from the courses he had taken on

> Pushkin, Lermontov, and Dostoyevsky, above all Dostoyevsky. The Russian novel, the novels of Dostoyevsky and Tolstoy appeared to me to be completely preoccupied with fundamental things. Books that were traversed by anxiety, by the essential, by religious unease; but that read like a quest for the meaning of life [sens de la vie] . . . It was certainly in the sentimental love of these novels that I found my first philosophical temptations.[13]

Levinas was not interested in the theoretical idealism of neo-Kantianism, which he felt was too abstract to deal with the fundamental things of everyday life, so he turned instead to the work of Henri Bergson and the fields of sociology, psychology, and theology. The work of Bergson and these other disciplines seemed much closer in their concerns to the issues that Levinas had been exploring in the work of Pushkin, Lermontov, Dostoyevsky, and Tolstoy.

His first years in the Department of Philosophy at Strasbourg were spent studying with Maurice Pradines, professor of general philosophy, and Henri Carteron, professor of ancient philosophy. But soon he had branched out to psychology under Charles Blondel and sociology under Maurice Halbwachs.

> In contact with these masters the great virtues of intelligence and intellectual probity were revealed to me, but also those of clarity and the elegance of the French university. Initiation into the great philosophers Plato and Aristotle, Descartes and the Cartesians, Kant. Not yet Hegel, in those twenties at the Faculty of Letters at Strasbourg! But it was Durkheim and Bergson who seemed to me especially alive . . . They had incontestably been the professors, our masters.[14]

Maurice Pradines was a contemporary of Max Scheler and Ernst Cassirer. A Bergsonian, Pradines's primary concern was the privileged position of ethics and morality, and specifically the relation of ethics to politics. One of the first courses Levinas took with Pradines was on just this topic, and as proof of the privileged position of ethics over politics Pradines gave the example of the Dreyfus Affair.[15] This was an essential moment in Levinas's decision to embrace French culture and society as his own.

For Levinas, as for most Jews in Eastern Europe, the Dreyfus Affair was an event of mythic proportions: "Everywhere in Eastern Europe, Jews knew about Dreyfus. Old Jewish men with beards who had never seen a letter of the Latin alphabet in their life, spoke of Zola as if he were a saint. And then, suddenly, there was a professor before me in the flesh who had chosen this [the Dreyfus Affair] as his example [of the superiority of ethics over politics]. What an extraordinary world!"[16] Pradines's investigation into the privileged position of rationality and ethics in relation to religion is evident in Levinas's later Talmudic lectures and his writings on Judaism. Perhaps most important was the emphasis on a rational investigation with recourse to universal claims that does not veer either into pure subjective revelation nor a positivist schematic of facts. The basis of this de-divinized and universal reason is ethics but the example Pradine offered, the Dreyfus Affair, was highly problematic. Levinas's decision to embrace French culture and the Republican tradition as the embodiment of the privileged position of ethics over politics neglected the very real aspects of that tradition that led to Dreyfus's arrest and incarceration. Indeed it was the implications of this early choice seen through the lens of Vichy France that in part led Levinas to reshape his philosophical project and turn to Talmud. But his Talmudic readings are a critique, not a rejection, of Western philosophy.

Through Pradines, Levinas was introduced to the works of Henri Bergson, a figure as inspirational to Levinas for his Jewish background as for his philosophical prowess. But while the realization that a man of Jewish origin could reach the summits of popularity in the field of philosophy was encouraging, if not seductive, to the young Jewish scholar, it was the realization of how the works of Bergson could guide the future of philosophy that truly sparked the interest of the young Levinas. For Levinas, Bergson seemed to represent all that was new in philosophy, and he was swept up in the novelty of this sensation. But soon Levinas came to see Bergson's philosophy as static in the sense that it had completed the task it set out to achieve. Bergson's work had opened up new horizons and new possibilities. It was the basis without which "all the new ideas developed by philosophers during the modern and postmodern periods, and in particular the venerable newness of Heidegger, would not have been possible."[17] But its impact lay in breaking the grip of positivism and rationalism by emphasizing the concept of free will.

For Levinas, Bergson's philosophy escaped pure objectivity but did so by going to the other extreme and was dangerously close to pure subjectivity. Levinas did not want to replace the emphasis on the object with an emphasis on the subject that was equally removed from our everyday interactions with things in the world in which we live. But here, too, his investigation was primarily concerned with the Western philosophical tradition, and Levinas would continue his search for the "concrete meaning of the very possibility of 'working in philosophy.'"[18]

While these eminent professors were responsible for the more formal aspects of Levinas's academic training and for instilling a connection between the tradition of the French "Enlightenment" and Levinas's own understanding of Judaism, perhaps the two most important figures in Levinas's development at Strasbourg were fellow student Gabrielle Peiffer and a young instructor and pastor named Jean Hering. It was Peiffer who first introduced Levinas to the work of Edmund Husserl.[19] The following year Levinas enrolled in the course of Jean Hering, who taught in the Faculty of Protestant Theology at Strasbourg. Hering had been a member of the Göttingen circle, one of the original phenomenological groups which gathered to study around Edmund Husserl.

At the time that Levinas enrolled in Hering's course, none of Husserl's work had been translated into French (Levinas and Peiffer's translation in 1931 would be practically the first). Hering's course and his use of the phenomenological method were inspired by his personal interest in the ontological investigation of man's relation to God. Here, too, the importance of religion in philosophy was not lost on Levinas, but while the *possibility* of religion was important to him at the time, the future of *philosophy* was Levinas's primary concern.

> It was with Husserl that I discovered the concrete meaning of the very possibility of "working in philosophy" without being straight away enclosed in a system of dogmas, but at the same time without running the risk of proceeding by chaotic intuitions.[20]

Husserlian phenomenology appeared to Levinas as a methodology that escaped the closed model of science that was the basis of French neo-Kantianism, while at the same time avoiding the slippery slope of spiritualism that bordered on pure subjectivity and "chaotic intuitions" toward which Bergson's work veered perilously close.

PHENOMENOLOGIST

Levinas spent the academic year of 1928–1929 studying with Husserl, who had just retired from the University of Freiburg but was continuing his courses until a replacement had been chosen. For Levinas, phenomenology was the possibility of moving beyond the systematic organization of knowledge under the rubric of reason to the interrogation of the dynamic act of knowing and the mechanism at its origin. In this way it moved past the subject-object split by emphasizing consciousness at the locus of the relationship between the subject and the object.

In Husserl, Levinas found a kind and rigorous professor and like Bergson, Husserl was of Jewish origin. But ultimately Levinas felt constricted by Husserl: "At the time conversation with him [Husserl], after some questions or replies by the student, was the monologue of the master concerned to call to mind the fundamental elements of his thought."[21] But this was Husserl's last year as a lecturer, and it was he who suggested to Levinas that he should remain in Freiburg to continue his studies with Husserl's successor, Martin Heidegger.

Levinas had already been introduced to the work of Heidegger on a trip back to Strasbourg. Levinas had gone to visit Jean Hering at his hotel, and Hering had given him a copy of *Being and Time* (first published in 1927). It was with Heidegger that Levinas finally discovered a means to explore the issues of metaphysical "unease" that had been his interest since his studies with Dr. Moses Schwabe in Kovno. Husserl's phenomenology had begun the radical interrogation that allowed for the possibility of "grasping oneself," of understanding relations to things as a "consciousness of," which always implies a Self that is conscience, but Heidegger took the investigation further by shifting the focus away from the intellectual activities of the specific self and toward an investigation into Being. Through *Being and Time* and then through the lectures of Heidegger himself, Levinas was introduced to

> the comprehension of the verb "to be." Ontology would be distinguished from all the disciplines which explore *that* which is, beings, that is, the "beings," their nature, their relations—while forgetting that in speaking of these beings they have already understood the meaning of the word Being, without, however, having made it explicit. These disciplines do not worry about such an explication.[22]

Heidegger's project, however, made that explication of Being its primary goal by extending and reshaping Husserl's phenomenological project. One could certainly tease out the theological implications of Levinas's pursuit of Being. It is also possible to draw a line between the hermeneutic exegesis of Heidegger and the Lithuanian Talmudic tradition but the line is clearly disturbing to Levinas after Heidegger's political choices of the 1930s.

For the young Levinas, the chief pursuit was philosophy and the work of Husserl seemed less convincing precisely because it "seemed less expected. This may sound paradoxical or childish but everything seemed unexpected in Heidegger, the wonders of his analysis of affectivity, the new access toward the investigation of everyday life, the famous ontological difference he drew between Being [*être*] and beings [*étant*]."[23] Levinas's philosophical transition from Husserlian phenomenology to Heideggerian ontological phenomenology can be best traced through two of Levinas's earliest works: his article, "Sur 'les Ideen' de M. Husserl," written for the *Revue philosophique de la France et de l'étranger* in 1929, and his doctoral dissertation published in 1930 as *The Theory of Intuition in Husserl's Phenomenology*. The latter introduced the philosophy of Heidegger into France by analyzing his critique of Husserl's concept of intentionality.

What is essential to our investigation is that it was in his use of Heidegger to critique Husserl that Levinas began to articulate the concerns that later surfaced in his Talmudic writings, concerns that were also fostered by his Strasbourg *maîtres*. In *The Theory of Intuition*, Levinas foreshadowed what would later become his foremost concern, ethics and the place of the Other:

> There is another reason why the phenomenological reduction, as we have interpreted it so far, does not reveal concrete life and the meaning that objects

have for concrete life. Concrete life is not the solipsist's life of a consciousness closed in upon itself. Concrete Being is not what exists for only one consciousness. In the very idea of concrete Being is contained the idea of an intersubjective world. If we limit ourselves to describing the constitution of objects in an individual consciousness, in an *ego*, the *egological reduction* can only be a first step toward phenomenology. We must also discover "others" and that intersubjective world.[24]

At this point in his career, Levinas saw Heidegger's displacement of the primacy of the ego as the possibility of an opening to "others." Therefore, Levinas's movement away from Husserl and toward Heidegger was derived through the realization that there was no place for "others" in Husserl's phenomenological program. These themes returned in Levinas's later writing and in his Talmudic readings when they were recast in relation to his renewed emphasis on Jewish thought.

PARISIAN

In 1930, Levinas moved to Paris and took an administrative job with the Alliance israélite universelle (AIU). Levinas's work with the AIU was more than a job; it was a return to Jewish culture but a return to Jewish culture under the rubric of the French-conceived "rights of man." Levinas described the origin and mission of the AIU as:

> constituted in 1860 with the express concern of working for the emancipation of Israelites in countries where they did not yet have the right of citizenship. The first of these Israelite institutions was inspired by the French Rights of Man. There were in this inspiration no Zionist sentiments. Its mission was simply to emancipate those Israelites living in countries where they were not recognized as citizens . . . Soon these activities became scholastic work; the founding of French schools of the highest level that would express above all the ideals of the nineteenth century . . . the elevation of universal culture and the affirmation of the glorious ideals of 1789.[25]

In this light we can view Levinas's embrace of Jewish culture via the AIU as more indebted to the influence of his professors at Strasbourg and the "glorious ideals of 1789" than to his own upbringing in Lithuania. Despite the foreign nature of his work in philosophy, or perhaps precisely because of it, Levinas adopted an allegiance of "literary chauvinism," a faith in the tolerance and equality of France as exemplified in the rights of man. His was not the nationalism of a Maurice Barrès or a Charles Maurras but of Emile

Zola. He believed in a France based not on race and roots but on culture. So while the post at the AIU did constitute a return to Judaism, it was in no way a turn to the study of Talmud in the Lithuanian tradition. Instead, Levinas's position at the AIU should be seen as a job that allowed him to move between the world of "Jewish thought" and Parisian philosophy.[26]

Ultimately, the mission of the AIU was as colonial as it was humanitarian, exporting both French and Jewish culture simultaneously to Northern Africa, Eastern Europe, and Asia. Here we see a conflation of the universal ideals of the French Enlightenment project and the particular identity of Judaism. Levinas was not unaware of the conflicts inherent in such a conflation and the desire to understand the tensions between assimilation and identity led him to the work of Franz Rosenzweig. Rosenzweig's *Star of Redemption* (1921) became a focal point for Levinas, who was trying to reconcile his own bifurcated existence—Jewish clerk for the AIU by day, French philosopher by night.

For Levinas, Rosenzweig led the way to a truly modern approach to Jewish thought, one that had gone through the process of assimilation and then returned to Judaism without rejecting European history. Thus his use of Rosenzweig was a shift of focus toward the investigation of Judaism that later culminated in his turn to Talmud after the war. Rosenzweig's *Star of Redemption* also led Levinas to the work of Søren Kierkegaard.[27] But more than this, Levinas's reading of Rosenzweig's work was an attempt to reconcile the tension between Christians and Jews in an increasingly unstable Europe.

Levinas was an avid reader of German newspapers as well as Jewish journals from Germany and Eastern Europe, so he was well aware of the rising trends of nationalism and anti-Semitism. He was also aware of the actions that his former professor, Heidegger, had taken in Germany, including his choice to join the National Socialist Party, his ascension to the rectorate at Freiburg, and the implementation on April 6, 1933, of the Baden Decree, which suspended all civil servants of non-Aryan origin, regardless of religious orientation, from office, including those, such as Edmund Husserl, already in retirement.[28] Furthermore, recent events in France had forced Levinas to accept the fact that this was not a phenomenon to which France was exempt, despite his hopes in the 1930s that anti-Semitism was a mere product of importation.

The work of Rosenzweig provided Levinas with a sort of optimism in alleviating the tensions between Jew and Christian through his understanding of Rosenzweig's concept of "the neighbor." Furthermore, it seems that through Rosenzweig, Levinas found an alternative to Heidegger that allowed him to conserve key aspects of Heidegger's philosophical project in the service of his reflections on what it meant to be a Jew in 1930s Europe. But Levinas's particular reading of Rosenzweig says far more about his own concerns than about Rosenzweig.

By the late 1930s the circle of intellectuals around Levinas had completely destabilized. Perhaps one of the most difficult blows for Levinas was the realization that at this time of rising fascism and xenophobia, even those whom he held in the highest regard were not immune to the seductions of this vulgar trend. Heidegger's political choice in Germany is the most obvious example, but equally troublesome were the assertions made by Maurice Blanchot, Levinas's best friend. By 1937 Blanchot had joined the ranks of the virulently anti-Semitic press, writing numerous articles for the journals *Combat* and *L'Insurgé*.[29] But while Blanchot's work paralleled the anti-Semitism of other right-wing intellectuals such as Pierre Drieu la Rochelle, Henri de Motherlant, and Robert Brassillach, it did not display the same concerns.[30]

In response to Blanchot and Heidegger, Levinas was forced to rethink his understanding of philosophy, the relation of ontology to the subject as "I," and to the relation of that subject to an Other. More germane to our discussion, Levinas was forced to consider his position as a Jew and his own proximity to two thinkers (one his friend) tainted by anti-Semitism. It is in the context of this uncertainty and instability that Levinas wrote "De l'évasion" in 1935 for *Recherches philosophiques*. While the majority of his work from the 1930s follows the works of Heidegger and Husserl fairly closely, using the phenomenological method to explore the ontological question of *Being*,[31] this piece intimated Levinas's growing concerns with the solipsistic nature of what he would later call the totalitarian project of ontology. But in 1935, the issue was escape, and here we can detect a growing unease with the Western philosophical tradition, which he had adopted, in light of its apparent rejection of Levinas as a Jew, as the Other.

In 1939 Levinas was mobilized to serve in the Tenth Army; but by June 16, 1940, his company had been captured by the German army and the soldiers sent to prisoner of war camps. It was due to his capture as a soldier in the French army that Levinas was not deported to the concentration camps as a Jew.[32] Despite the segregation, the derogatory remarks from the inhabitants of the local village, and the constant reminder of his subhuman status inscribed on his uniform, the war passed for Levinas without incident and, according to him, without the slightest news of the atrocities committed at the camp in Bergen-Belsen.

In the POW camp, Levinas began to reformulate his position in relation to ontology in the form of an article entitled "Il y a" ("There Is"). Upon his return to Paris after the war this article would become the basis for *De l'ex-istence à l'existant* (1947), and it would be with this work that Levinas would break with the ontological project and uncover an opening to ethics that would coincide with his discovery of Talmud. Levinas describes the *il y a*, the "there is," as

> something resembling what one hears when one puts an empty shell close to the ear, as if the emptiness were full, as if the silence were a noise. It is some-thing one can also feel when one thinks that even if there were nothing, the fact that "there is" is undeniable. Not that there is this or that; but the very scene of Being is open: there is. In the absolute nothing that one can imagine before creation-there is.[33]

In the impersonal, anonymous Being of the "there is," Levinas attempted to explore the space prior to the posting of a subject. But here, too, we see evidence of the growing importance of counterhistoricism. The basic prem-ise of counterhistoricism is that meaning transcends time. The *il y a* sug-gests a source that lies outside of time and whose meaning is transcendent.

RETURN

When Levinas returned to Paris in 1945, his first concern was for his fam-ily in France. Then, slowly he began to take stock of the events that hap-pened in Europe. Over the next few months, stories of death camps became more and more real and unbelievable. Before long, Levinas would find out the fate of his own family in Kovno. In June 1941 the Germans had taken control of Lithuania; on June 24, Kovno fell into German hands, and the Jews were immediately rounded up. Pogroms were incited by the Germans, and after several days of intensive violence 5,000 Jews were dead. By July 13 the Jews had been segregated, and Lithuanian groups working with German *Einsatzkommandos* shot 500 Jews every day around the clock. For the following months the Jews were systematically shot in groups of 1,000. On November 1, the detention center was converted into a "proper camp," and the survivors were held until they were deported to camps in Germany.[34]

After the Shoah, Levinas's emphasis on the philosophical interrogation into the question of Being no longer sufficed. He believed that for philosophy to make sense in the wake of the Shoah, it would have to move beyond Hei-degger's emphasis on Being, but it could not return to the investigation of the individual being and that being's own personal horizon. Instead, philosophy

had to work through the question of Being to the relation of an individual being to an Other. But how could this undertaking be possible given the historical reality of the Shoah? For Levinas, the answer lay in the equally important
question of what it meant to be a Jew after the Shoah. Levinas realized that
the Western philosophical tradition he had so readily embraced in the years
prior to the war had been implicated, if not indicted by the Shoah. In the
years following the war he also suffered a crisis of conviction as a Jew. On the
one hand, he took a position as director of the École normale israélite orien-
tale. This institution, modeled after the French variant, was charged with the
mission of teaching teachers who would then serve as instructors at the various schools of the AIU. Indeed, one can see this as a commitment to revital-
ize the Jewish community by providing knowledgeable instructors who could
guarantee the perseverance of Jewish thought. On the other hand, it appears
that Levinas's commitment to the practice of Judaism was in doubt and that
for a period of time he even stopped keeping kosher.[35] It was at this time that
Levinas became close with a certain Henri Nerson, and Nerson brought Levinas back to Judaism and to the reading of Talmud in the Lithuanian tradition. Nerson was an observant Jew raised in a Jewish community in Strasbourg. He had been studying Talmud with a mysterious foreigner named
Shushani who had purportedly been trained in the Lithuanian Talmudic tradition of the Gaon of Vilna. It was Nerson who introduced Levinas to
Shushani and to the study of Talmud that would remain a central focus for
the rest of Levinas's life.

   Shushani was a drifter who appeared and disappeared for months at a
time. No one knew where he came from or even his real name. He claimed
to have been trained in the Lithuanian Talmudic tradition, but he was not
from Lithuania—Levinas noted that he spoke the Yiddish of Lite with a
strong foreign accent.[36] Levinas was taken by this Talmudic scholar who, he
said, could cite Torah, Talmud, and Zohar by heart. Shushani often stayed
with Levinas and would teach courses in Talmud until one day when he
would mysteriously depart. The courses were taught in French and were
not cheap, but for Levinas, Shushani represented a "new way to approach
rabbinic wisdom and to understand what it meant to be human."[37] Here we
should take seriously Levinas's statement that Shushani represented a *new*
way to approach rabbinic wisdom.

   One can only imagine the impact that Shushani must have had on Emmanuel Levinas. For Levinas, Shushani was the embodiment of a tradition
associated with his childhood, his parents, his family, and his community in
Lithuania. All of which Levinas had lost. Furthermore, Shushani represented a tradition that at some level Levinas had rejected in his desire to as-

similate into European culture through the pursuit of the Western philosophical tradition. This tradition had now been placed in question by the
event of the Shoah. As Levinas states, his turn to Talmud had far more to
do with the Shoah than with Shushani: "Certainly the history of the Holocaust played a much larger role in what happened to my Judaism than my
encounter with this man [Shushani]. But through this man I regained my
confidence in these books."[38]

Here we see a double move by Levinas. At the same time that Levinas
began to question the viability of Western philosophy and to break definitively with the philosophy of Heidegger we also see a questioning of what it
means to be a Jew after Auschwitz. Both of these questions led Levinas to
the study of Talmud through the ghost of his Lithuanian past as embodied
in the mysterious figure of Shushani. Levinas's study with Shushani thus
marked the beginning of his own Talmudic readings and lectures. But here,
too, we should see this turn to Talmud through the lens of his education and
training in the Western metaphysical tradition. While his study of the Talmud began in the years following World War Two, he presented his first
"Talmudic Lesson" at the Third Colloquium for Francophone Jewish Intellectuals in 1960. The goal of the lesson, and the conference in general, was
to present traditional Jewish thought to assimilated French-Jewish intellectuals. As we will see, the lessons were given in French, and Levinas selected
texts that spoke to contemporary issues on larger philosophical questions. It
is myth to believe Levinas was trained as a Talmudic scholar in Lithuania
and thus can serve as the fountainhead for the reclamation of that tradition.
But perhaps more important is the way that Levinas's Talmudic readings
serve as a historical record that documents his attempt to construct a bridge
between the traditions of Eastern European Jewry and the conditions of
modern Jewishness and in doing so opens a new way of interpreting the Talmud, forging a new link in the chain of tradition.

TALMUD

There is a certain irony in emphasizing the utility of Levinas's Talmudic readings as historical documents, given his own counterhistoricism and its claim
that meaning transcends time. But further investigation will show that it was
this emphasis on the transcendence of meaning that allowed Levinas to re-
claim the lost Talmudic traditions of his youth and that the source of Levinas's
counterhistoricism was the very historical event of the Shoah. Samuel Moyn
has effectively demonstrated that "Levinas's 'counterhistoricism' is among the

most prominent and remarkable elements of his methodology," yet it is "not one that he claimed to derive from the Talmud as an insider, but instead one that enabled him access to these texts as a philosopher and an outsider."[39] Furthermore, Moyn's investigation illuminates the ways that Levinas's inaugural Talmudic readings were inextricably tied to contemporary events. "The eternal debate" found in Levinas's exegesis of several passages from the Tractate *Sanhedrin* "about the comprehensive finality at the end of history thus turns out to have been a temporary obsession around the very moment that Levinas pronounced his reading."[40]

Following Moyn's lead, we can read in light of contemporary historical events Levinas's reference to Rabbi Chaim of Volozhin's interpretation of a passage from the *Sayings of the Fathers* in his 1979 essay "On the Jewish Reading of Scriptures." In the *Saying of the Fathers*, the rabbinical scholars compare the Torah to "glowing coals" and "Rabbi Chaim Volozhiner interpreted this remark approximately as follows: the coals light up by being blown on, the glow of the flame that thus comes alive depends on the interpreter's length of breath."[41] Levinas's counterhistoricism allows him to rekindle the coals through the force of his breath. The meaning remains in the coals, and what seems to matter most is not the blower's training but his or her engagement with the coals. Thus, as Levinas states in his introduction to *Quatre lectures talmudiques* of 1968 (translated in English as the introduction to *Nine Talmudic Readings*), "Our approach assumes that the different periods of history can communicate around thinkable meanings, whatever the variations in the signifying material which suggests them." The contemporary reference becomes more clear as Levinas continues: "For we assume the permanence and continuation of Israel and the unity of its self-consciousness throughout the ages."[42] Even in the face of the most horrible temporal disaster the "permanence" and "continuation" of Israel is guaranteed. What was lost can be found. The coals still hold the fire. Levinas's logic of transcendence also holds as long as the key to understanding is personal revelation. But here, too, the source of Levinas's method is not derived from the Talmud but from the philosophy of Søren Kierkegaard.[43]

In Kierkegaard's presentation, the story of Abraham and Isaac is as meaningful to us today as it was to the first Hebrews because "no generation begins other than where its predecessor did, every generation begins from the beginning, the succeeding generation comes no further than the previous one, provided the latter was true to its task and didn't betray it."[44] One need only read the text, but one must read closely and critically. Thus the close and skeptical reader (the philosopher?) is particularly suited to the task of coaxing meaning from sacred texts, but he or she must be willing to accept that there is meaning beyond his or her intellect or evolution. Levinas refers to this as the paradigmatic method.[45] For Kierkegaard and for Levinas, it only takes one man to restore meaning to the text, but whereas Kierkegaard is content to allow the Knight of Faith to bask in his personal salvation, Levinas is not. For Levinas, the figure of emulation is not Abraham, who could not explain his act, but Moses who is given the daunting challenge of translating divine will into human law.

Levinas tells a story from the Tractate *Shabbath* about a Sadducee who "saw Raba buried in study, holding his fingers beneath his foot so tightly that blood spurted from it."[46] Levinas interprets this passage as a template for his own Talmudic methodology when he states: "to rub in such a way that blood spurts out is perhaps the way one must 'rub' the text to arrive at the life it conceals. Many of you are undoubtedly thinking, with good reason, that at this very moment, I am in the process of rubbing the text to make it spurt blood—I rise to the challenge!" But Levinas also concedes and embraces the violent nature of such a task: "to the degree that it rests on the trust granted the author, it can only consist in this violence done to words to tear from them the secret that time and conventions have covered over with their sedimentations."[47] Levinas's self-proclaimed violent reading of the story of Raba becomes the very justification for his methodology of Talmudic exegesis. In essence he has granted himself authority based on his own reading of the Talmud.

There is a second Moses story to which Levinas refers almost every time he discusses his method of Talmudic interpretation.[48] In this story, Moses wants to know the future of the Torah and is transported to the academy of Rabbi Akiba. Upon entering the school Moses is disconsolate to discover that he does not understand anything of the lessons being taught. His mood is lifted, however, when at the end of the lesson Rabbi Akiba attributes his teachings to the teachings of Moses at Mount Sinai. Here the eternal message is delivered within the context of temporal change, and the authority of Rabbi Akiba is not questioned despite the incomprehensibility of his teachings to Moses. In Levinas's presentation it is the intellectual milieu of Akiba that is incomprehensible to Moses while the teachings are somehow constant. In these two stories we see how Levinas's counterhistoricism and emphasis on the transcendence of meaning enable him to restore life to a tradition, his tradition, that was lost, but it also allows him to do so in a way that conserves his own particular talents and interests. Perhaps upon entering one of Levinas's Talmudic lessons the Gaon of Vilna would have had the same reaction as Moses? In any case Levinas forges a forced continuity based on transcendence and justified by his reading of the Talmud. Here we see the inversion of Levinas's prewar emphasis on the primacy of philosophy over religion in an effort to confront the most troubling issues of his times and his past. But this inversion also allows Levinas to conserve his philosophical interests in the service of his "religious" discourse.

Here I would like to turn to a specific Talmudic reading because it is particularly useful in understanding Levinas's inversion of emphasis and the context that led to this reevaluation of his own project. The reading in question is entitled "Toward the Other" and was presented at a conference on the theme "Forgiveness" in October 1963.[49] In this reading, Levinas examines several passages from the Tractate *Yoma*. The issue at hand is indeed forgiveness, and the text consists of two parts: "an excerpt from the Mishna (the name given to the oral teachings collected by Rabbi Judah Hanassi toward the end of the second century); and an excerpt from the Gamara (the oral teachings of the period following the writing down of the Mishna and themselves recorded in writing by Rav Ashi and Ravina, toward the end of the fifth century)."[50] The Mishna is about the Day of Atonement (Yom Kippur) and the passage reads: "The transgressions of man toward God are forgiven him by the Day of Atonement; the transgressions against other people are not forgiven him by the Day of Atonement if he has not first appeased the other person."

Levinas is careful to distinguish that there are two types of transgressions that require two different types of forgiveness and spends the first portion of his reading differentiating between the two. The first of the transgressions are those against God, and Levinas suggests that perhaps these "ills that must heal inside the Soul without the help of others are precisely the most profound ills, and that even where our social faults are concerned, once our neighbor has been appeased, the most difficult part remains to be done. In doing wrong toward God, have we not undermined the moral conscience as moral conscience?" This is certainly a possible reading of the aforementioned tract, but I would like to suggest that this is also a deeply personal confession. The transgression against God is Levinas's own transgression of his youth: his movement away from the Judaism of Vilna and toward Western philosophy. Levinas continues, "the ritual transgression that I want to erase without resorting to the help of others would be precisely the one that demands all my personality; it is the work of *Teshuvah*, of Return, for which no man can take my place."[51] But we must also note that this transgression is forgiven by God on the Day of Atonement.

Levinas then shifts his focus to confront the second kind of transgression and the seeming contradiction that the more profound transgression against God can be forgiven while the temporal offense against another person is not. Here Levinas turns from Mishna to Gemara and examines Rabbi Joseph bar Helbe's objection to the Mishna as voiced to Rabbi Abbahu. Rabbi Joseph bar Helbe said, "How can one hold that faults committed by man against another are not forgiven him by the Day of Atonement when it is written (1 Samuel): If a man offends another man, Elohim will reconcile."[52]

Levinas concedes that Rabbi Joseph bar Helbe's criticism is not only in opposition to the Mishna but is also substantiated by biblical verse. In this version it is God that forgives, and thus the distinction in the Mishna is denied. But Levinas does not agree with Helbe and instead rubs the text until it spurts blood to produce a counter-reading. Levinas takes a portion of Helbe's discourse and finds that the "solution consists in inserting these italicized words into the biblical verse to bend it toward the spirit of the Mishna." After Levinas's subtle manipulation the verse reads, "If a man commits a fault toward another man and *appeases him*, God will forgive; but if the fault concerns God, who will be able to intercede for him, *if not repentance and good deeds*."

Levinas interprets this to mean that the matter of forgiveness depends on the offended party and that "one finds oneself in his hands. There can be no forgiveness that the guilty party has not sought! The guilty party must recognize his fault. . . . Further, no person can forgive if forgiveness has not been asked him by the offender, if the guilty party has not tried to appease the offended."[53] The differentiation between the two types of transgression has been re-established, but why the emphasis on these two variants?

The answer again brings us back to the context of Levinas's lecture. Levinas himself leads us there via the story of Rab, who insulted his master when he would not repeat his lesson and then was *refused* forgiveness. The verse reads:

> Then Rab Hanina bar Hama came in and Rab said: How many times am I to repeat myself? He did not go back to the beginning. Rab Hanina was wounded by it. For thirteen years, on Yom Kippur eve, Rab went to ask forgiveness, and Rab Hanina refused to be appeased.[54]

This story also seems to contradict the Mishna as interpreted by Levinas where forgiveness is predicated on the offending party's attempt to appease the offended. In this story the offended Rab Hanina never forgives Rab, and that is the end of the story. The Gemara refers to Rab Hanina's dream where he saw Rab hanging from a palm tree, which according to the story indicates that Rab is destined to sovereignty. The explanation in the

Gemara thus assumes that Rab Hanina, having guessed that Rab would succeed him, preferred to make him leave by denying his forgiveness. Levinas
is ill at ease with the Gemara's explanation of Rab Hanina's behavior, so with
recourse to the tools of psychoanalysis, he produces a counter-reading
compatible with his earlier exegesis. Here we must be clear that Levinas
employs a psychoanalytic dream analysis to revise the explanation provided
by the Gemara. Levinas states:

> Whenever we have dreams, we are in the realm of psychoanalysis and the un-
> conscious, of a psychoanalysis before the letter, to be sure . . . Now in the story
> that is troubling us, what is at stake? Rab recognizes his faults and asks Han-
> ina for forgiveness. The offended party can grant forgiveness when the of-
> fender becomes conscious of the wrong he has done.[55]

But if we are in the realm of the unconscious then perhaps Rab is not actually conscious of the wrong he has done. Levinas believes that Rab Hanina's dream reveals "more about Rab than Rab knew himself. The dream revealed Rab's secret ambitions, beyond the inoffensive gesture at the origin
of the incident. Rab, without knowing it, wished to take his master's
place."[56] Thus Levinas concludes that Rab Hanina could not forgive Rab.
For how is one to forgive the offender if, unaware of his deeper thoughts,
the offender cannot ask forgiveness?

But it turns out Levinas's meditation on forgiveness has a target more recent than the rabbis of yore. Levinas asks at the beginning of this section
"Would an offense between intellectuals be the most irreparable?" and now
he is ready to give his reply.[57]

> But perhaps there is something altogether different in all this. One can if
> pressed to the limit, forgive the one who has spoken unconsciously. But it is
> very difficult to forgive Rab, who was fully aware and destined for a great fate,
> which was prophetically revealed to his master. One can forgive many Ger-
> mans, but there are some Germans it is difficult to forgive. *It is difficult to for-*
> *give Heidegger.* If Hanina could not forgive the just and humane Rab because
> he was also the brilliant Rab, it is even less possible to forgive Heidegger. Here
> I am brought back to the present.[58]

To make the connection obvious, one need only substitute the names
Husserl and Heidegger for Hanina and Rab and replace the inoffensive
gesture at the origin of the incident with the deeply offensive gesture of the
Baden Decree.

Now the emphasis on the differentiation of transgression becomes clear.
Levinas is guilty of a transgression against God. This is the most serious of-

fense, but one he can repair through the work of *Teshuvah*, of Return, for which no man can take his place.[59] But central to the work of *Teshuvah* for Levinas is a continued engagement with the Western philosophical tradition. One can already see the tension in this formulation, as it was this very tradition that led Levinas astray. This is the focus of a later Talmudic reading where Levinas refers to philosophy as the "temptation of temptation."[60] This necessarily leads us to Levinas's former teacher Martin Heidegger. Levinas's intellectual relationship to Heidegger is itself a transgression, but one that Levinas is able to resolve in his Talmudic discourse. And this is why it was so incredibly important for Levinas to establish the differentiation of transgression and to justify it with the authority of the Talmud. Unlike Levinas whose transgression against God will be forgiven on the Day of Atonement, Heidegger's transgression will not. Heidegger's transgressions were against his fellow man for which he never asked forgiveness. Like Rab, Heidegger repressed his offense, through equivocations and justifications, and because he never took responsibility for his actions he will never be forgiven.

So let us take stock of this particular lesson. In this lesson Levinas distanced himself from Heidegger and the transgressions of the Western philosophical tradition by embracing the transcendent meaning of the Torah. But in so doing he conserved his own use of Western philosophy, albeit subordinated to Torah, by means of his own *Teshuvah*.

CONCLUSION

It is a noble mission to rethink the project of Western philosophy through the critical and transcendent wisdom of Talmudic discourse. But one must wonder about the authority of Levinas's readings and the legitimacy of his use of psychoanalyis and modern hermeneutic exegesis in the reading of these texts. If one accepts the logic of Levinas's counterhistoricism, then one must accept that the "aim is to refer to a context which allows the level of discussion to be raised and to make one notice the true import of the data from which the discussion derives its meaning. The transfer of an idea to another climate—which is its original climate—wrests new possibilities from it."[61] But who or what is to keep this multiplicity of meaning from falling into pure perspectivalism or subjective musing? Levinas realizes that his emphasis on transcendence is always in danger of allowing everyone equal authority over the texts and combats it with comments that infer an appropriate course of training:

> It is certain that, when discussing the right to eat or not to eat "an egg hatched on a holy day," or payments owed for damages caused by a "wild ox," the sages of the Talmud are discussing neither an egg nor an ox but are arguing about fundamental ideas without appearing to do so. *It is true that one needs to have encountered an authentic Talmudic master to be sure of it.*[62]

Statements like this lead readers to the conclusion that Levinas himself was trained by an "authentic Talmudic master" (Shushani?) or that he himself is just such a master. They are a key source of the "myth of Emmanuel Levinas." Conversely, one could argue that Levinas's reading and interpretation of Talmud and the Torah is as indebted to his studies at Strasbourg and his training with Husserl and Heidegger as it is to Shushani (or certainly his early childhood in Lithuania). But statements like this are also seemingly at cross purposes with Levinas's other statements such as:

> the lines you are reading are about forgiveness. But this is only one of countless texts the Talmud devotes to this subject. Therefore, one should not think after hearing me that the Jewish intellectuals of France now know what the Jewish tradition thinks of forgiveness. This is the danger of sporadic explanations of Talmudic texts, like ours, the danger of premature bad conscience, by the very sources of Jewish thought.[63]

The tension one finds in these conflicting passages point to the precarious nature of Levinas's attempt to build a bridge to his Lithuanian past. In his reading and use of Talmud, Levinas is working through his own understanding of what it means to be Jewish in relation to the choices made in the years prior to the war. He did not set out to be a Talmudic master and thus the "debt to Torah" of which Levinas speaks in *Beyond the Verse*, for example, is one that he did not attempt to pay in the years before the war.

Levinas's Talmudic lectures are the continuation of his lifelong mission to find a universal statement but now based on the transcendent authority of Jewish scripture. In his Talmudic readings, Levinas wanted to reread the "essential books" of the Jewish tradition in order to "translate them into Greek." Thus his use of Talmud owes a debt to the Lithuanian tradition, the Gaon of Vilna, and Chaim of Volozhin in the attempt to provide a rational commentary on the traditional books that eschews the "mysticism" and "superstition" of the Hassidim. But it is equally in debt to his understanding of the French Enlightenment, the counterhistoricism of Søren Kierkegaard and Franz Rosenzweig, and Martin Heidegger's method of hermeneutic exegesis. Thus the most cynical reader would say that Levinas's turn to Talmud and emphasis on the transcendence of meaning allowed him to conserve the methods and emphases of Heidegger and his Strasbourg *maîtres* even after the Shoah and Vichy France. The most optimistic reader could claim that Levinas sought out philosophies compatible with the Talmudic environment he absorbed in his youth. In either case, what seems most important to Levinas in his Talmudic readings is the attempt to rethink, revise, and rehabilitate the Western tradition of philosophy in the wake of the Shoah through recourse to the eternal meaning of Jewish scripture. Thus his project is to confront the tradition that has given us modern philosophy with the ethical concerns of the Jewish religion.

But through his published Talmudic lessons and his smaller Talmudic teachings on Saturdays, as well as comments attempting to justify his readings beyond the realm of personal revelation, the "myth" of Emmanuel Levinas as a Lithuanian Talmudic scholar came to be. In a sense, it is no myth since Levinas has become a post-rabbinic authority on Talmud. But it is mythical in that Levinas has become a legitimating authority for thinkers like Alain Finkelkraut, Benny Lévy, and Richard Cohen seeking to fashion a notion of "authentic" Jewish identity. The fact that Lévy felt as comfortable citing Levinas as the source of his religious conversion as Finkelkraut and Cohen do as the source of their rehabilitation of Enlightenment thought and the project of humanism shows that Levinas's Talmudic readings have become more important as a legitimating source than for their actual content. Furthermore, this use of Levinas does not take into account Levinas's own journey.

Levinas's journey took him away from the Talmudic schools of Lithuania and back to the study of Talmud in Paris after the Shoah. As a legitimating authority of "authentic" Jewish practice, Levinas becomes a replication of the Western tradition he is attempting to criticize.[64] Despite many of his own claims, Levinas did not turn to Talmud to provide authority but to investigate the possibility of responsibility. It is from this liminal position where one has renounced one's position as an authority of the text that one can truly begin to question and allow the text to say more than it says. For Levinas, this is the basis of his critique of the Western metaphysical tradition and the opening to infinity and morality. It is in this sense that he speaks of Judaism as a religion for adults.

NOTES

This chapter is based on research presented in chapters 1 and 7 of my monograph, *Generation Existential: The Reception of Heidegger in France, 1927–1961* (Ithaca:

Cornell University Press, forthcoming). I would also like to thank the Tauber Institute for the Study of European Jewry and Julian Bourg, Peter Gordon, and Samuel Moyn for their thoughtful comments. I would especially like to thank Eugene Sheppard for his insight, suggestions, and support.

1. Emmanuel Levinas, "Damages Due to Fire," in *Nine Talmudic Lectures*, trans. Annette Aronowicz (Bloomington: Indiana University Press, 1990).

2. Judith Friedlander, *Vilna on the Seine* (New Haven: Yale University Press, 1990), 3.

3. Stuart L. Charmé, "From Maoism to Talmud (With Sartre Along the Way): An Interview with Benny Lévy," *Commentary* 78, no. 6 (December 1984): 50.

4. I intend to provide a detailed investigation into Levinas and the post-rabbinic chain of tradition in a forthcoming monograph but the topic is beyond the scope of the present article.

5. For an overview of the intellectual and religious climate in Lithuania, see Friedlander, *Vilna on the Seine*.

6. Marie-Anne Lescourret, *Emmanuel Levinas* (Paris: Flammarion, 1994), 32–33.

7. Levinas cited in François Poirié, *Emmanuel Lévinas: qui êtes-vous?* (Lyon: La Manufacture, 1987), 67.

8. Levinas cited in François Poirié, *Emmanuel Lévinas*, 68.

9. Myriam Anissimov, "Emmanuel Levinas se souvient," *Les Nouveaux Cahiers* 82 (Fall 1985): 32.

10. Poirié, *Emmanuel Lévinas*, 69.

11. Poirié, *Emmanuel Lévinas*, 69.

12. Lescourret, *Emmanuel Levinas*, 51.

13. Poirié, *Emmanuel Lévinas*, 69. We will return to the question of why Levinas came to see philosophy as a "temptation."

14. Levinas, *Éthique et infini: dialogues avec Phillipe Nemo* (Paris: Fayard, 1982), 16.

15. Lescourret, *Emmanuel Levinas*, 61–62.

16. Poirié, *Emmanuel Lévinas*, 70. My additions in brackets.

17. Poirié, *Emmanuel Lévinas*, 72.

18. Levinas, *Ethics and Infinity*, trans. Richard A. Cohen (Pittsburgh: Duquesne University Press, 1985), 28.

19. Levinas, *Ethics and Infinity*, 29.

20. Levinas, *Ethics and Infinity*, 29.

21. Levinas, *Ethics and Infinity*, 32–33.

22. Levinas, *Ethics and Infinity*, 38–39.

23. Poirié, *Emmanuel Lévinas*, 75.

24. Levinas, *Theory of Intuition in Husserl's Phenomenology*, trans. André Orianne, 2nd ed. (Evanston, Ill.: Northwestern University Press, 1995), 150.

25. Poirié, *Emmanuel Lévinas*, 79–80.

26. We might also speculate that, as in the case of the return to the Jewish gymnasium in Kovno, Levinas's decision to take the post at the AIU was not based on

choice but on a lack of choice. In this sense Levinas's embrace of Jewish culture via the AIU takes on a Sartrean character as his position as the administrator of a Jewish organization was dictated by others.

27. We will explore the impact of Kierkegaard's counterhistorical presentation of the transcendence of meaning on Levinas's Talmudic readings later in this chapter.

28. Hugo Ott, *Martin Heidegger: A Political Life* (New York: Harper Collins, 1993), 177.

29. The right-wing journal *Combat* has no relation to the daily newspaper *Combat* that was clandestinely published by the Resistance throughout the war and which Camus directed after 1944.

30. See Jeffrey Mehlman, "Of Literature and Terror: Blanchot at *Combat*," *Modern Languages Notes* 95 (1980): 808–29; Dianne Rubinstein, *What's Left? The École Normale Supérieure and the Right* (Madison: University of Wisconsin Press, 1990), 113; Michael Holland, "Bibliographie I" and "Bibliographie II," in *Gramma* 3/4 and 5 (1976): 223–45, 124–32; Phillipe Mesnard, "Maurice Blanchot, le sujet et l'engagement," *L'Infini* 48 (Winter 1994): 103–28.

31. Many of these articles were collected and published in a 1957 volume entitled *En découvrant l'existence avec Husserl et Heidegger* (Paris: Vrin, 1957).

32. Raul Hilberg, *The Destruction of the European Jews* (Chicago: Quadrangle Books, 1961), 401. This policy did not apply to Jewish members of the Red Army, nor to former members of the Reich of Jewish origin who were serving in any army. These prisoners of war were either shot or sent to camps.

33. Levinas, *Ethics and Infinity*, 48.

34. Hilberg, *The Destruction of the European Jews*, 196–208.

35. Lescourret, *Emmanuel Levinas*, 142

36. Anissimov, "Emmanuel Levinas se souvient," 32.

37. Poirié, *Emmanuel Lévinas*, 127–28.

38. Poirié, *Emmanuel Lévinas*, 130.

39. Samuel Moyn, "Emmanuel Levinas's Talmudic Readings: Between Tradition and Invention," *Prooftexts* 23, no. 3 (Fall/Winter 2003): 42–68. Moyn also persuasively demonstrates that even "context denying ideas originate in context" as he situates Levinas within a tradition of counterhistoricism that had its origins in the extra-Talmudic European philosophical and religious discussion of the interwar period. Specifically, Moyn cites the influence of Rosenzweig and Kierkegaard.

40. Moyn, "Emmanuel Levinas's Talmudic Readings," 357. Moyn is referring to Levinas's "initial forays" into Talmudic exegesis prior to 1963, published in *Difficult Freedom: Essays on Judaism*, trans. Sean Hand (Baltimore: Johns Hopkins University Press, 1990).

41. Levinas, *Beyond the Verse: Talmudic Readings and Lectures*, trans. Gary D. Mole (Bloomington: Indiana University Press, 1994), 109, 210 n. 8.

42. Levinas, *Quatre lectures talmudiques* [*Nine Talmudic Lectures*] (Paris: Éditions de Minuit, 1968).

43. For the influence of Kierkegaard on Levinas and other intellectuals in post-war France, see Moyn, *Selfhood and Transcendence: Emmanuel Levinas and the Origins of Intersubjective Moral Theory 1928–1961* (Ph.D. diss., University of California, Berkeley, 2000), 270–319. For the relation of Kierkegaard to Heidegger and the impact of Kierkegaard on the reception of Heidegger in France, see Kleinberg, *Generation Existential*.

44. Søren Kierkegaard, *Fear and Trembling*, trans. Alastair Hannay (New York: Penguin Putnam, 1985), 145–46.

45. Levinas, *Nine Talmudic Lectures*, 21.

46. Levinas, *Nine Talmudic Lectures*, 31. Levinas examined this story from the Tractate *Shabbath*, 88*a* and 88*b*, in his Talmudic reading, "The Temptation of Temptation," presented at a December 1964 colloquium on "The Temptations of Judaism." The reading is translated in *Nine Talmudic Lectures*, 30–50.

47. Levinas, *Nine Talmudic Lectures*, 46–47.

48. Ira F. Stone, *Reading Levinas Reading Talmud* (Philadelphia: The Jewish Publication Society, 1998), 20.

49. This lecture was originally published in *La Conscience juive face à l'histoire: le pardon*, eds. Éliane Amado Lévy-Valensi and Jean Halperin (Paris: PUF, 1965), and repub. in Levinas, *Quatre lectures talmudiques* (Paris: Éditions de Minuit, 1968), trans. as *Nine Talmudic Lectures*.

50. Levinas, *Nine Talmudic Lectures*, 15.

51. Levinas, *Nine Talmudic Lectures*, 17.

52. Levinas, *Nine Talmudic Lectures*, 18.

53. Levinas, *Nine Talmudic Lectures*, 19.

54. Levinas, *Nine Talmudic Lectures*, 23.

55. Levinas, *Nine Talmudic Lectures*, 24–25.

56. Levinas, *Nine Talmudic Lectures*, 25.

57. Levinas, *Nine Talmudic Lectures*, 23.

58. Levinas, *Nine Talmudic Lectures*, 23. My emphasis.

59. Levinas, *Nine Talmudic Lectures*, 17.

60. Levinas, *Nine Talmudic Lectures*, 30–50. Here Levinas seeks to demonstrate that it is Revelation that conditions Reason and that the Torah as revelation is actually the basis for rational choice and not vice versa.

61. Levinas, *Nine Talmudic Lectures*, 21.

62. Levinas, *Nine Talmudic Lectures*, 4. My emphasis.

63. Levinas, *Nine Talmudic Lectures*, 14.

64. Levinas makes this clear in his lesson, "The Temptation of Temptation."

9

RAYMOND ARON: NATIONALISM AND SUPRANATIONALISM IN THE YEARS FOLLOWING THE SECOND WORLD WAR

Lucia Bonfreschi

Raymond Aron (1905–1983) was fully involved in the intellectual *engagement* that took place in postwar France. He wanted to help politicians comprehend the reality of their times and have no illusions that they could completely foresee or control the evolution of history. He maintained that politics could not be viewed in moral terms, that it was not a struggle between right and wrong, because what was good for the collectivity could not be determined a priori. This concept, contrary to what Aron defined as Jean-Paul Sartre's "moralism," implied a refusal of any type of philosophy that distinguished between good and bad and that tended to view the political opponent as embodying absolute evil. Choosing, as he said, the role of "King's counsel" over that of "confident of Providence," Aron based his constructions on the precept that the state and democracy could not be safeguarded by a political community that was lacerated by moralizing "holy wars."

A useful approach for understanding Aron's work, then, is to follow the rational line of his *engagement*, his preoccupation with the French political community, and the value of liberty that community expressed and guaranteed. Only in this way can the reader grasp the dialectic between the national and the supranational in his works. The term "supranationalism" has been used instead of others, such as internationalism or cosmopolitanism, since the latter do not express the notion that Aron felt himself to be above all a French citizen while at the same time able to overcome the simply nationalist viewpoint.[1] Aron's project went beyond national horizons; indeed he was one of the few postwar French intellectuals possessing sufficient cultural depth to see beyond the frontiers of the homeland. His intellectual formation was mainly derived from the German school of social thought, especially Max Weber and Karl Marx, for whom he had great admiration. He was sympathetic to the Anglophile school, and he made special reference to liberal social thinkers including Montesquieu, Alexis de Tocqueville, and Elie Halévy, declaring himself to be a late successor of these three.[2] Aron's cosmopolitanism was further broadened by his marked linguistic abilities: he studied German at school and then in Germany, while he learned English in his first few months in London during World War Two. This absence of language barriers gave him the opportunity to follow foreign debates, to publish numerous articles abroad, and to keep up important dialogues with the principal intellectuals of his times.[3] He also learned much from the ongoing developments in the social sciences, mainly an Anglo-American discipline at the time, against the backdrop of the Greek and Latin classics and the great thinkers of the nineteenth century.

This analysis concentrates on the postwar period, when Aron, for both personal and intellectual reasons, developed his reflections on national crisis. The problem of nationhood is an Ariadne's thread running through almost all of Aron's mature works, and we might understand better his activism in the 1940s and 1950s by following the evolution of this problem and his analyses of the international situation. The return to power of Charles de Gaulle in 1958 signaled not only an institutional change—the creation of the Fifth Republic—but also a return to a nationalistic vision on the question of European construction, a vision that contrasted the Fourth Republic's attitudes to foreign policy.

BEFORE THE WAR: GERMANY IN THE 1930S

To understand the development of Aron's thinking we must consider a change brought about by the expansion of national sentiment at the beginning of the 1930s. Aron's stay in Germany between 1930 and 1933 represented a turning point in his intellectual formation and self-conception. The historian must, of course, contextualize the importance of the stay in Germany in order to establish continuity between the student Aron who left for Cologne and the twenty-eight year old who came back three years later. At the same time, Aron's lifelong interest and commitment to the freedom of man were already apparent in these early years. In his own reconstruction of this period, he himself strictly connected his discovery of Germany with his discovery of politics.[4] He described his decision, both philosophical and existential, taken on the banks of the Rhine, regarding what would be his two main tasks in life: to understand his own times "as honestly as possible," never losing sight of the limitation of his knowledge; and to detach himself from what was going on around him without ever becoming a mere spectator, to be, in other words, a *spectateur engagé*.[5]

German philosophy was largely ignored at the Sorbonne in the 1920s when Aron studied there. His years of study at the École normale supérieure (1924–1928) were passed in the shadow of Léon Brunschvicg and Alain (Emile Chartier). The former, the mandarin of the Sorbonne during that period, interpreted Kantianism as a theory of knowledge. The latter was the guru of an entire generation of pacifists that had emerged after World War One. His opinion was that temporal power was a thankless necessity, though inevitable. Obeying temporal power was inevitable, but the first duty of the citizen was not to respect but to resist it. The resistance of individuals, all protesting against the abuses of administrators and the government, was a valid form of eternal resistance by the ruled against the rulers. What Brunschvicg and Alain had in common, apart from their strong morality, was their non-historical approach and belief in an immutable concept of man: for Brunschvicg, man caught in the act of knowing; for Alain, man caught in the act of his struggle against power. In Alain's politics, this non-historical approach was accompanied by a typically French supposition that the democracy of the Third Republic would endure.

The period Aron spent in Germany brought about an encounter with contemporary German philosophy, but also and crucially, an encounter with history, a shock Aron described using Toynbee's words: "History is again on the move." An emotional rejection of war and the conformation of the followers of Alain's ideology were gradually replaced by political reflection.[6] Certainly Aron's political activities during the 1920s had already revealed his interest in the subject and the desire to participate in the life of the *res publica*. The École normale supérieure years saw him in a more politicized light than his *petit camarade* and fellow student, Sartre. He participated in the Paris group of the Étudiants socialistes, and like the majority of non-Catholic Normaliens, he leaned toward the Left and declared himself a socialist.[7]

Aron's development can be charted by reading his articles between 1930 and 1933 in *Libres Propos*, the Alainist review. In the first of a series of "Lettre d'Allemagne," conscious of the tragic situation in Germany, he showed early signs of the state of uncertainty that would characterize those years, agonizing between pacifist ideals and the inability of those ideals to

provide a solution to Hitler. The young French *assistant* refused to acknowledge "the right of force" but understood that it was not clear "which
principles to apply in solving the international difficulty."[8] These first writings were characterized by a categorical "*non*" to war, pleas for disarmament, and calls for a revision of the Treaty of Versailles (erroneously
"founded on the sole guilt" of Germany) and for a reconciliation with
France's defeated neighbor based on equality of rights among nations.[9]
Faced with the spasms of the final years of the Weimar Republic, however,
he was led to reconsider his interpretation of politics. In his final articles
(1933) his doubts about disarmament became ever stronger; he was no
longer sure whether it was the solution that would lead to peace, or if rearmament was a surefire road to war. Aron was disillusioned with pacifist
and internationalist efforts, which he considered to have failed: "the pacifist
ideology, as an autonomous faith and moral will, has failed. Let us have the
courage to recognize this! Peace will be made notwithstanding everything,
we want to believe this and we shall, but it shall be first and foremost the
fruit of the politics of realism."[10]

His time in Germany, which has been described as a loss of innocence,
left its mark on Aron both intellectually and existentially.[11] He was able to
compare contemporary German thought, especially Weber's, with his
own, and to discover the struggle between his pacifist values and the
Hobbesian concept of international relations as *bellum omnium contra
omnes*. Moreover, firsthand experience of the final difficult years of the
Weimar Republic, with the "national revolution" of the Nazis brought before his very eyes the evidence of the aggressive aspects of German nationalism and the danger that Hitler represented to France, not only with
regard to her borders but to her very existence.[12] The discovery of the fact
that moral refusal of Nazism did not resolve the problem of its existence,
that politics was not morally based, was, however, to be taken hand-in-
hand with a distancing from the socialist and pacifist internationalism of
his student days.[13] He abandoned the idea of "an international understanding among the working class" as a main weapon against the absolute
evil of war.[14] This is not to suggest that Aron embraced a form of nationalism (as an alternative to "pacifism"), but that he gained a new appreciation for the relevance of the national aspect in politics. "The same deep
values moved me," he wrote about the 1930s, "but now we were dealing
with matters going beyond the Left or anti-fascism; we were dealing with
France and her salvation."[15]

Over the following years Aron still considered himself as leaning toward
the Left, and refused all compromises with the Right. The 1930s were for

Aron the years of French decadence: national interests were overcome by tumultuous passions. He indeed felt that France as such no longer existed, that its only expression of being was the hatred of one political faction for another.[16] Content in his private life—he was married and had his first child—the young philosophy professor was, however, desperate about the situation in his homeland and filled with obsessive dread of civil war and external threats. He was by now "cured" of internationalism based on pacifist and socialist ideology, but preoccupied by the problem of a France torn apart by ideologies. "I wish that intellectuals, who have inflicted much ill on France by encouraging civil hatred, would at last realize that the salvation of the homeland is just as important, indeed more important than the ideologies they exalt. It is perhaps too late to avert the catastrophe."[17]

DURING THE WAR

During World War Two and in the months immediately following the end of the hostilities, Aron, who regularly commented on war events, developed his own reflections on the changes in the international scene. This analysis was undertaken in the pages of *La France libre*, a magazine published in London. Aron had been appointed its chief secretary in late summer 1940 by director André Labarthe. This monthly review's aim was "national"; it supported the battle of the Français Libres who proclaimed their faith in the destiny of the homeland. At the same time, going beyond the question of a war among nations, the review spoke in universalistic tones and opposed the Nazis' "crusade of brute force" with a "crusade of ideas" fueled by democratic thinkers and societies.[18]

   The articles Aron regularly wrote for the review were aimed at helping his countrymen to take stock of the historical significance of the moment, to understand their place in the world, and also to formulate a draft reply to the overwhelming question: did France still have a future?[19] France would have to re-adapt its thinking and actions in a world that had completely changed, a world that would no longer tolerate attitudes of isolation in some nations.[20] In Aron's eyes France represented the crisis of the European nations: whereas national crisis in the nineteenth century had essentially been caused by domestic reasons, after the outbreak of World War Two, the French crisis was a particular case of the crisis of European nations.[21] The political and economic disadvantages of France could be held up as examples of an extreme form of backwardness that might be manifested in all European nation-states.

The changes brought about by the war had both strategic and political aspects. Above all they had led to unification in the diplomatic field. As the theater of war covered the whole planet, the European balance, to which the nations of the Old Continent had grown accustomed after the Peace of Westphalia (1648), was overtaken by a world balance, with no space remaining for localized or regional equilibrium, and by a diplomacy that covered all sectors of existence. This change was strictly interconnected with the transformation of the nature of war, beginning in 1914, from traditional to industrial and scientific: modern military weaponry needed very highly developed industrial and scientific approaches.[22] Only those nations able to unite material and human resources at very high technical levels would become main actors in what Aron, echoing Tocqueville, baptized in May 1945 *l'âge des empires,*" drawing on the European notion of empire as that which surpasses the cultural and linguistic community of the nation. After unification in the diplomatic field, a second salient characteristic of the international order that would emerge was the disappearance of the traditional distinction between diplomacy and politics. This was a consequence of Hitler's imperial plans: the Führer had reawakened national sentiment in the European peoples, but had also caused the Resistance to take on an ideological shape because in defeated countries internal regimes had been given power: "We are not struggling only against Germany; we are fighting against ideas."[23]

The question concerning France related therefore to the type of existence that nations would have in a totally reworked worldwide context. In the eyes of a European observer, the two new superpowers, the United States and the Soviet Union, were in fact entities that had gone beyond the political concept of nationhood in the sense that both were multinational. Aron knew very well that the nation, in the modern sense of the term, was a historical concept. Only since the French Revolution had a necessary coincidence between the cultural community and political unity been identified, bringing about the concept of nationhood. But even in this new worldwide context, the old European nations were not condemned to die. What had undermined the system between 1919 and 1939 was not so much the existence of nations as such, the division of the Old Continent into many distinct states, but rather the economic nationalism they had adopted. The principle of nationality was not in itself a guarantee of peace—contrary to the illusionary visions of the Treaty of Versailles—but, as in the nineteenth century, nor did it ineluctably lead to war or economic crisis. The principle of nationality could survive on one condition: that international organizations would be set up to coordinate the development of the various states and set down regulations to govern exchanges between them.

Within this conceptual framework it can be understood what new role the secretary of *La France libre* attributed to France in his writings. Noting that the foreign policy of a country had to be measured using the means it had at its disposal, because military potency depended on industrial wealth, the first urgent postwar task for France was to make internal reforms, both economic and political. France could thus avoid recreating a disproportionate relationship between international obligations and the human and material resources the country could call upon, as had been the case throughout the first half of the twentieth century. France, which had been the model for nation-states, and which now participated in their decline, had the mission of saving those nations, which would continue to be the political actors in the Old Continent, being a political and spiritual pivot around which the smaller nations would group together. This project would restore to France a *rayonnement* and influence of a high order, and the country would return to its position as a great power.[24] France would have two aims surpassing national confines: to restore to Europe a sense of unity, without sacrificing its rich and fertile inheritance of diversity; and to maintain the solidarity of the French Empire, since North Africa and, to a lesser extent, Western Africa were of fundamental importance to the future of a great power.

INTO THE COLD WAR

What prevented postwar analysis from being in line with analyses made during the war years was the decline and fall of what Aron himself described as "the fatal illusion of the victors, of believing that after the German problem there was no Russian problem."[25] In May 1945 he stated that although there was a divergence between the two conceptions of democracy possible in the twentieth century, represented, on the one hand, by the Soviet Union and, on the other hand, by the Anglo-Saxon model, de facto collaboration between these countries was possible.[26] A year later, after he had started writing for the daily publication, *Combat*, Aron insisted that any kind of international agreement now seemed inaccessible; the divisions between the ex-allies were such that there was even a risk of World War Three. "The world is no more united than our country. . . . Humanity no longer has the time to be joyful in the defeat of the Germanic Caesar, because it is already wondering about the possibility of a new Caesar."[27] There was absolutely no need for the contending powers to have a conscious will to dominate the other; it was sufficient that each suspected the other's intentions. Gradually, between 1945 and 1947, Aron shifted his explanation of the Soviet Union's isolation from one which indicated a structural factor—the Soviet Union's poverty in relation to Europe—to one which cited an ideological factor— that Stalin and his comrades, believing that no peaceful coexistence could exist between capitalism and communism, reasoned with a Marxist logic that envisaged the destruction of the capitalist system. Thus Russia was preparing for the conflict that would decide the future of the world.[28] The ideological factor remained a constant in Aron's analysis of international politics, as in one of his most famous theoretical works, *Paix et guerre entre les nations* (1962).[29]

However, the absence of peace did not necessarily mean war. For this reason Aron defined the postwar situation in 1946 using the term "bellicose peace."[30] The dividing-up of the world between the two superpowers, which was the basis of peace, was made impossible by the fear that each power had of the other. At the same time, neither Washington nor Moscow had any determined desire for a bloody war, which would have been total war and total destruction. Thus, in Aron's opinion, "peace was impossible, but war was improbable."[31]

This was the new context in which Aron was attempting to find a place for the nation. In 1946–1947, the main problem emerging from his analyses, first in *Combat* and then in *Le Figaro*, was the laceration of the body of the nation: the nations of Europe were now Balkanized. It was not by chance that his first book published after the war was entitled *Le Grand Schisme* (1948). Communist parties were conceived as being different from other parties. They were the fifth columnists of a foreign power that dictated political policy to them, so when a communist party came to power, for the Americans it was equivalent to an expansion of the Soviet zone.

The presence of a strong Communist Party in France in the postwar period—the Parti communiste français achieved more than twenty-five percent in all national elections during the Fourth Republic, thus being the biggest party in terms of votes—meant that there was no national community, as the citizens were not in agreement over the country's vocation, nor over where to stand in a war scenario, nor even over the principles of social and political order.[32] The Bolshevik parties, which as a precept required solidarity with the elective homeland, the Soviet Union, over and above adhesion to the de facto homeland, France, were machines of civil war. "By definition the Communist Party is not a party like the others. It provisionally suppresses its revolutionary will, but is not changed for this reason. It is a half-warlike sect; it sees in the exercise of power a step toward total possession of the state."[33]

The liberal state, which Europe had come to know during the nineteenth and twentieth centuries, was a very rare phenomenon in overall historical terms and had become possible only through the triumph of the national state. Only when national identity had prevailed over other identities in the minds of the citizens had the state succeeded in becoming a *supra partes* entity. Consequently, democracy could function only among citizens and parties who had fully accepted its methodologies. While a large Communist Party was exercising an influence on the political system, French democracy would find itself adapting its ideals to a situation of diplomatic and ideological schism: "A communist, by dint of this very fact, subordinates the commands of the Republican state to those of his party. . . . The French Communists are not citizens of the Fourth Republic; we cannot be citizens of the French Soviet Republic (and they would never give us the time to hesitate). They betray our France; we would betray their France."[34]

Aron's analysis of the international constellation in terms of schism led him to identify the need, both for individuals and for nations, to choose between "the universe of free countries and the universe subjected to crude Soviet law."[35] This choice was a total one, just as the diplomacy of the second half of the twentieth century was total. Neutralism was not only an illusion, but blindness: starting from the recognition that the European states were not on the same level as the United States or the Soviet Union, and that, as Communists themselves admitted, if you were not with the USSR, you were against it, it was perfectly impossible to avoid this radical political choice. By refuting one of the two centers of power one was perforce obliged to work together with the other. Both superpowers saw the situation in these terms.[36] From his analysis of the internal and international situation of France, Aron coherently chose the Atlantic alliance, and remained faithful to it to the end of his life, as the Soviet risk, though modified over time, was still there at his death.

His sense of urgency in relation to the need to line up with the Atlantic camp also led to his joining the Rassemblement du peuple français (RPF), the party founded by Charles de Gaulle on April 7, 1947.[37] The RPF, in Aron's eyes, was the only party present on the French scene that had fully understood the polarizing international situation and the need to reform French democracy. "There was the classic parliamentary conception that even today maintains that traditional parliamentary mechanisms can be used to guide the economy. And then there are others who say: to govern a modern society, especially in the face of a Communist opposition, another governmental method is needed."[38] The RPF pursued a revision of the constitution in favor of a more solid organization of executive power, in contrast with the practices of the Fourth Republic, which was characterized by weak and unstable governments. Alongside this proposed reform, which would reinforce the effectiveness of French democracy and thus provide a domestic bulwark against communism, was added a clear preference for the Atlantic alliance, a choice made by De Gaulle between 1947 and 1953, and in clear contrast with other French governments, who had sought to mediate between East and West. Historians have now reconstructed the "Atlantic" choice made by the RPF.[39]

Aron's position was confirmed in his defense of the Atlantic Treaty, declared in the columns of *Le Figaro* in 1949 against neutralists such as Étienne Gilson. Europe was not able to rearm alone and therefore had no protection against the Soviet threat if not that offered by the United States.[40] At the same time Aron did not mean that Europe should be completely dominated by the United States. Europe was an ally, not a satellite, of the United States and should resist falling victim to the risk of passively accepting American power and, at the same time, should avoid the total refusal of alliance typical of neutralists.[41] Conceiving of the world as being divided into two blocks meant placing the fact of safety in the collectivity before independence of choice in foreign policy.

IN THE SEARCH FOR EUROPE

In the new international context, France was a second-level entity, having "lost control over its own destiny"; it was destined to "express the disputes of the universe rather than shape them." Aron knew that it would not be easy to get used to this new status, but he felt it was necessary.[42] In 1946, the search for a solution to the crisis of the European nations meant, for many, an approach to a supranational reordering. The crisis was, therefore, at the origin of the "demand for a Europe." In *Le Figaro*, Aron wrote that this was the first time a politically serious expression had been given to this idea. Politicians, the masses, and intellectuals all felt "that European unity, in a way that still needs to be shaped, represents one of the necessities of the age."[43] A supranational demand did not mean, however, that the answer was readily available. First, there could not be a rigorous delimitation of the idea of Europe, from either a historical or geographical point of view. Europe had never been a political unit; in the Middle Ages it had a vague consciousness of its unity and vocation, without seeing itself as being able to tend toward unity as a continent. "Maybe there exists a Europe *in se*," Aron wrote in a purely Hegelian idiom, "there is certainly not a Europe *per se*."[44]

World War Two had made the feeling of apartness and single nationhood among the states more acute. The division of Europe into around twenty independent nations (or who believed themselves independent) was a fundamental reality in the postwar period.

For Aron, that nationality should be the exclusive subject of European political life was an excessive statement: Europe had always had the concept of a cultural community, and Aron defined the originality of Europe as a sort of dialectic, stretched between two opposing terms—the single nation and the supranational community. "This means that Europeans deny their true vocation when they attempt to radicalize in one of the two concepts but can justify this only in terms of opposition to the other," he wrote.[45] In the definition of Europe, it was not possible either to affirm that Europe should become a unit—because there was neither the will to unite nor a consciousness of unity—or to deny that this should be so—because there was really and truly the draft copy of a unity, a certain number of common cultural threads drawing the continent together.

Between 1946 and 1948, however, the reply he gave to the question of the crisis of nationhood changed, becoming more pro-European. In a cycle of conferences held at the École nationale d'administration in Paris in November 1946—just a few weeks after Winston Churchill had spoken of the need to recreate the "European family"—Aron declared himself skeptical about building a European unit independent of both Russia and the United States. First of all, he realized that the two superpowers would raise strong objections to the creation of a European unity. Then, the internal situation in each nation was not favorable to this unity, as there were no representatives of a European idea as such and the concept of European patriotism simply did not exist. In order to build a European union there would have to be a power capable of creating a federation, and such a power simply did not yet exist.[46] Thus in 1946 his historical-political analysis led him to see Europe as condemned to remain divided into single nations.

The Marshall Plan, announced on June 5, 1947, changed the whole scene that had given birth to Aron's concept of European union. A fundamental piece at the base of Aron's analysis at the end of 1946 was now gone: it was no longer true that both superpowers were opposed to a European unity; in fact one of them was actively promoting it. Aron was very much in favor of American help, in order to resuscitate the French economy rapidly without imposing privations on the French people that were too rigorous.[47] The other fundamental aspect of the Marshall Plan was the appeal for common European action. It demonstrated the willingness of the United States to sustain a process of European integration. It opened to France and Europe vast horizons, capable of re-awakening enthusiasm and opposing the universalism which, notwithstanding his nationalistic tactics, Stalin's communism vaunted as the good moral aim. And in the long run, a customs union offered Europe its last chance for prosperity. Thus the best chance for Europe of attaining real autonomy through unity lay in following the impulse that came from across the Atlantic Ocean.

Aron knew that this unity could not be achieved in a few weeks or months.[48] Recognizing the daunting difficulties hindering its realization, he insisted its opponents had not understood the degree of misery, if not an unstoppable decline, a closure of the frontiers would inflict on the European nations.[49] Within this "consciousness of necessity" there lay a paradox: the desire for European unity contained a kind of admission of Europe's misfortune, linked to "what each of us feels most deeply, that is, national passion."[50] This desire for unity was born of reason rather than sentiment, of conscious recognition of a necessity rather than common passion, since European patriotism did not exist (existing supranational sentiment was, generally speaking, connected to ideologies). It was to be hoped that one day a European passion would emerge and would replace reason as the motivating force for unity. Aron did not think that unification of Europe was incompatible with traditional patriotism. Europeans would not be asked to forget their own nations. Instead they would be invited to recognize, little by little, the reality and value of a greater structure, and would consent to certain decisions being made by a European commission, over and above national governments. Europe as a reality needed to exist in the hearts of its citizens.[51]

In 1947–1948 Aron sought to identify an idealistic impulse that would sustain the idea of Europe, replacing the mere impotence of nations and the economic advantages offered by integration of a large territory. He ascribed to Europe an anti-totalitarian role: totalitarianism was not compatible with the European spirit in its most authentic form.[52] The conditions in which the European nations found themselves, materially and morally exhausted by the war, were favorable to the rise of totalitarianism, which in the postwar period was embodied by communism. The Soviet communist regime represented anew the Machiavellian mechanism of Nazism—ends justifying the use of any means.[53]

Aron was forced to concede, though, that "beyond economic utility and a vague resistance to Soviet influence, we haven't a lot of cards to play with."[54] The difficulty of his position is obvious: he was maintaining that the main task of Europeans was to give a sense to "being European" in order to avoid becoming satellites of either Russia or America, but at the same time he was unable to define a concept in the name of which Europe could be constructed. Furthermore, he could not find a political entity to whom this task could be entrusted, believing that the birth of ideas and passions necessary to unite Western Europe was more difficult to achieve than a necessary economic unity.

In sum, the construction of Europe and the question of the future of Germany were to be understood in the context of the Cold War. Europe to the west of the Iron Curtain would strongly resist any impulse to become Sovietized, to avoid both economic decline and the establishment of a political police. Since it could in no way remain neutral without re-arming, Europe would have need of American defense, the only deterrent as long as it could not defend itself from Soviet attack.[55] At the same time, since the ideal for the nations of Europe within the Western world was to gain the maximum level possible of independence or autonomy, it seemed probable to Aron that the countries outside the Soviet sphere would achieve this best by consenting to a certain form of unity rather than by closing in on themselves. The need to overcome nationalism in a world dominated by two powers meant, for Aron, building Europe within an Atlantic perspective, quite distinct from any concept of the Old Continent as a Third Power.

Aron's united Europe, however, did not at all coincide with the concept expressed by the European federalists—the many movements and associations that flourished in the late 1940s—as it was more pessimistic than theirs. The Europe envisaged by them simply was not possible to achieve. Only after common institutions had been constructed could a European sentiment be born. Furthermore, Aron's "construction of Europe" was essentially moderate. Apart from his writings, we can see this from the associations he belonged to in support of the idea of Europe. For example, he adhered to the French Committee for a United Europe [Comité français pour l'Europe unie] and later to the Executive French Committee of the European Movement [Comité exécutif français du mouvement européen]. The former was organized by René Courtin, co-director of *Le Monde*, and was affiliated with the "United Europe Movement" inspired by Churchill and considerably more moderate than the continental federalist movements: the European nations must decide simply to "*coordinate* their political and economic activities."[56]

AN ATTEMPT AT INTEGRATION: THE EUROPEAN DEFENSE COMMUNITY

In 1949 Aron recognized that the revolution needed by the nations of the Old Continent to transform the European economic zone into a wide area of free circulation of goods, men, and capital, regulated by a federal authority—this revolution had not come about in any meaningful way, since the two main obstacles had not been overcome: British hesitation and French chaos.[57] The Organization for European Economic Cooperation had put both liberal integration and interventionist liberation to the test, and both had failed because each national government had continued to concentrate its powers on its own interests, in monetary and customs policy and also in investment planning.[58] The disappointment caused by the nationalist egotism in the European political circles brought Aron to welcome the Schuman Plan as a "third way" for overcoming the obstacles impeding structural unification. It placed supranational power, in a limited field (coal and steel), at the level of a high authority appointed by national governments but independent from them. The unity of the continent became a long-term desirable objective, but not an indispensable condition for European resurgence.[59]

In another field, however, in Aron's opinion, European integration was becoming even more urgent, namely, the military. The Korean War, which broke out in June 1950, imposed a change in military attitudes. In the climate of fear of a further global conflict—even Aron wondered whether the years preceding the Cold War had been a preparation rather than a substitute for total war—the rearmament of Europe became the prime question in the Atlantic relationship. Technology made some form of European integration necessary in the military field: in fact, the research and manufacturing of arms needed to put an army on the field would cost more than any of the European nations could afford. So Aron applauded talk of an integration of laboratories, military schools, and the general staff and armies of the "Little Europe" of six nations (France, Germany, Italy, the Netherlands, Belgium, and Luxembourg). This was the only field in which a transfer of sovereignty could be achieved, although the transfer of sovereign power should depend less on the definition of common institutions than on concrete collaboration, which would be followed by integration of military institutions.[60]

European rearmament invoked the question of the participation of Germany in the defense of Europe, raising the thorny problem of French people's acceptance of an old enemy's rearmament. To remove this obstacle, on October 24, 1950, the French prime minister, René Pleven, drew up a plan for a European army: the European Defense Community (EDC). In his plan, the German contingent would be split up and integrated into European divisions, formed and equipped by a supranational European organization, a body formed by nine commissars entrusted to enact policies decided by the EDC counsel of ministers and placed under Atlantic command in Europe.[61] Aron, who since 1947 had insisted on the necessity of an authentic reconciliation between France and Germany, immediately supported the idea of German rearmament, since a Europe without Germany would be undefended and prey to Russian aggression.[62] Thus, initially, he approved of Pleven's proposal.[63]

It was not long, however, before aspects of the Pleven plan came out that attracted Aron's criticism. He realized that the projected European army meant that French sovereignty would be damaged, principally by a European administration, following the orders of an American general. The very authorities that considered themselves supranational were in fact without the necessary powers to be authoritative. Furthermore, a true federal unification presupposed a common foreign policy among the members of the federation. In France's case this would have created special problems regarding the relations between the French Union (the ex-empire) and the *métropole* (territorial France in Europe). Once France had entered the federation of "the Six" it could have conserved rights and responsibilities in the territories of the union, but the resulting dualism in foreign policy and in the management of the army would have been difficult to reconcile with a federal army. The alternative solution involved extending powers of European authority to the overseas territories. Aron held that the public was not ready to sacrifice the old empire for the sake of "the Six." French autonomy in foreign policy was still too attached to the French Union and to the possibility of "radiance" [*rayonnement*] in international politics offered by overseas possessions. The political idea of European unity clashed with the reality of the French Union.

Moreover, Aron believed in the essentiality of a federal construction that would obtain citizens' support. The lack of a moral pact, a community sentiment among the peoples of "the Six," would undermine the federation at its base. "Constitutions have never been sufficient to create sentiments," Aron said pointedly, "They can precede sentiments, but excessive anticipation causes the risk of failure of the entire enterprise."[64] The tasks Aron assigned to a united Europe (coordinating diplomatic action, creating a free trade zone, and exorcizing memories of a tragic past) did not imply the need for a federal government, which would have required unification of foreign policy—not possible—and moral cohesion—nonexistent. Thus, Aron supported a project for a European army that would maintain technical integration within Europe, would set aside the national aspects of the military administrations, and would reduce the supranational powers of the European Commissariat.[65]

Notwithstanding his doubts, when in August 1954 the EDC Treaty was debated before the French National Assembly, Aron was worried that it might be thrown out and, once this had happened, feared that the defeat of the EDC would become the symbol of defeat for all attempts to achieve European integration. This eventuality would cause a crisis in the Atlantic coalition by favoring the American party least supportive of military involvement in Europe as well as giving fuel to the neutralist tendencies in France. Aron also feared this would lead to a dispute over the German contribution to the defense of Europe.[66] Thus, he wanted the EDC Treaty to be approved by the French National Assembly. It was not. His fears, though, were allayed by the Paris Agreements of October 1954, which cleared the way for West German entry into the Atlantic Alliance.

NATION BETWEEN DECOLONIZATION AND THE END OF IDEOLOGIES

During 1953 and 1954, France faced up to the possibility of dissolution of the French Union, first with the bloody end to the war in Indochina (1954), then with the granting of independence to Tunisia and Morocco (1956). The process of decolonization would change the international status of France as well as the perception the country had of itself. The claims of the African and Asian nations against their colonizers were based on the very European concept of nationality. For this reason the dissolution of the empires of the European nations, in Aron's opinion, was inscribed in reality. Beyond the fact of whether each single nation had agreed voluntarily to the independence of its colonies or not, the empires were transitory precisely because the nations of the Old Continent were based on the national ideal and could only partially divorce themselves from it.[67] The European empires and the consequent decolonization had therefore a different meaning from the empires of the past and the empire built by the czar and inherited by the Bolsheviks.

The France of the Fourth Republic did not go peacefully into the phase of decolonization. Though one must not understate the extent of the wounds inflicted by the war in Indochina, it was principally the Algerian War, which broke out at the end of 1954, that placed the very existence of the Fourth Republic in jeopardy. Our overview of the national-supranational relationship in Aron's thinking helps explain the strong position he took up from the beginning of the Algerian War and which caused scandal in the right-wing parties, from the Gaullists to the Mouvement républicain populaire and beyond.[68] The politics of "pacification" adopted by Minister Robert Lacoste excluded liberalism, that is, respect for human rights. This meant going against the identity of the French political community, which recognized human rights as fundamental. For this reason France was acting in bad faith when it pursued the Algerian insurgents, the Front de libération nationale rebels. At the same time, France was divided by the conflict, between those who felt that continuing the repression was in contrast with French identity and those who saw Algeria as an integral part of the nation. The conflict brought France to the very brink of civil war, and placed the French community in jeopardy, because it touched on the question of identity. Whatever decision the government took went against half its citizens.

Unlike the 1930s, during which he had been unable to warn French opinion on the risk of Nazism, now Aron, professor of sociology at the Sorbonne since 1955, promoted the idea that Algeria was not part of France. Integration of Algerians into the French body politic was impracticable: the population of the *métropole* and the population of Algeria (apart from the Algerian residents of French ancestry, the *pieds-noirs*) did not belong to the same "demographic type," nor were they at the same economic level. "Algeria is not part of France, must not be so, cannot be so: excess of population, poverty, make of it an underdeveloped country which must be treated as such."[69] French legislation could not be applied to a population that was socially, economically, and culturally different from the country for which the legislation had been devised. French advocates of remaining in Algeria should be aware of these facts. Integration presupposed a stronger state and supranational ideology that France simply did not possess. In the dissolution of the European empires, Aron saw a whole new future prospect opening up: the triumph of the nation and the recognition of the right of all peoples to take their place in universal society and to govern themselves. In the longer run, communist totalitarianism could even be overturned by the same kinds of nationalistic claims; even the supranationalism at the base of its philosophy might be cast into doubt by the emergence of the new spirit of African and Asian nationalism.

Acceptance of decolonization did not mean that Aron no longer believed in France's African "mission." He clearly stated: "I believe in the African vocation of France," going on to specify that France's duty was to spread its beliefs and culture, but that this was not compatible with a refusal on France's part to recognize Africans' right to self-government.[70] What future awaited the European nations after the independence of the colonies? Europe did not necessarily have to abdicate all pretenses to *grandeur*, since it was power, not wealth, that was gravely hurt by loss of empire and the formation of new nation-states. European nations could be historically great without returning to great power status. Their size precluded them from aspiring to positions of prime importance, but they were big enough to function as industrial civilizations, self-conscious enough to be tolerant of differences, and rich enough to support dialogue among free men. They were close to the "realization of the idea of industrial civilization" and were ahead of other nations in this consciousness and development.[71]

The way in which Aron conceived of the future of the European nations in the second half of the 1950s is strictly connected with his elaborations on the theme of the end of ideologies, the historical exhaustion of the ideological systems.[72] He dealt with this theme in *L'Opium des intellectuels* (1955). Based on the hypothesis that the Marxist-Leninist interpretation of history was losing its momentum in the context of the transformations occurring in the Western-style or capitalist societies, no other ideological system would remain to replace it, not even a nation-based ideology, at least in Europe.

The United States and the USSR had (in very different ways) suppressed ideological debate, integrating workers and imposing unanimous adhesion to the principles of the city.[73] Coexistence, inaugurated by Nikita Khruschev's speech at the Twentieth Congress of the Soviet Communist Party in 1956, and the emergence of liberation movements in Asia and Africa, which confounded the bipolar logic of the Cold War, brought Aron to hypothesize the end of the era of ideologies at the international level.[74]

Concerning the sphere of internal politics within a nation, in the West public and private property, state-planned and market economies, were now combined as much as opposed. Treating property or market systems as absolute goods or radical evils was becoming more and more difficult. If none of the social actors were strongly ideological, if all of them sought reasonable solutions to problems, then according to widely accepted objectives, politics became removed from ideology and moved toward pragmatism (although the most pragmatic political approach was inspired, in the final analysis, by values, ideals, or principles).[75]

In Aron's view the real discriminating element among twentieth-century societies was the distinction between stationary economies and industrial economies, and not between collective property and private property. Countries with a highly developed industrial civilization were societies in which collective resources increased year after year, rather than being approximately fixed, as in stationary economies. In industrial economies the old question of social class was transformed; it was commonly accepted that increased productivity was useful to all, the standard of living of the masses depending on economic expansion rather than on laws governing redistribution of income. This situation had repercussions for politics, since it opened a space, not for a general agreement, but for debates between Left and Right, planners and liberals, radicals and traditionalists.[76]

Aron made a distinction between highly developed democracies that were "at peace with themselves" [*apaisées*], like Great Britain, the United States, and Germany, and those which were "lacerated" [*déchirées*], such as France and Italy. The latter had a "Weimar-type" political scene: the regime had to face up to a double opposition, sandwiched between communism, on one side, and the anti-parliamentary right-wing, on the other side. Lacerated democracies presented ideological conflicts that were typical of socially heterogeneous countries, in which industrial civilization still had to win over "the resistances born from social inertia." Aron wrote, "The more the diversity of the real problems prevents the formation of two parties, the more the theorists are inclined to substitute abstract antitheses for the complexities of the interests in question. . . . Ideological transfiguration of debates is contemporary to the first steps of industrialization."[77] However, in the daily business of politics, the classic Left and Right parties were able to collaborate over decolonization, management of an expanding economy, and the formulation of social laws. Verbal extremism, arguments, attitudes of obstinate opposition, all tended to hide both from the public and from the politicians themselves the fact that there was agreement, only half-conscious, over what was seen as inevitable.

According to Aron, many of the tasks France in the final years of the Fourth Republic ought to have performed had a meaning above and beyond the confines of the nation: organizing an authentic community of French and Muslims in North Africa, uniting the nations of Western Europe so that they would be less dependent on American power, and making up for lost time in the economy. None of these tasks, however, would make France into a champion of ideals, and none would have the apparent universality of the socialist or nationalist ideologies. "By putting our country in its true place on the planet, and acting according to the teachings of the social sciences," he commented, "we would reach the only politically universal situation acceptable in our times."[78]

Aron therefore criticized the attitudes of French intellectuals homesick for the universal idea and national pride. Even if nationalist ideology was doomed, at least in Europe, patriotic sentiment must remain the cement of the collectivity, and a government should defend the interests and rights of the country against a too-invasive influence of allies. Nonetheless, Aron asked, "Is it possible to exalt the temporal greatness of a collectivity when it is incapable of manufacturing its own arms?"[79]

Following these arguments, he approved of the Common Market, founded by the Treaty of Rome in 1957, because it responded to the logic of the historical process he saw underway. He nevertheless held that what would determine the future of Europe was not the form of cooperation among the countries of Western Europe, but the responses Europe would give to three challenges: resistance to the Soviet empire and, one day, the liberation of Eastern Europe; supply and production of raw materials and energy; and the maintaining of good relations between Europe and its ex-colonies or, more generally, with the underdeveloped world. The federal state, whose creation in the long run was implied by the Common Market, did not directly respond to any of these three challenges, but was justified to the extent that its existence provided the chance for a positive response to them.[80]

LOOKING AHEAD TO THE FIFTH REPUBLIC

The return of General de Gaulle to power in 1958 meant a return to the classical concept of foreign policy, in which nationalistic interests counted more than ideologies in conducting of diplomacy. France moved into a new era. The framework of the diplomacy of the 1960s and 1970s was, for Aron, unchanged: since 1945 there had been neither peace nor war in Europe; the victors of World War Two could not reach agreement but had no wish to go to war directly. Especially after 1962 the common interest of the United States and the USSR to maintain their own nuclear arms and their own powers in their relative spheres of influence became utterly clear. France and China sought to oppose this, by abandoning the policy of non-proliferation and dependency in military matters. De Gaulle could not accept the partition of Europe and the apparent world stability, which did much to consecrate the dominion of the Soviet Union and the United States. He could not accept the existence of two "empires" over and above nations.

The erosion of ideological dogmatism, even in the face of the events of 1968, which Aron interpreted as a "crisis of civilization" and not as the rise of a new ideological system, was accompanied by a certain resuscitation of national passions: "the concept, the idea, the reality, or the myth of the nation (and not of social class) dominates the twentieth century," he noted.[81] Aron, though, feared a return to nationalistic diplomacy. The reality of an

Old Continent, which, thanks also to De Gaulle, was irremediably divided and incapable of deciding on a policy to follow, had to be overcome. The mission of European countries in Aron's view was to provide the example of nations overcoming problems without selling out, nations that could dissociate consciousness of their own cultural specificity and their desire for power. He augured that cooperation among European countries would eventually form a sort of confederate state. Europe had tasks to perform: definitive liquidation of the consequences of World War Two, in other words, re-unification of Germany; realization of a common and coordinated political approach to the Soviet sphere, the United States, and the Third World; and a safeguarding of liberal institutions and the maintenance of high economic growth. Europe would not return to being one of the main players on the international scene, but it was duty-bound to contribute to the formation of a universal society and to aid the diffusion of the social formula expressed by an industrial society with a liberal-democratic system.

NOTES

1. The problem assumes a deeper meaning still for a Jewish intellectual such as Aron, as the foundation of Israel posed, even for "integrated" Jews, the problem of belonging to two nations. For Aron, the question emerged in his writing only when Charles de Gaulle's foreign policy contrasted with that of Israel during the 1960s; this is therefore beyond the scope of the present article.

2. Raymond Aron, *Les Etapes de la pensée sociologique* (Paris: Gallimard, 1967), 21, 295.

3. Nicolas Baverez, *Aron* (Paris: Flammarion, 1993), 75.

4. Aron, *Mémoires: 50 ans de réflexion politique* (Paris: Julliard, 1983), 67.

5. Aron, *Mémoires*, 53.

6. Aron, *Mémoires*, 55.

7. Jean-François Sirinelli, "Aron avant Aron (1923–1933)," *Vingtième siècle: revue d'histoire* 2 (1984): 22–23.

8. Aron, "Lettre d'Allemagne," *Libres Propos* (1930): 570.

9. On disarmament, see Aron, "Simples propositions du pacifisme," *Libres Propos* (1931): 81–83. On reconciliation with Germany, see Aron, "Lettre d'Allemagne," *Libres Propos* (1931): 138–140.

10. Aron, "Désarmement ou union franco-allemande?" *Libres Propos* (1932): 424.

11. Jean-François Sirinelli, *Deux intellectuels dans le siècle, J.-P. Sartre et R. Aron* (Paris: Fayard, 1995), 115.

12. Aron, "La révolution nationale en Allemagne," *Europe* (1933): 125–38.

13. Aron wrote, "Le problème politique n'est pas un problème moral." Aron, "Réflexions sur le pacifisme intégral," *Libres Propos* (1933): 96–99.

14. Sirinelli, *Deux intellectuels dans le siècle*, 61.

15. Aron, *Mémoires*, 81.

16. Aron, *L'etica della libertà: memorie di mezzo secolo: colloqui con Jean-Louis Missika e Dominique Wolton*, trans. M. Le Cannu (Milano: Mondadori, 1981), 68.

17. Letter from Aron to Jean Paulhan (15 March 1938). Institut mémoires de l'édition contemporaine, Paris, Fonds Jean Paulhan, PLH2.C4-03.07.

18. [Leading article, no title], *La France libre* 1 (1940): 3.

19. The majority of Aron's articles for *La France libre* are collected in *Chroniques de guerre: La France libre 1940–1945* (Paris: Gallimard, 1990).

20. Aron, "Remarques sur la politique étrangère de la France," in *Chroniques de guerre*, 968.

21. Aron, "Signification des problèmes français," in *Chroniques de guerre*, 891.

22. Aron, "Conclusion," in *Chroniques de guerre*, 420.

23. Aron, "Destin des nationalités," in *Chroniques de guerre*, 612–13. Aron, "La stratégie totalitaire et l'avenir des démocraties," in *Chroniques de guerre*, 571.

24. Aron, "Redevenir une grande puissance," in *Chroniques de guerre*, 746.

25. Aron, "Du gaullisme au RPF," in *Les Conséquences sociales de la guerre*, Cours au Collège libre des sciences sociales et économiques (1948), inédit. Archives Raymond Aron, École des hautes études en sciences sociales, Paris, AP 3, 7. The author thanks Madame Dominique Schnapper for having given permission to consult and use unpublished papers in the Archives Aron.

26. Aron, "L'âge des empires," in *Chroniques de guerre*, 975–76. In the August 1945 *Point de vue*, Aron declared himself to be greatly disappointed by the Potsdam agreements and denounced the bipolar clash that would follow. Again in November of the same year he had refused a bipolar alignment along the lines of communism/anti-communism.

27. Aron, "Anniversaire," *Combat*, 14 May 1946.

28. Aron, "Le monde déchiré," in *Trente ans d'histoire: de Clemenceau à de Gaulle, 1918–1948* (Paris: Editions Sant'Andréa, 1949), 334.

29. Aron, *Paix et guerre entre les nations* (Paris: Calmann-Lévy, 1962; repr. 1984), 108–13.

30. Aron, "La paix belliqueuse," *Promotions: revue de l'École nationale d'administration* 3 (1946); repr. in *Commentaire* 76 (1996).

31. Aron, "Stupide résignation," *Le Figaro*, 21–22 September 1947; and *Le Grand Schisme* (Paris: Gallimard, 1948).

32. Aron, "Stupide résignation," 174. Charles de Gaulle, in a 27 July 1947 speech at Rennes, explained that national unity was in danger due to "a group of men whose leaders place service toward a foreign state above all other things," qualifying communists as "separatists." De Gaulle, *Discours et messages: dans l'attente, février 1946–avril 1958* (Paris: Plon, 1970), 98.

33. Aron, "L'unique problème," *Combat*, 3–4 November 1946.

34. Aron, "La cité déchirée, l'Etat et les communistes," *Le Figaro*, 11 April 1948.

35. Aron, "La fin des illusions," *Le Figaro*, 5 July 1947.

36. Aron, "La structure de la politique mondiale et le destin de l'Europe," in Aron, *Les Conséquences sociales de la guerre*, 7.

37. De Gaulle did not call the RPF a "party." For a reconstruction of the RPF affair, see Jean Charlot, *Le Gaullisme d'opposition 1946–1958* (Paris: Fayard, 1983).

38. Aron, "Du gaullisme au RPF," in Aron, *Les Conséquences sociales de la guerre*, 19.

39. Gaetano Quagliariello, "Prospettiva atlantica e prospettiva europea nel pensiero e nell'azione di Charles de Gaulle," in *Atlantismo e europeismo*, eds. Piero Craveri and Gaetano Quagliariello (Soveria Mannelli: Rubbettino, 2003).

40. Aron, "Le Pacte Atlantique," *Liberté de l'esprit* 3 (1949): 52–54.

41. Aron, "Allies-Not Satellites!" *American Mercury* 345 (1952): 10–14.

42. Aron, "Stupide résignation."

43. Aron, *Y a-t-il une civilisation européenne?* Savennières, semaines étudiantes internationales, 5 août 1947. Archives Aron, inédit, 1.

44. Aron, "Discours à des étudiants allemands sur l'avenir de l'Europe," *La Table ronde* 1 (1948): 66. Aron did not agree with Denis de Rougemont who, in his work *Vingt-huit siècles d'Europe* (Paris: Payot, 1961), stated that Europe is much older than its nations.

46. Aron, *Perspectives sur l'avenir de l'Europe, conférence donnée à l'École nationale d'administration (26 et 27 Novembre 1946)*, inédit, Archives Aron, AP 1: Ière journée, 31.

47. Aron, "La fin des illusions."

48. Aron, "Responsabilité historique," *Le Figaro*, 31 August 1947.

49. Aron, "Le Plan Marshall est-il artificiel?" *Le Figaro*, 4 October 1947.

50. Aron, *Y a-t-il une civilisation européenne?* 3–4.

51. Aron, *France and Europe* (Hinsdale, Ill.: Henri Regnery Company, 1949), 23.

52. Aron, "Discours à des étudiants," 76.

53. Aron, "Vers un nouveau reniement?" *Le Figaro*, 10 December 1947.

54. Aron, *Y a-t-il une civilisation européenne?* 14.

55. Aron, "Le Pacte Atlantique," 53.

56. Archives Michel Debré, Fondation nationale des sciences politiques, Paris, 1DE 25. Jean-Pierre Gouzy, "I movimenti per l'unità europea in Francia," in *I movimenti per l'unità europea dal 1945 al 1954*, ed. Sergio Pistone (Milano: Jaca Book, 1992), 68.

57. Aron, "Plan Marshall et unité européenne," *Le Figaro*, 1 November 1949.

58. Aron, "L'unité économique de l'Europe," *La Revue libre* 2 (1952): 18–19.

59. Aron, "L'unité économique," 21. His approval of the European Coal and Steel Community did not prevent Aron from criticizing it.

60. Aron, *Les Guerres en chaîne* (Paris: Gallimard, 1951), 414.

61. Georges-Henri Soutou, *La Guerre des cinquante ans: les relations Est-Ouest 1943–1990* (Paris: Fayard, 2001), 248.

62. Aron, "Le réarmement de l'Allemagne," *Le Figaro*, 16 September 1950.

63. Aron, "L'armée européenne: un pari sur l'avenir qu'on ne peut refuser," *Le Figaro*, 17 September 1951.

64. Aron, "Ce que peut être la fédération des Six," *Le Figaro*, 4 December 1952.

65. Aron, "A propos de l'unité de l'Europe: la dialectique du politique et de l'économique," *Mitteilungen der List Gesellschaft E.V.* 11–12 (1957): 274.

66. Aron, "La fin de la CED ne doit pas être la fin de l'Europe," *Le Figaro*, 3 September 1954.

67. Aron, "La désagrégation des empires," *Pensée française* 1 (1956): 23.

68. Jean-Pierre Rioux and Jean-François Sirinelli, *La Guerre d'Algérie et les intellectuels français* (Bruxelles: Editions Complexe, 1991), 120.

69. Aron, *La Tragédie algérienne* (Paris: Plon, 1957), 43–44.

70. Aron, *La Tragédie algérienne*, 50–51.

71. Aron, "La désagrégation des empires," 25.

72. This debate developed especially in the United States in the second half of the 1950s and in the early 1960s. See Chaim J. Waxman, ed., *The End of Ideology Debate* (New York: Funk & Wagnalls, 1968).

73. Aron, *L'Opium des intellectuels* (Paris: Calmann-Lévy, 1955), 324.

74. Aron, "Coexistence: The End of Ideology," *Partisan Review* 25 (1958): 230–40. Aron reaffirmed that there was no reason to believe that the Soviet strategy had changed or that Khrushchev had abandoned the dogma of the Leninist-Stalinist creed.

75. In the 1970s Aron recognized that the absence of an ideological system to substitute for Marxism did not authorize forecasting pragmatic politics or maintaining consensus. Furthermore, the expression "end of ideologies" was a sign of the years between 1955 and 1965. However, he maintained that the 1960s and 1970s had not seen new ideological systems, that is, meaning systematic constructions of a global interpretation of the historical or social world. Such interpretations would enable the ideologue both to understand the society to which he or she belonged and to make a lucid choice of the objectives of his actions. Marxism-Leninism remained in 1969, as in 1955, the latest Western ideological system. Aron, "Remarques sur le nouvel âge idéologique," in *Theory and Politics: Theorie und Politik*, ed. Klaus von Beyme (The Hague: Martinus Nijhoff, 1972).

76. Aron, *Espoir et peur du siècle: essais non partisans* (Paris: Calmann-Lévy, 1957), 70.

77. Aron, *Espoir et peur du siècle*, 87.

78. Aron, *L'Opium des intellectuels*, 328.

79. Aron, *L'Opium des intellectuels*, 317.

80. Aron, "A propos de l'unité," 280.

81. Aron, *Plaidoyer pour l'Europe décadente* (Paris: Robert Laffont, 1977), 469–514.

III

CULTURAL STRUGGLES/
POLITICAL STAKES

FRENCH INTELLECTUALS AND THE REPRESSION OF THE HUNGARIAN REVOLUTION OF 1956: THE POLITICS OF A PROTEST RECONSIDERED

Michael Scott Christofferson

Historians commonly recognize the Soviet Union's November 1956 repression of the Hungarian Revolution as a turning point in French intellectual politics. Among non-communist left-wing intellectuals the Soviet Union lost its status as a political model, and the French Communist Party (PCF), which supported the repression, became an unacceptable political partner. Communist front organizations hemorrhaged members as fellow-traveling collapsed. Within the PCF the repression led between 1956 and 1958 to the formation of party factions opposed to the leadership and ultimately to large-scale resignations.[1]

Existing historical accounts of this episode in French intellectual politics have generally been limited to published sources and have focused on the initial reactions to the revolution's repression. This has allowed some to claim that the wave of revulsion following the Soviet intervention was inconsequential. For example, Tony Judt asserts that shortly after the Hungarian Revolution French intellectuals abandoned Eastern Europe and reflection on East European communism and instead focused their attention on decolonization, transferring their political enthusiasm to third-world revolutionary utopias. Likewise, Pierre Grémion assumes that French intellectuals did little to support East European dissidents until the late 1970s.[2]

This chapter investigates the impact of the repression of the Hungarian Revolution on French intellectual politics by focusing closely on the crisis within the Comité national des écrivains (CNE) and the long-term efforts of intellectuals in the Comité Tibor Déry to free imprisoned Hungarian intellectuals. Based on archival sources, this chapter reveals the full extent of the collapse of fellow-traveling. It also demonstrates (contrary to Grémion) that numerous intellectuals of the non-communist Left—as well as some communist intellectuals—were determined to protest repression by communist regimes after 1956 and (contrary to Judt) that this protest involved significant reflection on East European communism and the relationship of French intellectuals to it. It was, to be sure, a political protest, in the name of socialism reconciled with liberty, unlike Amnesty International's later campaign for human rights. Still, protest was not solely instrumental to the political projects of French intellectuals. Motivated to build a socialism free from Stalinist repression, based on genuine feelings of solidarity, including close personal ties with Hungary in some cases, the mobilization against the repression of the Hungarian Revolution was central to French intellectual politics.

THE COMITÉ NATIONAL DES ÉCRIVAINS AND THE PCF BEFORE THE HUNGARIAN REVOLUTION

Founded in 1941, the CNE was the leading association of Resistance writers by the time of France's Liberation in 1944, after which it led the purge of French writers by blacklisting those who had collaborated during the war. Although communists (notably Louis Aragon) played key roles in the CNE's formation, it was a national organization dedicated to defending Resistance values, promoting French intellectual and creative production, and aiding France's postwar revival.[3] In 1946, however, the CNE lost its ecumenical outlook. At the 1946 General Assembly, Louis Aragon became the CNE's general secretary, and the Gaullist Jacques Debû-Bridel lost the presidency to fellow traveler Jean Cassou, thereby bringing the CNE under PCF control.[4] In late 1946 Jean Paulhan and a number of prominent older writers (including Jean Schlumberger, Georges Duhamel, and Gabriel Marcel) resigned from the CNE—in part out of anti-communism—dealing a serious blow to its legitimacy and ability to enforce the blacklist. Still, the CNE remained important. Its membership rose from fifty at the Liberation to 230 in May 1947, and its annual book sale became a major literary event.[5]

Following the 1946 communist takeover, the CNE was careful about intervening in politics, yet it followed the PCF in supporting the peace movement and communist writers such as Pablo Néruda, Howard Fast, and Roger Vailland. These positions contributed to an erosion of membership to 176 in March 1952, and culminated in a full-scale crisis of fellow-traveling in early 1953 when Serge Groussard demanded that the CNE denounce the anti-Semitism and anti-Zionism of the Czechoslovak purge trials. When the CNE did not act, around twenty members resigned, including the former CNE presidents Jean Cassou and Louis Martin-Chauffier. In order to prevent the remaining non-communist members from using the CNE to criticize the PCF or the Soviet Union, Elsa Triolet—who was, alongside her husband Aragon, the real force behind communist control of the CNE—pushed through an amendment to the association's charter that prohibited it from addressing purely political questions or issues that did not directly concern writers. This depoliticization of the CNE was reinforced when CNE President Vercors (celebrated author of the Resistance novel *Le Silence de la mer*) discontinued the "Page du C.N.E." in *Les Lettres françaises* after failing to obtain an open debate in it on Groussard's demands. Thus, come 1956 the CNE was in decline. Having lost many of its leading non-communist members, it was identified as a tool of the PCF. To stave off future crises, it had restricted severely its ability to intervene politically. Yet, even this cautious approach would not shelter it from the upheaval of 1956.[6]

The 1956 crisis of the CNE began in May when President Vercors demanded in a speech before the CNE General Assembly that the CNE and, more broadly, communist relations with fellow-traveling intellectuals like himself be reformed in line with the spirit of the February 1956 Khrushchev report at the USSR Communist Party Congress. Raising the 1949 show trial of the Hungarian communist Lázló Rajk, Vercors argued that the communists had blindly accepted Rajk's guilt because they had habitually lied to themselves and had not listened to fellow travelers like himself. To prevent a new Rajk affair, Vercors called upon the PCF to accept friendly criticism by friendly intellectuals. For the CNE, this would mean reopening the "Page du C.N.E." in *Les Lettres françaises* so writers could say "from day to day what they think and if necessary express one of these days their disagreement."[7]

Vercors did not succeed. The "Page du C.N.E." was not reopened, and his presidential address—contrary to tradition—was not published in *Les Lettres françaises*. The CNE General Assembly deferred to Aragon, who refused to repoliticize *Les Lettres françaises*. This, plus further efforts by Aragon to squelch discussion of the Khrushchev report, led Vercors to resign the CNE presidency because he felt he was no longer "an element of cohesion of our association." At the June CNE Comité directeur (CD) meeting the elderly communist writer Francis Jourdain reluctantly accepted the presidency at Aragon's suggestion, an appointment that closely identified the CNE with the PCF on the eve of the Hungarian Revolution.[8]

THE CNE AND THE SHOCK OF NOVEMBER 1956

Given the Hungarian Revolution's significance in the history of communism, the key role played in it by Hungarian writers in the Petöfi Circle, and the Hungarian writers' appeals for assistance from their Western counterparts, the repression of the revolution was uniquely important for French intellectuals, who responded to it with protests and petitions. Beyond seeking to impact events in Hungary, these asserted an interpretation of the revolution and its repression while legitimizing certain choices in French politics and rejecting others. French intellectuals' mobilizations against the Hungarian Revolution's repression were as much about French domestic politics as anything else.

Anti-communist intellectuals, who tended to interpret the revolution as an attempt to establish Western democracy and a vindication of their rejection of communism, protested to denounce communism and fellow-traveling. A petition organized by Suzanne Labin and signed by a number of prominent French intellectuals including François Mauriac and Albert Camus charged that the Soviet leaders "remade Moscow, as in the time of Czarism, the capital of world absolutist reaction, taking up . . . the role of the bloody superpolice that the Holy Alliance and the Versaillais had played." The signatories added that they "consider these butchers to be the pariah of humanity and stigmatize the communist leaders of the free world who in following in their footsteps cover their hands with the blood of the Hungarian people."[9] Although the anti-communist Congress for Cultural Freedom's initial statement was relatively mild,[10] Denis de Rougemont, who had a regular column in the Congress's journal *Preuves*, was not. In *Le Figaro littéraire* of November 10, 1956, he demanded action "against those who applaud the crime, who will try to have it be forgotten or to find excuses for it." In *Preuves* he called for a severing of relations with those who approved of the repression, including "the 'objective' accomplices of this crime, the Soviet intellectuals," made the case for banning the PCF, and accused left-wing intellectuals who had previously been silent on repression in Eastern Europe of being "accomplices of everything that prepared" the repression of the revolution.[11]

While De Rougemont tried to score points against the Left and make his case against communism, left-wing intellectuals protested in the name of socialism and proclaimed the Right's protests to be hypocritical. A statement written by Vercors and signed by important fellow-traveling and communist intellectuals such as Jean-Paul Sartre, Simone de Beauvoir, and Claude Roy sought, Vercors later explained, to "bring together outraged consciences without coming to the aid of Western imperialism and its hypocritical condemnations" in reaction to "the overzealous protest of a group of old enemies of communism."[12] Vercors's statement established the right of the signatories to protest the repression because they had never "shown unfriendly feelings toward the USSR or socialism" and denied the right to protest to "the hypocrites" who "kept quiet—if they did not applaud—when the United States smothered in blood the liberty conquered in Guatemala" and "to all those who dare speak of a 'Prague coup' at the same moment that they loudly applaud the 'Suez coup.'" Further, it protested "against the use of guns and tanks to break the revolt of the Hungarian people and their desire for independence, even if reactionary elements were mixed in with this revolt," proclaimed their belief that neither socialism nor liberty "are brought about at the point of bayonets," raised their voices "in advance against the legal proceedings to which they [Hungarian writers] might be subjected," and demanded "the truth" from the Soviet government.[13] However defensive they were, this and similar protests by left-wing intellectuals marked a new stage in their reflection on socialism by explicitly condemning the Soviet Union for betraying it. It was a position that most would maintain, even in the face of criticism from the PCF and the Soviet Union.[14]

This and other petitions and protests put pressure on the PCF and the CNE. The PCF was unable to rally nonparty intellectuals to its position that the revolution was a fascist coup and also lost support in its own ranks. Four communist intellectuals (Claude Roy, Roger Vailland, Jacques-Francis Rolland, and Claude Morgan) signed the Vercors petition. And, in late November, ten leading communist intellectuals and artists, including the CNE President Francis Jourdain, questioned the party's interpretation of events in Hungary and called for an extraordinary party congress on the issue.[15]

Aragon and Triolet, who defended the PCF on the Hungarian Revolution, were hard pressed in the CNE. Shortly after the Soviet military intervention a letter by Louis de Villefosse and the CD members Vercors, Stanislas Fumet, Jacques Madaule, Jean-Paul Sartre, and Janine Bouissounouse called for a CD meeting, stating that they would only participate in the CNE's annual book sale later that month "if the position of the CNE is clearly defined with regard to this distressing problem."[16] The threat to the book sale was serious; even before the CD could meet and distribute a statement on the events, authors wrote the CNE to announce their withdrawal from it.[17]

At the November 6 CD meeting most of those present were critical of the PCF's position (at least eight of the fifteen had signed or would soon sign protests to this effect),[18] yet the meeting ended in a victory of sorts for the PCF. Vercors began it by suggesting a letter to Hungarian writers and the Hungarian government that "would be written in measured terms, but would show our concern." Sartre, who declared himself to be "less moderate" than Vercors, felt that the Soviet government should also be an addressee. Marc Beigbeder and Bouissounouse agreed with this, but Madaule and Aragon contended that it would be a political act foreign to the CNE's mission. Aragon, playing the role of conciliator, argued that they should not focus on questions of form, but rather concentrate on "our common concern": "the survival and liberty of Hungarian writers." Claiming that "the most important thing in all this is the life of these men," Aragon asserted that a text addressed to the USSR would not be accepted by any Hungarian government, yet a text addressed to the government of János Kádár might yield results. It would be a "courteous, non-accusatory text that clearly implies that we are loyal to that which incarnates the CNE, the defense of culture," and "that constitutes on the eve of the CNE sale a response to the provocations of which we have been the target." Following this gesture Sartre withdrew his proposal that they address the Soviet government, but he maintained that they should address Soviet writers and the writers' associations in the popular democracies. This was shot down by Triolet who called it a "perfidious gesture." The final statement, signed by all present except Beigbeder—who found it too soft—and published on the front page of *Les Lettres françaises*, did not condemn the invasion, but, while noting that they were "profoundly divided" over their interpretation of it, simply asked Kádár to protect Hungarian writers and intellectuals. Although relatively anodyne, the text was hardly insignificant. For the first time the CNE had expressed concern about repression in Eastern Europe. It would be followed on December 4 by another telegram to Kádár asking "to be reassured of the fate" of four writers (including Georg Lukács) and on December 11 by a telegram to the Union of Soviet Writers asking it to associate itself with the CNE's November 6 communiqué.[19]

The November 6 communiqué did little to stem discontent as measured by cancellations for the annual book sale and resignations from the association. In fact, it may have done more damage than good to the efforts of

Aragon and Triolet to hold the CNE together on the PCF's terms. More than one writer cited the document as a reason to distance himself from the CNE. Upon resigning from the CNE, Alla Budin wrote that "the Appeal of Hungarian Intellectuals deserved from your Comité directeur better than the petition without teeth that you addressed to President Kádár," and Claude Couffon held that "the ambiguity, the lack of warmth and of conviction of the communiqués published recently by the CNE do not allow me to remain anymore one of its members." Jean Rousselot, who opted out of CNE events until a General Assembly discussed the issues, considered the November 6 communiqué to be "not sufficient" and asked that "the CNE reexamine its attitude toward Hungarian intellectuals and not limit itself to asking in their favor for objectivity, indeed indulgence, from a government whose authority depends on the goodwill of a foreign power."[20]

Developments in November and December threatened the existence of the CNE. Anti-communist riots in Paris on November 7 led the CD to decide the next day to call off the book sale—already threatened by authors' cancellations—in order to protect the public.[21] Given the importance of the sale to the CNE's finances, this endangered the association's economic future. In February 1957 it decided to reduce the monetary award for its annual literary prize, the "Prix du CNE." Without a successful book sale in 1957, Léon Moussinac warned in May, "we can close up the shop; we do not have any more money."[22]

Increasingly, the future of the CNE was threatened from within and without. In November, Louis de Villefosse, frustrated by the CNE's position on Hungary, circulated a collective letter of resignation, ultimately obtaining seven signatures.[23] Taking advantage of the CNE's crisis, former CNE President Louis Martin-Chauffier called for the creation of a new CNE, the Union des écrivains pour la vérité, that would respect the spirit of its charter. *France observateur*'s article on Martin-Chauffier's effort was entitled "Death of the CNE?"—an eventuality that the left-wing weekly clearly did not oppose.[24]

In early December Aragon agreed to an extraordinary General Assembly, citing the resignations of CD members Beigbeder and Fumet as the reason. The resignation of Fumet, who had been the CNE's vice president, was significant. A well-known Gaullist Catholic, he had helped the CNE maintain its claim to be ecumenical.[25] Intent on keeping the crisis under control, Aragon successfully delayed the meeting until January 12—thereby allowing passions to cool down—and otherwise blunted the meeting's impact. The meeting's agenda did not mention the Hungarian question, and the proposal that all CD members resign before the meeting was rejected as

were Vercors's suggestions that they reinstate CNE members who had resigned "for valid reasons" and consider negotiating with Martin-Chauffier's
dissident CNE. Rather than compromise with the dissidents, the CD took
a hard line, selecting as a new CD member Pierre de Lescure, the only former CNE member to rejoin it in late 1956 out of solidarity with the communists.[26]

Although Aragon and Triolet maintained control of the CNE at the January
General Assembly, the last remaining CNE fellow travelers of significance—
notably Vercors and Sartre—were clearly discontented. After an introductory
statement by Triolet in which she accused De Villefosse of seeking to destroy
the CNE, discussion began with critiques by De Villefosse, Vercors, and Sartre
of the inadequacy of the CNE's response to events. De Villefosse, who came
to the meeting armed with a motion that had the approval of Bouissounouse,
Michel Leiris, Rousselot, and André Spire, wanted the CNE to go beyond
stating its "concern" to protest events in Hungary. He claimed that its failure
to act followed from its undemocratic mode of operating. Pointing to the efficacy of the International PEN Club's protest, De Villefosse asserted that "the
prestige of French writers in the world is at stake." Vercors, who spoke next,
accused the CNE of being emasculated and announced that, although he
would remain in the CNE out of fidelity and because he wanted to be in it
when it revived, he would quit the CD and attempt to lead an internal opposition to it. Sartre echoed Vercors, stating that although he believed in "the necessity of remaining in it [the CNE], if only in the capacity of opposition," he,
too, would not be a candidate for reelection to the CD. Regretting that the
PEN Club had been more effective and that Hungarian writers did not address themselves to the CNE, Sartre also believed that "one must try to make
the CNE virile again." He did not think that the CNE should condemn the Soviet intervention because that would be a political position contrary to its mission, but he argued that the CNE had to defend men of culture. Thus, Sartre
proposed a motion condemning the illegal use of violence against Lukács and
intellectuals in general. De Villefosse, aware that his motion lacked support,
withdrew it in favor of Sartre's, which was acceptable to him because it contained the words "condemnation" and "indignation."[27]

The communists Pierre Courtade and Aragon rejected Sartre's proposal.
Courtade reminded Sartre of their support for violence after the Liberation and argued that Lukács had been arrested for being a member of the
government and should be treated as a politician. By contending that the
Hungarian government had turned reactionary and the Soviet intervention
was therefore justified, Courtade suggested that Lukács deserved to be
punished. Aragon, more subtle than Courtade, argued that they should not

act precipitously in the Lukács case because the facts were unclear. Recalling the November 6 communiqué, Aragon called upon them to compromise and agree to disagree. He would not accept a condemnation and demanded that their statement on Lukács be limited to a request for information.

This was unacceptable to De Villefosse who contested Courtade's claim that the Hungarian Revolution had turned reactionary and attacked him for his judgment in the Rajk affair: "If I had written what you wrote on the Rajk trial I would not have spoken today." At this point Aragon scolded De Villefosse for being "too talkative today." De Villefosse replied that he had a right to speak because "we are not in Moscow." When Aragon shot back, "I will shove that back down your throat!" and called De Villefosse and his supporters a "gutter minority [*minorité de la canaille*]," both Aragon and De Villefosse left the room.[28]

The meeting ended in victory for Aragon. After Triolet pleaded with Sartre to stay in the CD to discuss matters with them, Sartre capitulated. The telegram sent to the Hungarian government asked only for reassurance on the fate of Lukács. Much more vigorous was the motion adopted denouncing "the pressures and threats" against writers due to participate in the CNE sale as "an effort to bring intellectuals to heel."[29]

With the conclusion of the January General Assembly the CNE had survived the crisis largely on the PCF's terms, but at a high price. With the resignation of Spire, Bouissounouse, and De Villefosse, the total loss of CNE members as a result of events in Hungary numbered at least sixteen and may have been nineteen or higher, in other words, roughly 10 percent of the membership.[30] Vercors and Sartre remained, but they were exceptional among leading intellectuals in their desire to maintain contact with the communists and keep the unity of the Resistance legacy alive. And, although Aragon could point to responses from Hungarian intellectuals to CNE telegrams as proof of the CNE's significance, there was a growing sense that the end result of the efforts to hold the CNE together was its loss of relevance.

THE CNE'S ONGOING HUNGARIAN AFFAIR

Although the shock of November 1956 was over by the end of January 1957, the Hungarian question would not disappear. Intellectuals outside of the CNE, including many former CNE members, kept it alive as did the CNE's "internal opposition," notably Vercors, whose persistence reflects his close ties with Hungary from which his father had immigrated to France.[31] Vercors believed that his past reticence to criticize communists for fear of aiding counterrevolutionaries was no longer acceptable after 1956. Still dedicated to the cause of socialism and unwilling to totally abandon the communists, Vercors sought to use his influence and the prestige of the CNE to fight for liberalization within the communist world. On a trip to Moscow in the spring of 1957 he endeavored to "bring a dissenting voice" about the repression of the Hungarian Revolution to Soviet writers. In France, he pushed the CNE to protest repression vigorously instead of continuing what he called "the little game of harmless motions, of 'requests for explanation' or 'to be reassured on the fate or such and such,' sent periodically to a government whose silence has already slapped us." By using his title of honorary president of the CNE, Vercors intended to "force the CNE to take a certain position or kick me out the door."[32] This effort began shortly after the January General Assembly when Vercors raised the issue of repression at the Hungarian embassy. The CD responded by prohibiting CNE members from mentioning their CNE affiliation when making public declarations. The CD even considered sending someone to Hungary "in order to gather information on the situation of Hungarian writers . . . in case this situation gives rise to marked dissent in the CNE."[33]

When news of the dissolution of the Hungarian Writers Association and the arrest of renowned writer and Petöfi Circle leader Tibor Déry reached France in April 1957, Vercors wrote two telegrams (one to Kádár and the other to Aleksii Surkov, general secretary of the Soviet Writers Union), signed both "Members of the C.N.E." and "Vercors Honorary President," and solicited signatures from selected CNE members. Beyond protesting the repression, the telegram to Kádár stated that "we are sure that these methods will be harmful to the future of socialism and will favor an intellectual resistance with which we will be in solidarity as with all oppressed progressive thought."[34] Vercors's telegrams, CD member Léon Moussinac feared, "could possibly break up the unity of the CNE."[35] The CD contemplated expelling Vercors from the CNE, but they recognized, Triolet said, that "he has lots of people behind him. Not in the Comité directeur, but among the members of the CNE. He is all the same something."[36] Kicking Vercors out would be the death of the CNE they surmised. Consequently, the CD limited its action to a letter reprimanding Vercors for his use of the title of honorary president in the telegrams. In addition, the CD sent, upon Claude Roy's suggestion, its own telegram to Kádár recalling the one sent November 6, 1956 and asking to be "reassured" about Déry.[37]

Despite its mildness, the telegram in support of Déry did not please Aragon, who had been absent from the meeting in which Vercors's action was first discussed and claimed that he would not have signed it if he had been present.[38] To ensure that nobody would be associated with communiqués with which they disagreed the CD decided that henceforth communiqués would list the CD members who supported them. Aragon, judging from what he would say the next time the Déry affair was raised in the CNE, apparently believed that Déry was guilty of serious crimes.[39] Although Aragon intervened on more than one occasion with the Hungarian authorities in favor of Hungarian intellectuals in prison, it appears that he was primarily interested in the favorable impact that his interventions would have on the communist cause in France and Hungary. Worried about his image, he denied that he had disapproved of the Déry telegram when his position was leaked to the press in August.[40]

Aragon's concern for the communist image can be seen most clearly in his intervention with the Hungarian authorities in favor of the writer József Gáli. Gáli and another writer, Gyula Obersovsky, had been condemned in April 1957 to brief prison terms (one year for Gáli and three for Obersovsky), only to have their sentences changed to the death penalty by a special court in June 1957. This raised a storm of protest from intellectuals in France and elsewhere.[41] In response Aragon wrote a letter to István Dobi, the official Hungarian head of state. He presented himself as "among those who have not for a minute doubted the pertinence and legitimacy of the action of today's Hungarian government" who was additionally "the constant object of attacks by the press" in 1956, all of which, Aragon wrote, authorized him to say that "the execution of the death sentence in the case of József Gáli would serve in France first and foremost to foster anti-Hungarian agitation and would risk enabling a mass action of French intellectuals deceived by certain appearances." Claiming that he did not want to interfere in the Hungarian judicial system or judge the culpability of the accused, Aragon begged Dobi "in the name of French writers who resisted the fascist occupation . . . to consider the deplorable results in France and therefore a large number of countries that the execution of the sentence might bring about. A measure of pardon on the contrary would greatly help the soothing of minds and might be used against the enemies of Hungary." Gáli, Aragon concluded his letter, "can be more useful by his survival than by his death to the cause to which I beg you to believe me to be unshakably devoted."[42]

When the death sentence of the two Hungarian writers was suspended on June 25 the CNE issued a communiqué that implied that it was responsible and claimed that Aragon's effort was, unlike others, apolitical. A little less than a year later in a speech before the May 1958 CNE General Assembly, Aragon took full credit for the commutation of the death sentence, which, he said, corrected an "error of viewpoint" of the Hungarian government that would have been "used against it [the CNE]." If the CNE was able "to make its voice heard with a government that does not respond to the commotion of the press or of the street" this was "due to the respect abroad that one still accords to an organization born in the French Resistance, representing French culture before and against fascism, and due to the representative character that the diversity of its membership gives it."[43]

The repression of the Hungarian Revolution intruded into the life of the CNE one last time before the amnesty of Déry in April 1960. In reaction to a *Le Monde* report that Déry's health had declined, CNE members Jean Rousselot—who had been in Hungary in October 1956 and defended Hungarian intellectuals on the basis of his personal knowledge of them[44]—and Herbert Le Porrier (both members of the Comité Tibor Déry discussed below), requested at the June 1959 General Assembly that the CNE ask the Hungarian government to pardon Déry. Aragon replied that he had already saved two lives and that Déry had been condemned to death before he had intervened. Claiming that any further intervention in Déry's favor would only hurt him, Aragon threatened to resign if they pushed the issue. The CNE took no action, but nineteen CNE members, including Sartre and a number of communists, signed a petition circulated at the General Assembly asking for Déry's pardon.[45]

The CNE survived the impact of the Hungarian Revolution's repression, but at a considerable price. It lost many of its leading non-communist members and never fully recovered either its pre-November 1956 reputation—as tarnished as that already was—or its finances. Its refusal to make political statements when dealing with the Hungarian question left it disarmed when facing the Algerian War. Criticized during the spring 1958 crisis of the Fourth Republic by Hélène Parmelin for being politically inactive and hence having its "influence diminish considerably," the CNE, led by Aragon, rejected her suggestion that it become more politically engaged. The cost in terms of quarrels and membership losses would be too great, Aragon argued.[46] Although the CNE would soldier on until Elsa Triolet's death in 1970, it had little weight in the intellectual or literary politics of the Fifth Republic.

BEYOND THE CNE AND FELLOW-TRAVELING: THE FORMATION OF THE COMITÉ TIBOR DÉRY

The repression of the Hungarian Revolution resonated far beyond the CNE, eliciting protests and appeals for clemency in France and elsewhere and focusing after 1956 on the fate of Tibor Déry, one of Hungary's greatest twentieth-century writers who had played a key role in the Hungarian Revolution and was, as a consequence, sentenced to a nine-year prison term in 1957. In France, intellectuals of all stripes protested Déry's arrest, trial, and sentence.[47] A sustained effort to mobilize support for him was launched in May 1958 by Jean-Marie Domenach, François Fejtö, and Louis de Villefosse from the offices of Domenach's journal *Esprit*. In a letter of May 6, 1958, they called upon specific "writers, journalists, and publishers to whom the name of Tibor Déry is familiar, who share a common admiration for him and his work, who find his conviction scandalous, and of whom a certain number have already intervened to ask for his liberation" to join a provisional committee in his support.[48] This committee would then launch an "appeal" for the formation of a permanent committee to liberate Déry. Although the provisional committee had a broad political base and the proposed "appeal" was—beyond its designation of the Kádár régime as a "government installed by an army of occupation"—politically agnostic, differences over the politics of protest soon risked to undermine the hoped-for unity of French intellectuals in defense of Déry.

Sartre's secretary responded on his behalf in a letter of May 14 that "he [Sartre] would have liked for this committee to have been established on a wider basis, and in the current conditions its composition does not allow him to join it." Domenach, Fejtö, and De Villefosse inferred that Sartre refused to support the committee because it did not include any communists. They replied to him with the question: "but how could we ask those who approved [of Déry's fate] to protest?" This and a letter by Domenach to convince Sartre to join the committee proved fruitless. Yet, Sartre did take action in favor of Déry. In addition to signing the petition circulated at the June 1959 CNE General Assembly, in the autumn of 1957 he and the editorial board of *Les Temps modernes* telegrammed Kádár to demand a fair and open trial for Déry and to protest in advance an "intolerable conviction of Déry for his beliefs."[49]

Jean Bloch-Michel, a novelist and essayist who was also the literary director of *Preuves* beginning in early 1958, refused to join the provisional committee for quite different political reasons.[50] His May 29 letter protested Claude Roy and Claude Bourdet's presence on the committee, explaining: "we cannot ask for a pardon for Déry or even undertake any action in his favor with someone like Claude Roy who just asked to reenter the Communist Party, or, for other reasons, with Claude Bourdet. . . . One must . . . remember that he [Bourdet] is one of the leaders of a party [the

Nouvelle Gauche] the candidates of which withdrew in favor of communists in the last elections." He added, "if the communists and their friends want to undertake an action in favor of Déry, I think that we must encourage them to do so, but not get ourselves mixed up in it." Bloch-Michel's letter, written on *Preuves* letterhead and addressed exclusively to Louis de Villefosse, reiterated the journal's absolute prohibition of compromises with communism.

Domenach, responding for the organizers of the committee, told Bloch-Michel in a June 20 letter that they did not understand his problem with Bourdet: "He [Bourdet] supported the communists on certain occasions, and that was the case of the quasi-totality of us, and that was the case of Tibor Déry himself. As for Imre Nagy, was he not a communist?" Domenach agreed that Roy's request to be reinstated in the PCF was problematic, but he believed that "Claude Roy's protest against the execution of Nagy places him without ambiguity in the camp of the enemies of murder by the state." Domenach concluded that they would not exclude Roy and Bourdet from the provisional committee.

Bloch-Michel's June 25 rejoinder addressed to Domenach revealed the true stakes of this quarrel. Although Sartre's position made him want to support the effort, "if only to protest against the reasons for his refusal," he would not because "things must be clear, otherwise one is condemned to ineffectiveness." Bloch-Michel agreed that people should not be judged by their past—"because this would purely and simply be McCarthyism"—but one must judge their present positions. Bourdet was unacceptable because "he proposes at the same time to protest against the murders and to bring us together with those who approve of the murderers." As for Roy, "this sort of ballet that he dances with communism is so complex that one never knows very well on which side he will find himself the next day." Since he doubted that his intervention would have a "decisive influence" on the fate of Déry, Bloch-Michel decided to maintain his "refusal of ambiguity" and avoid the committee. He explained:

> Any action against the crimes of a state undertaken with those who at the same time declare themselves ready to collaborate with those who represent it, with those who approve of these crimes, or with those who only refuse to condemn them is ambiguous, condemned to failure, and destined only to increase confusion. However, I think that only a certain rigor is effective. This is why, for example, I will never associate myself with a protest against torture and massacres in Algeria by men who do not become indignant over torture and massacres in Soviet Russia.

The exchange between Domenach and Bloch-Michel also revealed that the identity of the victim was as important as who protested for him. Domenach proclaimed that Déry had supported the communists when, in fact, he was a communist. Bloch-Michel held that "you do not summon us to the aid of Déry as a communist, but as a victim of communism." In fact, the appeal did not describe Déry as a victim of communism, although Bloch-Michel clearly believed that it should have. Neither did the appeal come to Déry's aid "as a communist," but Bloch-Michel rightly suspected that the committee's political agenda was not his.

The campaign for Déry was partially justified and defended on the grounds that Déry was on the Left. The committee's biography of him spoke at length of his politics—his communism, his difficulties with the Horthy régime, his participation in the Resistance, and his role in the 1956 revolution in which he "took the side of the insurgents while inviting the nation at arms to abstain from pronouncing summary judgments." This biographical sketch argued implicitly that, beyond humanitarian considerations, Déry deserved the solicitude of the intellectual Left because, as De Villefosse's open letter to Henri Martin stated, "he was never reactionary."[51] Although the committee would later defend the more moderate István Bibó, it did not support reactionaries such as Cardinal József Mindszenty, who took refuge in the American embassy in 1956.

Bloch-Michel, Sartre, and the organizers of the committee in support of Déry were all engaging in a complex game of controlling the political signification of the campaign on his behalf. Bloch-Michel, like many within the Congress for Cultural Freedom, wanted the campaign to repudiate all forms of communism, whereas Sartre refused anything close to anticommunism. Claude Roy, who knew the Hungarian revolutionaries of 1956 well, defended his protest against Déry's treatment from a socialist perspective.[52] Roy rejected communists and fellow travelers who held that one must be "realistic" and defend Soviet socialism against its enemies. Citing Benjamin Constant in support of his case, Roy argued that socialism and liberty cannot be established through tyranny. His appeal was not to Kantian moralism, but to a realism dosed in idealism, a realism that also involved establishing "the grievance books of humanity." Referring to the latest Soviet achievement, Roy concluded "man does not live by Sputnik alone, but also by justice and by liberty."[53]

It is important to note that the campaign to liberate Déry was orchestrated by individuals like Domenach and De Villefosse, that is, intellectuals who had recently broken with fellow-traveling. Their efforts, like Claude Roy's, proceeded from the conviction that true socialism must be based on liberty, justice, and the rights of man.[54] Although Déry was a communist and they had only been fellow travelers, his itinerary closely paralleled theirs: in his anti-fascism, his brief bewitchment by Stalinism, and his more recent struggle for a free and democratic socialism. By defending Déry they were—as suggested by Domenach's misidentification of Déry as a supporter of the communists rather than a communist—defending their own politics. But they were also defending the core of the Hungarian Revolution because, as the Hungarian Social Democrat Paul Ignotus recognized, the Hungarian Revolution "did not come from the anti-Communists but from disenchanted Communists" like Tibor Déry.[55] Déry symbolized the hope for an internal transformation of communism; this was a hope that many French intellectuals of the non-communist Left held dear in the late 1950s.

The Comité Tibor Déry got off to a slow start, undoubtedly because it had the misfortune of being launched while the Fourth Republic was in its final death throes. By mid-June 1958 only about half of those invited to join the provisional committee had responded. Some, like the anticolonial activist Robert Boudry, rejected the committee because they believed that it would divide the Left and distract attention from the crisis of the republic. No doubt in reaction to people like Boudry, the Trotskyist and sociologist of labor Pierre Naville complained to the committee that "the wind behind this effort appears to me to be deplorably too weak if one compares it to what is justly written against the jails of Algeria, America, or elsewhere." Still, hostility to the committee seems to have been exceptional within the non-communist intellectual Left. Other than Sartre and Bloch-Michel, the only intellectuals invited to join the provisional committee who were not members by October 1958 were Albert Camus, René Char, and Daniel Mayer, none of whom were likely to have refused their patronage for the reasons articulated by Sartre or Boudry. The membership of the committee included many of the CNE dissidents of 1956 (Henri d'Amfreville, Marc Beigbeder, Jean-Jacques Bernard, Janine Bouissounouse, Jean Cayrol, Stanislas Fumet, Herbert Le Porrier, Claude Morgan, Jean Rousselot, Claude Roy, Pierre Seghers, André Spire, and Louis de Villefosse), some of those who had resigned from the CNE over the Groussard affair in 1953 (Claude Aveline, Jean Cassou, Louis Martin-Chauffier, and Armand Salacrou), and others who had been communists or fellow travelers after the Liberation (Claude Bourdet, Jean-Marie Domenach, Jean Duvignaud, Pierre Emmanuel, François Fejtö, Pierre Fougeyrollas, André Frénaud, Georges Friedmann, Pierre Hervé, Agnès Humbat, Bernard Lecache, Henri Lefebvre, Clara Malraux, Edgar Morin, René Tavernier, and Edith Thomas). When the Comité Tibor Déry met for the first time on October 17, 1958, it elected

Jean Cassou president and confirmed Domenach and De Villefosse as its secretaries; all three were former fellow travelers.

TOWARD THE LIBERATION OF DÉRY: THE WORK OF THE COMITÉ TIBOR DÉRY

The Comité Tibor Déry's efforts included letters to Hungarian and Soviet authorities as well as international organizations and the translation, publication, and performance of works by imprisoned authors. Its most important action, however, was probably its intervention at the Thirtieth Congress of the International PEN club held in Frankfurt, Germany in July 1959.[56] At that meeting, the Comité Tibor Déry, represented by De Villefosse (whose activism reflects his ties with Hungary from a 1954 trip there[57]) armed with the committee's recently published brochure, *Pour Tibor Déry et les 24 intellectuels hongrois en prison*, unsuccessfully sought to prevent the reintegration of the Hungarian PEN center into the international organization. In doing so, it found common ground with the Congress for Cultural Freedom, which also assumed that the Hungarian center's reintegration would serve the cause of repression.[58] By contrast, the leadership of the International PEN Club, although very critical of repression in Hungary, fought to keep the organization apolitical and the Hungarian center within the international organization. Although, for example, Jean de Beer, general secretary of the French PEN center, agreed with Georges Paloczy-Horvath, who criticized the Frankfurt Congress in *Preuves*, that "none of the centers in the Popular Democracies respected the charter of the PEN Club and its statutes," which called for national centers to defend freedom of expression, he believed that Paloczy-Horvath in his opposition to the Hungarian center's reintegration "ignored the true objectives of PEN," the most important of which was the promotion of dialogue across borders between writers. Keeping the centers in the popular democracies in the international organization was important because it allowed Eastern European writers, "many of which think like us and are reduced to silence," to maintain contact with the West. De Beer, who had close family ties in and traveled frequently to Hungary, believed that this contact, which he identified with détente, was vital for Hungarian intellectuals and could even be given some credit for sparking the Hungarian Revolution. It was, he wrote in response to a call for an end to cultural contacts with the East by Denis de Rougemont and *Le Figaro littéraire*, "because the doors were half-opened, . . . because certain confrontations and comparisons were possible, that the immensity of the failure into which their country sank became apparent."[59]

The Frankfurt Congress did not end the question of the Hungarian center's membership in the International PEN Club. A growing international campaign for Déry, which included a protest by American writers in December 1959 and the formation of a Tibor Déry Committee in London in early 1960 (both of which the Paris Comité Tibor Déry claimed to have inspired); violations of the PEN Club's charter by the Hungarian center; and the failure of the Hungarian center to secure the release of imprisoned writers—all these factors helped put reconsideration of the Hungarian center's membership on the agenda of the International Pen Club's Executive Committee meeting of April 4, 1960.[60] The April 1 amnesty of a number of Hungarian writers including Déry was in all likelihood in response to this pressure, which the Kádár regime could not ignore given the importance it attached to intellectuals in Hungarian politics and its efforts to gain international legitimacy.[61]

CONCLUSION

From the November 1956 Soviet intervention to the April 1960 amnesty of Déry the Hungarian Revolution resonated profoundly in French intellectual politics. A source of serious and continuing crisis in the CNE and more generally of the collapse of fellow-traveling, the repression occupied French intellectuals in campaigns in support of Hungarian intellectuals that ultimately found institutional expression in the Comité Tibor Déry. Largely due to the efforts of intellectuals, the case of Déry and other Hungarian intellectuals remained in the French press. This contrasts dramatically with the situation in the United States where, after a spate of articles about Déry's ordeal in 1957, nothing more appeared in *The New York Times* until his amnesty.[62]

Although close ties with Hungary clearly motivated individuals like Vercors, De Villefosse, Rousselot, Roy, De Beer, and Fejtö (a Hungarian émigré who did much of the legwork for the Comité Tibor Déry), the resonance of the repression of the Hungarian Revolution among French intellectuals was largely a consequence of its political significance. Many intellectuals were led by their commitment to socialism not to abandon Eastern Europe for more promising revolutionary possibilities in the Third World—as Tony Judt would have it—but rather to protest the travesty of socialism, notably the lack of liberty, that they saw in communist Europe. This critique of the failures of "really existing socialism" in the name of a humane socialism reconciled with liberty was central to French intellectual politics for twenty years after 1956 and would motivate protests of other instances of repression in Eastern Europe such as the 1966 trial of the Soviet dissidents Iuli Daniel and Andrei Siniavski and the "normalization" of Czechoslovakia in the 1970s. This critique and the various efforts to revise Marxism and the revolutionary project to enlarge the place of liberty within them are—as this author has argued elsewhere—key to understanding both the content of the revolutionary politics of 1968 and the nature of the post-revolutionary antitotalitarian moment of the 1970s. Unfortunately, the discrediting of this revisionism since the 1970s has blinded historians to its important role in the third quarter of the twentieth century, crippled historical understanding, and consequently made the origins of both the intellectual politics of 1968 and the 1970s French critique of totalitarianism something of a mystery.[63]

This post-1956 protest in the name of socialism marks a turning point in French intellectual politics. To be sure, intellectuals protested in the name of socialism against repression in Eastern Europe before 1956, but this earlier protest was often apologetic. In the protest of the Hungarian Revolution's repression, on the other hand, one finds very little in the way of apologetics and much in the way of challenges to the communist position that put its representatives like Aragon on the defensive. Given the diversity of positions in French intellectual politics, there were, of course, exceptions to this generalization. Sartre, for example, came close to apologetics in his *The Ghost of Stalin*, but his position was, as Pierre Grémion rightly contends, "against the current."[64] Indeed, many of those most active in protesting the repression in Hungary expressed remorse regarding their past silences about and support for repression in Eastern Europe. For Vercors, Roy, and De Villefosse, for example, protesting the Hungarian Revolution's repression involved significant reflection on the recent past of French intellectual politics and an attempt to make up for their past failings with untiring mobilization against repression.[65] While they reserved their most serious criticisms of past conduct for the PCF and its intellectuals, which were repeatedly reminded of what they had said during the Rajk affair of 1949, the months and years after November 1956 were clearly a time of reckoning with the past of fellow-traveling.

NOTES

Parts of this chapter were presented at the Annual Meeting of the Society for French Historical Studies of March 2001 and the Eleventh International Conference of

Europeanists of February 1998. The author thanks the participants of those conferences and Thomas Christofferson for their comments as well as the Penn State Institute for the Arts and Humanistic Studies, which funded research on the Comité national des écrivains and the International PEN Club.

1. See notably Peter Deli, *De Budapest à Prague: les sursauts de la gauche française* (Paris: Anthropos, 1981); Florence Grandsenne, "Les Intellectuels français face aux crises du communisme en Europe du Centre-Est: perception et interprétation des mouvements et de leur répression, 1956–1981," vol. 1, "Budapest, 1956" (doctoral thesis, Institut d'études politiques, Paris, 1998); and Michel Dreyfus, "1956: l'année terrible," *Communisme* 29–31 (1992): 237–47.

2. Tony Judt, *Past Imperfect: French Intellectuals, 1944–1956* (Berkeley: University of California Press, 1993), 280–92; and Pierre Grémion, *Paris-Prague: la gauche face au renouveau et à la régression tchécoslovaques (1968–1978)* (Paris: Julliard, 1985).

3. "Charte du Comité national des écrivains," and "Statuts de l'Association du Comité national des écrivains," in Fonds Elsa Triolet-Aragon, Centre nationale de la recherche scientifique, Paris. Henceforth FETA.

4. Vincent Feré, "Le Comité national des écrivains et les compagnons de route du parti communiste français (février 1946–avril 1953)" (DEA thesis, Institut d'études politiques, Paris, 1998), 1, 38–40.

5. Vincent Feré, "Le Comité national des écrivains," 68. Gisèle Sapiro, *La Guerre des écrivains, 1940–1953* (Paris: Fayard, 1999), 659–60 and *passim*; and Sapiro, "La Politique culturelle d'Elsa Triolet au CNE (1949–1951)," in *Elsa Triolet un écrivain dans le siècle: actes du colloque international 15–17 novembre 1996 Maison Elsa Triolet-Aragon-Saint-Arnoult-en-Yvelines*, ed. Marianne Gaudric-Delfranc (Paris: L'Harmattan, 2000), 205, 208.

6. Sapiro, "La Politique culturelle d'Elsa Triolet au CNE," 218–19; Feré, "Le Comité national des écrivains," 83–90, 111, 123; Sapiro, *La Guerre des écrivains*, 672–80; and Suzanne Ravis, "L'Année 1956 dans l'orientation des *Lettres françaises*," in *Aragon 1956: actes du colloque d'Aix-en-Provence 5–8 septembre 1991*, ed. Suzanne Ravis (Aix-en-Provence: Publications de l'Université de Provence, 1992), 15.

7. Vercors, *P.P.C. ou le concours de Blois* (Paris: Albin Michel, 1957), 36–46, 44 for the citation.

8. Citation from June 1, 1956 letter of Vercors to "Mon cher ami," CNE Comité directeur règlements, FETA, CD 57; Vercors, *P.P.C.*, 47–50; and Janine Bouissounouse, *La Nuit d'Autun: le temps des illusions* (Paris: Calmann-Lévy, 1977), 262–64. The minutes of the CD meetings of May 31 and June 20, 1956 do not mention this dispute between Vercors and Aragon. Comptes rendus du Comité Directeur CNE, FETA, CD-46 in-f°.

9. Grandsenne, "Budapest, 1956," 140–41.

10. Jean-François Sirinelli, *Intellectuels et passions françaises: manifestes et pétitions au XXe siècle* (Paris: Gallimard, 1990), 311–12.

11. This last statement was in response to the Vercors protest discussed below. Pierre Grémion, *L'Intelligence de l'anticommunisme: Le Congrès pour la liberté de la culture à Paris* (Paris: Fayard, 1995), 229; Denis de Rougemont, "Sur la honte et l'espoir de l'Europe," *Preuves* 71 (January 1957): 55–56; and De Rougemont, "Sur Voltaire," *Preuves* 72 (February 1957): 68–70.

12. Vercors, *P.P.C.*, 119.

13. "Contre l'intervention soviétique," *France observateur* 339 (8 November 1956): 4.

14. "La Lettre des écrivains soviétiques," and "La Réponse des écrivains français," *France observateur* 342 (29 November 1956): 13–14. A milder appeal (signed by Jean-Marie Domenach, Claude Bourdet, and Edgar Morin among others) accused the USSR of having "delivered a terrible blow to the cause of peace and of socialism." *France observateur* 339 (8 November 1956): 4.

15. Sirinelli, *Intellectuels et passions françaises*, 297–98.

16. November 5, 1956, letter to "Mon cher Président," in "Événements de Hongrie 1956," FETA, HONG. Marc Beigbeder also demanded a CD meeting and a CNE General Assembly to address the issue in a November 4, 1956, letter to "Mon cher Président et ami," FETA, CD 57.

17. At the November 6 CD meeting, Triolet announced that five writers had cancelled their participation in the sale, and Fumet said that he would not participate either. "Réunion du Comité Directeur, 6 novembre 1956," FETA, CD 46 in-f°.

18. Marc Beigbeder, Bouissounouse, Fumet, Jourdain, Madaule, Morgan, Sartre, and Vercors.

19. "Réunion du Comité Directeur, 6 novembre 1956," FETA, CD 46 in-f°; and "Le Comité national des écrivains s'adresse au Président Kadar," *Les Lettres françaises* 644 (8–14 November 1956): 1. The December telegrams are in FETA, HONG.

20. November 1956 letters in FETA, ADH 44–69.

21. November 8 CNE communiqué in FETA, HONG. See also "Réunion du Comité Directeur—8 Novembre 1956," FETA, CD 46 in-f°.

22. "Réunion du Comité Directeur—Séance du 7 Février 1957," FETA, CD 46 in-f°; and "Comité Directeur du 27 Mai 1957," FETA, CD 57.

23. Louis de Villefosse, *L'Oeuf de Wyasme: récit* (Paris: Julliard, 1962), 210.

24. M. N., "Mort du C.N.E.?" *France observateur* 342 (29 November 1956): 16.

25. De Villefosse, *L'Oeuf de Wyasme*, 207.

26. "Réunion du Comité Directeur—3 Décembre 1956," and "Réunion du Comité Directeur—Séance du 11 Décembre 1956," FETA, CD46 in-f°; letter from Vercors to Aragon dated November 24, 1956, in FETA; letter of December 21, 1956, by Francis Jourdain announcing the General Assembly and its order of the day in FETA, AG57; and Pierre de Lescure's November 30, 1956, letter to Francis Jourdain in FETA, ADH 44-69.

27. "Assemblé Générale C.N.E.—12.I.56"; and Vercors, "Assemblé Générale du C.N.E.," both in FETA, AG57.

28. "Assemblé Générale C.N.E.—12.I.56"; and "Le C.N.E. et la Hongrie," *France observateur* 349 (17 January 1957): 15–16.

29. "Assemblé Générale C.N.E.—12.I.56." The texts of motions passed by the assembly can be found in "Communiqué," FETA, AG57; and *Les Lettres françaises* 654 (17 January 1956): 8. Although Sartre continued to be a CD member, he rarely attended CD meetings either before or after November 1956.

30. Based on texts in FETA, ADH 44-69, notably "MEMBRES DU CNE AYANT DEMISSIONE EN 1956," dated January 20, 1962; and "Liste du Comité directeur du CNE et liste des membres du CNE 1957?" a document evidently created shortly before November 1956 and which lists 186 members.

31. Tivadar Gorilovics, "Vercors et la Hongrie," in *Vercors (Jean Bruller) et son oeuvre*, eds. Georges Cesbron and Gérard Jacquin (Paris: L'Harmattan, 1999), 311–22

32. Vercors, "Colloques Moscovites. I. L'Intervention en Hongrie," *Le Monde*, May 8, 1957; May 4, 1957, letter to Francis Jourdain in Vercors, *P.P.C.*, 65; and Alain Prevost quoting Vercors in "COMITE DIRECTEUR DU 27 MAI 1957," FETA, CD57.

33. "Réunion du Comité Directeur—Séance du 7 Février 1957," FETA, CD46 in-f°.

34. Telegrams quoted in a letter of April 25, 1957, from Marinette Amar to the members of the Comité directeur. FETA, HONG.

35. "Comité Directeur—Réunion du 1er Mai 1957," FETA, HONG.

36. Triolet quoted in "Comité Directeur du 27 Mai 1957," FETA, CD 57.

37. Letter from Jacques Madaule to Vercors; and May 2, 1957, press release by A. M. Amar, both in FETA, HONG.

38. "Réunion du Comité Directeur—Séance du 27 Mai 1957," FETA, CD in-f°; and "Comité Directeur du 27 Mai 1957," FETA, CD 57.

39. See Aragon's comments at the June 1959 General Assembly in the untitled handwritten pages in FETA, AG59.

40. "Réunion du Comité Directeur—Séance du 2 Octobre 1957," FETA, CD in-f°.

41. Protests from intellectuals all across the political spectrum can be found in the press on June 24, 1957. According to François Fejtö "the quasi-totality of French intellectuals" protested the death sentence. Fejtö, "Une lettre de Budapest," *France observateur* 372 (27 June 1957): 7.

42. Draft of a letter from Aragon to "Monsieur le Président Istvan Dobi," FETA. The political logic of Aragon's letter is repeated in "Assemblé Générale du 22 Mai 1958: Allocution prononcée par le Président Aragon," in "CNE Archives 1958 General Assembly," FETA, AG58. According to István Majoros, there is a 1959 letter from Aragon in favor of Tibor Déry in the Hungarian archives ("Les Relations franco-hongroises [1956–1964]," *Revue d'histoire moderne et contemporaine* 43, supplément 3–4 [1996]: 77).

43. "Communiqué" dated June 25, 1957, FETA, HONG; "Assemblé Générale du 22 Mai 1958; and Allocution prononcée par le Président Aragon," FETA, AG58.

44. Jean Rousselot, "Les Intellectuels hongrois méritent notre amitié et notre respect," *France observateur* 343 (9 December 1956): 20.

45. Untitled handwritten pages in "CNE Archives 1959 General Assembly," FETA, AG59; "Réunion du Comité Directeur—Séance du 10 juin 1959," FETA, CD46 in-f°; and "Le C.N.E. et Tibor Déry," *France observateur* 475 (11 June 1959): 19.

46. Letter of March 15, 1958 from Hélène Parmelin to "Chers Amis," FETA, CD57; and "Procès Verbal assemblée gle Jeudi 22 Mai 58," FETA, AG58.

47. See the protests collected in *Pour Tibor Déry et les 24 intellectuels hongrois en prison* (Paris: Comité Tibor Déry, 1959), 13–21, in the *Esprit* archives of the Institut mémoires de l'édition contemporaine, Paris (henceforth IMEC), ESP2 E2-02.01.

48. Archival sources on the committee used in the following pages are, unless otherwise noted, from IMEC ESP2 folder E2-01.01 for 1958; folder E2-01.02 for 1959; and folder E2-02.02 for 1960.

49. *Pour Tibor Déry*, 21. See also "Pièces pour le procès Déry," *Les Temps modernes* 136 (June 1957): 1972–88.

50. On Bloch-Michel's place at *Preuves* see Grémion, *Intelligence de l'anticommunisme*, 390–91.

51. Louis de Villefosse, "Lettre à un ancien martyr," *Esprit* 260 (April 1958): 641.

52. Claude Roy, *Somme toute* (Paris: Gallimard, 1976), 118.

53. Roy, "L'Homme ne vit pas seulement de spoutnik," *France observateur* 396 (12 December 1957): 17, repr. in *Pour Tibor Déry*, 39–41. Roy repeated this argument that one needed to speak the truth about socialist regimes and protest in the name of a socialism reconciled with liberty on many occasions. See, for example, his "P.P.C. du P.C.," *France observateur* 397 (19 December 1957): 15–16; and "'Effet calmant sur le peuple'," *France observateur* 425 (26 June 1958): 6.

54. For a further discussion of Domenach's politics in this period see Michael Scott Christofferson, "The Antitotalitarian Moment in French Intellectual Politics, 1975–1984" (Ph.D. diss., Columbia University, 1998), 89–91. For Louis de Villefosse's break with fellow-traveling see his "Et maintenant?" *Preuves* 79 (September 1957): 3–8; and "La Collaboration impossible," *France observateur* 342 (22 November 1956): 18.

55. Paul Ignotus, *Political Prisoner* (London: Routledge and Kegan Paul, 1959), 180. For confirmation of Ignotus's thesis see György Litván, ed., English version eds. and trans. János M. Bak and Lyman H. Legters, *The Hungarian Revolution of 1956: Reform, Revolt, and Repression 1953–1963* (New York: Routledge, 1996), 33–34.

56. On the PEN Club and the Hungarian Revolution see Nicole Racine, "L'Action européenne des PEN Clubs de 1945 aux années soixante," in *Les Intellectuels et l'Europe de 1945 à nos jours*, eds. Andrée Bachoud, Josefina Cuesta, and Michel Trebitsch (Paris: Publications universitaires Denis Diderot, 2000), 109–14; and the PEN Club archives in IMEC.

57. De Villefosse, *L'Oeuf de Wyasme*, ch. 12

58. Georges Paloczy-Horvath, "La Politique des apolitiques," *Preuves* 103 (September 1959): 51–54; and Louis de Villefosse, "Déry va-t-il mourir au secret?" *Le Monde*, August 8, 1959.

59. Letter of November 10, 1956, from Jean de Beer to David Carver, IMEC PN2 G02.01; letter of October 28, 1959, from De Beer to Carver, IMEC PN2 G02.02; letter of November 12, 1957, from De Beer to Carver, and letter of November 11, 1956, from De Beer to *Le Figaro littéraire*, both in IMEC PN2 I06.01.

60. "Memorandum Concerning the Hungarian P.E.N. Centre" of March 31, 1960; and Letter of Carver to the secretaries of the centers of the International PEN Club of 27 January 1960, both in IMEC PN2 I06.02.

61. Litván, *The Hungarian Revolution*, 137–38. Anthony Krause, "Les Écrivains hongrois face à la normalisation kadarienne: le cas Tibor Déry," *Revue d'histoire moderne et contemporaine* 49, no. 2 (April–June 2002): 205 n. 8.

62. Based on an analysis of *The New York Times Index*, vols. 45–48 (New York: The New York Times Company, 1958–1961).

63. See Michael Scott Christofferson, *French Intellectuals Against the Left: The Antitotalitarian Moment of the 1970s* (New York: Berghahn Books, 2004), on these later developments and the role played by revisions of the revolutionary socialist project.

64. Grémion, *L'Intelligence de l'anticommunisme*, 260–61. Jean-Paul Sartre, *The Ghost of Stalin*, trans. Marta H. Fletcher with the assistance of John R. Kleinschmidt (New York: George Braziller, 1968).

65. Roy, *Somme toute*, 24, 151; Vercors, *P.P.C.*, 37 and *passim*; De Villefosse, "La Collaboration impossible"; and Bouissounouse, *La Nuit d'Autun*, 283.

FROM *L'UNIVERS CONCENTRATIONNAIRE* TO THE JEWISH GENOCIDE: PIERRE VIDAL-NAQUET AND THE *TREBLINKA* CONTROVERSY

Samuel Moyn

Writing in 1995, the eminent classical historian and important public intellectual Pierre Vidal-Naquet pointed out a fact noticed by many other observers about the evolution of the perception of Nazi criminality in recent years. In 1945, few—next to no one in Vidal-Naquet's France—drew a meaningful distinction between concentration camps and extermination camps, between Western sites like Buchenwald and Eastern death installations like Treblinka. Now, such a difference is deeply ingrained in the consciousness of historians and, to some extent, even that of the public; but, as Vidal-Naquet emphasized, "The distinction, now strongly drawn, between the system of concentration camps and the exterminatory project is an acquisition of contemporary history."[1] In this chapter, I attempt, in a deliberately focused way, to reconstruct the circumstances in which Vidal-Naquet first acquired the distinction himself, pregnant as they are for understanding both postwar French culture as a whole and Vidal-Naquet's own metamorphosis into the principal academic commentator in France on the Nazi Holocaust that he became. The chapter is thus an inquiry into the origins of Vidal-Naquet's second career, a study in how he became eligible to author his justifiably famous attacks on the Holocaust denial of Robert Faurisson and to act as ubiquitous and knowledgeable French commentator on the Nazi genocide.[2] For what is striking about Vidal-Naquet's evolution is that—in spite of his parents' deportation to and murder in Auschwitz and his own hiding during the war to avoid capture and deportation himself—he did not intuitively grasp the distinction between the so-called *univers concentrationnaire* of Nazi internment and work facilities and the different project of Jewish extermination now so central to perceptions of the World War Two events. He had to learn it, and he did so, many years after the war, as part of the affair unleashed by the publication of Jean-François Steiner's lurid and sensationalizing book, *Treblinka*, in 1966.

In the first edition of *The Destruction of the European Jews*, published in 1961, Raul Hilberg could decry "the constant emphasis in the literature and in speeches upon 'concentration camps,' often including the epitomization of Dachau and Buchenwald but rarely embracing any mention of Auschwitz, let alone the faraway camps of Treblinka and Sobibor or Belzec."[3] This emphasis on the Western concentration camps occluded in particular the special fate of the Jews and the singularity of the purpose at work in the Eastern sites centered on their destruction. Now, things are different. In this sense, it is perhaps emblematic of the change under study in this essay that, late in his book exclusively on the Jewish fate during the war, Daniel Jonah Goldhagen is led, because of his correction of emphasis, to remind the reader that "not only Jews inhabited the concentration camp system."[4] Where once the concentration camps subsumed the death camps, now the reverse often occurs. While—as multinational research has shown—this perceptual shift occurred in nearly all countries, the French case presents its own specificity; and its study illuminates a surprisingly long-lasting moral conflict that continues to be felt even in current debates.

The immediate postwar emphasis in France on concentration instead of extermination had many causes. First and perhaps foremost, the many non-Jewish deportees who returned to France upon the Liberation were visible and vocal, unlike the Jewish victims of deportation. While roughly equivalent numbers of Jews and non-Jews were deported from France, nearly all of the former perished during the war where about half of the latter survived. For these two reasons, non-Jewish deportees to western concentration were more visible, after the war, than Jewish deportees to eastern extermination. In the second place, the western concentration camps were highly visible—indeed, spectacular—in their liberations and in the documentations immediately produced graphically (often photographically) illustrating their horror, while the discovery of the extermination camps did not provide the same spectacle.[5] (Though some of these camps had been reception sites for remaining Jewish prisoners when they were relocated, many in the infamous "death marches," from the Auschwitz region in early 1945, many of the longer-term inhabitants of the western camps interpreted their arrival as evidence of the further extent of the Nazi project, not

that their own suffering in the west had to be classed as a lesser, or at least
different, crime.) Finally, of course, there may have been persisting anti-
Semitism (not only right- but also left-wing in provenance), which certainly
played a role in the occlusion of the nature of victimhood, as well as the
penchant of Jewish survivors and communities, in all countries, for avoiding
a topic that (they believed) may have obstructed their reintegration.[6] The
result is that in the years leading up to the publication of Steiner's *Treblinka*
the main struggle over the legacy of World War Two amongst victims of the
Nazis occurred not over the recognition of the genocide but between
Gaullists and leftists over the political implications of the more general phenomenon of "deportation."[7]

No one contributed more than the Frenchman David Rousset to the perception that Nazi criminality consisted, at its most grave and extreme, in the
establishment of a vast network of concentration camps for a wide variety
of enemies (as opposed to, or rather including, the exterminatory project it
undertook against a particular group). He did not coin the expression "concentration camp," but he popularized it; and in the title of his immediate
postwar book *L'Univers concentrationnaire*, he inaugurated the notion of a
separate and isolated world constituted by the archipelago of exclusionary
institutions constructed by the Nazi regime to contain their enemies.[8] As
Annette Wieviorka has put it, Rousset

> introduced to the larger public the idea of a "concentration camp," no longer
> simply a repressive tool like a prison, but a world apart governed by its own
> laws. He thus allowed the concentration camp system to be conceived glob-
> ally, and made it possible—going beyond the testimonies on the Nazi camps
> published already before the war and, in great quantities, after 1945—for
> common principles of organization to be perceived. . . . It was not a matter any
> longer of the mere evocation of individual tragedies or of limited insights into
> a given camp—Dachau or Buchenwald—but of a global reflection. Even if
> David Rousset's analyses can seem partially obsolete today, a whole mode of
> reflection still operative is owed to him.[9]

Like Eugen Kogon's *Der SS-Staat*, the other report of the period that had
major international resonance, *L'Univers concentrationnaire* was written by
a non-Jew and extrapolated from personal experience in different western
camps, notably Buchenwald, to dwell more generally on the system as a total phenomenon. The title bespeaks the thesis, arguing for the universality
of an experience across a wide swath of territory. The book, like its vast se-
quel *Les Jours de notre mort* of the following year, aimed to capture the

sheer immensity of the camp system that grew up in Europe from shortly after the Nazi seizure of power.[10] It also presented such a system as in principle iterable in other times. Rousset epitomized, in France, the broadly universalist and specifically antifascist interpretation of Nazi criminality.

Rousset's work influentially described the camp experience as absurd and fictitious. The closest parallel he found to the camp was in Alfred Jarry's absurdist play *Ubu the King*: "Ubu and Kafka lost their original literary association," Rousset wrote, "and became component parts of the world in which we live."[11] In terms that, we will see, became central to both contemporary and very recent theoretical interpretations of the camps, Rousset emphasized the prisoners as not only literally but also existentially naked as a result of their internment and in the midst of a life no different from death.

But what is perhaps most striking, in rereading Rousset's work in light of Jean-François Steiner's later enterprise, is how much they shared, how close they were even as they believed they so fundamentally diverged. Steiner, we will see, claimed that the notion of a *univers concentrationnaire* obscured the exterminatory enterprise; and he focused on the specificity of the drive for survival among those targeted for death as a community. Rousset, in his early text, showed himself more than happy to admit inward differentiation within the overall *univers concentrationnaires*—even to the point of acknowledging the obvious differences between concentration and extermination. "The camps," he wrote,

> were not all identical or equivalent. The *univers concentrationnaire* was organized on different planes. . . . Buchenwald, Neuengamme, Sachsenhausen, Dachau, each and all fitted into the same plan, and were types of the "normal" camps which made up the essential framework of the concentration camp world. In utterly different latitudes lay the reprisal camps . . . for Jews . . . in the shape of Auschwitz. . . . The camps for Jews . . . were a large scale industry for torture and extermination.

This proximity alerts us to the fact that the claim of unity of and not differences in Nazi criminality is at bottom not an empirical dispute to be resolved by appeal for factual resolution. In any case, the factual distinction Rousset willingly drew did not lead to any more serious analytical fragmentation of the universal syndrome he depicted. "Between these extermination camps and the 'normal' camps there was no fundamental difference: only a difference in degree," he affirmed.[12] Rousset also shared Steiner's later perception of the moral difficulties that internees faced in the camps through their "collaborative" activity, and the zest for life that explained it.

Only the "ludicrous determination to hold on to life" is for Rousset no eth-
nic or religious principle, reserved to the Jews in particular, but a human
need that operates everywhere. Long before Steiner, he endorsed a "principle of life" that warred against the "principle of death" unleashed by the
SS camp masters, referring to "a dynamic awareness of the strength and
beauty of being alive, self-contained, brutal, entirely stripped of all superstructures, of being able to live even in the midst of the most appalling catastrophes or the most serious setbacks."[13]

Where Rousset ultimately differed from his later antagonist, we will
see, is in the moral consequence that flowed from a depiction of the
camps. For Rousset, the unforgettable portrait of the camps he achieved
served as a "warning" to the present of the easy and perhaps imminent
iterability of the evil that Nazis had unleashed most spectacularly but
that lurked near in any modern (capitalist and imperialist) society. "It
would be duplicity, and criminal duplicity, to pretend that it is impossible for other nations to try a similar experiment because it would be contrary to their nature," Rousset concluded his work. "Under a new guise,
similar effects may appear tomorrow."[14] Indeed, a few years later Rousset became one of the first to decry the Soviet Gulag in the postwar
years, appealing to other survivors to join his cause, only to be greeted by
communist denunciation.[15]

Rousset's conception of a unified system of Nazi criminality under which
many suffered had an enormous impact, within antifascist circles but also
far beyond them. It found illustrious readers both in France and outside.
Indeed, though her many commentators have failed to note it, Hannah
Arendt depended almost entirely on Rousset's interpretation as a source on
camp life in *The Origins of Totalitarianism*, which is worth examining in order to understand the drift of Rousset's universalizing and homogenizing
views. Arendt praised Rousset for perceiving the radical novelty of the
camps in European history. There was a caesura in European history, only
it was the camp system as a whole and not simply the particular fate of the
Jews in it. The Nazis had, Arendt argued, realized in practice the scope of
possible human crimes that European moralists and immoralists had first
achieved in theory. Ordinary social life excluded the terrifying fact that
Rousset had been (Arendt affirmed) "the first to understand" that "everything is possible." Far from denying extremity, Rousset alone first captured
its dimensions. Fiction, she repeated from Rousset's presentation, had become reality. (Arendt herself used the word "fictitious" several times to describe the world of the aims and achievements of totalitarian regimes.)
Most important, Rousset's analysis pushed Arendt to a striking and explicit

argument that the suffering of the Jews in the extermination camps needs to be understood as *continuous* with the rest of the Nazi camp system, its natural outgrowth or furthest consequence rather than a phenomenon in a different and alternative category.[16] Drawing on his depiction of living death, she understood extermination camps such as Treblinka as a consequence of concentration camps, not as a new and different formation. As Arendt put matters, it is the camp system, rendering human beings superfluous through killing them juridically and morally, which deserves the most attention; having become "living corpses," it is as if they are already dead.[17] Only a regime that produces living death, she suggested, can reach the last consequence of producing actual death.

Arendt's extraordinary rendition indicates some of the originality and fecundity of Rousset's intervention. But in many respects, it is the consistency of the interpretation of the World War Two events that Rousset crystallized with its age that invites comment. It certainly struck a continuity with interwar antifascist discourse, notably important in French politics, reviving its themes without allowing the novelty of genocide the force of interruption. Just as important, in France, the antifascist narrative that Rousset provided allowed a left-wing inflection to interpretation of events shared by Left and Right, which presented the search for a postwar patriotic order as the principal legacy of the victory against "concentrationist" regimes, and a set of protagonists who, by virtue of their experience, could testify about the past and lead into the future. And yet it would not be fair to say that the antifascist interpretation always and by definition "suppressed" the terrible fact of the Jews' victimhood in the Holocaust. Instead, at least some of the time, the Jewish persecution is given a great deal of attention *as part of* a more general "theory and practice of hell" (the English title of Eugen Kogon's book). Drawing on Rousset, Arendt actually gave an argument—persuasive or not—for why the camp system explains the genocide (the superfluity which totalitarianism confers on human beings also makes their elimination an expectable next step). And by and large Rousset, like Arendt and some of the other contributors to the discourse, never denied the disproportionate Jewish victimhood in the war, even as they integrated it into a larger picture of Nazi criminality. The thesis of continuity coexisted perfectly well with that of epitome: as Rousset put it in an early postwar article published in the Jewish journal *Évidences*, funded by the American Jewish Committee, the Jews' fate in the genocide, epitomizing the horror of the more general *univers concentrationnaire*, showed the need for more change to avoid in the present for others what in the past the Jews had suffered.[18]

As Henry Rousso comments in mentioning the *Treblinka* controversy in passing in his classical work on "the Vichy syndrome," the "furor" that the curious figure of Jean-François Steiner—in 1966 a twenty-eight year old first-time author—instigated occurred more thanks to the theses he announced in a prepublication interview than to his book itself.[19] The cover of the issue of *Le Nouveau Candide* in which the interview appeared, dated March 14, must have been designed to shock—though not to sell, for the magazine made this issue available free of charge. In large block letters, surrounding a swastika, the headline announces: THE JEWS: WHAT NO ONE EVER DARED TO SAY.[20] As of Steiner's response to the first question put him by the interviewer, Pierre Démeron, it is clear that an important moment of transition in French discourse about Nazi criminality has arrived:

> Q: Many books have been written on the death camps. Why a new one?
> A: There have been many books on concentration camps, on what used to be called the "camp universe" [*l'univers concentrationnaire*] . . . And there have been thousands upon thousands of testimonies. But on the death camps specifically there has been very little, actually.

Steiner's abrupt answer is important because it denies the premise of the question. Steiner set out to end the assimilation of the Holocaust to other Nazi crimes, helping to usher in a new regime of memory in which the Holocaust received specific attention as a phenomenon in its own right, separate from and irreducible to the continental war during which it took place or the more general Nazi system of terror that it consummated. Steiner's book alleged a descriptive failure, shared by many contributors to the first international regime of memory, such as Rousset and many others, that—he contended—led to a massive explanatory loss in confronting the past.[21]

Steiner opposed this tendency in many ways. In the first place, disrupting any sense of linear continuation from concentration camp to extermination camp along Rousset's lines, Steiner instead began his book with a set-piece on Jewish Vilna. This emplotment implied that ghettoization rather than concentration is the genuine (and specifically Jewish) precursor to the Nazis' ultimate crime. Then, of course, he set his drama in one of the principal death camps of the Nazi regime; like his narrative arc, Steiner's choice of setting—and inclusion of the phrase "extermination camp" in the subtitle of his book—underlined his opposition to the universalizing interpretation of Nazi criminality that he inherited.

But the book itself is no mere defense, with a historian's probity, of a factual distinction neglected in an earlier age. Instead it is itself a moral project, no different in this sense than Rousset's enterprise, even though opposite in spirit.[22] The following treatment of the book itself, by an author himself a Jew, like Vidal-Naquet, whose father had likewise died in Auschwitz, must necessarily be brief. Reversing Rousset's whole strategy in *L'Univers con-centrationnaire*, Steiner emphasized the difference and specificity of the Jewish fate at Nazi hands. Crucially, however, he did so as part of an equal and opposite moral insistence about what moral lesson that fate teaches. Steiner argued that the Jews who revolted in Treblinka, at the end of his book, illustrated a specifically Jewish existential imperative to survive—to follow the biblical command and "choose life" (Deut. 30: 19).

A hypothetical, literary reconstruction untroubled by academic scruples, *Treblinka* took liberties with the testimonial sources on which it relied that proved highly controversial; this method allowed Steiner, however, to give full flight to his imagination and to his interpretation. For though dedicated, like several other early treatments of the Holocaust, to Jewish resistance—the book is essentially a narrative of the origins of the Jewish revolt that destroyed the extermination camp on August 2, 1943—Steiner's *Treblinka* is only superficially martial in subject matter. It is more fundamentally moral. It is not just that the Treblinka Jews, in boldly planning and successfully executing their resistance, adopted an aim Steiner characterized as "insane, grandiose, and almost unique in the history of the camps of Nazi Europe: an armed revolt." It was the spirit in which they adopted this purpose, for Steiner, that truly mattered.[23] He made this clear in the one of the numerous reflective (and often grandiloquent) asides that littered his narrative. "For the Jews," he argued,

the real enemy was not Hitler . . ., it was death . . . Wars may be made with men, they are declared in the name of principles, and the victor is not the one who has lost the least men, but the one whose principle is saved. The real stake of the war that the Nazis made on the Jews was life itself.

He followed this reflection with a factual assertion often repeated in the controversy that followed:

When people talk about the war of 1939–45, they confuse two wars that have absolutely nothing in common: a world war, the one Germany made on the world, and a universal war, the war of the Nazis against the Jews, the war of the principle of death against the principle of life.[24]

In this way, then, Steiner insisted that concentration had "absolutely nothing in common" with extermination. This distinction was indeed one of the reasons Steiner wanted finally, against the overwhelming tendency of the initial postwar decades, to distinguish the Holocaust from the war that merely (he suggested) provided the occasion for the Holocaust to occur. The assault of death on life had been, for Steiner, the true conflict at the heart of the war, a struggle to be recognized only through isolating it from its apparently happenstance preconditions.

As for the "principle of life," the principle the Treblinka Jews opposed to the Nazis' morbidity, Steiner linked it not with humanity—as Rousset had in his own reflections on the imperative of survival—but with particularity. Where Rousset uncompromisingly integrated Jewish resistance into the larger antifascist fight, Steiner just as uncompromisingly separated them off from it, so that their behavior, both passive and active, had to be explained according to specific and incomparable principles. In the event, he concocted a seemingly dubious explanation for their behavior, relying most heavily on the Hasidic saying, "One must descend very low, in order to find the strength to rise again."[25] On Steiner's reconstruction of the revolt, the Treblinka Jews, initially passive to a man, slowly, out of the extremity of abjection, conceive the plan to revolt in order to remain true to the sempiternal Jewish imperative of communal survival.[26] In the passage that probably counted as his deepest explanation of the Jewish refusal, during the Treblinka revolt that destroyed the camp, to submit to the fate Nazism had decreed for them, Steiner suggested that there

> is a mystery here whose explanation can only be found in another and greater mystery, which is the survival of the Jewish people. Reason can enumerate a certain number of causes for this phenomenon—devotion to a faith, sense of solidarity, familial fanaticism, and so on—but other nations in which these same conditions applied have disappeared, at best leaving behind only a few fragments of stone. Heirs of this age-old mystery, the Jews of Treblinka revived it once again. And yet this time all of the conditions seemed to point to its not being renewed. Perhaps it is in this individual denial of death, this congenital inability to imagine it, that one can find the underlying cause of this miracle or survival. The Jew, more than any other man, realizes himself within his national community; as a Jew he can exist only insofar as he belongs to it. As soon as he leaves it he loses himself in the broader species of man. If the individual Jew remains mortal in spite of himself, his will to deny death renders the community immortal.[27]

Accordingly, the "mad idea" of a central figure to stage the revolt "had germinated in a Jewish brain."[28] Most important, then, the book illustrates a particular Jewish fate in the war, and a particularly Jewish principle of response.

Rousset's fiery review of Steiner's work, published a few weeks later in the same publication as Steiner's controversial interview, tasked his target with a "mystical, racist, and confusing" thesis.[29] What vexed Rousset into so enraged a reply to Steiner was that *Treblinka*'s particularizing interpretation destroyed the actual universalism that a study of the concentration camps should, he thought, promote. In this sense, Rousset perfectly recognized that Steiner's attempt to *entirely separate* Jewish from other victimhood at Nazi hands also destroyed the basis for postwar solidarities (of both Left and Right). Rousset acknowledged that the Jews suffered particular straits in the Nazi years, but he insisted that one erred in absolutely distinguishing the Jews from other kinds of victims, for "[t]he anti-Jewish enterprise of the Nazis was integrated in their general enterprise against fundamental liberties. It was one of the means of spreading terror and enforcing subjugation. They also eliminated the Gypsy people. They wanted to exterminate the Slavs. They pretended to make of the French a minor population." But even if the Nazis singled out the Jews to some extent (a fact Rousset never flatly denied, though of course it did not occupy the center of his thinking), this fact did not suggest, as Steiner had fantastically supposed, that the Jews responded in kind, and that the motives for their behavior during the war, including their resistance, involved the mystical drive for communal self-perpetuation. In this, most charitably read, Rousset did not so much deny the *fact* of special victimhood as the *significance* of this fact for making sense of the Nazi years as well as crafting a moral program in response.

In this vein, Rousset vehemently rejected the romanticized and sentimental view of Eastern European Jewry on which, he argued, Steiner had based his book, and emphasized instead the diversity of their political identities in the years prior to the genocide. Not surprisingly, he took special care to emphasize their participation in radical politics. Rooted in the workers' movement, Jews according to Rousset were primed, not for the mystical perpetuation of their communities, but solidarity in the common antifascist fight. "The struggle against Nazism was first of all and fundamentally an antifascist enterprise in which tens of thousands of Jews in Europe engaged because they were communists, socialists, and democrats," Rousset averred. It would be hard to say who erred through exaggeration more in the name of his ideology, Rousset or Steiner, traducing the complexity of the facts of prewar life in the name of his own thesis. But Rousset's opposite view led him to complain that Steiner's "confused lucubrations regarding the mystical necessity of the biological survival of God's people," which motivated Steiner's attempt to categorically distinguish the European war from the Holocaust that the war merely made possible, falsified not simply the unity of the Nazi enterprise but also the unity of the resistance to it. "Without underestimating the effects of an undeniable anti-semitism, the Jews did not fight alone, in Poland or elsewhere: . . . Their motivations were just as diverse as those of non-Jews. All the same, many, and not the least important, battled on behalf of a social and political ideal that they shared with all those who presented themselves in Europe as democrats, as socialists, and revolutionaries."[30] In this way, Rousset read the wartime in a manner that understood Jewish resistance as part of the larger war between the Nazis and their enemies.

Though the foregoing only scratches the surface of the *Treblinka* controversy, it presents the basic circumstances—the contrasting arguments of Steiner on one side and Rousset on the other—in which Vidal-Naquet's activation as a scholar of the genocide occurred, contingent as that turn was on the perception of the genocide as something different and other than the concentration camp universe.

In light of his personal history, accessible now thanks to the recent publication of his memoirs, it is easier to understand why the *Treblinka* controversy could have been a transformative moment in his life. The universalist, republican, and Dreyfusard content of his French-Jewish identity were ones which initially led to the suppression of the Holocaust as an important theme in Vidal-Naquet's life and work, in spite of how closely it touched him. As he describes it, while endogamy had persisted until his generation, he had no introduction to the spiritual or practical content of Judaism as a child (including even circumcision). He remembers his father as "what Raymond Aron called a 'de-Judaized Jew,' a perfect example of the abstract citizen." In 1940, Vidal-Naquet gained a sense of himself as a Jew, but only as a target; and his father, in an affiliation that would profoundly mark the son, responded by introducing him to the Dreyfus Affair, which most French Jews understood as a confirmation (not, as in much Zionist literature, a falsification) of their inherited Jewish republicanism.[31] "I am still proud," Vidal-Naquet wrote in his memoirs, "to affiliate with this tradition (which does not mean that I did not at times mistakenly apply the categories of the [Dreyfus] affair to causes that did not fit them)."[32] He came to see his famed engagement during the Algerian War largely in these Dreyfusard terms; indeed, Vidal-Naquet reflects that he may have singled out torture for his early interventions out of patriotic anger as well as in response to his memory of his father's torture at French hands before his deportation.[33] His republican-style identity, rooted in a defense of the rights of man, conformed perfectly with the tradition of Jewish republicanism. As a result, insofar as he considered himself to have a

Jewish identity, Vidal-Naquet shared the perception of Jean-Paul Sartre's *Anti-Semite and Jew*, published in 1946 and immediately purchased and read by Vidal-Naquet as clarifying his own sense of himself as one of the "inauthentic" Jews "whom other men take for Jews and who have decided to run away from this insupportable situation."[34] He lived his Jewish identity in the postwar period by being more universalist than the next person. For these reasons, as well as because of his affiliation with leftist politics, Vidal-Naquet did not differ initially from the consensus view (which provided the terms of debate between Left and Right) of the nature of Nazi criminality.

That is, until the *Treblinka* controversy. In an archival letter, written before the controversy allowed *Le Monde* to solicit a review from him (it had already printed one), Vidal-Naquet apologized to Steiner that he would not publish the article he envisioned writing upon reading the book. "I read your book with admiration—admiration for the men who revolted, of course, but also admiration for the author." He explained that "professional historians (and as you know I belong to their guild) would criticize you, asking, for example, how you were able to reconstitute dialogue and interior monologue." But this professionalizing objection could not really impair the success of Steiner's project, Vidal-Naquet observed. He also expressed exasperation about the leftist interpretation of Jewish resistance, for it ignored Steiner's central insight. "I fail to grasp," Vidal-Naquet suggested, "how [a] rather rudimentary Marxism can succeed in explaining how it is that the revolt was organized precisely by those whom the Germans put in charge of the camp. But what your book makes so clear is that it is only these actors who could have achieved anything."[35] Vidal-Naquet, then, entirely accepted not simply Steiner's insistence that the Nazis particularized the Jews for extermination rather than concentration, but also his particularizing theory of the nature of their response—precisely the "mysticism" of communal self-perpetuation for the purposes of witnessing that Rousset, for his part, angrily rejected.

When, as a result of the controversy, he published a review in *Le Monde* after all, Vidal-Naquet offered an all-out defense of Steiner's text. It reveals much about Vidal-Naquet's conversion to one of the book's central premises: the factual difference between concentration and extermination. "This book which others have violently criticized, I read with admiration," Vidal-Naquet began. He politely disagreed with those who rejected it on the grounds that it falsified the past. One needed the proper standard to appreciate it, for though "it narrates history," *Treblinka* never pretends to be "a book of history." Nothing invalidated the project of novelizing history in order to make it more vivid and instructive, Vidal-Naquet commented, citing John Hersey's *The Wall* and Rousset's own *Les Jours de notre mort.*[36] More importantly, however, Vidal-Naquet defended not just the "novelistic" form but also the moral content of Steiner's project. He agreed with Steiner—implicitly against Rousset's attack—that the Treblinka inmates were not "simply combatants in the antifascist fight." Instead, they were specifically Jewish in their submission and, finally, in their rebellion, too. In the major section of his review, Vidal-Naquet affirmed that Steiner had perceived the aims and nature of the camp inmates' actions with great moral exactitude. "Even a French, Marxist, and atheist Jew like myself will have noticed such tendencies in his own family traditions," Vidal-Naquet noted. Steiner had succeeded in documenting the limitations of the antifascist point of view, Vidal-Naquet concluded. In particular, Vidal-Naquet responded to Rousset's claim that Jews in extermination camps—as everywhere else in the concentration camp world—inserted themselves in a unitary war rather than singularizing their particular straits. For Vidal-Naquet, however, "[n]o doubt some of the men and women at Treblinka followed the progress of the Red Army and rejoiced at Mussolini's fall," finding grounds for revolt in a universalist ideology of resistance; but

> [t]he immense majority [of the Treblinka inmates] had no refuge but the pride in being Jews that they slowly regained. . . . The sources show that it is only in returning to their function as *witnesses*, the role in which the medieval church had thought to imprison them, only in wanting to make themselves witnesses of horror in the world and to play Israel's role among the nations that the Jews of Treblinka found the strength to survive. Let us not make them "Antifascist Poles of the Mosaic Confession."

It is as particularist Jews, not as universalist citizens or as antifascist resisters, that Steiner had properly captured both the intent and the success of the Treblinka insurrectionaries.

But perhaps most importantly, the implication that victims were not universalists led to another, and in postwar France epoch-making, implication: as Steiner had correctly insisted, the perpetrators were not universalists either. The genocide of the Jews occurred in some different category than Rousset's *univers concentrationnaire*. Not just the revolt of the Jews, but the genocide visited on the Jews, escaped the dominant universalist (and especially the antifascist) rubric of the time. "To imagine Treblinka, Sobibor, Majdanek, Belzec, Chelmno, Auschwitz just as particular cases of the *univers concentrationnaire*," Vidal-Naquet insisted, referring directly to Rousset's paradigm, "is to betray the reality of the Nazis who organized [the genocide as well as] the free world that allowed it." For this reason, he finished,

The Treblinka revolt (like that of the *Sonderkommando* at Auschwitz) is no longer possible to compare to the seizure of power by the Buchenwald deportees on 10 April 1945 any more than the Warsaw ghetto insurrection of April–May 1943 is possible to compare to the Parisian insurrection of 19 August 1944. The Nazis attempted, with the Jews, a complete and final obliteration [*une mise en condition totale*]. . . . If the Treblinka revolt reveals the truth about the nature of this horror, is it too much to ask that the Jews receive the credit?

These are, in the context, striking affirmations. The emphasis in Vidal-Naquet's homage to Steiner is, if not on the singularity of the genocide, then at least on the difference between concentration and extermination, a difference that by and large eluded the antifascist paradigm, and one which the act of witnessing of the Treblinka Jews—abetted (or invented) by Steiner's attempt to ventriloquize their voices—made clear for the first time.

A debate organized by the newspaper *Combat*, in which Vidal-Naquet and Rousset participated, makes a fitting conclusion to this chapter because it casts light on the contest of paradigms that the *Treblinka* affair encouraged. Vidal-Naquet affirmed, once again, that "the Hitlerian massacre of the Jews is without any common measure with any other crime committed by them,"[37] and that this point, the one "on which David Rousset criticizes Steiner most violently," survived all of the other difficulties of the book. Just as strikingly, Vidal-Naquet accepted Steiner's particularizing account of Jewish identity and its role in the *Treblinka* affair; Steiner convinced him of the descriptive difference between concentration and extermination not independently but as part of his evaluative project of insisting on Jewish moral particularity.[38] "I believe, contrary to David Rousset," Vidal-Naquet concluded, "that Steiner is right when he describes the dramatic solitude of the Jews and especially of the Polish Jews who formed a relatively homogeneous community." For his part, Rousset, all while claiming that he had never denied that Jews and non-Jews had experienced different suffering, and that the terror visited on the first group had been "still deeper" than for the second, nevertheless concluded that *"this difference should not create any distinction in the moral problem under debate."* Vidal-Naquet replied that "there was not a difference of terror," between the two kinds of camps, "but one of nature, since the ends were different [*la finalité n'étant pas le même*]."

Beyond any sociological claim about the homogeneity of the victim population, however, Vidal-Naquet also endorsed Steiner's argument for the existential commitment that must have driven them in their revolt. In this regard, it is interesting to find an assimilated Jew insisting, against the Jewish historians on the panel such as Léon Poliakov and Michel Borwicz, that the imperative Steiner had underlined must indeed have played a role in the revolt.[39] Against these and other critics of the book assembled by *Combat*, Vidal-Naquet continued to insist on "a Jewish specificity in the revolt." In a striking comment, in light of his prior engagements during the Algerian war, Vidal-Naquet likened his discovery of Jewish specificity during the Holocaust to his discovery of Arab nationalism rather than Enlightenment universalism among the population whose revolt he had famously advocated a few years before. Rousset, in reply, dismissed Steiner's book as "a serious step backward. Steiner returns us to the conditions of a world which was a world entirely focused on the Jewish question, and in which the Jew always felt he was the particular victim of particular circumstances." To which Vidal-Naquet replied: "That's because he was!"

Vidal-Naquet's conversion proved the turning point in his career, and, more broadly, in French culture. Soon after the controversy, to be sure, Vidal-Naquet's evaluation of Steiner's book changed drastically. Provoked by the controversy into studying the genocide with the same academic and scientific rigor he brought to ancient Greece, his professional specialty, Vidal-Naquet soon realized that he had been badly fooled by Steiner and his book, a concoction of truth and falsehood, fact and legend that skillful marketing, abetted by the ignorance of the reading public, had made a literary event. Indeed, when Steiner's next book appeared, Vidal-Naquet told its author that he would not allow himself to be duped by the same person twice in a lifetime.[40] In "A Paper Eichmann," his celebrated attack on Faurisson, Vidal-Naquet grouped *Treblinka* together with the "vast subliterature representing a truly obscene appeal to consumption and sadism" that has to be "pitilessly denounced."[41] In a note, Vidal-Naquet admitted that he "fell into the trap laid by Steiner's book," and though he did not "retract the substance" of his *Le Monde* review, he insisted that he had atoned for his mistake by attacking later sensationalizations and falsifications of the genocide.[42] But he did not reverse his own insistence during the *Treblinka* affair that Steiner had, whatever his faults, properly forced on France the all-important distinction between concentration and extermination.

For it remains true, all the same, that it is the "trap" laid by Steiner that proved the decisive catalyst for Vidal-Naquet's entry into his celebrated and far-reaching career as a scholar (and public intellectual) of the genocide, a topic so long ignored in the French academy, but since increasingly central thanks to his work. What is so ironic, then, is that the book Vidal-Naquet eventually rejected played such a significant role in catalyzing his interest in the subject he accepted. It played this role, it is fair to say, not just in a general way but on a specific point. In a pregnant and important passage in his recollections, Vidal-Naquet observes that it was Steiner's book that pushed him to insist on the difference between the antifascist conception of a unitary system of repression and the insistence that, whatever the horrors of Rousset's "concentration camp universe," the extermination camps were in a different category. "The text I wrote differentiated," Vidal-Naquet recalled of his *Le Monde* intervention in the Steiner affair, "between the concentration camps and the places which were just for killing pure and simple." While at the time, he continued, many "refused to make an important distinction between Auschwitz and Treblinka, on the one hand, and Buchenwald or Dachau, on the other," and while Rousset, in his various attacks on Steiner's book, "acknowledged that the terror was much deeper at Auschwitz than at the western camps but refused to distinguish between the war declared by the SS against the Jews and the war pursued by the Wehrmacht against the Allies," Vidal-Naquet insisted on the difference. This insistence, he wrote, "proved to be a nodal point, even if my own researches on it became much richer."[43]

The *importance* of the distinction between concentration and extermination, of course, remains a matter of intense controversy, not simply in French culture but also in Vidal-Naquet's own subtle thinking as it has evolved since the *Treblinka* controversy. Indeed, in a different place in his memoirs, written in the years of the culmination of the penchant for separating concentration and extermination, Vidal-Naquet added that he believes that

> the two systems, that of concentration and that of extermination, . . . are, I now think, closer cousins of one another than it is sometimes thought. Why do I say this? Not at all in order to deny that Treblinka and Dachau had distinct ends: killing on the one hand, isolating from the world and, possibly, extinguishing, on the other. But one must add that the machine for killing was born in proximity to the machine for extinguishing and that at Auschwitz and Majdanek the two systems were combined.[44]

The recent period in French intellectual life, indeed, has been the period of Rousset's posthumous return and perhaps of his belated revenge. After many years, a group of European (and especially French) intellectuals has begun an attempted—no doubt qualified and far more theoretically sophisticated—return to the immediate postwar perception of a universe of camps and the present-day engagement on behalf of humanity that traditionally followed from it.[45] Many tendencies nourished this challenge to the perception of the singularity and differentiation of extermination that grew slowly but powerfully in France beginning in the 1960s, not least the new penchant for comparing Nazi and Stalinist horror, a comparison evidently facilitated by a shift in emphasis to their common camp universes—a commonality Rousset, after all, stressed early on.[46]

It is easy to adopt one of the two obvious perspectives on this recent development—that it is a salutary return to Rousset's universalism, mistakenly suppressed by excessive attention to the Jewish genocide, or that it sacrifices exactly the descriptive clarity about the past gained by the crisis and decomposition of Rousset's perspective.[47] Each of the rival paradigms obscures some aspects of the past even as it highlights others, though they are surely not equal in virtue of that fact. It is, in any event, more difficult to admit that we are probably witnesses to the same imbrication of moral ideology and historical perception now, in selecting between the paradigms, as a study of the *Treblinka* affair reveals. And yet, there is no question that the acquisition of the factual distinction between concentration and extermination, due to Steiner in Vidal-Naquet's biography and through him in French culture, is a permanent corrective to the prior manner of thinking that forces the project of its revival to take a new form if it is to be persuasive.

If the legacy of the *Treblinka* affair is understood as a historical problem, Vidal-Naquet's reflections on the relation of the historian's perception to public memory, offered at the same time that he narrated the emergence of the distinction between concentration and extermination, can serve as my own concluding remark as well. "The formation of a historian," he wrote,

> does not happen simply thanks to magisterial studies. Even in the work of a historian—and, naturally, in his life—the irrational plays a role. When I speak of the changes in historical consciousness, I cannot pretend that the historiography of the destruction of the European Jews has progressed in a linear fashion beginning with the simple gathering of testimonies and documents through the scientific elaboration to be found in the most recent edition of Hilberg's book. That would be a totally oversimplified picture of the evolution of the historiography. The idea of progress has to be put in question in the study of historiography just as it must in the study of history.[48]

But was Vidal-Naquet questioning the possibility of progress or only underlining the unexpected ways in which it may occur? In light of the centrality in French memory of the distinction it had once lacked between concentration and extermination—a distinction on which Steiner insisted—it is only fair to say that his book, though rejected, is among the factors catalyzing an important revolution in France in thinking about the nature of Nazi criminality. At the same time, the emergence of the *factual* distinction between concentration and extermination, though doubtless analytically independent from Steiner's idiosyncratic views about Jewish existence, nevertheless required them in Vidal-Naquet's own biography. One may wonder, then, if falsehood is sometimes the indispensable ally of truth.

NOTES

This chapter is a small portion of my study *A Holocaust Controversy: The Treblinka Affair in Postwar France* (University Press of New England, forthcoming).

1. Pierre Vidal-Naquet, *Les Juifs, la mémoire et le présent*, vol. 3, *Réflexions sur le génocide* (Paris: La Découverte, 1995), 12.

2. For his attack on "negationism," see Vidal-Naquet, *Les Assassins de la mémoire: "Un Eichmann de papier" et autres essais sur le révisionnisme* (Paris: La Découverte, 1987); in English as *Assassins of Memory: Essays on the Denial of the Holocaust*, trans. Jeffrey Mehlman (New York: Columbia University Press, 1992). Most of his other contributions—which often took the form of prefaces to the most important books on the subject of the genocide—are gathered in his *Les Juifs, la mémoire et le présent* series, partially translated as *The Jews: History, Memory, and the Present*, trans. David Ames Curtis (New York: Columbia University Press, 1995).

3. Raul Hilberg, *The Destruction of the European Jews* (Chicago: Quadrangle Books, 1961), 681.

4. Daniel Jonah Goldhagen, *Hitler's Willing Executioners: Ordinary Germans and the Holocaust* (New York: A.A. Knopf, 1996), 330.

5. Of the camps purely for extermination, only Majdanek (Lublin) survived long enough for Soviet capture. On the western liberations, see Robert Abzug, *Inside the Vicious Heart: Americans and the Liberation of the Nazi Concentration Camps* (New York: Oxford University Press, 1985). On photographs, but without the necessary distinction between concentration and extermination camps, see Barbie Zelizer, *Remembering to Forget: Holocaust Memory through the Camera's Eye* (Chicago: University of Chicago Press, 1998).

6. See Maud S. Mandel, *In the Aftermath of Genocide: Armenians and Jews in Twentieth-Century France* (Raleigh, N.C.: Duke University Press, 2003), chap. 2.

7. See Pieter Lagrou, *The Legacy of Nazi Occupation: Patriotic Memory and National Recovery in Western Europe, 1945–1965* (Cambridge: Cambridge University Press, 2000); and earlier, see Annette Wieviorka, *Déportation et génocide: entre la mémoire et l'oubli* (Paris: Plon, 1992).

8. The term "concentration camp" appears to date from 1901, while the consensus is that the institution itself dates from 1896. See Andrzej Kaminski, *Konzentrationslager 1896 bis heute: Geschichte, Funktion, Typologie* (Munich: Piper, 1990);

and Joël Kotek and Pierre Rigoulot, *Le Siècle des camps: détention, concentration, extermination: cent ans de mal radical* (Paris: Lattès, 2000). On the inception of the Nazi camps, see, in a large literature, Wolfgang Benz and Barbara Distel, eds., *Terror ohne System: die ersten Konzentrationslager im Nationalsozialismus 1933–1935* (Berlin: Metropol, 2001).

9. Wieviorka, "L'Expression 'camp de concentration' au 20e siècle," *Vingtième siècle* 54 (April–June 1997): 4–12 at 10, an article in which she contends that the lability of the term "concentration camp" makes it overly dangerous for historical use.

10. David Rousset, *L'Univers concentrationnaire* (Paris: Éditions du Pavois 1946); and *Les Jours de notre mort* (Paris: Éditions du Pavois, 1947). For the translations of the former, both long out of print, see *The Other Kingdom*, trans. Ramon Guthrie (New York: Reynal and Hitchcock, 1947); and *A World Apart*, trans. Yvonne Moyse and Roger Senhouse (London: Secker and Warburg, 1951). Eugen Kogon, *Der SS-Staat: das System der deutschen Konzentrationslager* (Berlin: Tempelhof, 1947).

11. Rousset, *L'Univers concentrationnaire*, 185; *The Other Kingdom*, 172; *A World Apart*, 111.

12. Rousset, *L'Univers concentrationnaire*, 48–51; *The Other Kingdom*, 58–61; *A World Apart*, 25–27.

13. Rousset, *L'Univers concentrationnaire*, 13, 184; *The Other Kingdom*, 29, 171; *A World Apart*, 2, 111.

14. Rousset, *L'Univers concentrationnaire*, 186–87; *The Other Kingdom*, 172–73; *A World Apart*, 112.

15. See Rousset, "Au secours des déportés dans les camps soviétiques: Un appel aux anciens déportés des camps nazis," *Le Figaro littéraire*, 12 November 1949; and, for the celebrated libel trial that followed, Rousset et al., *Le Procès concentrationnaire pour la vérité des camps: extraits des débats* (Paris: Editions du Pavois, 1951). Cf. Jean-Paul Sartre and Maurice Merleau-Ponty, "Les Jours de notre vie," *Les Temps modernes* 51 (January 1950): 1153–68.

16. It is also important to remark, in Arendt's case, that the continuity between concentration and extermination is balanced by a separate argument (absent in Rousset's work) about why Jews in particular ended up the victims of the latter rather than simply of the former. A revised version of her overall view has most recently been presented by Enzo Traverso, *The Origins of Nazi Violence*, trans. Janet Lloyd (New York: The New Press, 2003).

17. In her depiction, as well as in her critique of human rights, Arendt also followed Rousset's stress on human nudity in the camp, a premise more recently taken up by Giorgio Agamben; see below. Arendt originally presented her interpretation of Rousset in "The Concentration Camps," *Partisan Review* (1948), and reprinted it in *The Origins of Totalitarianism*, 2nd ed. (New York: Meridian, 1958), chap. 12, esp. 436–37, 441 n. 125. See also Arendt, "Social Science Techniques and the Study of the Camps," *Jewish Social Studies* 12 (1950), repr. in Arendt, *Essays in Understanding*,

ed. Jerome Kohn (New York: Harcourt, Brace, 1994). She also sent Rousset's book to her friends Karl Jaspers and Hermann Broch.

18. Rousset, "Les menaces ne sont pas mortes," *Évidences* 1 (March 1949): 17–19.

19. Henry Rousso, *The Vichy Syndrome: History and Memory in France since 1944*, trans. Arthur Goldhammer (Cambridge, Mass.: Harvard University Press, 1991), 164; cf. 139.

20. Pierre Démeron, "Les Juifs: Ce qu'on n'a jamais osé dire," *Le Nouveau Candide*, 14–20 March 1966.

21. Samuel Moyn, "Two Regimes of Memory," *American Historical Review* 103, no. 4 (October 1998): 1182–86.

22. Jean-François Steiner, *Treblinka: la révolte d'un camp d'extermination*, preface by Simone de Beauvoir (Paris: Fayard, 1966); the English translation (New York: Simon and Schuster, 1967) is by Helen Weaver. It also quickly appeared in German, Portuguese, Spanish, Italian, and Japanese.

23. Steiner, *Treblinka*, 167; English ed., 181.

24. Steiner, *Treblinka*, 277; English ed., 296.

25. The most famous invocation of this notion is in S. Ansky's play *The Dybbuk*, in which it is prominently cited at the outset. In a recent edition, it is translated as follows: "The seed of redemption / is contained within the fall." Ansky, *The Dybbuk and Other Writings*, ed. David G. Roskies (New York: Schocken Books, 1992).

26. Scandalously, in the *Nouveau Candide* interview that set off the controversy, Steiner explained that he had opted against a study of the Warsaw uprising because it seemed "very 'goy' as a revolt. The heroes of Warsaw chose the manner of their death but, in choosing death, they accepted it in a certain sense. There they sinned." As David Halberstam correctly understood in his *New York Times* coverage of the controversy, "the more frail and less-known Treblinka uprising was Jewish in the sense that it was first and foremost for survival." David Halberstam, "'Treblinka': An Author Finds Himself," *New York Times*, 17 April 1966.

27. Steiner, *Treblinka*, 136–37; English ed., 149.

28. Steiner, *Treblinka*, 313; English ed., 332.

29. Rousset, "L'affaire Tréblinka: les Juifs accusent," *Le Nouveau Candide*, 18 April 1966; and Rousset, "L'affaire Tréblinka: 'Nous ne sommes pas morts comme des moutons'," *Le Nouveau Candide*, 29 April 1966.

30. Similarly, Martine Monod, a communist writing in *L'Humanité*, suggested: "It is as if these Jews," as Steiner presented them, "came from nowhere, suddenly parachuting into Treblinka, springing from a mystical universe where there was no fascism, no world war, no Red Army, no Resistance, no occupied Europe, no nothing. . . . [Steiner] has developed the kinds of arguments most dangerous to the incessant combat that people must fight for their liberation, today as yesterday." Review of Steiner, *L'Humanité dimanche*, 12 June 1966.

31. Vidal-Naquet later published his father's diary from this period. See Lucien Vidal-Naquet, "Journal, 15 septembre 1942–29 février 1944," *Annales E.S.C.* 48, no. 3 (1993): 513–44, with Vidal-Naquet's "Préface," 501–12, in English as "Pre-

sentation of a Document: The Journal of Attorney Lucien Vidal-Naquet," in *The Jews*.

32. Vidal-Naquet, *Mémoires*, vol. 1, *La Brisure et l'attente, 1930–1955* (Paris: Le Seuil, 1995), 41–46 at 43, 113.

33. Vidal-Naquet, *Mémoires*, vol. 2, *Le Trouble et la lumière, 1955–1998* (Paris: Le Seuil, 1998), 33; and *Torture: Cancer of Democracy, France and Algeria, 1954–62*, trans. Barry Richard (Baltimore: Penguin Books, 1963), later published in French in 1972. See Vidal-Naquet's collection, *Face à la raison d'État: un historien dans la guerre d'Algérie* (Paris: La Découverte, 1989), for his influential typology of intellectual response, including his own Dreyfusard category. Vidal-Naquet's interventions are covered in the many works on French intellectuals and the Algerian war, such as Hervé Hamon and Patrick Rotman, *Les Porteurs de valises: la résistance française à la guerre d'Algérie*, 2nd ed. (Paris: Albin Michel, 1982); or Jean-Pierre Rioux and Jean-François Sirinelli, eds., *La Guerre d'Algérie et les intellectuels français* (Brussels: Éditions Complexe, 1991).

34 Vidal-Naquet, *Mémoires*, 2: 167; Sartre, *Anti-Semite and Jew*, trans. George J. Becker (New York: Schocken, 1948), 93; and cf. Vidal-Naquet, "Remembrances of a 1946 Reader," *October* 87 (Winter 1999): 7–23.

35. Letter of Vidal-Naquet to Steiner of April 4, 1966, in private archival files that Jean-François Steiner generously allowed me to consult.

36. Vidal-Naquet, "Treblinka et l'honneur des juifs," *Le Monde*, 2 May 1966. It is perhaps worth noting, in this connection, that Raul Hilberg welcomed the book with high praise upon its American translation, likewise not allowing a historian's scruples to serve as exclusive criteria for judging a book of imaginative reconstruction.

37. Jan-Claude Kerbourc'h, et al., "*Treblinka*, de Jean-François Steiner," *Combat*, 10 June 1966.

38. Vidal-Naquet's affirmation that this singularity placed the Treblinka Jews in a religious history stretching back to the Jewish revolt against the Romans strongly suggests that it is in the *Treblinka* affair that one must also seek the origins of perhaps Vidal-Naquet's most famous study in Jewish history, his lengthy treatment of Josephus's *Jewish War*. See Flavius Josephus, *La Guerre des juifs, précedé par "Du bon usage de la trahison," de Pierre Vidal Naquet* (Paris: Éditions de Minuit, 1977).

39. Poliakov, the reigning expert on Jewish history of the period, also made himself one of Steiner's most implacable critics. Borwicz, a forgotten figure, had been among the founding members of the Jewish Historical Commission in postwar Poland and subsequently established himself as a French scholar of the war (and especially of the camps) before the topic became popular. See Michael C. Steinlauf, *Bondage to the Dead: Poland and the Memory of the Holocaust* (Syracuse: Syracuse University Press, 1997), 55–56; and Michel Borwicz, *Écrits des condamnés à mort sous l'occupation allemande (1939–1945): étude sociologique* (Paris: Presses Universitaires, 1954).

40. He told me this in an interview of March 17, 1999.

41. Vidal-Naquet, *Assassins of Memory*, 14.

42. Vidal-Naquet, *Assassins of Memory*, 149–50 n. 24. Three years after the *Treblinka* affair, in 1969, Vidal-Naquet documented the plagiarism of an earlier testimony involved in another sensationalistic book, Sylvain Reiner's *Et la terre sera pure* (Paris: Fayard, 1969), and succeeded in having the publisher pull it from the market.

43. Vidal-Naquet, *Mémoires*, 2: 246.

44. Vidal-Naquet, *Mémoires*, 2: 242–43. Cf. for a similar point, Vidal-Naquet, "Réflexions sur trois *Ravensbrück*," in *Les Juifs, la mémoire et le present*, vol. 3; in English as "Reflections on Three *Ravensbrücks*," trans. David Ames Curtis, *South Atlantic Quarterly* 96, no. 4 (Fall 1997): 881–94 at 888–89.

45. See esp. Giorgio Agamben, "What Is a Camp?" (originally published in French in *Libération*, 3 October 1994), in *Means without End: Notes on Politics*, trans. Vincenzo Binetti and Cesare Casarino (Minneapolis: University of Minnesota Press, 2000); Agamben, *Homo Sacer: Sovereign Power and Bare Life*, trans. Daniel Heller-Roazen (Stanford: Stanford University Press, 1998), pt. III, chapter 7 ("The Camp as Nomos of the Modern"), a study also included in Hent de Vries and Samuel Weber, eds., *Violence, Identity, and Self-Determination* (Stanford: Stanford University Press, 1997).

46. See esp. Stéphane Courtois, ed., *Le Livre noir du communisme: crimes, terreurs, répression* (Paris: R. Laffont, 1997); in English as *The Black Book of Communism: Crime, Terror, Repression*, trans. Jonathan Murphy and Mark Kramer (Cambridge, Mass.: Harvard University Press, 1999), and the debate provoked by it. In this context, several writers suggested in the 1990s that the focus on Jewish extermination had not only served to obscure what Nazism and Stalinism shared, but had also led to the minimization of the suffering under communist regimes (and perhaps elsewhere as well). See notably Alain Brossat, *L'Épreuve du désastre: le XXe siècle et les camps* (Paris: Albin Michel, 1996); and Catherine Coquio, ed., *Parler des camps, penser les génocides* (Paris: Albin Michel, 1999). For French critiques of this perspective, see Henri Raczymow, "D'un 'détail' qui masque le tableau," *Le Monde*, 21 January 1998; or Robert Redeker, "Un autre révisionnisme?: Alain Brossat et les camps," *Les Temps modernes* (November–December 1997): 125–32; in English, see Omer Bartov, "The Proof of Ignominy: Vichy France's Past and Presence," *Contemporary European History* 7, no. 1 (1998): 107–31; and his *Germany's War and the Holocaust: Disputed Histories* (Ithaca: Cornell University Press, 2003), chap. 4, 160–71. Cf. Tzvetan Todorov, "Je conspire, Hannah Arendt conspirait, Raymond Aron aussi," *Le Monde*, 31 January 1998; and *Les Abus de la mémoire* (Paris: Arléa, 1998).

47. Not surprisingly, Rousset's rediscovery has coincided with the focus on the camp phenomenon. See the recent collection of essays on him by Alain Brossat, Catherine Coquio, Tzvetan Todorov, and others in *Lignes*, n.s., 2 (May 2000): 5–232. Todorov's reflections on Rousset also figure in *Mémoire du mal, tentation du bien: enquête sur le siècle* (Paris: R. Laffont, 2000); now available in English as *Hope and Memory: Lessons from the Twentieth Century* (Princeton: Princeton University Press, 2003).

48. Vidal-Naquet, "Qui sont les assassins de la mémoire?" in *Les Juifs, la mémoire et le présent*, 3: 284; cf. Wieviorka, "Pierre Vidal-Naquet face aux 'assassins de la mémoire'," in *Pierre Vidal-Naquet: un historien dans la cité*, eds. François Hartog, Pauline Schmitt, and Alain Schnapp (Paris: La Découverte, 1998). In this text, Vidal-Naquet repeated once again that it was "nonetheless the execrable book of Jean-François Steiner" that "led me to understand what a camp for pure extermination was."

(12)

FRENCH CULTURAL POLICY
IN QUESTION, 1981–2003

Philippe Poirrier

The guiding role played by the French government in regulating cultural and artistic affairs is often regarded, within the family of Western democracies, as a curiosity.[1] The institution of an official policy for culture was consecrated in 1959, in the early days of the Fifth Republic, by the creation of a ministry for cultural affairs headed by André Malraux. The fledgling administration was, however, able to draw on a long history with a substantial body of theory and legislation, and could count on a large number of cultural institutions concentrated in and around Paris.[2]

Malraux had been the target of much criticism, especially from adult educationists [*l'éducation populaire*] who disputed the elitist nature of his policies.[3] But a principal debate was triggered by the action of the left-wing government beginning in the early 1980s. Our contribution is intended to clarify the pattern of this debate from the 1980s to the present day, and to describe the main developments that have shaped France's cultural policy.[4]

A digression into historiography will help us understand how the French academic world has viewed the issues. Cultural policy studies, often government-sponsored, for a long time limited themselves to examining or assessing the socio-economic aspects of past and future policy.[5] Interest in the history of cultural policies and institutions is comparatively recent in France.[6] The social history of cultural habits is the field of action preferred by "modernist" historians.[7] Scholars of the "contemporary" period who claim for themselves the cultural history label are usually recycled political historians.[8] The Ministry of Culture's History Committee, headed since 1993 by Augustin Girard and Geneviève Gentil, has done much to promote research in the field by holding conferences and seminars, compiling oral records, and issuing a score of publications. The effect has been to extend the field to all the social science disciplines.[9]

THE CULTURAL IMPERATIVE: A POLICY UNDER DEBATE, 1981–1993: GOAL-ORIENTED POLICY

When the Left came to power in 1981, a threefold break with the past occurred. The major change was the doubling of the Ministry of Culture's budget.[10] Second, this change of scale was fittingly embodied in the public mind in the person of the new minister of culture, Jack Lang, who had the unswerving support of the president. Third, the intentional linkage of culture with the economy amounted to a Copernican revolution in socialist thinking. While every policy department benefited from these quantitative and qualitative changes, creative activities and the performing arts received more attention than the heritage sector [*le patrimoine*]. Further evidence of the presidential role in cultural policy was provided by the grand-scale works program [*les Grands Travaux*], essentially devoted to heritage institutions.[11]

The original 1959 decree was officially amended for the first time under Mitterrand. The text promulgated on May 10, 1982, considerably altered the tasks allotted to the Ministry of Culture:

> The Ministry of Culture serves the following purposes: to let all French citizens develop their inventive and creative abilities, freely exercise their talents and receive their choice of artistic training; to preserve national and regional heritage and the heritage of the various social groups for the common benefit of the entire community; to foster the creation of works of art and of the mind and offer them the widest possible audience; to help propagate French culture and art in an unrestricted interchange of all the world's cultures.

The idea of culture for all was replaced by that of individual self-expression through creativity, each type of culture being respected. The intentional broadening of the culture field brought recognition—although not everyone approved—to cultural activities that had previously been considered unimportant. Jazz, pop music, break dancing, and cartoon

strips all became worthy objects of government cultural support. Two remarks need to be made here. This cultural relativism was not invented in
the 1980s. In the heritage field, for example, the Ministry of Culture had
begun to include "ethnological" and "industrial" heritage in the mid-
1970s.[12] Furthermore, the nod given to the cultural activities listed above
did not basically modify the system for defining cultural legitimacy. As
Vincent Dubois points out, "Quite a distance separated the 'everything is
culture' line and any real undermining of the established cultural ranking
system."[13] Still, the growing role and independence of the various cultural
occupations helped to strengthen the legitimacy of newly promoted activities and instill in them their own ways of doing things. Government,
moreover, was only one factor contributing to a broader transformation of
the cultural landscape. Also at work were mass education, the decline of
a humanities education that had provided the food for the "cultivated
mind," and the rising power of the media as a standard of reference for
art and culture.

The linking of culture with the economy was an equally central element.
At a Mexico City conference in 1982, Jack Lang outlined his hopes for this
new alliance. Commentators have put the accent on the speech's Third
World and anti-American aspects while glossing over the minister's new line
of reasoning. Whereas Augustin Girard's ideas on cultural industries' role in
democratizing culture had raised a storm of protest on the Left, and especially among French communists, in 1978,[14] Jack Lang could now calmly
list the positive effects expected from the new collaboration:

> Economy and culture. The issue is the same. I should like to mention two
> seemingly contradictory facts in this connection. The first is that creation in
> culture and the arts suffers from a system of multinational financial domina-
> tion that needs to be fought. The second, which seems to contradict the first,
> is that the international crisis can be solved by artistic and scientific creativity
> and invention. . . .
>
> There is another aspect: creativity can drive an economic recovery. . . . To
> quote Nietzsche, "Art should not be a bauble hung up here and there to look
> pretty." Art and creation must, on the contrary, occupy a central, and not just
> ornamental or decorative place in our society.[15]

Cultural policy, through support for cultural industries [*les industries culturelles*], took on an economic and industrial dimension. Its central administration assumed a double charge: on the one hand, it was the ministry for
artists and artistic institutions and occupations; on the other hand, it was the
ministry for cultural industries.

LANG VERSUS MALRAUX

Comparison with the July 24, 1959, decree defining the assignments of the
Ministry for Cultural Affairs under André Malraux is instructive. It reveals
how much government theory had changed in the space of twenty years:

> The Minister in charge of cultural affairs has the task of giving the largest pos-
> sible number of French citizens access to the great works of mankind, and of
> France in particular; of ensuring the widest possible audience for our cultural
> heritage; and of fostering the creation of those works of art and mind which
> enrich that heritage.

The implementing paragraphs of this initial decree consecrated the ideology of equality. The all-important intention was to democratize and give
equal access to culture, a policy which formed part and parcel of the welfare state. Equal treatment for all was to be a matter of practice, not only
words. The goal of the welfare state was to make cultural assets equally
available to everyone. That goal was expressed in two parallel policies: giving citizens at large access to works of culture; and extending welfare benefits to the artistic community. Cultural policy was, in addition, molded by
the Gaullist republic's ideal of modernization. The state was required to
play a driving role of guidance, incentive, and regulation. It would be a mistake, however, to think of this policy as an over-arching and carefully
thought-out product of Gaullist ambition. The setting-up of the Ministry for
Cultural Affairs resulted also in part from De Gaulle's desire to keep André
Malraux inside his cabinet.

In Malraux's eyes, only art had the power to rally people within a society
dominated by cold reason and machines. Having access to culture meant
putting works of art and the public in direct touch with one another, in an
act of revelation and communion. The stricture requiring artistic creation
of the highest level shut out the adult education movement's didacticism
and amateurism. Last, the support given to the avant-garde was evidence of
the intention to weaken the influence of the university crowd.[16]

Despite its merits, the Ministry for Cultural Affairs was a fragile construction. It had been set up in difficult conditions, with a small budget and
persistent feuding between the Finance and Education Ministries. The
Foreign Ministry kept a tight rein over France's external cultural policy and
would continue to do so. The events of May 1968 severely shook the Ministry for Cultural Affairs, and it found itself under attack from the Left and
Right. Leftists derided the fiction of cultural democracy, while order-lovers
denounced government support for artists considered as subversive. The

bond between creative artists and the ministry was torn asunder. Furthermore, at a time when mass consumption and mass culture were gathering momentum, the Ministry for Cultural Affairs was not paying the kind of attention to cultural industries demanded by the situation. The rift with adult education confirmed an impression of culture being reserved for an elite, out of touch with the cultural habits of ordinary French people.[17] The ministry, still strongly centralized and opposed to decentralization, was thinly present across the country, even though the few cultural centers [*les maisons de la culture*] that had been built were beginning, not without difficulty, to establish a partnership with the larger towns.

The 1970s were turbulent times for the ministry. Georges Pompidou, who did not want to be hemmed in by his strictly presidential functions, became a new actor on the scene.[18] In spite of the instability of the era, the ministry's structure was given permanent form. The idea of "cultural development" provided a response to the destabilization fomented by the events of May 1968. The Jacques Duhamel ministry (1971–73) attempted to modernize cultural policy by working on an interministerial basis, obtaining a substantially bigger budget, and acknowledging the importance of local governments. "Cultural development" [*le développement culturel*], the third component of Prime Minister Jacques Chaban-Delmas's "New Society," expressed a philosophy in sharp contrast with André Malraux's cherished doctrine of cultural action [*l'action culturelle*]. While the goal of democratizing "culture" remained, two fresh approaches modified the concept itself. The anthropological sense of the word replaced the usual meaning of "high" culture, and the admission that many paths lead to democratization replaced the "aesthetic shock" principle. The state, though, continued to occupy a leading role. Its task was to foster the propagation of culture and refuse market-economy rules. Although the Duhamel ministry's policy sowed seeds for the future, it was seriously affected by the political misfortunes of Chaban-Delmas.[19]

The more economically liberal philosophy that prevailed after 1974 led to a wind-down in state funding, and President Valéry Giscard d'Estaing showed less passion for cultural policy. The public service vocation of the ministry lost strength as liberalism took hold. The period was notable for the growth of urban cultural policies, varyingly in line with state directives. By the end of President Giscard's seven-year term, the state's guardianship of culture had greatly weakened, and it found itself confined essentially to heritage protection. Cultural policy, much to the discontent of cultural professionals, was no longer a government priority. Meanwhile, the opposition, and especially the revitalized Socialist Party, was offering a different sort of program. The socialist culture platform had two highly political purposes: first, to pry the people working in the cultural field away from the still-strong influence of the French Communist Party and, second, to rally these people behind presidential candidate François Mitterrand, at a time when the polemic over "totalitarianism" had estranged the intellectuals from the socialists.[20] At the end of Giscard's term, the culture-state was a mere shadow of the "juggernaut" excoriated by its foes. Under the Ministers Françoise Giroud, Michel d'Ornano, and Jean-Philippe Lecat, the "system" dreamt of by Malraux was quietly but purposefully dismantled.

PUBLIC MEDIA: A DEFEAT FOR THE MINISTRY OF CULTURE

The public media scene also went through a revolution in the 1980s. After Canal + (encrypted pay-TV) and two private channels (La Cinq and TV6) had been created and Channel One was privatized in 1986, competition among the several channels intensified. The Ministry of Culture was unable to impose its views. Jack Lang spoke out vigorously, but in vain, against the handing over of La Cinq to the Seydoux-Berlusconi consortium. The film industry also opposed this choice, which ushered in a television service subordinated to the rule of money. Silvio Berlusconi, the Italian TV magnate, was seen as the incarnation of low-grade television consisting of variety programs, game shows, and sitcoms. What the minister of culture did obtain was a European TV channel focused on culture. The idea he proposed in 1984 grew into "La Sept" (February 1986), later to become Arte (Association relative à la télévision européenne). Arte, a Franco-German cultural channel broadcasting on the open air-waves since 1992, was something of an odd-man-out in a media world now dominated by commercial thinking. Certain commentators deplored the institution of a cultural "ghetto," which would serve as a perfect pretext for commercial abuses by the other public channels.[21] In 2003, the philosopher Catherine Clément, author of a report for the minister of culture, was obliged to acknowledge a state of affairs in which commercial pressures had been aggravated over the previous twenty years. Television had become French people's main cultural practice, but programs labeled as "cultural" were consigned to non-primetime—"at night or in summer."[22]

French intellectuals—using the term in its broad sense of members of the intellectual professions—had for a long time had mixed feelings toward the audiovisual media, especially television. They were divided between condemning the propagation of a mass culture that watered down real culture [*la culture légitime*] and wanting to use the media for popularizing that same culture.[23] In academia, the cultural purism of French scholars had blocked the inclusion of these new issues in social science studies. British cultural studies, initiated outside of university circles, had been much bolder in exploring the subject.

The Lang ministry had nevertheless thrown all its weight into binding the film and television industries together. This singular combination had been in the works since the early 1970s. Under the act of July 29, 1982, television was constrained to accept a certain quota of French movies, and the way in which the different channels could broadcast outside-produced movies was defined in detail. The creation of the pay-per-view channel Canal + in 1985 provided the movie industry with a solid source of funds. Canal +, in exchange for an exceptionally generous operating charter, was to occupy a key position in French movie production for more than ten years. Television became the cinema industry's main funder and production outlet. Movie theater screenings were looked upon only as showcases and launch pads. In 1997, the creation of the TPS satellite bouquet spelled the end of the Canal + monopoly. A third party, the communication industry, with its trans-frontier outlook and strategies, was about to upset an already delicate balance.[24]

CRITICISM FROM THE INTELLIGENTSIA: FROM CULTURAL PESSIMISM TO THE CONTEMPORARY ARTS CRISIS

The main charges made by the intelligentsia bore on cultural relativism. The publication of Alain Finkielkraut's *La Défaite de la pensée* in 1987 unleashed a storm of controversy. The philosopher and essayist lamented the decline of culture. His polemic was, in fact, an attack on cultural laxity. It is true that the policy conducted by Jack Lang since 1981 and continued in its general outlines by François Léotard in 1986 under the "cohabitation" government was not the principal subject of debate. Finkielkraut was nonetheless of the opinion that the policy had, by incorporating fields hitherto ignored by the ministry (rock music, fashion, advertising, etc.), done much to dilute culture in a sort of everything-goes cultural broth.[25] Bernard-Henri Lévy, in his *Eloge des Intellectuels* (1987), wrote in a similar vein. Lévy, the standard-bearer of the *nouveaux philosophes*, mentioned the "sick spirit in culture." The Ministry of Culture was accused of compounding the sickness by giving respectability to the "minor" fringes of culture.[26] Perhaps it was a sign of the times but, the same year, the French translation of *The Closing of the American Mind* by American scholar Allan Bloom was published. The book criticized the United States' education system which, in incorporating minority culture, was responsible for muddying values. The more or less simultaneous publication of the three books—and the stir created by the first two—provided theoretical ammunition for launching attacks against the ministry. The subject of the dispute was not, however, multiculturalism. In this respect, the French debate differed considerably from the one going on in the United States and Canada.

In 1990 the ministry published a survey on the French population's "cultural practices" that rekindled and expanded the debate.[27] The survey conclusions, which revealed the persistence of material and symbolic barriers restricting access to "high" culture, were interpreted as proof that cultural democratization had failed. Minister Jack Lang was shaken by the findings and by the way the survey was exploited, considering that the government had committed itself to an extremely bold policy over the previous ten years. Sociological studies, which had for a long time been a valuable adjunct to democratization policies, were now feeding the skepticism of the foes of the state as cultural arbiter.

In the fall of 1991 the publication of Marc Fumaroli's *L'État culturel* gave a new twist to the controversy.[28] The French press, soon followed by television and radio, gave wide coverage to the argument generated by the author's ideas. Two of France's most eminent intellectual magazines, *Esprit* and *Le Débat*, gave space to partisans on both sides of the fence. The public at large, especially after all the media treatment, also showed interest in the subject. The book remained on top of the specialized press' best-seller lists for many weeks.

It needs to be said that the author of *L'État culturel* is a member of one the most honorable of all French academic institutions, the Collège de France. Fumaroli, a historian of literary and artistic forms in modern Europe, has held the chair of rhetoric and society in sixteenth- and seventeenth-century Europe since 1986, and is the author of a series of works respected by the international scholarly community; they include *L'Age de l'éloquence* (1980) and *Héros et orateurs, rhétorique et dramaturgie cornéliennes* (1990). Little-known by the public at large for his academic work, Fumaroli chose to tackle the subject of cultural policy in contemporary France by writing not a scholarly treatise but a lively broadside. His academic standing indeed carried more weight than the style he chose to employ. He is considered, wrongly, by many critics as a reputable specialist on the issue under discussion.

His argument should not, however, be dismissed lightly. Cultural policy, he argues, has transformed the state into a mass supplier of "popular recreation" and "consumer products." This makes the welfare state, using public money, a competitor in the culture market. The conflict of interest inherent in an everything-goes culture stems from confusing cultural action with a form of tourism. Culture of this kind, spread by a growing army of cultural bureaucrats, takes on the proportions of a modernist religion. The nationwide music festival held annually on June 21 [*la Fête de la musique*], the *Fureur de Lire*, commemorative celebrations (notably the bicentenary of the French Revolution in 1989), along with the presidential "*Grands Travaux*," are manifestations of state-inspired manipulation, the state being a neo-Leviathan of culture serving a political party and an ideology. What is not said is that this "culture state" is the product of policies initiated well before the socialists came to power in 1981. As a worthy disciple of the political philosophy of Tocqueville and Raymond Aron, Fumaroli assumes the role of preacher for a "liberal" state that would equip our leisure and consumer societies with a certain number of firewalls—principally an education system and some legal and tax safeguards. Culture in this scheme of things would become an essentially personal matter. "The arts are not dishes that can be divided into an infinite number of equal portions," he writes. "They are the rungs of an ascent; to be desired, not meted out." In other words, the main enemy of liberal democracy is mass culture.

Marc Fumaroli's book may be seen as a weather vane, symptomatic of the uncertainty concerning the place and conception of culture in today's societies. It also expresses the will to defend the fine arts and the humanities against the ravages of mass culture. The work thus belongs to a long-established polemical tradition, even though its media exposure was exceptional. Indeed, the ideas are not new, and Fumaroli himself aired most of them in a 1982 article in the magazine *Commentaire*. But their extensive popularization in France and abroad gave them an added impact. Although some historians seriously question the sequence of events recounted by Fumaroli, certain media reproduced his thesis without comment. The novel element was the fierce contestation of the Ministry of Culture's very legitimacy. Fumaroli refrained from demanding the complete dismantling of the ministry, but he argued for its being limited to the heritage field [*le patrimoine*]. The success of *L'Etat culturel*—23,000 copies sold in the original printing and over 20,000 in the paperback edition—probably amplified by the disputes over the Bibliothèque nationale de France and the run-up to the March 1993 parliamentary elections, revivified an already simmering debate. The book's success was further evidence that the cultural policy propelled by Jack Lang was losing steam, and this at a time when the second seven-year term of François Mitterrand was marred by a spate of scandals. Last, the confirmation in 1991 of a darkening in the economic and social forecast made it difficult to defend a cultural policy based on support for creative artists.

In 1992, *L'Utopie française: essai sur le patrimoine*, by Jean-Michel Leniaud, with a preface by Fumaroli, proved that the debate was still very much alive.[29] With the presidential elections only a few months away, books by Henry Bonnier—*Lettre recommandée à Jack Lang et aux fossoyeurs de la culture*—and Zadig, a pen-name for a group of intellectuals belonging to right-leaning university clubs—*L'Implosion française*— gave extreme and somewhat oversimplified form to the ideas of Fumaroli.[30] The goal was perfectly clear: suppression of the Ministry of Culture. Zadig promptly listed the authors who were required reading: "It is vital to culture that those who tomorrow will hold the destiny of France in their hands should have read and pondered [George] Steiner, [Allan] Bloom, [Bruno] Lussato, Finkielkraut, Fumaroli, on the return of true culture."

As 1993 dawned, a critique not only from the nominal Left but from within the cultural administration fold itself joined the chorus of protests from the "liberals" close to what was then the political opposition. Michel Schneider, a senior civil servant, Director of Music and Dance at the Ministry of Culture from 1988 to 1991, an authority on Robert Schumann and Glenn Gould, conceded to Fumaroli a number of points: the dissolution of art in "culture"; the political exploitation of the arts by a ministry turned toward the "creators"; and the disproportionate attention paid to media use. In his *La Comédie de la culture*, Schneider countered the free-choice solutions proposed by Fumaroli with the necessity for public service, that is, the obligation for a democratic nation to provide education in the arts in order to attenuate unequal access to works of culture.[31] This vital education function would round out a Ministry of Culture limited to two other duties: heritage protection and the democratic propagation of art. The book—regarded by some as a settling of scores—received plentiful coverage in the national and regional press. It also was a resounding public success, with over 32,000 copies sold. A year later, *Culture et contre-cultures*, by the jurist Jean-Louis Harouel, revisited the subject but in a broader framework. Harouel wrote of the "decline" in Western culture dating from the advent of avant-gardism up until the alleged clash with the lower forms of "counter-culture." The author tied up his argument with the conclusion that the Ministry of Culture should be scrapped and replaced with a Ministry for Heritage flanked by a small-scale national arts fund.[32]

A second line of criticism, again well-publicized by the media, had to do with the *Grands Travaux*. Jean-François Revel attacked them as "the President's private playground" and held them up as an example of what his essay denounced as "inefficient absolutism."[33] What struck many observers were the personal nature of *Grands Travaux* policy decisions, their attachment to a political agenda, and their staggering cost. The three factors kept the controversy alive. Once his decision was taken, the president kept a close eye on each project's progress.

The opponents of the *Grands Travaux* castigated the fortunes spent on the different programs. *Le Canard enchaîné* called them Pharaonic and derided the choices of "Tontonkhamen."[34] Over a period of ten years, the "Grand Works" ended up costing roughly 34 billion francs. More than the initial outlay, it was the operating budget needed for running the new cultural facilities that was to cause a problem in the following years. Although a few projects were located in the provinces, local officeholders berated a policy which, as always, mostly benefited Paris.

The Grand Louvre, later acclaimed as a model of its kind, was at first the subject of heated controversy. The plans of American architect Ieoh Pei for the Louvre pyramid stirred intense debate. Among those taking sides were former minister of culture, Michel Guy, and the authors (Bruno Foucart, Antoine Schnapper, and Sébastien Loste) of *Paris mystifié*, published in 1985.[35] The favorable opinion expressed by the curators of the Louvre in 1984 was a deciding factor. With the agreement of the mayor of Paris, Jacques Chirac, and the unwavering support of Mitterrand, the team led by Emile Biasini was able to carry the project through to completion. The violent debate over the daring construction of a glass pyramid at the heart of the old Louvre palace buildings was soon forgotten when its public success became apparent.

Table 12.1. Cost of the *Grands Travaux*[36]

Name	Architect(s)	Cost in Billions of French Francs	Year
Musée d'Orsay	Gae Aulenti	1.3	1986
Parc de la Villette	Bernard Tshumi	1.3	1986
Musée des Sciences	Adiren Fainsilber	5.4	1986
Institut du Monde Arabe	Jean Nouvel	0.424	1987
Opéra Bastille	Carlos Ott	2.8	1989
Arche de la Défense	Paul Andreu, Otto von Spreckelsen	3.175	1989
Ministry of Finance	Paul Chemetov, Borja Huidobro	3.7	1989
Cité de la Musique	Christian de Portzamparc	1.1	1994
Muséum	Paul Chemetov, Borja Huidobro	1	1994
Grand Louvre	Ieoh Pei	5.7	1995
Bibliothèque de France	Dominique Perrault	7.8	1995
Total		**34.239**	

During Mitterrand's second seven-year term, it was the new Biblio-thèque nationale de France which set passions aflame. This time, the op-position came less from political factions, as had been the case with the Grand Louvre, than from the scientific community. The supervising team, the architect, Dominique Perrault, and the eventual researchers argued at length over the functions and shape of the future building. The researchers organized themselves into a pressure group, with the journal *Le Débat* play-ing an active role, and obtained significant alterations to the original plans. The dispute reshaped the intellectual landscape, one of its side effects be-ing to harmonize the positions on cultural matters of the magazines *Com-mentaire* and *Le Débat*. Two different conceptions of the future library, which many commentators believed to be incompatible, underlay the di-vergence: it was conceived, on the one hand, as a public library offering a sort of agora for cultural interaction, and, on the other hand, as a new Bib-liothèque nationale with a primarily heritage mission catering to scholars. This twin purpose, set out in the decree of January 3, 1994, defining the li-brary's tasks, was to prove extremely difficult to manage institutionally in terms of everyday running.

Beginning in 1991, another polemic hatched up by the magazines *Esprit* and *Télérama* on the "crisis in contemporary art" had an influence on the Ministry of Culture's fine arts policy. The nub of this very "in-house" French debate turned on an attack against avant-garde aesthetics. Govern-ment policy was cited as evidence for the prosecution; the state was accused of aesthetic partiality. It has always been tempting to belittle "official art." The neo-liberals Marc Fumaroli and Yves Michaud believed that the state should retire from the field and allow more independence to other institu-tions. Philippe Dagen was one of the few protagonists to state that govern-ment support for the fine arts was still inadequate. He did not deny that a certain official academicism existed, but he felt that it was of minor impor-tance and was not sure that the market would fill the void if the state pulled out.[37] The debate took a more political turn in November 1996 when an is-sue of the review *Krisis*, sympathetic to the far-right, edited by Alain de Benoist, expatiated on the subject. Upholders of contemporary art, such as the magazine *Art Press*, edited by Catherine Millet, or *Le Monde*'s art critic, Philippe Dagen, quickly assimilated the attack on contemporary art with conservative reaction and fascism. Admittedly, the political context of the day, marked by the gains of the National Front in town council elections, tended to make parties on all sides exaggerate their positions.[38]

The three controversies—cultural relativism debates (Fumaroli), the *Grands Travaux*, and the "crisis of contemporary art" controversy—

crisscrossing from time to time, were instrumental in casting doubt on cultural policy's purpose and legitimacy. But their impact, outside a small coterie of intellectuals and specialists, should not be overstated. The artists themselves had no say in the proceedings. Polls bore out the fact that the great majority of the French population did not contest the government's cultural policy. That policy, especially from 1993 on, was basically one of continuity. The fact remains that the principles used to adjust cultural policy to a gloomier financial outlook and the onslaughts of globalization were grounded partly in argumentation heard during the 1980s.

TOWARD A NEW CULTURAL POLICY MODEL, 1993–2003: CULTURAL POLICY AND "SOCIAL FRACTURE"

The return to power of the parliamentary Right in 1993 ushered in a new period. Cultural policy was definitely no longer a government priority, and presidential backing was less in evidence after Jacques Chirac's election in 1995. The trimming of the budget was felt all the more keenly in that the overheads of the *Grands Travaux* monuments and institutions made heavy inroads into the Ministry of Culture's finances. The desire for a new cultural policy model was illustrated by the idea of "reformulation" [*la refondation*] elaborated by Jacques Rigaud for Minister Philippe Douste-Blazy in 1996. Discussion had shifted to mending the "social fracture." Cultural policy at the approach of the twenty-first century seemed destined to take a more "liberal" turn.

After the 1993 parliamentary elections, the ministerial policy pursued by Jacques Toubon was quick to follow the path traced by his predecessor Jack Lang. The first *cohabitation*, from 1986 to 1988, had to a large degree remained faithful to the policy in place since 1981. François Léotard, who advocated a "retiring state," to use Michel Crozier's term, had sought to push cultural policy in a more rightward direction. The emphasis was placed back on heritage; education in the arts was promoted; and "cultural development" lost its priority status. In 1993 the Ministry of Culture adopted three guiding principles: territorial development (one of the avowed hobbyhorses of Prime Minister Édouard Balladur's government), intensified projection of French culture abroad, and education and promotion of culture for all. The debate in the fall of 1993 over Europe's right to "cultural exception" forged broad agreement among the public and politicians alike. The minister of culture drew attention, over and above the technical issues and the trade imbalance between Europe and the

United States—in the latter's favor—to broader questions of symbolic importance and the defense of a cultural identity under threat:

> We do not want our spirits to be stifled, our eyes blinded, our industries enslaved. We want to breathe freely, to breathe our own air, the air that has vivified every culture in the world, and could tomorrow be lacking to mankind. On both sides of the Atlantic and the Pacific, let us mobilize for this battle for survival.[39]

The return of the Right, in other words, picked up the thread of the earlier concerns of the Left. There was no longer any question of a financial upturn or a priority proclaimed by the government. Moreover, the absence of presidential backing, combined with the traditional stinginess of the Ministry of Finance, weakened the Ministry of Culture's position. In retrospect, the two major advances of the 1980s could be better appreciated: the budget increases won for the ministry by Jack Lang, and the backing, sometimes distant but unfailing, of President Mitterrand.

The 1995 presidential campaign was not concerned with cultural policy. Philippe Douste-Blazy, the centrist minister of culture in Prime Minister Alain Juppé's cabinet, ordered a remodeling of the ministry's policy. The deliberations were the first step toward establishing a new type of policy for culture that would take account together of the advances made in the previous decade, the criticisms that had been expressed, and the international economic situation as affected by rising globalization. The Rigaud Report submitted to the minister in October 1996 reasserted the validity of the French system of cultural action as a public service. The state's role as an instrument for government action, in consultation with local bodies, was firmly asserted. The ministry's financial muscle should be restored, and the report noted the Ministry of Finance's mistrust, if not downright hostility, toward government spending on culture. There were several suggestions for reorganizing the Ministry of Culture's central administration. Education in art and culture was termed a "national cause." Another priority was the harmonization of state policies concerning cultural industries.[40] The "remodeling" process was brutally interrupted in the spring of 1997, when President Chirac chose to dissolve the National Assembly.[41]

RESTORING THE REPUBLICAN SOCIAL PACT

Catherine Trautmann, minister of culture and communication in the new cabinet headed by socialist Lionel Jospin, tailored her action to the pattern devised by her predecessor. An administrative overhaul was accompanied by a "reconstruction" budget (15.1 billion French francs in 1998). Further deconcentration and the signing of contracts with local bodies showed that the ministry was willing to take part in the reform of the state's structure. A "Charter on the Public Service Duties of the Performing Arts" stressed the need to write public service clauses into contracts covering public aid for cultural institutions. The charter was a genuine attempt to break with past practices. In the same vein, a charter signed in June 1999 with the main adult education federations endeavored to end the divorce, dating back to Malraux's time, between cultural action and further education.[42] The new partnership satisfied two of the Ministry of Culture's primary objectives: to strengthen education in arts and culture, and to encourage amateur artistic activity. On the political far-right, populism was again on the rise. Catherine Trautmann, like Douste-Blazy before her, took action to assert the state's role in preserving cultural pluralism. The authority of the minister, who had tried to escape from interest-group domination, was irremediably sapped, however, by pressure from the performing arts lobbies, abetted by the national press.

Catherine Tasca, who took over from Catherine Trautmann following a Jospin cabinet shuffle in March 2000, geared her action to three main principles: promoting cultural diversity, improving access to culture, and advancing cultural decentralization. The political background was also of great importance—with an eye to the next elections, the minister had to defuse the rebellion of the performing arts movement leaders. The Ministry of Culture's participation in the new round of decentralization demanded by the government was expressed through a set of "cultural decentralization protocols." One of the protocols' goals was to establish a clear apportionment of responsibilities between central and local government. The late parliamentary term also saw the conclusion of several long-awaited legislative measures, including those on rescue archeology, museums, and the art market. The intention to support education in the arts, which politicians had been talking about since the early 1990s, led to closer cooperation between the Ministry of Culture and the Ministry of Education.[43] The Ministry of Culture, having noted the nationwide proliferation of locally based artistic endeavors that owed little to institutions or the market, set about alerting public authorities to the scale of the phenomenon and introducing measures to support these ventures, since they promised to play a major role in local cultural life and the development of art activities.[44] The media scene continued to be occupied by the war between haters and admirers of cultural policy *à la française*.[45] In the field, the prevailing discussion had turned to the new problems, nearly all relating to globalization, facing French cultural policy. The sharp debate over paying for borrowing in public libraries, which had the book trade divided, showed how much the public cultural services were being buffeted by the commercial logic of increasingly transnational cultural industries—television in particular—and the globalized habits of individual cultural consumption.[46]

FROM CULTURAL EXCEPTION TO CULTURAL DIVERSITY

During international trade talks, France did not budge from its position and shaped the European Union's attitude. In 1998, in negotiations with the Organization for Economic Co-operation and Development over a Multilateral Investment Agreement, France pleaded for what it called "cultural exception." The Jospin government decided to oppose any inclusion of a culture clause and refused to take part in the negotiations. In 1999, on the eve of the World Trade Organization (WTO) meetings in Seattle, France strove in the European Union to retain its "cultural exception." The commission's mandate, approved by member states on October 26, 1999, endorsed the French position: "The Union will, during the forthcoming WTO negotiations, take care to guarantee, as in the Uruguay Round, the possibility for the Community and its member states to preserve and develop their capacity to determine and implement their cultural and audiovisual policies so as to conserve their cultural diversity." Catherine Trautmann added, "Cultural exception is the legal tool; cultural diversity is our objective." This semantic shift enabled a frail consensus to be reached within the European Union. "Cultural diversity" continued to be defended. On October 15, 2001, President Chirac in his speech at the opening of the Thirty-First UNESCO General Conference solemnly reiterated France's position: "The answer to culture-crushing globalization is cultural diversity. Diversity based on the conviction that each people has a unique message to transmit to the world, and that each people can enrich humanity by contributing its share of beauty and its share of truth."

The shift toward cultural diversity was not universally appreciated by art and culture professionals. The exact meaning of the phrase remained highly ambiguous. On December 17, 2001, when taking control of USA Networks, Jean-Marie Messier, then CEO of Vivendi-Universal, declared in New York: "The French cultural exception is dead . . . and domestic French anxieties are archaisms." The declaration quickly had culture professionals up in arms; they denounced what they saw as an attack on the

French system for funding movie-making. Politicians of every stripe—from the Communist Party to the far-right—also castigated Messier's pronouncement. Everyone was wondering in private what would now be the policy of Canal+, part of Messier's empire, which was a vital partner in French movie production.

The official reaction "at the state's highest level" shows just how important this question was. Prime Minister Jospin, who had already raised the point in presenting his greetings to the press on January 15, 2002, took the opportunity six days later when inaugurating the Palais de Tokyo site for contemporary creation to restate the government's position. He implicitly condemned Jean-Marie Messier's remarks: "Our vision in no way implies retiring into our national shell; on the contrary, it betokens a desire to reach out to the world. Through culture, we celebrate all cultures. Their diversity is mankind's priceless heritage." President Chirac, for his part, formally confirmed France's position regarding cultural diversity, on February 12:

> As we can well see, in these times of uncertainty, when traditional borders are becoming blurred, when there are justified fears that the rule of the market will replace the rule of governments, when people no longer feel that they are in charge of their agenda, the need to assert one's identity is making a strong comeback all over the world. It is like a vital instinct, since everyone feels that the snuffing out of traditions, languages, cultures and knowledge is akin to throwing away chances, or closing doors that we shall never be able to open again. Let us then be vigilant. Uniformization, when it acts like a steamroller, has the backlash effect of encouraging ghetto attitudes and fanaticism. Affirming diversity is quite the opposite: it is one of the keys to assuaging contemporary fears. . . . That is why not everything can be a tradable good, and why not everything can be abandoned to market rule.

Until the official opening of the presidential election campaign, the battle of views swirled. On March 9, certain artists, incensed by business mogul Jean-Marie Messier's statements, took advantage of the *Victoires de la musique* ceremony to make their opinions known. Messier had quoted as an example of cultural diversity the inclusion of "rebels" such as Noir Désir and Zebda in the catalogue of the music major he had just acquired. From the mid-1990s, the government received support from the main professional organizations as well as from the associations opposed to globalization. The sociologist Pierre Bourdieu, who had become a new icon of intellectual activism, on several occasions warned against reducing culture to the status of merchandise, "To reintroduce commercialism into systems crafted, piece by piece, . . . is to endanger mankind's noblest achievements: art, literature, and even science."[47]

Jacques Chirac, following his reelection as president in 2002, returned more than once to the theme of defending cultural diversity, increasingly presented as the backbone of France's cultural policy. France also did its best to change the forum of discussion from the WTO to UNESCO.[48] On February 2, 2003, President Chirac, speaking at the Second International Meeting of Cultural Professional Organizations, proposed "establishing [cultural] diversity as a principle in international law" and called for the "adoption by the international community of a world convention on cultural diversity." France also wanted "promotion of and respect for cultural diversity" to be included in the future Treaty on European Unity.

A MODEL IN SEARCH OF ITS BEARINGS

The election campaign in the spring of 2002 was not notable, however, for the public attention accorded to cultural policy, although all the candidates mentioned it in their platforms. The qualification of the populist leader, Jean-Marie Le Pen, for the second round of the presidential elections triggered an "antifascist" reflex on the part of the art and culture world. In the following weeks, the discussions on the condition of French society included references to the limits of cultural democratization. Cultural institutions were blamed for having deepened the cultural divide between the "*cognoscenti*" and the "people" because of their highbrow policies.

The appointment of the former curator of the Georges Pompidou Center, Jean-Jacques Aillagon, as minister of culture and communication in the Jean-Pierre Raffarin cabinet was on the whole well-received by arts professionals. The text setting out the minister's terms of reference indicated that there would be no break with previous policy. Still, the reduction in the culture budget (2,490,72 million euros, or a 4.3 percent cut) was perceived in culture circles as a worrying sign. Several priorities were set, backed by official reports: heritage and decentralization (Bady Report), violence on television (Kriegel Report), and cultural content on television (Clément Report). The ministerial agenda displayed right from the first months an intention to encourage private patronage and allow greater independence to the major cultural institutions. A symposium held in March 2003 by the French-American Foundation and the *Centre français des fondations* under the auspices of the minister of culture and the minister for the budget and state reform—"Culture Funding and

Management in the United States and France: New Synergies and Interdependences of Private and Public Sources"—produced arguments for a shift toward liberalism in France's cultural policy model. In April 2003, the minister of culture and communication told the National Assembly that reform of patronage and the status of foundations was a necessity, "expressing, alongside deconcentration and decentralization, the government's trust in an assumption of responsibility by civil society, individuals, business institutions, and foundations, since it aims at associating their commitments more closely with the action of the state." He drew attention to France's backwardness in this respect, comparing the situation to that in the United States where patronage contributed roughly 217 billion euros, or 2.1 percent of GDP, as against only 0.09 percent in France.

These first measures produced mixed reactions. Debate focused on two topics. The first was the question of non-salaried performing artists.[49] Employers and unions asked questions of the government concerning the special unemployment insurance scheme applying to performing arts professionals. At stake was the survival of a large section of the country's cultural activity. The minister of culture, who expressed his attachment to the scheme, failed to convince labor representatives opposed to the employers' demands that he had the capacity to act. The second topic concerned the decentralization process set in motion by Prime Minister Jean-Pierre Raffarin. The prime minister, a proponent of a "decentralized France," hoped to strengthen the cultural prerogatives of the regions. Art and culture professionals, especially in the performing arts, criticized a possible divestment by the state at the very moment when many urban cultural systems were being threatened by the reluctant attitudes of certain local authorities.[50] Local officeholders themselves appeared afraid of a transfer of expenditures in their disfavor and a retreat by the state toward institutions having exclusively national stature. Some voices pointed out that the government's program remained silent about other projects in the works, such as "intercommunality" (partnerships among several communes), particularly in rural districts, of "home areas" and "settled communities." The hesitancy could also have been a sign of the local authorities' difficulty in assimilating and practicing the new rules of the game imposed by the growing localization of government action.[51] The Ministry of Culture's own staff began to worry. The "culture" inter-union group at the Ministry of Culture issued a strike call for April 24, 2003, to protest what it called a "scheduled dismantling of the ministry" by a "bogus decentralization which does not pursue any goal of improving and consolidating public service."

The government continued, however, to present state commitment to art and culture as a fundamental requirement of democracy. The primary objective remained the popularization of cultural habits. It was equally important to guarantee maximum freedom for the citizen in his or her choice of cultural activities. To that end, the state has proclaimed its determination to support artists, while ensuring them absolute freedom in their work of creation and dissemination. A seeming contradiction may be noted here. The defense of cultural diversity in the international arena has been accompanied domestically by an avowed "liberal" shift, which many observers have seen as a serious threat to the public service cultural ideal.

For nearly half a century now, government cultural policies in France seem, despite certain changes in trajectory, to have followed a continuous path. There can be no denying their role in regulating the national culture scene; yet this can in no way be likened to a "straitjacketing" of the country's art and culture. The small size of official budgets, the growing influence of world-scale cultural industries, and highly eclectic cultural habits have prevented the state from becoming the string-puller of France's cultural life. Arguing over cultural policy has never really stopped since the early 1980s, from the condemnation of the all-is-culture credo to criticism of decentralization, experienced by art and culture professionals as a whittling away of state-guided policy. In truth, these disputes have had little impact on the nature of public policies as practiced, and the public in general has always seemed quite happy with them. At the beginning of the twenty-first century, one trend seems to be emerging: criticism is giving way to defense of state policy, recognized as a bulwark against the erosion of cultural identities and the resurgence of populist philistinism.

NOTES

Our gratitude goes to the Ministry of Culture's History Committee for financing the translation, and to Augustin Girard and Julian Bourg for their thoughtful revision of the French text.

1. Robert Wangermée, "Tendances de l'administration de la culture en Europe occidentale," *Revue française d'administration publique* 65 (January–March 1993): 11–24. Kevin Mulkahy, "Cultural Patronage in Comparative Perspective: Public Support for the Arts in France, Germany, Norway, and Canada," *The Journal of Arts Management Law and Society* 27, no. 4 (Winter 1998): 247–63.

2. See my anthology, Philippe Poirrier, ed., *Les Politiques culturelles en France* (Paris: La Documentation Française, 2002).

3. Brian Rigby, *Popular Culture in Modern France: A Study of Cultural Discourse* (London: Routledge, 1991).

4. For details, see David Looseley, *The Politics of Fun: Cultural Policy and Debate in Contemporary France* (Oxford: Berg Publishers, 1995). *Dictionnaire des politiques culturelles de la France depuis 1959* (Paris: Larousse-CNRS, 2001).

5. A. J. Wiesand, "Comparative Cultural Policy Research in Europe: A Change of Paradigm," *Canadian Journal of Communication* 27 (2002): 369–78. J. M. Schuster, *Informing Cultural Policy: The Research and Information Infrastructure* (New Brunswick, N.J.: Center for Urban Policy Research, 2002).

6. See my essay, Poirrier, *Les Enjeux de l'histoire culturelle* (Paris: Seuil, 2004).

7. The most representative author, whose work is easily available in English, is Roger Chartier, *Cultural History: Between Practices and Representations* (Ithaca: Cornell University Press, 1988.); and *On the Edge of the Cliff: History, Language, and Practices* (Baltimore: The Johns Hopkins University Press, 1996).

8. Jean-Pierre Rioux and Jean-François Sirinelli, *Pour une histoire culturelle* (Paris: Seuil, 1997).

9. See Poirrier, "L'histoire des politiques culturelles: un territoire pour l'historien," in *Bibliographie de l'histoire des politiques culturelles: France, XIXe–XXe siècles* (Paris: La Documentation Française—Comité d'histoire du Ministère de la Culture, 1999), 7–27. For a description of the History Committee's action, see "L'historien, la culture et les institutions," Dossier in *Culture & Recherche* 95 (March–April 2003).

10. The budget approved for the fiscal year 1982 amounted to 5.99 billion French francs, up from 2.97 billion in 1981. The 1993 budget rose even further, to 13.79 billion FF.

11. Pascal Ory, "La décision en politique culturelle: l'exemple de la présidence Mitterrand," in *Les Années Mitterrand: les années du changement, 1981–1984*, eds. Serge Berstein, Pierre Milza, and J. L. Bianco (Paris: Perrin, 2001), 818–38.

12. Poirrier, "Heritage and Cultural Policy in France under the Fifth Republic," *The International Journal of Cultural Policy* 9, no. 2 (2003): 215–26.

13. Vincent Dubois, "Une politique pour quelle(s) culture(s)," *Les Cahiers français* 312 (January–February 2003): 22.

14. Augustin Girard, "Industries culturelles," *Futuribles* 17 (September–October 1978): 598–605; trans. as "Cultural Industries," in *French Cultural Policy Debates: A Reader*, ed. Jeremy Ahearne (London: Routledge, 2002), 102–8.

15. Repr. in Poirrier, *Les Politiques culturelles en France*, 391–95.

16. Philippe Urfalino, *L'Invention de la politique culturelle* (Paris: Comité d'histoire du Ministère de la Culture-La Documentation Française, 1996). Augustin Girard and Geneviève Gentil, eds., *Les Affaires culturelles au temps d'André Malraux* (Paris: Comité d'histoire du Ministère de la Culture-La Documentation Française, 1996).

17. Jean-Pierre Rioux and Jean-François Sirinelli, eds., *La Culture de masse en France: de la Belle Epoque à aujourd'hui* (Paris: Fayard, 2002).

18. Jean-Claude Grohens and Jean-François Sirinelli, *Culture et action chez Georges Pompidou* (Paris: PUF, 2000).

19. *Les Affaires culturelles au temps de Jacques Duhamel: 1971–1973* (Paris: La Documentation Française, 1995).

20. Pierre Gremion, "Ecrivains et intellectuels à Paris: une esquisse," *Le Débat* 103 (January–February 1999): 74–99.

21. Dominique Wolton, "Télévision culturelle: 'l'apartheid' distingué," *Pouvoirs* 51 (1989): 99–113. Jean Cluzel, "Une ambition justifiée, une réalisation contestable," *Le Débat* 121 (September–October 2002): 178–83.

22. Catherine Clément, *La Nuit et l'été: rapport sur la culture à la télévision* (Paris: Seuil-La Documentation Française, 2003).

23. See Hélène Eck, "Médias audiovisuels et intellectuels," in *L'Histoire des intellectuels aujourd'hui*, eds. Michel Leymare and Jean-François Sirinelli (Paris: PUF, 2003), 201–25.

24. Laurent Creton, *Le Cinéma à l'épreuve du système télévisuel* (Paris: CNRS Editions, 2002).

25. Alain Finkielkraut, *La Défaite de la pensée* (Paris: Gallimard, 1987).

26. Bernard-Henri Lévy, *Eloge des intellectuels* (Paris: Grasset, 1987).

27. Olivier Donnat and Denis Cogneau, *Les Pratiques culturelles des français* (Paris: La Découverte-La Documentation Française, 1990). The poll was based largely on attendance at and use of cultural facilities. Not much detail was given on audio-visual media habits.

28. Marc Fumaroli, *L'État culturel: une religion moderne* (Paris: Editions de Fallois, 1991).

29. Jean-Michel Leniaud, *L'Utopie française: essai sur le patrimoine* (Paris: Mengès, 1992).

30. Henri Bonnier, *Lettre recommandée à Jack Lang et aux fossoyeurs de la culture* (Monaco: Editions du Rocher, 1992). Zadig, *L'Implosion française* (Paris: Albin Michel, 1992).

31. Michel Schneider, *La Comédie de la culture* (Paris: Seuil, 1993).

32. Jean-Louis Harouel, *Culture et contre-cultures* (Paris: PUF, 1994).

33. Jean-François Revel, *L'Absolutisme inefficace ou contre le présidentialisme à la française* (Paris: Plon, 1992).

34. A play on word, *tonton*, meaning "uncle," the popular nickname for François Mitterrand.

35. Bruno Foucart, Antoine Schnapper, and Sébastien Loste, *Paris mystifié: la grand illusion du Grand Louvre* (Paris: Julliard, 1985).

36. F. Benhamou, *L'Économie de la culture* (Paris: La Découverte, 1996), 60.

37. Philippe Dagen, *La Haine de l'art* (Paris: Grasset, 1997).

38. The arguments used in the dispute are set out in Yves Michaud, *La Crise de l'art contemporain: utopie, démocratie et comédie* (Paris: PUF, 1997). The main texts can be found in an anthology compiled by Patrick Barrer, ed., *(Tout) l'art con-*

temporain est-il nul? le débat sur l'art contemporain en France avec ceux qui l'ont lancé: bilan et mise en perspective (Lausanne: Favre, 2000).

39. Jacques Toubon, "Laisser respirer nos âmes!" *Le Monde*, 1 October 1993, repr. in Poirrier, *Les Politiques culturelles en France*, 486–89.

40. Jacques Rigaud, *Pour une refondation de la politique culturelle* (Paris: La Documentation Française, 1996).

41. See Jacques Rigaud's account, *Les Deniers du rêve: essai sur l'avenir des politiques culturelles* (Paris: Grasset, 2001).

42. The two texts may be found in Poirrier, *Les Politiques culturelles en France*, 537–39, 551–59.

43. Pascale Lismonde, *Les Arts à l'école: le plan de Jack Lang et Catherine Tasca* (Paris: Cndp-Gallimard, 2002).

44. Fabrice Lextrait, *Une Nouvelle Étape de l'action culturelle* (Paris: La Documentation Française, 2001); and "Les valeurs de l'art: entre marché et institutions," *Mouvements* 17 (September–October 2001).

45. Two books published in the fall of 1999 were received with great interest: Maryvonne de Saint-Pulgent, *Le Gouvernement de la culture* (Paris: Gallimard, 1999); and Claude Mollard, *Le Cinquième Pouvoir: la culture et l'État de Malraux à Lang* (Paris: Armand Colin, 1999).

46. Jean-Yves Mollier, *Où va le livre?* (Paris: La Dispute, 2002).

47. Pierre Bourdieu, "Questions aux vrais maîtres du monde," *Le Monde*, 14 October 1999. See also Bourdieu, "La culture est en danger," in *Contre-feux 2: pour un mouvement social européen* (Paris: Raisons d'agir éditions, 2001), 75–91.

48. The adoption in November 2001 of the UNESCO Universal Declaration on Cultural Diversity was a success for this strategy. It should be recalled that the United States had not yet rejoined UNESCO at that point.

49. This French peculiarity—an unemployment benefits scheme for performing artists (singers, actors, musicians, dancers, producers, directors, technicians, set designers, etc.)—is explained by the insecure nature of their work and the number of their employers. The sharp rise in beneficiaries—up from 41,000 in 1991 to 96,500 in 2001—is responsible for the scheme's deficit (739 million euros in 2001). Unemployment insurance thus indirectly funds the performing arts sector.

50. Periodicals have reflected this fear: "Quelle culture de la décentralisation?" *Mouvement: revue interdisciplinaire des arts vivants* 19 (November–December 2002); and "La décentralisation culturelle pervertie," *Cahier du Groupe reflex[e]* 1 (March–April 2003).

51. The most recent account of the territorial game in action: Guy Saez, "L'action des collectivités territoriales en matière culturelle," *Les Cahiers français* 312 (January–February 2003): 12–18.

⑬

RELIGION, REPUBLICANISM, AND DEPOLITICIZATION: TWO INTELLECTUAL ITINERARIES— RÉGIS DEBRAY AND MARCEL GAUCHET

Michael Behrent

When French republicans think, they speak about religion—often enough, at least, to merit reflection. During the nineteenth century, republicans engaged in a complex dialectic with religion: their goal of building a republican state committed them to reversing the authority of a reactionary church, yet their concern with finding a spiritual authority to replace the church led them to embrace what one historian has called "not the negation of religion, but a new religion."[1] In recent times, after a near half-century during which most self-respecting intellectuals deemed the *"idée républicaine"* dull and quaint at best, the ideological and social mutations of the 1970s and 1980s led to a rekindling of interest in republicanism that has been accompanied, like a reflex, by renewed attention to religion and its political uses.

This preoccupation with religion and republicanism has been evident, in recent decades, in the work of two prominent thinkers of the 1968 generation: the political philosopher Marcel Gauchet, and the philosopher, critic, and occasional political courtier Régis Debray. From the perspective of the dialectic between religion and republicanism, their intellectual itineraries reveal some striking parallels. Having come of age in the feverishly political environment of 1960s student radicalism, both Debray (born in 1940) and Gauchet (born in 1946) sought, in the 1970s, to come to terms with their early induction into political *militantisme* by reflecting on the conditions of possibility of politics. For both thinkers, this project brought religion into their philosophical crosshairs. During the 1980s (to periodize somewhat schematically), Debray and Gauchet both favorably reappraised the French republican ideal at a time when its traditional appeal appeared to be fading. Finally, since the early 1990s, both Debray and Gauchet have argued that the strident secularism of French republicanism has become outdated, and they have asserted that traditional religion has a relevant public role in modern democracy.

What inner coherency do these two itineraries share? The answer, I shall argue, lies less in Debray's or Gauchet's normative commitments to either religion or republicanism *per se*, than in an unwavering belief that politics is the primordial basis of social cohesion. In the 1970s, Gauchet and Debray each employed religion as a philosophical category for explaining the fact that no human society can exist in a state of immanence, but inevitably yields some form of transcendence that opens up the possibility of politics. In the 1980s, both thinkers praised the French republican tradition precisely because they deemed it to have acknowledged explicitly the transcendence of the state over society—thus instantiating their earlier analysis of the essential nature of politics. However, faced with what they perceived as the dangers of an increasingly depoliticized society in the 1990s, both thinkers appealed to religion—not as a philosophical concept or as a historical example, but in its contemporary, institutional forms—as a means for mending the frayed public bonds of French society. Religion and republicanism could have such an ultimately similar meaning for both thinkers because each began his intellectual career obsessed with the centrality of politics to social existence, only to observe—and bemoan—the steady decline of its primacy.

1971–1981: TOWARD A CRITIQUE OF PURE POLITICS

For Régis Debray, the shift from political activism to meditation on politics was abrupt and beyond his control: in 1967, during the same forest ambush that felled his companion, Che Guevera, Debray, the brilliant young *normalien* who had made his name as a theorist of South American insurgency, was arrested by the Bolivian military and, in a widely publicized trial, sentenced to prison. Retrospectively, Debray presented his internment as a liberation of sorts: prevented by the prison walls from being politically active, he now had time to take stock of his precocious *militantisme* and to contemplate the nature of politics as such. "The *being* of politics (or its nature) would perhaps never have posed a problem in my eyes had I not found myself for many years in the physical incapacity of *doing* any."[2] While serving his time, Debray devoured classic works in the history of religion, willingly supplied by chaplains and conveniently authorized by censors. These readings allowed him to "cross the wires" of the sacred and the profane. While Parisian radicals preached Marx in 1968 only to turn, in their subsequent despair, to the solace of spirituality in the 1970s, Debray mused that he was awoken to religion's importance at precisely the moment when he was keen to decipher the nature of politics. Politically incapacitated as a result of his own militancy, Debray inchoately glimpsed, while wallowing in Camiri, the religious underpinnings of politics.

Following his release from jail and his return to France in 1971, Debray's investigations into the nature of politics led him to revise his commitment to Marxism. In particular, he expressed unease with Marxism's theoretical rationalism. Contemplating Marxism's mobilizing role in South American political movements and its legitimating function in Eastern European states, Debray was troubled that historical materialism proved incapable of accounting for the politics that existed in its name. As he later explained, "The 'International' has produced more Marxists than the reading of *Capital*."[3] Rather than merely critiquing Marxism, Debray now sought to understand the irrational allegiances which, he sensed, lurked beneath all political action, however rational it aspired to be.

Debray synthesized his views in a long tome, the title of which cast his thinking about politics in an explicitly Kantian light: *The Critique of Political Reason*. The book was published in 1981, shortly after Debray formally brought his radical days to a close by joining the presidential staff of the newly elected François Mitterrand. In the introduction, Debray described the historical moment that had made his own reflections possible. The contrast between the 1960s, a period of intense political ferment, and the 1970s, when activism dissipated, had made him almost physically aware of the specificity of "the political"; he defined it as a "level of reality specifically delimited by the formation and disaggregation of large human groups."[4] In the spirit of critical philosophy, he divided his exploration of the transcendental conditions of the political into a "dialectic" and an "analytic." Significantly, whereas Kant had first analyzed the conditions of knowledge before exploring how the mind can dialectically stray beyond its proper boundaries, Debray *began* with a dialectic, describing the constitutive ignorance of political action, *before* analyzing the concepts without which politics would be impossible. With this exposition, Debray made it clear that, far from delineating the proper scope of political reason, his *Critique* would show that politics was no reason at all.

One of political reason's greatest paralogisms, proving the irrational underpinnings of politics, was the Marxist concept of ideology. Debray's critique of ideology testifies to years of experience with the concept's insidious potency in political debate. A *"diabolus ex machina"* for disqualifying an adversary's claims, ideology is also the measuring rod for tracing "the limit of our lost illusions," accompanying each step of the never-ending flight from self-deception.[5] Thus while any particular use of the term could only ever be strategic, political reason's unwavering need for ideology as a conceptual war machine suggested that it was a basic form of political thinking. The "truth" of ideology lay in the omnipresence of the need that it revealed: to assure ourselves of the rationality of our own political views, we must be able to unmask everyone else's as ideological.

Ideology, Debray argued, thus shed light on something essential about politics: the irrational blind spots upon which collective unity depends. "Wherever there quivers a 'we'," he wrote, "there will be an 'ideology.'"[6] It is ideology that makes politics drift off into a dialectic that no analytic can tug back to the peaceful waters of reason. Though ideology thus understood becomes little more than a generic term for any irrational belief eliciting social cohesion, Debray endowed it with the status of a transcendental category: belief is an "a priori form of sociability."[7]

Moreover, once he had jettisoned the Marxist concept of ideology in favor of a transcendental one, Debray claimed that he had entered the sphere of religion. "The anatomy of religion is the key to the anatomy of 'ideology'; however, it is not religion which apes 'ideology,' but the contrary."[8] For Debray, the concepts of society, politics, and ideology each fit snugly, like so many Russian dolls, into "religion" understood as the non-rational condition of collective existence.

But if ideology can be so neatly collapsed into it, what then is the specificity of the concept of religion? Debray distinguished religion from ideology *tout court* by what he called the "axiom of incompleteness." Drawing somewhat speciously on Kurt Gödel's mathematical theories, Debray argued that no collectivity could account for its existence solely in its own terms. To exist, a community must achieve "closure" through a set of symbolic reference points allowing it to seal off its own identity. The meaning of these symbols cannot be straightforwardly accessible to the members of the group, but must in some way transcend them. Consequently, a community's cohesion inheres not in the horizontal relations between its members, but in their shared subordination to a symbolic summit, or *"foundational gap."*[9] By demonstrating that the purely immanent relations of a group are inadequate to constitute it as a community, a transcendental theory of the

political, Debray hoped, provided a cure to the fantasies of political rationalism and showed that there is no way out of the dialectic of ideology. Moreover, by subsuming ideology under belief and by demonstrating the necessary non-immanence of communities, Debray believed he had established
that politics is defined by questions that only religion can answer. "God does
not exist," he wrote, "but we are all politically condemned to a collective existence that is theological in essence, and to make theologians of ourselves
to understand something about our immediate political life."[10]

Though never indulging in the kind of swashbuckling Marxism practiced
by Debray, Marcel Gauchet, too, by his own recollection, traced the origin
of his reflections on the nature of politics to the heady days he spent immersed in the *militantisme* of the 1960s. Indeed, Gauchet first encountered
the politics of the far-left as a high school student in Normandy around
1962; by his own account, he was a teenage anti-Stalinist.[11] In his later remarks about this period, one detects a lingering exasperation with the suf-
focating culture of the *groupuscules* of the far-left, as well as a visceral dis-
comfort with their unavowed contradictions—between the freedom they
embraced in theory and the rigidity of their practice, between their self-
confidence in their historical task and their willingness to ape outdated revolutionary antics. In 2003, Gauchet recalled:

> I was twenty-two in 1968, and I belonged to a *militant* generation. . . . To use
> a conventional typology, I belonged to the libertarian far-left, which butted
> against the considerable power of the French Communist Party and of the
> various Trotskyist and Maoist denominations that contested it in the name of
> an even more pure and glowing Marxist-Leninism. This situation weighed on
> the direction of my studies and of my life. It determined my choice to study
> history and philosophy, with the idea that the key to the political situation in
> which we found ourselves resided in a *theory of history* capable of effectively
> giving the lie to Marxism, not only by attempting to critique it on specific
> points, . . . but by proposing an alternative vision.[12]

Gauchet would later describe the theory that he proceeded to elaborate as
a "transcendental anthropo-sociology" laying bare, through an examination
of politics, the "transcendental conditions of the social."[13] Thus Gauchet,
like Debray, sought to come to terms with his experiences in the 1960s
through a transcendental theory of politics that accorded a prominent role
to religion.

Gauchet's philosophical starting point was to ask: why it is that something
like politics happens to human societies? This question arose out of
Gauchet's encounter with Claude Lefort at the University of Caen in 1966.

A leader (with Cornelius Castoriadis) of the dissident Trotskyist group So-cialisme ou Barbarie in the 1950s and a student of the phenomenologist Maurice Merleau-Ponty, Lefort challenged the Marxist reduction of politics to a superstructural reflection of class struggle by proposing an analysis of the autonomy of what he called *"le politique"*—"the political." The political, Lefort taught, is not a specialized sphere of power relations within society, but is the name of human efforts to overcome the inherent intangibility of social relations and to grasp society as a phenomenon. As Lefort wrote, "the political" is the "'form' in which the symbolic dimension of the social is un-veiled."[14] Gauchet became the most brilliant member of Lefort's circle, which consisted, as one contemporary recalled, of a "nebula of students" who were discovering "political philosophy, or even just philosophy *tout court*, in what was officially a sociology course."[15]

Deeply influenced by Lefort's teachings, Gauchet, in his earliest writings, explored the implications of understanding the political as the perspective from which society can be grasped as a whole. In an extensive essay from 1971 summarizing Lefort's 1966–1967 lecture course, Gauchet asserted that the political is the answer a society offers to the question of its own self-definition. This answer, however, can only be articulated in a different id-iom than that of the social. "The logic that organizes a political regime," he maintained, "is that of an articulated *response* to the interrogation opened by the coming-to-being and in the coming-to-being of the social as such." Through the political, "a society communicates in a singular manner with the fact that there is society, that there is *appearance of the social*."[16] In other words, the sheer fact that humans coexist together necessitates an an-gle from which the meaning of their coexistence can come into relief. This perspective is "the political." Yet while the space of the political emerges out of society's phenomenological need to grasp itself, the political cannot be coextensive with society itself: in order to make society visible, it must be distinct from society. The political, in short, is the "other" through which society becomes its "own."

Following on these insights, Gauchet sought to describe the different possibilities according to which a society could arrange its political space. The dynamic structuring of these basic options was what he called the prob-lem of the "occupiability" of political space. Society lays out the space of the political, from which it can be viewed as a meaningful whole; yet because this place emerges out of society's interest in grasping itself as a phenome-non, it can never be fully occupied by a specific individual, for to do so would be to equate a social need with a personal attribute. "For none," Gauchet writes, "is installed with the solidity of a fact in the place of power."[17] He demonstrated this point in a dense article from 1971 analyzing the varieties of Indo-European kingship. The institution of the *rex*, he maintained, depends on a practical paradox: through his status as the contemporary incarnation of society's mythical founder, the *rex* occupies a space outside the community of his subjects, thus establishing power on the basis of his exteriority from society. Yet a *rex* confined to a place outside society would be incapable of being an active force within that society. Moreover, even his claim to occupy this external space requires that he must simultaneously situate himself within society, if only to draw the line separating the profane interior from the sacred exterior. As the embodiment of power, the *rex* represents "the exteriority of the social body" from which it could be "purely circumscribed," but at the same time lays bare the "impossibility of attaining this outside." Similarly, power "provides the collectivity with the 'knowledge' that there is society," yet, by virtue of its role in this process, deprives society of this knowledge.[18] Gauchet's philosophical "wager" was to show that "the stake of the political is the impossible juncture of the social with itself through the impossible erasure of the *difference* between power and civil society."[19]

The logic of the relationship between the political and society allowed for only a finite number of variations. In Gauchet's estimation, the basic alternative was between a premodern form, in which society suppressed its divisions, acquiring unity by submitting itself to a political system based on the personal rule of an individual who claims to embody power *per se*, and a modern one, in which society, laying bare its divisions, gives form to them through a depersonalized, representative political space that is indefinitely open to competition among candidates seeking to occupy it temporarily.

It was in trying to explain this premodern form of power that Gauchet was led to consider religion as a political category. In his very first allusion to religion, Gauchet viewed it as a mere exercise in political imagination: religion is the ideological means through which a monarch attempts to legitimate his shaky occupation of a political space outside and above society. As such, religion was atavistic: with "the disappearance of all transcendent guarantees . . . the radical invention of society by itself" would be recognized as the "fundamental demand of politics."[20] With the advent of the modern representative political space, the religious imaginary would yield, in short, to the political reality principle.

Yet Gauchet soon came to realize that religion constituted a fundamental political form in its own right. Shifting his emphasis from the figure of the absolute monarch, for whom religion represented the fantastic pretension to *fuse* with the unoccupiable space of the political, Gauchet, drawing heavily on the work of the ethnologist Pierre Clastres, concocted a theory of prehistoric society. Primitive religion, he argued, was a deliberate social mechanism for *preventing* any member of society from attempting to occupy the space of the political. By ingeniously filling up the space of the political with gods rather than humans, Gauchet contended, primitive peoples denied themselves the right to meddle in their collective self-definition, thus ensuring that none amongst them could lay claim to power. By warding off all claims to occupying the political, the "choice of the imaginary is the realism of the savages' politics and of its implications."[21] The recognition that more was at stake in religion than a failed act of imaginary fusion made it possible for Gauchet to unmask religion as a thoroughly political phenomenon.

Yet the true originality of Gauchet's position consisted in his assertion that religion is not simply political, but that it is a form of pure politics. This became evident in his succinct statement of the problem in a 1977 article entitled "The Debt of Meaning and the Roots of the State." Why, Gauchet asked, were "exteriority, dispossession, indebtedness" so central to the institutions of primitive society?[22] Reformulating his earlier argument, Gauchet asserted that no society was ever simply "given" as a natural entity. To exist as a meaningful whole, the members of a society must identify "a point of view of absolute power" in relation to which the nature of their association is defined.[23] Thus, paradoxically, it is through an act of self-dispossession that a society acquires a grasp on its own nature. "Any society is destined, in order to be, to decode itself in something that is for it, but not of it," Gauchet insisted. "Indebtedness is a way of being oneself. . . . The enigma of political separation is the enigma of social being."[24] Moreover, far from being unique to primitive society, dispossession is constitutive of social existence as such. This "need, as mysterious as it is universal, that has pushed men ever since their beginnings to depend on something other than themselves or on men other than themselves" arises out of the "radical imperative to be in society."[25] The political, now understood as the self-dispossessing medium through which society relates to its own meaning, thus assumes its purest form in primitive religion. Hence Gauchet's stunning conclusion: *"religion was historically the condition of possibility of the state."*[26] The Kantian resonance of this language is no mere flourish: Gauchet believed that he had identified the fundamental structure of politics, of which all other forms were transmutations.

There are thus some striking similarities in the ways in which Debray and Gauchet encountered the problem of religion. The hyperpoliticization of French student culture of the 1960s brought each to his own Kantian moment: the inevitable slide into dogmatism to which leftist ideology appeared to lead could only be halted by an interrogation into what made politics possible at all. Terminologically, this move was reflected in an emphasis on *le politique*, or "the political," over *la politique*—mere "politics." Furthermore, it was by thinking about religion that each awoke from his dogmatic slumbers. What they believed they had learned from anthropological literature on religion was that humans could not gather together in society without defining their horizontal relationships in terms of a vertical relationship to a transcendent order. What Debray described as the "axiom of incompleteness" and Gauchet called "the debt of meaning" both referred to the impossibility for society to exist as a purely immanent entity. While each drew significantly different conclusions from this position—Debray, despite protestations to the contrary, effectively equated politics to religion, while Gauchet argued that religion was the historical precondition for the state—both nonetheless located the condition of possibility of the political in the symbolic breach opened up by society's incapacity simply to be itself.

1981–1990: THE RETURN OF THE REPUBLICAN REPRESSED

Though France has enjoyed republican constitutions without interruption since the Liberation, not until the 1980s did a series of circumstances coalesce to create a context ripe for a new era of republican ferment. The 1981 victory of François Mitterrand's Socialist Party brought to power a group of leaders, who, for all their talk of a "rupture with capitalism," staunchly espoused the republican tradition. Moreover, increasing public awareness of the evolution of French society toward multiculturalism brought the universalistic model of republican citizenship under sharp scrutiny, notably during the infamous *chador* (or Islamic veil) affair of 1989. Furthermore, as France diligently cleared each successive hurdle on its race toward European integration, skeptics invoked the republican principle of the nation as the sole bearer of popular sovereignty to mobilize opposition against a seemingly inexorable process. Finally, the national celebration of the bicentennial of the French Revolution in 1989 brought considerable public reflection on the specificities of France's republican democracy.

These events and trends were accompanied by a renewal of interest in republicanism on the part of intellectuals. The critique of Marxism and the rebirth of antitotalitarian and liberal thought in the 1970s had remained largely indifferent to republicanism. In the 1980s, however, republicanism reentered the pantheon of political philosophy. Claude Nicolet, a historian

of ancient Rome, published *L'Idée républicaine en France*, the standard
text on the topic, in 1982.[27] Following the socialist government's adoption
of austerity measures in 1983, which marked its abandonment of the ideological aspirations upon which it had campaigned, contributors to a special
issue of *Intervention*, a journal associated with the "Second Left," wondered whether republicanism might not be an ideological alternative to politically bankrupt socialism.[28] Two years later, Luc Ferry and Alain Renaut,
the budding stars of French political philosophy, devoted the final volume
of their reappraisal of the liberal tradition to the "republican ideal."[29] Just
in time for the 1989 bicentennial, François Furet, Jacques Julliard, and
Pierre Rosanvallon welcomed the end of the "French exception," typified
by the revolution's republican legacy, in a volume polemically entitled *The
Republic of the Center*.[30] Whether celebrated or decried, republicanism became, in the 1980s, a key idiom for discussing the specificity of French political culture.

   A major voice in the renewal of republicanism was Régis Debray. Having
largely set aside his political reflections during the seven years he served on
François Mitterrand's staff, his return to political thought in the late 1980s
revealed a dramatic conversion to the republican ideal. In an article from
Le Nouvel Observateur, appearing in late 1989, responding to the question,
"Are you are a democrat or a republican?" Debray defended an austere
breed of republicanism that appeared to depart dramatically from the positions he had defended earlier in his *Critique*. With a litany of pithy distinctions between ideal-typical republicans and democrats, Debray defined a
model of republicanism that would serve as a vantage point from which to
critique the decadent (read: American) tendencies of French democracy.
Republics, he asserted, embrace a rational conception of man as well as citizenship, a unitary state, public education, civic consciousness, the primacy
of law, and political principles. Democracies, on the other hand, adhere to
a conception of man as mere producer as well as communitarianism, feder-
alism, multiculturalism, the primacy of contracts, and political compromise.
Democracy, in Debray's view, was clearly a republic gone soft.

   Even more striking was Debray's defense of republican laicism. In a re-
putedly secular European community, Debray complained, "the political
has not truly conquered its full autonomy over the religious."[31] The reason
was that most European countries were—whatever their official names—
democracies, not republics. Democracies need God to aggregate the dispersed "particularisms" that even a federal system can never make cohe-
sive. Republics, however, by embracing a universalist conception of
humanity, unite their citizens over and above their differences by placing

them on equal footing in relation to a unitary state. In short, Debray appeared in 1989 to be singing the praises of laïc French republicanism, whereas in 1981 he had argued that religion was the core of all politics. Had he changed his position?

Debray's position had not dramatically changed, because his understanding of the nature of politics remained constant: the value of republicanism lay for him precisely in the fact that it existed in a transcendent relationship to society. He made this clear in a polemical open letter entitled *Que vive la République!* (also from 1989), admonishing President Mitterrand to rally to the republic's defense. Debray alerted Mitterrand to the dangerous implications of the contemporary fetishization of the idea of "civil society." A prominent faction of the president's own party had adopted it as its mantra. The socialist Michel Rocard, whom Mitterrand, following his reelection in 1988, had appointed prime minister, began his tenure by calling for a reduction in the chasm separating the "state apparatus" from "civil society," immediately setting the example by naming a contingent of "civil society" figures to his government.[32] The implication of this discourse, as Debray interpreted it, was that the spontaneous, "natural" bonds within society itself were more determinant of social identity than the deliberately political bond of citizenship. Consequently, self-management socialism—the socialism of Rocard's "Second Left"—was "radically antirepublican."[33] To be a republican meant affirming the state's role in creating bonds that transcended society's particularisms. This required distinguishing the state as much as possible from, rather than collapsing it into, society. Just as the First Republic, representing "the function of the universal in society," set out to uproot the remnants of aristocratic and clerical privilege, so the Fifth Republic needed to fight off monetary greed and mindless entertainment—the new "idols of society."[34]

The rise of democracy at the republic's expense was due, in Debray's analysis, to a crisis of the state, and notably the state's abandonment of its role in producing *le lien social*. The notion of *le lien social* is an often unnoticed, yet peculiarly pervasive mainstay of mainstream political discourse in France. *Lien*, in this context, means both "bond" and "relationship"— "tie" is perhaps the best way to translate it. The problem of "*how to make ties*," Debray observed, is a fundamentally "religious interrogation."[35] Already in his *Critique*, while discussing different etymologies of the word religion, he had remarked: "A religion ties us to one another in tying us to an external element (the 'divinity')."[36] As the republic faded into democracy, Debray explained, the state had ceased to generate the superordinating ties needed to create relations over and above the "natural" ones born spontaneously within society. Drawing on his earlier argument that the constitutive "incompleteness" of social existence assigns politics the task of filling it with meaning, Debray denounced the contemporary decline in the symbolic importance of citizenship. By minimizing the worth of citizenship, which had previously been republican France's over-arching social tie, the state had created a symbolic void destined to be filled by the "churches and tribes" of society—for "there is no *lien social* without symbolic references."[37] From the perspective of Debray's republicanism, in opposition to liberalism or "Second Left" socialism, this retreat of the state entailed not the emancipation of society, but its refeudalization. "When a Republic leaves the room on the tips of its toes, it is not the free and triumphant individual who occupies the terrain. . . . [T]he decline of political power is paid for by the political advance of religious authorities, and by a new arrogance of money's fiefdoms."[38] The connection between Debray's earlier religious interpretation of politics and his newfound laic republicanism thus becomes clear: if politics is social unity achieved through common adherence to a transcendent authority, then the degeneration of the republic into democracy, in Debray's terms, represents a process of desacralization, even—and, indeed, all the more so—if the retreat of the republican state leads individuals to seek substitute forms of social ties in churches. To say that laicity is "sacred" for a republican is not to speak metaphorically: it means that the state must always transcend the society from which it emerges. As Debray wrote in 1991: "The Republic guarantees the self-management of different forms of the sacred. But in order to respect a 'to each his own transcendence,' the protective agent must itself be recognized as transcending these particular transcendences."[39]

Unlike Debray, Gauchet has never, in the course of his career, described himself as a republican. As his political thought reached a wider audience—notably with the 1985 publication of *The Disenchantment of the World*, the major statement of his philosophy of history—many promptly identified him with the strident secularism associated with the republican tradition. Moreover, without straying from his argument that religion was a condition of the possibility of the state, Gauchet insisted in the mid-1980s that his project consisted in demonstrating democracy's complete "viability" outside of any religious or transcendent references. Responding to an article written by Gauchet in January 1984 entitled "The End of Religion," the editor of the Jesuit journal *Études*, Paul Valadier, expressed consternation at Gauchet's thoroughgoing secularism, even suggesting that Gauchet's vision of political modernity as thoroughly disenchanted was totalitarian. Gauchet dug in his heels, insisting that modern societies demonstrate "the perfect viability of human existence, on a personal as well as social level, without the gods." He added: "If God doesn't exist—then nothing happens."[40] Yet, by the decade's end, Gauchet had, without completely abandoning it, significantly tempered his laic stridency. Tellingly, this shift followed a period of reflection on the French republican tradition.

As with Debray, Gauchet's favorable reevaluation of French republicanism emerged, at least in part, out of a critique of the liberal conception of society. Gauchet's position on this question has long been complex. The high-water mark of Gauchet's liberalism was reached around the late 1970s. In an article for *Annales* in 1979, he expressed considerable sympathy for the liberal account of society as a self-regulating mechanism eliciting equilibrium through the confrontation of competing individual interests. The advent of this conception of society in the eighteenth century constituted a major historical threshold; it acknowledged, he believed, the fundamental truth that society is the product of human creativity, not of transcendent design.[41] The liberal conception of society was thus thoroughly compatible with the "viability" of the democratic age.

In the 1980s, however, Gauchet's attention shifted from a defense of liberalism's crucial insights to a preoccupation with its constitutive tensions. While admitting that the notion of a self-regulating society was the unsurpassable horizon of political modernity, Gauchet criticized contemporary liberals for ignoring liberal society's "unconscious": its origin in the political dynamics of the state. Such an insight was particularly germane in the early 1980s: two years following their historic victory in 1981, the governing socialists made a dramatic about-face in March 1983, announcing a draconian austerity plan that laid the groundwork for economic liberalization. As Gauchet observed in 1984, "the battle for modernization has begun," but "this national imperative comes to us from above, via a mobilizing state."[42] In this context, Gauchet considered that the order of the day was less to embrace liberalism than to offer a "critical reevaluation" of it. As he observed in 1986, the very year in which a liberal coalition beat the socialists in parliamentary elections: "Hayek is as inept and as inapplicable as the *programme commun* [the joint electoral platform of the Socialist and Communist parties from 1972–1977]."[43]

Liberals, Gauchet argued, found it difficult to overcome the illusory dimension of their ideology. While rightly insisting upon society's capacity for self-regulation, they blinded themselves to the fact that this autonomy could not exist without a degree of heteronomy, of which obligations to the state were the prototype. In short, to understand the true nature of *le lien social* under modern conditions, one needed to be conscious of the heteronomy repressed by liberal autonomy. In 1986, Gauchet stated emphatically:

> The *lien social* is, in general, the result in our society of a compromise between the dimension of obligation and the dimension of the autonomy of persons. It is this compromise that the ideologues of elementary liberalism and the despisers of decadent modernity agree amongst themselves not to see. The problem is thus to make it more visible and more conscious. . . . One must think together, in a sense, Rousseau and Bonald, while refuting both.[44]

Properly understood, liberal autonomy should affirm the heteronomous dimension of social life upon which it depends, over the naive objections of "elementary" liberals.

While bringing the obligatory repressed back into liberal consciousness, it was equally necessary to temper triumphant liberal individualism. During the 1980s, Gauchet became particularly preoccupied with this problem in the realm of education. The 1980s represented, in many respects, an important turning point in French educational policy. The socialists' attempt, in 1984, to bring private schools under state tutelage met with a massive popular mobilization in defense of the freedom to choose between state and private schools. Around the same time, a book by the psychoanalyst Jean-Claude Milner critiquing the inanities of contemporary pedagogy sparked an intense intellectual exchange concerning the purpose of education. Intervening in this debate in 1985, Gauchet argued that the contemporary educational crisis had to be traced back to the "dynamic constraints flowing from the paradoxical mode of composition of a *society of individuals*."[45] The dominance within schools of a pedagogy of "personal fulfillment," which increasingly gave priority to the expression of the student's personality over the transmission of the canon, belonged, Gauchet maintained, to the ever-increasing intensification of individualism as the primary organizing principle of modern societies. Yet in upholding the "private right to ignore the *lien* of society," a society of individuals confronted the "difficulty of representing itself as a society."[46] This was a problem because, despite the leeway given to individual preferences, the reality of society persisted at the "invisible" level of the mechanisms needed to integrate individuals into the whole. Schools were situated along the fault line of these tensions: whatever pressures they faced from the demands of ambient individualism, they remained the one social space in which "it has always been impossible to ignore the fact that it is society that produces individuals."[47] Schools, in short, give the lie to the liberal myth of the autonomous individual.

Partial relief to the dilemmas of liberal society that democratic education dramatized could be found, Gauchet decided, by pondering the republican school as its founders conceived it. The educational system established by Jules Ferry and his fellow republicans in the 1880s rested, Gauchet maintained, on an appealing compromise: to produce the autonomous individuals necessary for a responsible citizenry, a pedagogical philosophy with no qualms about its own authority was required. In this sense, historic republicanism was conscious that individualism is a socially instilled value in a way that liberalism is not. Gauchet wrote: "This is why, retrospectively, the Republic is so beautiful; it holds before us the emblem that we are in fact missing: namely, a successful connection between social inscription and the right of the individual—achieved, notably, *in* and *through* schools."[48] The pedagogy of "personal fulfillment," which Gauchet believed had poisoned French education, sought to liberate students from the stodgy discipline of traditional schooling, but in fact left them at sea in society by depriving them of the resources to negotiate their social embeddedness. The republican model, by contrast, brought sharply into focus the fact that "one does not function effectively as an individual except under the condition of having an in-depth grasp of one's society."[49] Gauchet's historicism prevented him from prescriptively advocating a return to the golden age of the Third Republic. However, by defending republicanism's avowal of the social origin of the individual, which liberalism is condemned to repress, he suggested a solution to the dilemmas of contemporary individualism.

In its contrast to liberalism, Gauchet's description of republicanism thus tellingly resembled his own account of religion. Describing primitive social organization, Gauchet had argued that religious "dispossession" was perfectly compatible with a strong sense of individuality: accepting that the key to one's existence is available from the community in which one lives makes it far more accessible than if one must face the daunting task of finding it within oneself. In 1988, Gauchet argued explicitly that the establishment of autonomous individuality had always depended on references to the value of "heteronomy"—a term which, in Gauchet's lexicon, is synonymous with religion.[50] While refusing to contemplate a return to religious values, he maintained that liberal society's great achievement of allowing individuals to think of themselves as existing independently of society could easily undermine itself if taken too far. By making visible the ineluctably heteronomous dimension of society, of which primitive religion was the purest form, republicanism could be therapeutically useful in coaxing liberal society to accept its repressed collective basis.

Though neither had previously paid it any attention, by the late 1980s both Debray and Gauchet had not only discovered French republicanism's appeal, but used it as a vantage point from which to criticize contemporary trends. This sympathetic reappraisal of republicanism was, moreover, intellectually consistent with their earlier positions, not because they took the question-begging view that republicanism was "like" a religion, but because they believed it verified the understanding of politics they had arrived at in the 1970s: namely, that because human society cannot exist in a purely immanent fashion, it yields a separate, transcendent order of the political. In a climate that was saturated with concerns about liberalism on the Left as well as the Right, republicanism became an appealing tradition to invoke for two thinkers whose fundamental philosophical commitments made them suspicious of the liberal idea of a self-regulating society. Their positions in this period were, as always, far from identical. Debray was so concerned with denouncing liberalism in the name of social transcendence that he never bothered to distinguish carefully between the republic and religion, or between the socially sacred and organized churches. Gauchet, always more complex, acknowledged that the autonomous conception of society was at least half true, and that, historically, it foreclosed any return to the instituted heteronomy of primitive religion. Yet because republicanism recognizes both the transcendent dimension of collective existence and the liberal insight into social autonomy, it is better suited to keep in focus the space of the political, which liberals tend to blur. In any case, Debray and Gauchet turned to republicanism in the 1980s because it instantiated, in their view, the thesis that society requires a transcendent dimension in order to exist.

1991–2003: BRINGING RELIGION BACK TO THE REPUBLIC

The late 1980s and early 1990s marked a moment of considerable political disenchantment in France, not unlike the "malaise" that characterized American politics of the late 1970s. As Mitterrand's reign passed the ten-year mark, political corruption became a staple of the news. Voters increasingly rejected mainstream political parties, turning their attention to more radical or simply novel faces. More generally, the French became increasingly less likely to vote at all in their frequent elections. Widespread unemployment throughout much of the 1990s, the acceleration of European construction, and globalization all suggested that the capacity of politicians to direct French society was also waning. Occasional outbursts of collective mobilization—notably the public sector strikes of 1995—only served to bring this broader phenomenon of depoliticization into sharper relief. The titles of Gauchet's writings during this period are revealing: "Malaise in Democracy" (1988); "Democratic Pacification, Civic Desertion" (1990); "The Democratic Illness" (1993); and "The Bogged-Down Republic" (1995).[51] For both Debray and Gauchet, the apparent decline in the status of politics as the primary reference point of collective life led both—surprisingly—to argue that institutional religion could play a greater role in the public sphere.

Debray reacted to the climate of depoliticization with a strident defense of the need for political communities to engender a sense of "belonging." In 1996, he gave a talk to the Société française de philosophie entitled "Incompleteness, the Logic of the Religious," in which he restated, fifteen years later, the basic thesis of his *Critique*. Yet his emphasis on the need for a transcendent basis for community clearly rankled the rationalist instincts of some in his audience. Catherine Kintzler, a prominent republican intellectual, pressed Debray on the compatibility between his political views and his philosophical argument, asking him whether republicans should not seek rational ties between autonomous individuals, rather than fusion into a transcendent community. Debray replied, confusingly, that republicanism properly conceived should steer clear of the twin dangers of a "rationalist idealism" that ignores the religious character of social life and of the communitarian impulse to denigrate rational universality in favor of "ethnological forms of belonging."[52] As if this were not hedging his bets enough, he added that the religious problem for the laic republican is one of knowing "how to incorporate the spiritual in the city while struggling against the confusion of the spiritual and the temporal."[53]

Despite the questionable coherency of this position, it informed a significant shift in recent French educational policy. In February 2002, Debray submitted a report, entitled "Teaching Religious Facts in a Laic School," which the socialist education minister Jack Lang had commissioned him to write. In a recommendation that caused immediate alarm among entrenched secularists, Debray argued that the French republic was now sufficiently mature to integrate religious knowledge into the curricula of its primary and secondary schools. His report is currently being implemented.

In addition to its policy recommendations, the Debray report asserts that introducing religious studies into the classroom will reinvigorate social ties of all kinds. The sorry state of "religious culture" in French society, Debray argues, creates the risk of a "collective disinheritance" and of a "rupture in the chains of national and European memory." What will happen, he asks, when *Trinité* will be thought of as nothing more than a *métro* station?[54] Moreover, religious ignorance could lead to "a communitarian dismemberment of civic solidarities." Furthermore, the poverty of religious awareness, which, Debray says, originates with the decline of the traditional role assumed by churches and families in the transmission of culture, means that it is incumbent upon the state to take responsibility for the "elementary tasks of orientation in space-time that civil society is no longer in a position to ensure." Debray thus seeks both to capture for the state, through its schools, some of the radiance that religions have acquired in a post-traditional society obsessed with "the search for meaning," and to mitigate the socially dissolving effects of communitarianism by bringing a frank discussion of religion into the classroom. As the perspective from which all religious beliefs appear particularistic, *laïcité* can thus be the transcendent value of the republic. Religious instruction becomes a circuitous route to a reinvigorated republic, in which the citizenry will perceive its polity, via the state, as the primary domain for meaningful reflection on life's dilemmas, while being properly equipped to engage with the particularistic temptations of civil society.

Even more than Debray, Gauchet was traumatized by the malaise of French civil life in the early 1990s. His writings show him obsessed with what he took to be the central paradox of contemporary democracy: the more democracy triumphs, taming the totalitarian demons of the early twentieth century, the more it meets with indifference. This paradox is a variation on the one he had encountered, years before, in the writings of the Restoration liberal Benjamin Constant: the triumph of the right to private enjoyments, and the freedom not to consider oneself as belonging to society, saps the taste for self-government, *which is nonetheless the only reliable guarantor that individual rights will ever find.*

In the early 1990s, Gauchet detected a new kind of individualism at play that made the social inscription of individuals even more invisible. Rather than simply privileging the private over the public realm, this "negative individualism" based itself on "distance and defiance towards the other and towards any engagement likely to constitute a tie [*lien*]."[55] This negative individualism did not limit itself to private activities, but expressed itself in paradoxical forms of public action. Firmly anchored in their democratic ways, many people were prepared to take to the streets to defend their rights, but without regard for how their actions could be integrated into a collective political agenda. Hence the phenomena of "political movement without politics, civic engagements without civic spirit."[56] Gauchet detected this dynamic at work in recurring waves of student protests, as well as in the burgeoning ecologist movement of the 1990s (upon which he heaped his scorn). The potential consequences of these developments were deeply disturbing:

> Will we have a democracy of little protesting islands, delegating to morally dis-qualified, but politically undisputed masters the impure task of administering in reality values cultivated in an exclusively sentimental mode? Or, rather, will we finally see the development of a responsible citizenry in which no one be-lieves himself obliged to rely on others—elsewhere, higher up—for the de-termination of constraints?[57]

Negative individualism and apolitical politics combined to make modern citizens curiously submissive to the very leaders whom they disdained too much even to bother voting them out.

Against this pessimistic backdrop, Gauchet enlisted his intellectual ener-gies, in the 1990s and 2000s, into the project of repairing the texture of French public life that depoliticization was tearing apart. Gauchet's public role during these years rested on a historical observation and a principle of action. The historical observation was that the latest twist in modernity's on-going extraction of itself from religious heteronomy consisted in a "secular-ization" of politics itself, which, in the French case, meant a loss of faith in the republican "religion." In 1991, Gauchet told an interviewer from *Projet*, a Je-suit journal, that the "black hole at the heart of the public sphere" can be ex-plained by "the erosion of the republican religion": "We continue to live amidst its rituals and symbols."[58] As Gauchet repeated throughout the 1990s, it was its very victory over the Catholic Church that had brought the repub-lic to the state of crisis in which it now found itself. During the nineteenth century, republicans had defended a "project of autonomy" against the church's "party of heteronomy." But now that the church had permanently ac-cepted its place within a democratic society, republicanism lost the very foil against which it had defined itself. In the process, the centrality of politics in defining collective life also faded, rendering its project of autonomy elusive.[59] In short, depoliticization itself belonged to the broader process of the "de-parture from religion." "We are living," he wrote in 2001, "a remarkable mo-ment in the history of religious belief and of political belief. Religious belief is ceasing to be political. . . . For its part, political belief is ceasing to be reli-gious."[60] Gauchet's gambit was to clarify how this historical observation could suggest new ways of conceiving political life in a disenchanted democracy.

The principle of action embraced by Gauchet consisted in aiming the floodlights of public discourse at the redoubts to which an individualistic society had confined the political. "The supreme function of politics," he wrote in 1990, "is to give a collectivity the feeling of a grasp on its destiny."[61]

Two years later, he explained to an interviewer from *Le Banquet*, a journal edited by public-spirited civil servants, that the French needed to reacquaint themselves with the political form that had made their precious individual rights possible: the nation. Furthermore, Gauchet outlined the role that "intermediary bodies" must play in articulating public opinion. This proved to be precisely the way in which Gauchet came to define a place for religion in republican politics:

> It is on the terrain of public deliberation that one must intervene. I think that intermediary structures must be created or recreated. . . . A lot depends . . . on the capacity to make existing institutions truly civic institutions. Once we had institutions that were unconscious of their public role. Let's take the example of the church. The goal of the church was not to be a civic or a cultural institution. Its purpose was to lead its faithful down the good path leading straight to heaven. In reality, it was something else, but only by accident, and not explicitly, not consciously. . . . One must inspire in society a consciousness of the true role of intermediary bodies. . . . Setting aside the question of whether people believe in God or not, the church must consider that it has social responsibility. In these institutions, a type of public education is delivered to people, even if its goal is not explicit.[62]

The levers upon which an intellectual could exert his limited pressure were thus representative bodies of the nation and the intermediary bodies through which public opinion was refracted.

Following his own advice, Gauchet, beginning around 2000, embarked on a discussion with the French educational community, in order to justify religion before laic republicans in the name of revitalizing public life. Speaking in 2002 to the staff of an educational journal devoted to middle-school reading, Gauchet tacitly approved the Debray report: "To be free of religions is not to ignore them; it is on the contrary to know and to recognize them; more than this, it is to seek to understand them, that is to say, to not content oneself with worn-out clichés on fanaticism and superstition or the opium of the people."[63] This was all the more true given that politics itself, more than ever, was in search of "final values." And yet, while accommodating religious values, schools needed to recognize that, in a modern democracy, they could only contribute to fostering civic consciousness on a rational basis—even if, in doing so, they had to integrate a heteronomous element. As Gauchet explained to the faculty of a teacher-training college:

> The enormous political and social task before us is the recomposition of an appropriate language to express rationally and democratically this order of con-

straint [that traditional republican civic education had articulated affectively]. This is the condition of democracy: one has no grasp on constraints unless they are recognized, articulated, and acknowledged.[64]

Around the same time, Gauchet entered into dialogue with religious organizations, admonishing them to take advantage of the opportunities for actively engaging in public debate that the "departure from religion" afforded them. As he explained to a Catholic colloquium in 2000: "The debacle of 'republican spirituality,' the rout of politics as an end in itself, have had the effect of reopening the problem of ends and the problem of morality at the level of each individual."[65] Religions can henceforth offer a kind of framework for the free exercise of autonomy, providing individuals with a far richer context for moral thinking than they could arrive at on their own. This role need not be confined to the private sphere, as intransigent republicans would have it. Precisely because religions provide vital frameworks through which individuals can structure their life choices, they are of public consequence. As Gauchet explained to the Catholic newspaper *Témoignage chrétien*:

> The separation between the spiritual and the political, which makes of each believer a citizen like any other, is no longer absolute. In other words, the superior values to which each individual refers have consequences on his conduct and his engagements in the city. I think, for example, that any Christian worthy of the name considers that the economy is simply a means; that its end is to serve the moral dignity of humanity. As an agnostic, I have the same conviction.[66]

Yet even while advocating a prominent role for religion in a democratic public sphere when addressing a Catholic audience, Gauchet warned that acceptance of pluralism was the entry fee for taking on this role—a condition that, when addressing secular audiences, he wondered if Catholics were prepared to accept. Religion was invited to stem the tide of individualism, but not to substitute itself for republican arrangements.

CONCLUSION

Only in late 2003 did Debray and Gauchet explicitly address one another in print. At a moment when religion loomed large culturally and politically, Debray and Gauchet readily agreed, in an exchange in *Le Débat*, that they had often approached it in a similar fashion. Gauchet observed that, as explanations of the origin of religion, his concept of "exteriority" was practically synonymous with Debray's notion of "incompleteness." At the same time, they noted their considerable divergences: While Debray maintained that religion and politics were essentially homogeneous, Gauchet claimed that, while often conflated in practice, they were analytically distinguishable. Consequently, whereas Debray held that modernity could be religious, Gauchet asserted that modernity was conceivable outside of any religious stricture—even fundamentalists, he suggested, are more secular than they realize. Yet more revealing than these agreements and disagreements was how much they took for granted the terms of the problem. They differed as to whether exteriority primarily characterized the political or the religious, but both agreed that the political arose out of the inherent incompleteness of social existence. Thus Gauchet, while rejecting Debray's argument that religion was compatible with modernity, was careful to point out that secularization did not eliminate social exteriority: "The crucial point," he averred, "is that exteriority is first of all in the political," which is why "it can function without religion."[67]

"Part of what it is to be on the Left in France," Tony Judt has written, "is to take very, very seriously the business of politics."[68] However one judges their complex relationship to the Left, the coherency of Debray's and Gauchet's basic commitments across their careers indeed lies in the constancy of their concern with the question of politics and in their belief that it is through politics that human societies acquire cohesion and meaning. Ironically, many of the reasons that led both to critique Marxism in the 1970s for failing to grasp the primacy of the political also made them uneasy with liberalism by the 1980s: whatever their differences, Marxism and liberalism can both imagine a society left to its own self-regulating devices. In their engagement with religion and republicanism as different signs of society's need to transcend itself, Debray and Gauchet provide trenchant examples of a still-pervasive view among French intellectuals that politics must be about something greater than the adjudication of competing social interests. Yet, having come of age in the 1960s, when politics seemed to be reinventing the scale of its possibilities, by the 1990s, when politics seemed ever more impotent, if not irrelevant for most people, Debray and Gauchet found themselves in the Cassandra-like position of observing a steady decline in political vitality. As Gauchet observed, the paradox of the political, understood as the perspective from which a society defines its collective meaning, was that its visibility was so glaring as to be almost blinding: it is not hidden, but "veiled in the visible, as it were, masked in the fullness of its effectuating power at the very heart of its exposition."[69] The question that neither has perhaps fully confronted is: what is the worth of continuing to define the political according to its primacy when one simultaneously registers its seemingly inexorable decline?

NOTES

1. Maurice Agulhon, *1848, ou l'apprentissage de la République* (Paris: Seuil, 1973; 1992), 249.

2. Régis Debray, *Critique de la raison politique* (Paris: Gallimard, 1981), 12. Significantly, only when the book was reprinted in 1987 was the subtitle, *ou l'inconscient religieux*, added.

3. Debray and Jean-Paul Enthoven, "La Longue marche de Régis Debray," *Le Nouvel Observateur* (10 October 1981): 109.

4. Debray, *Critique*, 43.

5. Debray, *Critique*, 89.

6. Debray, *Critique*, 205.

7. Debray, *Critique*, 178.

8. Debray, *Critique*, 123–24.

9. Debray, *Critique*, 258.

10. Debray, *Critique*, 263.

11. See Gauchet's remarks in François Dosse, *L'Empire du sens: l'humanisation des sciences humaines* (Paris: La Découverte, 1995), 76.

12. Marcel Gauchet, "Une Histoire de confection: entretien avec Marcel Gauchet," *Tissage* 2 (2003): 5.

13. Gauchet, "On n'échappe pas à la philosophie de l'histoire: réponse à Emmanuel Terray," *Le Genre humain* 23 (May 1991): 130–31.

14. Claude Lefort, "Esquisse d'une genèse de l'idéologie dans les sociétés modernes," in *Les Formes de l'histoire* (Paris: Gallimard, 1978), 490.

15. Marcel Jaeger, "L'esprit de fronde," *L'Information psychiatrique* 10 (December 1993): 970.

16. Gauchet and Claude Lefort, "Sur la démocratie: la politique et l'institution du social," *Textures* 2–3 (1971): 8–9.

17. Gauchet and Lefort, "Sur la démocratie," 14.

18. Gauchet, "Figures de la souveraineté: à propos de 'La Royauté et ses privilèges,' livre I, volume II, du *Vocabulaire des institutions Indo-européens*, d'Emile Benvéniste," *Textures* 2–3 (1971): 142.

19. Gauchet, "Figures de la souveraineté," 138.

20. Gauchet, "Figures de la souveraineté," 154.

21. Gauchet, "Politique et société: la leçon des sauvages (I)," *Textures* (1975): 78.

22. Gauchet, "La Dette du sens et les racines de l'état: politique de la religion primitive," *Libre* 2 (1977): 26.

23. Gauchet, "La Dette du sens et les racines de l'état," 27.

24. Gauchet, "La Dette du sens et les racines de l'état," 29–30.

25. Gauchet, "La Dette du sens et les racines de l'état," 30.

26. Gauchet, "La Dette du sens et les racines de l'état," 23.

27. Claude Nicolet, *L'Idée républicaine en France* (Paris: Gallimard, 1982).

28. See, notably, Bernard Manin, "Pourquoi la République?" *Intervention* 10 (August–December 1984): 7–25.

29. Luc Ferry and Alain Renaut, *Philosophie politique*, vol. 3, *Des Droits de l'homme à l'idée républicaine* (Paris: PUF, 1985).

30. François Furet, Jacques Julliard, and Pierre Rosanvallon, *La République du centre: la fin de l'exception française* (Paris: Calmann-Lévy, 1988).

31. Debray, "République ou démocratie," repr. in *Contretemps: éloge des idéaux perdus* (Paris: Gallimard, 1992), 20.

32. Jean-Jacques Becker and Pascal Ory, *Crises et alternances: 1974–2000* (Paris: Seuil, 1998), 465, 475.

33. Debray, *Que vive la République!* (Paris: Odile Jacob, 1989), 34. Debray is quoting his former teacher, Jacques Muglioni.

34. Debray, *Que vive la République!* 32, 29.

35. Debray, *Que vive la République!* 89.

36. Debray, *Critique*, 380.

37. Debray, "République ou démocratie," 51.

38. Debray, "République ou démocratie," 51–52.

39. Debray, *Cours de médiologie générale* (Paris: Gallimard, 1991; 2001), 489.

40. Gauchet and Paul Valadier, "Sur la religion," *Le Débat* 32 (November 1984): 190.

41. Gauchet, "De l'Avènement de l'individu à la découverte de la société," *Annales E.S.C.* 34, no. 3 (May–June 1979): 458–59.

42. Gauchet, "Renouveau de la nation?" *L'Histoire* 73 (December 1984): 9.

43. Gauchet, "La Nature du lien social," *La Cité: revue de la nouvelle citoyenneté* 12 (1986): 8.

44. Gauchet, "La Nature du lien social," 16.

45. Gauchet, "L'École à l'école d'elle-même: contraintes et contradictions de l'individualisme démocratique," *Le Débat* 37 (November 1985): 56.

46. Gauchet, "L'École à l'école d'elle-même," 57.

47. Gauchet, "L'École à l'école d'elle-même," 58.

48. Gauchet, "L'École à l'école d'elle-même," 60.

49. Gauchet, "L'École à l'école d'elle-même," 60–61.

50. Gauchet and Alain Finkielkraut, "Malaise dans la démocratie: l'école, la culture, l'individualisme," *Le Débat* 51 (September–November 1988): 151.

51. Gauchet, "Malaise dans la démocratie," and "Pacification démocratique, désertion civique," *Le Débat* 60 (May–August 1990): 87–98; "Le Mal démocratique," *Esprit* 195 (October 1993): 67–89; and "La République enlisée," *Le Banquet* 6 (1995): 174–88.

52. Debray, "L'Incomplétude, logique du religieux," *Bulletin de la Société française de philosophie* 90, no. 1 (January–March 1996): 24.

53. Debray, "L'Incomplétude," 23.

54. Debray, *Rapport à M. le Ministre de l'Education nationale: l'enseignement du fait religieux dans l'école laïque*, available online from the French Education Ministry at: www.education.gouv.fr/rapport/debray (11 March 2004).

55. Gauchet, "Le Mal démocratique," *Esprit* 195 (October 1993): 77.

56. Gauchet, "Malaise dans la démocratie," 149.

57. Gauchet, "Sous l'amour de la nature, la haine des hommes," *Le Débat* 60 (May–August 1990): 281.

58. Gauchet, "Religion civile, croyance, morale," *Projet* 225 (Spring 1991): 44.

59. See Gauchet, *La Religion dans la démocratie: parcours de laïcité* (Paris: Gallimard, 1998).

60. Gauchet, "Croyances religieuses, croyances politiques," *Le Débat* 115 (May–August 2001): 12.

61. Gauchet, "Les Mauvaises surprises d'une oubliée," *Le Débat* 60 (May–August 1990): 298.

62. Gauchet, "L'intellectuel et l'action politique," *Le Banquet* 1 (1992). This passage was excised from the original, but is available in the online version at: www.revue-lebanquet.com (11 March 2004).

63. Gauchet, "Quelle laïcité pour quelle modernité?" *Lire au collège* 63 (Fall 2002): 9.

64. Gauchet, "Laïcité et éducation civique," *Présences de la recherche à l'IUFM de Paris* 2 (February 2000): 17.

65. Gauchet, René Rémond, and Paul Valadier, "Place du religieux dans les sociétés modernes," in Semaines sociales de France, *D'un siècle à l'autre: l'évangile, les chrétiens et les enjeux de la société* (Paris: Bayard, 2000), 132.

66. Gauchet, "Il n'y a plus péril de chrétienneté en la demeure!" "Cahier spécial" of *Témoignaige chrétien*, 18 January 2001, vi.

67. Debray and Gauchet, "Du Religieux, de sa permanence et de la possibilité d'en sortir," *Le Débat* 127 (November–December 2003): 13.

68. Tony Judt, *Marxism and the French Left: Studies in Labor and Politics in France, 1830–1981* (Oxford: Clarendon Press, 1986), 22.

69. Gauchet, "Changement de paradigme en science sociale?" *Le Débat* 50 (May–August 1988): 169.

AFTERWORD

AFTERWORD:
FOR INTELLECTUAL HISTORY

François Dosse

Periodically accused of treason, if not a conspiracy against culture, since the time of Julien Benda, torn among roles (Cassandra or Creon) in the political city, taken up in the tournament of oppositional or mandarin engagements, alternately guardians against state reason and counselors to the prince—intellectuals have lost the Ariadne's thread that had consistently identified them with the image of activist indignation since the Dreyfus Affair. Here and there, people take pleasure in proclaiming the end of the era of intellectuals—after the end of history and without doubt before the end of the world. From mobilization in favor of Captain Dreyfus to Jean-Paul Sartre, the figure of the critical intellectual dominated the French scene, seemingly imposing itself as the only possible intellectual posture. The catastrophic destiny of those utopias embraced by twentieth-century intellectuals, as well as the frustration of all global projects by the technicization and specialization of knowledge, have led to the triumph of an expert culture tending to undermine democratic control and to rob citizens of the opportunity to control their own future. Facing this danger, which is not a conspiracy, but seems instead the inexorable consequence of the increasing complexity of requisite knowledge, a new chance is offered to intellectuals: to engage in real society in order to sort out the multiple stakes of the present and to contribute to citizens rebuilding collective hope on new foundations. It is up to us, therefore, to historicize the figure of the intellectual in its many metamorphoses.

The history of ideas does not receive good press in France. In fact, it has been practiced more openly outside of France. There are many reasons for this "French exception." First, one might consider the important role played by proper philosophical teaching in the formation of an educated public. Such teaching has stabilized a field of philosophers tied to a corpus and its history. Furthermore, the development of French social sciences and the success of the "history of mentalities" in the 1970s inhibited the emergence of either the history of ideas or intellectual history (with the exception of a marginal movement in the history of literature, under the influence of Jean Ehrard, who pursued the history of ideas).[1]

Since then, the study of the history of intellectuals in France has rarely become a specific and autonomous research field within sociology and political, social, and cultural history. A marginal domain since the 1960s and 1970s, when the models of the *longue durée* and "serial history" completely dominated historical studies, intellectual history has been considered too close to devalued objects of historical study, such as individuals, biography, and politics. Intellectual culture's "narrow, little world," as Sartre put it following Albert Camus's death on January 7, 1960, remained inappropriate for statistical dissection or long-term quantitative analysis.[2] It was thus irremediably castigated as an "impressionism" incapable of being transformed into a scientific object. Moreover, the limits of the intellectual group seemed so blurred and derivative of conventional modes of analysis that the object became elusive. To this drawback was added a pervasive interest in mass phenomena over elite groups, if one recalls the program defined by the *Annales* historical school, which followed the 1903 injunction of the Durkheimian sociologist, François Simiand, when he called on historians to attack the three "idols" of biography, chronology, and politics. We have thus had to wait for a more recent period to see an interest in the history of intellectuals emerge in France. This history, though, has had two faults: setting its sights on the political short term, and disqualifying itself as a simple return to a traditional history of ideas, along the lines of the slogans "It's Rousseau's fault" or "It's Voltaire's fault" of French revolutionary historiography. This opprobrium is a very French phenomenon, since, as François Azouvi has noted, "outside of France being a historian of ideas in no way implies national indignity."[3]

Thus only in the 1980s did one begin to see this domain of scholarship develop, specifically with the creation of the Groupe de recherche sur l'histoire des intellectuels in 1985, directed first by Jean-François Sirinelli under the auspices of the Institut d'histoire du temps présent. The research field acquired even greater visibility when Sirinelli and Pascal Ory's now-

classic *Les Intellectuels en France: de l'affaire Dreyfus à nos jours* was published by Armand Colin in 1986. Soon after, in 1988 Sirinelli published his
important *Génération intellectuelle: khâgneux et normaliens dans l'entre-
deux-guerres.* The appearance of the *Dictionnaire des intellectuels français*
(1996) and Michel Winock's *Le Siècle des intellectuels* (1997), among other
publications, confirms the dynamism of this historiographical field.[4] The
emergence of this field is certainly related to a broader paradigm shift in the
human sciences.[5] It has perhaps also been related to the "beautiful death"
and disappearance of the figure of the universally engaged intellectual that
Emile Zola incarnated during the Dreyfus Affair in 1898. Michel Foucault
had already observed this mutation when he described the modernity of the
"specific" intellectual who, renouncing his or her universal vocation, sought
"to be respectful when a singularity rises up, intransigent when power in-
fringes upon the universal."[6] Pierre Nora has raised the question of the possible disappearance of the figure of the intellectual altogether: "The epoch
that corresponds to the figure of the 'intellectual' is without a doubt past.
The very word, adorned with all its prestige, withering with disgrace, full of
confusion and misunderstanding, has become almost unbearable. . . . Today, almost in the same breath, one can mourn the death of the intellectual
and deplore the proliferation of the species."[7]

In the same way that one could celebrate during the 1970s a popular culture all the more discernible since it was dying, contemporary fascination
for intellectuals and their history may turn on their disappearance. Thanks
to historians, intellectuals will have their swan song. One hastens to count
them, classify them, prepare a list, before definitively burying them. An object for which enthusiasm has cooled, the "intellectual" has become a historical object for lack of having a real claim on the present. Intellectuals
have paid a high price for their compromises over the course of the tragic
twentieth century. However, this may only be a presentist illusion with regard to a figure who took successive forms over time and whose effacement
might only be a temporary avatar in an already long history.

Alongside this history of intellectuals, a proper intellectual history has developed at the crossroads of a traditional history of ideas, the history of philosophy, the history of mentalities, and cultural history. This research space
has become autonomous. Without imperial ambitions, intellectual history
simply aims to bring together works, their authors, and the context that
bore them, and to do so in a way that refuses the apparent alternative between an internalist reading of works and an externalist approach that privileges networks of sociability. Intellectual history intends, beyond disciplinary boundaries, to take account of works, trajectories, and itineraries.

This intellectual history is already rich in debates among diverse tendencies. Some privilege contextualism (Quentin Skinner), others a historical semantics (Reinhart Koselleck), or hermeneutics (Paul Ricoeur). In recent decades intellectual history has contended with challenges from cultural and social history in their many forms (histories of mentalities, print, reading, bodies, practices, and discourses); from the anthropology of daily life; from psychoanalysis; and from the interpretive strategies and worries linked to the "linguistic turn."[8] The wager is showing the fecundity of an approach to works and their production in history while avoiding the pitfalls of historicism. Many avenues are open, between the history of concepts, social history, and the history of intellectuals in the political city. On the condition of postulating a form of epistemological indistinction and renouncing a posture of the bird's-eye view, all these possibilities provide their distinctive illuminations. Intellectual history investigates the life of ideas through a constant back-and-forth movement between the past and the present.

In the very plurality of its orientations, intellectual history challenges reductive explanatory schemas that are incapable of grasping heterogeneous and contingent parts of the proverbial explanatory stewpot. It requires a genuine reduction in explanatory arguments. A certain number of "connectors" are useful for taking into account such arguments, but they are merely imperfect mediations that let a good deal of what makes the essence of intellectual history escape.

This intellectual history, locked in a vise between the diachronic logics of the history of ideas and synchronic logics of cartographies and sociocultural "cuts," is an uncertain domain, an interlacing between the plurality of possible approaches and the will to redesign the contours of a global history. To this tension is further added intellectual history's proximity to sociology and philosophy, since its object is similar to theirs. The result is what Christian Delacroix has called "epistemological indeterminism," which I would submit as a heuristic principle in intellectual history.[9] This indeterminism refers to the necessary interlacing between a purely internalist approach that takes into consideration only the endogenous logic of a work or an idea's content, and an externalist approach that is satisfied with purely external explanations and the contextualization of ideas. Intellectual history is only possible from the moment when it begins to think these two poles together, overcoming a false alternative. It is useless to envisage an intellectual history that stops at the threshold of a work, standing clear of interpretation and privileging only external manifestations of intellectual life. How could one avoid intellectual work itself, its books and wagers?

Certainly, in order to define a space proper to this intellectual history, privileging the externalist approach was for a time necessary, for reasons of visibility and in order to escape a traditional history of ideas. However, it seems to me appropriate to penetrate the content of intellectual life and its wagers, which are not limited to the reactions of intellectuals to exterior events. The study of their modes of engagement is at once pertinent and illuminating for a better understanding of how intellectuals are implicated in or distanced from the political city. But this study only accounts for part of intellectual activity, which also includes worldviews, representations, practices born by schools of thought, paradigms that inspire converging orientations linked to singular moments, and so forth. From one pole to the other, from the externalist to the internalist point of view, it is not a question of finding strict and reductive causal relations, such as a logic of suspicion that reduces someone to his or her social position, or to the question of how one handles one's libido. Such an approach has often served disqualifying and lazy enterprises that judge without understanding and misrecognize content in the name of that which speaks without knowing. Jean-François Sirinelli cautions with good reason against the temptation of escaping the "heart of the intelligent act" in studies that limit themselves to restoring the micro-social effects of the networks of intellectual sociability. "There is," he writes, "a categorical imperative in the history of cultural elites: Don't make a blind alley of the study of works and currents."[10]

Mechanisms of causality cannot emerge from an approach at once internalist and externalist. More modestly, one finds evidence of correlations, simple and possible links on the order of hypotheses between, on one hand, expressed content and what is said, and on the other hand, the existence of networks, generational membership, adherence to a school, or a period and its stakes. The historian puts down a trump card when faced with these difficulties by elaborating an intellectual *history*, thanks to his or her capacity to sketch a plot and construct a complex story that permits this correlation, while preserving indetermination and the probabilist character of the proposed hypotheses. This is what I attempted to realize in my publications that, over time, seem to me united by the concern to construct this intellectual history with the help of the narrative strategies of the *Annales* school of French historiography, the structuralist paradigm, and the biographical itineraries of the likes of Paul Ricoeur and Michel de Certeau.[11]

Epistemological indeterminism is appropriate to this interlacing of relations within the intellectual field. Individuals are engaged in relations that inextricably interweave the defense of their values (their self-understood interests) with—I dare say, above all—a subjective dimension of intense affectivity, fluctuating according to friendships or felt intimacies. There is an entire part of affect that is difficult to bring to light, and, furthermore, entirely essential. Oral interviews and collected testimonies can touch on it. As Jean-Claude Passeron has noted, intellectual groups "always have needed to be in step with the 'pathetic' content of their times, century, and 'contemporaneousness'." This dimension is so important that Passeron even suggests that the sociology of intellectuals could only be a "sociology of the affects of rationalization."[12]

Taking into account the interweaving among theory, writing, and affect in all intellectual history, my *History of Structuralism* neither presupposed its object as a method or an ideology, nor mechanically correlated it to classical historical macro-determinations (political conjuncture, social forces, etc.).[13] Program, concept, ideology, method, paradigm, project, rallying point, generation, fashion—structuralism was all of these things at once, a "skein of yarn difficult to untangle, if one does not take into account moments, concepts, and stakes." The question asked was less "What was structuralism?" than "When and how did structuralism begin to function as a historical object?" This object was understood as irreducible to either a single apparent context or its explicit content alone. This exercise in emplotment allowed me to escape the game of "determinations in the last instance" and an Althusserian sophistry I had adopted earlier, as well as to eschew the schema of the "relative autonomy" of intellectual authority. The plurality of determinations emerges from the very movement of exposition, being inside a historical narrative that institutes its own object. Nevertheless, I was reproached for not making hierarchies, of not delimiting a body of texts dependent on a single scientific culture, and to have given too much place to media echoes and the press. It nevertheless seems to me that an intellectual history that takes seriously the reception of works cannot abandon this dimension, which is described or denounced as playing an increasingly central role. Considering this reception aims at bypassing the illusion that it suffices to begin with authorial intention and the content that it signifies, since intellectual history is also fashioned from this explicit content as well as from the misinterpretations and the successive and subsequent reappropriations it invites. As Léon Robin had already indicated in the 1930s, philosophical doctrines continue to exercise influence by the misinterpretations which they occasion as much as by their declared content.

A certain number of "operators" were at work in this historicization. Structuralism was imagined first of all in my narrativization as a moment that necessitates the use of the notion of the period as a first connector. The two volumes each corresponded to a different "respiration": that of the growing conquest of the "field of the sign" leading up to its apogee in what I called the structuralist year: 1966. From this ascendant phase came a progressive deconstruction that corresponded to the second volume, translated into English as *The Sign Sets*.[14] As a historian, I investigated each of these scansions in order to gauge its pertinence and effects. Making works pertinent requires resituating them in chronological order.

The second connector I used was that of the paradigm, in the general sense of an intellectual orientation that traversed the frontiers of any particular discipline. Structuralism was a hypercritical paradigm, a thought of suspicion that presupposed a truth always hidden and ready to be unmasked. This progressively unitary program of general semiology attempted to demystify *doxa*, ordinary opinion assigning delusion. It withheld apparent meanings in order to dislodge bad faith and thus radicalize the famous "rupture" delivered by the French epistemological tradition from Jean Cavaillès to Gaston Bachelard and the epistemological "break" in Louis Althusser, Foucault, and other structuralist master thinkers. In the name of this break, it was necessary to decouple common sensical meaning from scientific positions and competences cleared of their ideological shell.

The third connector deployed was the study of conflictual relations between the university field and the world of letters. This conflict shed light on a major stake in this new battle of ancients and moderns that saw the emancipation of what Wolf Lepenies called "the third culture," namely, the human sciences, whose confinement in marginal places until 1968 benefited the classical humanities in the old Sorbonne. Structuralism became in this respect the standard of emancipation, a form of socialization for the human sciences that, following the explosion of May 1968, undertook a coup d'état under the structuralist banner.

The fourth connector, which I found particularly useful, was that of generation. The actors of the structuralist action were marked by datable events, which Marc Bloch considered as markers of an "imprinted community." The famous master thinkers of this moment promoted a dehistoricized vision in which Clio was exiled, in favor of a chilled and structuralized temporality, thus effecting a radical questioning of all *telos* and all Eurocentric and evolutionary vision of history.[15] World War Two manifestly engendered this flattening, which led to an evacuation of the subject and the referent. Decolonization also radicalized these positions to the point of absolutizing differences. The "discovery" of the Gulag by French intellectuals in the 1970s furthermore accentuated this propensity to leave behind an enchanted vision of history, making room for a double relation of, on one hand, fascination with science as an anchor, whence the scientism of the era of the human sciences, and on the other hand, a self-hatred to the point of betrayal, as Roland Barthes expressed when he called writing a form of fascism: "I profoundly refuse my civilization, to the point of nausea."[16]

All these connectors helped me to characterize and describe the process of the human sciences' emancipation, a process that took structuralism as an instrument in elaborating a vast program of general semiology. It enlisted an anthropology wrested from its biological anchorage by Claude Lévi-Strauss, a Saussurean linguistics severed by speech, a demedicalized psychoanalysis under Jacques Lacan's inspiration, and a literary criticism more attentive to discursivity than to the content of what was written. This elaboration was completed by an often contingent rhythm of meetings, such as that between Lévi-Strauss and Roman Jakobson in New York during World War Two, as well as apparatus battles that privileged the notion of rupture and took on the allure of institutional disputes, whether by Althusser standing up against the French Communist Party apparatus, Lacan against the International Psychoanalytic Association, or Barthes, the iconoclast against the old Sorbonne. These were largely conscious strategies of deviation by the periphery that permitted prospering of the programs of certain very eccentric universities, the Sixth Section of the École pratique des hautes etudes, or a highly legitimating institution like the Collège de France, which welcomed a number of these master thinkers and helped them prosper. Above all, however, the attention to the content of works marking this structuralist moment evidenced how concepts circulated and how they transformed in their passage from one discipline to another. Thus, the Saussurean algorithm from the *Course in General Linguistics*, which defined the sign as the equation of signifier/signified, was taken as the very nucleus of modern structural rationality, but it was transformed by changing the field of application: with Lévi-Strauss, Lacan, or Barthes, it took on a definition very different than that which Saussure had initially given it.

The moment of knotting around this common structuralist program was characterized in particular by the games of interdisciplinary exchanges, loans, and poachings, as Michel de Certeau would have put it. Thus Lacan's notion of the unconscious was close to that of the symbolic unconscious used by Lévi-Strauss; Lacan's *"petit objet a"* was refound in the "a" of Derrida's written difference—*"différance"*—and sent back to the object of lack. Althusser threw himself into a symptomatic readings of Marx and used the notion of "overdetermination," which was also borrowed from Lacan and from the world of analytic listening. The signifying chain gave rise to a constant slipping of the signifier, whether in the Lévi-Straussian approach to myths, the Lacanian listening to the subject of the unconscious, or in Derridean deconstruction. Michel Foucault's 1969 conference, "What is an Author?" was fundamental in the Lacanian elaboration of the theory of the "four discourses."[17] The way Foucault imagined a "general history" as a space of dispersion in his introduction to the *Archaeology of Knowledge* (1969) was entirely essential to the tenor of the *Annales'* historical discourse during the 1970s. One could easily multiply examples of this conceptual circulation that marked this moment of French thought.

Such a conception of intellectual history presupposes an entry point into the content of what is written, inside works themselves, an immersion at the same time as a distancing in a constant hermeneutical suspicion in the understanding of others. This presupposition was basic to the viewpoint, for example, of Olivier Mongin, director of the review *Esprit*, in his book on the period between 1976 and the recent past.[18] The great merit of his book was to take actors of intellectual life seriously, to enter inside their works in order to get a fix on their theoretical stakes and the diverse, opposing currents that animate the life of ideas, exemplifying Marcel Gauchet's contention that "ideas don't engender historical reality as much as they are secreted by it; they are in history."[19]

The notion of the intellectual moment seems to me essential. It is particularly crucial at the present hour, marked as it is by a spectacular enfeeblement of historical experience, a situation in which the future is blocked as much as the past is tragic, and in which the only possible entry into history is according to the model of the transparency of communication. The resulting crisis is omnipresent and affects all the domains of knowledge and creation. According to Mongin, it is tangible as well in the movement of political dereliction, in the collapse of culture into identity, in the crisis of inspiration in novelistic fiction, in the substitution of the image by the visual, and in the effacement of communication by information.

The current displacement of the historian's way of seeing toward the memorial dimension of history, toward a social history of memory, corresponds exactly to a historiographical turn that we have made. According to this turn, tradition is only as good as "traditionality," inasmuch as it affects the present. Temporal distance is no longer a handicap but an asset for appropriating the diverse stratifications of the meaning of past events that have become "oversignified."[20] This discontinuist conception of historicity, privileging the irreducible character of the event, leads to a questioning of the teleological vision of historical reason realizing itself according to an oriented axis. This attention to "event-alization" evokes a line of reflection developed in Germany during the 1920s by Franz

Rosenzweig, Walter Benjamin, and Gershom Sholem, with the idea of a discontinuous present time, escaping progressive continuism and the idea of causality.[21] These figures shared, as Stéphane Mosès has shown, the move from a "time of necessity to a time of possibilities."[22] The messianic Judaism of these three figures, who experienced the disappointments of their times, avoided finality in order to privilege the tearing apart of history. The aesthetic paradigm served Walter Benjamin in defining "a link that is not a relation of causality" between diverse moments in time.[23] From a discontinuous temporality, meaning reveals itself through a hermeneutic work strongly dependent on a present instance that finds itself foregrounded and veritably constitutive of the past. It is only in the aftermath, in the trace, that one attempts to seize again a meaning that is not a priori: "The aesthetic model of history questions the postulates of historicism's basis: continuity of historical time and causality governing the linkage of past events to the present and the present toward the future."[24]

This discontinuist approach to history questions the distance germane to most historiographical traditions between a dead past and the historian who makes it objective. In fact, to write history is to recreate, and the historian is the mediator, the bearer of this recreation. History realizes itself in the work of the interpreter [herméneute] who reads reality as a writing in which meaning displaces itself within the flow of time in its diverse phases of actualization. The object of history is thus a construction always reopened by inscription. History is first of all "event-ality"; its inscription in a present gives it a renewable actuality, since it is situated in a singular configuration. Walter Benjamin already opposed historicism to the transposition of a model borrowed from mechanical causality in which the cause of an effect is found in the immediately anterior position in the temporal chain. Benjamin substituted to this scientific model "a hermeneutic model, tending toward the interpretation of events, that is, toward the illumination of their meaning."[25]

This reflexive reprise of the oversignified event is the basis for the narrative construction of foundational identities, like the taking of the Bastille for France, or the arrival of the *Mayflower* for the United States. It could also become, when facing radical evil, a negative identity for the international collectivity, as remains the case for Auschwitz. This displacement of the look that, without denying the relevance of the necessary methodological and critical moment, prioritizes the interpretive part of history, is described by Pierre Nora when he characterizes the present historiographical moment: "The way is open for an entirely different history: no longer determining causes, but their effects; no longer memorized and commemorated actions, but the trace of actions in the game of these commemorations; not events for themselves, but their construction in time, the effacement and resurgence of their meanings; not the past as past, but in its successive re-uses; not tradition, but the manner in which it is constituted and transmitted."[26]

What is at play is historians gaining consciousness of the "second-degree" status of their discourse. Between history and memory, the gap is hardly bridged. One can avoid both the impasse of too great a separation and also the overlapping of these two notions. To the expertise of historians, who valorize the status of truth in their efforts, for example, to tear negationists to shreds and thus give memory the function of fidelity, one could ask what a truth without fidelity or fidelity without truth is worth? It is by way of narrative mediation that an articulation between these two dimensions can be realized.

This reflexive turn of a second-degree history opens a vast site of investigative work, pursuing new convergences between the history of thought and history *tout court*. As Marcel Gauchet has written, "Another intellectual history is possible than that which has been written until recently; a history attentive to the participation of thought in events, without giving up anything on the analysis of thought."[27] The actual context of the human sciences, favorable to a reflexive and historiographical turn, could in effect facilitate the flowering of this new intellectual history that is neither internalist nor externalist: "We are fortunate to find ourselves in the moment where a double opening becomes possible, relativizing a counterproductive division. It is possible to place works in history without sacrificing anything of their internal reading, adding, in fact, to their internal intelligibility."[28]

None of the possible avenues for the construction of intellectual history— contextualism, intentionalism, hermeneutics, conceptualism, sociography, politics—is to be rejected on the condition that each remain open to others. The typical illusion for intellectual history would be to shut itself up in an enclosure of meaning, either in the name of a past to rediscover in its original purity (in the way that Fustel de Coulange understands himself as saying nothing other than what is dictated by archive documents), or in the name of a presentism of meaning.[29] It remains, on the contrary, for intellectual history to weigh the positivity of temporal distance in order to question the ideal world in its social density, a density that emerges from a back and forth movement between the past and the questions that we ask of the past from our standpoint in the present.

NOTES

This chapter was translated from the French by Julian Bourg and Arline Cravens.

1. Jean Ehrard, "Histoire des idées et histoire littéraire," in *Problèmes et methods de l'histoire littéraire* [18 November 1972] (Paris: Armand Colin, 1974), 68–80.

2. See Jean-François Sirinelli, "Les intellectuels," in *Pour une histoire politique*, ed. René Rémond (Paris: Seuil, 1998), 199–231.

3. François Azouvi, "Pour une histoire philosophique des idées," *Le Débat* 72 (November–December 1992): 20.

4. Sirinelli and Pascal Ory, *Les Intellectuels en France: de l'affaire Dreyfus à nos jours* (Paris: Armand Colin, 1986). Sirinelli, *Génération intellectuelle: khâgneux et normaliens dans l'entre-deux-guerres* (Paris: Fayard, 1988). Jacques Julliard and Michel Winock, eds., *Dictionnaire des intellectuels français* (Paris: Seuil, 1996). Winock, *Le Siècle des intellectuels* (Paris: Seuil, 1997).

5. See François Dosse, *L'Empire du sens: l'humanisation des sciences humaines* (Paris: La Découverte, 1995), trans. Hassan Melehy as *Empire of Meaning: The Humanization of the Social Sciences* (Minneapolis: University of Minnesota Press, 1999).

6. Michel Foucault, "La fonction critique de l'intellectuel," *Politique-Hebdo* (19 November 1976); repr. in *Dits et écrits*, 4 vols. (Paris: Gallimard, 1994), 3: 109–14.

7. Pierre Nora, "Adieux aux intellectuals?" *Le Débat* 110 (May–August 2000): 13–14.

8. For an analysis of these themes in relation to intellectual history and the history of intellectuals, including an assessment of Franco/Anglo-American debates involving the researches and methodological reflections of scholars such as Robert Darnton, Michel de Certeau, Roger Chartier, Lynn Hunt, William Sewell, Richard Biernacki, Hayden White, Gareth Stedman-Jones, Steven Kaplan, Dominick LaCapra, Mark Poster, and Richard Rorty, among others, see my *La Marche des idées: histoire des intellectuels–histoire intellectuelle* (Paris: La Découverte, 2003).

9. Christian Delacroix, [n.t.], *Esquisses psychanalytiques* 18 (Fall 1992): 211–15.

10. Sirinelli, "Les elites culturelles," in *Pour une histoire culturelle*, eds. Jean-Pierre Rioux and Sirinelli (Paris: Seuil, 1997), 288.

11. Dosse, *L'Histoire en miettes: des "Annales" à la "nouvelle histoire"* (Paris: La Découverte, 1987), trans. Peter V. Conroy, Jr. as *New History in France: The Triumph of the Annales* (Urbana, Ill.: University of Illinois Press, 1994); *L'Empire du sens*; *Histoire du structuralisme*, 2 vols. (Paris: La Découverte, 1991–92), trans. Deborah Glassman as *History of Structuralism*, 2 vols. (Minneapolis: Minnesota University Press, 1997); *L'Histoire: le temps réflechi* (Paris: Haiter, 1999); *Paul Ricoeur: les sens d'une vie* (Paris: La Découverte, 2000); *Michel de Certeau: le marcheur blessé* (Paris: La Découverte, 2002); and *La Marche des idées*.

12. Jean-Claude Passeron, "Quel regarde sur le Populaire?" *Esprit* (March–April 2002): 151.

13. Dosse, *The History of Structuralism*.

14. [The French title, *Le Chant du cygne*, plays on the expression "swan song" and the homonym between *cygne* [swan] and *signe* [sign]. –Ed.]

15. Dosse, "*Clio* en exil," *L'Homme et la société* 95–96 (1990): 103–18.

16. Roland Barthes, [Interview with Raymond Bellour], *Les Lettres françaises* (20 May 1977); repr. in *Le Grain de la voix: entretiens, 1962–1980* (Paris: Seuil, 1981), 82.

17. Dosse, "Barthes, Lacan, Foucault: L'auteur, la structure," in *L'Auteur à l'oeuvre*, ed. Patrick du Mascio (Fontenay/Saint-Cloud: ENS Éditions, 1996), 11–43.

18. Olivier Mongin, *Face au scepticisme: les mutations du paysage intellectuel* (Paris: La Découverte, 1994).

19. Marcel Gauchet, "Changement de paradigme en sciences sociales," *Le Débat* (May–August 1988): 169.

20. Paul Ricoeur, "Événements et sens," *Raisons politiques* 2 (1991): 55.

21. See Ricoeur, "Le 'figure' dans *L'Etoile de la Rédemption* de Franz Rosenzweig," *Esprit* (1988); repr. in *Lectures 3* (Paris: Seuil, 1994), 63–81.

22. Stéphane Mosès, *L'Ange de l'histoire* (Paris: Seuil, 1992), 23.

23. Mosès, *L'Ange de l'histoire*, 122.

24. Mosès, *L'Ange de l'histoire*, 126.

25. Mosès, *L'Ange de l'histoire*, 161.

26. Pierre Nora, "Comment on écrit l'histoire en France?" in *Les Lieux de mémoire*, ed. Pierre Nora, 3 vols. (Paris: Gallimard, 1993), 1: 24.

27. Marcel Gauchet, "L'Élargissement de l'objet historique," *Le Débat* 103 (January–February 1999): 141.

28. Gauchet, "L'Élargissement de l'objet historique," 141. See also Dosse, *L'Empire du sens*.

29. [See, for instance, Numa-Denis Fustel de Coulanges, *Histoire des institutions politiques de l'ancienne France* (Paris: Hachette, 1875). –Ed.]

BIBLIOGRAPHY

ARCHIVES

Raymond Aron Archives, École des hautes études en sciences sociales, Paris
Centre d'accueil et de recherche des archives nationale (CARAN), Paris
Centre audiovisuel Simone-de-Beauvoir, Paris
Michel Debré Archives, Fondation nationale des sciences politiques, Paris
Esprit Archives, Institut mémoires de l'édition contemporaine (IMEC), Paris
Daniel Guérin Archives, Bibliothèque de documentation internationale
    contemporaine (BDIC), Nanterre
Jean Paulhan Archives, Institut mémoires de l'édition contemporaine, Paris
Jean-François Steiner (personal papers)
Elsa Triolet-Aragon Archives, Centre nationale de la recherche scientifique
    (CNRS), Paris

WEBSITES

online.stcharles.ac.uk/courses/business/economic_growth.htm
www.eurofound.eu.int/emire/FRANCE/NATIONALIZATION-FR.html
www.lib.bke.hu/gt/2000-4/towse.pdf
www. pbs.org/wgbh/commandingheights/lo/countries/fr/fr_economic.html
www.knowtv.com/primetime/conflicting/mouffe.html
www.ekemel.gr/deapiliotis5.htm

nyartsmagazine.com/72/letter.htm
www.brookes.ac.uk/schools/apm/publishing/culture/2001/tregomai.html
www-staff.lboro.ac.uk/~eudgb/DG.htm
www.magazine-litteraire.com/archives/ar_anar.htm
www.education.gouv.fr/rapport/debray
www.revue-lebanquet.com

JOURNAL AND NEWSPAPER ARTICLES

Adorno, Theodor. "Fragments." *Arguments* 14 (1959).
———. "Hegel et le contenu de l'experience." *Arguments* 14 (1959).
———. "Musique et technique, aujourd'hui." *Arguments* 19 (1960).
"L'Agrégation de philosophie." *Bulletin de la Société française de philosophie* 38 (1938).
"The American Production of French Theory." Special Issue of *SubStance* 31, no. 1 (2002).
"Les Anarchistes et l'autogestion." Special Issue of *Autogestion et socialisme* 18–19 (1972).
Anissimov, Myriam. "Emmanuel Levinas se souvient." *Les Nouveaux Cahiers* 82 (fall 1985).
Arendt, Hannah. "The Concentration Camps." *Partisan Review* (1948).
———. "Social Science Techniques and the Study of the Camps." *Jewish Social Studies* 12 (1950).
Aron, Raymond. "Lettre d'Allemagne." *Libres Propos* (1930).
———. "Simples propositions du pacifisme." *Libres Propos* (1931).
———. "Lettre d'Allemagne." *Libres Propos* (1931).
———. "Désarmement ou union franco-allemande?" *Libres Propos* (1932).
———. "La révolution nationale en Allemagne." *Europe* (1933).
———. "Réflexions sur le pacifisme intégral." *Libres Propos* (1933).
———. [n.t.]. *La France libre* 1 (1940).
———. "Anniversaire." *Combat*, 14 May 1946.
———. "L'unique problème." *Combat*, 3–4 November 1946.
———. "La paix belliqueuse." *Promotions: revue de l'École nationale d'administration* 3 (1946); repr. in *Commentaire* 76 (1996).
———. "La fin des illusions." *Le Figaro*, 5 July 1947.
———. "Responsabilité historique." *Le Figaro*, 31 August 1947.
———. "Stupide résignation." *Le Figaro*, 21–22 September 1947.
———. "Le Plan Marshall est-il artificiel?" *Le Figaro*, 4 October 1947.
———. "Vers un nouveau reniement?" *Le Figaro*, 10 December 1947.
———. "La cité déchirée, l'Etat et les communistes." *Le Figaro*, 11 April 1948.
———. "Discours à des étudiants allemands sur l'avenir de l'Europe." *La Table ronde* 1 (1948).

———. "Plan Marshall et unité européenne." *Le Figaro*, 1 November 1949.

———. "Le Pacte Atlantique." *Liberté de l'esprit* 3 (1949).

———. "Le réarmement de l'Allemagne." *Le Figaro*, 16 September 1950.

———. "L'armée européenne: un pari sur l'avenir qu'on ne peut refuser." *Le Figaro*, 17 September 1951.

———. "Ce que peut être la fédération des Six." *Le Figaro*, 4 December 1952.

———. "Allies-Not Satellites!" *American Mercury* 345 (1952).

———. "L'unité économique de l'Europe." *La Revue libre* 2 (1952).

———. "La fin de la CED ne doit pas être la fin de l'Europe." *Le Figaro*, 3 September 1954.

———. "La désagrégation des empires." *Pensée française* 1 (1956).

———. "A propos de l'unité de l'Europe: la dialectique du politique et de l'économique." *Mitteilungen der List Gesellschaft E.V.* 11–12 (1957).

———. "Assemblé Générale C.N.E.—12.I.56." *France observateur* 349 (17 January 1957).

———. "Coexistence: The End of Ideology." *Partisan Review* 25 (1958).

Axelos, Kostas. "Y a-t-il une philosophie marxiste?" *Arguments* 4 (June–September 1957).

———. "Adorno et l'école de Francfort." *Arguments* 14 (1959).

———. "Présentation bio-bibliographique de Karl Korsch." *Arguments* 16 (1959).

———. "Une déclaration de G. Lukács." *Arguments* 20 (1960).

———. "L'errance érotique: problématique de l'amour." *Arguments* 21 (1961).

———. "Les marxistes et l'amour." *Arguments* 21 (1961).

———. "Le jeu de l'autocritique." *Arguments* 27–28 (1962).

———. "Planetary Interlude." Trans. Sally Hess. *Yale French Studies* 41 (1968).

———. "Play as the System of Systems." Trans. Robert Emmett Chumbley. *SubStance* 25 (1980).

———. "Arguments et pensées." In Jean-Philippe Milet, ed., "Kostas Axelos et la question du monde." Special Issue of *Rue Descartes* 18 (1997).

Axelos, Kostas, and Olivier Corpet. "Le fonctionnement." *La Revue des revues* 4 (fall 1987).

Azouvi, François. "Pour une histoire philosophique des idées." *Le Débat* 72 (November–December 1992).

Badia, Gilbert, et al. "Rosa Luxemburg et nous: Débat." *Politique aujourd'hui: recherches et pratiques socialistes dans le monde* (1972).

Barthes, Roland. "Les taches de la critique brechtienne." *Arguments* 1 (December 1956–January 1957).

———. [Interview with Raymond Bellour]. *Les Lettres françaises* (20 May 1977).

Bartov, Omer. "The Proof of Ignominy: Vichy France's Past and Presence." *Contemporary European History* 7, no. 1 (1998).

Bellamy, Elizabeth. "Discourses of Impossibility: Can Psychoanalysis be Political?" *Diacritics* 1, no. 23 (spring 1993).

Birchall, Ian. "Sartre's Encounter with Daniel Guérin." *Sartre Studies International* 2, no. 1 (1996).

Bottigelli, E. "Une protestation de G. Lukács." *Arguments* 5 (December 1957).

Bourdieu, Pierre. "Questions aux vrais maîtres du monde." *Le Monde*, 14 October 1999.

Bourdieu, Pierre, and Jean-Claude Passeron. "Sociology and Philosophy in France Since 1945: Death and Resurrection of a Philosophy without a Subject." *Social Research* 34, no. 1 (spring 1967).

Bouwsma, William. "Intellectual History in the 1980s: From the History of Ideas to the History of Meaning." *Journal of Interdisciplinary History* 12, no. 2 (1981).

Brockelman, Thomas. "The Failure of the Radical Democratic Imaginary: Zizek versus Laclau and Mouffe on Vestigial Utopia." *Philosophy & Social Criticism* 29, no. 2 (2003).

Canguilhem, Georges. "Hegel en France." *Revue d'histoire et de philosophie religieuses* 27 (1948).

Chaperon, Sylvie. "Kinsey en France: les sexualités féminine et masculine en débat." *Mouvement social* 198 (2002).

———. "Le fonds Daniel Guérin et l'histoire de la sexualité." *Journal de la BDIC* 5 (2002).

Charmé, Stuart L. "From Maoism to Talmud (With Sartre Along the Way): An Interview with Benny Lévy." *Commentary* 78, no. 6 (December 1984).

Cluzel, Jean. "Une ambition justifiée, une réalisation contestable." *Le Débat* 121 (September–October 2002).

Cohen, Sande. "Structuralism and the Writing of Intellectual History." *History and Theory* 17 (1978).

Colomb, Phillipe. "Le Rose du destin et le noir de la politique." *La Revueh* 3 (winter 1996–97).

Comité national des écrivains. "Le Comité national des écrivains s'adresse au Président Kadar." *Les Lettres françaises* 644 (8–14 November 1956).

Corpet, Olivier. "Au fil d'*Arguments*." In Jean-Philippe Milet, ed., "Kostas Axelos et la question du monde." Special Issue of *Rue Descartes* 18 (1997).

Crimp, Douglas. "The New French Culture: An Interview with Guy Hocquenghem." *October* 19 (winter 1981).

"Daniel Guérin." Special Issue of *Alternative libertaire* (2000).

Daster, Françoise. "Monde et jeu: Axelos et Fink." In Jean-Philippe Milet, ed., "Kostas Axelos et la question du monde." Special Issue of *Rue Descartes* 18 (1997).

Debray, Régis. "L'Incomplétude, logique du religieux." *Bulletin de la Société française de philosophie* 90, no. 1 (January–March 1996).

Debray, Régis, and Jean-Paul Enthoven. "La Longue marche de Régis Debray." *Le Nouvel Observateur* (10 October 1981).

Debray, Régis, and Marcel Gauchet. "Du Religieux. de sa permanence et de la possibilité d'en sortir." *Le Débat* 127 (November–December 2003).

"La décentralisation culturelle pervertie." *Cahier du Groupe reflex[e]* 1 (March–April 2003).

Delacroix, Christian. [n.t.]. *Esquisses psychanalytiques* 18 (fall 1992).

Delannoi, Gil. "*Arguments*. 1956–1962 ou la parenthèse de l'ouverture." *Revue française de science politique* 34, no. 1 (February 1984).

———. "Les voyages de la raison: Sartre, 'Arguments,' Morin." *Esprit* 5 (May 1984).

Delbos, Victor. "Husserl: Sa critique du psychologisme et sa conception d'une Logique pure." *Revue de métaphysique et de morale* (1911).

Deleuze, Gilles. "Faille et feux locaux. Kostas Axelos" [Review of *Vers la pensée planetaire*, *Arguments d'une recherche*, and *Le jeu du monde*]. *Critique* 275 (April 1970).

Démeron, Piere. "Les Juifs: Ce qu'on n'a jamais osé desire." *Le Nouveau Candide*, 14–20 March 1966.

Domench, Jean-Marie, et al. [n.t.]. *France observateur* 339 (8 November 1956).

Dosse, François. "Clio en exil." *L'Homme et la société* 95–96 (1990).

Doyle, Natalie. "The End of a Political Identity: French Intellectuals and the State." *Thesis Eleven* 48 (February 1997).

Dreyfus, Michel. "1956: l'année terrible." *Communisme* 29–31 (1992).

Dubois, Vincent. "Une politique pour quelle(s) culture(s)." *Les Cahiers français* 312 (January–February 2003).

Eaubonne, Françoise d'. "Le FHAR." *La Revue h* 2 (fall 1996).

Fejtö, François. "Une lettre de Budapest." *France observateur* 372 (27 June 1957).

"FHAR: il y a 10 ans." *Gai Pied* 25 (April 1981).

Forgacs, Don. "Gramsci and Marxism in Britain." *New Left Review* 176 (1989).

Foucault, Michel. "La fonction critique de l'intellectuel." *Politique-Hebdo* (19 November 1976).

Fougeyrollas, Pierre. "Thèses sur la mondialisation." *Arguments* 15 (1959).

Fougeyrollas, Pierre, Kostas Axelos, Jean Duvignaud, Edgar Morin, and Olivier Corpet. "Le sabordage." *La Revue des revues* 4 (fall 1987).

Fraser, Nancy. "The French Derrideans: Politicizing Deconstruction or Deconstructing the Political?" *New German Critique* 33 (1984).

Gauchet, Marcel. "Figures de la souveraineté: à propos de 'La Royauté et ses privilèges,' livre I, volume II, du *Vocabulaire des institutions Indo-européens*, d'Emile Benvéniste." *Textures* 2–3 (1971).

———. "Politique et société: la leçon des sauvages (I)." *Textures* (1975).

———. "La Dette du sens et les racines de l'état: politique de la religion primitive." *Libre* 2 (1977).

———. "De l'Avènement de l'individu à la découverte de la société." *Annales E.S.C.* 34, no. 3 (May–June 1979).

———. "Renouveau de la nation?" *L'Histoire* 73 (December 1984).

———. "L'École à l'école d'elle-même: contraintes et contradictions de l'individualisme démocratique." *Le Débat* 37 (November 1985).

———. "La Nature du lien social." *La Cité: revue de la nouvelle citoyenneté* 12 (1986).

———. "Changement de paradigme en science sociale?" *Le Débat* 50 (May–August 1988).

———. "Malaise dans la démocratie." *Le Débat* 60 (May–August 1990).

———. "Pacification démocratique, désertion civique." *Le Débat* 60 (May–August 1990).

———. "Sous l'amour de la nature: la haine des hommes." *Le Débat* 60 (May–August 1990).

———. "Les Mauvaises surprises d'une oubliée." *Le Débat* 60 (May–August 1990).

———. "Religion civile, croyance, morale." *Projet* 225 (spring 1991).

———. "On n'échappe pas à la philosophie de l'histoire: réponse à Emmanuel Terray." *Le Genre humain* 23 (May 1991).

———. "L'intellectuel et l'action politique." *Le Banquet* 1 (1992).

———. "Le Mal démocratique." *Esprit* 195 (October 1993).

———. "La République enlisée." *Le Banquet* 6 (1995).

———. "L'Élargissement de l'objet historique." *Le Débat* 103 (January–February 1999).

———. "Laïcité et éducation civique." *Présences de la recherche à l'IUFM de Paris* 2 (February 2000).

———. "Croyances religieuses. croyances politiques." *Le Débat* 115 (May–August 2001).

———. "Quelle laïcité pour quelle modernité?" *Lire au collège* 63 (fall 2002).

———. "Une Histoire de confection: entretien avec Marcel Gauchet." *Tissage* 2 (2003).

Gauchet, Marcel, and Alain Finkielkraut. "Malaise dans la démocratie: l'école, la culture, l'individualisme." *Le Débat* 51 (September–November 1988).

Gauchet, Marcel, and Claude Lefort. "Sur la démocratie: la politique et l'institution du social." *Textures* 2–3 (1971).

Gauchet, Marcel, and Paul Valadier. "Sur la religion." *Le Débat* 32 (November 1984).

Girard, Augustin. "Industries culturelles." *Futuribles* 17 (September–October 1978).

Gremion, Pierre. "Écrivains et intellectuels à Paris: une esquisse." *Le Débat* 103 (January–February 1999).

Guérin, Daniel. "Faisons le point." *Le Libérateur politique et social pour la nouvelle gauche* (12 February 1956).

———. "Le Nouveau monde amoureux de Fourier." *Arcadie* 168 (1967), and 169 (1968).

Halberstam, David. "'Treblinka': An Author Finds Himself." *New York Times*, 17 April 1966.

Hazera, Hélène. "Petits prouesses avec des mort: 'Le rose et le noir.'" *Libération*, 30 May 1996.

———. "Enterrements." *La Revue h* 2 (fall 1996).

Heidegger, Martin. "Principe d'identité." Trans. Gilbert Kahn. *Arguments* 7 (April–May 1958).

———. "Le mot de Nietzsche 'Dieu est mort'." Trans. W. Brokmeier. *Arguments* 15 (1959).

———. "Principes de la pensée." Trans. François Fédier. *Arguments* 20 (1960).

———. "Au-dèla de la métaphysique." Trans. Roger Munier. *Arguments* 24 (1961).

Helvig, Jean-Michel. [Review of Guy Hocquenghem, *Lettre ouverte à ceux qui sont passés du col Mao au Rotary*]. *Libération*, 1 June 1986.

"L'historien, la culture et les institutions." Dossier in *Culture & Recherche* 95 (March–April 2003).

Hocquenghem, Guy. ["The Wonderful Life of the Gauchistes"]. *Actuel* 29 (March 1973).

———. [Interview with Hugo Marsan]. *Gai Pied Hebdo* 130–31 (4 August 1984).

———. "Le dégoût du siècle." *Traverses* 33–34 (1985).

———. "Les premières lueurs du Fhar" [Interview]. *Gai Pied Hebdo* (12 March 1988).

———. "Le sacerdoce de l'activiste" [Interview with Guy Chevalier]. *Têtu* 54 (March 2001).

Holland, Michael. "Bibliographie I." *Gramma* 3/4 (1976).

———. "Bibliographie II." *Gramma* 5 (1976).

"L'Homosexualité, ce douloureux problème" [Ménie Grégoire radio program] (10 March 1971). *La Revue h* 1 (summer 1996).

Internationale Situationniste. *Aux poubelles de l'histoire* (Paris: IS. 1963); repr. in *Internationale Situationniste* 12 (September 1969).

———. "Les mois les plus longs (février 1963–juillet 1964)." *Internationale Situationniste* 9 (August 1964).

———. "Quand Axelos avait trouvé un disciple." *Internationale Situationniste* 11 (October 1967); org. pub. *Bulletin of the International Centre of Poetic Studies* (June 1966).

Jacoby, Russell, and Dominick LaCapra. *American Historical Review* 97, no. 2 (April 1992).

Jaeger, Marcel. "L'esprit de fronde." *L'Information psychiatrique* 10 (December 1993).

James, C. L. R. "L'actualité de la Révolution française." *Perspectives socialistes: revue bimensuelle de l'Union de la gauche socialiste* 4 (15 February 1958).

Janover, Louis. "Guérin, le trouble-fête." *Débattre* 10 (spring 2000).

Kelly, Michael. "Demystification: A Dialogue between Barthes and Lefebvre." *Yale French Studies* 98 (2000).

Kerbourc'h, Jan-Claude, et al. "*Treblinka*, de Jean-François Steiner." *Combat*, 10 June 1966.

Korsch, Karl. "Thèses sur Hegel et la révolution." *Arguments* 16 (1959).

———. "Dix thèses sur le marxisme aujourd'hui." *Arguments* 16 (1959).

Krause, Anthony. "Les Écrivains hongrois face à la normalisation kadarienne: le cas Tibor Déry." *Revue d'histoire moderne et contemporaine* 49, no. 2 (April–June 2002).

Lefebvre, Henri. "Les rapports de la philosophie et de la politique dans les premières oeuvres de Marx (1842–1843)." *Revue de métaphysique et de morale* 63, nos. 2–3 (April–September 1958).

———. "Marxisme et technique." *Esprit* 307 (1962).

———. "La signification de la commune." *Arguments* 27–28 (1962).

———. "Kostas Axelos: *Vers la pensée planétaire: le devenir-pensée du monde et le devenir-homme* [sic] *de la pensée* (Ed. de Minuit)." *Esprit* 338 (1965).

Lefort, Claude. "L'analyse Marxiste et le fascisme." *Les Temps modernes* 2 (November 1945).

Le Goff, Yann. "Le FHAR." *Têtu* 54 (March 2001).

"La Lettre des écrivains soviétiques." *France observateur* 342 (29 November 1956).

Lextrait, Fabrice. "Les valeurs de l'art: entre marché et institutions." *Mouvements* 17 (September–October 2001).

"Liste de 343 femmes qui ont eu le courage de signer le manifeste 'je me suis fait avorter.'" *Le Nouvel Observateur* (5 April 1971).

Löwith, Karl. "Les implications politiques de la philosophie de l'existence chez Heidegger." *Les Temps modernes* 14 (November 1946).

Lukács, Georg. "Qu'est-ce que le marxisme orthodoxe?" *Arguments* 3 (April–May 1957).

———. "Qu'est-ce que le marxisme orthodoxe?" *Arguments* 5 (December 1957).

———. "Rosa Luxembourg, Marxiste." *Arguments* 5 (December 1957).

———. "Le phénomène de la reification." *Arguments* 11 (December 1958).

———. Letter from Budapest (28 June 1960), in Kostas Axelos, "Une declaration de G. Lukács." *Arguments* 20 (1960).

Majoros, István. "Les Relations franco-hongroises [1956–1964]." *Revue d'histoire moderne et contemporaine* 43, supplément 3–4 (1996).

"Manifeste." *Arguments* 1 (December 1956–January 1957).

Maniglier, Patrice. "Penser la culture gay." *Magazine littéraire* 426 (December 2003).

Manin, Bernard. "Pourquoi la République?" *Intervention* 10 (August–December 1984).

Mathy, Jean-Philippe. "The Resistance to French Theory in the United States: A Cross-Cultural Inquiry." *French Historical Studies* 19, no. 2 (fall 1995).

Mehlman, Jeffrey. "Of Literature and Terror: Blanchot at *Combat*." *Modern Languages Notes* 95 (1980).

Merleau-Ponty, Maurice. "Hegel's Existentialism." *Les Temps modernes* 1, no. 7 (April 1946).

Mesnard, Phillipe. "Maurice Blanchot, le sujet et l'engagement." *L'Infini* 48 (winter 1994).

Milet, Jean-Philippe, ed. "Kostas Axelos et la question du monde." Special Issue of *Rue Descartes* 18 (1997).

M. N. "Mort du C.N.E.?" *France observateur* 342 (29 November 1956).

Monod, Martine. [Review of Jean-François Steiner, *Treblinka*]. *L'Humanité dimanche*, 12 June 1966.

Morin, Edgar. "La fin d'un commencement." *Arguments* 27–28 (1962).

———. "Une tribune de discussion." In Jean-Philippe Milet, ed., "Kostas Axelos et la question du monde." Special Issue of *Rue Descartes* 18 (1997).

Morin, Edgar, Franco Fortini, Jean Duvignaud, and François Fejtö. "Les origines." *La Revue des revues* 4 (fall 1987).

Mouffe, Chantal, and Anne Showstack Sassoon. "Gramsci in France and Italy—A Review of the Literature." *Economy and Society* 6 (1977).

Moyn, Samuel. "Two Regimes of Memory." *American Historical Review* 103, no. 4 (October 1998).

———. "Emmanuel Levinas's Talmudic Readings: Between Tradition and Invention." *Prooftexts* 23, no. 3 (fall/winter 2003).

Mulkahy, Kevin. "Cultural Patronage in Comparative Perspective: Public Support for the Arts in France, Germany, Norway, and Canada." *The Journal of Arts Management Law and Society* 27, no. 4 (winter 1998).

Nora, Pierre. "Adieux aux intellectuals?" *Le Débat* 110 (May–August 2000).

Norris, Andrew. "Against Antagonism: On Ernesto Laclau's Political Thought." *Constellations* 4, no. 9 (December 2002).

[n.t.]. *Revue universitaire* 65, no. 5 (November–December 1956).

Padova, Mariateresa. "Testimonianze su 'Arguments.'" *Studi Francesci* 73 (January–April 1981).

Paloczy-Horvath, Georges. "La Politique des apolitiques." *Preuves* 103 (September 1959).

Passeron, Jean-Claude. "Quel regard sur le Populaire?" *Esprit* (March–April 2002).

Poirrier, Philippe. "Heritage and Cultural Policy in France under the Fifth Republic." *The International Journal of Cultural Policy* 9, no. 2 (2003).

"Quelle culture de la décentralisation?" *Mouvement: revue interdisciplinaire des arts vivants* 19 (November–December 2002).

Raczymow, Henri. "D'un 'détail' qui masque le tableau." *Le Monde*, 31 January 1998.

Redeker, Robert. "Un autre révisionnisme?: Alain Brossat et les camps." *Les Temps modernes* (November–December 1997).

"La Réponse des écrivains français." *France observateur* 342 (29 November 1956).

[Review of Edmund Husserl, *Méditations cartésiennes*]. *Revue de métaphysique et de morale* 39 (1932).

[Review of Edmund Husserl, *Méditations cartésiennes*]. *Revue philosophique de la France et de l'étrangère* 115 (1933).

Ricoeur, Paul. "Le 'figure' dans *L'Etoile de la Rédemption* de Franz Rosenzweig." *Esprit* (1988).

———. "Evénements et sens." *Raisons politiques* 2 (1991).

Ross, Kristin. "Lefebvre on the Situationists: An Interview." *October* 79 (winter 1997).

Rougemont, Denis de. "Sur la honte et l'espoir de l'Europe." *Preuves* 71 (January 1957).

———. "Sur Voltaire." *Preuves* 72 (February 1957).

Rousselot, Jean. "Les Intellectuels hongrois méritent notre amitié et notre respect." *France observateur* 343 (9 December 1956).

Rousset, David. "Les menaces ne sont pas mortes." *Évidences* 1 (March 1949).

———. "Au secours des déportés dans les camps soviétiques: Un appel aux anciens déportés des camps nazis." *Le Figaro littéraire*, 12 November 1949.

———. "L'affaire Tréblinka: les Juifs accusent." *Le Nouveau Candide*, 18 April 1966.

———. "L'affaire Tréblinka: 'Nous ne sommes pas morts comme des moutons.'" *Le Nouveau Candide*, 29 April 1966.

Roy, Claude. "L'Homme ne vit pas seulement de spoutnik." *France observateur* 396 (12 December 1957).

———. "P.P.C. du P.C." *France observateur* 397 (19 December 1957).

———. "'Effet calmant sur le peuple.'" *France observateur* 425 (26 June 1958).

Rubel, Maximilien. "Présentation des 'Dix thèse sur le marxisme.'" *Arguments* 16 (1959).

Saez, Guy. "L'action des collectivités territoriales en matière culturelle." *Les Cahiers français* 312 (January–February 2003).

Sanzio, Alain. "Une Décennie mouvementée." *Masques* 9/10 (summer 1981).

Sartre, Jean-Paul, and Maurice Merleau-Ponty. "Les Jours de notre vie." *Les Temps modernes* 51 (January 1950).

Sartre, Jean-Paul, et al. "Le C.N.E. et la Hongrie." *France observateur* 349 (17 January 1957).

Sartre, Jean-Paul, et al. "Pièces pour le procès Déry." *Les Temps modernes* 136 (June 1957).

Schérer, René. "Guy Hocquenghem: la passion de l'étranger." *Sociétés* 21 (December 1988).

Sedgwick, Peter. "Out of Hiding: The Comradeships of Daniel Guérin." *Salmagundi* 58, no. 9 (June 1982).

Sirinelli, Jean-François. "Aron avant Aron (1923–1933)." *Vingtième siècle: revue d'histoire* 2 (1984).

Soulié, Charles. "Anatomie du goût philosophique." *Actes de la recherche en sciences sociales* 109 (October 1995).

"Symposium on Intellectual History in the Age of Cultural Studies." *Intellectual History Newsletter* 18 (1996).

Toews, John E. "Intellectual History after the Linguistic Turn: The Autonomy of Meaning and the Irreducibility of Experience." *American Historical Review* 92, no. 4 (October 1987).

"Trois millards de pervers: grande encyclopédie des homosexualités." Special Issue of *Recherches* 12 (March 1973).

Vandemborghe, Jacques. "Mai 68 dans la Sorbonne Occupée." *Mec Magazine* 1 (1988).

Vercors. "Colloques Moscovites: I. L'Intervention en Hongrie." *Le Monde*, 8 May 1957.

Vercors et al. "Contre l'intervention soviétique." *France observateur* 339 (8 November 1956).

La Veuve Cycliste. "Martel en tête, pas en mémoire." *La Revue h* 1 (summer 1996).

Vidal-Naquet, Lucien. "Journal, 15 septembre 1942–29 février 1944." Preface by Pierre Vidal-Naquet. *Annales E.S.C.* 48, no. 3 (1993).

Vidal-Naquet, Pierre. "Treblinka et l'honneur des juifs." *Le Monde*, 2 May 1966.

———. "Remembrances of a 1946 Reader." *October* 87 (winter 1999).

———. "Reflections on Three *Ravensbrücks*." Trans. David Ames Curtis. *South Atlantic Quarterly* 96, no. 4 (fall 1997).

Villefosse. "La Collaboration impossible." *France observateur* 342 (22 November 1956).

———. "Et maintenant?" *Preuves* 79 (September 1957).

———. "Lettre à un ancien martyr." *Esprit* 260 (April 1958).

———. "Déry va-t-il mourir en secret?" *Le Monde*, 8 August 1959.

Wangermée, Robert. "Tendances de l'administration de la culture en Europe occidentale." *Revue française d'administration publique* 65 (January–March 1993).

Wiesand, A. J. "Comparative Cultural Policy Research in Europe: A Change of Paradigm." *Canadian Journal of Communication* 27 (2002).

Wieviorka, Annette. "L'Expression 'camp de concentration' au 20e siècle." *Vingtième siècle* 54 (April–June 1997).

Wolton, Dominique. "Télévision culturelle: l'apartheid' distingué." *Pouvoirs* 51 (1989).

Zivancevic, Nina. "Letter from Paris." *NY Arts* 8, no. 1 (January 2003).

BOOKS

Abensour, Miguel. *La Démocratie contre l'État: Marx et le moment machiavélien.* Paris: PUF, 1997.

Abzug, Robert. *Inside the Vicious Heart: Americans and the Liberation of the Nazi Concentration Camps.* New York: Oxford University Press, 1985.

Ahearne, Jeremy, ed. *French Cultural Policy Debates: A Reader.* London: Routledge, 2002.

Agamben, Giorgio. *Homo Sacer: Sovereign Power and Bare Life*, translated by Daniel Heller-Roazen. Stanford: Stanford University Press, 1998.

———. *Means without End: Notes on Politics*, translated by Vincenzo Binetti and Cesare Casarino. Minneapolis: University of Minnesota Press, 2000.

Agulhon, Maurice. *1848, ou l'apprentissage de la République.* Paris: Seuil, 1973; 1992.

Alain [Émile-Auguste Chartier]. *Les Philosophes.* Paris: Delaplane, 1901.

Althusser, Louis. *Pour Marx.* Paris: Maspéro, 1965.

———. *Essays in Self-Criticism*, translated by Grahame Lock. London: NLB, 1976.

Althusser, Louis, Jacques Rancière, Pierre Macherey, Étienne Balibar, and Roger Establet. *Lire "Le Capital".* 2 vols. Paris: Maspéro, 1965. Partially translated by Ben Brewster as *Reading Capital.* London: NLB, 1970.

Alquié, Ferdinand. *Nature et vérité dans la philosophie de Spinoza.* Paris: Centre de documentation universitaire, 1965.

———. *Le Rationalisme de Spinoza.* Paris: PUF, 1981.

Alternative Libertaire. *Un Projet de société communiste libertaire.* Paris: Alternative libertaire, 2002.

Anderson, Kevin. *Lenin, Hegel, and Western Marxism: A Critical Study.* Urbana, Ill.: University of Illinois Press, 1995.

Anderson, Perry. *Arguments Within English Marxism.* London: Verso, 1980.

———. *A Zone of Engagement.* London: Verso, 1992.

Ansky, S. *The Dybbuk and Other Writings*, edited by David G. Roskies. New York: Schocken Books, 1992.

Arendt, Hannah. *The Origins of Totalitarianism.* 2nd ed. New York: Meridian, 1958.

———. *Essays in Understanding*, edited by Jerome Kohn. New York: Harcourt, Brace & Co., 1994.

Arguments 1956–1962: édition intégrale, prefaces by Kostas Axelos, Edgar Morin, and Jean Duvignaud. Toulouse: Privat, 1983.

Aron, Raymond. *Le Grand Schisme.* Paris: Gallimard, 1948.

———. *France and Europe.* Hinsdale, Ill.: Henri Regnery Company, 1949.

———. *Les Guerres en chaîne.* Paris: Gallimard, 1951.

———. *L'Opium des intellectuels.* Paris: Calmann-Lévy, 1955. Translated by Terence Kilmartin as *The Opium of the Intellectuals.* New York: Doubleday, 1957.

———. *Espoir et peur du siècle: essais non partisans.* Paris: Calmann-Lévy, 1957.

———. *La Tragédie algérienne.* Paris: Plon, 1957.

———. *France Steadfast and Changing: The Fourth to the Fifth Republic.* Cambridge, Mass.: Harvard University Press, 1960.

———. *Paix et guerre entre les nations.* Paris: Calmann-Lévy, 1962; 1984.

———. *Les Étapes de la pensée sociologique.* Paris: Gallimard, 1967.

———. *Plaidoyer pour l'Europe décadente.* Paris: Robert Laffont, 1977.

———. *L'etica della libertà: memorie di mezzo secolo: colloqui con Jean-Louis Missika e Dominique Wolton*, translated by M. Le Cannu. Milano: Mondadori, 1981.

———. *Mémoires: 50 ans de réflexion politique.* Paris: Julliard, 1983.

———. *Chroniques de guerre: la France libre 1940–1945.* Paris: Gallimard, 1990.

Atack, Margaret. *May '68 in French Fiction and Film: Rethinking Society, Rethinking Representation.* Oxford: Oxford University Press, 1999.

Axelos, Kostas. *Marx, penseur de la technique: de l'aliénation de l'homme à la conquête du monde.* 2 vols. Paris: Éditions de Minuit, 1961; 1974. Translated and introduced by Ronald Bruzina as *Alienation, Praxis, and Techne in the Thought of Karl Marx*. Austin: University of Texas Press, 1976.

———. *Héraclite et la philosophie: la première saisie de l'être en devenir de la totalité*. Paris: Éditions de Minuit, 1962.

———. *Vers la pensée planétaire: le devenir-pensée du monde et le devenir-monde de la pensée*. Paris: Éditions de Minuit, 1964.

———. *Einführung in ein künftiges Denken: Über Marx und Heidegger*. Tübingen: Max Niemeyer, 1966.

———. *Arguments d'une recherche*. Paris: Éditions de Minuit, 1969.

———. *Le Jeu du monde*. Paris: Éditions de Minuit, 1969.

———. *Pour une éthique problématique*. Paris: Éditions de Minuit, 1972.

———. *Entretiens: "reéls," imaginaires, et avec "soi-même"*. Montpellier: Fata Morgana, 1973.

———. *Horizons du monde*. Paris: Éditions de Minuit, 1974.

———. *Contribution à la logique*. Paris: Éditions de Minuit, 1977.

———. *Problèmes de l'enjeu*. Paris: Éditions de Minuit, 1979.

———. *Systématique ouverte*. Paris: Éditions de Minuit, 1984.

———. *Métamorphoses: clôture–ouverture*. Paris: Éditions de Minuit, 1991.

———. *L'Errance érotique*. Paris: Éditions de Minuit, 1992.

———. *Lettres à un jeune penseur*. Paris: Éditions de Minuit, 1996.

———. *Notices "autobiographiques"*. Paris: Éditions de Minuit, 1997.

———. *Ce Questionnement: approche–éloignement*. Paris: Éditions de Minuit, 2001.

Bachoud, Andrée, Josefina Cuesta, and Michel Trebitsch, eds. *Les Intellectuels et l'Europe de 1945 à nos jours*. Paris: Publications universitaires Denis Diderot, 2000.

Bataille, Georges. *The Bataille Reader*, edited by Fred Botting and Scott Wilson. Oxford: Blackwell, 1997.

Balibar, Étienne. *Masses, Classes, Ideas: Studies on Politics and Philosophy Before and After Marx*, translated by James Swenson. New York: Routledge, 1994.

Barkat, Sidi Mohammed, ed. *Des Français contre la terreur d'État: Algérie 1954–1962*. Paris: Éditions Reflex, 2002.

Barrer, Patrick, ed. *Tout l'art contemporain est-il nul? le débat sur l'art contemporain en France avec ceux qui l'ont lancé: bilan et mise en perspective*. Lausanne: Favre, 2000.

Barthes, Roland. *Writing Degree Zero*, translated by Annette Lavers and Colin Smith. New York: Hill and Wang, 1968.

———. *Le Grain de la voix: entretiens, 1962–1980*. Paris: Seuil, 1981.

Bartov, Omer. *Germany's War and the Holocaust: Disputed Histories*. Ithaca: Cornell University Press, 2003.

Bataille, Georges. *L'Érotisme*. Paris: Éditions de Minuit, 1957.

Baverez, Nicolas. *Aron*. Paris: Flammarion, 1993.

Beaufret, Jean. *Dialogue avec Heidegger*. 4 vols. Paris: Éditions de Minuit, 1973–85.

Beauvoir, Simone de. *The Prime of Life*, translated by Peter Green. New York: World Publishing Co., 1962.

Becker, Jean-Jacques, and Pascal Ory. *Crises et alternances: 1974–2000*. Paris: Seuil, 1998.

Benhamou, Françoise. *L'Économie de la culture*. Paris: La Découverte, 1996.

Benjamin, Walter. *Paris: capitale du XIXe siècle: le livre des passages*. Paris: Les Éditions du Cerf, 1989.

Benz, Wolfgang, and Barbara Distel, eds. *Terror ohne System: die ersten Konzentrationslager im Nationalsozialismus 1933–1935*. Berlin: Metropol, 2001.

Berman, Marshall. *All that is Solid Melts into Air: The Experience of Modernity*. New York: Penguin Books, 1982.

Berstein, Serge, Pierre Milza, and Jean-Louis Bianco, eds. *Les Années Mitterrand: les années du changement, 1981–1984*. Paris: Perrin, 2001.

Bertens, Hans. *The Idea of the Postmodern: A History*. London: Routledge, 1995.

Bertram, Christopher, and Andrew Chitty, eds. *Has History Ended? Fukuyama, Marx, Modernity*. Aldershot: Avebury, 1994.

Beyme, Klaus von, ed. *Theory and Politics: Theorie und Politik*. Haag: Martinus Nijhoff, 1972.

Blanchot, Maurice. *Lautréamont et Sade*. Paris: Éditions de Minuit, 1949.

Bonnier, Henri. *Lettre recommandée à Jack Lang et aux fossoyeurs de la culture*. Monaco: Éditions du Rocher, 1992.

Borwicz, Michel. *Écrits des condamnés à mort sous l'occupation allemande 1939–1945: étude sociologique*. Paris: Presses universitaires, 1954.

Bougnoux, Daniel, Jean-Louis Le Moigne, and Serge Proulx, eds. *Arguments pour une méthode: autour d'Edgar Morin: colloque de Cerisy*. Paris: Éditions du Seuil, 1990.

Bouissounouse, Janine. *La Nuit d'Autun: le temps des illusions*. Paris: Calmann-Lévy, 1977.

Bourdieu, Pierre. *La Distinction: critique sociale du jugement*. Paris: Éditions de Minuit, 1979. Translated by Richard Nice as *Distinction: A Social Critique of the Judgement of Taste*. Cambridge, Mass.: Harvard University Press, 1984.

———. *Homo Academicus*. Paris: Éditions de Minuit, 1984.

———, ed. *La Misère du Monde*. Paris: Seuil, 1993.

———. *Contre-feux 2: pour un mouvement social européen*. Paris: Raisons d'agir éditions, 2001.

Bourseiller, Christophe. *Les Maoïstes: la folle histoire des gardes rouges français*. Paris: Plon, 1996.

Brillant, Bernard. *Les Clercs de 68*. Paris: PUF, 2003.

Brossat, Alain. *L'Épreuve du désastre: le XXe siècle et les camps*. Paris: Albin Michel, 1996.

Brunschvicg, Léon. *Spinoza*. Paris: F. Alcan, 1894.

———. *Spinoza et ses contemporains*. Paris: F. Alcan, 1923.

Castiglione, Dario, and Iain Hampsher-Monk, eds. *The History of Political Thought in National Context*. Cambridge: Cambridge University Press, 2001.

Castoriadis, Cornelius. *World in Fragments: Writings on Politics, Society, Psychoanalysis, and the Imagination*, edited and translated by David Ames Curtis. Stanford: Stanford University Press, 1997.

———. *La Société bureaucratique*. Vol. 1, *Les Rapports de production en Russie*. Paris: Union générale d'éditions, 1973.

———. *La Société bureaucratique*. Vol. 2, *La Révolution contre la bureaucratie*. Paris: Union générale d'éditions, 1973.

———. *L'Expérience du mouvement ouvrier*. Vol. 1, *Comment lutter*. Paris: Union générale d'éditions, 1974.

———. *L'Expérience du mouvement ouvrier*. Vol. 2, *Prolétariat et organisation*. Paris: Union générale d'éditions, 1974.

———. *L'Institution imaginaire de la société*. Paris: Seuil, 1975.

———. *Les Carrefours du labyrinthe*. Paris: Seuil, 1978.

———. *Capitalisme moderne et révolution*. Vol. 2, *Le Mouvement révolutionnaire sous le capitalisme moderne*. Paris: Éditions 10/18, 1979.

———. *La Société française*. Paris: Union générale d'éditions, 1979.

———. *Les Carrefours du labyrinthe*. Vol. 2, *Domaines de l'homme*. Paris: Seuil, 1986.

———. *Les Carrefours du labyrinthe*. Vol. 4, *La Montée de l'insignifiance*. Paris: Seuil, 1996.

———. *Les Carrefours du labyrinthe*. Vol. 5, *Fait et à faire*. Paris: Seuil, 1997.

———. *Les Carrefours du labyrinthe*. Vol. 6, *Les Figures du pensable*. Paris: Seuil, 1999.

———. *Sur Le Politique de Platon*. Paris: Seuil, 1999.

———. *La Création humaine*. Vol. 1, *Sujet et vérité dans le monde social-historique: séminaire 1986–1987*. Paris: Seuil, 2002.

Canguilhem, Georges. *The Normal and the Pathological*, introduction by Michel Foucault, translated by Carolyn R. Fawcett in collaboration with Robert S. Cohen. New York: Zone Books, 1991.

Cesbron, Georges, and Gérard Jacquin, eds. *Vercors (Jean Bruller) et son œuvre*. Paris: L'Harmattan, 1999.

Charle, Christophe. *Naissance des "intellectuels," 1880–1900*. Paris: Éditions de Minuit, 1990.

Charlot, Jean. *Le Gaullisme d'opposition 1946–1958*. Paris: Fayard, 1983.

Chartier, Roger. *Cultural History: Between Practices and Representations*. Ithaca: Cornell University Press, 1988.

———. *On the Edge of the Cliff: History, Language, and Practices*. Baltimore: The Johns Hopkins University Press, 1996.

Châtelet, François. *Logos et praxis: recherches sur la signification théorique du marxisme*. Paris: Société d'Édition d'Énseignement Supérieur, 1962.

Cheval, André. *Histoire de l'agrégation: contribution à l'histoire de la culture scolaire*. Paris: Éditions Kimé, 1993.

Christofferson, Michael Scott. "The Antitotalitarian Moment in French Intellectual Politics, 1975–1984." Ph.D. diss., Columbia University, 1998.

———. *French Intellectuals Against the Left: The Antitotalitarian Moment of the 1970s*. New York: Berghahn Books, 2004.

Chun, Lin. *The British New Left*. Edinburgh: Edinburgh University Press, 1993.

Clément, Catherine. *La Nuit et l'été: rapport sur la culture à la télévision*. Paris: Seuil-La Documentation Française, 2003.

Cohn-Bendit, Daniel, and Gabriel Cohn-Bendit. *Le Gauchisme, remède à la maladie sénile du communisme*. Paris: Seuil, 1968.

Coquio, Catherine, ed. *Parler des camps, penser les genocides*. Paris: Albin Michel, 1999.

Coston, Henry. *Les 200 familles au pouvoir*. Paris: Henry Coston, 1977.

Cotta, Alain. *Le Capitalisme dans tous ses états*. Paris: Fayard, 1991.

Courtois, Stéphane, ed. *Le Livre noir du communisme: crimes, terreurs, repression*. Paris: R. Laffont, 1997. Translated by Jonathan Murphy and Mark Kramer as *The Black Book of Communism: Crime, Terror, Repression*. Cambridge, Mass.: Harvard University Press, 1999.

Coward, Rosalind, and John Ellis. *Language and Materialism: Developments in Semiology and the Theory of the Subject*. London: Routledge, 1977.

Craipeau, Yvan. *Mémoires d'un dinosaure trotskyste: secrétaire de Trotsky en 1933*. Paris: L'Harmattan, 1999.

Craveri, Piero, and Gaetano Quagliariello, eds. *Atlantismo e europeismo*. Soveria Mannelli: Rubbettino, 2003.

Creton, Laurent. *Le Cinéma à l'épreuve du système télévisuel*. Paris: CNRS Éditions, 2002.

Critchley, Simon, Jacques Derrida, Ernesto Laclau, and Richard Rorty. *Deconstruction and Pragmatism*, edited by Chantal Mouffe. New York: Routledge, 1996.

Crozier, Michel. *La Société bloquée*. Paris: Seuil, 1971.

Cusset, François. *French Theory: Derrida, Foucault, Deleuze et Cie. et les mutations de la vie intellectuelle aux Étas-Unis*. Paris: La Découverte, 2003.

Dagen, Philippe. *La Haine de l'art*. Paris: Grasset, 1997.

Darnton, Robert. *The Kiss of Lamourette: Reflections in Cultural History*. New York: Norton, 1990.

Debord, Guy. *La Société du spectacle*. 3rd ed. Paris: Gallimard, 1992.

Debray, Régis. *Teachers, Writers, Celebrities: The Intellectuals of Modern France*, translated by David Macey. London: New Left Books, 1981.

———. *Critique de la raison politique*. Paris: Gallimard, 1981.

———. *Que vive la République!* Paris: Odile Jacob, 1989.

———. *Cours de médiologie générale*. Paris: Gallimard, 1991; 2001.

———. *Contretemps: éloge des idéaux perdus*. Paris: Gallimard, 1992.

Delbos, Victor. *Le Problème moral dans la philosophie de Spinoza et dans l'histoire du spinozisme*. Paris: F. Alcan, 1893.

———. *La Philosophie française*, preface by Maurice Blondel. Paris: Librairie Plon, 1919.

Deleuze, Gilles. *Présentation de Sacher-Masoch: la Vénus à la fourrure*. Paris: Éditions de Minuit, 1967.

———. *Spinoza et le probleme de l'expression*. Paris: Éditions de Minuit, 1968.

Deleuze, Gilles, and Félix Guattari, *Anti-Oedipus: Capitalism and Schizophrenia*. Minneapolis: University of Minnesota Press, 1985.

———. *A Thousand Plateaus: Capitalism and Schizophrenia*. London: Continuum, 1988.

Deli, Peter. *De Budapest à Prague: les sursauts de la gauche française*. Paris: Anthropos, 1981.

Derrida, Jacques. *Of Grammatology*, translated by Gayatri Chakravorty Spivak. Baltimore: Johns Hopkins University Press, 1976.

———. *L'Autre cap*. Paris: Éditions de Minuit, 1991.

———. *Specters of Marx: The State of the Debt, the Work of Mourning, & the New International*, translated by Peggy Kamuf. New York: Routledge, 1994.

Desan, Wilfred. *The Planetary Man: A Noetic Prelude to a United World*. Washington, D.C.: Georgetown University Press, 1961. Translated by Hans Hildenbrand and Alex Lindenberg as *L'Homme planétaire: prélude théorique a un monde uni*. Paris: Éditions de Minuit, 1968.

Descombes, Vincent. *Le Même et l'autre*. Paris: Éditions de Minuit, 1979. Translated by L. Scott-Fox and J. M. Harding as *Modern French Philosophy*. Cambridge: Cambridge University Press, 1980.

Diels, Hermann. *Die Fragmente der Vorsokratiker*, edited by Walther Kranz. 3 vols. 6th ed. Berlin-Grunewald: Weidmannsche Verlagsbuchhandlung, 1951.

Donnat, Olivier, and Denis Cogneau. *Les Pratiques culturelles des français*. Paris: La Découverte-La Documentation Française, 1990.

Dosse, François. *L'Histoire en miettes: des "Annales" à la "nouvelle histoire"*. Paris: La Découverte, 1987. Translated by Peter V. Conroy, Jr. as *New History in France: The Triumph of the Annales*. Urbana, Ill.: University of Illinois Press, 1994.

———. *L'Empire du sens: l'humanisation des sciences humaines*. Paris: La Découverte, 1995. Translated by Hassan Melehy as *Empire of Meaning: The Humanization of the Social Sciences*. Minneapolis: University of Minnesota Press, 1999.

———. *Histoire du structuralisme*. 2 vols. Paris: La Découverte, 1991–92. Translated by Deborah Glassman as *History of Structuralism*. 2 vols. Minneapolis: Minnesota University Press, 1997.

———. *L'Histoire: le temps réflechi*. Paris: Haiter, 1999.

———. *Paul Ricoeur: les sens d'une vie*. Paris: La Découverte, 2000.

———. *Michel de Certeau: le marcheur blessé*. Paris: La Découverte, 2002.

———. *La Marche des idées: histoire des intellectuels–histoire intellectuelle*. Paris: La Découverte, 2003.

Drake, David. *Intellectuals and Politics in Post-War France*. Houndmills: Palgrave, 2002.

Dworkin, Dennis. *Cultural Marxism in Postwar Britain: History, the New Left, and the Origins of Cultural Studies*. Durham, N.C.: Duke University Press, 1997.

Eagleton, Terry. *After Theory*. New York: Basic Books, 2003.

Easthope, Antony. *British Post-Structuralism: Since 1968*. London: Routledge, 1991.

Ehrard, Jean. *Problèmes et methods de l'histoire littéraire*. Paris: Armand Colin, 1974.

Elden, Stuart. *Mapping the Present: Heidegger, Foucault and the Project of a Spatial History*. London: Continuum, 2001.

———. *Understanding Henri Lefebvre: Theory and the Possible*. London: Continuum, 2004.

Eley, Geoff. *Forging Democracy: The History of the Left in Europe, 1850–2000*. New York: Oxford University Press, 2002.

Engels, Friedrich, and Karl Marx. *La Première Critique de l'économie politique*, translated by Kostas Papaioannou. Paris: Union générale d'éditions, 1972.

Eribon, Didier, ed. *Dictionnaire des cultures gays et lesbiennes*. Paris: Larousse, 2003.

Fanon, Frantz. *The Wretched of the Earth*, preface by Jean-Paul Sartre, translated by Constance Farrington. New York: Grove Press, 1968.

Farías, Victor. *Heidegger and Nazism*, translated by Paul Burrell and Gabriel R. Ricci. Philadelphia: Temple University Press, 1989.

Feré, Vincent. "Le Comité national des écrivains et les compagnons de route du parti communiste français février 1946–avril 1953." DEA Thesis, Institut d'études politiques, Paris, 1998.

Ferry, Luc, and Alain Renaut. *Philosophie politique*. Vol. 3, *Des Droits de l'homme à l'idée républicaine*. Paris: PUF, 1985.

———. *La Pensée 68: essai sur l'anti-humanisme contemporain*. Paris: Gallimard, 1985. Translated by Mary H. S. Cattani as *French Philosophy of the Sixties: An Essay on Antihumanism*. Amherst: The University of Massachusettes Press, 1990.

French, Patrick. *The Time of Theory: A History of Tel quel 1960–1983*. Oxford: Clarendon Press, 1995.

FHAR: Rapport contre la normalité. Paris: Champs Libre, 1971.

Fields, A. Belden. *Trotskyism and Maoism: Theory and Practice in France and the United States*. New York: Autonomedia, 1998.

Fink, Eugen. *La Philosophie de Nietzsche*, translated by Hans Hildenbrand and Alex Lindenberg. Paris: Éditions de Minuit, 1965.

———. *Le Jeu comme symbole du monde*, translated by Hans Hildenbrand and Alex Lindenberg. Paris: Éditions de Minuit, 1966.

———. *De la phénoménologie*, translated by Didier Franck. Paris: Éditions de Minuit, 1975.

Finkielkraut, Alain. *La Défaite de la pensée*. Paris: Gallimard, 1987.

Flavius Josephus, *La Guerre des juifs, précedé par "Du bon usage de la trahison,"* de Pierre Vidal Naquet. Paris: Éditions de Minuit, 1977.

Flood, Christopher, and Nick Hewlett, eds. *Currents in Contemporary French Intellectual Life*. New York: St. Martin's Press, 2000.

Fontenis, Georges. *Changer le monde: histoire du mouvement communiste libertaire, 1945–1997*. Paris: Le Coquelicot/Alternative libertaire, 2000.

Forrester, Viviane. *L'Horreur économique*. Paris: Fayard, 1996.

Foucart, Bruno, Antoine Schnapper, and Sébastien Loste. *Paris mystifié: la grand illusion du Grand Louvre*. Paris: Julliard, 1985.

Foucault, Michel. *The Order of Things*. New York: Random House, 1970.

———. *Power/Knowledge: Selected Interviews and Other Writings, 1972–1977*, edited and translated by Colin Gordon. New York: Pantheon 1980.

———. *Politics, Philosophy, Culture: Interviews and Other Writings, 1977–1984*, edited by Lawrence Kritzman. New York: Routledge, 1988.

———. *Dits et écrits*. 4 vols. Paris: Gallimard, 1994.

Fourastié, Jean. *Les Trentes glorieuses*. Paris: Pluriel, 1975.

Fourier, Charles. *Vers la liberté en amour*, edited by Daniel Guérin. Paris: Gallimard, 1975.

Franck, Didier. *Chair et corps: sur la phénomenologie de Husserl*. Paris: Éditions de Minuit, 1981.

———. *Heidegger et le problème de l'espace*. Paris: Éditions de Minuit, 1986.

Freedeman, Charles E. *The Triumph of Corporate Capitalism in France, 1867–1914*. Rochester, N.Y.: University of Rochester Press, 1993.

Frickey, Gene H. *The Origins of Phenomenology in France, 1920–1940*. Ph.D. diss., Indiana University, 1979.

Fridenson, Patrick, and André Strauss, eds. *Le Capitalisme français XIXe–XXe siècles: blocages et dynamismes d'une croissance*. Paris: Fayard, 1987.

Friedlander, Judith. *Vilna on the Seine*. New Haven: Yale University Press, 1990.

Fumaroli, Marc. *L'État culturel: une religion moderne*. Paris: Editions de Fallois, 1991.

Furet, François. *Interpreting the French Revolution*, translated by Elborg Forster. Cambridge: Cambridge University Press, 1981.

———. *In the Workshop of History*, translated by Jonathan Mandelbaum. Chicago: The University of Chicago Press, 1984.

Furet, François, Jacques Julliard, and Pierre Rosanvallon. *La République du centre: la fin de l'exception française*. Paris: Calmann-Lévy, 1988.

Fustel de Coulanges, Numa-Denis. *Histoire des institutions politiques de l'ancienne France*. Paris: Hachette, 1875.

Gallois, William. *Zola: The History of Capitalism*. Bern: Peter Lang, 2000.

Gauchet, Marcel. *La Religion dans la démocratie: parcours de laïcité*. Paris: Gallimard, 1998.

Gaudric-Delfranc, Marianne, ed. *Elsa Triolet un écrivain dans le siècle: actes du colloque international 15–17 novembre 1996, Maison Elsa Triolet-Aragon-Saint-Arnoult-en-Yvelines*. Paris: L'Harmattan, 2000.

Gaulle, Charles de. *Discours et messages*. 5 vols. Paris: Omnibus/Plon, 1993.

Gentil, Geneviève and Augustin Girard, eds. *Les Affaires culturelles au temps de Jacques Duhamel: 1971–1973*. Paris: La Documentation Française, 1995.

Geras, Norman. *Discourses of Extremity: Radical Ethics and Post-Marxist Extravagances*. New York: Verso, 1990.

Gilot, Françoise, and Carlton Lake. *Life with Picasso*. New York: McGraw Hill, 1964.

Girard, Augustin, and Geneviève Gentil, eds. *Les Affaires culturelles au temps d'André Malraux*. Paris: Comité d'histoire du Ministère de la Culture-La Documentation Française, 1996.

Goldhagen, Daniel Jonah. *Hitler's Willing Executioners: Ordinary Germans and the Holocaust*. New York: A.A. Knopf, 1996.

Gombin, Richard. *The Origins of Modern Leftism*, translated by Michael K. Perl. Harmondsworth: Penguin, 1975.

Gottraux, Philippe. *'Socialisme ou Barbarie': un engagement politique et intellectuel dans la France de l'après-guerre*. Lausanne: Éditions Payot Lausanne, 1997.

Grandsenne, Florence. "Les Intellectuels français face aux crises du communisme en Europe du Centre-Est: perception et interprétation des mouvements et de leur répression, 1956–1981." 2 vols. Doctoral Thesis, Institut d'études politiques, Paris, 1998.

Grémion, Pierre. *Paris-Prague: la gauche face au renouveau et à la régression tchécoslovaques 1968–1978*. Paris: Julliard, 1985.

———. *L'Intelligence de l'anticommunisme: Le Congrès pour la liberté de la culture à Paris* Paris: Fayard, 1995.

Griffiths, A. Phillips, ed. *Contemporary French Philosophy*. Cambridge: Cambridge University Press, 1987.

Grohens, Jean-Claude, and Jean-François Sirinelli, *Culture et action chez Georges Pompidou*. Paris: PUF, 2000.

Guérin, Daniel. *La Peste brune a passé par là*. Paris: Librairie du Travail, 1933; Paris: Spartacus, 1996. Translated as *The Brown Plague: Travels in Late Weimar and Early Nazi Germany*. Durham, N.C.: Duke University Press, 1994.

———. *Fascisme et grand capital*. Paris: Gallimard, 1936. Preface by Alain Bihr; Paris: Syllepse, 1999. Translated as *Fascism and Big Business*. New York: Monad Press, 1973.

———. *La Lutte de classes sous la Pemière République, 1793–1797*. 2 vols. Paris: Gallimard, 1946; 1968.

———. *Où va le peuple américain?* Paris: Julliard, 1950–51. Part. repub. as *Décolonisation du noir américain*. Paris: Éditions de Minuit, 1963; *Le Mouvement ouvrier aux États-Unis*. Paris: Maspero, 1968; and *De l'Oncle Tom aux Panthères: le drame des noirs américains*. Paris: Union générale d'éditions, 1973. Translated by Duncan Ferguson as *Negroes on the March: A Frenchman's Report on the American Negro Struggle*. New York: George L. Weissman, 1956; and translated by Alan Adler as *100 Years of Labor in the USA*. London: Ink Links, 1979.

———. *Au Service des colonisés: 1930–1953*. Paris: Éditions de Minuit, 1954.

———. *Kinsey et la sexualité*. Paris: Julliard, 1955; repub. EDI, 1967.

———. *L'Algérie n'a jamais été la France*. Paris: [published by the author], 1956.

———. *Les Antilles décolonisées*, introduction by Aimé Césaire. Paris: Présence africaine, 1956.

———. *Jeunesse du socialisme libertaire*. Paris: Rivière, 1959.

———. *L'Algérie qui se cherche*. Paris: Centre d'étude socialiste, 1964.

————. *L'Anarchisme, de la doctrine à la pratique.* Paris: Gallimard, 1965. Translated as *Anarchism: From Theory to Practice*, introduction by Noam Chomsky. New York: Monthly Review Press, 1970.

————. *Ni dieu ni maître, anthologie de l'anarchisme.* Lausanne: La Cité-Lausanne, 1965. Translated as *No Gods No Masters: An Anthology of Anarchism.* Edinburgh: AK Press, 1998.

————. *Un Jeune Homme excentrique: essai d'autobiographie.* Paris: Julliard, 1965.

————. *Essai sur la révolution sexuelle après Reich et Kinsey.* Paris: Belfond, 1969.

————. *Rosa Luxemburg et la spontanéité révolutionnaire.* Paris: Flammarion, 1971.

————. *Autobiographie de jeunesse, d'une dissidence sexuelle au socialisme.* Paris: Belfond, 1972.

————. *Les Assassins de Ben Barka, dix ans d'enquête.* Paris: Guy Authier, 1975.

————. *La Révolution française et nous.* Paris: Maspero, 1976.

————. *Le Feu du sang: autobiographie politique et charnelle.* Paris: Grasset & Fasquelle, 1979.

————. *Quand l'Algérie s'insurgeait, 1954–1962: un anticolonialiste témoigne.* Paris: La Pensée sauvage, 1979.

————. *Ben Barka, ses assassins, seize ans d'enquête.* Paris: Plon, 1982.

————. *Homosexualité et révolution.* Paris: Le Vent du ch'min, 1983.

————. *À la recherche d'un communisme libertaire.* Paris: Spartacus, 1984; 2003.

————. *Front populaire, révolution manquée? témoignage militant.* Arles: Actes Sud, 1997.

Guérin, Daniel, Boris Fraenkel, Michel Cattler, Constantin Sinelnikoff, Marc Kravetz, and Jacques Delattre, eds. *Société et répression sexuelle: l'œuvre de Wilhelm Reich.* Bruxelles: Éditions Liaisons 20, 1968.

Guéroult, Martial. *Spinoza.* Vol. 1, *Dieu Éthique, I.* Paris: Aubier-Montaigne, 1968.

————. *Spinoza.* Vol. 2, *L'Âme Éthique, II.* Paris: Aubier-Montaigne, 1974.

Guiral, Pierre. *La Vie quotidienne en France à l'Age d'Or du capitalisme 1852–1879.* Paris: Hachette, 1976.

Gutting, Gary. *French Philosophy in the Twentieth Century.* Cambridge: Cambridge University Press, 2001.

Gurvitch, Georges. *Les Tendances actuelles de la philosophie allemande*, preface by Léon Brunschvicg. Paris: Librairie Vrin, 1930.

Hamon, Hervé, and Patrick Rotman. *Les Porteurs de valises: la résistance française à la guerre d'Algérie.* 2nd ed. Paris: Albin Michel, 1982.

————. *Génération.* 2 vols. Paris: Seuil, 1988.

Harbi, Mohammed. *Une Vie debout: mémoires politiques.* Vol. 1, *1945–1962.* Paris: La Découverte, 2002.

Harouel, Jean-Louis. *Culture et contre-cultures.* Paris: PUF, 1994.

Hartog, François, Pauline Schmitt, and Alain Schnapp, eds. *Pierre Vidal-Naquet: un historien dans la cité.* Paris: La Découverte, 1998.

Haviland, Eric. *Kostas Axelos: une vie pensée, une pensée vécue.* Paris: L'Harmattan, 1995.

Hebdige, Dick. *Subculture: The Meaning of Style*. London: Metheun, 1979.

Hegel, G. W. F. *La Raison dans l'histoire*, translated by Kostas Papaioannou. Paris: Union générale d'éditions, 1965.

Heidegger, Martin. *Identität und Differenz*. Pfulligen: Neske, 1957.

———. *Being and Time*, translated by John Macquarrie and Edward Robinson. Oxford: Blackwell, 1962.

———. *Le Principe de raison*, translated by André Préau. Paris: Gallimard, 1962.

———. *What is Philosophy?/Was ist das—die Philosophie?* [English-German edition], translated by William Kluback and Jean T. Wilde. London: Vision Press, 1963.

———. *Questions I et II*, translated by Kostas Axelos, Jean Beaufret, Dominique Janicaud et al. Paris: Gallimard, 1968.

———. *The Question Concerning Technology and Other Essays*, translated by William Lovitt. New York: Harper & Row, 1977.

———. *Einführung in die Metaphysik, Gesamtausgabe Band 40*. Frankfurt am Main: Vittorio Klostermann, 1983.

———. *The Principle of Reason*, translated by Reginald Lilly. Bloomington: Indiana University Press, 1991.

———. *Nietzsche: Der europäische Nihilismus, Gesamtausgabe Band 48*. Frankfurt am Main: Vittorio Klostermann, 1986. A shorter version is translated as *Nietzsche*. 4 vols. San Francisco: Harper Collins, 1991.

———. *Essais et conférences*, translated by André Préau. Paris: Gallimard, 1992.

———. *Pathmarks*, edited by William McNeill. Cambridge: Cambridge University Press, 1998.

Heidegger, Martin, and Eugen Fink, *Heraclitus Seminar 1966/67*, translated by Charles E. Seibert. University, Ala.: University of Alabama Press, 1979.

Heraclitus, *Les Fragments d'Héraclite d'Ephèse*, edited and translated by Kostas Axelos. Paris: Éditions Estienne, 1958.

Raul, Hilberg. *The Destruction of the European Jews*. Chicago: Quadrangle Books, 1961.

Hirsch, Arthur. *The French New Left: An Intellectual History from Sartre to Gorz*. Boston: South End Press, 1981; Montreal: Black Rose Books, 1982.

Hobsbawm, Eric. *Interesting Times: A Twentieth-Century Life*. New York: Pantheon, 2002.

Hocquenghem, Guy. *L'Après-mai des faunes*. Paris: Grasset, 1974.

———. *Homosexual Desire*, preface (1978) by Jeffrey Weeks, translated by Daniella Dangoor. Durham: Duke University Press, 1993.

———. *L'Amphithéâre des morts: mémoires anticipées*, preface by Roland Surzur. Paris: Gallimard, 1994.

———. *Oiseau de la nuit*. Paris: Albin Michel, 1998.

———. *Lettre ouverte à ceux qui sont passes du col Mao au Rotary*, introduction by Serge Halimi. Marseille: Agone, 2003.

———, and René Schérer. *L'Âme atomique*. Paris: Albin Michel, 1986.

Hollier, Denis, and Jeffrey Mehlman, eds. *Postwar French Thought*. Vol. 2, *Literary Debate: Texts and Contexts*. New York: The New Press, 1999.

Hourmant, François. *Le Désenchantement des clercs: figures de l'intellectuel dans l'après-mai 68.* Rennes: Presses universitaires de Rennes, 1997.

Hunt, Lynn, ed. *The New Cultural History.* Berkeley: University of California Press, 1989.

Husserl, Edmund. *Méditations cartésiennes: introduction à la phénoménologie,* translated by Gabrielle Peiffer and Emmanuel Levinas. Paris: Armand Colin, 1931.

———. *Husserliana 1: Cartesianische Meditationen und Pariser Vorträge,* edited by Stephen Strasser. The Hague: Martinus Nijhoff, 1950; 1973. Translated by Dorion Cairns as *Cartesian Meditations: An Introduction to Phenomenology* [The Hague: Martinus Nijhoff, 1960].

———. *The Paris Lectures.* Translated by Peter Koestenbaum. The Hague: Martinus Nijhoff, 1964.

Hilberg, Raul. *The Destruction of the European Jews.* Chicago: Quadrangle Books, 1961.

Hjemslev, Louis. *Essais linguistiques.* Paris: Éditions de Minuit, 1971.

Hyppolite, Jean. *Genèse et structure de la "Phénoménologie de l'esprit" de Hegel.* Paris: Aubier, 1946. Translated by Samuel Cherniak and John Heckman as *Genesis and Structure of Hegel's Phenomenology of Spirit.* Evanston, Ill.: Northwestern University Press, 1974.

Ignotus, Paul. *Political Prisoner.* London: Routledge and Kegan Paul, 1959.

Internationale Situationniste. *Aux poubelles de l'histoire.* Paris: IS, 1963.

Internationale Situationniste 1958–1969, edition augmentée, edited by Patrick Mosconi. Paris: Librarie Artheime Fayard, 1997.

Jameson, Fredric. *Late Marxism: Adorno, or, The Persistence of the Dialectic.* London: Verso, 1990.

Janicaud, Dominique. *L'Ombre de cette pensée.* Grenoble: Jérome Millon, 1990.

———. *Heidegger en France.* 2 vols. Paris: Albin Michel, 2001.

Jakobson, Roman. *Essais de linguistique generale,* translated by Nicolas Ruwet. 2 vols. Paris: Éditions de Minuit, 1963–1973.

———. *Selected Writings.* 8 vols. The Hague: Mouton, 1971–88.

Jaspers, Karl. *Strindberg et van Gogh, Swedenborg, Hölderlin.* Paris: Éditions de Minuit, 1970.

Jay, Martin. *Downcast Eyes: The Denigration of Vision in Twentieth-Century French Thought.* Berkeley: University of California Press, 1993.

———. *Force Fields: Between Intellectual History and Cultural Critique.* New York: Routledge, 1993.

———. *Refractions of Violence.* New York: Routledge, 2003.

Jennings, Jeremy, ed. *Intellectuals in Twentieth-Century France: Samuris and Mandarins.* New York: St. Martin's Press, 1993.

Judt, Tony. *Marxism and the French Left: Studies in Labor and Politics in France, 1830–1981.* Oxford: Clarendon Press, 1986.

———. *Past Imperfect: French Intellectuals, 1944–1956.* Berkeley: University of California Press, 1992.

———. *The Burden of Responsibility: Blum, Camus, Aron, and the French Twentieth Century*. Chicago: The University of Chicago Press, 1998.

Julliard, Jacques, and Michel Winock, eds. *Dictionnaire des intellectuals français*. Paris: Seuil, 1996.

Kaenel, André, Catherine Lejeune, and Marie-Jeanne Rossignol, eds. *Études culturelles–Cultural Studies*. Nancy: Presses universitaires de Nancy, 2003.

Kaminski, Andzrej. *Konzentrationslager 1896 bis heute: Geschichte, Funktion, Typologie*. Munich: Piper, 1990.

Kaplan, Alice Yaeger. *The Collaborator: The Trial & Execution of Robert Brasillach*. Chicago: The University of Chicago Press, 2000.

Kaplan, Steven. *Farewell Revolution: The Historians' Feud*. Ithaca: Cornell University Press, 1995.

Kauppi, Niilo. *French Intellectual Nobility: Institutional and Symbolic Transformations in the Post-Sartrean Era*. Albany: The State University of New York Press, 1996.

Kelly, Michael. *Modern French Marxism*. Baltimore: The Johns Hopkins University Press, 1983.

Khilnani, Sunil. *Arguing Revolution: The Intellectual Left in Postwar France*. New Haven: Yale University Press, 1994.

Kierkegaard, Søren. *Fear and Trembling*, translated by Alastair Hannay. New York: Penguin Putnam, 1985.

Kitson, Simon, and Hanna Diamond, eds. *Vichy, Resistance, Liberation: Festschrift in Honour of H. R. Kedward*. Oxford: Berg, forthcoming.

Kockelsman, Joseph, and Theodore Kisiel, eds. *Phenomenology and the Natural Sciences*. Evanston, Ill.: Northwestern University Press, 1970.

Kofman, Myron. *Edgar Morin: From Big Brother to Fraternity*. London: Pluto, 1996.

Kogon, Eugen. *Der SS-Staat: das System der deutschen Konzentrationslager*. Berlin: Tempelhof, 1947.

Kojève, Alexandre. *Introduction à la lecture de Hegel: leçons sur la Phénoménologie de l'Esprit*, edited by Raymond Queneau. Paris: Gallimard, 1947. Translated by James H. Nichols, Jr. as *Introduction to the Reading of Hegel*. New York: Basic Books, 1969.

Kotek, Joël, and Pierre Rigoulot. *Le Siècle des camps: détention, concentration, extermination: cent ans de mal radical*. Paris: Lattès, 2000.

Koyré, Alexandre. *Études d'histoire de la pensée philosophique*. Paris: Éditions Gallimard, 1971.

Kraus, Chris, and Sylvère Lotringer. *Hatred of Capitalism: A Semiotexte Reader*. Los Angeles: Semiotexte, 2002.

Kremer-Marietti, Angèle. *Thèmes et structures dans l'œuvre de Nietzsche*. Paris: Lettres modernes, 1957.

Kristeva, Julia. *The Kristeva Reader*, edited by Toril Moi. New York: Columbia University Press, 1986.

Lacan, Jacques. *Écrits*, translated by Alan Sheridan. New York: Norton, 1977.

LaCapra, Dominick. *A Preface to Sartre*. Ithaca: Cornell University Press, 1978.

LaCapra, Dominick and Steven L. Kaplan, eds. *Modern European Intellectual History: Reappraisals and New Perspectives*. Ithaca: Cornell University Press, 1982.

Laclau, Ernesto, and Chantal Mouffe. *Hegemony & Socialist Strategy: Towards a Radical Democratic Politics*. London: Verso, 1985.

Laclau, Ernesto, ed. *New Reflections on the Revolutions of Our Time*. London: Verso, 1990.

———. *Emancipations*. London: Verso, 1996.

Lacoue-Labarthe, Philippe, and Jean-Luc Nancy. *Retreating the Political*, edited by Simon Sparks. New York: Routledge, 1997.

Lagrou, Pieter. *The Legacy of Nazi Occupation: Patriotic Memory and National Recovery in Western Europe, 1945–1965*. Cambridge: Cambridge University Press, 2000.

Lalande, André. *Vocabulaire technique et critique de la philosophie*. Paris: PUF, 1928.

Lapassade, Georges. *Groupes, organisation et institutions*. Paris: Gauthier-Villars, 1970.

Larousse, Pierre, ed. *Grand Dictionnaire Universel du XIXe siècle*. Paris: Larousse, 1866–76.

Lechte, John. *Fifty Key Contemporary Thinkers: From Structuralism to Postmodernity*. London: Routledge, 1994.

Lecourt, Dominque. *Les Piètres Penseurs*. Paris: Flammarion, 1999. Translated by Gregory Elliott as *The Mediocracy: French Philosophy since the Mid-1970s*. London: Verso, 2001.

Lefebvre, Georges. *The Coming of the French Revolution*, translated by R. R. Palmer. Princeton: Princeton University Press, 1947.

Lefebvre, Henri. *La Somme et le reste*. 3rd ed. Paris: Méridiens Klincksieck, 1959; 1989.

———. *Introduction à la modernité: préludes*. Paris: Éditions de Minuit, 1962.

———. *Marx*. Paris: PUF, 1964.

———. *Métaphilosophie: prolégomènes*. Paris: Éditions de Minuit, 1965.

———. *La Proclamation de la Commune*. Paris: Gallimard, 1965.

———. *La Fin de l'histoire*. Paris: Éditions de Minuit, 1970.

———. *De l'État*. 4 vols. Paris: Union générale d'éditions, 1976–78.

———. *Qu'est-ce que penser?* Paris: Publisad, 1985.

———. *Méthodologie des sciences: inédit*. Paris: Anthropos, 2002.

Lefebvre, Henri, and Pierre Fougeyrollas. *Le Jeu de Kostas Axelos*. Paris: Fata Morgana, 1973.

Lefort, Claude. *Éléments d'une critique de la bureaucratie*. Paris: Gallimard, 1971.

———. *Democracy and Political Theory*, translated by David Macey. Minneapolis: University of Minnesota Press, 1988.

——. *Les Formes de l'histoire*. Paris: Gallimard, 1978.

——. *Sur une colonne absente*. Paris: Gallimard, 1978.

——. *The Political Forms of Modern Society: Bureaucracy, Democracy, Totalitarianism*, ed. John Thompson. Cambridge, Mass.: The MIT Press, 1986.

Le Goff, Jean-Pierre. *Mai 68, l'héritage impossible*. Paris: La Découverte, 2002.

Leymare, Michel, and Jean-François Sirinelli, eds. *L'Histoire des intellectuels aujourd'hui*. Paris: PUF, 2003.

Leniaud, Jean-Michel. *L'Utopie française: essai sur le patrimoine*. Paris: Mengès, 1992.

Lescourret, Marie-Anne. *Emmanuel Levinas*. Paris: Flammarion, 1994.

Levinas, Emmanuel. *En découvrant l'existence avec Husserl et Heidegger*. Paris: Vrin, 1957.

——. *Quatre lectures talmudiques*. Paris: Les Éditions de Minuit, 1968. Translated by Sean Hand as *Difficult Freedom: Essays on Judaism*. Baltimore: Johns Hopkins University Press, 1990.

——. *Éthique et infini: dialogues avec Phillipe Nemo*. Paris: Fayard, 1982. Translated by Richard A. Cohen as *Ethics and Infinity*. Pittsburgh: Duquesne University Press, 1985.

——. *Nine Talmudic Lectures*, translated by Annette Aronowicz. Bloomington: Indiana University Press, 1990.

——. *Theory of Intuition in Husserl's Phenomenology*, translated by André Orianne. 2nd ed. Evanston, Ill.: Northwestern University Press, 1995.

——. *Beyond the Verse: Talmudic Readings and Lectures*, translated by Gary D. Mole. Bloomington: Indiana University Press, 1994.

Lévi-Strauss, Claude. *Structural Anthropology*, translated by Claire Jacobson and Brooke Grundrest Schoepf. New York: Basic Books, 1963.

——. *The Savage Mind*. Chicago: The University of Chicago Press, 1966.

Lévy, Bernard-Henri. *Éloge des intellectuels*. Paris: Grasset, 1987.

Lévy-Valensi, Éliane Amado and Jean Halperin, eds. *La Conscience juive face à l'histoire: le pardon*. Paris: PUF, 1965.

Lextrait, Fabrice. *Une Nouvelle Étape de l'action culturelle*. Paris: La Documentation Française, 2001.

Leymaire, Michel, and Jean-François Sirinelli, eds. *L'Histoire des intellectuels aujourd'hui*. Paris: PUF, 2003.

Lichtheim, George. *Marxism in Modern France*. New York: Columbia University Press, 1966.

Lilla, Mark, ed. *New French Thought: Political Philosophy*. Princeton: Princeton University Press, 1994.

——. *The Reckless Mind: Intellectuals and Politics*. New York: The New York Review of Books Press, 2001.

Lismonde, Pascale. *Les Arts à l'école: le plan de Jack Lang et Catherine Tasca*. Paris: Cndp-Gallimard, 2002.

Litván, György, *The Hungarian Revolution of 1956: Reform, Revolt, and Repression 1953–1963*, edited and translated by János M. Bak and Lyman H. Legters. New York: Routledge, 1996.

Looseley, David. *The Politics of Fun: Cultural Policy and Debate in Contemporary France*. Oxford: Berg Publishers, 1995.

Lourau, René. *L'Analyse institutionnelle*. Paris: Éditions de Minuit, 1970.

———. *L'État-inconscient*. Paris: Éditions de Minuit, 1978.

———. *Autodissolution des avant-gardes*. Paris: Éditions Galilée, 1980.

———. *La Clé des champs: une introduction à l'analyse institutionnelle*. Paris: Anthropos, 1997.

Lotringer, Sylvère, and Sande Cohen, eds. *French Theory in America*. New York: Routledge, 2001.

Lukács, Georg. *Histoire et connaissance de classe: essais de dialectique marxiste*, translated by Kostas Axelos and Jacqueline Bois. Paris: Éditions de Minuit, 1960.

———. *History and Class Consciousness: Studies in Marxist Dialectics*, translated by Rodney Livingstone. London: Merlin, 1971.

Lutz, Vera. *Central Planning for the Market Economy: An Analysis of the French Theory and Experience*. London: Longman, 1969.

Luxemburg, Rosa. *Le Socialisme en France, 1898–1912*, introduction by Daniel Guérin. Paris: Belfond, 1971.

Lyotard, Jean-François. *The Postmodern Condition: A Report on Knowledge*. Manchester: Manchester University Press, 1984.

———. *Political Writings*. London: UCL Press, 1994.

Macherey, Pierre. *Pour une théorie du production littéraire*. Paris: Maspéro, 1966.

———. *Histoires de dinosaure: faire de la philosophie 1965–1997*. Paris: PUF, 1999.

Macpherson, C. B. *The Political Theory of Possessive Individualism: Hobbes to Locke*. Oxford: Clarendon Press, 1962.

Mandel, Maud S. *In the Aftermath of Genocide: Armenians and Jews in Twentieth-Century France*. Raleigh, N.C.: Duke University Press, 2003.

Marcuse, Herbert. *Éros et civilisation: contribution à Freud*, translated by Jean-Guy Nény and Boris Fraenkel. Paris: Éditions de Minuit, 1963.

———. *L'Homme unidimensionel: étude sur l'idéologie de la société industrielle*, translated by Monique Wittig. Paris: Éditions de Minuit, 1968. In English as *One-Dimensional Man*. Boston: Beacon Press, 1991.

Marshall, Bill. *Guy Hocquenghem: Beyond Gay Identity*. Durham: Duke University Press, 1997.

Martel, Frédéric. *Le Rose et le noir: les homosexuels en France depuis 1968*. Paris: Seuil, 2000. Translated by Jane Marie Todd as *The Pink and the Black: Homosexuals in France since 1968*. Stanford: Stanford University Press, 1999.

Marx, Karl. *The Poverty of Philosophy*. New York: International Publishers, 1963.

———. *Writings of the Young Marx on Philosophy and Society*, edited by Loyd D. Easton and Kurt H. Guddat. New York: Doubleday, 1967.

————. *Critique de l'État hégélien*, translated by Kostas Papaioannou. Paris: Union générale d'éditions, 1976.

————. *Écrits de jeunesse*, translated by Kostas Papaioannou. Paris: La République des Lettres, 1994.

Marx, Karl, and Friedrich Engels. *The German Ideology*, edited by C. J. Arthur. London: Lawrence & Wishart, 1970.

Marx-Scouras, Danielle. *The Cultural Politics of Tel Quel: Literature and the Left in the Wake of Engagement*. University Park, Pa.: Pennsylvania State University Press, 1996.

Mascio, Patrick du, ed. *L'Auteur à l'oeuvre*. Fontenay/Saint-Cloud: ENS Éditions, 1996.

Mathy, Jean-Philippe. *Extrême Occident: French Intellectuals and America*. Chicago: The University of Chicago Press, 1993.

————. *French Resistance: The French-American Culture Wars*. Minneapolis: The University of Minnesota Press, 2000.

Memmi, Albert. *The Colonizer and the Colonized*, translated by Howard Greenfeld. New York: Orion Press, 1965.

Merleau-Ponty, Maurice. *Phenomenology of Perception*, translated by Colin Smith. London: Routledge and Kegan Paul, 1962.

————. *In Praise of Philosophy*, translated by John Wild and James M. Edie. Evanston, Ill.: Northwestern University Press, 1963.

————. *Sense and Non-Sense*, translated by Hubert L. Dreyfus and Patricia Allen Dreyfus. Evanston, Ill.: Northwestern University Press, 1964.

————. *Signs*, translated by Richard C. McCleary. Evanston, Ill.: Northwestern University Press, 1964.

Michaud, Yves. *La Crise de l'art contemporain: utopie, démocratie et comédie*. Paris: PUF, 1997.

Minc, Alain. *www.capitalisme.fr*. Paris: Grasset, 2000.

Mollard, Claude. *Le Cinquième Pouvoir: la culture et l'État de Malraux à Lang*. Paris: Armand Colin, 1999.

Mollier, Jean-Yves. *Où va le livre?* Paris: La Dispute, 2002.

Mongin, Olivier. *Face au scepticisme: les mutations du paysage intellectuel 1976–1998*. 2nd ed. Paris: Hachette, 1998.

Montefiore, Alan, ed. *Philosophy in France Today*. New York: Cambridge University Press, 1983.

Morin, Edgar. *Autocritique*. 2nd ed. Paris: Seuil, 1959; 1970.

————. *Le Cinema ou l'homme imaginaire: essai d'anthropologie*. Paris: Éditions de Minuit, 1978.

————. *Pour sortir du vingtième siècle*. Paris: Nathan, 1981.

————. *Reliances*. Paris: Éditions de l'Aube, 2002.

Morin, Edgar, Claude Lefort, and Jean-Marc Coudray [Cornelius Castoriadis]. *Mai 68: La Brèche*. Paris: Complexe, 1988.

Mosès, Stéphane, *L'Ange de l'histoire*. Paris: Seuil, 1992.

Mouffe, Chantal, ed. *Gramsci and Marxist Theory*. London: Routledge, 1977.

Moyn, Samuel. *Selfhood and Transcendence: Emmanuel Levinas and the Origins of Intersubjective Moral Theory 1928–1961*. Ph.D. diss., University of California, Berkeley, 2000.

Nancy, Jean-Luc. *The Inoperative Community*, edited by Peter Connor. Minneapolis: University of Minnesota Press, 1991.

Negri, Antonio. *The Savage Anomaly: The Power of Spinoza's Metaphysics and Politics*, translated by Michael Hardt. Minneapolis: University of Minnesota Press, 1991.

Nicolet, Claude. *L'Idée républicaine en France*. Paris: Gallimard, 1982.

New York Times Index. New York: The New York Times Company, 1958–61.

Nora, Pierre, ed. *Les Lieux de mémoire*. 3 vols. Paris: Gallimard, 1984–92.

Noir et Rouge (Cahiers d'études anarchistes révolutionnaires): anthologie 1956–1970. Paris: Spartacus, 1982.

Ory, Pascal, and Jean-François Sirinelli. *Les Intellectuels en France de l'affaire Dreyfus à nos jours*. Paris: Armand Colin, 1992.

Ott, Hugo. *Martin Heidegger: A Political Life*. New York: Harper Collins, 1993.

Palmade, Guy P. *Capitalisme et capitalistes français au XIXe siècle*. Paris: Armand Colin, 1901.

Papaioannou, Kostas. *Hegel*. Paris: Agora, 1962.

———. *De Marx et du marxisme*. Paris: Gallimard, 1983.

———. *La Consécration de l'histoire*. Paris: Ivréa, 1996.

———. *De la critique du ciel à la critique de la terre*. Paris: Allia, 1998.

Pasteur, Paul, Sonja Niederacher and Maria Mesner, eds. *Sexualität, Unterschichtenmilieu und ArbeiterInnenbewegung*. Vienna: ITH & Akademische Verlagsanstalt, 2003.

Payne, Michael and John Schad, eds. *Life.After.Theory: Jacques Derrida, Frank Kermode, Toril Moi, and Christopher Norris*. London: Continuum, 2003.

Picq, Françoise. *Libération des femmes: les années-mouvement*. Paris: Seuil, 1993.

Pistone, Sergio, ed. *I movimenti per l'unità europea dal 1945 al 1954*. Milano: Jaca Book, 1992.

Poel, Ieme van der, et al., eds. *Traveling Theory: France and the United States*. Madison, N.J.: Fairleigh Dickinson University Press, 2000.

Poirié, François. *Emmanuel Lévinas: qui êtes-vous?* Paris: La Manufacture, 1987.

Poirrier, Philippe, ed. *Bibliographie de l'histoire des politiques culturelles: France, XIXe–XXe siècles*. Paris: La Documentation Française—Comité d'histoire du Ministère de la Culture, 1999.

———, ed. *Les Politiques culturelles en France*. Paris: La Documentation Française, 2002.

———. *Les Enjeux de l'histoire culturelle*. Paris: Seuil, 2004.

Poster, Mark. *Existential Marxism in Postwar France*. Princeton: Princeton University Press, 1975.

Power and Opposition in Post-Revolutionary Societies, translated by Patrick Camiller and Jon Rothschild. London: Ink Links, 1979.

Poulantzas, Nicos. *State, Power, Socialism.* Rev. ed. London: Verso, 2000.

Pouthas, Charles H. *Démocraties et capitalisme 1848–1860.* Paris: PUF, 1948.

Prochasson, Christophe. *Les Intellectuels, le socialisme et la guerre, 1900–1938.* Paris: Seuil, 1993.

Rajsfus, Maurice. *Mai 68: sous les pavés, la repression (mai 1968–mars 1974).* Paris: Le cherche midi éditeur, 1998.

Ravis, Suzanne, ed. *Aragon 1956: actes du colloque d'Aix-en-Provence 5–8 septembre 1991.* Aix-en-Provence: Publications de l'Université de Provence, 1992.

Reader, Keith. *Intellectuals and the Left in France since 1968.* New York: St. Martin's Press, 1987.

Reiner, Sylvain. *Et la terre sera pure.* Paris: Fayard, 1969.

Rémond, René, ed. *Pour une histoire politique.* Paris: Seuil, 1998.

Revel, Jacques, and Lynn Hunt, eds. *Postwar French Thought.* Vol. 1, *Histories: French Constructions of the Past.* New York: The New Press, 1995.

Revel, Jean-François. *L'Absolutisme inefficace ou contre le présidentialisme à la française.* Paris: Plon, 1992.

Ricoeur, Paul. *Freud and Philosophy: An Essay on Interpretation,* translated by Denis Savage. New Haven: Yale University Press, 1970.

———. *Lectures 3: aux frontières de la philosophie.* Paris: Seuil, 1994.

Rieffel, Rémy. *Les Intellectuels sous la Ve République.* 3 vols. Paris: Calmann-Lévy, 1993.

Rigaud, Jacques. *Pour une refondation de la politique culturelle.* Paris: La Documentation Française, 1996.

———. *Les Deniers du rêve: essai sur l'avenir des politiques culturelles.* Paris: Grasset, 2001.

Rigby, Brian. *Popular Culture in Modern France: A Study of Cultural Discourse.* London: Routledge, 1991.

Rioux, Jean-Pierre, and Jean-François Sirinelli, eds. *La Guerre d'Algérie et les intellectuels français.* Brussels: Éditions Complexe, 1991.

———. *Pour une histoire culturelle.* Paris: Seuil, 1997.

———., eds. *La Culture de masse en France: de la Belle Époque à aujourd'hui.* Paris: Fayard, 2002.

Robertson, Gillian, and John Rundell, eds. *Rethinking Imagination: Culture and Creativity.* New York: Routledge, 1994.

Ross, George, Stanley Hoffmann, and Sylvia Malzacher, eds. *The Mitterrand Experiment: Continuity and Change in Modern France.* New York: Oxford University Press, 1987.

Ross, Kristin. *Fast Cars, Clean Bodies: Decolonization and the Reordering of French Culture.* Cambridge, Mass.: The MIT Press, 1995.

———. *May '68 and Its Afterlives.* Chicago: The University of Chicago Press, 2002.

Roth, Michael S. *Knowing and History: Appropriations of Hegel in Twentieth-Century France* Ithaca: Cornell University Press, 1988.

———. *The Ironist's Cage: Memory, Trauma, and the Construction of History*. New York: Columbia University Press, 1995.

Roudinesco, Elisabeth. *La Bataille de cent ans: histoire de la psychanalysme en France*. 2 vols. rev. ed. Paris: Fayard, 1994. Vol. 2 translated by Jeffrey Mehlman as *Jacques Lacan & Co.: A History of Psychoanalysis in France, 1925–1985*. Chicago: The University of Chicago Press, 1990.

———. *Jacques Lacan: esquisse d'une vie, histoire d'une système de pensée*. Paris: Fayard, 1993. Translated by Barbara Bray as *Jacques Lacan*. New York: Columbia University Press, 1997.

Rougemont, Denis de. *Vingt-huit siècles d'Europe*. Paris: Payot, 1961.

Rousset, David, *L'Univers concentrationnaire*. Paris: Éditions du Pavois 1946. Translated by Ramon Guthrie as *The Other Kingdom*. New York: Reynal and Hitchcock, 1947.

———. *Les Jours de notre mort*. Paris: Éditions du Pavois, 1947. Translated by Yvonne Moyse and Roger Senhouse as *A World Apart*. London: Secker and Warburg, 1951.

Rousset, David, et al. *Le Procès concentrationnaire pour la vérité des camps: extraits des débats*. Paris: Éditions du Pavois, 1951.

Rousso, Henry. *The Vichy Syndrome: History and Memory in France since 1944*, translated by Arthur Goldhammer. Cambridge, Mass.: Harvard University Press, 1991.

Roy, Claude. *Somme toute*. Paris: Gallimard, 1976.

Rubinstein, Dianne. *What's Left? The École Normale Supérieure and the Right*. Madison: University of Wisconsin Press, 1990.

Saint-Pulgent, Maryvonne de. *Le Gouvernement de la culture*. Paris: Gallimard, 1999.

Salvaresi, Élisabeth. *Mai en héritage*. Paris: Syros, 1988.

Samuelson, François-Marie. *Il était une fois Libération . . .* Paris: Seuil, 1979.

Sapiro, Gisèle. *La Guerre des écrivains, 1940–1953*. Paris: Fayard, 1999.

Sartre, Jean-Paul. *Critique de la raison dialectique*. Paris: Gallimard, 1960.

———. *Search for a Method*, translated by Hazel Barnes. New York: Alfred A. Knopf, 1963.

———. *The Ghost of Stalin*, translated by Marta H. Fletcher with the assistance of John R. Kleinschmidt. New York: George Braziller, 1968.

———. *Anti-Semite and Jew*, translated by George J. Becker. New York: Schocken, 1948.

Scheler, Max. *Nature et formes de la sympathie: contribution à l'étude des lois de la vie émotionnelle*, translated by M. Lefebvre. Paris: Payot, 1928.

Schmidt, James, ed. *What is Enlightenment? Eighteenth-Century Answers and Twentieth-Century Questions*. Berkeley: University of California Press, 1996.

Schrift, Alan D., and Gayle L. Ormiston, eds. *Transforming the Hermeneutic Context: From Nietzsche to Nancy*. Albany, N.Y.: SUNY Press, 1990.

Schuster, J. M. *Informing Cultural Policy: The Research and Information Infrastructure*. New Brunswick, N.J.: Center for Urban Policy Research, 2002.

Schneider, Michel. *La Comédie de la culture*. Paris: Seuil, 1993.

Semaines sociales de France. *D'un siècle à l'autre: l'évangile, les chrétiens et les enjeux de la société*. Paris: Bayard, 2000.

Senghor, Léopold. *Anthologie de la nouvelle poésie nègre et malgache de langue française*. Paris: PUF, 1948.

Serres, Michel, with Bruno Latour. *Conversations on Science, Culture, and Time*, translated by Roxanne Lapidus. Ann Arbor: University of Michigan Press, 1995.

Simonin, Anne. *Les Éditions de Minuit 1942–1955: le devoir d'insoumission*. Paris: IMEC Éditions, 1994.

Sirinelli, Jean-François, *Deux intellectuels dans le siècle, J.-P. Sartre et R. Aron*. Paris: Fayard, 1995.

———. *Intellectuels et passions françaises: manifestes et pétitions au XXe siècle*. Paris: Gallimard, 1990.

———. *Génération intellectuelle: khâgneux et normaliens dans l'entre-deux-guerres*. Paris: Fayard, 1988.

Soubise, Louis. *Le Marxisme après Marx 1956–1965: quatre marxistes dissidents français*. Paris: Aubier Montaigne, 1967.

Soboul, Albert. *The French Revolution, 1787–1799: From the Storming of the Bastille to Napoleon*, translated by Alan Forrest and Colin Jones. New York: Vintage, 1975.

Soutou, Georges-Henri. *La Guerre des cinquante ans: les relations Est-Ouest 1943–1990*. Paris: Fayard, 2001.

Spiegelberg, Herbert. *The Phenomenological Movement: A Historical Introduction*. 3rd rev. ed. The Hague: Martinus Nijhoff, 1960; 1982.

Sprinker, Michael, ed. *Ghostly Demarcations: A Symposium on Jacques Derrida's Specters of Marx*. London: Verso, 1999.

Smith, Douglas. *Transvaluations: Nietzsche in France 1872–1972*. Oxford: Clarendon Press, 1996.

Steiner, Jean-François. *Treblinka: la révolte d'un camp d'extermination*, preface by Simone de Beauvoir. Paris: Fayard, 1966. Translated by Helen Weaver as *Treblinka*. New York: Simon and Schuster, 1967.

Steinlauf, Michael C. *Bondage to the Dead: Poland and the Memory of the Holocaust*. Syracuse, N.Y.: Syracuse University Press, 1997.

Stoekl, Allan. *Agonies of the Intellectual: Commitment, Subjectivity, and the Performative in the 20th Century French Tradition*. Lincoln, Neb.: University of Nebraska Press, 1992.

Stone, Ira F. *Reading Levinas Reading Talmud*. Philadelphia: The Jewish Publication Society, 1998.

Thompson, E. P. *The Poverty of Theory and Other Essays*. London: Merlin, 1978.

Todorov, Tzvetan. *Les Abus de la mémoire*. Paris: Arléa, 1998.

——. *Mémoire du mal, tentation du bien: enquête sur le siècle*. Paris: R. Laffont, 2000. Translated as *Hope and Memory: Lessons from the Twentieth Century*. Princeton: Princeton University Press, 2003.

Tosel, André. "Les philosophies de la mondialisation" (public lecture, Université René Descartes, Paris V, 7 July 2003).

Torfing, Jacob. *New Theories of Discourse: Laclau, Mouffe, and Zizek*. Oxford: Blackwell, 1999.

Traverso, Enzo. *The Origins of Nazi Violence*, translated by Janet Lloyd. New York: The New Press, 2003.

Trente ans d'histoire: de Clemenceau à de Gaulle, 1918–1948. Paris: Éditions Sant'Andréa, 1949.

Turkle, Sherry. *Psychoanalytic Politics: Jacques Lacan and Freud's French Revolution*. 2nd ed. New York: The Guilford Press, 1992.

——. *Life on the Screen: Identity in the Age of the Internet*. New York: Simon & Schuster, 1995.

Union des travailleurs communistes libertaires. *Le Droit à la caresse: les homosexualités et le combat homosexuel*. Paris: UTCL, n.d.

Urfalino, Philippe. *L'Invention de la politique culturelle*. Paris: Comité d'histoire du Ministère de la Culture-La Documentation Française, 1996.

Vercors. *P.P.C. ou le concours de Blois*. Paris: Albin Michel, 1957.

Vidal-Naquet, Pierre. *Torture: Cancer of Democracy, France and Algeria, 1954–62*, translated by Barry Richard. Baltimore: Penguin Books, 1963. Pub. as *La Torture dans la République: essai d'histoire et de politique contemporaines (1954-1962)*. Paris: Éditions de Minuit, 1972.

——. *Les Assassins de la mémoire: "Un Eichmann de papier" et autres essais sur le révisionnisme*. Paris: La Découverte, 1987. Translated by Jeffrey Mehlman as *Assassins of Memory: Essays on the Denial of the Holocaust*. New York: Columbia University Press, 1992.

——. *Face à la raison d'État: un historien dans la guerre d'Algérie*. Paris: La Découverte, 1989.

——. *Les Juifs, la mémoire et le présent*. 3 vols. Paris: La Découverte, 1995. Partially translated by David Ames Curtis as *The Jews: History, Memory, and the Present*. New York: Columbia University Press, 1995.

——. *Mémoires*. Vol. 1, *La Brisure et l'attente, 1930–1955*. Paris: Le Seuil, 1995.

——. *Mémoires*. Vol. 2, *Le Trouble et la lumière, 1955–1998*. Paris: Le Seuil, 1998.

Villefosse, Louis de. *L'Oeuf de Wyasme: récit*. Paris: Julliard, 1962.

Vries, Hent de, and Samuel Weber, eds. *Violence, Identity, and Self-Determination*. Stanford: Stanford University Press, 1997.

Wahl, Jean. *Vers le concret*. Paris: Vrin, 1932.

Waresquiel, Emmanuel de, ed. *Dictionnaire des politiques culturelles de la France depuis 1959*. Paris: Larousse-CNRS, 2001.

Waxman, Chaim J., ed. *The End of Ideology Debate*. New York: Funk & Wagnalls, 1968.

Wieviorka, Annette. *Déportation et génocide: entre la mémoire et l'oubli*. Paris: Plon, 1992.

Wievorka, Olivier, and Christophe Prochasson, eds. *La France du XXe siècle: documents d'histoire*. Paris: Seuil, 1994.

Williams, Raymond. *Keywords*. London: Fontana, 1983.

Winock, Michel. *Le Siècle des intellectuals*. Rev. ed. Paris: Seuil, 1997; 1999.

Wright, Gordon. *France in Modern Times*. 5th ed. New York: W.W. Norton, 1995.

Wolin, Richard. *Labyrinths: Explorations in the Critical History of Ideas*. Amherst: University of Massachusetts Press, 1995.

Wood, Ellen Meiksins. *The Retreat from Class: A New "True" Socialism*. London: Verso, 1986.

Zadig. *L'Implosion française*. Paris: Albin Michel, 1992.

Zelizer, Barbie. *Remembering to Forget: Holocaust Memory through the Camera's Eye*. Chicago: The University of Chicago Press, 1998.

Zizek, Slavoj. *Did Somebody Say Totalitarianism? Five Interventions in the Misuse of a Notion*. London: Verso, 2001.

Zizek, Slavoj, Ernesto Laclau, and Judith Butler. *Contingency, Hegemony, Universality: Contemporary Dialogues on the Left*. London: Verso, 2000.

INDEX

ABOUT THE CONTRIBUTORS

Michael Behrent is a doctoral candidate in history at New York University. A recipient of a 2001–2002 Fulbright Fellowship and a 2003–2004 Charlotte W. Newcombe Dissertation Fellowship, he is writing his dissertation, entitled "Society Incarnate: The Religious Current in Nineteenth-Century French Republicanism." He has taught extensively in France and New York.

David Berry is lecturer in French in the Department of European and International Studies, Loughborough University, United Kingdom. Author of *A History of the French Anarchist Movement, 1917–1945* (2002), he is a member of the editorial committee of the *Journal of Contemporary European Studies*. He is currently working on a biography of Daniel Guérin, entitled *Fire in the Blood: A Personal and Political Biography of Daniel Guérin, 1904–1988*, and his articles have been published in *Contemporary European History*, *Modern and Contemporary France*, *French History*, *Dissidences*, and *Anarchist Studies*.

Lucia Bonfreschi is a doctoral candidate at the Università di Bologna, Italy. A contributing editor to the Italian political history review, *Ricerche di Storia Politica*, she is writing her dissertation, entitled "Raymond Aron and Gaullism, 1940–1958." She has published an article on anti-Americanism in France under the Fourth Republic in *Atti del Convegno: L'antiamericanismo in Italia e in Europa nel secondo dopoguerra*.

Julian Bourg is visiting assistant professor of history at Bryn Mawr College. From 2002–2004, he was a Mellon Postdoctoral Fellow in Interdisciplinary Studies at Washington University in St. Louis. His articles have appeared in *The Journal of the History of Ideas, The Modern Schoolman, Actuel Marx,* and *French Cultural Studies.* He has completed a manuscript on the ethical turn in post-1968 intellectual-cultural politics.

Warren Breckman is associate professor of history at the University of Pennsylvania. A recent fellow at the Institute for Advanced Study, Professor Breckman is the author of *Marx, the Young Hegelians and the Origins of Radical Social Theory: Dethroning the Self* (1999). In 2001, he was the recipient of the Selma V. Forkosch Prize for the Best Article Published in the *Journal of the History of Ideas.* The article was "Eduard Gans and the Crisis of Hegelianism," *Journal of the History of Ideas* 62, no. 3 (July 2001). He is currently working on a book entitled *Adventures of the Symbolic: French Post-Marxism and Democratic Theory.*

Michael Scott Christofferson is assistant professor of history at Penn State Erie. He is the author of *French Intellectuals Against the Left: The Antitotalitarian Moment of the 1970s* (2003). His articles have appeared in the journals *French History* and *French Historical Studies.*

François Dosse is professor in history at l'IUFM de Créteil and at the Institut d'études politiques de Paris as well as a researcher associated with the Institut d'histoire du temps présent and the Centre d'histoire culturelle des sociétés contemporaines de l'université Saint-Quentin-en-Yvelines. He is the author, among other works, of *L'Histoire en miettes: des "Annales" à la "nouvelle histoire"* (1987), translated as *New History in France: The Triumph of the Annales* (1994); *L'Empire du sens: l'humanisation des sciences humaines* (1995), translated as *Empire of Meaning: The Humanization of the Social Sciences* (1999); *Histoire du structuralisme,* 2 vols. (1991–1992), translated as *History of Structuralism,* 2 vols. (1997); and *La Marche des idées: histoire des intellectuels–histoire intellectuelle* (2003).

Stuart Elden is lecturer in political geography at the University of Durham, United Kingdom. He is the author of *An Introduction to Henri Lefebvre: Theory and the Possible* (2004); and *Mapping the Present: Heidegger, Foucault, and the Project of a Spatial History* (2001). He is the co-editor of *Henri Lefebvre: Key Writings* (2003), and has contributed articles on French and

German thought to journals such as *Political Geography*, *boundary 2*, *Antipode*, *Historical Materialism*, and the *European Journal of Political Theory*.

William Gallois is assistant professor of history at the American University of Sharjah, United Arab Emirates. He is the author of *Zola: The History of Capitalism* (2000); and *Wittgenstein and History* (forthcoming). His articles have appeared in the *Biographical Dictionary of Literary Influences: The Nineteenth Century, 1800-1914* (2000); and the *Encyclopedia of Capitalism* (2004).

Ron Haas is a doctoral candidate in history at Rice University. He is the recipient of a 2002–2003 Charlotte W. Newcombe Dissertation Fellowship. His dissertation is entitled "Maoism in France: A History of the French Cultural Revolution after May 1968."

Ethan Kleinberg is assistant professor of history at Wesleyan University. The assistant editor of the journal *History and Theory*, he is author of *Generation Existential: The Reception of Martin Heidegger's Philosophy in France, 1927–1961* (forthcoming). He recently contributed an article on Alexandre Kojève and Frantz Fanon to the collection *French Civilization and Its Discontents*, eds. Tyler Stovall and George Van Den Abbeele (2003).

Samuel Moyn is assistant professor of history at Columbia University. He is the author of *Origins of the Other: Emmanuel Levinas and Interwar Philosophy* (forthcoming). His articles have appeared in the *Leo Baeck Institute Year Book*, *History and Memory*, *The American Historical Review*, *Yale French Studies*, *The Journal of Modern History*, *Prooftexts*, and *The Journal of the History of Ideas*.

Philippe Poirrier is maître de conférences in contemporary history at the Université de Bourgogne, France. He is author, among other works, of *Les Politiques culturelles en France* (2002); *L'État et la culture en France au XXe siècle* (2000); *Société et culture en France depuis 1945* (1998); and *Histoire des politiques culturelles de la France contemporaine*, 2nd ed. (1998).

Christophe Premat is a doctoral candidate (Allocataire-moniteur normalien) at the Institut d'Études Politiques, Bordeaux, France. His principal research is on the referendum process in post-1945 Europe. He has taught and lectured in Sweden and the United States, and his articles have appeared in *Tracés* and *Tissages*.

Alan D. Schrift is professor of philosophy at Grinnell College. He is the author of *Nietzsche and the Question of Interpretation: Between Hermeneutics and Deconstruction* (1990); and *Nietzsche's French Legacy: A Genealogy of Poststructuralism* (1995). He has edited the collections *The Logic of the Gift: Toward an Ethic of Generosity* (1997); and *Why Nietzsche Still? Reflections on Drama, Culture, and Politics* (2000).